October 27–28, 2013
Indianapolis, Indiana, USA

I0034590

Association for Computing Machinery

Advancing Computing as a Science & Profession

SPLASH
INDIANAPOLIS 2013

GPCE'13

The Proceedings of the 12th International Conference on
Generative Programming: Concepts & Experiences

Sponsored by:
ACM SIGPLAN

Supported by:
Microsoft Research, NSF, Cisco, Oracle Labs, Intel, Google, IBM Research, Purdue University, & Typesafe

**Association for
Computing Machinery**

Advancing Computing as a Science & Profession

The Association for Computing Machinery
2 Penn Plaza, Suite 701
New York, New York 10121-0701

Notice to Past Authors of ACM-Published Articles

ISBN: 978-1-4503-2373-4 (Digital)

ISBN: 978-1-4503-2680-3 (Print)

Additional copies may be ordered prepaid from:

ACM Order Department
PO Box 30777
New York, NY 10087-0777, USA

Phone: 1-800-342-6626 (USA and Canada)
+1-212-626-0500 (Global)
Fax: +1-212-944-1318
E-mail: acmhelp@acm.org
Hours of Operation: 8:30 am – 4:30 pm ET

Printed in the USA

Foreword

Welcome to the Twelfth International Conference on Generative Programming: Concepts & Experiences (GPCE'13). GPCE continues to provide the premiere venue for researchers and practitioners interested in techniques that use program generation, domain-specific languages, and component deployment to increase programmer productivity, improve software quality, and shorten the time-to-market of software products. In addition to exploring cutting-edge techniques of generative software, our goal is to foster further cross-fertilization between the software engineering and the programming languages research communities. This year, GPCE is co-located with OOSPLA, the premier conference on object-oriented programming, with SLE, the conference on software language engineering, and with various other events under the SPLASH umbrella. GPCE participants are invited to visit other sessions on the same day and vice versa. This provides the attendees of all events with a comprehensive overview of current research at the intersection of programming languages and software engineering.

This volume contains the papers presented at the conference as well as the abstracts of the keynote presentations. GPCE'13 attracted 59 submissions with authors from 23 different countries. Each submission was reviewed by at least three members of the program committee. In 17 cases we reached out to external experts for an additional review. The submissions were discussed intensively during a week-long electronic program committee meeting. As a result of this meeting, 17 full research papers and 3 short research papers were selected for presentation at the conference, covering all topic areas of the call for papers, from domain-specific languages, to empirical results, and to program synthesis. The conference program also includes two keynote presentations shared with SLE, one by Don Batory titled "Dark Knowledge and Graph Grammars in Automated Software Design" and another by Ras Bodik titled "Solver-Aided Languages".

Putting together GPCE'13 was a team effort. We would like to thank the authors and keynote speakers for providing the content of the program, and the program committee and external reviewers for their hard work in reviewing the papers and contributing to the program committee meeting discussions. We would also like to thank Norbert Siegmund for helping with publicity and maintaining the GPCE'13 web site, Vibeke Nielsen for designing the poster, and the GPCE steering committee and prior chairs and various colleagues for their advice. We are grateful to SPLASH for the general organization and full support for flexible deadlines and help with local organization. Finally, we would like to thank ACM SIGPLAN for their continued support of this conference.

We hope that you will find this program inspiring and compelling, and that the conference will provide you with a valuable opportunity to share ideas with other researchers and practitioners from institutions around the world.

Jaakko Järvi
GPCE13 General Chair,
Texas A&M University, USA

Christian Kästner
GPCE'11 Program Chair
Carnegie Mellon University, USA

The Fourth Annual ACM International Conference on *Systems, Programming, Languages, and Applications: Software for Humanity*

It is our great pleasure to welcome you to Indianapolis and SPLASH 2013, the umbrella venue for the 28th *OOPSLA*, plus *Onward!*, *Wavefront*, and the *Dynamic Languages Symposium*. Moreover, SPLASH 2013 is proud to host the *ACM SIGPLAN Conference on Generative Programming: Concepts & Experiences* (GPCE), co-locating with the *International Conference on Software Language Engineering* (SLE). SPLASH this year revives the former educator's symposium in its new guise as SPLASH-E, for discussion of Computer Science education uniquely embedded within the culture of visionary research and practice embodied by *OOPSLA*, *Onward!*, and *Wavefront*. SPLASH-E is timely in that it coincides with the finalization of the ACM/IEEE Computer Science Curriculum 2013. This year also sees the return to SPLASH of tutorials and tech-talks, plus a new twist in the form of the synergistic SPLASH-I as a forum for acclaimed speakers from industry, all offered free to SPLASH attendees.

Drawing on the long tradition of *OOPSLA*, and with the addition of *Onward!* and *Wavefront*, SPLASH embraces all aspects of software construction and delivery to make it the premier conference at the intersection of programming, languages, and software engineering. *OOPSLA* was the incubator for CRC cards, CLOS, design patterns, Self, the agile methodologies, service-oriented architectures, wikis, Unified Modeling Language (UML), test driven design (TDD), refactoring, Java, dynamic compilation, and aspect-oriented programming, just to name a few. *Onward!* focuses on everything to do with programming and software: including processes, methods, languages, communities, and applications. *Onward!* is more radical, more visionary, and more open than other conferences to not yet well-proven but well-argued ideas. *Wavefront* is about how industry applies the lessons learned from the software development community in deploying today's software and systems, and how the community can learn from what is happening in the trenches of software engineering. The *Dynamic Languages Symposium* is the place where researchers and practitioners come together to discuss the new crop of wildly successful dynamic languages, their implementation, and their applications.

Guest conferences at SPLASH this year include GPCE and SLE. The *ACM SIGPLAN International Conference on Generative Programming: Concepts & Experiences* (GPCE) is a venue for researchers and practitioners interested in techniques that use program generation, domain-specific languages, and component deployment to increase programmer productivity, improve software quality, and shorten the time-to-market of software products. The *International Conference on Software Language Engineering* (SLE) is devoted to topics related to artificial languages in software engineering. SLE's mission is to encourage and organize communication among communities that have traditionally looked at software languages from different and yet complementary perspectives.

This year we are extremely fortunate to have four keynote speakers who tap into broad and deep SPLASH themes. Kathryn McKinley looks at the impact that heterogeneous hardware is having on the design and implementation of software abstractions for parallelism. Greg Wilson asks why the gap between research and practice remains so wide, and suggests how to narrow it. Molham Aref explores declarative programming for the cloud to combine rapid prototyping with performance in the deployment of large-scale cloud applications. Gilad Bracha ponders the history of innovation in programming languages and what is yet to come, asking how the elegance of Lisp, Simula, Actors, Beta, Smalltalk and Self led to the reality of C++, Java, Javascript, Perl, Python and PHP.

Organizing SPLASH has been a long march, alleviated greatly by the enthusiasm and talent of all those who have volunteered their time to make it a success. We are especially grateful to all the members of the Organizing Committee, comprising the committee chairs of all the conferences and events, and to our corporate supporters for their generosity. All the program chairs, aided by their program committees and reviewers, are to be congratulated on putting together such a strong program of papers and presentations. We thank the authors and presenters for their research, experiences, and valuable insights, which above anything else are the only reason for a conference like SPLASH in the first place. Finally, we thank you, the attendees, for being here to experience the wonder and excitement of SPLASH! We hope that you find the resulting program to be interesting and thought-provoking, and that your interactions at SPLASH with other researchers, educators, students, and practitioners from around the world are stimulating and fruitful.

Antony Hosking
SPLASH'13 General co-Chair
Purdue University, USA

Patrick Eugster
SPLASH'13 General co-Chair
Purdue University, USA

Table of Contents

Staging and Synthesis

Session Chair: Sebastian Erdweg (TU Darmstadt)

Industrial Applications

Session Chair: Yannis Smaragdakis (University of Athens)

GPCE 2013 Conference Organization

General Chair: Jaakko Järvi *(Texas A&M University, USA)*

Program Chair: Christian Kästner *(Carnegie Mellon University, USA)*

Publicity Chair: Norbert Siegmund *(Unversity of Passau, DE)*

Steering Committee Chair: Eelco Visser *(Delft University of Technology, NL)*

Steering Committee:
Bernd Fischer *(University of Stellenbosch, ZA)*
Jaakko Järvi *(Texas A&M University, USA)*
Julia Lawall *(Inria/LIP6, FR)*
Jeremy Siek *(Indiana University, USA)*
Ulrik Pagh Schultz *(University of Southern Denmark, DK)*
Eelco Visser *(Delft University of Technology, NL)*

Program Committee:
Jonathan Aldrich *(Carnegie Mellon University, USA)*
Sven Apel *(University of Passau, DE)*
Emilie Balland *(Inria, FR)*
Don Batory *(University of Texas at Austin, USA)*
Paulo Borba *(Federal University of Pernambuco, BR)*
Sebastian Erdweg *(TU Darmstadt, DE)*
Martin Erwig *(Oregon State University, USA)*
Bernd Fischer *(Stellenbosch University, ZA)*
Matthew Flatt *(University of Utah, USA)*
Mark Grechanik *(University of Illinois at Chicago, USA)*
Stefan Hanenberg *(Universität Duisburg-Essen, DE)*
Julia Lawall *(Inria/LIP6, FR)*
Marjan Mernik *(U. of Maribor, SI; U. of Alabama at Birmingham, USA)*
Emerson Murphy-Hill *(North Carolina State University, USA)*
Markus Püschel *(ETH Zürich, CH)*
Derek Rayside *(University of Waterloo, CA)*
Ina Schaefer *(Technische Universität Braunschweig, DE)*
Ulrik Pagh Schultz *(University of Southern Denmark, DK)*
Jeremy G. Siek *(Indiana University, USA)*
Yannis Smaragdakis *(University of Athens, GR)*
Tijs van der Storm *(Centrum Wiskunde & Informatica, NL)*
Walid Taha *(Halmstad University, SE)*
Eelco Visser *(Delft University of Technology, NL)*
Jan Vitek *(Purdue University, USA)*
Andrzej Wąsowski *(IT University of Copenhagen, DK)*

Additional reviewers:

Paola Accioly
Wyatt Allen
Nada Amin
Paul Anderson
Rodrigo Andrade
Suparna Bhattacharya
Goetz Botterweck
Paul Brauner
Sheng Chen
Charles Consel
Maxime Cordy
Jan Corfixen Sorensen
Robert Dyer
Nil Ergin
Prodromos Gerakios
Paolo Giarrusso
Jeff Gray
Danny Groenewegen
Torsten Hoefler
Alexandru Florin Iosif-Lazar
Deepal Jayasinghe
Gabriël D.P. Konat
Matthias Kowal

Duc Le
Joerg Liebig
Amir M Sharifloo
Jean Melo
David Naumann
Richard Paige
Helge Pfeiffer
Sebastian Proksch
Alexander von Rhein
Guido Salvaneschi
Klaus Schmid
Pierre Yves Schobbens
Sandro Schulze
Karl Smeltzer
Stefan Catalin Stanciulescu
Leopoldo Teixeira
Sam Tobin-Hochstadt
Társis Tolêdo
Vlad Vergu
Guido Wachsmuth
Eric Walkingshaw
Ben Wiedermann

Conference Organizers

General Chairs: Antony Hosking & Patrick Eugster *(Purdue University, USA)*

OOPSLA Program: Crista Lopes *(University of California, Irvine, USA)*

OOPSLA Artifacts: Matthias Hauswirth *(University of Lugano, Switzerland)*
Steve Blackburn *(Australian National University, Australia)*

Onward! Program: Robert Hirschfeld *(Hasso-Plattner-Institut Potsdam, Germany)*

Onward! Essays: Bernd Brügge *(TU München, Germany)*

Wavefront Program: Dennis Mancl *(Alcatel Lucent, USA)*

Wavefront Experience: Eduardo Guerra *(National Institute for Space Research, Brazil)*

DLS Program: Carl Friedrich Bolz *(Heinrich-Heine U Düsseldorf, Germany)*

SPLASH-E Program: Kim Bruce *(Pomona College, USA)*

SPLASH-I Program: Jan Vitek *(Purdue University, USA)*

Tutorials: Jonathan Aldrich *(Carnegie Mellon University, USA)*

Workshops: Stephanie Balzer *(Carnegie Mellon University, USA)*
Ulrik Schulz *(University of Southern Denmark)*

Panels: Steven Fraser *(Cisco, USA)*

Demonstrations: Floréal Morandat *(LaBRI, France)*
Igor Peshansky *(Google, USA)*

GPCE Chairs: Jaakko Järvi *(Texas A&M University, USA)*
Christian Kästner *(Carnegie Mellon University, USA)*

SLE Chairs: Eric Van Wyk *(University of Minnesota, USA)*
Martin Erwig *(Oregon State University, USA)*
Richard Paige *(University of York, UK)*

Posters: Emina Torlak *(University of California, Berkeley, USA)*
K. R. Jayaram *(HP Labs, USA)*

Publicity: Konstantin Beznosov *(Institute of British Columbia, Canada)*

Doctoral Symposium: Lukasz Ziarek *(SUNY Buffalo, USA)*

ACM Student Research Competition: Isil Dillig *(College of William and Mary, USA)*
Sam Guyer *(Tufts University, USA)*

Proceedings: Danny Dig *(University of Illinois Urbana-Champaign, USA)*

Web: Henry Baragar *(Instantiated Software, Canada)*
Chuck Matthews *(Fifth Generation Systems, Canada)*
Jan Havel *(Catch Exception, Czech Republic)*

Corporate Support: Jeff Foster *(University of Maryland, USA)*
Jan Vitek *(Purdue University, USA)*

Social Media: Emery Berger *(University of Massachusetts Amherst, USA)*

Local Arrangements: Rajeev Raje *(IUPUI, USA)*

Steering Committee Chairs: Crista Lopes *(University of California, Irvine, USA)*
William Cook *(University of Texas at Austin, USA)*

Conference Management: Annabel Satin *(PCK, UK)*

SPLASH INDIANAPOLIS 2013 OCTOBER 26-31

SPLASH 2013 Supporters

Diamond Supporters: Microsoft Research   NSF

Silver Supporters: CISCO   (intel) Oracle Labs

Friends: Google   IBM Research

PURDUE UNIVERSITY   Typesafe

Modeling Biology with Solver-Aided Programming Languages

Rastislav Bodik
EECS
UC Berkeley
bodik@cs.berkeley.edu

A good model of a biological cell exposes secrets of the cell's signaling mechanisms, explaining diseases and facilitating drug discovery. Modeling cells is fundamentally a programming problem --- it's programming because the model is a concurrent program that simulates the cell, and it's a problem because it is hard to write a program that reproduces all experimental observations of the cell faithfully.

In this talk, I will introduce solver-aided programming languages and show how they ease modeling biology as well as make programming accessible to non-programmers. Solver-aided languages come with constructs that delegate part of the programming problem to a constraint solver, which can be guided to synthesize parts of the program, localize its bugs, or act as a clairvoyant oracle.

I will describe our work on synthesis of stem cell models in c. elegans and then show how our framework called Rosette can rapidly implement a solver aided language in several domains, from programming by demonstration to spatial parallel programming.

Categories and Subject Descriptors

D.3.3 PROGRAMMING LANGUAGES: Language Constructs and Features; Constraints -- CSP.

Keywords

program synthesis.

GPCE '13, October 27–28, 2013, Indianapolis, Indiana, USA.
ACM 978-1-4503-2373-4/13/10.
http://dx.doi.org/10.1145/2517208.2517229

A Framework for Extensible Languages

Sebastian Erdweg

TU Darmstadt, Germany

Felix Rieger

TU Darmstadt, Germany

Abstract

Extensible programming languages such as SugarJ or Racket enable programmers to introduce customary language features as extensions of the base language. Traditionally, systems that support language extensions are either (i) agnostic to the base language or (ii) only support a single base language. In this paper, we present a framework for language extensibility that turns a non-extensible language into an extensible language featuring library-based extensible syntax, extensible static analyses, and extensible editor support. To make a language extensible, our framework only requires knowledge of the base language's grammar, the syntax for import statements (which activate extensions), and how to compile base-language programs. We have evaluated the generality of our framework by instantiating it for Java, Haskell, Prolog, JavaScript, and System F_ω, and by studying existing module-system features and their support in our framework.

Categories and Subject Descriptors D.2.11 [*Software Architectures*]: Languages; D.3.2 [*Language Classifications*]: Extensible languages; D.3.3 [*Language Constructs and Features*]: Frameworks

Keywords Macros; syntactic extensibility; compiler framework; module system; SugarJ

1. Introduction

Extensible programming languages enable programmers to introduce customary language features as language extensions of the base language. This serves two main purposes. First, a programmer can define language extensions for language constructs that are missing in the base language, such as tuples and first-class functions in Java. Second, extensible programming languages serve as an excellent base for language embedding, because the syntax, static analysis, and sometimes even the editor support of the embedded language can be realized as a language extension of the base language. This way, extensible languages combine the simplicity, composability, and base-language integration of internal DSLs with the flexibility of external DSLs [7]. To be unambiguous, when referring to extensible languages in this paper, we mean programming languages that at least provide some form of syntactic abstraction. Examples of extensible languages include Racket [14], SugarJ [10], and OCaml with camlp4 [4].

GPCE '13, October 27–28, 2013, Indianapolis, Indiana, USA.
Copyright is held by the owner/author(s). Publication rights licensed to ACM.
ACM 978-1-4503-2373-4/13/10... $15.00.
http://dx.doi.org/10.1145/2517208.2517210

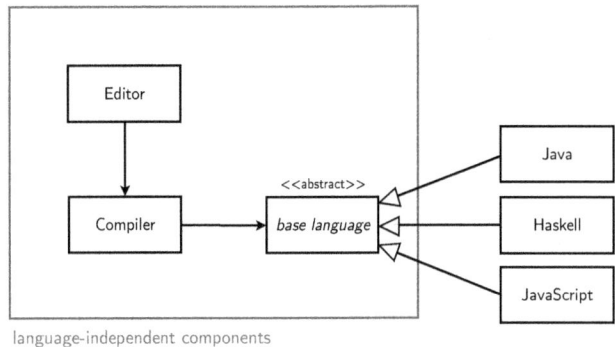

Figure 1. Architecture of the extensibility framework Sugar*.

In existing extensible languages, different techniques for syntactic abstraction have been applied. Most prominently, syntactic macros are compile-time functions that take syntactic objects as arguments and produce another syntactic object as output. Syntactic macros exist for many language, such as Scheme [5], Racket [15], C [31], Java [1, 26], Scala [2], Nemerle [24], or Haskell [23]. While the corresponding macro engines share many design decisions and implementation techniques, each system has its own implementation fully independent of the others. An alternative to syntactic macros are lexical macros, which take token sequences as input and produce another token sequence. Since lexical macros can be run before parsing takes place, the execution of lexical macros is agnostic to the base language. For example, the lexical macros of the C preprocesor (CPP) do, in fact, not depend on the C programming language and have been applied in many base languages including C++, Java, and Haskell. However, lexical macros are an unsatisfying mechanism for language extensibility since they cannot provide standard guarantees on the syntactic correctness of programs [9].

As an alternative to syntactic and lexical macros, in our prior work we proposed grammar-based language extensibility in the SugarJ programming language [10]. Instead of compile-time functions with explicit invocation syntax, SugarJ extensions extend the grammar of the base language with new productions that lead to extension-specific nodes in the abstract syntax tree (AST). In addition, a SugarJ language extension defines program transformations that transform the extension-specific parts of the AST into a base-language AST (the transformations may change base-language ASTs as well). Optionally, a SugarJ extension can define static analyses and editor services that SugarJ automatically executes. However, like existing syntactic macro systems, our implementation of SugarJ was specific to Java as a base language.

In this paper, we present Sugar*, a generalization of the SugarJ compiler as a framework for language extensibility that supports many different base languages with relatively little additional effort. To the best of our knowledge, Sugar* is the first reusable implementation for extensible languages and syntactic abstraction. The basic architecture of our framework is illustrated in Figure 1. The core innovation is the abstract component base language that abstracts from concrete base languages. Essentially, the abstract base-language component abstracts from the following aspects of the base language: the grammar and pretty printer, the syntax for import statements (which activate extensions), and how to compile programs that result from an extension's program transformations. Since only these aspects have to be provided to the framework, the implementation effort to support a new base language is low. All extension-specific tasks are handled by the framework. We refactored the original SugarJ compiler such that it only depends on the abstract base-language component, but not on any specific base language such as Java or Haskell.

One important design decision that enabled the generalization of SugarJ into Sugar* was to use metalanguages independent of the base language. Specifically, we use SDF2 [29] for the declaration of syntax, Stratego [30] for the declaration of static analyses and program transformations, and Spoofax [19] for the declaration of editor services. We reuse these metalanguages for all base languages.

We have realized our framework for language extensibility in Java. The abstract base-language component is encoded as an abstract Java class whose abstract methods must be implemented for each concrete base language. To evaluate the generality of our framework, we have developed extensible languages based on Java, Haskell, Prolog, JavaScript, and System F_ω by instantiating the framework. We furthermore conducted a study of module-system features to identify the limits of our framework. In summary, we make the following contributions:

- We present the design of an abstract base-language component that can represent many different base languages, yet is detailed enough to realize syntactic extensibility on top of it.

- We present the design and implementation of a framework for language extensibility that provides extensibility support for syntax, static analyses, and editor support for a wide range of base languages.

- We instantiate the framework to realize extensible variants of Java, Haskell, Prolog, JavaScript, and System F_ω.

- We present a study of existing module-system features and discuss to which extent our framework supports these features.

2. Source-code processing with Sugar*

The Sugar* infrastructure distinguishes five separate phases: parsing, analysis, desugaring, generation, and editing. Figure 2 shows how these phases are connected in a pipeline to form a compiler and development environment. Sugar* applies this pipeline to a source file incrementally one toplevel declaration at a time, so that import statements (which activate language extensions) can affect the parser, etc. for the rest of the file. User extensions can customize all phases except for the final code-generation phase. In this section, we briefly describe the different phases and their respective responsibilities, and how users can apply customizations. This section is important to understand the interaction between the Sugar* processing and the base-language definition.

Parsing. The parser translates a textual source file into a structured syntax tree. We employ SDF2 and its scannerless GLR parser [29], which we have extended with support for layout-sensitive syntax [11] to enable base languages such as Haskell [12]. A user can customize parsing by leveraging SDF's support for grammar composition. In particular, it is possible to provide additional productions for a nonterminal of the base language. For

example, the following SDF fragment extends the nonterminal JavaExpr from the base language Java:

```
context-free syntax
  XMLDoc -> JavaExpr {"XMLExpr"}
  XMLElem -> XMLDoc
  "<" Id Attr* "/>" -> XMLElem {"XMLEmptyElem"}
```

Sugar* composes user extensions with grammar of the base language and other extensions to obtain a parser for the composed language. This way it is possible to deeply intertwine syntax from different extensions in a single program. Accordingly, the Sugar* parser results in a syntax tree that contains nodes from the Sugar* base language and nodes specific to different extensions, such as XMLEmptyElem.

Technically, it is important that Sugar* performs incremental parsing: It parses a source file one toplevel declaration at a time. This is important because we want to change the current parser when encountering an import statement that refers to a language extension. When encountering such an import statement, we compose the imported grammar with the current grammar, regenerate a parser for the composed grammar (we use caching for performance), and continue with this parser.

Analysis. After parsing, Sugar* applies any static analyses that are defined as part of the base language. For example, for Java, we would define type checking as part of the base language. A Sugar* analysis receives the parsed syntax tree as input and is not allowed to change the structure of the parsed syntax tree; it may only add metadata to the syntax tree as annotations (illustrated by * in Figure 2). For example, the Java type checker would annotate types to expressions and variables in the syntax tree, but would not rewrite class references to fully qualified names. Such transformations can be realized in the next phase.

We use the strategic rewriting language Stratego [30] for implementing Sugar* analyses on top of syntax trees. Importantly, Stratego supports the composition of equally named rewrite rules that define alternative rewritings for some input. This allows Sugar* users to extend the analyses of the base language or to define additional ones specific to their language extension. Sugar* forwards the annotated syntax tree to the desugaring.

Desugaring. A desugaring implements the actual semantics of a user-defined language extension by translating programs of the extended syntax into programs of the base language. Like analyses, Sugar* desugarings are implemented in Stratego. The composition support of Stratego is essential for desugarings, because it allows Sugar* to compose desugarings of different extensions into a single one. Sugar* applies this composed desugaring bottom-up to the syntax tree until a fixed point is reached (rewriting strategy *innermost*). This way, Sugar* combines the semantics of different language extensions to form a single semantics for the composed extension.

Desugaring transformations can use the analysis information acquired in the previous phase (type-driven translation) and are free to translate any part of the syntax tree. This is unlike and more expressive than macros of most macro systems, which perform top-down expansion starting at the macro application. In particular, a Sugar* desugaring can also transform base-language programs, for example, to implement a custom optimization or to inject code for runtime monitoring (logging). However, whatever desugarings do, when a fixed point is reached, the resulting program may only consist of syntax-tree nodes of the Sugar* base language so that the subsequent generation phase can focus on the base language alone.

Generation. A Sugar* base-language syntax tree may describe a regular base-language program and/or a language extension. The generation phase receives such a tree and generates various artifacts

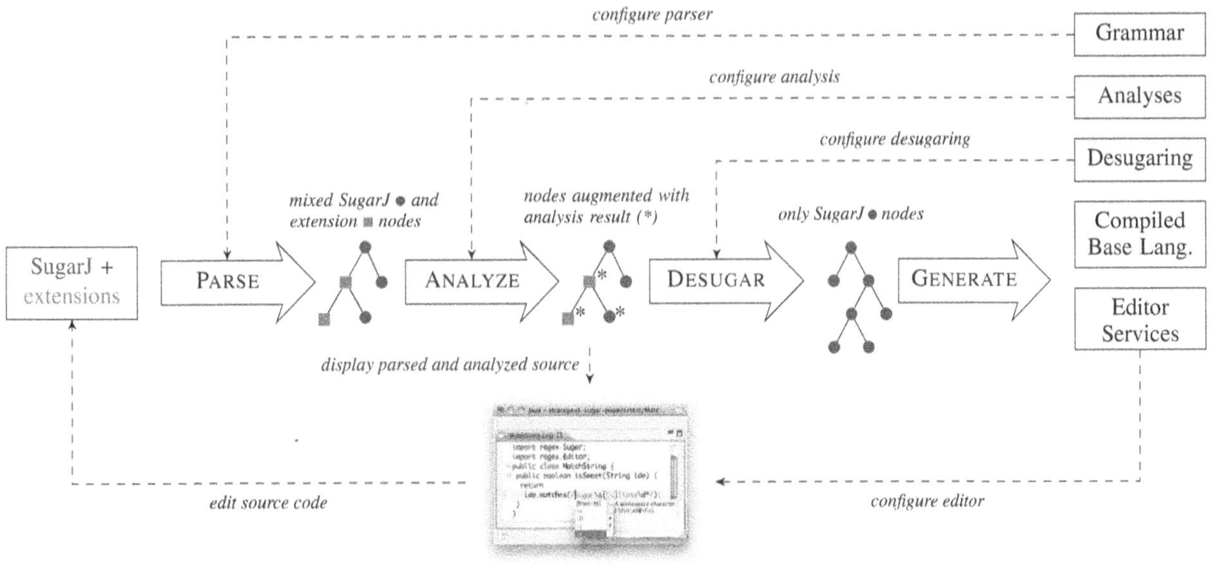

Figure 2. The SugarJ infrastructure: The result of processing is used to configure the parser, analysis, transformation, and editor.

depending on the nature of the syntax tree: If the syntax tree represents a base-language program, Sugar* calls the base-language compiler (if existent) to generate base-language binaries. For example, for Java, we call *javac* and write the corresponding *.class* files. For interpreted languages such as Prolog, we simply store the pretty-printed syntax tree for later execution. If the syntax tree represents a language extension, Sugar* generates separate artifacts for the different kind of extensions. If the extension defines an extended grammar, we generate a corresponding SDF module; if the extension defines an analysis, we generate a corresponding Stratego module; and so on. Since, at the time of writing, SDF and Stratego do not support separate compilation, we only generate pretty-printed artifacts and only call the respective compilers when we require the updated parser, analysis, or desugaring.

The generation phase is the only phase of Sugar* that is not customizable: The semantics of the base language is fixed once and for all in the definition of the base language (see next section), and the semantics of extensions is defined in terms of the base language. Thus, a customization of the generation phase is not required.

Editing. Language extensions break existing tools such as IDEs, which typically only support the unchanged base language. Sugar* builds on Spoofax [19] to automatically derive a simple Eclipse-based editor for the base language [8]. This editor can be further adapted to realize syntactic services (for example, syntax coloring, outline view, template-based code completion) and semantic services (for example, hover help or reference resolution) for the base language. Sugar* users can extend the editor support of the base language to accommodate, for example, extension-specific syntax coloring, hover help, or reference resolution. Sugar* editor services operate on the annotated syntax tree resulting from the analysis phase. Therefore, many editor services really are only concerned with the presentation of annotated information, such as showing type information in hover help or providing jump-to-definition support for resolved names.

Extension activation. Sugar* lifts a base language into an extensible language: Extensions of the lifted language can be defined *within* the lifted language itself as part of regular modules. For activating language extensions, Sugar* promotes the use of regular import statements. If an import statement refers to a module that

declares a language extension, Sugar* adapts the current parser, analysis, desugaring, and editor by reconfiguring them. However, since imports are scoped, extensions are never activated globally but at most on a file-by-file basis.

The processing of the Sugar* framework is not independent of the base language. In the following section, we describe how the Sugar* processing interacts with the base language via an abstract representation.

3. An abstract representation of base languages

To support syntactic extensibility for a large number of programming languages, we define an abstract representation of programming languages. Our abstract representation captures the features needed for language extensibility, yet is generic enough to permit the instantiation with many different base languages. We split our abstraction into two parts: a base language and a base-language processor. The former is stateless and provides methods that reveal details about the base language in general, whereas the latter is stateful and provides methods for processing a single source file. We display our abstract representation for base languages and base-language processors in Figure 3.

3.1 Base language

The abstract base-language representation IBaseLanguage provides information per language and is independent of the processing of concrete source files. However, the base language gives rise to fresh base-language processors via the method createNewProcessor. The Sugar* compiler calls this method once for each source file it compiles.

File extensions. Sugar* distinguishes three kinds of files required respective file extensions from a base-language definition: Files that contain possibly extended base-language code and extension declarations (getSugarFileExtension), files that contain desugared, plain base-language code (getBaseFileExtension), and compiled base-language source files (getBinaryFileExtension). For the last one, a base language may return **null** to indicate that the language is interpreted and no compiled files exists. As example, our Java implementation returns "sugj", "java", and "class" as file extensions, respectively.

```
public interface IBaseLanguage {
  public IBaseProcessor createNewProcessor();
  public String getLanguageName();

  public String getSugarFileExtension();
  public String getBaseFileExtension();
  public String getBinaryFileExtension();

  public Path getInitGrammar();
  public String getInitGrammarModuleName();
  public List<Path> getPackagedGrammars();
  public Path getInitTrans();
  public String getInitTransModuleName();
  public Path getInitEditor();
  public String getInitEditorModuleName();

  public boolean isImportDecl(IStrategoTerm decl);
  public boolean isExtensionDecl(IStrategoTerm decl);
  public boolean isBaseDecl(IStrategoTerm decl);
}
```

```
public interface IBaseProcessor {
  public IBaseLanguage getLanguage();
  public void init(RelativePath sourceFile, Environment env);

  public void processModuleImport(IStrategoTerm toplevelDecl);
  public List<String> processBaseDecl(IStrategoTerm decl);

  public String getNamespace();
  public String getModulePathOfImport(IStrategoTerm decl);
  public boolean isModuleExternallyResolvable(String module);

  public String getExtensionName(IStrategoTerm decl);
  public IStrategoTerm getExtensionBody(IStrategoTerm decl);

  public Path getGeneratedSourceFile();
  public String getGeneratedSource();
  public List<Path> compile(List<Path> generatedSourceFiles,
                            Path targetDir,
                            List<Path> classpath);
}
```

Figure 3. Abstract representations for base languages (stateless) and their processors (stateful: one processor per source file).

Initialization. We make few assumptions about the structure of a language's programs and no assumptions about their syntax or tooling. Instead, a base language provides its own grammar, initial transformation (desugaring and analysis), and editor declaration. These provide the initial configurations for all customizable phases in Section 2: parsing, analysis, desugaring, and editing.

The initial grammar (getInitGrammar) must point to an SDF2 module, which typically requires other, pre-packaged SDF2 modules (getPackagedGrammars). In particular, the base-language grammar must define nonterminal ToplevelDeclaration, which Sugar* uses as the start symbol to parse the next toplevel declaration as explained in Section 2. The initial grammar must include productions for the declaration of syntactic extensions. To this end, the Sugar* standard library provides a pre-defined nonterminal ExtensionElem that can be integrated into the initial grammar. For example, the SugarJ grammar contains the following production in addition to standard Java:

```
JavaMod* "extension" JavaId "{" ExtensionElem* "}"
-> ToplevelDeclaration
```

The initial transformation (getInitTrans) must point to a Stratego module. Sugar* uses Stratego for analyses and desugarings, both of which can get initially defined here by implementing Stratego strategies start-analysis and desugar, respectively. In contrast to SDF2, Stratego modules do not occur pre-packaged, so that this additional method is only required for grammars.

Finally, the initial editor (getInitEditor) must point to a Spoofax editor-service module. This way, a base language can specify standard editor services such as syntax coloring or code completion. The user of the extensible language later can extend the initial grammar, transformation, and editor with custom rules.

AST predicates. Sugar* distinguishes only three kinds of toplevel declarations: import statements, extension declarations, and base-language declarations. These declarations have an abstract syntax that is specific to the base language. For example, import statements in Java look different from module-use statements in Prolog. Accordingly, we require the base language to provide predicates that allow us to distinguish imports, extensions, and base-language declarations. The AST predicates are used as the first step of the generation phase described in Section 2.

Importantly, the Sugar* compiler fully handles the processing and activation of extensions as well as the resolution and sub-compilation of imported modules. For handling language-specific declarations such as a Java package, a Java class, a Haskell module header, or a Haskell module body, our compiler uses the base-language processor.

3.2 Base-language processor

The abstract base-language processor IBaseProcessor provides methods for source-file handling specific to the base language. A base-language processor is a stateful component that, in particular, is used to accumulate desugared source-file fragments during compilation of a sugared file. The Sugar* compiler acquires and uses exactly one base-language processor per source file and initializes it (init) with the path to the sugared source file and the compiler's environment. The environment contains common information such as the source path or the include path.

Base-language processing. In case the Sugar* compiler encounters a base-language declaration or an import statement that refers to another base-language module, the compiler requires the base-language processor to handle them (processModuleImport and processBaseDecl). Typically, these methods just pretty-print the abstract declaration term and store it until the source file is completely processed and the base-language compilation is triggered.

Our design permits a base-language declaration to establish further module dependencies. For example, a Java class can contain qualified names to that reference external classes or a Scala declaration can contain nested import statements. For this reason, processBaseDec yields a (possibly empty) list of additional module dependencies. Our compiler ensures that these additional dependencies are satisfied and, if needed, compiles the corresponding source files first.

Namespace. The Sugar* compiler requires base-language support for correctly treating the base-language's namespace. Generally, we assume that modules are organized in a hierarchical namespace that follows the file/directory structure. However, a base language can customize this behavior by providing non-standard implementations of getNamespace and getModulePathOfImport.

The compiler calls getNamespace to retrieve the namespace of the currently processed source file. In languages with hierarchical module systems that reflect the file/directory structure like Java or Haskell, getNamespace returns the directory path of the source file

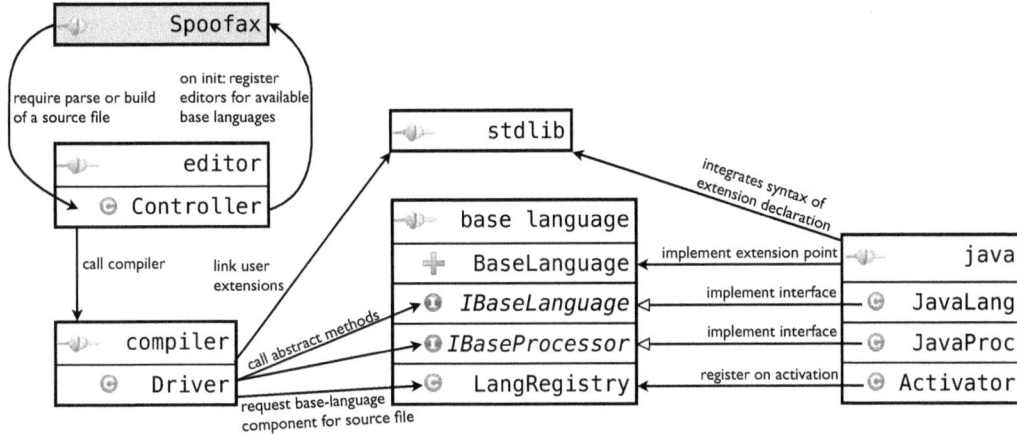

Figure 4. Detailed architecture of the extensibility framework Sugar*: OSGi modules ⇥, classes ◉, interfaces ❶, extension points ✛.

relative to the root location of source files. In contrast, a language with a flat namespace returns the empty string or a constant string.

Conversely, to locate imported modules, the Sugar* compiler queries the base-language processor to retrieve the module path referred to by an import statement (getModulePathOfImport). Depending on the nature of the base-language module system, the returned path may reflect the hierarchical namespace. Our compiler will try to locate binaries, extensions, and source files of the returned module path. If this fails, the compiler would usually mark an illegal import statement. However, some languages like Haskell employ a package manager to resolve imported modules if no source/binary artifact exists. To allow for such module resolution, our compiler checks with the base-language processor if a module is externally resolvable (isModuleExternallyResolvable). We treat an import of an externally resolvable module just like an import of a pre-compiled base-language module.

Extensions. Sugar* handles all aspects of extensions independent of the base language. The only assistance the compiler needs, is to extract the name (getExtensionName) and the body (getExtensionBody) of an extension from its abstract-syntax representation, which may be base-language specific. For example, language extensions in Java occur in their own **public extension** declaration, whereas SugarHaskell extensions are regular modules containing grammar, transformation, and editor artifacts.

Generation. After processing all toplevel declarations of a source file, the Sugar* compiler queries the base-language processor for the generated base-language source code as a string (getGeneratedSource) and the path of a file into which the generated source code should be written. Typically, a base-language processor simply returns a concatenation of the pretty-printed, desugared toplevel declarations.

Finally, a base-language processor must define a method for compiling base-language source files (compile). This method receives a list of base-language source files that should be compiled, a target directory for the compiler output, and a classpath. The method receives a list of source files because the Sugar* compiler automatically detects cyclic imports. For each cycle, the compile method is only called once with all modules of the cycle as argument. This way, the base-language compiler can treat the cycle appropriately, for example, by rejecting it.

4. Technical realization of Sugar*

To realize Sugar*, we significantly reengineered the original SugarJ compiler at different levels. First, we introduced the abstract base-language component from the previous section as a level of indirection to parameterize the compiler over different base languages. Second, we used OSGi [21] to impose a large-scale module structure that separates the compiler, the editor, and the different base languages into separate but interdependent modules. Finally, we employed Eclipse extension points [17] to realize a central language registry that eliminates the dependency from the compiler to the concrete base languages. The final architecture is shown in Figure 4, which is a detailed version of the overview shown in Figure 1.

Parameterizing the compiler. The original SugarJ compiler incorporated specific knowledge about Java in various places. For example, it required a Java grammar to build the initial SugarJ grammar, it did a case distinction over different kinds of Java AST nodes, and it called the Java compiler to compile desugared programs. At all such places, we changed the implementation to call a corresponding method from the abstract base-language component BaseLang instead of using the Java-specific code. Simultaneously, we moved the old Java-specific code into a class JavaLang that instantiates BaseLang. After refactoring, we can use the refactored compiler and the extracted language component JavaLang to compile SugarJ files by instantiating the compiler with JavaLang: Driver.compile(**new** JavaLang(), sourceFile).

Imposing modules. Our framework should permit adding additional base languages independent of the compiler implementation. To this end, we decomposed the different artifacts of Sugar* into OSGi modules as follows:

editor: Operates as a bridge between the compiler of Sugar* and the Spoofax Eclipse plugin. In particular, registers the file-name extensions of available Sugar* languages with Spoofax and receives corresponding parse requests and compilation requests.

compiler: Contains classes that realize the processing explained in Section 2. In particular, the compiler contains code to build and execute the user-defined parsers and desugarings. Since the compiler has no dependency on the editor, it is possible to apply the Sugar* compiler as a batch compiler without a supporting editor.

stdlib: Contains the grammars of the metalanguages used by Sugar*: SDF2, Stratego, and Spoofax editor services. For defin-

SugarJ	SugarHaskell	SugarProlog	SugarJS	SugarFomega
| ```
package test;
import foo.Foo;
public sugar Bar {
  syntax
    A -> B {"Cons"}
}
``` | ```
module test.Bar
import foo.Foo

syntax
  A -> B {"Cons"}
``` | ```
:- sugar_module(test/Bar).
:- use_module(foo/Foo).

:- syntax
   A -> B {"Cons"} .
``` | ```
module test/Bar
import foo/Foo
sugar {
  syntax
    A -> B {"Cons"}
}
``` | ```
module test.Bar
import foo.Foo

syntax
  A -> B {"Cons"}
``` |

Figure 5. Extension declarations in different instantiations of Sugar*.

ing an extensible base language, developers mix these metalanguages with their base-language grammar. The standard library furthermore defines some commonly used Stratego operations, such as functions for performing analysis and annotating the result in a syntax tree. The compiler links extensions defined by the user against the standard library.

base language: Contains the abstract base-language component and the language registry. This module is used by the compiler and refined by concrete base languages.

concrete base language (java, etc.): Extends the abstract base-language component and, in particular, defines an initial grammar, an initial desugaring, and initial editor services for the extensible variant of the base language.

Language registry. OSGi employs a lazy activation policy of modules to minimize the number of loaded modules: A module is only loaded when the first class of this module is required [21]. Since the compiler of Sugar* should be independent of concrete base-language implementations, the compiler does not refer to any class from a base-language module. Thus, no base-language module would ever be activated by OSGi.

To circumvent this problem, we define an Eclipse *extension point* [17] and use Eclipse's *buddy policy* [17] to activate all concrete base-language modules whenever the abstract base-language module is activated. On activation, concrete base-language modules register themselves with the language registry. The compiler queries this language registry to receive a base-language component. This way, we achieve the decoupling of compiler and base languages:

1. The compiler can process any source file for which a base-language module is available.

2. The compiler is defined fully independently of any concrete base-language module.

5. Evaluation: SugarJ, SugarHaskell, SugarProlog, SugarJS, SugarFomega

To evaluate the generality of Sugar*, we instantiated the Sugar* framework by developing 5 extensible languages based on Java [10], Haskell [12], Prolog [22], JavaScript[1], and System F_ω [20]. Despite the significant difference between these languages regarding their syntax, semantics, and building, Sugar* successfully accommodates each of them. More yet, the design of Sugar* provides sufficient freedom for base languages to allow the integration of extensibility in a way that feels native to the language. For example, in Figure 5 we illustrate extension declarations in all 5 extensible languages we developed. Notably, for Java, Haskell, and Prolog we use standard-like module headers and import statements, and integrate extensibility declarations in a natural way. SugarJS and SugarFomega were implemented by others to provide extensibility for JavaScript and System F_ω, respectively. Since JavaScript and

System F_ω do not have a standard module system, the respective developers designed a module system themselves. For example, the module system of SugarFomega syntactically resembles the module system of Haskell.

To realize an extensible variant of a base language, the interfaces presented in Section 3 had to be implemented. Specifically, for each base language, we defined or reused the following artifacts:

- A grammar of the pure base language specified with SDF2 [29].

- An SDF2 grammar module that integrates extension declarations (nonterminal ExtensionElem) into the base language and defines nonterminal ToplevelDeclaration for the base language. This module can serve as initial grammar.

- A Spoofax module that defines the initial editor services for the base language.

- An instance of IBaseLanguage.

- An instance of IBaseProcessor.

Except for Java, we did not define any initial transformations.

To illustrate the implementation of an extensible language with Sugar*, we present the relevant details of the SugarHaskell implementation. The SugarHaskell grammar is defined as follows:

```
module org/sugarj/languages/SugarHaskell
imports org/sugarj/languages/Haskell
        org/sugarj/languages/Sugar
exports context-free syntax
  ModuleDec          -> ToplevelDeclaration
  OffsideImportdecl  -> ToplevelDeclaration
  OffsideTopdeclList -> ToplevelDeclaration {cons("HSBody")}
  ExtensionElem+     -> ToplevelDeclaration {cons("ExtBody")}
```

This grammar defines the ToplevelDeclaration nonterminal by forwarding existing definitions for Haskell modules, Haskell imports, and Haskell toplevel declarations from the Haskell grammar org/sugarj/languages/Haskell and extension declarations from the grammar org/sugarj/languages/Sugar, that comes with the standard library of Sugar*. In Figure 6, we sketch the implementation of IBaseLanguage and IBaseProcessor for SugarHaskell using pseudo code.

The implementation shows that HaskellLanguage is stateless and simply functions as a body of knowledge about SugarHaskell. In contrast, HaskellProcessor stores the namespace and module name of the currently processed source file and accumulates the desugared source code when processModuleImport or processBaseDecl is called. For this, HaskellProcessor uses a pretty printer, which we generated from the Haskell base grammar (not shown). To check for externally resolvable modules, we call on the GHC packet manager ghc-pkg. Finally, compile runs the standard GHC compiler on the list of desugared files.

Implementation effort. As the implementation in Figure 6 indicates, the implementation effort for realizing an extensible variant of base language is modest using our framework. In Table 1, we summarize the source lines of code (SLOC: excluding empty

---

[1] https://github.com/bobd91/sugarjs/

8
```

```
public class HaskellLanguage implements IBaseLanguage {
  name = "Haskell"
  sugarFileExtension = "shs"
  baseFileExtension = "hs"
  binaryFileExtension = "o"
  initGram = Path("org/sugarj/languages/SugarHaskell.sdf")
  initTrans = Path("org/sugarj/languages/SugarHaskell.str")
  initEditor = Path("org/sugar/languages/SugarHaskell.serv")
  isImportDecl(x) = x.nodeName == "Import"
  isExtensionDecl(x) = x.nodeName == "ExtBody"
  isBaseDecl(x) = x.nodeName == "ModuleDec"
              || x.nodeName == "HSBody"
}
```

```
public class HaskellProcessor implements IBaseProcessor {
  var namespace; var moduleName; var source = ""
  processModuleImport(t) = source += prettyPrint(t)
  processBaseDecl(t) =
    source += prettyPrint(t)
    if t.nodeName == "ModuleDec"
      (namespace, moduleName) = splitName(prettyPrint(t))
    return [ ]
  modulePathofImport(t) = prettyPrint(t.subterm(1))
  isExternallyResolvable(s) = exec "ghc-pkg find-module $s"
  extensionName(t) = moduleName
  extensionBody(t) = t.subterm(1)
  genSourceFile = Path("$BIN/$namespace/$moduleName.hs")
  genSource = source
  compile(files, target, cp) =
    exec "ghc -outputdir $target -i $cp $files"
}
```

Figure 6. Instantiation of Sugar* for SugarHaskell.

	Base Grammar	Initial Grammar	IBase Language	IBase Processor
Java	1164	52	113	182
Haskell	923	10	92	168
Prolog	266	26	93	140
JavaScript	542	39	88	149
System F_ω	163	39	94	123

Table 1. SLOC for realizing extensible languages with Sugar*.

Feature	Base	Extensions
Flat namespace	●	●
Hierarchical namespace	●	●
Nested modules	●	○
First-class modules	●	○
External module management	●	○
Lexical imports	●	n/a
Qualified names	●	○
Selective import/renaming	●	○
Module reexport	●	◐
Nested imports	●	○
Cyclic imports	●	○
Dynamic module loading	●	○
Global compilation	◐	○
Incremental compilation	●	●
Separate compilation	◐	○
Interpreted	●	n/a

Table 2. Module system features and their support in Sugar*.

lines and comments) that were necessary to realize the different languages. As the table shows, the implementation effort per language is low. For all languages we considered, most effort actually had to be spent in developing a grammar for the base language. In particular for syntactically more complex languages like Java, Haskell, or JavaScript, developing a grammar for the base language is comparably laborious. The implementation of a new base language involves additional artifacts, such as constructor signatures, a pretty-printer, and static analyses for the base language.

This data suggests that the abstraction we designed for representing base languages is adequate in the sense that the instantiation is straight-forward and does not require involved coding. Especially, if one considers the boilerplate imposed by Java even for implementing simple functions, as opposed to the more concise pseudo-code implementation of Figure 6. Note that the numbers shown in Table 1 do not include the definition of a pretty-printer, which can be generically derived from the base-language grammar [3, 28]. Furthermore, we did not count the effort for developing static analyses of the base language since running these analyses inside Sugar* is optional and can be left to the base-language compiler. However, a reimplementation of base-language analyses in Stratego is required if they should be extended inside Sugar*.

In summary, Sugar* enables a full-fledged extensible language with little effort. The extensible language supports extensible syntax, extensible static analyses, extensible desugarings, and an extensible IDE. Moreover, even without any actual language extension, a base language realized with Sugar* already benefits from the dependency management of the Sugar* compiler and from the Spoofax-based Eclipse plugin that we provide [8, 19]. To show the generality of Sugar*, we successfully instantiated Sugar* with 5 base languages that employ diverse module-system features. In the subsequent section, we present a more general study of module-system features and their support in Sugar*.

6. A study of module-system features

We developed a framework for adding syntactic extensibility to existing programming languages. In our design of Sugar*, our main goal was generality: We want to support as many base languages as possible. Since Sugar* is largely module-driven (modules encapsulate extensions and extensions are activated through import statements), a deciding factor in the generality of Sugar* is whether it is possible to encode the module system of the base language as implementations of the interfaces IBaseLanguage and IBaseProcessor shown in Section 3. To better understand the generality of Sugar*, we investigate a subset of the module-system features of mainstream programming languages and discuss their support in Sugar*.

Table 2 gives an overview of the module-system features we studied. We distinguish whether Sugar* supports a module-system feature for base-language modules and whether it supports a feature for modules containing extension declarations. In the following, we describe the studied module-system features, name example languages that support the features, and discuss their support in Sugar* in detail.

Namespace (Flat: Prolog; Hierarchical: Haskell, Java): A module system's namespace can be either flat or hierarchical. In a flat namespace, modules only have a name that identifies them. In a hierarchical namespace, modules are organized in a hierarchical structure and are identified by their name and their path through this hierarchy. Sugar* was originally designed to support a base language with hierarchical namespaces (Java) for both language and extension modules. In our generalization, we retained this feature through method getModulePathOfImport of interface IBaseProcessor. This method takes the syntax tree of an import statement and returns a relative *path* to the referenced module. A flat namespace can be modeled as hierarchical namespaces with an empty path prefix.

Nested modules (Java, Scala): Nested modules are submodules of a module which are defined in a module's body itself. Sugar* supports nested base-language modules as they do not expose any dependency to additional source files and can be fully handled by processBaseDecl. Since a nested module may be compiled to a separate binary (as is the case in Java and Scala), method compile returns a list of all generated files, which enables Sugar* to keep track of them and initiate a recompilation when necessary. However, we do not support extension declarations as nested modules, since we have no means of extracting the extension declaration from the outer module. Thus, extensions can only be declared as toplevel declarations.

First-class modules (Python, ML, Newspeak): First-class modules are modules that can be created dynamically, manipulated, and passed around as first-class values of the language. Similar to nested modules, we support first-class base-language modules, since they can be fully handled by processBaseDecl. Extensions cannot be declared in first-class modules since we cannot extract the extension declaration and we require extension declarations statically for parsing source code that uses the extension.

External module management (Haskell): External module management is a feature that some programming languages support to load pre-installed modules from external locations. An external location in this sense is any location outside the sourcepath and classpath used for compilation. For example, the Glasgow Haskell Compiler (ghc) looks up pre-installed modules in a package manager. We support external module management for base modules through method isModuleExternallyResolvable. However, externally resolved modules cannot define extension declarations, as we need to actually load and process extension declarations but we have no way of requesting the extension declaration from the external location.

Lexical imports (C, C++, Ruby): A lexical import inserts the source code of the imported module literally into the source file where the import occurs. The method processModuleImport in our interface is concerned with handling module imports. Implementations of a base language can choose to implement lexical import behavior for the base language, since we do not require that an import statement itself occurs in the final generated source code provided by getGeneratedSource. Lexical imports are not applicable for extensions, since an import of an extension declaration has a fixed semantics in Sugar*, namely to activate the extension in the scope of the importing module.

Qualified names (Java, Scala): Qualified names allow using members of a module without explicitly importing the containing module. For example, in Java this is accomplished by providing the hierarchical path to the module and the name of the member. Sugar* supports qualified names for base modules even though this entails dependencies to additional source files. To this end, method processBaseDecl returns a list of paths to additional module dependencies that occurred in the base declaration. For Java, processBaseDecl returns a list of all modules accessed through qualified names in the base declaration. We do not support qualified names for extension modules, as dependencies to extension declarations have to be explicit via import statements.

Selective import/renaming (Haskell, Prolog, Scala): A selective import allows to select which members are imported from a module. Renaming allows such members to be locally renamed. We support selective imports and renaming for base language modules, because we are only interested in the module dependency and allow method getModulePathOfImport to extract the path to the module from arbitrarily complex import statements. The selection and renaming of module members can be either realized by method processBaseDecl or simply forwarded to the base-language compiler. We do not support import selection/renaming for extension modules. Importing an extension will always bring the full extension into scope. We plan to investigate more fine-grained extension activation in our future work.

Module reexport (Haskell, Prolog): A reexport statement allows to export module members that have been imported from other modules. This way a module can collect and package functionality from multiple modules into a single module. We support module reexports for base-language modules, which can be handled as a standard base-language declaration by method processBaseDecl. We do not support customizable reexport of extension modules. Instead, an extension is never reexported by a base-language module, and an extension is always reexported by an extension module. Technically, the latter is due to transitive imports in the metalanguages SDF, Stratego, and Spoofax editor specifications, which underlie Sugar*.

Nested imports (Scala): A nested import is an import that occurs nested inside a code block. Specifically, a nested import is not a toplevel declaration. While Sugar* has special support for handling toplevel import statements, we also support nested imports for base-language modules. In principle, these nested imports can be handled by method processBaseDecl. However, since we want to keep track of module dependencies, we require processBaseDecl to provide a list of additional module dependencies, so that Sugar* can ensure these dependencies are resolvable and can initiate the compilation of the required modules. We do not support nested imports for extensions, when method processBaseDecl is called, the base declaration has already been parsed, analyzed, and desugared. Hence, it is too late for activating any language extension.

Cyclic imports (Java): Cyclic imports occur when two or more modules require features from each other so that a cyclic dependency graph is imposed. Cyclic imports are relevant for the Sugar* compiler because they essentially prevent incremental or separate compilation: In order to compile modules with cyclic dependencies, all involved modules have to be processed simultaneously. Sugar* supports cyclic dependencies of base-language modules by detecting cyclic dependencies and forwarding minimal strongly connected components to the method compile of interface IBaseProcessor. We do not support cyclic dependencies for language extensions, because the compilation of these extensions would depend on themselves, which is a circular definition.

Dynamic module loading (Python, Java): Languages that support dynamic module loading provide facilities for loading a module at runtime of a program. Accordingly, these module dependencies are not resolved statically at Sugar* compile time, but when the compiled program is executed. For example, Python resolves imports at runtime, which can be used to realize conditional import depending on some runtime computation. In Java, a class loader enables the dynamic loading of pre-compiled modules at runtime. We support base languages that feature dynamic loading of modules, because they do not influence compilation and no dependency tracking is necessary: The binary of a module does not change when a dynamically loaded module changes. We do not support dynamic loading of extension modules, as an extension influences the static parts of language processing: parsing, static analysis, desugaring, and editor support.

Global compilation (Stratego): Global compilation simultaneously processes all modules of a program. For example, Stratego collects all source modules and weaves them into a single module before continuing code generation. Sugar* partially supports global compilation of base-language source modules, because we do not enforce the compilation of single modules. However, Sugar* lacks a mechanism for adding a global-compilation phase after all modules have been processed. We will investigate better support for global compilation as described below for separate compilation. For language extensions, we do not support global compilation, since extensions have to be compiled before they can be used.

Incremental compilation (Java, Haskell): Incremental compilation first processes all imported modules before processing the a module itself. Sugar* supports incremental compilation for both base-language modules and extensions. In particular, Sugar* keeps track of module dependencies to initiate recompilation whenever a required module changes.

Separate compilation (C): Separate compilation processes source modules independently from each other by only relying on the interfaces of required modules. For example, a C source file typically does not import any other C source files but only header files from other modules. The C compiler compiles each source module independently and links the resulting binaries. Sugar* partially supports separate compilation, because method compile is free to compile modules that do not require other source modules. However, like for global compilation, Sugar* currently lacks a post-processing phase that could be used to collect all compiled modules and call the linker. In a sense, such global linking contradicts the modular extension-activation nature that Sugar* promotes. However, it would be possible to include some sort of *linker module* in a base language with the mere purpose of connecting otherwise unrelated modules. The method compile could implement a special handling for linker modules that initiates global compilation or linking for all required modules. This way we would circumvent the global nature of global compilation and would not require a closed world assumption. We will investigate this as part of our future work. For language extensions, we do not support separate compilation, since this would require an interface for the extensions against which clients of the extension can be compiled. Our extensions do not possess an interface useful for that purpose.

Interpreted (Ruby, Prolog): In interpreted languages, a module is not compiled but stored as source code for later execution. We support this feature by declaring method getBinaryFileExtension from interface IBaseLanguage as being optional and by allowing method compile to simply do nothing.

Summary. As our study of module-system features shows, Sugar* is able to support a large range of module-system features. This means that many base languages can be made extensible by instantiating Sugar*. However, for extension modules we are currently much more restrictive. To emphasize this difference, for some instantiations of Sugar* it would make sense to distinguish statements for base-language import from statements for extension import syntactically, for example using different keywords. In our future work, we want to investigate support base languages that use global or separate compilation as well as more flexible usage of extension modules.

7. Related work

Existing systems for syntactic abstraction typically fall into one of two categories: Either a system only supports a single base language, or it supports multiple base languages but is agnostic to the base language.

A prominent example of the first category are Scheme macros [5]. Scheme macros provide syntactic abstraction via compile-time functions that operator on abstract syntax trees. While the conceptual idea has been transferred to many base languages, the implementation of the Scheme macro system only supports Scheme as a base language. One of the reasons is that Scheme itself is used for implementing writing transformations of abstract syntax trees. In contrast, Sugar* employs metalanguages SDF, Stratego, and Spoofax editor specifications that are independent of the base language.

A prominent example of the second category is the C preprocessor (CPP) [25]. CPP supports the definition of lexical macros (#define) and compile-time conditionals (#ifdef). CPP supports multiple base languages; for example, it has been successfully applied in C, Java, and Haskell. However, CPP is agnostic to the base language. CPP operates on a stream of lexical tokens and is completely oblivious to the syntactic structure of the source code. In contrast, we require the definition of a parser for the base language and our transformations operate on abstract syntax trees of the base language.

Also most existing language workbenches fall into the second category. A language workbench [13, 16] is a tool that facilitates the definition of languages. While a language workbench allows the definition of multiple languages, the language workbench itself is agnostic to the actual workings of the defined language. Any language-specific functionality needs to be defined as part of the language definition itself, and the language workbench simply executes this functionality. In contrast, Sugar* has internal compilation logic that resolves modules of the base language, ensures sound recompilation schemes, and extracts and activates base-language extensions according to extension declarations and extension imports.

Polymorphic embedding [18] of domain-specific languages defines the notion of a language interface, but with a different meaning. In polymorphic embedding, the language interface declares the operators of the language and is parametric over the semantic domain that these operators result in. This allows the implementation of different semantics for a single language interface. In contrast, the language interface of Sugar* abstracts over the syntax and semantics of *different* base languages, where each base language is a separate instantiation of this interface.

Racket [14] allows the implementation of custom programming languages on top of Racket. Languages are defined as libraries [27]. They can later be used by using the #lang statement at the top of a source file. In Racket, the internal representation of each programming language is identical. The implementation of a language needs to provide a transformation that takes the source code as an input and outputs a transformed representation in Racket's internal language. Sugar* does not have an internal representation of programs written in a base language. Instead, the Sugar* compiler only interacts with the base language's module system and compiler via interfaces IBaseLanguage and IBaseProcessor.

Xbase [6] is a generic expression language for programming languages written using Xtext. Xbase abstracts over programming languages by offering a language-independent representation of expressions. We chose a different abstraction approach for Sugar* by offering a language-independent language-extension mechanism and compiler.

8. Conclusion

We presented Sugar*, a framework for syntactic language extensibility. Sugar* leverages the module system of the base language to encapsulate extensions as modules and to activate extensions via module import statements. To support language extensibility for many different base languages, we designed an abstract base-language representation that provides sufficient information for tracking module dependency and for activating language extensions. Simultaneously, our abstract base-language representation is highly versatile and supports base languages with many different module-system features. To the best of our knowledge, Sugar* is the first system that supports syntactic language extensibility for a wide range of languages.

Acknowledgments

We are grateful to Florian Lorenzen for the development of SugarFomega and Bob Davison for the development of SugarJS. We thank the anonymous reviewers for their helpful remarks.

References

[1] J. Bachrach and K. Playford. The Java syntactic extender (JSE). In *Proceedings of Conference on Object-Oriented Programming, Systems, Languages, and Applications (OOPSLA)*, pages 31–42. ACM, 2001.

[2] E. Burmako. Scala macros: Let our powers combine! In *Scala Workshop*, 2013. to appear.

[3] M. de Jonge. A pretty-printer for every occasion. In *Proceedings of Symposium on Constructing Software Engineering Tools (CoSET)*, pages 68–77, 2000.

[4] D. de Rauglaudre. Camlp4 reference manual. http://caml.inria.fr/pub/docs/manual-camlp4/index.html, accessed Mar. 26 2013, 2003.

[5] R. K. Dybvig, R. Hieb, and C. Bruggeman. Syntactic abstraction in scheme. *Lisp and Symbolic Computation*, 5(4):295–326, 1992.

[6] S. Efftinge, M. Eysholdt, J. Köhnlein, S. Zarnekow, R. von Massow, W. Hasselbring, and M. Hanus. Xbase: implementing domain-specific languages for java. In *Proceedings of Conference on Generative Programming and Component Engineering (GPCE)*, pages 112–121. ACM, 2012.

[7] S. Erdweg. *Extensible Languages for Flexible and Principled Domain Abstraction*. PhD thesis, Philipps-Universiät Marburg, 2013.

[8] S. Erdweg, L. C. L. Kats, T. Rendel, C. Kästner, K. Ostermann, and E. Visser. Growing a language environment with editor libraries. In *Proceedings of Conference on Generative Programming and Component Engineering (GPCE)*, pages 167–176. ACM, 2011.

[9] S. Erdweg and K. Ostermann. Featherweight TeX and parser correctness. In *Proceedings of Conference on Software Language Engineering (SLE)*, volume 6563 of *LNCS*, pages 397–416. Springer, 2010.

[10] S. Erdweg, T. Rendel, C. Kästner, and K. Ostermann. SugarJ: Library-based syntactic language extensibility. In *Proceedings of Conference on Object-Oriented Programming, Systems, Languages, and Applications (OOPSLA)*, pages 391–406. ACM, 2011.

[11] S. Erdweg, T. Rendel, C. Kästner, and K. Ostermann. Layout-sensitive generalized parsing. In *Proceedings of Conference on Software Language Engineering (SLE)*, volume 7745 of *LNCS*, pages 244–263. Springer, 2012.

[12] S. Erdweg, F. Rieger, T. Rendel, and K. Ostermann. Layout-sensitive language extensibility with SugarHaskell. In *Proceedings of Haskell Symposium*, pages 149–160. ACM, 2012.

[13] S. Erdweg, T. van der Storm, M. Völter, M. Boersma, R. Bosman, W. R. Cook, A. Gerritsen, A. Hulshout, S. Kelly, A. Loh, G. Konat, P. J. Molina, M. Palatnik, R. Pohjonen, E. Schindler, K. Schindler, R. Solmi, V. Vergu, E. Visser, K. van der Vlist, G. Wachsmuth, and J. van der Woning. The state of the art in language workbenches. In *SLE*, 2013. to appear.

[14] M. Flatt. Creating languages in Racket. *Communication of the ACM*, 55(1):48–56, 2012.

[15] M. Flatt, R. Culpepper, D. Darais, and R. B. Findler. Macros that work together—Compile-time bindings, partial expansion, and definition contexts. *Functional Programming*, 22(2):181–216, 2012.

[16] M. Fowler. Language workbenches: The killer-app for domain specific languages? Available at http://martinfowler.com/articles/languageWorkbench.html, 2005.

[17] O. Gruber, B. J. Hargrave, J. McAffer, P. Rapicault, and T. Watson. The Eclipse 3.0 platform: Adopting OSGi technology. *IBM Systems Journal*, 44(2):289–300, 2005.

[18] C. Hofer, K. Ostermann, T. Rendel, and A. Moors. Polymorphic embedding of DSLs. In *Proceedings of Conference on Generative Programming and Component Engineering (GPCE)*, pages 137–148. ACM, 2008.

[19] L. C. L. Kats and E. Visser. The Spoofax language workbench: Rules for declarative specification of languages and IDEs. In *Proceedings of Conference on Object-Oriented Programming, Systems, Languages, and Applications (OOPSLA)*, pages 444–463. ACM, 2010.

[20] F. Lorenzen and S. Erdweg. Modular and automated type-soundness verification for language extensions. In *Proceedings of International Conference on Functional Programming (ICFP)*, 2013. to appear.

[21] OSGi Alliance. Osgi core release 5, 2012.

[22] F. Rieger. A language-independent framework for syntactic extensibility. Bachelor's Thesis, University of Marburg, June 2012.

[23] T. Sheard and S. Peyton Jones. Template meta-programming for Haskell. In *Proceedings of Haskell Workshop*, pages 1–16. ACM, 2002.

[24] K. Skalski, M. Moskal, and P. Olszta. Meta-programming in nemerle. http://nemerle.org/metaprogramming.pdf, accessed Oct. 01 2012., 2004.

[25] R. Stallman and Z. Weinberg. The C Preprocessor. Available at http://gcc.gnu.org/onlinedocs/cpp/, accessed Nov. 08, 2012., 1987.

[26] M. Tatsubori, S. Chiba, M.-O. Killijian, and K. Itano. OpenJava: A class-based macro system for Java. In *Proceedings of Workshop on Reflection and Software Engineering*, volume 1826 of *LNCS*, pages 117–133. Springer, 2000.

[27] S. Tobin-Hochstadt, V. St-Amour, R. Culpepper, M. Flatt, and M. Felleisen. Languages as libraries. In *Proceedings of Conference on Programming Language Design and Implementation (PLDI)*, pages 132–141. ACM, 2011.

[28] M. van den Brand and E. Visser. Generation of formatters for context-free languages. *Transactions on Software Engineering Methodology (TOSEM)*, 5(1):1–41, 1996.

[29] E. Visser. *Syntax Definition for Language Prototyping*. PhD thesis, University of Amsterdam, 1997.

[30] E. Visser, Z.-E.-A. Benaissa, and A. P. Tolmach. Building program optimizers with rewriting strategies. In *Proceedings of International Conference on Functional Programming (ICFP)*, pages 13–26. ACM, 1998.

[31] D. Weise and R. F. Crew. Programmable syntax macros. In *Proceedings of Conference on Programming Language Design and Implementation (PLDI)*, pages 156–165. ACM, 1993.

Submodules in Racket

You Want it *When*, Again?

Matthew Flatt

PLT and University of Utah
mflatt@cs.utah.edu

Abstract

In an extensible programming language, programmers write code that must run at different times—in particular, at compile time versus run time. The module system of the Racket programming language enables a programmer to reason about programs in the face of such extensibility, because the distinction between run-time and compile-time phases is built into the language model. *Submodules* extend Racket's module system to make the phase-separation facet of the language extensible. That is, submodules give programmers the capability to define new phases, such as "test time" or "documentation time," with the same reasoning and code-management benefits as the built-in distinction between run time and compile time.

Categories and Subject Descriptors D.3.3 [*Programming Languages*]: Language Constructs and Features

Keywords Macros, modules, language tower

1. Introduction

Racket's module system is similar to the module systems of other languages. Modules are static, they reside in a global namespace with hierarchical names, and they statically declare their dependencies on other modules. These properties of the module system simplify compilation and linking tasks; for example, the `raco make` tool can traverse and compile the dependencies of a program as needed, and `raco exe` can combine all needed modules into a single executable.

A distinguishing feature of Racket's module system is the way that it interacts with macro-based "languages." Each module explicitly declares its language, so that different modules in the same program can have different syntaxes or different semantics for a given syntactic form. Such languages are implemented by macros via arbitrary Racket code that runs at compile time, and the module-and-macro system ensures that run-time and compile-time evaluation are kept separate (Flatt 2002). The separation of run time from compile time enables compilation, analysis, and reasoning about programs in general, as well as limiting evaluation at each phase to only the code that is needed for that phase.

GPCE '13, October 27–28, 2013, Indianapolis, Indiana, USA.
Copyright is held by the owner/author(s). Publication rights licensed to ACM.
ACM 978-1-4503-2373-4/13/10... $15.00.
http://dx.doi.org/10.1145/2517208.2517211

The original design for modules in Racket allows module declarations only at the top level. Our new extension to Racket's module system enables modules to contain nested module declarations, which are called *submodules*. In most module systems that support nesting, lexically nested modules merely define a local namespace, and they are instantiated along with their enclosing modules. Racket submodules, in contrast, have a lifetime that can be independent of the enclosing module. The code of a submodule need not even be loaded when the enclosing module is used, or vice versa—unless the submodule imports from the enclosing module, or vice versa, in which case the usual phase-sensitive module loading and instantiation rules apply.

Submodules solve a number of practical problems for Racket programmers. They provide a natural way to express a "main" routine that is used only when the module is run as a program and ignored when the module is used as a library. Submodules provide a place for testing internal functions without making the functions public and without causing the tests to run on all uses of the module. Submodules enable abstraction over sets of modules, which is not possible when modules and only modules exist at the top level. Submodules also provide a communication channel for static semantic information about a module, such as whether the module is implemented in Typed Racket (Tobin-Hochstadt and Felleisen 2008) and the types of its exports.

More generally, submodules give a programmer the ability to define new phases along the same lines as the built-in run-time and compile-time phases. We can think of tests, for example, as "test-time" code, as opposed to run-time code. Unlike the distinction between the compile and run phases, the test phase subsumes the run phase, but not vice versa. As another example, when documentation is written as part of the library that it documents, then the code to produce the documentation is document-time code, which is independent of run-time code. In much the same way that run-time code and compile-time code can coexist within a module and benefit from a shared lexical scope (so that the macro's expansion can conveniently refer to bindings in the same module), document-time code can coexist with run-time code and benefit from a shared scope (so that the documentation can conveniently refer to bindings in the module, where the references are rendered as links to the bindings' documentation).

In this paper, we describe Racket's module system, its handling of different phases, and its support for submodules. We show how submodules are used for tasks such as testing and documentation. Finally, we provide a formal model that specifies the interaction of macro expansion, module declarations, compilation, and evaluation.

2. Modules and Phases

Before introducing submodules, we begin with a recap of Racket's design for modules and phases (Flatt 2002). In particular, we motivate Racket's module system in terms of compilation, but we mean "compilation" in a broad sense—as a proxy for any task that requires understanding what a program means without actually running the program. In a macro-extensible language, any such compilation involves running code for macro expansion. At the same time, when running code can have a side effect, running the code only at the right time is particularly important.

In a traditional Lisp or Scheme setting, a program is constructed by loading code into a `read-eval-print` loop (REPL). For example, if a program is implemented across four files, then it is linked together by having files `load` other files:[1]

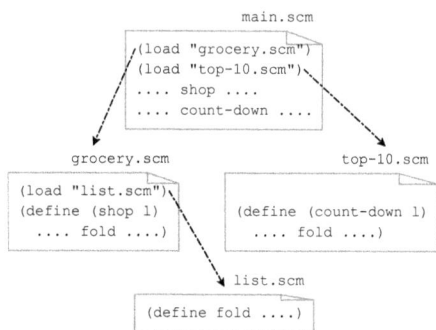

In this example, note that the `"top-10.scm"` file uses `fold` without explicitly `loading "list.scm"`. The program works, anyway, because the files are effectively flattened into a linear sequence as they are loaded, and `"list.scm"` gets loaded via `"grocery.scm"`, which is in turn loaded before `"top-10.scm"`.

Relying on load-order side effects for program structuring is clearly a bad idea. Reversing the initial loads of `"top-10.scm"` and `"grocery.scm"` will break the program, even though a programmer may be tempted to think of the files as modules that can be imported in either order. Indeed, the lack of an explicit dependency for `"top-10.scm"` on `"list.scm"` is likely to be a mistake that will be discovered unfortunately late. As the number of implementors and "module" files grows, the problem becomes acute.

A step in the right direction is to introduce a concept of "packages" and constrain access to a variable to those in packages that are explicitly imported with, say, a `use` declaration:[2]

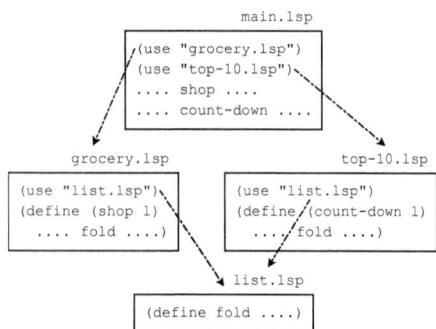

This hypothetical `use` declaration plays two roles: it makes the target package's bindings available in the current package, and it ensures that the target package is loaded before the current package. In other words, it helps avoid the mistakes possible with `load` by

---

[1] We use a `".scm"` suffix in the figure because many pre-R^{6}RS Scheme implementations often worked as illustrated.

[2] We use a `".lsp"` suffix in the figure because the Common Lisp package system works roughly as illustrated.

---

enforcing a connection between the lexical structure of the program and it dynamic evaluation; the `use` form leverages lexical scope.

Unfortunately, in a macro-extensible language, simply declaring dependencies on bindings does not cover the full dependency story. Suppose that a `"kitchen.lsp"` package depends on a `"grocery.lsp"` package to supply both a function `shop` and a macro `groceries` (to simplify the construction of grocery lists), while `"grocery.lsp"` depends on `"gui.lsp"` to implement a graphical list manager:

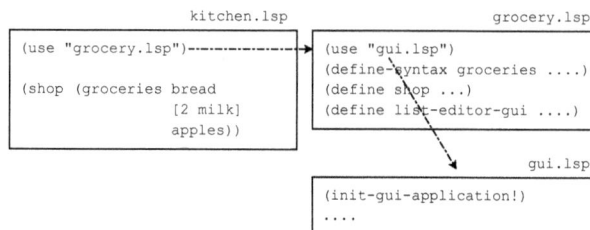

On the one hand, if `use` means only that `"grocery.lsp"` must be loaded before `"kitchen.lsp"` is run, then the implementation of the `groceries` macro will not be available at compile time for `"kitchen.lsp"`, which is when its macros must be expanded. On the other hand, if `use` means that a package is loaded at both run and compile times, then compiling `"kitchen.lsp"` means that `"gui.lsp"` will be loaded to start a graphical interface even at compile time, but the graphical interface should start only at run time.

The traditional solution to this problem is to annotate `use` declarations with an `eval-when` declaration to say when the corresponding package should be loaded. Such annotations, however, are a return to `load`-style scripting of dependencies, which are difficult to get right when many packages are involved. Furthermore, compile-time code must be split into separate packages from run-time code, so that the packages can be loaded at different times.

Racket modules with `require` look essentially the same as our hypothetical packages with `use`:

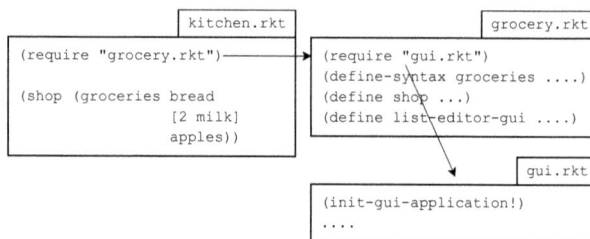

The meaning of `require`, however, is to *run the compile-time portions of the imported modules at compile time*, and to *run the run-time portion of the imported modules at run time*. Thus, the compile-time implementation of `groceries` is available to expand the body of `"kitchen.rkt"`, while `shop`, `list-editor-gui`, and `init-gui-application!` are deferred until run time.

The `require` form triggers the right code at the right time by leveraging lexical scope to determine which parts of a module are for compile time and which parts are for run time. To a first approximation, macro definitions in a module are part of the module's compile time, while function definitions and top-level expressions are part of the module's run time. The following variant of our example illustrates this difference, where solid outlines highlight runtime code, and the dashed outline highlights compile-time code:

○ = run time   ⟨⟩ = compile time

```
                                          kitchen.rkt
(require "list.rkt"
         "grocery.rkt")
(define weekly (groceries ....))
(shop .... fold ....)
```

```
                                          grocery.rkt
(require "gui.rkt"
         (for-syntax "list.rkt"))
(define-syntax groceries (.... fold ....))
(define shop (....))
(define list-editor-gui (....))
```

```
                                          list.rkt
(define fold (....))
```

In "kitchen.rkt", the run-time regions include references to groceries and fold, and therefore they are imported with a plain require. Whether fold is a macro, function, or variable, all that matters is that fold is referenced from a run-time position. In contrast, "grocery.rkt" uses fold in a compile-time position, so it must use require with for-syntax to import fold from "list.rkt". If "grocery.rkt" used require without for-syntax to import "list.rkt", then fold in "grocery.rkt" would be unbound for compile-time code, and its use as shown would trigger a syntax error.

The difference between require with for-syntax and eval-when with use is subtle but crucial: with eval-when, a programmer attempts to say when code should run to make identifiers available; with require, a programmer says in which phase an identifier should be bound, leaving the questions of loading and running up to the language. That is, with require, programmers reason about scope, instead of reasoning about side-effecting loads.

If the groceries macro in "grocery.rkt" expands to a run-time use of fold instead of using fold at compile time, then "grocery.rkt" should import "list.rkt" normally, instead of for-syntax. Put another way, a syntax-quoting #' in a macro embeds a run-time region within compile-time code, and a #'-quoted reference to fold in a macro is the same as a direct reference in a run-time position:

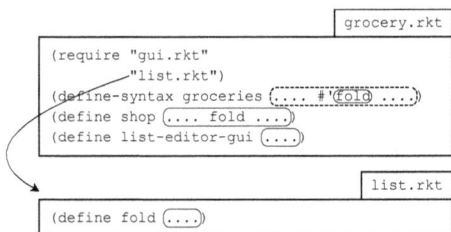

```
                                          grocery.rkt
(require "gui.rkt"
         "list.rkt")
(define-syntax groceries (.... #'fold ....))
(define shop (.... fold ....))
(define list-editor-gui (....))
```

```
                                          list.rkt
(define fold (....))
```

Some libraries, such as a list-processing library like "list.rkt", may even be useful at both compile time and run time. In that case, the module can be required both normally and for-syntax:

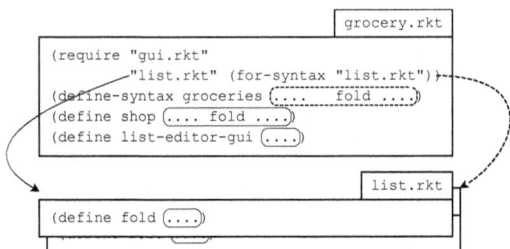

```
                                          grocery.rkt
(require "gui.rkt"
         "list.rkt" (for-syntax "list.rkt"))
(define-syntax groceries (.... fold ....))
(define shop (.... fold ....))
(define list-editor-gui (....))
```

```
                                          list.rkt
(define fold (....))
```

When a module is used in multiple phases, then it is instantiated separately in each phase. Furthermore, to ensure that all-at-once compilation is consistent with separate compilation of modules, a module that is used at compile time is instantiated separately for each module to be compiled. Separate instantiations avoid cross-phase interference and help tame state enough to make it useful for communication among macros (Culpepper et al. 2007; Flatt 2002).

Using lexical scope to determine and manage evaluation phases fits naturally with hygienic macros (Kohlbecker et al. 1986), which also obey lexical scope. For example, if the groceries macro expands to a use of a private function that is defined within "grocery.rkt", then hygiene ensures that the expanded reference is bound by the definition in "grocery.rkt" and not a definition in the client module where the groceries macro is used. Furthermore, the fact that groceries was bound for use in a certain position implies "grocery.rkt" was imported for that position's phase, which in turn implies that the private definition from "grocery.rkt" will be ready by the time that the position is evaluated.

Preserving lexical scope across module boundaries ultimately leads to the need for an import form that is like require with for-syntax but that works in the other direction. For example, imagine that the core implementation of the groceries macro is both sophisticated and general enough that it should be put in its own module, "gen-list-code.rkt" that is required with for-syntax for use by the groceries macro:

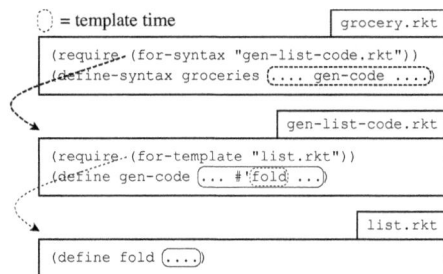

⟨⟩ = template time

```
                                          grocery.rkt
(require (for-syntax "gen-list-code.rkt"))
(define-syntax groceries (.... gen-code ....))
```

```
                                          gen-list-code.rkt
(require (for-template "list.rkt"))
(define gen-code (... #'fold ...))
```

```
                                          list.rkt
(define fold (....))
```

As gen-code constructs an expression for the expansion of groceries, it uses a syntax-quoted fold. The gen-code implementation exists at the run-time phase relative to its enclosing module, while the reference to fold is generated for sometime further in the future—when the result of gen-code is run as part of a generated program. Using require with for-template enables a reference to a binding that exists in that future (as opposed to for-syntax, which enables a reference to a binding that exists in the past, relative to run time), and so "gen-list-code.rkt" requires the "list.rkt" module with for-template.

Following the dependencies from "grocery.rkt" through "list.rkt", the for-syntax and for-template phase shifts effectively cancel each other. A for-syntax import implies a phase shift of +1 (toward the past), and a for-template import implies a phase shift of -1 (toward the future), so that the combination gives $+1 + -1 = 0$.[3] Consequently, a phase-0 (i.e., run time) use of "grocery.rkt" triggers a phase-0 use of "list.rkt", which means that a use of groceries and its expansion to fold are consistent. Reasoning about such phase shifts as a dynamic process is difficult, but reasoning locally about a reference to a future fold within "gen-list-code.rkt" is easy.

Using a macro inside of a compile-time context, such as the right-hand side of a define-syntax form, means that the macro runs at compile time relative to compile time—that is, at phase 2. In require, for-syntax and for-template specifications can be nested to import bindings into arbitrary phase levels. Furthermore, begin-for-syntax allows compile-time defini-

---

[3] Our phase numbers are negated compared to phase numbers in the staged-computation literature. The negation reflects our emphasis on macros instead of run-time code generation.

tions to be written within a module whose macros need the definitions. For example, if `gen-code` is needed only by macros within `"grocery.rkt"`, it might be better implemented within the `"grocery.rkt"` module instead of in a separate module:

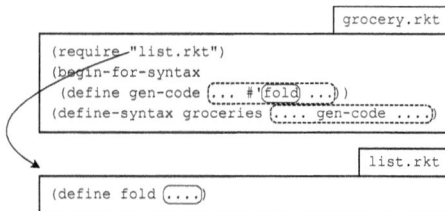

```
                                        grocery.rkt
  (require "list.rkt")
  (begin-for-syntax
    (define gen-code (... #'fold ...))
    (define-syntax groceries (.... gen-code ....))

                                        list.rkt
  (define fold (....))
```

This variant of `"grocery.rkt"` effectively inlines the earlier `"gen-list-code.rkt"` module, shifting the inlined code with `begin-for-syntax` instead of `require` with `for-syntax`.

In the same way that a module can import bindings at multiple phases, it can also *export* bindings at multiple phases. The most prominent example of multi-phase exports is the `racket` module, which is implicitly imported in the above module pictures. The `racket` module re-exports all of the bindings of a more primitive `racket/base` module, and it re-exports the bindings at both phase 0 and phase 1. That's why a module that imports `racket` can include a definition of the form

```
  (begin-for-syntax (define gen-code ...))
```

The `racket` module exports `define` at phase 1, so the `define` above is bound for the phase where it is used. If the module's initial import is `racket/base`, instead of `racket`, then the macro definition above is a syntax error unless `define` is explicitly imported `for-syntax`.

Naturally, `begin-for-syntax` forms can be nested to implement a function that is needed for a macro that is used on the right-hand side of a macro implementation, and so on, provided that `begin-for-syntax` itself is imported into each phase where it is used. Despite many possibilities for phases and nesting, the lexical and phase-sensitive constraints on each variable ensure that evaluation times are properly kept in sync.

3. Testing Time And Documentation Time

We can deploy the principles of lexical scope and phase separation to distinguish phases other than just run time and compile time. For example, suppose that we implement a function that uses the Racket `current-seconds` function to implement a `current-hours` function, and suppose that the implementation uses a private `seconds->hours` function:

```
                                        hours.rkt
  (provide current-hours)

  (define (current-hours)
    (seconds->hours (current-seconds)))

  (define (seconds->hours s)
    (quotient s (* 60 60)))
```

The internal `seconds->hours` function should be tested:

```
  (require rackunit)
  (check-equal 0 (seconds->hours 0))
  (check-equal 1 (seconds->hours 3600))
  (check-equal 42 (seconds->hours 151200))
```

Where should we put these tests? If we put them in a separate module, then `seconds->hours` must be exported, but we wanted to keep that function private. If we add the tests to the end of `"hours.rkt"`, then the private function `seconds->hours` is available, but the tests will run every time that the `"hours.rkt"`

module is used, and the dependency on `rackunit` means that every program that uses `"hours.rkt"` must carry along the testing framework.

The Racket `module+` form offers a solution that lets a programmer include tests with the code, which makes the most sense in terms of scoping, but puts the code in a separate *submodule* that effectively implements a testing phase (in the dashed box):

```
                                        hours.rkt
  (provide current-hours)

  (define (current-hours)
    (seconds->hours (current-seconds)))

  (define (seconds->hours s)
    (quotient s (* 60 60)))

  (module+ test
    (require rackunit)
    (check-equal 0 (seconds->hours 0))
    (check-equal 1 (seconds->hours 3600))
    (check-equal 42 (seconds->hours 151200)))
```

When `"hours.rkt"` is imported into another module with `require`, then the `test` submodule is ignored; the code for the `test` module is not even loaded in that case, assuming that the file has been compiled ahead of time. If the `"hours.rkt"` module is run with the `raco test` command-line tool or run in DrRacket, then the `test` module is also run.[4]

The testing example uses a submodule relatively explicitly. As an example of a new phase that looks more like compile time, consider the problem of documenting library exports at the site of their implementations. Common Lisp supports documentation in the form of *docstrings*, which are string literals that start the body of a function:

```
  (define (current-seconds)
    "reports the time in seconds since the Epoch"
    ....)
  (define (current-days)
    "reports the time in days since the Epoch"
    ....)
```

Docstrings are often accessed at run time, but they are required to be literal strings so that they can be recognized syntactically. With the restriction to literal docstrings, a tool can build a documentation index without running a program. Constraining docstrings to literal strings, however, prevents abstraction:

```
  (define (docs-for-current what)
    (format "reports the time in ~a since the Epoch"
            what))

  (define (current-seconds)
    (docs-for-current "seconds")
    ....)

  (define (current-days)
    (docs-for-current "days")
    ....)
```

The `docs-for-current` abstraction doesn't work if docstrings are restricted to literal strings. In Racket, we can address the problem by developing a macro-based extension of the language: a `begin-for-doc` form for documentation-time code along with a keyword syntax (in a macro replacement of `define`) to identify a part of a function definition as documentation:

---

[4] Sometimes you do want to run tests when a particular library is used. For example, this paper depends on the implementation of the model that is presented in section 5, and the paper explicitly imports the implementation's `test` submodule so that the model is tested whenever the paper is rendered (Klein et al. 2012).

```
(begin-for-doc
  (define (docs-for-current what)
    (format "reports the time in ~a since the Epoch"
            what)))

(define (current-seconds)
  #:doc (docs-for-current "seconds")
  ....)
```

With this approach, documentation need not be constrained to plain text. Figure 1 provides a more complete example that uses Scribble (Flatt et al. 2009) syntax for writing documentation, and where the `begin-for-doc`, `for-doc`, and `define` forms are implemented in `"doc-define.rkt"`. The `require...for-doc` import binds Scribble typesetting forms such as `code` for use in writing documentation, where `code` in turn uses the same scope information as used at run-time to hyperlink the documentation's mention of `current-seconds` to the documentation of `current-seconds`. Similarly, the contract expressions after `#:contract` are mainly run-time code, but they are also incorporated into the documentation, where `->` is hyperlinked to documentation on the contract-construction form and `exact-integer?` is hyperlinked to documentation of the number-testing predicate.

The example in figure 1 does not use submodules explicitly, but the `for-doc` imports, `begin-for-doc` forms, and documentation-time `#:doc` expressions are all macro-expanded into a `srcdoc` submodule (as we sketch later in section 4). The submodule is then available for use by documentation tools. The module that provides `current-hours`, etc., does not itself depend on the Scribble libraries or use the code for `current-docs` when the module is loaded.

4. Submodules

Our pictorial representation of modules so far omits the `#lang` line that starts an actual Racket module. For example, the module

```
┌─────────────┐
│ clock.rkt   │
├─────────────┤
│ "tick"      │
└─────────────┘
```

represents the file `"clock.rkt"` whose content is

```
#lang racket
"tick"
```

The initial `#lang racket` line, in turn, is a shorthand for using the parenthesized `module` form:

```
(module clock racket
  "tick")
```

The `racket` here indicates a module to supply the initial bindings for the `clock` module body. The `clock` module does not use any of those bindings (except for the implicit literal-expression form), but it could use any `racket` function or syntactic form—and only those syntactic forms, until it uses `require` to import more. Running the `clock` module prints the result of the expression in its body, so it prints `"tick"`.

To a first approximation, a *submodule* is simply a nested `module` form.

```
(module clock racket
  "tick"
  (module tock racket
    "tock"))
```

Running the `clock` module still prints just `"tick"`. Similarly, evaluating `(require "clock.rkt")` in the Racket REPL prints `"tick"`. In those cases, the `tock` submodule is declared, but it is not instantiated and run. Evaluating `(require (submod "clock.rkt" tock))` in the Racket REPL prints `"tock"` and does not print `"tick"`. Submodule nesting implies a

```
#lang at-exp racket/base
(require "doc-define.rkt"
         racket/contract/base
         (for-doc racket/base
                  scribble/manual))

(define (seconds->hours secs)
  #:contract (-> exact-integer? exact-integer?)
  #:doc @{Takes @code{secs}, a number of seconds
          since the Epoch, and converts it to a
          number of days since the Epoch.

          For example, compose with with the
          @code{current-seconds} function to get
          @code{current-hours}.}
  (quotient secs (* 60 60)))

(begin-for-doc
 (define (current-docs what)
   @list{Returns @what since the epoch.}))

(define (current-seconds)
  #:contract (-> exact-integer?)
  #:doc @{@current-docs["seconds"]}
  (inexact->exact
   (floor (/ (current-inexact-milliseconds) 1000))))

(define (current-hours)
  #:contract (-> exact-integer?)
  #:doc @{@current-docs["hours"]}
  (seconds->hours (current-seconds)))
```

Figure 1: Example program with documentation time

kind of nesting of module names, but it does not imply any run-time relationship between a submodule and its enclosing module.

A module can explicitly run one of its submodules using `require`, the same as it would trigger any other module. A module can reference one of its submodules using the relative form `(submod "." ....)`:

```
(module clock racket
  (module tock racket
    "tock")
  (require (submod "." tock))
  "tick")
```

Running this module prints both `"tock"` and `"tick"`, since the module explicitly `requires` its submodule and therefore creates an instantiation relationship.[5]

A submodule declared with `module` cannot import from its enclosing module. The `module*` form is the same as `module` for declaring submodules, but it allows the submodule to import from its enclosing module and not vice versa. (Module dependencies in Racket must be acyclic.) Thus, with the `clock` variant

```
(module clock racket
  "tick"
  (module* tock racket
    (require (submod ".."))
    "tock"))
```

evaluating `(require (submod "clock.rkt" tock))` in the Racket REPL prints `"tick"` followed by `"tock"`.

For the same reason that module nesting does not imply a connection in instantiation times, module nesting alone does not imply a lexical-binding connection. For example,

```
(module clock racket
```

---

[5] The `require` form is a dependency declaration, not a side-effecting statement, and its placement relative to the `"tick"` expression does not matter. Putting `"tick"` before the `tock` submodule declaration will still print `"tock"` first, since a `required` module is instantiated before the importing module.

```
(define sound "tick")
(module* tick racket
  sound))
```

is a syntax error, because the `tock` module starts with only the bindings of `racket`, just like any module that declares `racket` as its language. Furthermore,

```
(module clock racket
  (define sound "tick")
  (module* tick racket
    (require (submod ".."))
    sound))
```

is also a syntax error, because `clock` does not export its `sound` binding. A submodule can specify `#f` as its initial language to indicate that the enclosing module body provides the submodule's bindings:

```
(module clock racket
  (define sound "tick")
  (module* tick #f
    sound))
```

In this case, `(racket (submod "clock.rkt" tock))` prints `"tick"`, which is the value of `sound`.

The `module+` form, which we used in section 3, is a macro that expands to `module*` with `#f` as its language. The `module+` form also collects multiple declarations with the same module name and concatenates the bodies in a single submodule declaration, so `(module+ test ....)` can be used multiple times in a module to build up one `test` submodule.

Submodules can be nested under `begin-for-syntax`. For a submodule declared with `module` or with `module*` and a non-`#f` initial import, the nesting has no effect on the submodule, since the submodule starts with a fresh lexical context. Nesting `module*` with a `#f` initial import under `begin-for-syntax` has the effect of shifting the enclosing module's bindings *down* by one phase in the body of the submodule. That is, a submodule's body by definition starts at phase 0 relative to the submodule, so if the submodule is lexically at phase *ph* relative to an enclosing module, then the enclosing module is at phase *-ph* relative to the submodule.

Relative phase shifts are useful in the case of documentation submodules, where all of the bindings inside of a module are relevant for the submodule, but the submodule should not have a direct execution dependence on the enclosing module. For example, building documentation should not require running the documented library. Figure 2 sketches the expansion of the module with documentation in figure 1. In the expansion, contracts for each function declaration are moved to a `provide...contract-out` form, the function definitions contain only the function implementations, and all documentation is moved into a `srcdoc` submodule. The submodule is declared under `begin-for-syntax`, so that the enclosing module is at template time—i.e., an unspecified time in the future—relative to the implementation of its documentation; the `code` form can then reflect on binding information inherited from the enclosing module to properly hyperlink references to identifiers that are used in the function contracts and documentation prose.

5. Model

Our model of submodules in Racket shows how modules are compiled and instantiated, including support for submodules, macros, and macros that expand to submodule declarations. The model is implemented in PLT Redex (Felleisen et al. 2010), and while we cover only the most relevant details here, the full model is available in executable and typeset forms at

http://www.cs.utah.edu/plt/submod3/

```
#lang at-exp racket/base
(require "doc-define.rkt"
         racket/contract/base)

(provide
 (contract/out
  [seconds->hours (-> exact-integer? exact-integer?)]
  [current-seconds (-> exact-integer?)]
  [current-hours (-> exact-integer?)]))

(define (seconds->hours secs) (quotient secs (* 60 60)))
(define current-seconds ....)
(define current-hours ....)

(begin-for-syntax
 (module srcdoc #f
  (require scribble/base
           scribble/manual)

  (define (current-docs what)
    @list{Returns @what since the epoch.})

  (define doc
   (list
    (format-function-doc
     @code{seconds->hour}
     (list @code{src})
     @code{(-> exact-integer? exact-integer?)}
     @{Takes @code{secs}, a number of seconds
       since the Epoch, ....})
    (format-function-doc
     @code{current-seconds}
     @code{()}
     @code{(-> exact-integer?)}
     @{@current-docs["seconds"]})
    (format-function-doc
     @code{current-hours}
     @code{()}
     @code{(-> exact-integer?)}
     @{@current-docs["hours"]}))))))
```

Figure 2: Sketch of macro expansion for figure 1

mod ::= **MODULE**(*mname*, *dep* ..., *defn* ...)

dep ::= *mname*@*ph*   *mname* ::= a module name
defn ::= ⟨*dname*@*ph*, *kind*, *ast*⟩   *dname* ::= a defined name

kind ::= **VALUE** | **MACRO**   *ast* ::= a compiled expression
ph ::= *integer*

M ::= a mapping from *mname* to *mod*
Σ ::= a store

Figure 3: Compiled-module representation

5.1 Running Modules

The representation of a compiled module, *mod*, is shown in figure 3. A *mod* contains the module's name, a set of modules that the module depends on, and a sequence of definitions for the module's body. Each dependency and definition is associated with a particular phase, *ph*. A normal `require` of a module creates a dependency with phase 0, while a `require` with `for-syntax` creates a dependency with phase 1, and a `require` with `for-template` creates a dependency with phase -1.

Each definition is either for a run-time value or a macro, as indicated by *kind*, and its associated phase. A value definition is evaluated at its associated phase and can be referenced in its associated phase. A macro definition at phase *ph* can be referenced from a phase *ph* context, although the macro itself runs at phase *ph*+1.

run : *mname ph M Σ → Σ*

Run *mname* (as declared in *M*) at phase ph_Δ and record in Σ, but only if *mname@ph$_\Delta$* is not already recorded as ran in Σ.

---

run[*mname*, ph_Δ, *M*, Σ] = Σ
  subject to $\Sigma(mname@ph_\Delta)$ = **READY**
run[*mname*, ph_Δ, *M*, Σ] = run-body[*defn* ..., *mname*, ph_Δ, Σ_{deps}]
  subject to *M*(*mname*) = **MODULE**(*mname*, *deps*, *defn* ...),
      $\Sigma\big[mname@ph_\Delta \leftarrow$ **READY**$\big] = \Sigma_{init}$,
      run*[*deps*, ph_Δ, *M*, Σ_{init}] = Σ_{deps}

run* : *dep ... ph M Σ → Σ*

Run each *dep* (which is a *mname@ph*) with phase shift *ph*.

---

run*[ε, ph_Δ, *M*, Σ]   = Σ
run*[*mname@ph dep* ..., ph_Δ, *M*, Σ] = run*[*dep* ..., ph_Δ, *M*, Σ_{new}]
  subject to run[*mname*, $ph_\Delta + ph$, *M*, Σ] = Σ_{new}

run-body : *defn ... mname ph Σ → Σ*

Evaluate each run-time *defn* with phase shift ph_Δ, as long as ph_Δ plus the enclosing module's instantiation phase lands at phase 0. Record definitions in Σ.

---

run-body[ε, *mname*, ph_Δ, Σ] = Σ
run-body[⟨*dname@ph$_{def}$*, **VALUE**, *ast*⟩ *defn* ..., *mname*, ph_Δ, Σ]
  = run-body[*defn* ..., *mname*, ph_Δ, Σ_{new}]
  subject to $ph_\Delta + ph_{def} = 0$, eval[shift[*ast*, ph_Δ], Σ] = *val*,
      $\Sigma\big[⟨0, mname, dname⟩ \leftarrow ⟨$**VALUE**, *val*$⟩\big] = \Sigma_{new}$
run-body[*defn$_{skip}$ defn* ..., *mname*, ph_Δ, Σ]
  = run-body[*defn* ..., *mname*, ph_Δ, Σ]

Figure 4: The run metafunction

A module is instantiated and run with the run metafunction, as shown in figure 4. A store Σ is updated with module instantiations and returned by run. The run metafunction evaluates a module body, but only after folding run across all dependencies of the module. For each dependency, if a module was imported `for-syntax`, then its definitions will be shifted higher by one phase, and if a module was imported `for-template`, then its definitions will be shifted lower by one phase.

A *mod* does not record the original module's submodules, if any. Instead, the module repository *M* contains all compiled module definitions, including those that were submodules. For simplicity, the model assumes that all modules and submodules in a program have globally distinct names. Any module–submodule or not–that is not a dependency of the initially run module will itself not run.

5.2 Compiling Modules

The *M* module repository used by run must be generated from a sequence of module declarations, except for the predefined module `base`. A module declaration starts as an S-expression, *s-exp*, which is either a name[6] or a parenthesized sequence of S-expressions, as shown in figure 5. The compiler must take an S-expression representation of a module, such as

```
(module m base (define x (quote ok)))
```

and turn it into an executable form, *mod*.

The entry point for compilation is cmodule, which takes an S-expression for a single module along with a repository of previously compiled modules and returns an updated repository:

s-exp ::= *name* | (*s-exp* ...)
name ::= a token such as x, clock, or lambda

mname ::= *name*
dname ::= *name*

stx ::= *id* | (*stx* ...)
id ::= **STX**(*name*, *bindings*)

binding ::= ⟨*ph*, *mname*, *dname*⟩
bindings ::= *binding* ...

body ::= *stx@ph*

import : *mname ph M → bindings*

Collect a module's exports into a set of *bindings*.

wrap : *s-exp bindings → stx*

Attach bindings to a raw S-expression.

strip : *stx → s-exp*

Strip bindings from a syntax object to get an S-expression.

resolve : *id ph → binding*

Find relevant binding at a given phase, *ph*.

Figure 5: Syntax objects and bindings

cmodule : *s-exp M → M*

---

cmodule[(module *mname mname$_{init}$ s-exp* ...), *M*]
  = cbody[*body* ..., *mname*, *mname$_{init}$@0*, ε, *M*, Σ_{init}]
  subject to visit[*mname$_{init}$*, 0, *M*, ∅] = Σ_{init},
      import[*mname$_{init}$*, 0, *M*] = *bindings*,
      wrap[*s-exp*, *bindings*]@0 ... = *body* ...

Compilation of a module begins by *visiting* the module for the new module's initial import. The visit metafunction is just like run, but instead of running only phase 0 value definitions, it runs all definitions for the given module in phase 1 or higher, as well as all macro definitions at phase 0. The visit metafunction is called with an empty store, which reflects that every module compilation starts with fresh state.

Meanwhile, the import metafunction extracts a set of bindings from the initial import, as shown in figure 5; the model omits `provide`, and instead assumes that all definitions of a module are exported. The collected bindings are then applied to the body of the module to be compiled via wrap, which converts the module's body from S-expressions to syntax objects, *stx*. In general, syntax objects enable lexically scoped macros (Dybvig et al. 1993; Flatt et al. 2012), but we simplify here by considering only model-level scope.

Finally, each syntax object for a module's body is paired with the phase at which it appears, producing a *body* element of the form *stx@ph*. Initially, all body forms are at phase 0, but `begin-for-syntax` may later move forms to a higher phase. This phase shifting is implemented in the cbody metafunction, which completes compilation of the module.

deps ::= *dep* ...
defns ::= *defn* ...

cbody : *body ... mname deps defns M Σ → M*

In addition to the *body* sequence, cbody receives the name of the module being compiled (which is eventually used to create a *mod* and add it to *M*), a sequence of dependencies to extended by `require` forms among the *body*s, a sequence of compiled *defn*s to

19

$$form ::= (\texttt{begin-for-syntax}\ form\ ...)$$
$$|\ (\texttt{define}\ dname\ expr)$$
$$|\ (\texttt{define-syntax}\ dname\ expr)$$
$$|\ (\texttt{require}\ req)$$
$$|\ (\texttt{module}\ mname\ mname\ form\ ...)$$
$$|\ (\texttt{module*}\ mname\ mname\ form\ ...)$$
$$|\ (\texttt{module*}\ mname\ (\ )\ form\ ...)$$
$$|\ (dname\ arb\ ...)$$
$$req ::= mname$$
$$|\ (\texttt{for-syntax}\ req)$$
$$|\ (\texttt{for-template}\ req)$$
$$expr ::= \text{an expression}$$
$$arb ::= \text{whatever the macro allows}$$

Figure 6: Module syntax recognized by cbody

be extended by `define` and `define-syntax` forms among the *body*s, the set of previously compiled modules M to be extended by submodule declarations among the *body*s, and the current store Σ.

The simplest case of cbody is when no more *body*s are left, in which case the accumulated dependencies and definitions are combined into a *mod* and added to the result M:

$$\text{cbody}[\![\varepsilon, mname, deps, defns, M, \Sigma]\!]$$
$$= M[\![mname \leftarrow \textbf{MODULE}(mname, deps, defns)]\!]$$

Otherwise, cbody dispatches on the shape of the first *body*, matching one of the *form* cases of figure 6. The grammar of *form* shows `begin-for-syntax` as its first case. More precisely, from the perspective of cbody, a *body* to match that case must have a syntax object containing an identifier whose binding is `begin-for-syntax` from the pre-defined `base` module. That is, the forms listed in the grammar for *form* are available only when `base` is imported or via macro expansion from a module that imports `base`. The last *form* production is a macro invocation, where macro expansion can produce any of the other forms (or another macro invocation).

The cbody rule for `begin-for-syntax` is thus

$$\text{cbody}[\![(id_{bfs}\ stx\ ...)@ph\ body_{rest}\ ..., mname, deps, defns, M, \Sigma]\!]$$
$$= \text{cbody}[\![stx@ph+1\ ...\ body_{rest}\ ..., mname, deps, defns, M, \Sigma]\!]$$

$$\text{subject to resolve}[\![id_{bfs}, ph]\!] = \langle ph, \texttt{base}, \texttt{begin-for-syntax}\rangle$$

The syntax objects within `begin-for-syntax` get shifted up by one phase and added back to the list of bodies for the module.

We omit the rules for `define`, `define-syntax`, and macro invocation. For the purpose of explaining submodules, an interesting aspect of the omitted rules is that definitions are evaluated only when they have a phase greater than 0, so that they can be used in macro implementations, while definitions at phase 0 are merely compiled.

The `require` case of cbody uses a parse-req metafunction (not shown) to turn nested `for-syntax` and `for-template` specifications into a phase shift:

$$\text{cbody}[\![(id_{req}\ stx_{in})@ph\ body_{rest}\ ..., mname, dep\ ..., defns, M, \Sigma]\!]$$
$$= \text{cbody}[\![body_{new}\ ..., mname, dep\ ...\ dep_{new}, defns, M, \Sigma_{new}]\!]$$

$$\text{subject to resolve}[\![id_{req}, ph]\!] = \langle ph, \texttt{base}, \texttt{require}\rangle,$$
$$\text{parse-req}[\![stx_{in}, ph]\!] = \langle mname_{in}, ph_\Delta\rangle,$$
$$\text{visit}[\![mname_{in}, ph_\Delta, M, \Sigma]\!] = \Sigma_{new},$$
$$\text{import}[\![mname_{in}, ph_\Delta, M]\!] = bindings_{new},$$
$$\text{add}[\![body_{rest}, bindings_{new}]\!]\ ... = body_{new}\ ...,$$
$$mname_{in}@ph_\Delta = dep_{new}$$

Having extracted a module name $mname_{in}$ and relative phase ph_Δ, the `require` rule of cbody is essentially the same as cmodule: the imported module is visited, its bindings are added to the rest of the module, and the module is recorded as a dependency.

$$\text{cbody}[\![(id_{mod}\ id_{sub}\ id_{init}\ stx\ ...)@ph\ body_{rest}\ ..., mname, deps, defns, M, \Sigma]\!]$$
$$= \text{cbody}[\![body_{rest}\ ..., mname, deps, defns, M_{new}, \Sigma]\!]$$

$$\text{subject to resolve}[\![id_{mod}, ph]\!] = \langle ph, \texttt{base}, \texttt{module}\rangle,$$
$$\text{strip}[\![id_{sub}]\!] = mname_{sub}, \text{strip}[\![id_{init}]\!] = mname_{init},$$
$$\text{cmodule}[\![(\texttt{module}\ mname_{sub}\ mname_{init}\ \text{strip}[\![stx]\!]\ ...), M]\!] = M_{new}$$

$$\text{cbody}[\![(id_{mod}\ id_{sub}\ id_{init}\ stx\ ...)@ph\ body_{rest}\ ..., mname, deps, defns, M, \Sigma]\!]$$
$$= \text{cmodule}[\![(\texttt{module}\ mname_{sub}\ mname_{init}\ \text{strip}[\![stx]\!]\ ...), M_{new}]\!]$$

$$\text{subject to resolve}[\![id_{mod}, ph]\!] = \langle ph, \texttt{base}, \texttt{module*}\rangle,$$
$$\text{strip}[\![id_{sub}]\!] = mname_{sub}, \text{strip}[\![id_{init}]\!] = mname_{init},$$
$$\text{cbody}[\![body_{rest}\ ..., mname, deps, defns, M, \Sigma]\!] = M_{new}$$

$$\text{cbody}[\![(id_{mod}\ id_{sub}\ (\ )\ stx\ ...)@ph\ body_{rest}\ ..., mname, deps, defns, M, \Sigma]\!]$$
$$= \text{cbody}[\![\text{shift}[\![stx, 0-ph]\!]@0\ ..., mname_{sub}, mname@0-ph, \varepsilon, M_{new}, \Sigma_{init}]\!]$$

$$\text{subject to resolve}[\![id_{mod}, ph]\!] = \langle ph, \texttt{base}, \texttt{module*}\rangle,$$
$$\text{strip}[\![id_{sub}]\!] = mname_{sub},$$
$$\text{cbody}[\![body_{rest}\ ..., mname, deps, defns, M, \Sigma]\!] = M_{new},$$
$$\text{visit}[\![mname, 0-ph, M_{new}, \varnothing]\!] = \Sigma_{init}$$

Figure 7: Submodule cases of cbody

5.2.1 Compiling Submodules

The remaining cases of cbody handle submodules, as shown in figure 7. The `module` rule and first `module*` rule are similar: the submodule is compiled using cmodule, and the difference is only whether the submodule is compiled before or after the rest of the body of the current module. A `module` form is compiled before the rest of the body, so that it can be used by a later `require` in the current module. A `module*` form is compiled after the rest of the current module's body, so that the submodule can `require` the current module.

The last rule in figure 7 handles (`module*` *mname* (`)` *form* ...), which represents a submodule that inherits all bindings of its enclosing module. (We use (`)` instead of `#f` in the model to avoid the need for boolean literals in S-expressions and syntax objects.) Inheriting all bindings of the enclosing module is different from importing the enclosing module, because it makes any imports of the enclosing module visible in the submodule, as opposed to only the definitions of the enclosing module. Therefore, instead of compiling the submodule via a context-stripping cmodule, the submodule's compilation uses cbody directly. At the same time, the bindings inherited by the submodule must be shifted by a negative amount that corresponds to the submodule's phase nesting within its enclosing module. Although the submodule inherits bindings of the enclosing module, it does not inherit the store; the submodule's compilation via cbody starts with a fresh store that is initialized by visiting the enclosing module at the appropriate phase offset.

As noted for the first cbody rule, the result of cbody is ultimately a set of compiled modules to act as the result of cmodule. Folding cmodule over a set of S-expressions that represent a program accumulates a set of compiled modules, which then can be passed to run with a main-module name to run the program. The full model on the web site includes several example programs as tests.

6. Implementation and Discussion

We added submodules to Racket in version 5.3 (August 2012), which is 10 years after originally adding modules to Racket (then PLT Scheme). To support nested scopes, the initial implementation of modules was soon paired with a `package` macro that imitates the nestable `module` form of Chez Scheme (Waddell and Dybvig 1999), but such nested scopes never found much use in the Racket code base. Submodules, in contrast, have found immediate and widespread use, solving many different problems that we did ·not originally recognize as related: how to have code that is run when the module is "main" (in a more principled way than a Python-style dynamic test), how to include test code with a library's implementation, how to manage documentation in a library's implementation, how to provide extra exports from a module that are available only when specifically requested (by importing the submodule in addition to its enclosing module), how to package a read-time parser for a new language alongside its compile-time and run-time implementation (where read time is represented by a submodule), and how to declare dynamic file dependencies for use by a packaging tool (where the packaging tool can run a submodule to get information about the needed files). Naturally, we take the fact that submodules are conceptually simple but solve many problems as evidence that the submodule design is on the right track.

The key idea in our design is to allow a nested namespace to have its own dynamic extent relative to its enclosing environment. In a sense, submodules are a "meta" form of closures: in the same way that `(define (f x) (lambda (y) x))` returns a function that has access to the argument x beyond the dynamic extent of a call to f, submodules provide a way for a nested module to refer to the bindings of an enclosing module without necessarily implying a connection on the module extents (depending on how the bindings are referenced). More generally, lexical scope converts a potentially complex temporal question—how to ensure that a binding is available when it is needed—into a spatial problem that is easier for humans to reason about; that benefit applies just as much to modules, phases, and submodules as to function closures.

Racket's submodule design would look simpler if `module` and the two `module*` variants (with and without an initial import) could be collapsed into a single syntactic form. It may be possible to collapse `module` and `module*` and have the compiler infer (based on later `requires`) whether a submodule must be compiled before or after the rest of the enclosing module's body. The difference between `#f` or a module name in the initial-import position of `module*` might also be managed by cleaner syntax. We leave these problems for future work, and as a practical matter, choosing `module` or `module*` is easy enough for a Racket programmer.

The Racket implementation of modules includes a primitive `for-label` form in addition to `for-syntax` and `for-template`. A `for-label` import corresponds to binding at phase -∞: arbitrarily far in the future. The `code` form for documentation looks for bindings at this label phase for generating hyperlinks, and in the expansion sketch of figure 2, the generated module's body has been shifted by -∞ (but that fact is invisible in the sketch). The label phase is a kind of optimization hint to the module system, where a `for-label` dependency implies that no execution of the module at any finite phase will require the execution of the dependency. The label phase seems useful, but we are not yet sure whether it is fundamentally necessary.

As suggested by the model, top-level `module` forms are the unit of compilation in Racket. When a program is run from source in Racket, then a module and all of its submodules must be compiled together. In the case of a library module that contains its own documentation, this compilation process involves much more code than is needed to just run the library, negating an intended benefit of submodules. Racket modules are normally compiled to bytecode in advance, and the bytecode for a module starts with a directory of all submodules separate from the main module code, so that the module or any individual submodule can be loaded independently. Thus, a key benefit of submodules in practice relies on bytecode compilation.

7. Related Work

By enabling programming at different layers, submodules play a role similar to Java annotations and C# attributes. JavaDoc, in particular, is a use of Java annotations in the same way that Racket uses submodules for in-source documentation. Java annotations allow the decoration of code with data, and they are preserved through run time, so that annotations can be inspected in source, compiled code or reflectively. Still, Java annotations are limited to data, so that any abstraction or programmatic interpretation of the data depends on yet another external tool and language, or else the code part (such as test to run for a `@Test` annotation) is difficult to separate from the main program. C# attributes can have associated methods, but attribute code is still mingled with run-time code. Submodules, in contrast, generalize annotations to make them "live," so that the language of annotations can include expressions, function, and even syntactic extension, without necessarily tangling the submodule code with the base code. At the same time, submodules allow these live annotations to connect with the lexical scope of the associated code, which is useful in cases such as testing and documentation.

Although the model of submodules in this paper uses a simplistic notion of scope for syntax objects, in practice and in spirit submodules build on a long line of work on hygienic macros (Dybvig et al. 1993; Flatt et al. 2012; Kohlbecker et al. 1986). The R^6RS standard for Scheme (Sperber 2007) also includes modules with phases, as directly influenced by our previous work, but R^6RS does not include submodules or `begin-for-syntax`, and it does not allow macro expansion to introduce new imports within a module. R^6RS also does not require implementations to enforce a phase distinction. Some implementations support implicit phasing (Ghuloum and Dybvig 2007), where `for-syntax` and `for-template` annotation on imports are inferred automatically based on the use of imported identifiers. In Racket, we stick with explicit phasing because it supports different bindings for the same name in different phases (which is useful, for example, when documenting the `define` form of some language in a document that is implemented with Racket's normal `define`) and because explicit phasing allows macro expansion to depend in a reasonable way on side effects (as a last resort, but a useful one). We also suspect that checking programmer expectations against actual references is more useful in our context than implicit phasing's inference.

In TemplateHaskell (Jones and Sheard 2002), macro implementations are restricted to pure functions, which perhaps lessens the need to track phases; there is no question, for example, of initializing a GUI subsystem as part of a macro expansion, and in the absence of side-effects as side channels, the code that is accessed at compile time can be more easily limited to that needed by the macro's implementation. Since functions used by macros can be implemented themselves with macros, TemplateHaskell effectively supports arbitrary phase levels, the phases are implicit, and bindings are the same across all phases. TemplateHaskell does not support phases other than the implicit phases of run and compile times, and in-source documentation with Haddock (Marlow 2002) is analogous to JavaDoc. The Converge programming language (Tratt 2005) infers phases for macro expansion in a similar way to TemplateHaskell.

The SugarJ (Erdweg et al. 2011) design for library-based language extensibility relies on a separation between parsing code and transformation code, while allowing the two parts to coexist in a library. In SugarJ, the languages of parsing and transformation are separate and distinct from the base language. Nevertheless, there is room for a scope connection that is currently absent in SugarJ, which would connect the output of the parser to specific transformations or binding references in transformations to particular base-language bindings.

Lightweight Module Staging (Rompf 2012; Rompf and Odersky 2010), or LMS, is an approach to code generation where the type system is used to separate code at different levels. While the details of LMS are different from Racket's macros—particularly the way that run-time values can be implicitly coerced to representations of values—LMS is effective for fundamentally the same reason as modules and phases: both rely on scope and binding to separate phases, and both allow phases to lexically overlap without destroying a programmer's ability to reason about the code.

More generally, multi-stage programming languages such as MetaML (Taha and Sheard 2000) include a notion of phases that is similar to the notion in Racket. Racket's tracking of phases differs in that a syntax object can accumulate bindings in many phases, and the determination of the relevant binding can be made late, when the identifier is used in an expression position. Staged languages more typically identify the phase of each expression and identifier statically. MetaML and other statically typed multi-stage languages not only ensure that an identifier is used at a suitable phase, but they ensure that the identifier is used in a suitable type context.

Nested modules in languages such as ML (OCaml, SML/NJ) and Chez Scheme (Waddell and Dybvig 1999) are namespace-management tools, where nested modules are always instantiated with the enclosing module. Racket submodules, in contrast, are separately loadable and separately instantiable in the same way that top-level modules are separately loadable and instantiable.

Java classes are related to submodules in that the declaration of two classes within a single compilation unit does not imply that both classes must be used together at run time. Instead, classes are loaded and initialized on demand in a Java implementation, which allows a Java implementation to avoid loading code that is unused, and it ensures dynamically that any code that is needed is loaded before it is used. With a macro-extensible Java in the style of Maya (Baker and Hsieh 2002), code that is used only at compile time will naturally not be loaded at run time. This approach has the same benefits and drawbacks as implicit scoping in Scheme (e.g., the difficulty of reasoning about initialization side effects).

In this paper, we have used in-source documentation as one motivation for submodules. We reported on in-source documentation for Racket in previous work (Flatt et al. 2009), but that report glosses over certain problems. Documentation was extracted via `include-extracted` by re-expanding the source module and pulling designated syntax objects out of the expansion. Besides being ugly and reporting syntax errors late, the implementation had quadratic complexity for extracting N sets of documentation from a single module. Our revised implementation of in-source documentation uses a submodule to avoid these problems.

8. Conclusion

Lexical scope is a powerful organizing principle. In the context of Racket, we believe that lexically scoped macros are the key to our ability to define a rich ecosystem of language variants and tools, from teaching dialects of Racket, to statically typed dialects of Racket, to documentation languages. Phasing is a natural extension of lexical scope that adds a new dimension to each identifier, allowing the identifier to have different meanings in different phases while relying on the surrounding context of an identifier to also determine the phase in which the identifier is used. Submodules continue that extension; they add new expressive power to Racket in line with the principles of lexical scope, they solve a variety of practical problems for Racket programmers, and they increase the ability of macros to implement new language constructs.

Acknowledgements I would like to thank Matthias Felleisen, Robby Findler, Ryan Culpepper, the Racket community, and anonymous reviewers for feedback and suggestions on the design of submodules and this presentation.

Bibliography

Jason Baker and Wilson C. Hsieh. Maya: Multiple-Dispatch Syntax Extension in Java. In *Proc. ACM Conf. Programming Language Design and Implementation*, pp. 270–281, 2002.

Ryan Culpepper, Sam Tobin-Hochstadt, and Matthew Flatt. Advanced Macrology and the Implementation of Typed Scheme. In *Proc. Wksp. Scheme and Functional Programming*, 2007.

R. Kent Dybvig, Robert Hieb, and Carl Bruggeman. Syntactic Abstraction in Scheme. *Lisp and Symbolic Computation* 5(4), pp. 295–326, 1993.

Sebastian Erdweg, Tillmann Rendel, Christian Kästner, and Klaus Ostermann. SugarJ: Library-Based Syntactic Language Extensibility. In *Proc. ACM Conf. Object-Oriented Programming, Systems, Languages and Applications*, pp. 391–406, 2011.

Matthias Felleisen, Robert Bruce Findler, and Matthew Flatt. *Semantics Engineering with PLT Redex*. MIT Press, 2010.

Matthew Flatt. Composable and Compilable Macros: You Want it *When?* In *Proc. ACM Intl. Conf. Functional Programming*, pp. 72–83, 2002.

Matthew Flatt, Eli Barzilay, and Robert Bruce Findler. Scribble: Closing the Book on Ad Hoc Documentation Tools. In *Proc. ACM Intl. Conf. Functional Programming*, pp. 109–120, 2009.

Matthew Flatt, Ryan Culpepper, Robert Bruce Findler, and David Darais. Macros that Work Together: Compile-Time Bindings, Partial Expansion, and Definition Contexts. *J. Functional Programming* 22(2), pp. 181–216, 2012.

Abdulaziz Ghuloum and ; R. Kent Dybvig. Implicit Phasing for R6RS Libraries. In *Proc. ACM Intl. Conf. Functional Programming*, pp. 303–314, 2007.

Simon Peyton Jones and Tim Sheard. Template metaprogramming for Haskell. In *Proc. ACM Wksp. Haskell*, pp. 1–16, 2002.

Casey Klein, John Clements, Christos Dimoulas, Carl Eastlund, Matthias Felleisen, Matthew Flatt, Jay McCarthy, Jon Rafkind, Sam Tobin-Hochstadt, and Robert Bruce Findler. Run Your Research: On the Effectiveness of Lightweight Mechanization. In *Proc. ACM Sym. Principles of Programming Languages*, 2012.

Eugene Kohlbecker, Daniel P. Friedman, Matthias Felleisen, and Bruce Duba. Hygienic Macro Expansion. In *Proc. Lisp and Functional Programming*, pp. 151–181, 1986.

Simon Marlow. Haddock, a Haskell Documentation Tool. In *Proc. ACM Wksp. Haskell*, pp. 78–89, 2002.

Tiark Rompf. Lightweight Modular Staging and Embedded Compilers: Abstraction without Regret for High-Level High-Performance Programming. PhD dissertation, École Polytechnique Fédérale de Lausanne, 2012.

Tiark Rompf and Martin Odersky. Lightweight Modular Staging: a Pragmatic Approach to Runtime Code Generation and Compiled DSLs. In *Proc. Generative Programming and Component Engineering*, pp. 127–136, 2010.

Michael Sperber (Ed.). The Revised [6] Report on the Algorithmic Language Scheme. 2007.

Walid Taha and Tim Sheard. MetaML and Multi-Stage Programming with Explicit Annotations. *Theoretical Computer Science* 248(1-2), pp. 211–242, 2000.

Sam Tobin-Hochstadt and Matthias Felleisen. The Design and Implementation of Typed Scheme. In *Proc. ACM Sym. Principles of Programming Languages*, pp. 395–406, 2008.

Laurence Tratt. Compile-time Meta-programming in a Dynamically Typed OO Language. In *Proc. Dynamic Languages Symposium*, pp. 49–63, 2005.

Oscar Waddell and R. Kent Dybvig. Extending the Scope of Syntactic Abstraction. In *Proc. ACM Sym. Principles of Programming Languages*, pp. 203–213, 1999.

Declarative Visitors to Ease Fine-grained Source Code Mining with Full History on Billions of AST Nodes

Robert Dyer   Hridesh Rajan   Tien N. Nguyen

Iowa State University

{rdyer,hridesh,tien}@iastate.edu

Abstract

Software repositories contain a vast wealth of information about software development. Mining these repositories has proven useful for detecting patterns in software development, testing hypotheses for new software engineering approaches, etc. Specifically, mining source code has yielded significant insights into software development artifacts and processes. Unfortunately, mining source code at a large-scale remains a difficult task. Previous approaches had to either limit the scope of the projects studied, limit the scope of the mining task to be more coarse-grained, or sacrifice studying the history of the code due to both human and computational scalability issues. In this paper we address the substantial challenges of mining source code: a) at a very large scale; b) at a fine-grained level of detail; and c) with full history information.

To address these challenges, we present domain-specific language features for source code mining. Our language features are inspired by object-oriented visitors and provide a default depth-first traversal strategy along with two expressions for defining custom traversals. We provide an implementation of these features in the Boa infrastructure for software repository mining and describe a code generation strategy into Java code. To show the usability of our domain-specific language features, we reproduced over 40 source code mining tasks from two large-scale previous studies in just 2 person-weeks. The resulting code for these tasks show between 2.0x–4.8x reduction in code size. Finally we perform a small controlled experiment to gain insights into how easily mining tasks written using our language features can be understood, with no prior training. We show a substantial number of tasks (77%) were understood by study participants, in about 3 minutes per task.

Categories and Subject Descriptors D.3.3 [*Programming Languages*]: Language Constructs and Features—Patterns

Keywords visitor pattern; source code mining; Boa

1. Introduction

An extremely large wealth of information exists in software repositories, such as open-source repositories like SourceForge which contain over 250k projects, metadata about those projects, source code repositories for those projects including revision history, bug artifacts, etc. Mining this wealth of information is important for researchers in order to detect problems with existing development practices or to use for quantifying proposed solutions to software engineering problems. Many previous works mine these open-source software projects and software repositories to support use cases that include:

- guiding software evolution [23, 24, 35],
- discovering API usage [14, 21, 25, 33],
- fault prediction [10, 13, 17, 22],
- discovering code characteristics [8, 31],
- language feature usage [7, 11, 30], etc.

Source code mining is similar in nature to compilation and program analysis techniques and such techniques often use the visitor pattern [9]. This pattern allows easily traversing the structure of the underlying source code, which is represented as a graph or tree. For example, compilers represent source code as an abstract syntax tree (AST) and typically have several visitors (e.g. for type checking, semantic analysis, code generation). Many developers are familiar with compilers and/or program analysis techniques and have seen/used visitors before.

Despite this, existing approaches for mining source code typically use relational databases [4, 11, 19] and query with SQL. Other approaches provide the ability to mine source code using Datalog [12], Program Query Language (PQL) [20], JQuery [15], or even natural language queries [18]. The motivating question for this work is: can we present a more familiar interface to people interested in mining source code data?

In this paper we present domain-specific language features for mining source code. These features are inspired by the rich body of literature on object-oriented visitor patterns [1, 9, 26, 27, 34]. A key difference from previous work is that we do not require the host language to contain object-oriented features. Our *visitor types* provide a default depth-first search (DFS) traversal strategy, while still maintaining the flexibility to allow custom traversal strategies. Visitor types allow specifying the behavior that executes for a given node type, *before* or *after* visiting the node's children. The language also provides abstractions for dealing with mining of source code history, such as the ability to retreive specific snapshots based on date. We also show several useful patterns for source code mining that utilize these domain specific language features.

We show the feasibility of supporting these domain-specific features by realizing them in the Boa research infrastructure for mining software repositories [6]. Boa provides support for running mining tasks on a very large set of software repositores (699,332 projects from Sourceforge as of February 2013 [32]). As of May 2013, full support for the features described in this work is available

GPCE '13,   October 27–28, 2013, Indianapolis, Indiana, USA.
Copyright © 2013 ACM 978-1-4503-2373-4/13/10... $15.00.
http://dx.doi.org/10.1145/2517208.2517226

in the Boa research infrastructure and is being actively used by ourselves and other researchers for various mining tasks.

To evaluate the language features proposed in this work, we have reproduced two previous large-scale empirical studies using these new features [7, 11]. Together these require writing over 40 software repository mining tasks as programs. Both of these studies require fine-grained access to source code, e.g. Grechanik *et al.* [11] accesses expressions in source code. The study by Dyer *et al.* also requires access to full history information to examine usage of Java language features over time [7]. Finally, both studies require processing large data sets for higher confidence in the results. Using our new language features, a single student was able to reproduce both of these large-scale studies in 2 person-weeks.

Besides these studies, we have also written several other small and medium size mining tasks that are available from the Boa website [32]. These other use cases further increase our confidence in the usefulness of the proposed language features.

We also show some initial insights into the ease of comprehension of mining tasks written in our framework, in which over 75% of tasks were understood in about 3 minutes with no prior training in our language.

In summary, this paper presents the following contributions:

- Domain-specific language abstractions for easily writing source code mining tasks on billions of AST nodes.

- A data schema for representing source code in a language-agnostic manner.

- An implementation of the language features in the Boa infrastructure for software repository mining [6, 32].

- A partial reproduction of a large-scale empirical study on the Java language [11], with over 10 times more projects than the initial study.

- Initial insights into the ease of comprehension of mining tasks written in our framework, in which over 77% of tasks were understood in about 3 minutes each, with no prior training in the language. The same tasks written in Java had only 62% comprehension.

In the next section we motivate the need for large-scale, fine-grained source code mining via an example. We give necessary background on the data representation in Section 3 and detail our approach in Section 4. Our code generation strategy is described in Section 5. We then evaluate our approach in Section 6. In Section 7 we discuss related works. Finally we conclude in Section 8.

2. Motivation

Mining source code is extremely useful for researchers, allowing them to investigate if potential problems exist in reality and test their hypotheses on real-world software. For example, Okur and Dig mine the source code to over 600 programs to see how programmers use parallel libraries and if they use those libraries correctly [25]. Pinto *et al.* mine source code to investigate how test suites evolve over time [31]. Gabel and Su mine over 6k projects to determine how unique source code is [8]. These are but a few example use cases for mining source code. In this section we motivate the need for a domain-specific language for source code mining via a simple task.

Consider testing a simple hypothesis: a large number of bug fixes add checks for `null`. Null-pointer exceptions are a common source of bugs in object-oriented programs. A possible fix for some of these bugs may be to simply guard access to the variable with a check to ensure it is non-null. To investigate such a hypothesis, one may perform the following tasks:

1. Download candidate source code repositories (for example, from SourceForge [2]).

2. Write a program to scan all repositories and locate revisions that potentially fixed bugs.

3. Check out source code snapshots from the identified revisions and the previous snapshots (if any) of the code.

4. Write a program to compare each pair of files, and determine if the number of null checks has increased since the previous snapshot. If so, these files potentially represent a bug fix that added a null check.

5. Parallelize the previous program to support mining tens or hundreds of thousands of projects.

For the purposes of this paper, we assume step 1 has already finished and the repositories are available in a format most suitable for each query language used. This step by itself represents a significant challenge, but for simplicity of this example we will not go into detail on that step at the moment and just assume the data is already available in a suitable format.

The remaining steps, while sounding relatively simple, are very complex as well. For now, let's focus on a small portion of just step 4: let's write queries to find null comparisons in source code. Once we have such a query, we can of course extend it to look for such comparisons occurring inside an if-statement and apply that query to different versions of files, completing step 4.

One possible implementation could be in Java, using Hadoop [3] MapReduce [5] to parallelize the mining task. Such a program is shown in Figure 1. As with most Hadoop programs, there are three main sections: the job setup (lines 2–15), the mapper class (lines 16–138), and the reducer class (lines 139–146). The main portion of the mining task is inside the mapper's `map` method (lines 126–136).

This code is a mixture of several different features: the Hadoop code for efficient data parallelization (lines 2–15 and 139–146), code for traversing the structure of the source being mined (lines 17–124), and code for performing the mining (lines 126–136). Even if you only focus on the mining portion of the code and ignore the rest, this is a complex program.

Another possible implementation in Boa [6, 32] is shown in Figure 2. This program takes a project as input (line 1). It then declares a single visitor (lines 3–8) named `nullCheck`. When the visitor reaches a node of type `Expression` (line 4), it checks if that expression is a comparison operator (line 5) and if one of the operands is `null` (line 6). If it is, then it increments a counter (line 7). This visitor is used by starting a visit on the project using the declared visitor (line 9).

This code avoids the boilerplate code and complexity of the Hadoop version by abstracting away the details of step 5 from the user. Similar to the Hadoop version, it offers a visitor syntax which is easy to understand (as shown in Section 6.2) and familiar to developers. Expanding this query is straight-forward: simply add additional visitors and/or add more clauses to the existing visitor.

3. Background: Representing Data in Boa

Our approach builds on top of Boa [6, 32], a domain-specific language and research infrastructure for efficient, scalable software repository mining. In Boa, users write simple queries in a language that has abstracted away the details of how to write a MapReduce program, thus allowing users to focus on the mining task and not on how to parallelize their programs. Boa's compiler automatically generates a Hadoop [3] program from the source code. Users submit their program to Boa's website via the web interface shown in Figure 3, which compiles and executes it on a cluster. This cluster

```
1   class AddNullCheck {
2     static void main(String[] args) {
3       ... /* create and submit a Hadoop job */

15    }
16    static class AddNullCheckMapper extends
         Mapper<Text, BytesWritable, Text, LongWritable> {
17    static class DefaultVisitor {
18      ... /* define default tree traversal */

124   }
125     void map(Text key, BytesWritable value,
             Context context) {
126       final Project p = ... /* read from input */
127       new DefaultVisitor() {
128         boolean preVisit(Expression e) {
129           if (e.kind == ExpressionKind.EQ ||
                 e.kind == ExpressionKind.NEQ)
130             for (Expression exp : e.expressions)
131               if (exp.kind == ExpressionKind.LITERAL
                     && exp.literal.equals("null")) {
132                 context.write(new Text("count"),
                           new LongWritable(1));
133                 break;
134               }
135         }
136       }.visit(p);
137     }
138   }
139   static class AddNullCheckReducer
         extends Reducer<Text, LongWritable,
                 Text, LongWritable> {
140     void reduce(Text key, Iterable<LongWritable> vals,
             Context context) {
141       int sum = 0;
142       for (LongWritable value : vals)
143         sum += value.get();
144       context.write(key, new LongWritable(sum));
145     }
146   }
147 }
```

Figure 1. Finding null checks in Java/Hadoop.

```
1   p: Project = input;
2   count: output sum of int;

3   nullCheck := visitor {
4     before e: Expression ->
5       if (e.kind == ExpressionKind.EQ
           || e.kind == ExpressionKind.NEQ)
6         exists (i: int; isliteral(e.expressions[i],
                           "null"))
7           count << 1;
8   };

9   visit(p, nullCheck);
```

Figure 2. Finding null checks in Boa.

already contains a cached copy of the software repositories to be mined. Once finished, the website provides the output to the user.

Boa represents all input data using a tree structure. This tree is rooted with the Project and contains information such as project metadata, the source code repositories (SVN, CVS, etc), and the actual source code data.

The types Boa provides for representing source code are: Namespace, Declaration, Method, Variable, Type, Statement, Expression, and Modifier. Several of these are shown in Figure 4 [1], along with the enumeration

---

[1] For a full list of all data types and their attributes, please visit Boa's online documentation:
http://boa.cs.iastate.edu/docs/dsl-types.php

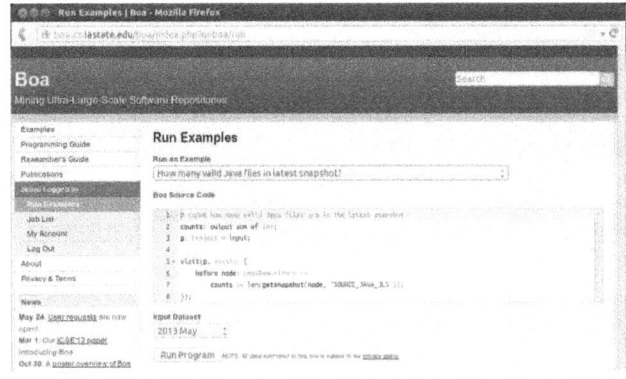

Figure 3. Boa's interface. Zero installation cost. Accessible interface to ease adoption in research, practice, and education.

StatementKind. The declaration, statement, and expression types are discriminated types, meaning they actually represent the union of many different record structures.

Namespace	
name	: string
modifiers	: Modifier[]
declarations	: Declaration[]

Declaration	
name	: string
kind	: TypeKind
modifiers	: Modifier[]
methods	: Method[]
fields	: Variable[]
generic_parameters	: Type[]
parents	: Type[]
nested_declarations	: Declaration[]

Statement	
kind	: StatementKind
statements	: Statement[]
initializations	: Expression[]
updates	: Expression[]
variable_declaration	: Variable?
type_decl	: Declaration?
expression	: Expression?

enum StatementKind
OTHER, BLOCK, TYPEDECL, RETURN, DO, FOR, ASSERT, SYNCRHONIZED, WHILE, IF, BREAK, THROW, TRY, CATCH, SWITCH, CASE, EXPRESSION, LABEL, CONTINUE, EMPTY

Figure 4. Discriminated types for representing source code.

For example, consider the type Statement shown in Figure 4. This type has an attribute kind, which is an enumerated value. Based on the kind of statement, different attributes in the record will be set. For example, if the kind is TYPEDECL then the type_decl attribute is defined. However if the kind is CATCH then the type_decl is undefined. Representing these types as discriminated types allows Boa to keep the number of types as small as possible. This makes supporting future languages easier by only needing to provide a mapping from the new language to the small set of types in Boa. Existing mining tasks would immediately be able to mine source code from these new languages.

While Boa keeps these types as simple as possible, they are still flexible enough to support more complex language features. For example, consider the enhanced-for loop in Java:

```
1   for (String s : iter)
2     body;
```

which says to iterate over the expression iter and for each string value s, run the body. Boa's types do not directly contain an ENHANCEDFOR kind for this language feature.

Despite this design decision, an enhanced-for statement can be easily represented in Boa's schema without having to extend it. First, Boa generates a Statement of kind FOR. Inside that statement, Boa sets expression to iter. Boa also sets the variable_declaration for String s in the statement. Thus, if a statement of kind FOR has its variable_declaration attribute set it is a for-each statement. If that attribute is not defined, then it is a standard for-loop.

Currently, we have fully mapped the Java language to Boa's schema, attempting to simplify the schema as much as possible. This gives a simple, yet flexible, schema capable of supporting the entire Java language (through Java 7). As additional support for other source languages is added, if the schema is not capable of directly supporting a particular language feature the `StatementKind` or `ExpressionKind` enumerations can be easily extended.

4. Fine-grained Source Code Mining

Users must be able to easily express source code mining tasks. For users who are intimately familiar with compilers and interpreters, the visitor style is well understood. However, other users may find two aspects of visitor-style traversals daunting. First, it generally requires writing a significant amount of boiler-plate code whose length is proportional to the complexity of the programming language being visited. Second, this strategy requires intimate familiarity with the structure of that programming language.

To make source code mining more accessible to all users, we investigated the design of more declarative features for mining source code. In this section, we describe our proposed syntax for writing source code mining tasks. The syntax was inspired by previous language features, such as the before and after visit methods in DJ [27] and case expressions in Haskell [16].

```
visitor ::= visitor { visitClause* }
visitClause ::= beforeClause | afterClause
beforeClause ::= before typeList -> beforeClauseStmt
afterClause ::= after typeList -> stmt
typeList ::= _ | identifier : type | type (, type)*
beforeClauseStmt ::= stmt | stopStmt | visit ( identifier ) ;
stopStmt ::= stop ;
```

Figure 5. Proposed syntax for easing source code mining.

The new syntax is shown in Figure 5. The top-level syntax for a mining task is a *visitor type*. Visitor types take zero or more *visit clauses*. A visit clause can be a *before* or an *after* clause. During traversal of the tree, a before clause is executed when visiting a node of the specified type. If the default traversal strategy is used, then the node's children will be visited. After all the children are visited, any matching after clause executes.

Before and after clauses take a *type list*. A type list can be a single type with an optional identifier, a list of types, or an underscore wildcard. The underscore wildcard provides default behavior for a visitor clause. This default executes for a node of type T if no other clause specifies T in its type list. Thus, the following code:

```
1  v := visitor {
2    before Project, CodeRepository, Revision -> { }
3    before _ -> counter++;
4  }
```

will execute the clause's body on line 2 when traversing nodes of type `Project`, `CodeRepository`, or `Revision`. When traversing a node of any other type, the default clause's body on line 3 executes. The result of this code is thus a count of all nodes, excluding those of the types listed. Thus we count only the source code AST nodes for a project.

Note that unlike pattern matching and case expressions in functional languages like Haskell, the order of the before and after clauses do not matter. A type may appear in at most one before clause and at most one after clause.

To begin a mining task, users write a `visit` statement:

```
visit(n, v);
```

that has two parts: the node to visit and a visitor. When this statement executes, a traversal starts at the node represented by `n` using visitor `v`.

4.1 Supporting Custom Traversals

To allow users the ability to override the default traversal strategy, two additional statements are provided inside `before` clauses. The first is the *stop statement*:

```
stop;
```

which when executed will stop the visitor from traversing the children of the current node. This is useful in cases where the mining task never needs to visit specific types further down the tree, allowing to stop at a certain depth. Note that stop acts similar to a return, so no statements after it are reachable.

If the default traversal is stopped, users may provide a custom traversal of the children with a *visit statement*:

```
visit(child);
```

which says to visit the node's `child` tree once. This statement can be called on any subset of the children and in any order. This also allows for visiting a child more than once, if needed.

Figure 6 illustrates a custom traversal strategy from one of our case studies [7]. This program answers the question *how many fields that use a generic type parameter are declared in each project?* To answer this question, the program declares a single visitor. This visitor looks for `Type` nodes where the name contains a generic type parameter (line 5). This visit clause by itself is not sufficient to answer the question, as generic type parameters might occur in other locations, such as the declaration of a class/interface, method parameters, locals, etc. Instead, a custom traversal strategy (lines 10–34) is needed to ensure only field declarations are included.

The traversal strategy first ensures all fields of `Declaration` are visited (lines 12–13). Since declarations can be nested (e.g. in Java, inside other types and in method declarations) we also must manually traverse to find nested declarations (lines 15–32). Finally, we don't want to visit nodes of type `Expression` or `Modifier` (line 34), as these node types can't possibly contain a field declaration but may contain a `Type` node.

Complex mining tasks can be simplified by using multiple visitors. For example, perhaps we only want to look for certain expressions inside of an if statement's condition. We can write a visitor to find if statements, and then use a second sub-visitor to look for the specific expression by visiting the if statement's children. We could perform this mining task with one visitor, however then we need to have flags set to track if we are in the tree underneath an if statement. Using multiple visitors keeps these two mining tasks separate and avoids using flags to keep it simple.

4.2 Mining Snapshots in Time

While our infrastructure contains data for the full revision history of each file, some mining tasks may wish to operate on a single snapshot. We provide several helper functions to ease this use case. For example, the function:

```
getsnapshot(CodeRepository [, time] [, string...])
```

takes a `CodeRepository` as its first argument. It optionally takes a time argument, specifying the time of the snapshot which defaults to the last time in the repository. The function also optionally takes a list of strings. If provided, these strings are used to filter files while generating the snapshot. The file's kind is checked to see if it matches at least one of the patterns specified. For example:

```
getsnapshot(CodeRepository, "SOURCE_JAVA_JLS")
```

says to get the latest snapshot and filter any file that is not a valid Java source file.

A useful pattern is to write a visitor with a before clause for `CodeRepository` that gets a specific snapshot, visits the nodes in the snapshot, and then stops the default traversal:

```
1   p: Project = input;
2   GenFields: output sum[string] of int;

3   genVisitor := visitor {
4     before t: Type ->
5       if (strfind("<", t.name) > -1)
6         GenFields[p.id] << 1;

7     # traversal strategy ensures we only reach Type
8     # if the parent is a Variable, and
9     # we only include Variable paths that are fields
10    before d: Declaration -> {
11    ######## check each field declaration ########
12      foreach (i: int; d.fields[i])
13        visit(d.fields[i]);

14    ########### look for nested types ############
15      foreach (i: int; d.methods[i])
16        visit(d.methods[i]);
17      foreach (i: int; d.nested_declarations[i])
18        visit(d.nested_declarations[i]);
19      stop;
20    }
21    before m: Method -> {
22      foreach (i: int; m.statements[i])
23        visit(m.statements[i]);
24      stop;
25    }
26    before s: Statement -> {
27      foreach (i: int; s.statements[i])
28        visit(s.statements[i]);
29      if (def(s.type_declaration))
30        visit(s.type_declaration);
31      stop;
32    }

33    ####### stop at expressions/modifiers ########
34    before Expression, Modifier -> stop;
35  };
36  visit(p, genVisitor);
```

Figure 6. Using a custom traversal strategy to find uses of generics in field declarations.

```
1   visitor {
2     before n: CodeRepository -> {
3       snapshot := getsnapshot(n);
4       foreach (i: int; def(snapshot[i]))
5         visit(snapshot[i]);
6       stop;
7     }
8     ...
9   }
```

This visitor will visit all code repositories for a project, obtain the last snapshot of the files in that repository, and then visit the source code of those files. This pattern is useful for mining the *current version* of a software repository.

4.3 Mining Revision Pairs

Often a mining task might want to locate certain revisions and compare files at that revision to their previous state. For example, our motivating example looks for revisions that fixed bugs and then compares the files at that revision to their previous snapshot. To accomplish this task, one can use the following pattern:

```
1   files: map[string] of ChangedFile;

2   v := visitor {
3     before f: ChangedFile -> {
4       if (def(files[f.name])) {
5         ... # task comparing f and files[f.name]
6       }
7       files[f.name] = f;
8     }
9   };
```

which declares a map of files, indexed by their path. The code on line 4 checks if a previous version of the file was cached. If it was, the code on line 5 executes where f refers to the current version of the file being visited and the expression files[f.name] refers to the previous version of the file. Finally, the code on line 7 updates the map, storing the current version of the file.

4.4 Bringing It All Together: Motivating Example

Recall the hypothesis in Section 2: a large number of bug fixes add checks for null. In that section, we focused on a very small sub-task of step 4. In this section, we describe a solution that incorporates all five steps required to answer the proposed hypothesis.

```
1   # STEP 1 - candidate projects as input
2   p: Project = input;
3   results: output collection[string] of string;

4   fixing := false;
5   count := 0;
6   files: map[string] of ChangedFile;

7   nullCheckVisitor := visitor {
8     before e: Expression ->
9       if (e.kind == ExpressionKind.EQ
            || e.kind == ExpressionKind.NEQ)
10        exists (i: int; isliteral(e.expressions[i],
                                    "null"))
11          count++;
12  };

13  visit(p, visitor {
14    before r: Revision ->
15      # STEP 2 - potential revisions that fix bugs
16      fixing = isfixingrevision(r.log);

17    before f: ChangedFile -> {
18      if (fixing && haskey(files, f.name)) {
19        count = 0;
20        # STEP 3a - check out source from revision
21        visit(getast(files[f.name]));
22        last := count;

23        count = 0;
24        # STEP 3b - source from previous revision
25        visit(getast(f));

26        # STEP 4 - determine if null checks increased
27        if (count > last)
28          results[p.id] << string(f);
29      }
30      files[f.name] = f;
31      stop;
32    }

33    before s: Statement ->
34      if (s.kind == StatementKind.IF)
35        visit(s.expression, nullCheckVisitor);
36  });
```

Figure 7. Finding in Boa fixing revisions that add null checks.

Consider the Boa program in Figure 7, which implements all five steps of the entire mining task. This program takes a single project as input. It then passes the program's data tree to a visitor (line 13). This visitor keeps track if the last Revision seen was a fixing revision (line 16). When it sees a ChangedFile it looks at the current revision's log message and if it is a fixing revision (step 2) it will get snapshots of the current file and the previous version of the file (step 3) and visit their AST nodes (lines 21 and 25).

When visiting the AST nodes for these snapshots, if it encounters a Statement of kind IF (line 34), it then uses a sub-visitor to check if the statement's expression contains a null check (lines 35 and 7–12) and increments a counter (line 11). Thus we will know the number of null checks in each snapshot and can compare (line

27

27) to see if there are more null checks (step 4). Note that this analysis is conservative and may not find all fixing revisions that add null checks, as the revision may also *remove* a null check from another location and thus give the same count.

This task illustrates several features mentioned earlier in this section. First, the second visitor shows use of a custom traversal strategy by utilizing a stop statement. Second, it makes use of a sub-visitor (nullCheckVisitor). Third, it uses the revision pair pattern to check several versions of a file.

Finally, writing this task required no explicit mention of parallizing the query. Writing the same task in Hadoop would require a lot of boilerplate code to manually parallelize the task, whereas the Boa version is automatically parallelized.

5. Code Generation Strategy

As noted previously, each Boa program is translated by the Boa compiler into a Map/Reduce program that runs using the Hadoop framework. We extended this compiler to support visitor types. In this section we outline the code generation strategy for supporting visitor types. For ease of illustration, we omit all code related to Map/Reduce to allow readers to focus on visitor types. The key to our strategy involves a default visitor (Figure 8) that we added to the Boa runtime.

```
1  public abstract class DeafultVisitor {
2    public final void visit(Project node) {
3      if (preVisit(node)) {
4        ... // call visit() on each of node's children

8        postVisit(node);
9      }
10   }
11   ... // similar visit() for each node type

205  /////////////////////////////////////////
206  // methods for before clauses

207  protected boolean defaultPreVisit() {
208    return true;
209  }

210  protected boolean preVisit(Project node) {
211    return defaultPreVisit();
212  }
213  ... // similar preVisit() for each node type

250  /////////////////////////////////////////
251  // methods for after clauses

252  protected void defaultPostVisit() { }

253  protected void postVisit(Project node) {
254    defaultPostVisit();
255  }
256  ... // similar postVisit() for each node type

295  }
```

Figure 8. Outline of the abstract default visitor.

The DefaultVisitor class contains a public visit method for each node type in the language. These methods contain a single if-statement which calls a preVisit method in the condition. If that method returns true, then the children of the current node are each visited and a postVisit method is called.

A preVisit and postVisit method is also generated for each node type in the language. The bodies of these methods simply call the defaultPreVisit/defaultPostVisit methods. These methods are virtual methods and are (possibly) overridden by the concrete visitor sub-classes.

Generating Visitors All visitors in the language:

```
var := visit { .. };
```

inherit from the DefaultVisitor (Figure 8):

```
var = new DefaultVisitor() { .. };
```

This inheritance provides the visitor with a default depth-first traversal strategy that will visit all nodes in the tree. The actions taken when visiting specific nodes are specified via the before and after visit clauses.

Generating Visit Clauses A before visit clause generates one or more method overrides for the preVisit methods. There are three possibilities for a before visit clause's type list. First, it may specify a specific type and an identifier:

```
before id: T -> body;
```

which is translated into:

```
1  protected boolean preVisit(T id) {
2    body;
3    [return true;] // if necessary
4  }
```

Since the method must return a value, the body is analyzed to determine if a stop statement occurs on all exit paths. If it does not, then a return statement is generated with a value of true.

The second form for a visit clause's type list is a list of types:

```
before T1, T2, .. -> body;
```

which is translated similar to before, where each type has its own preVisit method generated and the id is a fresh name.

The third form is an underscore wildcard:

```
before _ -> body;
```

which is translated into:

```
1  protected boolean defaultPreVisit() {
2    body;
3    [return true;] // if necessary
4  }
```

similar to the previous translation strategy.

Generation of after visit clauses is almost identical to before clauses, with two slight differences. First, the name of the generated method is changed to postVisit/defaultPostVisit. Second, since the method has a void return type no return statements are generated.

Generating Stop Statements Before visit clauses return a boolean value to indicate if the DefaultVisitor should visit the children of the node. Since stop statements can only appear in before visit clauses, they are transformed into:

```
return false;
```

which makes the if condition (Figure 8, line 3) false and stops the default traversal of the node's children. It also stops the execution of the before visitor.

Generating Nested Visit Calls There is no need to transform a nested visit call, as both the method name and arguments are identical in the generated code.

Optimizing Traversals By default, the generated code visits every node in the tree. For some visitors, this may not be optimal. By analyzing the visit clauses, we can determine the lowest type being visited and ensure the traversal stops at that point.

Stopping is accomplished by adding a stop statement to the end of the before clause for that type. If the type only has an after clause, then an empty before clause is first generated. If that type also has an after clause, it is merged into the body of the before clause, immediately before the stop statement.

6. Evaluation

We now evaluate the utility and comprehensibility of new features.

6.1 Utility of Declarative Visitors

To evaluate the language features proposed in this work, we reproduced two previous large-scale empirical studies [7, 11] using these new features. Together these require writing over 40 software repository mining tasks as programs. Both of these studies require fine-grained access to source code, e.g. Grechanik *et al.* [11] access expressions in source code. The study by Dyer *et al.* also requires access to full history information to examine usage of Java language features over time [7]. Finally, both studies require processing large data sets for higher confidence in the results.

Using our new language features, a single student was able to reproduce both of these large-scale studies in 2 person-weeks. Grechanik *et al.*'s study [11] took a bit over 1 person-week and Dyer *et al.*'s study [7] took under 1 person-week. This included the time to formulate, write, execute, debug, and analyze results.

6.1.1 Java Language Feature Usage

Dyer *et al.*'s study [7] performed a large-scale study on the use of Java language features. In that study, they wrote several mining tasks to identify the use of Java language features over time. For example, one such task mined source code to track the use of `assert` statements over time. These tasks were written in Boa without the syntax proposed in Section 4. For this paper, we rewrote those tasks using the new syntax and then measured the lines of code for both versions. The results are shown in Table 1.

Task	LOC (visitor)	LOC (old [7])
Annotations-define	17	63 (3.7x)
Annotations-use	17	80 (4.7x)
Assert	17	63 (3.7x)
Binary-lit	17	63 (3.7x)
Diamond	17	82 (4.8x)
EnhancedFor	17	63 (3.7x)
Enums	17	63 (3.7x)
Generics-define-field	39	77 (2.0x)
Generics-define-method	17	63 (3.7x)
Generics-define-type	17	63 (3.7x)
Generics-wildcard-extends	17	82 (4.8x)
Generics-wildcard-super	17	82 (4.8x)
Generics-wildcard	17	82 (4.8x)
Multicatch	17	63 (3.7x)
Safe-varargs	38	83 (2.2x)
Try-resources	17	63 (3.7x)
Underscore-lit	18	64 (3.6x)
Varargs	17	63 (3.7x)
Total	**350**	**1,262 (3.6x)**
Mean	**19**	**70 (3.6x)**

Table 1. Mining tasks on Java language feature usage.

The results clearly show that our proposed syntax improves the writing of fine-grained source code mining tasks. On average, the tasks required almost 73% fewer lines of code. Most of the difference in lines came from the lack of needing to manually specify the traversal strategy. These results give some insight into the utility and potential ease of declarative visitors for mining tasks.

6.1.2 Reproducing the Treasure Study

Grechanik *et al.* performed a large-scale empirical study on Java source code from 2,080 open-source projects [11]. The dataset used in their study were randomly selected projects from SourceForge. For their study they built an SQL database containing tables and attributes for storing (non)terminals from Java's grammar. They posed 32 different research questions and queried their database to answer those questions. To show the usefulness of our approach, we reproduced a portion of this study using Boa.

As the actual queries used are not available, we had to make a few assumptions about their study. First, we assumed that none of the projects in their study were empty and all contained at least one valid Java source file. This assumption was made on the basis that their minimum value for number of classes per application is 1. Thus, we filter our dataset to exclude any projects without at least one valid Java source file. This left 23,510 projects in our study.

Second, although their paper only mentions parsing the source code, we assume that since they were only working with releases of each project that they also had type resolution and bindings. This information is not yet available in Boa[2], so we do not reproduce the six tasks that rely on that information for accuracy.

Finally, we assume that the versions of each project used in their study were the latest versions. As Boa contains all revisions for projects but does not currently know what revision(s) map to specific releases, for our version of the study we simply take the latest snapshot of each project. We also filter out any obvious branches (in SVN, branches typically are rooted in the 'branches' folder). This gave a total of 8,360,673 changed files in this snapshot, or about one third of the total dataset.

The results of our study, as well as the values from the previous study, are shown in Table 2. The statistical values (mean, median, max, and min) are computed using the most logical container for each question. For example, the container for classes are projects, the container for methods are classes, etc. As can be seen, most values differ between the studies. This is to be expected, as there are over 11 times more projects in our study. However, note that the general trends are similar and in particular the order of magnitude between rows is maintained.

For our version of the study, some of the values in the max column seemed like they might be too high. We manually verified[3] these values to be correct. Some interesting results:

- Despite the Java VM having a limit of 255 arguments for a method, we located a class constructor with 262 arguments!

- We located a test class with over 32k (hopefully generated) `void` methods in it to exhaustively test a method's 16-bit integer argument.

- A compiler-generated X10 file with over 7k local variables.

- A class with 10k static fields as constant strings.

The one task where we differ substantially is for nested classes. Note the mean value is almost 1k times higher. We believe this is because their study averages nested classes by number of methods. However we disagree with this, as the most common container for a nested class is another class. Thus we opted to compute this value slightly different.

6.2 Comprehension of Mining Tasks

In this section, we outline a small controlled experiment to determine if our proposed framework and language extensions make it easier to understand source code mining tasks. Each participant was shown, one at a time, a set of 5 source code mining tasks written in Boa. For each task, they were asked to describe in their own words what the task does. They were given up to five minutes to study each task and forced to move on if no answer was given after five minutes. The five tasks were:

---

[2] This is a limitation of the data and types available in Boa, and not of the visitor syntax described in this paper.

[3] http://goo.gl/bwGGC http://goo.gl/jf0Fy
http://goo.gl/zuYoh http://goo.gl/ZgamQ

Question	Total		Mean		Median		Max		Min	
	Boa	Treasure	Boa	Treasure	Boa	Treasure	Boa	Treasure	Boa	Treasure
Classes	11,822,321	270,973	503.68	96.8	89	33	139,668	2,071	1	1
Static Classes	569,501	7,368	24.25	6.7	0	0	23,744	1,035	0	0
Anonymous Classes	3,772,130	29,237	0.05	0.04	0	0	724	136	0	0
Nested Classes	1,218,213	14,270	51.86	0.06	3	0	30,576	61	0	0
`assert` Statements	612,166	2,047	0.01	0	0	0	374	9	0	0
Methods	68,062,962	938,779	5.89	3.5	2	4	32,774	1,175	1	1
Static Methods	5,696,065	231,647	0.48	0.36	0	0	4,853	289	0	0
Methods (interfaces)	4,712,116	84,130	6.13	3.4	3	3	10,000	558	1	1
Method Arities	66,778,747	544,324	1.59	1.5	1	1	262	30	1	1
`void` return Methods	35,988,971	414,953	3.54	5.1	2	3	32,772	1,172	1	1
Methods Returning Arrays	1,334,259	24,744	1.87	2	1	1	383	137	1	1
non-`void` return Methods	32,073,991	523,826	4.93	5.8	2	3	4,854	888	1	1
Fields	31,682,721	448,898	2.68	1.9	0	0	10,000	1,457	0	0
`this` Expressions	51,933,214	840,937	0.72	2.2	0	1	6,294	785	0	0
Static Fields	10,949,191	154,067	0.93	0.7	0	0	10,000	1,457	0	0
Volatile Fields	48,471	492	0	0	0	0	97	9	0	0
Conditional Statements	118,557,128	620,419	1.63	0.76	0	0	5,294	750	0	0
`String` Fields	6,425,161	231,647	0.54	0.3	0	0	3,473	432	0	0
`try` Statements	14,080,420	93,714	0.19	0.11	0	0	1,722	90	0	0
Exceptions Thrown From `catch`	4,559,274	110,740	0.3	0.26	0	0	34	5	0	0
Exceptions	12,631,996	818,358	0.17	0.9	0	0	1,086	40	0	0
Local Variables	79,057,404	818,358	1.09	0.87	0	0	7,005	1,055	0	0

Table 2. Reproducing a portion of the Treasure study [11], at a much larger scale.

Q1 Count AST nodes (Section 4)

Q2 Assert use over time (Table 1, Assert)

Q3 Annotation use, by name (Table 1, Annotations-use)

Q4 Type name collector, by project and file (not shown)

Q5 Null check (Section 2, motivating example)

Q1	Q2	Q3	Q4	Q5	Total	Time
N	Y	Y	Y	Y	80%	12m32s
-Y	Y	Y	Y	Y	100%	11m22s
?	Y	Y	Y	Y	80%	19m22s
-Y	Y	Y	Y	Y	100%	18m21s
?	+N	Y	Y	N	40%	11m40s
N	Y	Y	Y	-Y	80%	23m01s
N	-Y	Y	Y	Y	80%	16m10s
N	+N	-Y	-Y	Y	60%	14m50s
				Mean	**77.5%**	**15m55s**

Table 3. Controlled experiment on comprehensibility of source code mining tasks in Boa.

Q1	Q2	Q3	Q4	Q5	Total	Time
-Y	-Y	N	-Y	-Y	80%	23m44s
?	-Y	-Y	-Y	N	60%	10m50s
-Y	Y	+N	Y	-Y	80%	23m48s
N	Y	N	-Y	N	40%	12m07s
N	-Y	N	N	N	20%	12m08s
-Y	Y	Y	Y	Y	100%	15m52s
N	N	Y	-Y	-Y	60%	18m14s
-Y	+N	Y	N	Y	60%	11m17s
				Mean	**62.5%**	**16m**

Table 4. Controlled experiment on comprehensibility of source code mining tasks in Java+Hadoop.

These answers were graded on a fixed set of criteria. For each question, we determined a list of criteria that must all be mentioned in order for the answer to be marked correct. For example, for Q1 they had to mention counting only AST nodes (not all nodes) and grouping the count by project.

Then they were shown the same set of 5 tasks again in a random order, only this time instead of a free-form entry they were given a choice of four descriptions and asked to choose the one that best fit. Only one of the four descriptions was accurate while the other four varied slightly (to make them inaccurate). For example, for Q1 only half the responses mention grouping by project. Also only two responses mention counting only AST nodes.

The results are shown in Table 3. A 'Y' indicates the participant answered correctly, both in the free-form and the multiple choice. Similarly a 'N' indicates they answered incorrectly in both. An entry marked '-Y' indicates their free-form answer was incorrect while their multiple choice was correct. Conversely, a '+N' indicates their free-form answer was correct and multiple choice answer incorrect. For the multiple choice, they were also given a choice of 'I am not sure what this task does' which is indicated in the table as '?'. We count this as an incorrect answer.

On average it took 16 minutes to study these five tasks, or around 3 minutes to comprehend a mining task in Boa. The accuracy of the comprehension was at 77.5% on average. Note however that one of the tasks in particular (Q1) seemed to give difficulty. Feedback suggested they failed to understand the semantics of the wildcard. Excluding that task, the accuracy jumps to over 90%.

We repeated this experiment with the same participants six months later. In the repeated experiment, the same five mining tasks were used as in the previous experiment, but this time the source code implementing the tasks was Java+Hadoop code (similar to

Figure 1). The results are shown in Table 4. Note that all results were anonymized so rows do not correlate to rows in Figure 3.

Again, participants spent 16 minutes on average to study these tasks. This time however, the accuracy of comprehension was lower at 62.5%, almost 15% lower than the Boa survey! Another interesting result was the number of '-Y' responses. There were 15 such responses in the second survey compared to only 6 in the Boa survey. This may indicate more guessing or possibly a memory effect where they recalled the answer from taking the Boa survey six months earlier.

The results from these studies are extremely promising for two reasons. First, it gives insight that in only a few minutes most people can comprehend a source code mining task using our approach. Second, this comprehension comes with **no training at all** in the new language features! Based on the feedback, we believe that even a short training session on Boa's language features would have helped the participants understand Q1 better.

6.3 Threats to Validity

For our usability evaluation in Section 6.1.1, there is potential construct bias as all of the code for our lines of code comparison in Table 1 was written by us. This was unavoidable as at the time no other researchers had access to our infrastructure.

The results of our reproduction of the Treasure study in Section 6.1.2 may not generalize to Java development practices in industry, as all of the code in our study comes from open-source. This same threat applies to the original study [11]. We avoid generalizing our results and instead focus on if the trends we observe are similar to the trends the previous study observed.

Our comprehension study in Section 6.2 suffers from selection bias as all participants were graduate students. We try to offset this bias by selecting participants from several sub-fields of SE/PL. The study also suffers from testing effects, since each task is given to the participants twice. We offset this effect by randomizing the presentation order the second time tasks were shown. There is also possible construct bias as we chose which tasks to present and might inadvertently select only simple tasks. To counter this, we chose what we considered to be a range from easy to difficult tasks. Finally, there are additional testing effects since the Java+Hadoop portion of the survey was performed after the Boa portion. This could actually bias the results in favor of the Java+Hadoop approach.

7. Related Works

Source code analysis is often performed using a visitor-style pattern [9]. The visitor pattern is intended to allow easily adding additional functionality to a hierarchy of types, without having to modify each type. This is typically accomplished via a double-dispatch where each type to be traversed contains an `accept` method and the new analysis contains `visit` methods. By default visitors perform a depth-first traversal of the tree. There are other forms of the pattern, such as hierarchical visitors [1] which allow controlling the traversal and visitor combinators [34] to compose more complex visitors. There are also reusable visitor pattern libraries [26]. Other approaches make use of visitors, such as Ovlinger and Wand who define a language for recursive traversals [29].

Our language is similar to many of these approaches, however while these approaches are typically for object-oriented languages our host language has no notion of object (only simple record types). Visitors make use of dynamic dispatch in the underlying language, which is not available in procedural languages like Boa. Also, since there is no notion of inheritance, the number of types in the language are fixed, making the analysis in our compiler implementation much simpler and allowed for the optimization mentioned in Section 5.

Orleans and Lieberherr provide the language DJ [27], a purely Java-based library implementation of Demeter/Java [28]. In DJ, users provide a traversal strategy and declare visitors with before and after visit methods, similar to our approach. DJ's implementation uses reflection to implement the traversals, while our implementation uses the `DefaultVisitor` and has no reflection in the source or generated code.

Both the work on DJ [27] and recursive traversals [29] provide syntax for specifying traversals separate from the visitor code. Our approach provides a default depth-first traversal and if users need a custom traversal strategy they must specify it intermixed with the visitor code by using `stop` statements and `visit` calls. In the

future we may investigate syntax for separating custom traversal strategies from the visitor syntax.

Martin *et al.* describe a program query language (PQL) [20] for easily analyzing source code. They provide a fixed set of events in the language, such as method call or field access and allow queries on those events. They provide static and dynamic matching algorithms. The query language lacks a visitor syntax.

There are also interactive tools for querying source code using natural language queries [18] and custom languages such as JQuery [15]. Since these tools are interactive, they are designed for searching a single codebase and not for mining source code across a large number of projects.

The Sourcerer project [19] provides project metadata source code for over 18k Java projects. Their data is stored in a SQL database, allowing for standard SQL queries on that data. They provide data on single snapshots of projects, including source code information which is represented in the database as entities and relationships. Entities include declarations, type references, and local variables. Relationships include full type resolution and binding of the entities, which our approach does not currently support. The Treasure study [11] built a database containing source code for over 2k projects. They take source code from releases of each project, and map it into their database schema. This schema is capable of representing the entire source code, down to the expression level. Bevan *et al.* proposed a centralized database and data schema called Kenyon [4] for storing mined software repository information. They provide an SQL interface for querying this dataset. All three of these approaches use SQL for mining source code, which gives the benefit of easily performing joins. However source code queries often require recursion (over the graph structure of the data), which is cumbersome to express in SQL [12].

Hajiyev *et al.* describe CodeQuest [12], which uses safe Datalog to query source code information. They map the Datalog queries to standard SQL and query a relational database containing source code information. Unlike SQL, Datalog allows easily specifying recursive style queries but lacks the visitor pattern that is familiar to researchers who have worked on or studied compilers and source code analysis previously.

Our previous work on the Boa language and infrastructure [6] provided a domain specific language for querying metadata on over 600k projects and an efficient infrastructure for executing those queries. The language abstracted away details of the underlying infrastructure such that users did not need to be aware of how to parallelize their queries. It also provided a set of domain-specific types for mining software repositories. Boa was extended to support source code mining on millions of Java files, however the language lacked the simple abstractions for easily traversing the structure of the data to perform source code mining tasks. This work has nicely filled that research gap.

8. Conclusion

Mining source code in large-scale software repositories should be easier! It is important for answering a large number of research questions [7, 8, 10, 11, 13, 17, 21, 23–25, 31]. In particular, having full history information for source code is necessary for research on fault prediction [10, 13, 17, 23], change dependency and change coupling analyses [14, 35], and temporal analysis on API and object usage [22, 33] among others.

This work described new domain-specific features to help with mining source code. Although host languages for mining source code may not always be object-oriented, we show how to build support for abstract syntax tree traversal in a style reminiscent of the familiar visitor design pattern. These features have a familiar look and semantics, but are flexible enough to support over 40 different mining tasks from two previous studies. We also give insights into the ease of comprehending tasks written using these domain-specific language features, which showed that over 77% of tasks can be understood in about 3 minutes even with no prior training in the new language features.

To date, previous works offer only a sub-set of: full source code history, enough data for mining down to the expression level, and being capable of scaling to a large number of projects. No previous work offers all of these features. The implementation presented in this work supports all of these features. We provide a flexible data schema for representing source code, including full history information and entities down to the expression level.

Since these features are now available in the Boa research infrastructure, and are actively being used on a daily basis, in the next few years we anticipate having hundreds more example uses. Feedback from this use would help drive their evolution and provide a larger validation of their design in practice.

Acknowledgments

This work was supported by NSF grants CCF-13-49153, CCF-13-20578, TWC-12-23828, CCF-11-17937, CCF-10-17334, and CCF-10-18600.

References

[1] Hierarchical visitor pattern, c2 pattern repository. http://c2.com/cgi/wiki?HierarchicalVisitorPattern, 2012.

[2] Sourceforge website. http://sourceforge.net/, 2012.

[3] Apache Software Foundation. Hadoop: Open source implementation of MapReduce. http://hadoop.apache.org/, 2013.

[4] J. Bevan, E. J. Whitehead, Jr., S. Kim, and M. Godfrey. Facilitating software evolution research with Kenyon. In *ESEC/FSE'05: 10th European Software Engineering Conference held jointly with 13th ACM SIGSOFT International Symposium on Foundations of Software Engineering*, pages 177–186, 2005.

[5] J. Dean and S. Ghemawat. MapReduce: simplified data processing on large clusters. In *OSDI'04: 6th Symposium on Operating System Design and Implementation*, pages 137–150, 2004.

[6] R. Dyer, H. A. Nguyen, H. Rajan, and T. N. Nguyen. Boa: A language and infrastructure for analyzing ultra-large-scale software repositories. In *ICSE'13: 35th International Conference on Software Engineering*, pages 422–431, 2013.

[7] R. Dyer, H. A. Nguyen, H. Rajan, and T. N. Nguyen. A large-scale empirical study of Java language feature usage. Technical report, Iowa State University, 2013.

[8] M. Gabel and Z. Su. A study of the uniqueness of source code. In *FSE'10: 18th ACM SIGSOFT International Symposium on Foundations of Software Engineering*, pages 147–156, 2010.

[9] E. Gamma, R. Helm, R. Johnson, and J. Vlissides. *Design Patterns: Elements of Reusable Object-Oriented Software*. Addison-Wesley Professional, 1994.

[10] T. L. Graves, A. F. Karr, J. S. Marron, and H. Siy. Predicting fault incidence using software change history. *IEEE Trans. Softw. Eng.*, 26 (7):653–661, 2000.

[11] M. Grechanik, C. McMillan, L. DeFerrari, M. Comi, S. Crespi, D. Poshyvanyk, C. Fu, Q. Xie, and C. Ghezzi. An empirical investigation into a large-scale Java open source code repository. In *ESEM'10: International Symposium on Empirical Software Engineering and Measurement*, pages 11:1–11:10, 2010.

[12] E. Hajiyev, M. Verbaere, and O. de Moor. Codequest: scalable source code queries with datalog. In *ECOOP'06: 20th European conference on Object-Oriented Programming*, pages 2–27, 2006.

[13] A. E. Hassan. Predicting faults using the complexity of code changes. In *ICSE'09: 31st International Conference on Software Engineering*, pages 78–88, 2009.

[14] K. Herzig and A. Zeller. Mining cause-effect-chains from version histories. In *ISSRE'11: 22nd IEEE International Symposium on Software Reliability Engineering*, pages 60–69, 2011.

[15] D. Janzen and K. De Volder. Navigating and querying code without getting lost. In *AOSD'03: 2nd international conference on Aspect-oriented software development*, pages 178–187, 2003.

[16] S. P. Jones. *Haskell 98 Language and Libraries: The Revised Report*. Cambridge University Press, 2003.

[17] S. Kim, T. Zimmermann, J. Whitehead, and A. Zeller. Predicting faults from cached history. In *ICSE'07: 29th International Conference on Software Engineering*, pages 489–498, 2007.

[18] M. Kimmig, M. Monperrus, and M. Mezini. Querying source code with natural language. In *ASE'11: 26th IEEE/ACM International Conference on Automated Software Engineering*, pages 376–379, 2011.

[19] E. Linstead, S. Bajracharya, T. Ngo, C. Rigor, C. Lopes, and P. Baldi. Sourcerer: mining and searching internet-scale software repositories. *Data Mining and Knowledge Discovery*, 18:300–336, April 2009.

[20] M. Martin, B. Livshits, and M. S. Lam. Finding application errors and security flaws using pql: a program query language. In *OOPSLA'05: 20th annual ACM SIGPLAN conference on Object-oriented programming, systems, languages, and applications*, pages 365–383, 2005.

[21] C. McMillan, D. Poshyvanyk, M. Grechanik, Q. Xie, and C. Fu. Portfolio: Searching for relevant functions and their usages in millions of lines of code. *TOSEM: ACM Transactions on Software Engineering and Methodology*, page To Appear, 2013.

[22] Y. Mileva, A. Wasylkowski, and A. Zeller. Mining evolution of object usage. In *ECOOP'11: 25th European Conference on Object-Oriented Programming*, 2011.

[23] N. Nagappan and T. Ball. Use of relative code churn measures to predict system defect density. In *ICSE'05: 27th International Conference on Software Engineering*, pages 284–292, 2005.

[24] I. Neamtiu, J. S. Foster, and M. Hicks. Understanding source code evolution using abstract syntax tree matching. In *MSR'05: International Workshop on Mining Software Repositories*, pages 1–5, 2005.

[25] S. Okur and D. Dig. How do developers use parallel libraries? In *FSE'12: 20th ACM SIGSOFT International Symposium on Foundations of Software Engineering*, pages 54:1–54:11, 2012.

[26] B. C. d. S. Oliveira, M. Wang, and J. Gibbons. The visitor pattern as a reusable, generic, type-safe component. In *OOPSLA'08: 23rd ACM SIGPLAN Conference on Object-Oriented Programming, Systems, Languages, and Applications*, pages 439–456, 2008.

[27] D. Orleans and K. J. Lieberherr. Dj: Dynamic adaptive programming in java. In *REFLECTION'01: 3rd International Conference on Metalevel Architectures and Separation of Crosscutting Concerns*, pages 73–80, 2001.

[28] D. Orleans and K. J. Lieberherr. DemeterJ. Technical report, Northeastern University, 2001. URL http://www.ccs.neu.edu/research/demeter/DemeterJava/.

[29] J. Ovlinger and M. Wand. A language for specifying recursive traversals of object structures. In *OOPSLA'99: 14th ACM SIGPLAN Conference on Object-Oriented Programming, Systems, Languages, and Applications*, pages 70–81, 1999.

[30] C. Parnin, C. Bird, and E. Murphy-Hill. Adoption and use of Java generics. *Empirical Software Engineering*, pages 1–43, 2012.

[31] L. S. Pinto, S. Sinha, and A. Orso. Understanding myths and realities of test-suite evolution. In *FSE'12: 20th ACM SIGSOFT International Symposium on Foundations of Software Engineering*, pages 33:1–33:11, 2012.

[32] H. Rajan, T. N. Nguyen, R. Dyer, and H. A. Nguyen. Boa website. http://boa.cs.iastate.edu/, 2012.

[33] G. Udding, B. Dagenais, and M. P. Robillard. Temporal analysis of API usage concepts. In *ICSE'12: 34th International Conference on Software Engineering*, pages 804–814, 2012.

[34] J. Visser. Visitor combination and traversal control. In *OOPSLA'01: 16th ACM SIGPLAN conference on Object-Oriented Programming, Systems, Languages, and Applications*, pages 270–282, 2001.

[35] T. Zimmermann, P. Weisgerber, S. Diehl, and A. Zeller. Mining version histories to guide software changes. In *ICSE'04: 26th International Conference on Software Engineering*, pages 563–572, 2004.

Open Pattern Matching for C++

Yuriy Solodkyy   Gabriel Dos Reis   Bjarne Stroustrup

Texas A&M University
College Station, Texas, USA
{yuriys,gdr,bs}@cse.tamu.edu

Abstract

Pattern matching is an abstraction mechanism that can greatly simplify source code. We present functional-style pattern matching for C++ implemented as a library, called *Mach7*[1]. All the patterns are user-definable, can be stored in variables, passed among functions, and allow the use of class hierarchies. As an example, we implement common patterns used in functional languages.

Our approach to pattern matching is based on compile-time composition of pattern objects through concepts. This is superior (in terms of performance and expressiveness) to approaches based on run-time composition of polymorphic pattern objects. In particular, our solution allows mapping functional code based on pattern matching directly into C++ and produces code that is only a few percent slower than hand-optimized C++ code.

The library uses an efficient type switch construct, further extending it to multiple scrutinees and general patterns. We compare the performance of pattern matching to that of double dispatch and open multi-methods in C++.

Categories and Subject Descriptors   D.1.5 [*Programming techniques*]: Object-oriented Programming;   D.3.3 [*Programming Languages*]: Language Constructs and Features

General Terms   Languages, Design

Keywords   Pattern Matching, C++

1. Introduction

Pattern matching is an abstraction mechanism popularized by the functional programming community, most notably ML [12], OCaml [21], and Haskell [15], and recently adopted by several multi-paradigm and object-oriented programming languages such as Scala [30], F# [7], and dialects of C++[22, 29]. The expressive power of pattern matching has been cited as the number one reason for choosing a functional language for a task [6, 25, 28].

This paper presents functional-style pattern matching for C++. To allow experimentation and to be able to use production-quality toolchains (in particular, compilers and optimizers), we implemented our matching facilities as a C++ library.

---

[1] The library is available at http://parasol.tamu.edu/mach7/

GPCE '13,   October 27–28, 2013, Indianapolis, Indiana, USA.
Copyright © 2013 ACM 978-1-4503-2373-4/13/10... $15.00.
http://dx.doi.org/10.1145/2517208.2517222

1.1 Summary

We present functional-style pattern matching for C++ built as an ISO C++11 library. Our solution:
* is open to the introduction of new patterns into the library, while not making any assumptions about existing ones.
* is type safe: inappropriate applications of patterns to subjects are compile-time errors.
* Makes patterns first-class citizens in the language (§3.1).
* is non-intrusive, so that it can be retroactively applied to existing types (§3.2).
* provides a unified syntax for various encodings of extensible hierarchical datatypes in C++.
* provides an alternative interpretation of the controversial n+k patterns (in line with that of constructor patterns), leaving the choice of exact semantics to the user (§3.3).
* supports a limited form of views (§3.4).
* generalizes open type switch to multiple scrutinees and enables patterns in case clauses (§3.5).
* demonstrates that compile-time composition of patterns through concepts is superior to run-time composition of patterns through polymorphic interfaces in terms of performance, expressiveness, and static type checking (§4.1).

Our library sets a standard for the performance, extensibility, brevity, clarity, and usefulness of any language solution for pattern matching. It provides full functionality, so we can experiment with the use of pattern matching in C++ and compare it to existing alternatives. Our solution requires only current support of C++11 without any additional tool support.

2. Pattern Matching in C++

The object analyzed through pattern matching is commonly called the *scrutinee* or *subject*, while its static type is commonly called the *subject type*. Consider for example the following definition of factorial in *Mach7*:

```
int factorial(int n) {
  unsigned short m;
  Match(n) {
    Case(0) return 1;
    Case(m) return m*factorial(m−1);
    Case(_) throw std::invalid_argument("factorial");
  } EndMatch
}
```

The subject n is passed as an argument to the *Match* statement and is then analyzed through *Case* clauses that list various patterns. In the *first-fit* strategy typically adopted by functional languages, the matching proceeds in sequential order while the patterns guarding their respective clauses are *rejected*. Eventually, the statement guarded by the first *accepted* pattern is executed or the control reaches the end of the *Match* statement.

The value 0 in the first case clause is an example of a *value pattern*. It will match only when the subject n is 0. The variable m in the second case clause is an example of a *variable pattern*. It will bind to any value that can be represented by its type. The name _ in the last case clause refers to the common instance of the *wildcard pattern*. Value, variable, and wildcard patterns are typically referred to as *primitive patterns*. The list of primitive patterns is often extended with a *predicate pattern* (e.g. as seen in Scheme [49]), which allows the use of any unary predicate or nullary member-predicate as a pattern: e.g. *Case*(even) ... (assuming **bool** even(**int**);) or *Case*([](**int** m) { **return** m^m−1; }) ... for λ-expressions.

The predicate pattern is a use of a predicate as a pattern and should not be confused with a *guard*, which is a predicate attached to a pattern that may make use of the variables bound in it. The result of the guard's evaluation will determine whether the case clause and the body associated with it will be *accepted* or *rejected*. Guards gives rise to *guard patterns*, which in *Mach7* are expressions of the form $P|=E$, where P is a pattern and E is its guard.

Pattern matching is closely related to *algebraic data types*. In ML and Haskell, an *Algebraic Data Type* is a data type each of whose values are picked from a disjoint sum of data types, called *variants*. Each variant is a *product type* marked with a unique symbolic constant called a *constructor*. Each constructor provides a convenient way of creating a value of its variant type as well as discriminating among variants through pattern matching. In particular, given an algebraic data type $D = C_1(T_{11}, ..., T_{1m_1})|\cdots|C_k(T_{k1}, ..., T_{km_k})$ an expression of the form $C_i(x_1, ..., x_{m_i})$ in a non-pattern-matching context is called a *value constructor* and refers to a value of type D created via the constructor C_i and its arguments $x_1, ..., x_{m_i}$. The same expression in the pattern-matching context is called a *constructor pattern* and is used to check whether the subject is of type D and was created with the constructor C_i. If so, it matches the actual values it was constructed with against the nested patterns x_j.

C++ does not directly support algebraic data types. However, such types can be encoded in the language in a number of ways. Common object-oriented encodings employ an abstract class to represent the algebraic data type and derived classes to represent variants. Consider for example the following representation of the terms of the λ-calculus in C++:

```
struct Term        { virtual ~Term() {} };
struct Var : Term { std::string name; };
struct Abs : Term { Var&  var;  Term& body; };
struct App : Term { Term& func; Term& arg; };
```

C++ allows a class to have several constructors, but it does not allow overloading the meaning of construction for use in pattern matching. This is why in *Mach7* we have to be slightly more explicit about constructor patterns, which take the form $C\langle T_i\rangle(P_1, ..., P_{m_i})$, where T_i is the name of the user-defined type we are decomposing and $P_1, ..., P_{m_i}$ are patterns that will be matched against members of T_i. 'C' was chosen to abbreviate "Constructor pattern" or "Case class" as its use resembles the use of case classes in Scala [30]. For example, we can write a complete (with the exception of bindings discussed in §3.2) recursive implementation of testing for the equality of two lambda terms as:

```
bool operator==(const Term& left, const Term& right) {
  var⟨const std::string &⟩ s; var⟨const Term&⟩ x,y;
  Match(left        , right          ) {
    Case(C⟨Var⟩(s)   , C⟨Var⟩(+s)    ) return true;
    Case(C⟨Abs⟩(x,y), C⟨Abs⟩(+x,+y)) return true;
    Case(C⟨App⟩(x,y), C⟨App⟩(+x,+y)) return true;
    Otherwise()                      return false ;
  } EndMatch
}
```

This == is an example of a *binary method*: an operation that requires both arguments to have the same type [3]. In each of the case clauses, we check that both subjects are of the same dynamic type using a constructor pattern. We then decompose both subjects into components and compare them for equality with the help of a variable pattern and an *equivalence combinator* ('+') applied to it. The use of an equivalence combinator turns a binding use of a variable pattern into a non-binding use of that variable's current value as a value pattern. We chose to overload unary + because in C++ it turns an l-value into an r-value, which has a similar semantics here.

In general, a *pattern combinator* is an operation on patterns to produce a new pattern. Other typical pattern combinators, supported by many languages, are *conjunction*, *disjunction* and *negation* combinators, which all have an intuitive Boolean interpretation. We add a few non-standard combinators to *Mach7* that reflect the specifics of C++, e.g. the presence of pointers and references.

The equality operator on λ-terms demonstrates both *nesting of patterns* and *relational matching*. The variable pattern was nested within an equivalence pattern, which in turn was nested inside a constructor pattern. The matching was also relational because we could relate the state of two subjects. Both aspects are even better demonstrated in the following well-known functional solution to balancing red-black trees with pattern matching due to Chris Okasaki [32, §3.3] implemented in *Mach7*:

```
class T{enum color{black,red} col; T* left; K key; T* right;};

T* balance(T::color clr, T* left, const K& key, T* right) {
  const T::color B = T::black, R = T::red;
  var⟨T*⟩ a, b, c, d; var⟨K&⟩ x, y, z; T::color col;
  Match(clr, left, key, right) {
    Case(B, C⟨T⟩(R, C⟨T⟩(R, a, x, b), y, c), z, d) ...
    Case(B, C⟨T⟩(R, a, x, C⟨T⟩(R, b, y, c)), z, d) ...
    Case(B, a, x, C⟨T⟩(R, C⟨T⟩(R, b, y, c), z, d)) ...
    Case(B, a, x, C⟨T⟩(R, b, y, C⟨T⟩(R, c, z, d))) ...
    Case(col, a, x, b) return new T{col, a, x, b};
  } EndMatch
}
```

The ... in the first four case clauses above stands for
return new T{R, **new** T{B,a,x,b}, y, **new** T{B,c,z,d}};.

To demonstrate the openness of the library, we implemented numerous specialized patterns that often appear in practice and are even built into some languages. For example, the following combination of regular-expression and one-of patterns can be used to recognize a toll-free phone number.

rex("([0−9]+)−([0−9]+)−([0−9]+)",any({800,888,877}),n,m)

The regular-expression pattern takes a C++11 regular expression and an arbitrary number of sub-patterns. It uses matching groups to match against the sub-patterns. A one-of pattern takes an initializer list with a set of values and checks that the subject matches at least one of them. The variables n and m are integers, and the values of the last two parts of the pattern will be assigned to them. The parsing is generic and will work with any data type that can be read from an input stream; this is a common idiom in C++. Should we also need the exact area code, we can mix in a variable pattern using the conjunction combinator: a && any(...).

3. Implementation

The traditional object-oriented approach to implementing first-class patterns is based on run-time compositions through interfaces. This "*patterns as objects*" approach has been explored in several different languages [11, 14, 34, 47]. Implementations differ in where bindings are stored and what is returned as a result, but in its most basic form it consists of the **pattern** interface with a virtual function match that accepts a subject and returns whether it was accepted or rejected. This approach is open to new patterns and pattern combinators, but a mismatch in the type of the subject and the type accepted by the pattern can only be detected at run-time. Furthermore, it implies significant run-time overhead (§4.1).

3.1 Patterns as Expression Templates

Patterns in *Mach7* are also represented as objects; however, they are composed at compile time, based on C++ concepts. *Concept* is the C++ community's long-established term for a set of requirements for template parameters. Concepts were not included in C++11, but techniques for emulating them with enable_if [18] have been in use for a while. enable_if provides the ability to *include* or *exclude* certain class or function declarations from the compiler's consideration based on conditions defined by arbitrary metafunctions. To avoid the verbosity of enable_if, in this work we use the notation for *template constraints* – a simpler version of concepts [42]. The *Mach7* implementation emulates these constraints.

There are two main constraints on which the entire library is built: PATTERN and LAZYEXPRESSION.

```
template ⟨typename P⟩ constexpr bool PATTERN() {
  return COPYABLE⟨P⟩          // P must also be COPYABLE
    && is_pattern⟨P⟩::value   // this is a semantic constraint
    && requires (typename S, P p, S s) {// syntactic reqs:
      bool = { p(s) };        // usable as a predicate on S
      AcceptedType⟨P,S⟩;      // has this type function
};      }
```

The PATTERN constraint is the analog of the pattern interface from the *patterns as objects* solution. Objects of any class P satisfying this constraint are patterns and can be composed with any other patterns in the library as well as be used in the *Match* statement.

Patterns can be passed as arguments of a function, so they must be COPYABLE. Implementation of pattern combinators requires the library to overload certain operators on all the types satisfying the PATTERN constraint. To avoid overloading these operators for types that satisfy the requirements accidentally, the PATTERN constraint is a *semantic constraint*, which means that classes claiming to satisfy it have to state that explicitly by specializing the is_pattern⟨P⟩ trait. The constraint also introduces some *syntactic requirements*, described by the **requires** clause. In particular, because patterns are predicates on their subject type, they require presence of an application operator that checks whether a pattern matches a given subject. Unlike the *patterns as objects* approach, the PATTERN constraint does not impose any restrictions on the subject type S. Patterns like the wildcard pattern will leave the S type completely unrestricted, while other patterns may require it to satisfy certain constraints, model a given concept, inherit from a certain type, etc. The application operator will typically return a value of type **bool** indicating whether the pattern is *accepted* on a given subject or *rejected*.

Most of the patterns are applicable only to subjects of a given *expected type* or types convertible to it. This is the case, for example, with value and variable patterns, where the expected type is the type of the underlying value, as well as with the constructor pattern, where the expected type is the type being decomposed. Some patterns, however, do not have a single expected type and may work with subjects of many unrelated types. A wildcard pattern, for example, can accept values of any type without involving a conversion. To account for this, the PATTERN constraint requires the presence of a type alias AcceptedType, which given a pattern of type P and a subject of type S returns an expected type AcceptedType⟨P,S⟩ that will accept subjects of type S with no or a minimum of conversions. By default, the alias is defined in terms of a nested type function accepted_type_for, as follows:

```
template⟨typename P, typename S⟩
  using AcceptedType = P::accepted_type_for⟨S⟩::type;
```

The wildcard pattern defines accepted_type_for to be an identity function, while variable and value patterns define it to be their underlying type. The constructor pattern's accepted type is the type it decomposes, which is typically different from the subject type. *Mach7* employs an efficient type switch [41] under the hood to convert subject type to accepted type.

Guards, n+k patterns, the equivalence combinator, and potentially some new user-defined patterns depend on capturing the structure (term) of lazily-evaluated expressions. All such expressions are objects of some type E that must satisfy the LAZYEXPRESSION constraint:

```
template ⟨typename E⟩ constexpr bool LAZYEXPRESSION() {
  return COPYABLE⟨E⟩          // E must also be COPYABLE
    && is_expression⟨E⟩::value // this is semantic constraint
    && requires (E e) {        // syntactic requirements:
      ResultType⟨E⟩;           // associated result_type
      ResultType⟨E⟩ == { eval(e) };// eval(E)→ result_type
      ResultType⟨E⟩ { e };     // conversion to result_type
};      }
```

```
template⟨typename E⟩ using ResultType = E::result_type;
```

The constraint is, again, semantic, and the classes claiming to satisfy it must assert it through the is_expression⟨E⟩ trait. The template alias ResultType⟨E⟩ is defined to return the expression's associated type result_type, which defines the type of the result of a lazily-evaluated expression. Any class satisfying the LAZYEXPRESSION constraint must also provide an implementation of the function eval that evaluates the result of the expression. Conversion to the result_type should call eval on the object in order to allow the use of lazily-evaluated expressions in the contexts where their eagerly-evaluated value is expected, e.g. a non-pattern-matching context of the right-hand side of the *Case* clause.

Our implementation of the variable pattern var⟨T⟩ satisfies the PATTERN and LAZYEXPRESSION constraints as follows:

```
template ⟨REGULAR T⟩ struct var {
  template ⟨typename⟩
  struct accepted_type_for { typedef T type; };
  bool operator()(const T& t) const // exact match
    { m_value = t; return true; }
  template ⟨REGULAR S⟩
  bool operator()(const S& s) const // with conversion
    { m_value = s; return m_value == s; }
  typedef T result_type; // type when used in expression
  friend const result_type& eval(const var& v) // eager eval
    { return v.m_value; }
  operator result_type() const { return eval(*this); }
  mutable T m_value; // value bound during matching
};
```

```
template⟨REGULAR T⟩struct   is_pattern⟨var⟨T⟩⟩:true_type{};
template⟨REGULAR T⟩struct is_expression⟨var⟨T⟩⟩:true_type{};
```

For semantic or efficiency reasons a pattern may have several overloads of the application operator. In the example, the first alternative is used when no conversion is required; thus, the variable pattern is guaranteed to be accepted. The second may involve a (possibly-narrowing) conversion, which is why we check that the values compare as equal after assignment. Similarly, for type checking reasons, accepted_type_for may (and typically will) provide several partial or full specializations to limit the set of acceptable subjects. For example, the *address combinator* can only be applied to subjects of pointer types, so its implementation will report a compile-time error when applied to any non-pointer type.

To capture the structure of an expression, the library employs a commonly-used technique called "expression templates" [45, 46]. In general, an *expression template* is an algebraic structure $\langle \Sigma_\zeta, \{f_1, f_2, ...\}\rangle$ defined over the set $\Sigma_\zeta = \{\tau \mid \tau \vDash \zeta\}$ of all the types τ modeling a given concept ζ. The operations f_i allow one to compose new types modeling the concept ζ out of existing types. In this sense, the types of all lazy expressions in *Mach7* stem from a set of a few (possibly-parameterized) basic types like var$\langle$T$\rangle$ and value$\langle$T$\rangle$ (which both model LAZYEXPRESSION) by applying type functors like plus and minus to them. Every type in the resulting family then has a function eval defined on it that returns a value of the associated type result_type. Similarly, the types of all the patterns stem from a set of a few (possibly-parameterized) patterns like wildcard, var$\langle$T$\rangle$, value$\langle$T$\rangle$, C$\langle$T$\rangle$ etc. by applying to them pattern combinators such as conjunction, disjunction, equivalence, address etc. The user is allowed to extend both algebras with either basic expressions and patterns or with functors and combinators.

The sets $\Sigma_{LazyExpression}$ and $\Sigma_{Pattern}$ have a non-empty intersection, which slightly complicates matters. The basic types var$\langle$T$\rangle$ and value$\langle$T$\rangle$ belong to both of those sets, and so do some of the combinators, e.g. conjunction. Since we can only have one overloaded **operator&&** for a given combination of argument types, we have to state conditionally whether the requirements of PATTERN, LAZYEXPRESSION, or both are satisfied in a given instantiation of conjunction$\langle T_1, T_2\rangle$, depending on what combination of these concepts the argument types T_1 and T_2 model. Concepts, unlike interfaces, allow modeling such behavior without multiplying implementations or introducing dependencies.

3.2 Structural Decomposition

Mach7's constructor patterns C$\langle$T$\rangle(P_1, ..., P_n)$ requires the library to know which member of class T should be used as the subject to P_1, which should be matched against P_2, etc. In functional languages supporting algebraic data types, such decomposition is unambiguous as each variant has only one constructor, which is thus also used as a *deconstructor* [2, 13] to define the decomposition of that type through pattern matching. In C++, a class may have several constructors, so we must be explicit about a class' decomposition. We specify that by specializing the library template class bindings. Here are the definitions that are required in order to be able to decompose the lambda terms we introduced in §2:

template()**class** bindings$\langle$Var$\rangle$\{*Members*(Var::name);\};
template()**class** bindings$\langle$Abs$\rangle$\{*Members*(Abs::var,Abs::body);\};
template()**class** bindings$\langle$App$\rangle$\{*Members*(App::func,App::arg);\};

The variadic macro *Members* simply expands each of its arguments into the following definition, demonstrated here on App::func:

static decltype(&App::func) member1()\{**return** &App::func;\}

Each such function returns a pointer-to-member that should be bound in position i. The library applies them to the subject in order to obtain subjects for the sub-patterns $P_1, ..., P_n$. Note that binding definitions made this way are *non-intrusive* since the original class definition is not touched. The binding definitions also respect *encapsulation* since only the public members of the target type will be accessible from within a specialization of bindings. Members do not have to be data members only, which can be inaccessible, but any of the following three categories:

- a data member of the target type T
- a nullary member function of the target type T
- a unary external function taking the target type T by pointer, reference, or value.

Unfortunately, C++ does not yet provide sufficient compile-time introspection capabilities to let the library generate bindings implicitly. These bindings, however, only need to be written once for

a given class hierarchy (e.g. by its designer) and can be reused everywhere. This is also true for parameterized classes (§3.4).

3.3 Algebraic Decomposition

Traditional approaches to generalizing n+k patterns treat matching a pattern $f(x, y)$ against a value r as solving an equation $f(x, y) = r$ [33]. This interpretation is well-defined when there are zero or one solutions, but alternative interpretations are possible when there are multiple solutions. Instead of discussing which interpretation is the most general or appropriate, we look at n+k patterns as a *notational decomposition* of mathematical objects. The elements of the notation are associated with sub-components of the matched mathematical entity, which effectively lets us decompose it into parts. The structure of the expression tree used in the notation is an analog of a constructor symbol in structural decomposition, while its leaves are placeholders for parameters to be matched against or inferred from the mathematical object in question. In essence, *algebraic decomposition* is to mathematical objects what structural decomposition is to algebraic data types. While the analogy is somewhat ad-hoc, it resembles the situation with operator overloading: you do not strictly need it, but it is so convenient it is virtually impossible not to have it. We demonstrate this alternative interpretation of the n+k patterns with examples.

- An expression n/m is often used to decompose a rational number into numerator and denominator.
- An expression of the form $3q + r$ can be used to obtain the quotient and remainder of dividing by 3. When r is a constant, it can also be used to check membership in a congruence class.
- The Euler notation $a + bi$, with i being the imaginary unit, is used to decompose a complex number into real and imaginary parts. Similarly, expressions $r(cos\phi + isin\phi)$ and $re^{i\phi}$ are used to decompose it into polar form.
- A 2D line can be decomposed with the slope-intercept form $mX + c$, the linear equation form $aX + bY = c$, or the two-points form $(Y - y_0)(x_1 - x_0) = (y_1 - y_0)(X - x_0)$.
- An object representing a polynomial can be decomposed for a specific degree: a_0, $a_1X^1 + a_0$, $a_2X^2 + a_1X^1 + a_0$, etc.
- An element of a vector space can be decomposed along some sub-spaces of interest. For example a 2D vector can be matched against $(0, 0)$, aX, bY, or $aX + bY$ to separate the general case from cases when one or both components of the vector are 0.

The expressions i, X, and Y in those examples are not variables, but rather are named constants of some dedicated type that allows the expression to be generically decomposed into orthogonal parts.

The linear equation and two-point forms for decomposing lines already include an equality sign, so it is hard to give them semantics in an equational approach. In our library that equality sign is not different from any other operator, like + or *, and is only used to capture the structure of the expression, while the exact semantics of matching against that expression is given by the user. This flexibility allows us to generically encode many of the interesting cases of the equational approach. The following example, written with use of *Mach7*, defines a function for fast computation of Fibonacci numbers by using generalized n+k patterns:

```
int fib(int n) {
  var⟨int⟩ m;
  Match(n) {
    Case(any({1,2})) return 1;
    Case(2*m)        return sqr(fib(m+1)) − sqr(fib(m−1));
    Case(2*m+1)      return sqr(fib(m+1)) + sqr(fib(m));
  } EndMatch                  // sqr(x) = x*x
}
```

The *Mach7* library already takes care of capturing the structure of lazy expressions (i.e. terms). To implement the semantics of their matching, the *Mach7* user (i.e. the designer of a concrete notation) writes a new function overload to define the semantics of decomposing a value of a given type S against a term E:

```
template ⟨LazyExpression E, typename S⟩
  bool solve(const E&, const S&);
```

The first argument of the function takes an expression template representing a term we are matching against, while the second argument represents the expected result. Note that even though the first argument is passed in with the **const** qualifier, it may still modify state in E. For example, when E is var⟨T⟩, the application operator for const-object that will eventually be called will update a mutable member m_value. The following example defines a generic solver for multiplication by a constant $c \neq 0$ of an expression $e = e_1 * c$.

```
template ⟨LazyExpression E, typename T⟩
  requires Field⟨E::result_type⟩()
bool solve(const mult⟨E,value⟨T⟩⟩&e,const E::result_type&r)
  { return solve(e.m_e1,r/eval(e.m_e2)); } // e.m_e2 is c

template ⟨LazyExpression E, typename T⟩
  requires Integral⟨E::result_type⟩()
bool solve(const mult⟨E,value⟨T⟩⟩&e,const E::result_type&r){
    T c = eval(e.m_e2); // e.m_e2 is c
    return r%c == 0 && solve(e.m_e1,r/c);
}
```

Intuitively, matching $e_1 * c$ against the value r in the equational approach means solving $e_1 * c = r$, which means that we should try matching the sub-expression e_1 against $\frac{r}{c}$.

The first overload is only applicable when the result type of the sub-expression models the Field concept. In this case, we can rely on the presence of a unique inverse and simply call division without any additional checks. The second overload uses integer division, which does not guarantee the unique inverse, and thus we have to verify that the result is divisible by the constant first. This last overload combined with a similar solver for addition of integral types is everything the library needs to support the fib example.

3.4 Views

Any type T may have an arbitrary number of *binding*s associated with it, which are specified by varying the second parameter of the bindings template: *layout*. The layout is a non-type template parameter of integral type; the layout parameter has a default value and is thus omitted most of the time. Our library's support of multiple bindings (through layouts) effectively enables a facility similar to Wadler's *views*[48]. Consider:

```
enum { cartesian = default_layout, polar }; // Layouts

template ⟨class T⟩ struct bindings⟨std::complex⟨T⟩⟩
  { Members(std::real⟨T⟩,std::imag⟨T⟩); };
template ⟨class T⟩ struct bindings⟨std::complex⟨T⟩, polar⟩
  { Members(std::abs⟨T⟩,std::arg⟨T⟩); };
template ⟨class T⟩ using Cart = view⟨std::complex⟨T⟩⟩;
template ⟨class T⟩ using Pole = view⟨std::complex⟨T⟩,polar⟩;

std::complex⟨double⟩ c; double a,b,r,f;
Match(c)
  Case(Cart⟨double⟩)(a,b)) ... // default layout
  Case(Pole⟨double⟩)(r,f)) ... // view for polar layout
EndMatch
```

The C++ standard effectively forces the standard library to use the Cartesian representation [17, §26.4-4], which is why we chose the Cart layout as the default. We then define bindings for each layout and introduce template aliases (an analog of typedefs for parameterized classes) for each view. The *Mach7* class view⟨T,l⟩

binds a target type with one of that type's layouts. view⟨T,l⟩ can be used everywhere the original target type T was expected.

The important difference from Wadler's solution is that our views can only be used in a pattern-matching context, not as constructors or as arguments to functions.

3.5 Match Statement

In functional languages with built-in pattern matching, *relational matching* on multiple subjects is usually reduced to *nested matching* on a single subject by wrapping multiple arguments into a tuple. In a library setting, we are able to provide a more efficient implementation if we keep the arguments separated. This is why our *Match* statement extends the efficient type switch for C++ [41] to handle multiple subjects (both polymorphic and non-polymorphic) (§3.5.1) and to accept patterns in case clauses (§3.5.2).

3.5.1 Multi-argument Type Switching

The core of our efficient type switch [41] is based on the fact that virtual table pointers (vtbl-pointers) uniquely identify subobjects in the object and are perfect for hashing. Open type switch maps these vtbl-pointers to jump targets and necessary this-pointer offsets and provides an amortized constant-time dispatch to the appropriate case clause. Its efficiency relies on the optimal hash function H_{kl}^V built for a set of vtbl-pointers V seen by a type switch. It is chosen by varying the parameters k and l to minimize the probability of conflict. The parameter k represents the logarithm of the size of cache, while the parameter l is the number of low bits to ignore.

A *Morton order* (aka *Z-order*) is a function that maps multidimensional data to one dimension while preserving the locality of the data points [26]. A Morton number of an N-dimensional coordinate point is obtained by interleaving the binary representations of all coordinates. The original one-dimensional hash function H_{kl}^V applied to arguments $v \in V$ produced hash values in a tight range $[0..2^k[$ where $k \in [K, K+1]$ for $2^{K-1} < |V| \leq 2^K$. The produced values were close to each other, which improved the cache hit rate due to increased locality of reference. The idea is thus to use Morton order on these hash values – not on the original vtbl-pointers – in order to preserve locality of reference. To do this, we retain a single parameter k reflecting the size of the cache, but we keep N optimal offsets l_i for each argument i.

Consider a set $V^N = \{\langle v_1^1, ..., v_1^N\rangle, ..., \langle v_n^1, ..., v_n^N\rangle\}$ of N-dimensional tuples representing the set of vtbl-pointer combinations coming through a given *Match* statement. As with the one-dimensional case, we restrict the size 2^k of the cache to be not larger than twice the closest power of two greater or equal to $n = |V^N|$: i.e. $k \in [K, K+1]$, where $2^{K-1} < |V^N| \leq 2^K$. For a given k and offsets $l_1,...,l_N$ a hash value of a given combination $\langle v^1, ..., v^N\rangle$ is defined as $H_{kl_1...l_N}(\langle v^1, ..., v^N\rangle) = \mu(\frac{v^1}{2^{l_1}}, ..., \frac{v^N}{2^{l_N}}) \bmod 2^k$, where the function μ returns the Morton number (bit interleaving) of N numbers.

As in the one-dimensional case, we vary the parameters $k,l_1,...,l_N$ in their finite and small domains to obtain an optimal hash function $H_{kl_1...l_N}^{V^N}$ by minimizing the probability of conflict on values from V^N. Unlike the one-dimensional case, we do not try to find the optimal parameters every time we reconfigure the cache. Instead, we only try to improve the parameters to render fewer conflicts in comparison to the number of conflicts rendered by the current configuration. This does not prevent us from eventually converging to the same optimal parameters, which we do over time, but is important for holding constant the amortized complexity of the access. We demonstrate in §4.3 that – similarly to the one-dimensional case – such a hash function produces few collisions on real-world class hierarchies, and yet it is simple enough to compute that it competes well with alternatives that can cope with relational matching.

3.5.2 Support for Patterns

Given a statement $Match(e_1,\ldots,e_N)$ applied to arbitrary expressions e_i, the library introduces several names into the scope of the statement: e.g. the number of arguments N, the subject types subject_type$_i$ (defined as **decltype**(e_i) modulo type qualifiers), and the number of polymorphic arguments M. When $M > 0$ it also introduces the necessary data structures to implement efficient type switching [41]. Only the M arguments whose subject_type$_i$ are polymorphic will be used for fast type switching.

For each case clause $Case(p_1,\ldots,p_N)$ the library ensures that the number of arguments to the case clause N matches the number of arguments to the $Match$ statement, and that the type P_i of every expression p_i passed as its argument models the PATTERN concept. For each subject_type$_i$ it introduces target_type$_i$ – the result of evaluating the type function AcceptedType$\langle P_i,$subject_type$_i\rangle$ – into the scope of the case clause. This is the type the pattern expects as an argument on a subject of type subject_type$_i$ (§3.1), which is used by the type switching mechanism to properly cast the subject if necessary. The library then introduces the names match$_i$ of type target_type$_i$& bound to properly casted subjects and available to the user in the right-hand side of the case clause in the event of a successful match. The qualifiers applied to the type of match$_i$ reflect the qualifiers applied to the type of the subject e_i. Finally, the library generates code that sequentially applies each pattern to properly-casted subjects, making the clause's body conditional:

if (p_1(match$_1$) **&&** $\ldots$ **&&** p_N(match$_N$)) { /* body */ }

When type switching is not involved, the generated code implements the naïve backtracking strategy, which is known to be inefficient as it can produce redundant computations [5, §5]. More-efficient algorithms for compiling pattern matching have been developed since [1, 21, 23, 24, 37]. Unfortunately, while these algorithms cover most of the typical kinds of patterns, they are not pattern-agnostic as they make assumptions about the semantics of concrete patterns. A library-based approach to pattern matching is agnostic of the semantics of any given user-defined pattern. The interesting research question in this context would be: what language support is required to be able to optimize open patterns?

The main advantage from using pattern matching in *Mach7* comes from the fast type switching weaved into the *Match* statement. It effectively skips case clauses that will definitely be rejected because their target type is not one of the subject's dynamic types. Of course, this is only applicable to polymorphic arguments; for non-polymorphic arguments, the matching is done naïvely with a cascade of conditional statements.

4. Evaluation

We performed several independent studies of our pattern matching solution to test its efficiency and impact on the compilation process. In the first study, we compare various functions written with pattern matching to functionally-equivalent manually-hand-optimized code in order to estimate the overhead added by the composition of patterns (§4.1). We demonstrate this overhead for both our solution and the *patterns as objects* approach. In the second study, we compare the impact on compilation times of both approaches (§4.2). In the third study, we looked at how well our extension of *Match* statement to N arguments using the Morton order deals with large real-world class hierarchies (§4.3). In the fourth study, we compare the performance of matching N polymorphic arguments against double, triple, and quadruple dispatch via visitor design pattern as well as open multi-methods extension to C++ (§4.4). In the last study, we rewrote the optimizer of an experimental language from Haskell into C++. We compare the ease of use, readability, and maintainability of the original Haskell code and its *Mach7* equivalent (§4.5).

The studies involving performance comparisons have been performed on a Sony VAIO® laptop with Intel® Core™i5 460M CPU at 2.53 GHz, 6GB of RAM, and Windows 7 Professional. All the code was compiled with G++ (versions 4.5.2, 4.6.1, and 4.7.2, all run under MinGW with -O2 and producing 32-bit x86 binaries) and Visual C++ (versions 10.0 and 11.0, both with profile-guided optimizations).

To improve accuracy, timing was performed using the x86 RDTSC instruction. For every number reported we ran 101 experiments timing 1,000,000 top-level calls each. (Depending on arguments, there may have been a different number of recursive calls). The first experiment served as a warm-up, and typically resulted in an outlier with the largest time. Averaged over 1,000,000 calls, the number of cycles per top-level call in each of the 101 experiments was sorted and the median was chosen. We preferred the median to the average to diminish the influence of other applications and OS interrupts as well as to improve reproducibility of timings between the application runs. In particular, in the diagnostic boot mode of Windows 7, where the minimum of drivers and background applications are loaded, we got the same number of cycles per iteration 70-80 out of 101 times. Timings in non-diagnostic boots had somewhat larger absolute values, but the relative performance remained unchanged and equally well-reproducible.

4.1 Pattern Matching Overhead

The overhead associated with pattern matching may come from:
- Naïve (sequential and often duplicated) order of tests due to a pure library solution.
- The compiler's inability to inline the test expressed by the pattern in a case clause's left-hand side (e.g. due to lack of [type] information or due to the complexity of the expression).
- The compiler's inability to elide construction of pattern trees when used in the right-hand side of a case clause.

To estimate the overhead introduced by the commonly-used *patterns as objects* approach and our *patterns as expression templates* approach (§3.1), we implemented several simple functions, both with and without pattern matching. The handcrafted code we compared against was hand-optimized by us to render the same results, without changes to the underlying algorithm. Some functions were implemented in several ways with different patterns in order to show the impact on performance of different patterns and pattern combinations. The overhead of both approaches on a range of recent C++ compilers is shown in Figure 1.

		Patterns as Expr. Templates					Patterns as Objects				
		G++			Visual C++		G++			Visual C++	
Test	Patterns	4.5.2	4.6.1	4.7.2	10.0	11.0	4.5.2	4.6.1	4.7.2	10.0	11.0
factorial$_0^*$	1,v,_	**15%**	**13%**	**17%**	85%	35%	347%	408%	419%	2121%	1788%
factorial$_1$	1,v	0%	6%	0%	83%	21%	410%	519%	504%	2380%	1812%
factorial$_2$	1,n+k	7%	9%	6%	78%	18%	797%	911%	803%	3554%	3057%
fibonacci*	1,n+k	17%	**2%**	2%	62%	15%	340%	431%	395%	2730%	2597%
gcd$_1$	v,n+k,+	21%	25%	25%	309%	179%	1503%	1333%	1208%	8876%	7810%
gcd$_2$	1,n+k,_	5%	13%	19%	373%	303%	962%	1080%	779%	5332%	4674%
gcd$_3$	1,v	**1%**	0%	**1%**	38%	15%	119%	102%	108%	1575%	1319%
lambdas^*	&,v,C,+	58%	54%	56%	**29%**	**34%**	837%	780%	875%	259%	289%
power	1,n+k	10%	8%	13%	50%	6%	291%	337%	338%	1950%	1648%

Figure 1. Pattern Matching Overhead

The experiments marked with $*$ correspond to the functions in §2 and §3.3. The rest of the functions, including all the implementations using the *patterns as objects* approach, are available on the project's web page. The patterns involved in each experiment are abbreviated as following: **1** – value pattern; **v** – variable pattern; **_** – wildcard pattern; **n+k** – n+k (application) pattern; **+** – equivalence combinator; **&** – address combinator; **C** – constructor pattern.

The overhead incurred by compile-time composition of patterns in the *patterns as expression templates* approach is significantly smaller than the overhead of run-time composition of patterns in the *patterns as objects* approach. In some cases, shown in the table in bold, the compiler was able to eliminate the overhead entirely. In the case of the "lambdas" experiment, the advantage was due to the underlying type switch, while in the other cases the generated code utilized the instruction pipeline and the branch predictor better.

In each experiment, the handcrafted baseline implementation was the same in both cases (compile-time and run-time composition) and reflected our idea of the fastest code without pattern matching describing the same algorithm. For example, gcd_3 was implementing the fast Euclidian algorithm with remainders, while gcd_1 and gcd_2 were implementing its slower version with subtractions. The baseline code was correspondingly implementing fast Euclidian algorithm for gcd_3 and slow for gcd_1 and gcd_2.

The comparison of the overhead incurred by both approaches would be incomplete without the details of our implementation of the *patterns as objects* solution. In particular, dealing with objects in object-oriented languages often involves heap allocation, subtype tests, garbage collection, etc., which can all significantly affect performance. To make this comparison applicable to a wider range of object-oriented languages, we took the following precautions in the *patterns as objects* implementations:

- All the objects involved were stack-allocated or statically allocated. This measure was taken to avoid allocating objects on the heap, which is known to be much slower. Many compilers of object-oriented languages perform the same optimization.
- Objects representing constant values as well – as patterns whose state does not change during pattern matching (e.g. wildcard and value patterns) – were all statically allocated.
- Patterns that modify their own state were constructed only when they were actually used, since a successful match by a previous pattern may return early from the function.
- Only the arguments that were actually pattern-matched were boxed into the object class hierarchy; e.g. in the case of the power function only the second argument was boxed.
- Boxed arguments were statically typed with their most derived type to avoid unnecessary type checks and conversions, e.g. object_of⟨int⟩&, which is a class derived from object and that represents a boxed integer, instead of just object&.
- No objects were returned as a result of a function, as in truly object-oriented approach that might require heap allocation.
- n+k patterns that effectively require evaluating the result of an expression were implemented with an additional virtual function that simply checks whether a result is a given value. This does not allow expressing all the n+k patterns of *Mach7*, but was sufficient to express all those involved in the experiments and allowed us to avoid heap-allocating the results.
- When run-time type checks were unavoidable (e.g. inside the implementation of pattern::match) we compared type IDs first, and only when the comparison failed we invoked the much slower **dynamic_cast** to optimize the common case.

With these precautions in place, the main overhead of the *patterns as objects* solution was in the cost of a virtual function call (pattern::match) and the cost of run-time type identification and conversion on its argument (the subject). Both are specific to the approach and not to our implementation, so similar overhead is present in other object-oriented languages following this strategy.

4.2 Compilation Time Overhead

Several people expressed concerns about a possible significant increase in compilation time due to the openness of our pattern-matching solution. While this might be the case for some patterns that require a lot of compile-time computations, it is not the case with any of the common patterns we implemented. Our patterns are simple top-down instantiations that rarely go beyond standard

overload resolution or the occasional enable_if condition. Furthermore, we compared the compilation time for each of the examples discussed in §4.1 with a handcrafted version.

		Patterns as Expr. Templates			Patterns as Objects		
		G++	Visual C++		G++	Visual C++	
Test	Patterns	4.7.2	10.0	11.0	4.7.2	10.0	11.0
factorial$_0^*$	1,v,_	1.65%	1.65%	2.95%	7.10%	**10.00%**	10.68%
factorial$_1$	1,v	2.46%	1.60%	10.92%	7.14%	0.00%	1.37%
factorial$_2$	1,n+k	2.87%	3.15%	3.01%	8.93%	4.05%	**3.83%**
fibonacci*	1,n+k	3.66%	1.60%	2.95%	11.31%	**4.03%**	1.37%
gcd$_1^*$	v,n+k,+	4.07%	4.68%	**0.91%**	9.94%	2.05%	8.05%
gcd$_2$	1,n+k,_	1.21%	1.53%	**0.92%**	8.19%	**2.05%**	**2.58%**
gcd$_3$	1,v	2.03%	3.15%	7.86%	5.29%	2.05%	0.08%
lambdas*	&,v,C,+	18.91%	7.25%	**4.27%**	4.57%	**3.82%**	0.00%
power	1,n+k	2.00%	6.40%	3.92%	8.14%	0.13%	4.02%

Table 1. Compilation Time Overhead

As can be seen in Table 1, the difference in compilation times was small: on average, 3.99% slower for open patterns and 4.84% slower for *patterns as objects*, with patterns compiling faster in a few cases (indicated in bold). The difference will be less in real-world projects with a larger amount of non-pattern-matching code.

4.3 Multi-argument Hashing

To check the efficiency of hashing in the multi-argument *Match* statement (§3.5) we used the same class hierarchy benchmark we used to test the efficiency of hashing in type switch [41, §4.4]. The benchmark consists of 13 libraries describing 15,246 classes. Not all the class hierarchies originated from C++, but all were written by humans and represent their respective problem domains.

While the *Match* statement works with both polymorphic and non-polymorphic arguments, only the polymorphic arguments are taken into consideration for efficient type switching and thus efficient hashing. It also generally only makes sense to apply type switching to non-leaf nodes of the class hierarchy. 71% of the classes in the entire benchmark suite were leaf classes. For each of the remaining 4,369 non-leaf classes we created 4 functions, performing case analysis on derived classes with 1, 2, 3 and 4 arguments, respectively. Each of the functions was executed with different combinations of possible derived types, including, in the case of repeated multiple inheritance, different sub-objects within the same type. There were 63,963 different subobjects when the class hierarchies used repeated multiple inheritance and 38,856 different subobjects with virtual multiple inheritance.

As with type switching, for each of the 4,369 functions (per same number of arguments) we measured the number of conflicts m in cache: the number of entries mapped to the same location in cache by the optimal hash function. We then computed the percentage of functions that achieved a given number of conflicts, shown in Figure 2.

N/m	[0]	[1]	···10]	···100]	···1000]	···10000]	>10000
Repeated 1	88.37%	10.78%	0.85%	0.00%	0.00%	0.00%	0.00%
Repeated 2	76.42%	5.51%	10.60%	4.89%	2.22%	0.37%	0.00%
Repeated 3	65.18%	0.00%	15.04%	8.92%	5.83%	5.03%	0.00%
Repeated 4	64.95%	0.00%	0.14%	14.81%	7.57%	12.54%	0.00%
Virtual 1	89.72%	9.04%	1.24%	0.00%	0.00%	0.00%	0.00%
Virtual 2	80.55%	4.20%	8.46%	4.59%	1.67%	0.53%	0.00%
Virtual 3	71.26%	0.37%	12.03%	7.32%	4.87%	4.16%	0.00%
Virtual 4	71.55%	0.00%	0.23%	11.83%	6.49%	9.90%	0.00%

Figure 2. Percentage of N-argument *Match* statements with given number of conflicts (m) in cache

We grouped the results in ranges of exponentially-increasing size because we noticed that the number of conflicts per *Match* statement for multiple arguments was not as tightly distributed around 0 as it was for a single argument. However, the main observation still holds: in most of the cases, we could achieve hashing without conflicts, as can be seen in the first column (marked [0]). The numbers are slightly better when virtual inheritance is used because the overall number of possible subobjects is smaller.

4.4 Comparison of Alternatives for Relational Matching

Relational matching on classes depends on the efficient discovery of the sought-after combinations of dynamic types of the subjects. This can be performed in a number of different ways including, for example, the techniques used to implement multiple dispatch. We compare the efficiency of type switching on multiple arguments in comparison to other relational matching alternatives based on double, triple and quadruple dispatch [16], as well as our own implementation of open multi-methods for C++ [36].

The need for multiple dispatch rarely happens in practice, diminishing with the number of arguments involved in dispatch. Muschevici et al [27] studied a large corpus of applications in 6 languages and estimate that single dispatch amounts to about 30% of all the functions, while multiple dispatch is only used in 3% of functions. In application to type switching, this indicates that we can expect case analysis on the dynamic type of a single argument much more often than on dynamic types of two or more arguments. However, this does not mean that pattern matching in general reflects the same trend, as additional arguments are often introduced into the *Match* statement to check some relational properties. These additional arguments are typically non-polymorphic and thus do not participate in type switching, which is why in this experiment we only deal with polymorphic arguments.

Figure 3 contains 4 bar groups corresponding to the number of arguments used for multiple dispatch. Each group contains 3 wide bars representing the number of CPU cycles per iteration it took the N-Dispatch, Open Type Switch and Open Multi-methods solutions to perform the same task. Each of the 3 wide bars is subsequently split into 5 narrow sub-bars representing performance achieved by G++ 4.5.2, 4.6.1, 4.7.2 and Visual C++ 10 and 11, in that order.

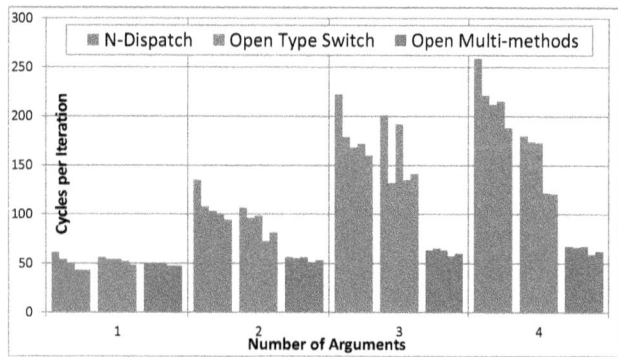

Figure 3. N-argument *Match* statement vs. visitor design pattern and open multi-methods

Open multi-methods give the best performance because the dispatch is implemented with an N-dimensional array lookup, requiring only $4N + 1$ memory references before an indirect call. N-dispatch runs the slowest, requiring $2N$ virtual function calls (accept/visit per each dimension). Open type switch falls between the two, thanks to its efficient hashing combined with a jump table.

In terms of memory, given a class hierarchy of n classes (actually n subobjects in the subobject graph) and multiple dispatch on N arguments, all 3 solutions require memory proportional to $O(n^N)$. More specifically, if δ is the number of bytes used by a pointer, then each of the approaches will use:

- Open Multi-methods: $\delta\left(n^N + Nn + N\right)$
- N-Dispatch: $\delta\left(n^N + n^{N-1} + \cdots + n^2 + n\right)$
- Open Type Switch: $\delta\left((2N + 3)\, n^N + N + 7\right)$

bytes of memory. In all 3 cases, the memory counted represents the non-reusable memory specific to the implementation of a single function dispatched through N polymorphic arguments. Note that n is a variable here since new classes may be loaded at run-time through dynamic linking in all 3 solutions, while N is a constant, representing the number of arguments to dispatch on.

The memory used by each approach is allocated at different stages. The memory used by the virtual tables involved in the N-dispatch solution as well as the dispatch tables used by open multi-methods will be allocated at compile/link time and will be reflected in the size of the final executable. Open multi-methods might require additional allocations and/or recomputation at load time to account for dynamic linking. In both cases, the memory allocated covers all possible combinations of n classes in N argument positions. In the case of open type switch, the memory is only allocated at run-time and grows proportionally to the number of actual argument combinations seen by the type switch (§3.5.1). Only in the worst case, when all possible combinations have been seen by the type switch, does it reach the size described by the above formula. This is an important distinction, as in many applications many possible combinations will never be seen: for example, in a compiler the entities representing expressions and types might all be derived from a common base class, but they will rarely appear in the same type switch together.

There is also a significant difference in the ease of use of these solutions. N-dispatch is the most restrictive solution as it is intrusive (and thus cannot be applied retroactively), hinders extensibility (by limiting the set of distinguishable cases), and is surprisingly hard to teach students. While analyzing Java idioms used to emulate multiple dispatch in practice, Muschevici et al [27, Figure 13] noted that there are significantly more uses of cascading instanceof in the real code than the uses of double dispatch, which they also attribute to the obscurity of the second idiom. Both N-dispatch and open multi-methods also introduce control inversion in which the case analysis is effectively structured in the form of callbacks. Open multi-methods are also subject to ambiguities, which have to be resolved at compile time and in some cases might require the addition of numerous overriders. Neither problem occurs with open type switch, where the case analysis is performed directly and ambiguities are avoided by the use of first-fit semantics.

4.5 Rewriting Haskell Code in C++

For this experiment, we took existing code written in Haskell and asked its author to rewrite it in C++ with *Mach7*. The code in question is a simple peephole optimizer for an experimental GPU language called *Versity*. We assisted the author along the way to see which patterns he used and what kind of mistakes he made.

Somewhat surprisingly to us, we found that the pattern-matching clauses generally became shorter, but their right-hand side became longer. The shortening of case clauses was perhaps specific to this application and mainly stemmed from the fact that Haskell does not support equivalence patterns or an equivalence combinator and had to use guards to relate different arguments. This was particularly cumbersome when the optimizer was looking at several arguments of several instructions in the stream, e.g.:

```
peep2(x1:x2:xs) =
  case (x1,x2) of
    ((InstMove a b),(InstMove c d)) | (a==d)&&(b==c) → ...
```

compared to the functionally-equivalent *Mach7* code:

```
Match(*x1,*x2) {
```

```
Case(C⟨InstMove⟩(a,b), C⟨InstMove⟩(+b,+a)) ...
```

Haskell also requires the programmer to use a wildcard pattern in every unused position of a constructor pattern (e.g. InstBin _ _ _ _), while *Mach7* allows the omission of all the trailing wildcards (e.g. C⟨InstBin⟩()). The use of named patterns avoided many repeated expressions and improved performance and readability:

```
auto either = val(src) || val(dst);
Match(inst) {
    Case(C⟨InstMove⟩(_,        either )) ...
    Case(C⟨InstUn⟩  (_, _,     either )) ...
    Case(C⟨InstBin⟩ (_, _, _, either )) ...
} EndMatch
```

Mach7 suffered a disadvantage in the code after the pattern matching, as we had to both explicitly manage memory when inserting, removing, or replacing instructions in the stream and explicitly manage the stream itself. Eventually we could hide some of this boilerplate behind smart pointers and other standard library classes.

4.6 Limitations

While our patterns can be saved in variables and passed to functions, they are not true first-class citizens as one cannot create a run-time data structure of patterns (e.g. a composition of patterns based on user input). This is similar to how polymorphic (template) functions are not considered first-class citizens in C++. This can potentially be solved by mixing in the *patterns as objects* approach, however the performance overhead we saw in §4.1 is too costly to be adopted.

5. Related Work

Language support for pattern matching was first introduced for string manipulation in COMIT [50], which subsequently inspired similar primitives in SNOBOL [10]. SNOBOL4 had string patterns as first-class data types, providing operations for concatenation and alternation. The first reference to modern pattern-matching constructs as seen in functional languages is usually attributed to Burstall's work on structural induction [4]. Pattern matching was further developed by the functional programming community, most notably ML [12] and Haskell [15]. In the context of object-oriented programming, pattern matching was first explored in Pizza [31] and Scala [9, 30]. The idea of first-class patterns dates back at least to Tullsen's proposal to add them to Haskell [44]. The calculus of such patterns has been studied in detail by Jay [19, 20].

There are two main approaches to compiling pattern-matching code: the first is based on *backtracking automata* and was introduced by Augustsson [1], and the second is based on *decision trees* and was first described by Cardelli [5]. The backtracking approach usually generates smaller code [21], whereas the decision tree approach produces faster code by ensuring that each primitive test is only performed once [24].

There have been several attempts to bring pattern matching into various languages by way of a library. They differ in which abstractions of the host language were used to encode the patterns and the match statement. *MatchO* was one of the first such attempts for Java [47]. The approach follows the *patterns as objects* strategy. *Functional C#* was a similar approach, bringing pattern matching to C# as a library [34]. The approach uses lambda expressions and chaining of method calls to create a structure that is then evaluated at run time for the first successful match. In the functional community, Rhiger explored the introduction of first-class pattern matching into Haskell as a library [38]. He uses functions to encode patterns and pattern combinators, which allows him to detect pattern misapplication errors at compile time through the Haskell type system. *Racket* has a powerful macro system that allows it

to express open pattern matching in the language entirely as a library [43]. The solution is remarkable in that unlike most of the library approaches to open pattern matching, it does not rely on naïve backtracking and, in fact, encodes the optimized algorithm based on backtracking automata [1, 21]. *Grace* is another programming language that provides a library solution to pattern matching through objects [14]. Similar to other control structures in the language, Grace encodes the match statement with partial functions and lambda expressions, while patterns are encoded as objects.

Multiple language extensions have been developed to provide pattern matching into a host language in a form of a compiler, preprocessor or tool. *Prop* brought pattern matching and term rewriting into C++ [22]. It did not offer first-class patterns, but supported most of the functional-style patterns and provided an optimizing compiler for both pattern matching and garbage-collected term rewriting. *App* was another pattern-matching extension to C++ [29] that mainly concentrated on providing syntax for defining algebraic data types and pattern matching on them. *Tom* is a pattern-matching compiler that brings a common pattern-matching and term-rewriting syntax into Java, C, and Eiffel. Thanks to its distinct syntax, it is transparent to the semantics of the host language and can be implemented as a preprocessor to many other languages. Tom neither supports first-class patterns, nor is open to new patterns. *Matchete* is a language extension to Java that brings together different flavors of pattern matching: functional-style patterns, Perl-style regular expressions, XPath expressions, Erlang's bit-level patterns, etc. [13]. The extension does not try to make patterns first-class citizens, but instead concentrates on implementing existing best practices and their tight integration into Java. *OOMatch* is another Java extension; it brings pattern matching and multiple dispatch close together [39]. The approach generalizes multiple dispatch by offering to use patterns as multi-method arguments and then orders overriders based on the specificity of their arguments. Similar to other such systems, the approach only deals with a limited set of built-in patterns.

Thorn is a dynamically-typed scripting language that provides first-class patterns [2]. The language defines a handful of atomic patterns and pattern combinators to compose them, and, similarly to Newspeak and Grace, uses the duality between partial functions and patterns to support user-defined patterns.

When a class hierarchy is fixed, we can design a pattern language that involves semantic notions represented by the hierarchy. Pirkelbauer devised a pattern language for Pivot [8] capable of representing various entities in a C++ program using syntax very close to C++ itself. The patterns were translated by a tool into a set of visitors implementing the pattern-matching semantics [35].

6. Conclusions and Future Work

The *Mach7* library provides functional-style pattern-matching facilities for C++. The solution is open to new patterns, with the traditional patterns implemented as an example. It is non-intrusive, so it can be applied retroactively. The library provides efficient and expressive matching on multiple subjects and compares well to multiple dispatch alternatives in terms of both time and space. We also offer an alternative interpretation of the n+k patterns and show how some traditional generalizations of these patterns can be implemented in our library. *Mach7* pattern matching code performs reasonably compared to open multi-methods and visitors, demonstrating the effectiveness of the library-based approach.

The work presented here continues our research on pattern matching for C++ [41]. Due to page limit, we had to omit many interesting details that provide a better insight into our solution. We refer the reader to the first author's PhD thesis [40] for an in-depth discussion of open type switching, open pattern matching and open multi-methods in the context of C++.

In the future, we would like to implement an actual language extension that will be capable of working with open patterns. Given such an extension and its implementation, we would like to look into how code for such patterns can be optimized without hardcoding the knowledge of the semantics of the patterns into the compiler. We would also like to experiment with other kinds of patterns (including those defined by the user), look at the interaction of patterns with both the standard library and other facilities in the language, and make views less ad-hoc.

Acknowledgments

We would like to thank Abe Skolnik, Peter Pirkelbauer, Andrew Sutton and numerous anonymous reviewers whose valuable feedback greatly helped us to improve this work. We would also like to thank Jason Wilkins for trying *Mach7* for *Versity*'s optimizer. This work was partially supported by NSF grants CCF-0702765, CCF-1043084, and CCF-1150055.

References

[1] L. Augustsson. Compiling pattern matching. In *Proc. of a conference on Functional programming languages and computer architecture*, pp 368–381, New York, USA, 1985. Springer-Verlag Inc.

[2] B. Bloom and M. J. Hirzel. Robust scripting via patterns. In *Proc. ACM DLS'12*, pp 29–40, NY, USA.

[3] K. Bruce, L. Cardelli, G. Castagna, G. T. Leavens, and B. Pierce. On binary methods. *Theor. Pract. Object Syst.*, 1(3):221–242, 1995.

[4] R. M. Burstall. Proving properties of programs by structural induction. *Computer Journal*, 1969.

[5] L. Cardelli. Compiling a functional language. In *Proc. ACM LFP'84*, pp 208–217.

[6] P. Cuoq, J. Signoles, P. Baudin, R. Bonichon, G. Canet, L. Correnson, B. Monate, V. Prevosto, and A. Puccetti. Experience report: Ocaml for an industrial-strength static analysis framework. In *Proc. ACM ICFP'09*, pp 281–286, New York, USA.

[7] S. Don, G. Neverov, and J. Margetson. Extensible pattern matching via a lightweight language extension. In *Proc. ACM ICFP'07*, pp 29–40.

[8] G. Dos Reis and B. Stroustrup. A principled, complete, and efficient representation of C++. In *Joint ASCM'09 and MACIS'09*, pp 407–421.

[9] B. Emir. *Object-oriented pattern matching*. PhD thesis, Lausanne, 2007.

[10] D. J. Farber, R. E. Griswold, and I. P. Polonsky. SNOBOL, a string manipulation language. *J. ACM*, 11:21–30, January 1964.

[11] F. Geller, R. Hirschfeld, and G. Bracha. *Pattern Matching for an object-oriented and dynamically typed programming language*. Technische Berichte, Universität Potsdam. Univ.-Verlag, 2010.

[12] M. Gordon, R. Milner, L. Morris, M. Newey, and C. Wadsworth. A metalanguage for interactive proof in LCF. In *Proc. ACM POPL'78*, pp 119–130, New York, USA.

[13] M. Hirzel, N. Nystrom, B. Bloom, and J. Vitek. Matchete: Paths through the pattern matching jungle. In *Proc. PADL'08*, pp 150–166.

[14] M. Homer, J. Noble, K. B. Bruce, A. P. Black, and D. J. Pearce. Patterns as objects in Grace. In *Proc. ACM DLS'12*, pp 17–28.

[15] P. Hudak, H. Committee, P. Wadler, and S. Jones. *Report on the Programming Language Haskell: A Non-strict, Purely Functional Language : Version 1.0*. ML Library. Haskell Committee, 1990.

[16] D. H. H. Ingalls. A simple technique for handling multiple polymorphism. In *Proc. ACM OOPSLA'86*, pp 347–349, New York, USA.

[17] International Organization for Standardization. *ISO/IEC 14882:2011: Programming languages: C++*. Geneva, Switzerland, 2011.

[18] J. Järvi, J. Willcock, H. Hinnant, and A. Lumsdaine. Function overloading based on arbitrary properties of types. *C/C++ Users Journal*, 21(6):25–32, June 2003.

[19] B. Jay. *Pattern Calculus: Computing with Functions and Structures*. Springer Publishing Company, Incorporated, 1st edition, 2009.

[20] B. Jay and D. Kesner. First-class patterns. *J. Funct. Program.*, 19(2):191–225, Mar. 2009.

[21] F. Le Fessant and L. Maranget. Optimizing pattern matching. In *Proc. ACM ICFP'01*, pp 26–37, New York, USA.

[22] A. Leung. Prop: A C++ based pattern matching language. Technical report, Courant Institute, New York University, 1996.

[23] L. Maranget. Compiling lazy pattern matching. In *Proc. ACM LFP'92*, pp 21–31, New York, USA.

[24] L. Maranget. Compiling pattern matching to good decision trees. In *Proc. ACM ML'08*, pp 35–46, New York, USA.

[25] Y. Minsky and S. Weeks. Caml trading – experiences with functional programming on wall street. *J. Funct. Program.*, 18(4):553–564, July 2008.

[26] G. M. Morton. A computer-oriented geodetic data base and a new technique in file sequencing. Technical report, IBM, Ottawa, Canada, 1966.

[27] R. Muschevici, A. Potanin, E. Tempero, and J. Noble. Multiple dispatch in practice. In *Proc. ACM OOPSLA'08*, pp 563–582.

[28] R. Nanavati. Experience report: a pure shirt fits. In *Proc. ACM ICFP'08*, pp 347–352, New York, USA.

[29] G. Nelan. An algebraic typing & pattern matching preprocessor for C++, 2000. http://www.primenet.com/ georgen/app.html.

[30] M. Odersky, V. Cremet, I. Dragos, G. Dubochet, B. Emir, S. Mcdirmid, S. Micheloud, N. Mihaylov, M. Schinz, E. Stenman, L. Spoon, and M. Zenger. An overview of the Scala programming language (2nd edition). Technical report, EPTF, 2006.

[31] M. Odersky and P. Wadler. Pizza into Java: Translating theory into practice. In *In Proc. ACM POPL'97*, pp 146–159.

[32] C. Okasaki. *Purely Functional Data Structures*. Cambridge University Press, 1999.

[33] N. Oosterhof. Application patterns in functional languages, 2005.

[34] E. Pentangelo. Functional C#. http://functionalcsharp.codeplex.com/, 2011.

[35] P. Pirkelbauer. *Programming Language Evolution and Source Code Rejuvenation*. PhD thesis, Texas A&M University, December 2010.

[36] P. Pirkelbauer, Y. Solodkyy, and B. Stroustrup. Open multi-methods for C++. In *Proc. ACM GPCE'07*, pp 123–134, New York, USA.

[37] L. Puel and A. Suarez. Compiling pattern matching by term decomposition. *J. Symb. Comput.*, 15(1):1–26, Jan. 1993.

[38] M. Rhiger. Type-safe pattern combinators. *J. Funct. Program.*, 19(2):145–156, Mar. 2009.

[39] A. Richard. OOMatch: pattern matching as dispatch in Java. Master's thesis, University of Waterloo, October 2007.

[40] Y. Solodkyy. *Simplifying the Analysis of C++ Programs*. PhD thesis, Texas A&M University, August 2013.

[41] Y. Solodkyy, G. Dos Reis, and B. Stroustrup. Open and efficient type switch for C++. In *Proc. ACM OOPSLA'12*, pp 963–982. ACM.

[42] A. Sutton, B. Stroustrup, and G. Dos Reis. Concepts lite: Constraining templates with predicates. Technical Report WG21/N3580, JTC1/SC22/WG21 C++ Standards Committee, 2013.

[43] S. Tobin-Hochstadt. Extensible pattern matching in an extensible language. September 2010.

[44] M. Tullsen. First class patterns. In *Proc. PADL'00*, pp 1–15.

[45] D. Vandevoorde and N. Josuttis. *C++ templates: the complete guide*. Addison-Wesley, 2003.

[46] T. Veldhuizen. Expression templates. *C++ Report*, 7:26–31, 1995.

[47] J. Visser. Matching objects without language extension. *Journal of Object Technology*, 5.

[48] P. Wadler. Views: a way for pattern matching to cohabit with data abstraction. In *Proc. ACM POPL'87*, pp 307–313, New York, USA.

[49] A. Wright and B. Duba. Pattern matching for Scheme. 1995.

[50] V. H. Yngve. A programming language for mechanical translation. *Mechanical Translation*, 5:25–41, July 1958.

Template Constructors for Reusable Object Initialization

Marko Martin

Technische Universität Darmstadt
MarkoMartin@gmx.net

Mira Mezini

Technische Universität Darmstadt
mezini@cs.tu-darmstadt.de

Sebastian Erdweg

Technische Universität Darmstadt
erdweg@cs.tu-darmstadt.de

Abstract

Reuse of and abstraction over object initialization logic is not properly supported in mainstream object-oriented languages. This may result in significant amount of boilerplate code and proliferation of constructors in subclasses. It also makes it impossible for mixins to extend the initialization interface of classes they are applied to. We propose *template constructors*, which employ template parameters and pattern matching of them against signatures of superclass constructors to enable a one-to-many binding of super-calls. We demonstrate how template constructors solve the aforementioned problems. We present a formalization of the concept, a Java-based implementation, and use cases which exercise its strengths.

Categories and Subject Descriptors D.3.2 [*Programming Languages*]: Language Classifications—object-oriented languages; D.3.3 [*Programming Languages*]: Language Constructs and Features—classes and objects, inheritance; D.3.1 [*Programming Languages*]: Formal Definitions and Theory

General Terms Languages, Theory

Keywords constructors, object initialization, reusability, mixins

1. Introduction

Reuse of and abstraction over object initialization logic is not properly supported in mainstream object-oriented languages.

First, mainstream object-oriented (OO) languages do not support constructor inheritance. In wide-spread languages like Java [2] and C# [11], to "inherit" the initialization logic encoded in some superclass constructor $BC(T_1\ p_1, ..., T_n\ p_n)$, subclasses must declare a constructor with the same number and type of formal parameters, $SC(T_1\ p_1, ..., T_n\ p_n)$, which just makes a *super*-call with its formal parameters as arguments. This *copy-down* pattern introduces boilerplate code and a high degree of rigidity because changes to constructors in such a hierarchy require all subclasses to adopt the changed constructor. Multiple inheritance often even worsens the problems of single-inheritance languages with respect to reusability of object initialization logic: In many built-in variants of multiple inheritance, e.g. non-virtual inheritance in C++ [8, 19], each constructor must call one constructor of each superclass, thereby establishing a hard coupling to the superclasses and to all referenced constructors. It is similar in Eiffel [14], although invocation

GPCE '13, October 27–28, 2013, Indianapolis, Indiana, USA.
Copyright is held by the owner/author(s). Publication rights licensed to ACM.
ACM 978-1-4503-2373-4/13/10...$15.00.
http://dx.doi.org/10.1145/2517208.2517212

of superclass constructors is not enforced (which may itself result in inconsistency problems). The situation is not better in Scala [17], where every class has a *primary* constructor implicitly encoded by the parameters and body of a class. All non-primary constructors must transitively call the primary constructor as first statement and only the primary constructor may call a constructor of the superclass. Consequently, even the copy-down reuse pattern is applicable to only one constructor of a superclass. Only languages that support the notion of classes as first-class objects and constructors as ordinary methods/features of these class-objects that are subject to inheritance, such as Smalltalk [10] and derivatives thereof, avoid the problems discussed so far.

Second, all languages mentioned above, including Smalltalk, do not offer mechanisms that enable a subclass to abstract over the initialization logic of the superclass. To extend the initialization logic of superclass constructors, a subclass needs to define constructors that propagate some of their parameters to superclass constructors and use the rest to initialize fields introduced by the subclass. If the superclass defines N constructors and the subclass wants to offer M different ways of initializing fields that it introduces, the subclass may end up defining $N \times M$ constructors in order to provide all possible initialization variants to clients, a phenomenon which we call *constructor explosion* in this paper.

To quantify the significance of the problem, we analyzed the Qualitas Corpus[1] [20], a carefully maintained collection of open-source Java systems. Altogether we analyzed 103 systems with a total number of 68,858 classes. We found 26,946 constructors that make a super-call with at least one argument. Of those, roughly 68% exhibit the problems outlined above: 53.3% propagate all parameters of the superclass constructor into their own parameter list, and another 14.6% do the same, but additionally declare some new parameters.

Lack of support for abstraction over object initialization logic represents an even more severe problem in languages with support for mixins [16], also called abstract subclasses [3]. Contrary to normal subclasses with statically known superclass(es), the superclass parameter of a mixin abstracts over an unlimited number of potential concrete superclasses to which the mixin applies.[2] Since the superclass is not statically known, for mixins it is not even possible to copy down the constructors of the superclass, which means that mixins have no way to extend or otherwise influence the initialization logic of their prospective superclasses.

In this paper, we propose *template constructors* – a linguistic means to address the problems outlined above. Template constructors support a powerful form of constructor inheritance, which goes beyond the normal OO inheritance of methods. Typically, a subclass inherits the public methods of its superclass and exposes their signatures to clients without change. An overriding method can

---

[1] Qualitas Corpus Version 20101126, http://qualitascorpus.com.

[2] In statically typed languages, an upper-bound can be given for the type of the superclass parameter.

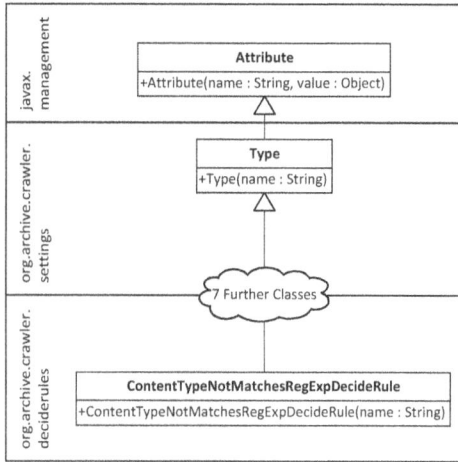

Figure 1. Copy-down Constructor Inheritance in Heritrix

call the overridden method of the superclass via a statically bound method call. For flexible constructors, this overriding technique is not sufficient for two reasons: 1. Subclasses commonly add new state that must be initialized with new constructor parameters. Yet, these new parameters and the associated initialization code should usually be an extension of *all* superclass constructors and not only of a single one. 2. For mixin constructors, the superclass constructor to be called is not known statically.

To overcome the limitations of normal OO inheritance, template constructors can employ *template parameters* to inherit/override superclass constructors based on pattern matching over constructor parameters. This way, template constructors effectively decouple *super*-calls in a subclass from the actual superclass constructors along two dimensions: A single template constructor can inherit/override multiple superclass constructors, and a template constructor can be used in a mixin to augment the initialization logic of different dynamically determined superclasses.

With this paper, we make the following contributions: 1. We motivate the need for more flexible constructors based on an empirical investigation of the the Qualitas Corpus (Sec. 2). 2. We provide an intuitive and a formal presentation of template constructors (Sec. 3 and 5) and an implementation of them as an extension of CaesarJ [1] (Sec. 6). 3. We demonstrate their usefulness by several use cases from the Qualitas Corpus and quantify potential improvements they bring to systems therein (Sec. 4).

2. Problem Statement

In this section, we demonstrate the problems of constructors in current OO languages by investigating real-world Java systems and by illustrating the problems with mixins.

2.1 Copy-down Constructor Inheritance

We exemplify the copy-down constructor inheritance phenomenon by its occurrence in a real system, quantify its frequency in the Qualitas Corpus, and discuss its problems.

Figure 1 shows a simplified version of the hierarchy of Heritrix, a Java web crawling API [15]. The class *ContentTypeNotMatches-RegExpDecideRule* is at the end of a nine-classes-deep hierarchy (the base class is *Attribute*, a subclass of *Object*). The *name* parameter of the *ContentTypeNotMatchesRegExpDecideRule* constructor is – without change – propagated by the constructors of all classes along the hierarchy up to *Attribute*, which handles and stores it.

The occurrences of the copy-down constructor inheritance phenomenon are significant in the Qualitas Corpus. Table 1 shows

the frequencies of copy-down constructors in the Qualitas Corpus grouped by hierarchy depths: Of all 53,937 analyzed constructors with at least one parameter, 27,613 (51.2%) forward at least one parameter to another constructor with a this-call or super-call. In 9,622 cases (17.8% of all), the invoked constructor forwards the parameter again. Hierarchies with a depth of five or more are rare (0.9%), but still appear in 22 (21.4%) of 103 analyzed systems.

The copy-down constructor inheritance results in a lot of boilerplate code. Consider the case, when *Attribute* in Figure 1 has not only one but N constructors that need to be copied down the hierarchy to *ContentTypeNotMatchesRegExpDecideRule*. For each of these N constructors, there will be $9 \cdot N$ copies only for the inheritance path in Figure 1. Depending on the depth and average fan out of the hierarchy, the overall number of constructor copies becomes overwhelming.

Copy-down constructor inheritance also impairs evolution. Consider the scenario, when a new design choice requires the *Type* constructor (Figure 1) to take another parameter, say *description*. In the worst case, *description* needs to be added to the list of constructor parameters of all classes down to *ContentTypeNotMatchesReg-ExpDecideRule and* of classes in other inheritance paths with *Type* as base. To avoid such ripple effects, changes to constructor signatures are typically avoided; instead, setter methods are introduced for new class attributes. However, a design with setter methods is (a) error-prone because calling them is not enforced and (b) inappropriate in case of conceptually immutable objects because clients get unlimited write access to fields that should rather be set only once: during object construction.

2.2 Constructor Explosion

The constructor explosion problem refers to the phenomenon of the exploding number of initialization variants in classes inheriting from superclasses with multiple constructors. For illustration, consider an example from Quartz[3], a Java framework for job scheduling. The class *BaseCalendar* is a basic implementation of a calendar. Its subclass *DailyCalendar* implements a daily time pattern. We list their constructors in Table 2. Each row lists the parameters of one constructor, i.e., *BaseCalendar* has four constructors and *DailyCalendar* has ten. Each of the *DailyCalendar* constructors forwards as many arguments as possible to the superclass constructor. For example, *DailyCalendar(TimeZone timeZone, long start-TimeInMillis, long endTimeInMillis)* calls *super(timeZone)*. Still, *DailyCalendar* adds some new state that can be initialized in different ways. By analyzing its constructors, we identify four variants: 1. String startTime, String endTime 2. int startHour, int startMinute, int startSecond, ... 3. Calendar startCalendar, Calendar endCalendar 4. long startTimeInMillis, long endTimeInMillis

For the first two *BaseCalendar* constructors in the table, all possible combinations have been declared, resulting in the first eight constructors of *DailyCalendar* given in the table. For the last two *BaseCalendar* constructors, only the last initialization variant with two longs has been implemented, resulting in the last two *DailyCalendar* constructors of the table. Yet, there is actually no reason for not having the other initialization variants for those constructors; writing them down is just tedious and error-prone.

The exploding number of constructors is not a rarity in the Qualitas Corpus. Table 3 shows how many superclass constructors are extended by how many different variants of initializing the subclass state: Most frequently, an initialization variant of the subclass extends exactly one superclass constructor. Yet, a significant number of initialization variants extend multiple constructors: In 3,321 cases, we found 2 subclass constructors that perform the same subclass initialization but call different superclass constructors, result-

---

[3] http://quartz-scheduler.org/

44

Depth	0	1	2	3	4	5	6	7	8	9
Frequency	26324	17991	6555	1886	692	358	85	30	12	4
Accumulated	53937	27613	9622	3067	1181	489	131	46	16	4
Percentage	100.0%	51.2%	17.8%	5.7%	2.2%	0.9%	0.2%	0.1%	< 0.1%	< 0.1%

Table 1. Frequencies of Constructor Hierarchy Depths in the Qualitas Corpus

BaseCalendar	DailyCalendar
(no parameters)	`String startTime, String endTime`
	`int startHour, int startMinute, int startSecond, int startMillis, int endHour, int endMinute, int endSecond, int endMillis`
	`Calendar startCalendar, Calendar endCalendar`
	`long startTimeInMillis, long endTimeInMillis`
`Calendar baseCalendar`	`Calendar baseCalendar, String startTime, String endTime`
	`Calendar baseCalendar, int startHour, int startMinute, int startSecond, int startMillis, int endHour, int endMinute, int endSecond, int endMillis`
	`Calendar baseCalendar, Calendar startCalendar, Calendar endCalendar`
	`Calendar baseCalendar, long startTimeInMillis, long endTimeInMillis`
`TimeZone timeZone`	`TimeZone timeZone, long startTimeInMillis, long endTimeInMillis`
`Calendar baseCalendar, TimeZone timeZone`	`Calendar baseCalendar, TimeZone timeZone, long startTimeInMillis, long endTimeInMillis`

Table 2. Constructors of Example Classes from the Quartz Framework

Extended Constructors	1	2	3	4	5	6	7	8	9	10	11	12	13	$\sum$
Frequency	35492	3321	349	292	26	23	9	2	4	1	0	2	1	
Possible Savings	0	3321	698	876	104	115	54	14	32	9	0	22	12	5257

Table 3. Absolute Frequency of Initialization Variants Extending a Certain Number of Constructors in the Qualitas Corpus

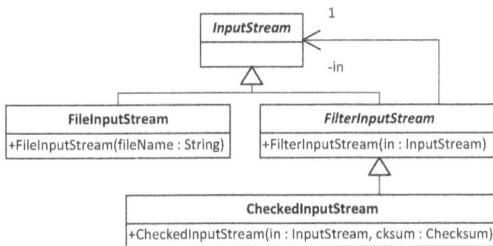

Figure 2. Extract of the *InputStream* Hierarchy from the Java API

ing in 6,642 constructors. In 349 cases, 3 superclass constructors were extended in a subclass, resulting in 1047 constructors.

The phenomenon described here has two main problems. The exploding number of constructors hampers understandability. Further, it causes the subclass-specific initialization logic to be repeated, causing boilerplate code and hampering maintainability and evolution.

2.3 Constructors in Mixins

The third problem we want to address is lack of support for mixin constructors. When a new class C' is generated by applying a mixin M to a superclass C, it is desirable to generate constructors in C' that combine the initialization logic of the superclass C with the initialization logic mixed in by M.

For illustration, consider a mixin variant of the *InputStream* hierarchy from the Java API (cf. Figure 2). *FileInputStream* is a basic implementation of *InputStream* providing access to a file. *FilterInputStream* is the basis for decorator functionality such as the *CheckedInputStream*, which calculates a checksum of the stream content according to a *Checksum* object provided as a parameter to its constructor.

An equivalent implementation with mixins would be to define *CheckedInputStream* as a mixin that can be applied to any *InputStream*. When applying it to *FileInputStream*, it would be desirable that the resulting new class has a constructor with two parameters: (a) *String fileName* to initialize the superclass part from *FileInputStream*, and (b) *Checksum cksum* to initialize the mixin part from *CheckedInputStream*. This constructor mixes the initialization logic from the superclass with the initialization logic from the mixin.

To the best of our knowledge, no OO language currently supports mixin constructors in this fashion. Instead, existing OO languages rely on implicit policies for the initialization of a mixin (for example, by calling setter methods) after the superclass initialization has completed.

3. Template Constructors in a Nutshell

A template constructor denotes a family of traditional Java-like constructors. Template constructors feature template parameters that abstract over any specific parameter list. By passing template arguments to the super-call, a single template constructor can extend many superclass constructors simultaneously. The targets of a super-call are determined based on pattern matching the super-call arguments against the parameter lists of superclass constructors. This abstraction over superclass constructors enables a single template constructor to implement an initialization variant of the subclass independently of the initialization variants of the superclass.

Table 4 compares Java constructors and template constructors with regard to parameters and arguments to super-calls. Like Java constructors, the declaration of a template constructor contains a comma-separated, ordered list of type/identifier pairs. Correspondingly, a super-call takes an ordered list of expressions as arguments, each with a certain type. The types of argument expressions are matched against the types of the formal parameter list of the superclass constructors in the order in which arguments appear.

	Java Constructor	Template Constructor
Parameter definition	identifier and type	identifier and type
		template parameter
Argument for super-call	expression	expression
		named expression
		template argument
Order of arguments	relevant	relevant (except for named expressions)

Table 4. Java Constructors versus Template Constructors

```
class DailyCalendar extends BaseCalender {
    private Calendar start;
    private Calendar end;
    public ? DailyCalendar(p*, Calendar start,
        Calendar end) {
        super(p*);
        this.start = start;
        this.end = end;
    }
}
```

Listing 1. Template Constructor for *DailyCalender*

3.1 Template Parameters and Arguments

In addition to type/identifier parameters, template constructor declarations may specify *template parameters*. A template parameter consists of an identifier followed by an asterisk (*). In addition to expression arguments, template constructors can use template arguments – the counterpart to template parameters – as arguments to a super-call. Each template parameter must appear as a template argument in the super-call and vice versa. The template argument matches an arbitrary list of parameters of a superclass constructor and propagates these into the parameter list of the constructor which contains the super-call. As a consequence, a super-call may match multiple superclass constructors – thereby enabling the desired one-to-many binding of constructor super-calls.

For illustration, consider the template constructor of the class *DailyCalender* in Listing 1. This constructor uses a template parameter $p*$ in its list of formal parameters and uses a template argument $p*$ in the super-call in its body. Accordingly, the template constructor accepts each list of arguments $p*$ followed by two objects of type *Calendar*, such that there is a superclass constructor accepting the list $p*$. The template constructor uses the other two arguments to initialize two fields that the class *DailyCalender* introduces. The question mark in the declaration of template constructors clarifies at a glance that there exist as many versions of the constructor as there are superclass constructors that match the template constructor's super-call. Since *super(p*)* matches all superclass constructors, one *DailyCalender* constructor is generated for each constructor of *BaseCalender*.

3.2 Named Expression Arguments

Template constructors also support *named expression arguments* of the form <*name*> : <*expression*> in super-calls. A named expression argument only matches a formal parameter with exactly the same name and, in contrast to unnamed expressions, the positions of the named expression and the matched parameter are irrelevant. The motivation for this feature is as follows.

Template parameters/arguments expose all parameters of superclass constructors as constructor parameters in subclasses. Sometimes, however, a subclass may want to set a certain parameter of a superclass constructor and stop delegating the initialization re-

```
class Type extends Attribute {
    public ? Type(p*) { super(p*, value : null); }
}
```

Listing 2. Template Constructor for *Type* with Named Expression

sponsibility to further subclasses or even to clients. For illustration, consider again Figure 1. The base class *Attribute* has a constructor parameter named *value*, which does not reappear in subclass constructors because it is set to a certain value by the *Type* constructor. To preserve this feature, template constructors must be able to set certain superclass parameters, while abstracting over the others.

In the example, the subclass wants to set the last parameter of the superclass constructor. The subclass can influence the initialization of the superclass by simply passing an expression argument in the last position of the super-call. For example, `super(p*, null);` would set the last parameter to `null` and forward the others. However, given that template constructors are made to cope with later changes of superclass constructors, assumptions about the position of a parameter in the super-constructor signature may render the design fragile in the presence of evolution. If the parameter list of *Attribute*'s constructor is modified by removing, adding, or reordering parameters, the subclass constructor setting only the *value* parameter should not break as long as the *value* parameter is still present in the modified list; instead, it should set the *value* parameter as before and forward the other – possibly new – parameters to subclass constructors. With a named expression argument, a parameter can be set regardless of its position in the superclass constructor. Listing 2 demonstrates this for the example of the *value* parameter, which is set to `null`.

It should be mentioned that named-based parameter matching, of course, requires stability of parameter names in superclass constructors. This means, in contrast to Java, programmers do not have to be careful with changes concerning the order of parameters but with changes concerning their names.

3.3 Instantiating Template Constructors

We call constructors that can be executed by a Java virtual machine *concrete* to distinguish them from template constructors. Template constructors are written to the binary class files during compilation. When the containing class is loaded, they are converted to concrete constructors. This two-step procedure allows a class C to adopt initialization variants of superclass C' without recompilation, which is particularly relevant if the source code of C is not available. We call the process of converting template to concrete constructors *constructor generation*; it is specified by Algorithm 1 and executed when loading a class C with superclass C'. *match(Con, Con')* matches the super-call arguments of a constructor *Con* against the formal parameter list of a concrete superclass constructor *Con'* and produces a matching σ as an output, if one exists. σ maps template arguments in the super-call of *Con* to parameters of *Con'*.

We formalize the matching semantics in Sec. 5. For an initial intuition, here we discuss some examples for matching super-calls against formal parameters of a superclass constructor (cf. Table 5). The first two columns denote the input to the matching procedure: The *Arguments* column shows the arguments of the super-call; the *Parameters* column shows the formal parameters the super-call is matched against. The column *Matching* shows the output of the matching procedure: either the possibly empty ($\emptyset$) mapping from template arguments to parameters, or "–" if the matching fails.

Rows 1 and 2 in Table 5 show examples that are equivalent to method parameter matching in Java. Examples with a named argument are given in rows 3 (matching is successful but empty because

Algorithm 1 ConstructorGeneration(C, superclass C')

> **if** C' contains template constructors **then**
>   **call** ConstructorGeneration(C', superclass(C'))
> **end if**
> **for all** template constructors Con in C **do**
>   **for all** concrete constructors Con' in C' **do**
> $\sigma \leftarrow$ match (Con, Con')
>   **if** matching succeeded **then**
> $CCon \leftarrow$ instantiate (Con, Con', σ)
>   Add $CCon$ to C.
>   **end if**
>   **end for**
>   Remove Con from C.
> **end for**

#	Arguments	Parameters	Matching
1	5, 0	int x, int y	$\emptyset$
2	5, 0	int x	−
3	x:5, 0	int x, int y	$\emptyset$
4	x:5, 0	int a, int b	−
5	p*	int x, int y	p*/(x, y)
6	p*, y:0	int x, int y	p*/(x)
7	p*, y:"s"	int x, int y	−
8	p*, c:4, 3	String a, int b, int c	p*/(a)

Table 5. Examples of Constructor Matching

there are no template arguments to be mapped) and 4 (matching fails due to wrong name). Rows 5 to 8 illustrate template arguments: The super-call argument *<name>** as in row 5 generally matches every possible parameter list completely. The pattern in row 6 uses one named argument (y) so that all other parameters (x) are mapped to the template argument $p*$. The matching in row 7 fails because the pattern requires parameter y to have type *String*, which is not true. Row 8 demonstrates the irrelevant position of named expressions. As the value 4 is assigned to parameter c, the residual argument list $p*, 3$ is matched against the residual parameter list *String a, int b*; hence, $p*$ is mapped to a.

If the matching is successful, *instantiate(Con, Con', σ)* (cf. Algorithm 1) instantiates a template constructor *Con* with a matching σ and a referenced superclass constructor *Con'* to a concrete constructor *CCon* in the following manner: 1. Replace each template parameter $p*$ of *Con* by the formal parameter list $\sigma(p)$. 2. For each template argument $p*$ of *Con*, add instructions which load the arguments provided for the parameters $\sigma(p)$. 3. Bind the super-call to *Con'*.

If there is no superclass constructor matching the super-call of a template constructor, the template constructor is just removed. If there are multiple matching superclass constructors, one concrete constructor is generated for each of them.

4. Template Constructors in Action

In this section, we discuss the benefits of template constructors on the design of programs.

4.1 Avoiding Copy-down Constructor Inheritance

In Sec. 2.1, we discussed two problems with the design of programs that employ copy-down constructor inheritance: Abundance of boilerplate code and fragility in the presence of evolution, because a change to a constructor signature may entail many cascading changes to subclass constructors. We first discuss how the application of template constructors fosters evolution.

For illustration, consider a version of the Heritrix example from Sec. 2.1, where all direct and indirect subclasses of *Type* (Figure 1) use template constructors. For example, the template constructor for *ContentTypeNotMatchesRegExpDecideRule* looks as follows:

```
public ? ContentTypeNotMatchesRegExpDecideRule(p*) {
    super(p*);
}
```

As a result, signature changes of *Type*'s constructors automatically propagate to the subclasses, which do not need to be adapted manually any more. Only clients of these classes that call the constructors still have to be adapted to provide the correct arguments to the constructor calls. This is unavoidable, given that the interface of the class used by these clients has changed. Compile-time errors can indicate instantiation sites in the code where modifications are necessary.

In the example of the *ContentTypeNotMatchesRegExpDecide-Rule* hierarchy, only one constructor is defined in the base class *Type* and entailed through the whole hierarchy. If there are more than one, template constructors are even more effective: Only one template constructor – analogous to the one above – has to be defined per class in order to expose all constructors of the superclass.

In the current design, a subclass developer has to define the trivial template constructor manually to enable constructor inheritance (see, e.g., the template constructor *ContentTypeNotMatchesReg-ExpDecideRule* again). An alternative design is to generate such a "trivial" template constructor by default. The former alternative resembles Java's strategy not to inherit constructors by default. The latter resembles Smalltalk's strategy to do so. There are trade-offs related to these alternatives: The explicit template constructors strategy enables subclass developers to decide on whether to expose superclass constructors in the instantiation interface of the subclass or not. When generating the trivial template constructor by default, the developer of the subclass does not have such control and the initialization interface may become wide, bearing the risk that clients are more exposed to constructor changes in the hierarchy.

There is another aspect of object instantiation in the presence of template constructors that needs closer consideration. In Java, the signatures of available constructors are explicitly specified in a class. Without dedicated tool support for template constructors, the programmer of a client class has to look at super-calls in the implementation of constructors in order to know which concrete constructors will be generated. While type safety is ensured by compiler checks at class instance expressions (cf. Sec. 6), lack of an explicit instantiation interface may impair understandability and modular reasoning. We believe these problems can be resolved by presenting a view of the concrete constructors to the programmer at class instantiation sites in an IDE.

4.2 Avoiding Constructor Explosion

Template constructors enable a subclass to define initialization variants for the fields it introduces as deltas that apply to all constructors (initialization variants) of its superclass. Four template constructors – two of them shown in the listing below – are, thus, sufficient to preserve all possible initialization variants of *DailyCalendar* from Sec. 2.2 in the combination with the superclass *BaseCalendar*: When *DailyCalendar* is loaded, the constructor generation process produces all 16 possible constructor variants automatically.

```
public ? DailyCalendar(p*, String start, String end) {
    super(p*);
    // initialize with Strings start and end
}
public ? DailyCalendar(p*, Calendar start, Calendar end){
    super(p*);
    // initialize with Calendars start and end
}
// similarly for the other two initialization variants
```

The example demonstrates how template constructors avoid an exploding number of constructors and the need for adapting constructors in subclasses to modifications of constructors in superclasses. To quantify the potential of template constructors to reduce the number of constructors in a larger scale, reconsider Table 3. The last row shows the number of constructors that could have been saved if the systems in the Qualitas Corpus used template constructors. For example, half of the constructors that combine the initialization logic of a subclass with two superclass constructors can be saved (3,321) because one template constructor can capture them both. In total, 5,257 constructors could have been saved, i.e., 11.7% of all 44,779 constructors in classes with a non-*Object* superclass in the analyzed systems of the Qualitas Corpus.

Template constructors also enable *DailyCalendar* to automatically adapt to changes in the constructor interface of the superclass *BaseCalendar*. If only a new constructor is added to *BaseCalendar*, no changes are required neither to *DailyCalendar* nor to its clients; yet, the new constructor is automatically inherited by *DailyCalendar* in all four combinations with its initialization variants. If the signatures of existing constructors change, only places in code, where *DailyCalendar* is instantiated, possibly have to be adapted to the new constructor signatures inherited from *BaseCalendar*.

Template constructors can also be used to reduce the number of constructors within one class with this-calls. Traditionally, a class that has n independent, optional parameters, requires 2^n distinct constructors. With template constructors, we can reduce the number of required constructors to $n + 1$: We need one constructor for the default instantiation that takes no optional arguments, and then one template constructor for each optional argument. For example, for *BaseCalendar* we define:

```
public BaseCalendar() { /* empty constructor */ }
public ? BaseCalendar(p*, Calendar baseCalendar) {
    this(p*);
    setBaseCalendar(baseCalendar);
}
public ? BaseCalendar(p*, TimeZone timeZone) {
    this(p*);
    setTimeZone(timeZone);
}
```

Constructor generation will produce four concrete constructors for *BaseCalendar*: no arguments, single *Calendar* argument, single *TimeZone* argument, two arguments *Calendar* and *TimeZone*. If we add one more optional class argument to *BaseCalendar*, we get four more constructors. For generated constructors that involve multiple arguments, the order of constructor arguments is defined by the order of template constructors. If two optional class arguments have the same type, constructor generation favors the argument whose template constructor precedes the other.

4.3 Template Constructors and Mixins

Template constructors are particularly suitable for mixins. While mixins abstract over a concrete superclass, template constructors abstract over both a concrete superclass and the constructors of the superclass. For example, we can define a template constructor for the mixin *CheckedInputStream* (cf. Sec. 2.3) in order to extend the constructor signature of the class that the mixin is applied to. For example, we can add an additional parameter *chksum*:

```
public ? CheckedInputStream(p*, Checksum chksum) {
    super(p*);
    this.chksum = chksum;
}
```

The main application of template constructors in the context of mixins is to propagate and extend parameter lists of superclass constructors. We do not allow mixins to set parameters of the superclass constructor. That is, template constructors of mixins always have the following form:

$e \in E$ expressions
$v \in V$ variable names
$t \in T$ types
$<: \subseteq T \times T$ subtyping relation
$\tau : E \to T$ mapping to most specific type

$p \in P ::= v : t$ formal parameters
$a \in A ::= e$ expression argument
         $| \; v : e$ named expression argument
         $| \; v*$ template argument

Figure 3. Syntax and notation for constructor matching

```
public ? C(<NewParams1>, p*, <NewParams2>)
{  super(p*); /* ... */ }
```

The super-call contains one single template argument, which propagates the constructor parameters of the unknown superclass. *<NewParams1>* are added before existing constructor parameters and *<NewParams2>* are added after them.

The design decision not to allow template constructors to set parameters of superclass constructors is motivated by the following two reasons:

1. A mixin does not know the semantics of superclass constructor parameters because it does not know its actual superclass. Hence, guarantees regarding positions and/or names of constructor parameters as required for setting super-constructor parameters (see Sec. 3) are hard to enforce for all classes that a mixin is possibly applied to.

2. When combining multiple mixins, it may quickly become confusing for the programmer which parameter is set by which mixin and which parameters are actually left for being set. Composabilty is fostered if mixins are only allowed to extend constructors of superclasses with new parameters but not to remove parameters by setting them.

5. Formalization of Constructor Matching

We presented some examples of constructor matching in Table 5. In this section, we formalize constructor matching with a calculus.

5.1 Definitions and Notations

Figure 3 introduces syntax relevant for constructor matching. We denote formal parameters P of a concrete constructor by their name and type $v : t$. For constructor arguments A, we distinguish simple expression arguments e, named expression arguments $v : e$, and template arguments $v*$ as illustrated in Section 3.

Based on these definitions, we define an *instance of the constructor matching problem* as a list of arguments to be matched against a list of formal parameters:

$$a_1, \ldots, a_n \doteq p_1, \ldots, p_k$$

The result of the constructor matching problem, if successful, is a matching function $\sigma \in V \rightharpoonup V^*$ which provides a mapping from names of the template arguments in $a_1, ..., a_n$ to names of matched formal parameters in $p_1, ..., p_k$. Note that we write M^* to denote the free monoid on a set M, thus the mapping retains the order of matched parameters V^*. We write ε for the empty sequence.

In addition, we require the following auxiliary definitions. We define the union of partial functions $f, g : A \rightharpoonup B$ as follows:

$$f \cup g : A \rightharpoonup B : x \mapsto \begin{cases} f(x) & \text{if } x \in \mathcal{D}(f) \\ g(x) & \text{if } x \in \mathcal{D}(g), x \notin \mathcal{D}(f) \\ \text{undefined} & \text{otherwise} \end{cases}$$

$\mathcal{D}\,(\mathrm{f})$ denotes the set of values for which the partial function f is defined. For the empty partial function f with $\mathcal{D}\,(\mathrm{f}) = \emptyset$, we write $\emptyset$. For the partial function f with finite $\mathcal{D}\,(\mathrm{f}) = \{x_1, ..., x_n\}$ and values $v_i = \mathrm{f}\,(x_i)$, we write $\{x_1/v_1, ..., x_n/v_n\}$.

5.2 Constructor Matching Calculus

We present constructor matching calculus through inference rules that relate a constructor matching problem to a matching function:

$$\mathcal{L} \quad ::= \quad a_1, \ldots, a_n \doteq p_1, \ldots, p_k \;\mapsto\; \sigma$$

We define $\bar{\mathcal{L}}$ as the subset of words in $\mathcal{L}$ that are derivable by the matching calculus.

Figure 4 displays the inference rules of the constructor matching calculus. Rule *type* (1) describes usual method parameter matching: Expression e can be used for a parameter with type t if the type of e is t or a subtype thereof. Since the mapping resulting from constructor matching maps template argument names to the corresponding constructor parameters, the reverse mapping of parameters to expressions is not recorded in the mapping. Rule *empty* (2) defines that the empty argument list matches the empty parameter list. Rule *template* (3) expresses that a single template argument matches an arbitrary list of formal parameters with mutually different labels ($S1$). Rule *name* (4) matches named expression arguments. A named expression argument can occur anywhere in the argument list and can match a constructor parameter of the expected name at any position. We delegate the type checking of the named expression to rule *type*. Rule *compos* (5) allows lists of arguments to match lists of formal parameters whose labels must be disjunct again. The side condition ($S2$) ensures that the first argument pattern always matches the longest possible sequence of formal parameters, and ($S3$) essentially expresses that each template argument may occur only once in a pattern list.

The calculus defines a matching which has a slight similiarity to unification: It aims at finding a substitution for template arguments to match the formal parameters. Yet, it is more than unification because it mixes matching with and without respecting the order of parameters – the order is ignored for named parameters whereas it is important for the others. Also, contrary to pure unification, the calculus respects types and names.

5.3 Properties of the Matching Calculus

The following two theorems lay down two key properties of the constructor matching calculus. Their proofs are available online.[4]

THEOREM 1 (Matching correctness). *If for an instance* $\mathcal{E} = a_1, \ldots, a_n \doteq p_1, \ldots, p_k$ *of the constructor matching problem* $\mathcal{E} \mapsto \sigma$ *is derivable, then applying* σ *to the template arguments in* $a_1, \ldots, a_n$ *and aligning the named expression arguments in* $a_1, \ldots, a_n$ *with the corresponding constructor parameters yields a valid argument list for the formal parameters* $p_1, \ldots, p_k$.

THEOREM 2 (Matching uniqueness). *If for an instance* $\mathcal{E}$ *of the constructor matching problem* $\mathcal{E} \mapsto \sigma$ *is derivable, then the matching function* σ *is unique, i.e., for all* σ' *with* $\sigma' \neq \sigma$, $\mathcal{E} \mapsto \sigma'$ *is not derivable.*

5.4 Solving the Constructor Matching Problem

Now that we have defined the constructor matching calculus, how can we apply it to the constructor matching problem? In formal terms, the matching procedure is specified by the sub-language $\bar{\mathcal{L}}$, consisting of the subset of words in $\mathcal{L}$ which can be derived with the constructor matching calculus. The theorems about the properties of the calculus show that the matching function σ is correct and

uniquely determined by a constructor matching problem instance $\mathcal{E}$. Moreover, it is easy to obtain an algorithmic implementation, for example, by resolving all named expressions first.

Figure 5 gives an example for the application of the calculus to the following instance of the constructor matching problem:

$$a*, z : 4, 3 \;\doteq\; x : \mathrm{String}, y : \mathrm{int}, z : \mathrm{int}$$

Since a derivation exists, a matching is possible, namely with the matching function in the root of the derivation tree: $\{a/\,(x)\}$.

The example illustrates that the position of named expressions is indeed arbitrary: With rule *name* in the last step of the tree, the argument $z : 4$ is inserted between the other arguments whereas the formal parameter $z : int$ is located at the last position. The unnamed expression 3 is assigned to the last formal parameter *except for z*, namely y, and the template argument $a*$ covers the rest, namely x.

6. Implementation

We have implemented template constructors in CaesarJ [1], a Java extension, which among other features also supports mixin-based inheritance. More specifically, the implementation extends the static type checking and the Java byte code generation phases of the JastAdd compiler [7] of CaesarJ. We exploit a custom class loader and the ASM bytecode toolkit [4] for applying transformations specific to template constructors. The implementation is available at GitHub; its main building blocks are detailed below.

Type Checking. The integration of template constructors affects the static type checking in two places of the abstract syntax tree generated by JastAdd: (a) class instance expressions (`new C(...)`) and (b) super-calls within constructors.

At *class instance expressions*, the implementation checks whether there is an appropriate constructor available for the class to be instantiated. To perform the check, the implementation partially executes the constructor generation process (cf. Sec. 3) only for the signatures of the template constructors. The check succeeds if one of the generated signatures or one of the non-template constructors contained in the class match the instance expression; otherwise, a compiler error is produced.

At *super-calls within constructors*, the implementation distinguishes between super-calls contained (a) in a template constructor and (b) in a non-template constructor. For super-calls of non-template constructors, the implementation checks whether they refer to an existing non-template constructor in the superclass. If this is not the case, a compiler error is produced. In contrast, super-calls of template constructors are not checked immediately, but rather at class instance expressions (see above).

Bytecode Generation. Figure 6 visualizes the process of compiling template constructors and loading them from a class file by means of the example in Listing 2. The compiled class file is saved with a special suffix that is recognized during class loading. The process of bytecode generation for template constructors (left part of the figure) deviates from that for normal Java constructors in following ways. First, the method signature does not declare any parameters. Second, the method code does not contain a super-call[5]. However, the super-call is prepared by loading the expression arguments of the super-call onto the stack. In the example, an instruction for loading null onto the stack is written to the code attribute (marked as 1 in Figure 6) because null is assigned to the parameter *value* in the super-call. The name *value* of the named argument expression is ignored in the code attribute as well as template arguments are. Third, a special template constructor attribute (marked

---

[4]   https://github.com/tud-stg-lang/caesar-jastadd/blob/mixin-constructors/
doc/TemplateConstructors%20-%20Matching%20Calculus.pdf?raw=true

[5] In standard bytecode, the code for super-calls is located between argument loading instructions and remaining constructor instructions.

$$\text{type} \quad \frac{}{e \doteq v : t \mapsto \emptyset} \; \tau(e) \leq t \quad (1) \qquad\qquad \text{empty} \quad \frac{}{\varepsilon \doteq \varepsilon \mapsto \emptyset} \quad (2)$$

$$\text{template} \quad \frac{}{v* \doteq v_1 : t_1, ..., v_n : t_n \mapsto \{v/(v_1, ..., v_n)\}} \; \begin{array}{c} n \geq 0 \\ (S1) \end{array} \quad (3)$$

$$\text{name} \quad \frac{e \doteq v_k : t_k \mapsto \emptyset \qquad a_1, ..., a_{q-1}, a_{q+1}, ..., a_m \doteq p_1, ..., p_{k-1}, p_{k+1}, ..., p_n \mapsto \sigma}{a_1, ..., a_{q-1}, v_k : e, a_{q+1}, ..., a_m \doteq p_1, ..., p_{k-1}, v_k : t_k, p_{k+1}, ..., p_n \mapsto \sigma} \; \begin{array}{c} m, n \geq 0 \\ 1 \leq q \leq m \\ 1 \leq k \leq n \\ (S1) \end{array} \quad (4)$$

$$\text{compos} \quad \frac{a_1 \doteq p_1, ..., p_k \mapsto \sigma_1 \qquad a_2, ..., a_m \doteq p_{k+1}, ..., p_n \mapsto \sigma_2}{a_1, ..., a_m \doteq p_1, ..., p_n \mapsto \sigma_1 \cup \sigma_2} \; \begin{array}{c} m \geq 2 \\ n \geq k \geq 0 \\ (S1), (S2), (S3) \end{array} \quad (5)$$

$(S1) : \forall i, j \in \{1, ..., n\} : i \neq j \Rightarrow v_i \neq v_j$ where $p_x = v_x : t_x$

$(S2) : \forall i \in \{k+1, ..., n\} : \forall \sigma_1', \sigma_2' \in V \rightharpoonup V^* :$
$$\begin{pmatrix} ((\quad a_1 \quad \doteq \quad p_1, ..., p_i), \sigma_1') \notin \bar{\mathcal{L}} \vee \\ ((a_2, ..., a_m \doteq p_{i+1}, ..., p_n), \sigma_2') \notin \bar{\mathcal{L}} \end{pmatrix}$$

$(S3) : \mathcal{D}(\sigma_1) \cap \mathcal{D}(\sigma_2) = \emptyset$

Figure 4. Rules of the Constructor Matching Calculus

$$\cfrac{(2) \; \cfrac{(1) \; \cfrac{}{(4 \doteq z : \text{int}), \emptyset} \quad (5) \; \cfrac{(4) \; \cfrac{}{(a* \doteq x : \text{String}), \{a/(x)\}} \quad (1) \; \cfrac{}{(3 \doteq y : \text{int}), \emptyset}}{(a*, 3 \doteq x : \text{String}, y : \text{int}), \{a/(x)\}}}{(a*, z : 4, 3 \doteq x : \text{String}, y : \text{int}, z : \text{int}), \{a/(x)\}}}{}$$

Figure 5. Applying the Constructor Matching Calculus

as 2 in Figure 6) is defined, which contains all the template constructor information that cannot be expressed in the code attribute: the parameters of the template constructor ($p*$ in the example), including identifiers of parameters and template parameters, and a complete list of the super-call arguments, which contains for each argument the type signature if it is a named or unnamed expression and the name if it is a named expression or a template argument.

Class Loading. Loading classes with template constructors is done by our custom classloader (cf. right-hand side of Figure 6). The template constructor attribute (2) contains all the information needed to perform constructor matching against superclass constructors at class load time. The constructor generation procedure (cf. Sec. 3) is now completely executed, resulting in zero, one or more concrete constructors for each template constructor. The process of matching a template constructor against a superclass constructor is as follows: First, the constructor signature (in the example *name : String*) is created using the full parameter list ($p*$) contained in the template constructor attribute and the mapping of template arguments to the matched parameters of the superclass constructor ($\{p*/(\text{name})\}$). Second, instructions are created to load the arguments to be forwarded to the superclass constructor (3); these instructions are interleaved with instructions for loading expression arguments already generated in the bytecode (1). Finally, instructions for invoking the matched superclass constructor are inserted (4) – the binding step of the constructor generation process. The remaining instructions are retained from the bytecode (5).

Since a template constructor can match multiple superclass constructors, the code generated for it is replicated and each replica is provided with specific super-call invocation instructions for each matching superclass constructor.

7. Related Work

Parameterized inheritance in C++ (PI) [18, 21] is a method to support mixins in C++: The mixin is defined as a subclass, which is parameterized by the superclass by using C++ templates. This approach has considerable restrictions regarding abstraction over initialization logic [6]. Mixins have to pass all initialization parameters of the original superclass as well as parameters of previously applied mixins. Hence, mixin constructors hard-code assumptions about constructors of their yet unknown superclasses/super-mixins. This restricts their applicability: One would have to define different constructors for different sets of possible superclasses and different orders of composition. Hence, constructor reusability is not properly supported, if at all only at the cost of a very complex design.

PI with virtual inheritance [6] is proposed as a countermeasure to the above problem with PI. Changing the inheritance mode of mixins to virtual inheritance makes it possible to abstract over the order in which mixins are applied (since, with virtual inheritance, the implementing subclass – instead of the mixin – is responsible for initializing them all). The drawback is that an implementing subclass together with all necessary calls to superclass constructors has to be written explicitly for every desired combination of mixins, yielding high design complexity. Also, the solution inherits the general weaknesses of virtual inheritance: Constructor invocations in mixins are ignored; particularly, mixins do not have any possibility to modify arguments passed to a superclass.

PI with argument class [19] is another workaround for the problems of the PI approach. The constructors of classes/mixins, which may be part of a (multiple) inheritance hierarchy, take an instance of an argument class as a parameter. The latter encapsulates data needed in any class/mixin, enabling a uniform constructor interface. Each mixin constructor can select the data it needs from the argument object and pass it through to the next superclass. This approach achieves flexibility at the cost of increasing design complexity and losing declarative expression of design intent. When many mixins exist, which may eventually not all be used in a certain hierarchy, the size of the argument class may constitute a significant overhead in memory. Also, the argument class must be extended for every new feature which is needed by any constructor of any mixin, completely defeating the open-closed principle [14].

The typed argument list approach [12] – like the argument class approach – is based on a standardized constructor interface; however, the type of the expected constructor parameter is now a heterogeneous value list. Based on C++ templates, the type of each list is generated automatically by the compiler, so that it defines the number and types of expected list elements according to the expected parameter types of the mixin and the inherited parameter types from other mixins. Constructor reusability is now achieved for mixins because changing the superclass of a mixin will not

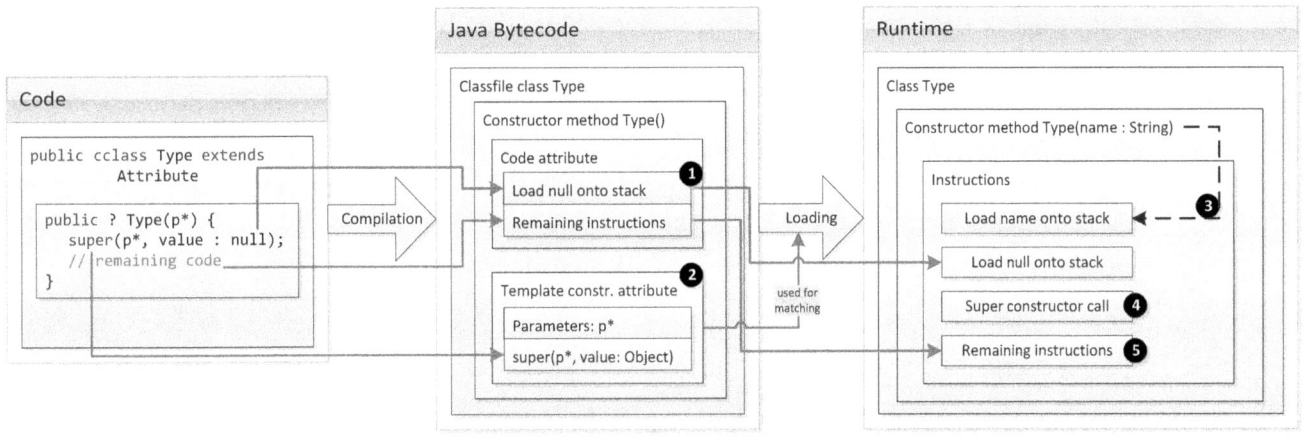

Figure 6. Process of Compiling and Loading the Template Constructor of the Example in Listing 2

render its constructor useless: The correct type of a heterogeneous value list is automatically generated for each possible hierarchy of mixins, which also makes the approach type-safe. The drawback is, however, the overhead for defining the mixins and the infrastructure needed to use the heterogeneous value lists. Design complexity remains high and design intent is still implicit.

Scala traits can have a parameterless default constructor encoding arbitrary initialization logic in the body of the trait after the opening bracket {. The order of trait constructor invocations is defined by the order in which traits are mixed in. The key disadvantage is that traits cannot be initialized with constructor parameters. Hence, initialization methods have to be used when creating trait-based objects. Also, traits cannot initialize their superclass, since *super* constructor calls are not allowed. Like with virtual inheritance in C++, if a trait extends a class without a default constructor, subclasses of the trait must explicitly invoke the superclass constructor. Unlike virtual inheritance, constructor reusability is, at least partially, achieved: A composition of a class with several traits can be created with one line of code, thereby reusing constructors of the class and parameterless constructors of mixins.

Object initializers in C# are a convenient notation to initialize object properties directly after object creation. An object initializer can set any combination of class properties without the necessity of defining a constructor for each combination. However, it is only syntactic sugar because it can be equivalently replaced by setting the properties on the object reference after creating the object: The constructor is entirely executed before the object initializer and can, thus, not perform initialization actions based on the values set in the object initializer. Therefore, object initializers do not bring advantages concerning constructor flexibility compared to Java.

CZ extends Java with multiple inheritance, but avoids the problems of diamond hierarchies [13]. In addition to *extends*, it introduces a new subtyping relationship, *requires*. Classes requiring other classes are abstract: They are not allowed to invoke constructors of required classes, but they can use their features as if they were subclasses. If a class *A* extends *B* and *B* requires *C*, *A* must require or extend *C* or a subclass of *C*. This ensures that *B* can rely on the existence of *C* in a concrete implementation. Superclass decoupling is simulated by only requiring, but not extending a certain class. E.g., *B* in the example above can be composed with any direct or indirect subclass of *C*. A weakness is that combining multiple classes always requires defining a new one, which must explicitly invoke constructors of all extended classes: There may be many of them if many classes requiring some other classes are extended. As

with Scala traits, the restriction that constructors of required classes may not be called limits expressiveness of constructors.

Object initialization in Common Lisp Object System (CLOS) [5] shares some similarity with template constructors. Basic constructors for setting object fields by name can be generated automatically. *:before*, *:after*, or *:around* method qualifiers – applied to the initialization function *initialize-instance* – can define additional constructor logic to be executed before, after, or around basic object initialization; in the latter case the arguments can also be modified. With the *&key* keyword, arguments can be extracted by name, and with the *&rest* keyword, other arguments can be forwarded to the wrapped initialization method called with the *call-next-method* keyword. Similarly to template parameters of template constructors, Lisp's *&rest* keyword enables forwarding some parts of the argument list to the next method, whereby the *&rest* concept applies to any method.[6] Its disadvantages in the context of object initialization are the quite complex syntax for forwarding and modifying arguments and the inherent lack of safety: With the *&key* keyword, argument names are conceptually contained in the list of arguments. Setting the argument of a method call is thus equivalent to adding the name of the argument to be set and its value to the list of arguments. A simple typo may leave the desired argument undefined. Also, other – possibly unknown – *:around*-qualified methods of a generic function may silently change the argument list. Hence, there is no safe way for a subclass-specific object initializer to fill an object slot with a certain value.

The Racket class system [9] circumvents many constructor pitfalls with its design to force exactly one initialization variant per class or mixin; unlike Java, multiple variants cannot be encoded in the form of multiple constructors. This is also the greatest drawback because it limits expressiveness of class definitions: For example, a class cannot create a file when a file name is provided for construction, and initialize an output stream when a stream is provided.

Instead, a class defines exactly one list of initialization arguments that must be provided during initialization. (Arguments with default values can be left out.) The arguments can be provided either by subclasses when calling the superclass initialization (`super -new`), or by clients when instantiating the class, which means that initialization arguments are aggregated down the inheritance hierarchy until they are set. As a consequence, subclasses and mixins

---

[6] In our approach, we restricted template parameters to constructors because we do not have evidence from existing systems that their main use case – abstracting over possibly multiple other constructors – is transferrable to normal methods. Nevertheless, further investigation of template parameters for normal methods might be an interesting aspect for future research.

Solution	Constr. inheritance	Constr. abstraction	No supercl. coupling	Expressiveness	Safety	Performance	Ease of use
Java, C#	−	−	−	+	+	+	0
Smalltalk	+	−	−	+	+	+	+
C++ default inherit.	−	−	−	+	+	+	0
C++ virtual inherit.	−	−	−	0	0	+	0
PI default inherit.	−	−	+	+	+	+	0
PI virtual inherit.	−	−	+	0	0	+	0
PI argument class	−	−	+	+	−	−	0
PI heter. val. lists	+	+	+	0	+	+	−
Scala classes	−	−	−	+	+	+	0
Scala traits	−	−	+	−	0	+	+
CZ *extends* relation	−	−	−	+	+	+	0
CZ *requires* relation	−	−	+	0	+	+	+
CLOS	+	+	+	+	0	+	0
Racket	+	+	+	0	+	+	+
Template constr.	+	+	+	+	+	+	0

Table 6. Comparison of Object Initialization Solutions

do not need to be aware of the initialization arguments of the superclass; if they do not set them, clients or subclasses will do.

Summary. Table 6 summarizes the advantages and weaknesses of various solutions for object initialization. "Constructor inheritance" refers to the ability of classes to inherit constructors from the superclass and to expose them to instantiating clients and subclasses. "Constructor abstraction" pertains to abstracting from superclass constructors in a way which allows to extend them with new parameters. "No superclass coupling" denotes the possibility to write constructors which are not restricted for application to a particular superclass. "Expressiveness" denotes the possibilities – even of mixins – to have constructors with parameters, to influence the initialization of the superclass, and to define multiple initialization variants per class. "Safety" indicates that super-calls are not ignored as for example with virtual inheritance and that initialization methods need not to be called separately because this is unsafe in the sense that it is not enforced by the compiler. "Performance" generally refers to a good runtime performance and requires that the solution does not impose a significant memory overhead. "Ease of use" indicates that boilerplate code is avoided and the particular solution is comfortable to use and does not require a large infrastructure to be applied. A "+" in the table indicates that the respective criterion is fulfilled (nearly) perfectly, "0" indicates partial validity, and "−" indicates that the criterion does not apply. Template constructors are rated with "0" concerning ease of use because the trivial template constructor, which just emulates constructor inheritance, must be written manually by the programmer. The reason was discussed in Sec. 4.1.

8. Summary

In this paper, we presented template constructors as a means to address the problems of object initialization in object-oriented programming languages. Template constructors abstract over concrete superclass constructors by employing named expressions and template arguments for use in super-calls besides unnamed expressions that are used in super-calls in mainstream OO languages such as Java and C++. Template parameters/arguments support matching super-calls against superclass constructors and abolish the need for static coupling super-calls to superclass constructors. A formal foundation of constructor matching was given and applicability and usefulness was shown by several use cases. The discussion in Sec.7 (cf. Tab. 6) indicates that from all existing solutions for object initialization, template constructors provide the best reusability without sacrificing other properties, such as safety and performance.

Acknowledgments

We would like to thank Vaidas Gasiunas for discussion on template constructors, and the anonymous reviewers for their helpful feedback.

References

[1] I. Aracic, V. Gasiunas, M. Mezini, and K. Ostermann. An overview of CaesarJ. In *Transactions on Aspect-Oriented Software Development*, LNCS, pages 135–173. Springer, 2006.

[2] K. Arnold, J. Gosling, and D. Holmes. *Java(TM) Programming Language, The (4th Edition)*. Addison-Wesley Professional, 2005.

[3] G. Bracha and W. Cook. Mixin-based inheritance. In *OOPSLA/ECOOP*, pages 303–311. ACM, 1990.

[4] E. Bruneton, R. Lenglet, and T. Coupaye. ASM: A code manipulation tool to implement adaptable systems. In *Adaptable and extensible component systems*, 2002.

[5] L. G. DeMichiel and R. P. Gabriel. The Common Lisp Object System: An overview. In *ECOOP*, pages 151–170. Springer, 1987.

[6] U. Eisenecker, F. Blinn, and K. Czarnecki. A solution to the constructor-problem of mixin-based programming in C++. In *GCSE'2000 Workshop on C++ Template Programming*, 2000.

[7] T. Ekman and G. Hedin. The JastAdd system – modular extensible compiler construction. *Sci. Comput. Program.*, 69(1-3):14–26, 2007.

[8] M. A. Ellis and B. Stroustrup. *The annotated C++ reference manual*. Addison-Wesley Longman Publishing Co., Inc., 1990.

[9] M. Flatt, R. B. Findler, and M. Felleisen. Scheme with classes, mixins, and traits. In *APLAS*, pages 270–289, 2006.

[10] A. Goldberg and D. Robson. *Smalltalk-80: the language and its implementation*. Addison-Wesley Longman Publishing Co., Inc., 1983.

[11] A. Hejlsberg, M. Torgersen, S. Wiltamuth, and P. Golde. *C# Programming Language*. Addison-Wesley Professional, 4th edition, 2010.

[12] J. Järvi. Tuples and multiple return values in C++. Technical report, Turku Centre for Computer Science, 1999.

[13] D. Malayeri and J. Aldrich. CZ: multiple inheritance without diamonds. In *OOPSLA*, pages 21–40, 2009.

[14] B. Meyer. Eiffel: A language and environment for software engineering. *Journal of Systems and Software*, 8(3):199–246, 1988.

[15] G. Mohr, M. Kimpton, M. Stack, and I. Ranitovic. Introduction to Heritrix, an archival quality web crawler. In *International Web Archiving Workshop*, 2004.

[16] D. A. Moon. Object-oriented programming with flavors. In *OOPLSA*, pages 1–8. ACM, 1986.

[17] M. Odersky, L. Spoon, and B. Venners. *Programming in Scala*. Artima, 2008.

[18] Y. Smaragdakis and D. S. Batory. Mixin-based programming in C++. In *GCSE*, pages 163–177. Springer, 2001.

[19] B. Stroustrup. *The design and evolution of C++*. ACM Press/Addison-Wesley Publishing Co., 1994.

[20] E. Tempero, C. Anslow, J. Dietrich, T. Han, J. Li, M. Lumpe, H. Melton, and J. Noble. Qualitas corpus: A curated collection of Java code for empirical studies. In *APSEC*, 2010.

[21] M. VanHilst and D. Notkin. Using role components in implement collaboration-based designs. In *OOPSLA*, pages 359–369. ACM, 1996.

Efficient High-Level Abstractions for Web Programming

Julien Richard-Foy   Olivier Barais   Jean-Marc Jézéquel

IRISA, Université de Rennes 1

{first}.{last}@irisa.fr

Abstract

Writing large Web applications is known to be difficult. One challenge comes from the fact that the application's logic is scattered into heterogeneous clients and servers, making it difficult to share code between both sides or to move code from one side to the other. Another challenge is performance: while Web applications rely on ever more code on the client-side, they may run on smart phones with limited hardware capabilities. These two challenges raise the following problem: how to benefit from high-level languages and libraries making code complexity easier to manage and abstracting over the clients and servers differences without trading this ease of engineering for performance? This article presents high-level abstractions defined as deep embedded DSLs in Scala that can generate efficient code leveraging the characteristics of both client and server environments. We compare performance on client-side against other candidate technologies and against hand written low-level JavaScript code. Though code written with our DSL has a high level of abstraction, our benchmark on a real world application reports that it runs as fast as hand tuned low-level JavaScript code.

Categories and Subject Descriptors   D.3.3 [*Programming Languages*]: Language Constructs and Features

Keywords   Heterogeneous code generation, Domain-specific languages, Scala, Web

1. Introduction

Web applications are attractive because they require no installation or deployment steps on clients and enable large scale collaborative experiences. However, writing large Web applications is known to be difficult [16, 18]. One challenge comes from the fact that the business logic is scattered into heterogeneous client-side and server-side environments [14, 19]. This gives less flexibility in the engineering process and requires a higher maintenance effort: there is no way to move a piece of code targeting the server-side to target the client-side – the code has to be rewritten. Even worse, logic parts that run on both client-side and server-side need to be duplicated. For instance, HTML fragments may be built from the server-side when a page is requested by a client, but they may also be built from the client-side to perform an incremental update

subsequent to a user action. How could developers write HTML fragment definitions once and render them on both client-side and server-side?

The more interactive the application is, the more logic needs to be duplicated between the server-side and the client-side, and the higher is the complexity of the client-side code. Developers can use libraries and frameworks to get high-level abstractions on client-side, making their code easier to reason about and to maintain, but also making their code run less efficiently due to *abstraction penalty*.

Performance is a primary concern in many Web applications, because they are expected to run on a broad range of devices, from the powerful desktop personal computer to the less powerful smart phone [10, 22].

Using the same programming language on both server-side and client-side could improve the software engineering process by enabling code reuse between both sides. Incidentally, the JavaScript language – which is currently the most supported action language on Web clients – can be used on server-side. Conversely, an increasing number of programming languages or compiler back-ends can generate JavaScript code (*e.g.* Java/GWT [5], SharpKit[1], Dart [8], Kotlin[2], ClojureScript [15], Fay[3], Haxe [4] or Opa[4]).

However, using the same programming language is not enough because the client and server programming environments are not the same. For instance, DOM fragments can be defined on client-side using the standard DOM API, but this API does not exist on server-side. How to define a common vocabulary for such concepts? And how to make the executable code leverage the native APIs, when possible, for performance reasons?

Generating efficient code for heterogeneous platforms is hard to achieve in an extensible way: the translation of common abstractions like collections into their native counterpart (JavaScript arrays on client-side and standard library's collections on server-side) may be hard-coded in the compiler, but that approach would not scale to handle all the abstractions a complete application may use (*e.g.* HTML fragment definitions, form validation rules, or even some business data type that may be represented differently).

On one hand, for engineering reasons, developers want to write Web applications using a single high-level language, abstracting over the target platforms differences and reducing code complexity. But on the other hand, for performance reasons, they want to keep control on the way their code is compiled to each target platform. We propose to solve this dilemma by providing high-level abstractions in compiled domain-specific embedded languages (DSELs) [7, 11]. Compiled DSELs allow the definition of domain-specific languages (DSLs) as libraries on top of a host language,

---

[1] http://sharpkit.net

[2] http://kotlin.jetbrains.org/

[3] http://fay-lang.org/

[4] http://opalang.org/

and to compile them to a target platform. Their deep embedding gives the opportunity to control the code generation scheme for a given abstraction and target platform.

Kossakowski *et al.* introduced *js-scala*, a compiled embedded DSL defined in Scala that generates JavaScript code, making it possible to write the client-side code of Web applications using Scala [13]. However, the authors did not discuss any specific optimization and did not consider performance issues of their approach. Our paper shows how js-scala has been extended to support a set of specific optimizations allowing our high-level abstractions for Web programming to be efficiently compiled on both client and server sides[5].

We validate our approach with a case study implemented with various candidate technologies and discuss the relative pro and cons of them. We also measured the individual impact of each of our optimizations using micro-benchmarks. Though the code written in our DSL is high-level and can be shared between clients and servers, it has the same runtime performance on client-side as hand-tuned low-level JavaScript code.

The remainder of this paper is organized as follows. The next section overviews the existing approaches defining high-level languages for Web programming. Section 3 presents the framework we used to define our DSLs. Section 4 presents our contribution. Section 5 compares our solution to common approaches. Section 6 discusses our results and section 7 concludes.

2. Related Work

We classified existing approaches providing high-level abstractions for Web programming in four categories, as shown in Figure 1.

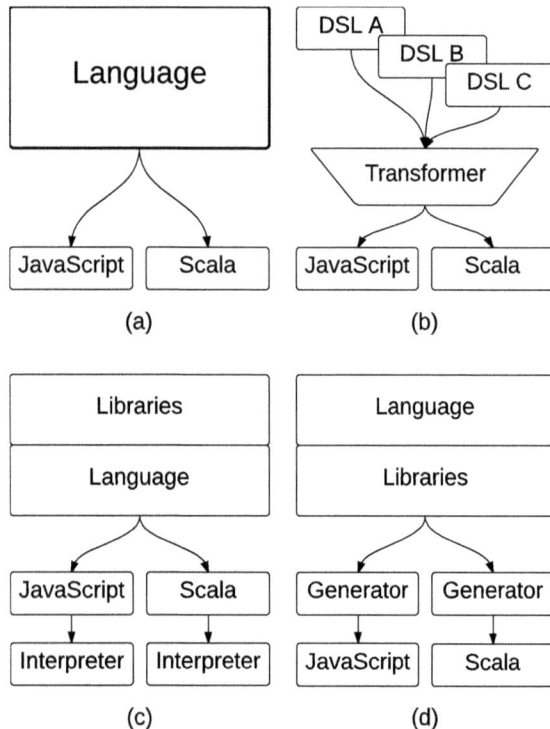

Figure 1. Language engineering processes

Fat Languages   The first approach for defining a cross-platform language consists in hard-coding, in the compiler, the code generation scheme of each language feature to each target platform. Figure 1 (a) depicts this process. In order to support a feature related to a specific domain, the whole compiler pipeline (parser, code generator, *etc.*) may have to be adapted. This approach gives *fat* languages because a lot of concepts are defined at the language level: general programming concepts such as naming, functions, classes, as well as more domain-specific concepts such as HTML fragment definition. Thus, implementing a fat language may require a high effort and adding support for these languages in development environments may require a even higher effort. Examples of such languages for Web programming are Links [6], Opa, Dart [8].

Domain-Specific Languages   Another approach consists in defining several independent domain-specific languages [23], each one focusing on concerns specific to a given problem domain, and then to combine all the source artifacts written with these language into one executable program, as shown in Figure 1 (b). Defining such languages requires a minimal effort compared to the previous approach because each language has a limited set of features. On the other hand, it is difficult to have interoperability between DSLs. [24] gave an example of such a domain-specific language for defining Web applications.

Thin Languages   Alternatively, one can define concepts relative to a specific domain as a library on top of a thin general purpose language (it is also referred to as a domain-specific *embedded* language [11]). Figure 1 (c) depicts this approach. Defining such a library requires minimal effort (though the syntax of the DSL is limited by the syntax flexibility of the host language) and several DSLs can interoperate freely within the host language. However, this approach gives no opportunity to efficiently translate a concept according to the target platform characteristics because the compiler has no domain-specific knowledge (though some compilers hard-code the translation of some common abstractions such as arrays to leverage the target platform characteristics). Examples of languages following this approach are Java/GWT, Kotlin, HaXe and SharpKit. Libraries written in JavaScript (*e.g.* jQuery [2]) also match this category though most of them do not support both client and server sides.

Deeply Embedded Languages   The last approach, shown in Figure 1 (d), can be seen as a middle-ground between the two previous approaches: DSLs are embedded in a host language but use a code generation process. This approach shares the same benefits and limitations as embedded DSLs for defining language units. However, the code generation process is specific to each DSL and gives the opportunity to perform domain-specific optimizations. In other words deeply embedded DSLs bring domain-specific knowledge to the compiler. Js-scala [13] is an example of deeply embedded DSL in Scala for Web programming. It makes it possible to produce JavaScript programs from Scala code that uses basic language concepts like arrays and control structures (`if` and `while`) as well as mechanisms specific to the Scala compiler like delimited continuations to handle asynchronous computations. Paper [13] presented the implementation of js-scala using staging, but did not discuss any specific optimization and did not consider performance issues of this approach. In this paper, we show how js-scala has been extended to support a set of specific optimizations allowing our high-level abstractions for Web programming to be efficiently compiled on heterogeneous platforms.

3. Lightweight Modular Staging

This section gives background material on the framework used to define js-scala.

Lightweight Modular Staging [20, 21] (LMS) is a framework for defining deeply embedded DSLs in Scala. It has been used to define high-performance DSLs for parallel computing [3] and to define JavaScript as an embedded DSL in Scala [13].

---

[5] The code is available at http://github.com/js-scala

LMS is based on staging [12]: a program using LMS is a regular Scala program that evaluates to an intermediate representation (IR) of a final program. This IR is a graph of expressions that can be traversed by code generators to produce the final program code. Expressions evaluated in the initial program and those evaluated in the final program (namely, staged expressions) are distinguished by their type: a Rep[Int] value in the initial program is a staged expression that generates code evaluating to an Int value in the final program. An Int computation in the initial program is evaluated during the initial program evaluation and becomes a constant in the final program.

Defining a DSL with LMS consists in the following steps:

- writing a Scala module providing the DSL vocabulary as an abstract API,
- implementing the API in terms of IR nodes,
- defining a code generator visiting IR nodes and generating the corresponding code.

4. Efficient High-Level Abstractions for Web Programming

This section presents some tasks typically performed in Web applications, either on client-side or server-side or on both, generalizes them in terms of high-level abstractions, and shows how they are implemented in js-scala to generate efficient code.

4.1 Selectors API

In a Web application, the user interface is defined by a HTML document that can be updated by the JavaScript code. A typical operation consists in searching some "interesting" element in the document, in order to extract its content, replace it or listen to user events triggered on it (such as mouse clicks). The standard API provides several functions to search elements in a HTML document according to their name or attribute values. Figure 2 summarizes the available functions and their differences.

Function	Description
querySelector(s)	First element matching the CSS selector s
getElementById(i)	Element which attribute id equals to i
querySelectorAll(s)	All elements matching the CSS selector s
getElementsByTagName(n)	All elements of type n
getElementsByClassName(c)	All elements which **class** attribute contains c

Figure 2. Standard selectors API. The querySelector and querySelectorAll are the most general functions while the others handle special cases.

Listing 1 gives an example of use of various functions from the native selectors API to retrieve a list of input fields within a form. The getWords function first finds in the document the HTML element with id add−user, then collects all its fieldset children elements, and for each one returns the list of its children elements having class word. The existence of several specialized functions in the API makes it possible to write efficient code, but forces users to think at a low abstraction level.

A high-level abstraction for searching elements in a document could be just one function finding all elements matching a given

```
function getWords() {
  var form = document.getElementById('add−user');
  var sections =
    form.getElementsByTagName('fieldset');
  var results = [];
  for (var i = 0 ; i < sections.length ; i++) {
    var words = sections[i]
      .getElementsByClassName('word');
    results[i] = words;
  }
  return results
}
```

Listing 1. Searching elements using the native selectors API

```
function getWords() {
  var form = $('#add−user');
  var sections = $('fieldset', form);
  return sections.map(function () {
    return $('.word', this)
  })
}
```

Listing 2. Searching elements using jQuery

CSS selector. In fact, most JavaScript developers[6] use the jQuery library that actually provides only one function to search for elements. Listing 2 shows an equivalent JavaScript program as Listing 1, but using jQuery. The code is both shorter and simpler, thanks to its higher level of abstraction. jQuery provides an API that is simpler to master because it has fewer functions, but this benefit comes at the price of a decrease in runtime performance.

Instead, we propose a solution that has a high-level API but generates JavaScript code using the specialized native API, when possible, in order to get both ease of engineering and performance. We achieve this by analyzing, during the first evaluation step, the selector that is passed as parameter and, when appropriate, by producing JavaScript code using the specialized API, and otherwise producing code using querySelector and querySelectorAll.

```
def find(selector: Rep[String]) =
  getConstIdCss(selector) match {
    case Some(id) if receiver == document =>
      DocumentGetElementById(Const(id))
    case _ =>
      SelectorFind(receiver, selector)
  }
```

Listing 3. Selectors optimization

Our API has two functions: find to find the first element matching a selector and findAll to find all the matching elements. Listing 3 gives the implementation of the find function. It is a Scala function that returns an IR node representing the JavaScript computation that will search the element in the final program. The getConstIdCss function analyzes the selector: if it is a constant String value containing a CSS ID selector, it returns the value of the identifier. So, if the find function is applied to the document and to an ID selector, it returns a DocumentGetElementById IR node (that is translated to a document.getElementById call by the code generator), otherwise it returns a SelectorFind IR node (that is translated to a querySelector call).

The same applies to the implementation of findAll: the selector passed as parameter is analyzed and the function returns

---

[6] According to http://trends.builtwith.com/javascript, jQuery is used by more than 40% of the top million sites.

a SelectorGetElementsByClassName in case of a CSS class name selector, a SelectorGetElementsByTagName in case of a CSS tag name selector, and a SelectorFindAll otherwise.

```
def getWords() = {
  val form = document.find("#add-user")
  val sections = form.findAll("fieldset")
  sections map (_.findAll(".word"))
}
```

Listing 4. Searching elements in js-scala

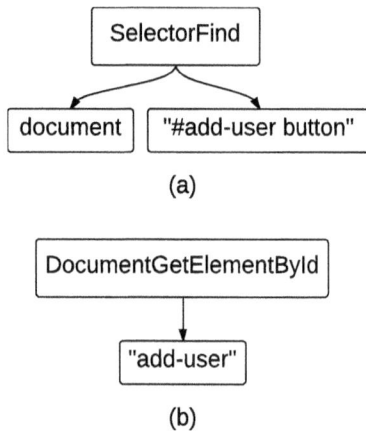

(a)

(b)

Figure 3. Intermediate representations returned by the evaluation of (a) document.find("#add-user button") and (b) document.find("#add-user")

Figure 3 shows the IRs returned by the evaluation of *document.find("#add-userbutton")* and *document.find("#add-user")*.

In the former case, the selector is parsed and does not match an ID selector (it is a composite selector matching button elements within the element having the add-user id), so a SelectorFind node is returned, then translated into a call to the general querySelector function. In the latter case, the selector matches an ID selector so a DocumentGetElementById node is returned, then translated into a call to the specialized getElementById function.

Finally, Listing 4 shows how to implement Listing 2 in Scala using js-scala. The code has the same abstraction level as with jQuery, however it generates a JavaScript program identical to Listing 1: the high-level abstractions (the find and findAll functions) exist only in the initial program, not in the final JavaScript program.

4.2 Monads Sequencing

This section presents an abstraction to handle **null** references and shows how this abstraction can be shared between client and server code.

null references are a known source of problems in programming languages [9, 17]. For example, consider Listing 5 finding a particular widget in the page and then a particular button within the widget. The native querySelector method returns **null** if no node matched the given selector in the document. If we run this code in a page where the widget is not present, it will throw an error and stop further JavaScript execution. Defensive code can be

written to handle **null** references, but leads to very cumbersome code, as shown in Listing 6.[7]

```
var loginWidget =
  document.querySelector("div.login");
var loginButton =
  loginWidget.querySelector("button.submit");
loginButton.addEventListener("click", handler);
```

Listing 5. Unsafe code

```
var loginWidget =
  document.querySelector("div.login");
if (loginWidget !== null) {
  var loginButton =
    loginWidget.querySelector("button.submit");
  if (loginButton !== null) {
    loginButton.
      addEventListener("click", handler);
  }
}
```

Listing 6. Defensive programming to handle null references

Some programming languages encode optional values with a monad (*e.g.* Maybe in Haskell and Option in Scala). In that case, sequencing over the monad encodes optional value dereferencing. If the language supports a convenient syntax for monad sequencing, it brings a convenient syntax for optional value dereferencing, alleviating developers from the burden of defensive programming.

In our DSL, we encode an optional value of type Rep[A] using a Rep[Option[A]] value, which can either be a Rep[Some[A]] (if there is a value) or a Rep[None.type] (if there is no value). An optional value can be dereferenced using the **for** notation, as shown in Listing 7, that implements in js-scala a program equivalent to Listing 6. The find function returns a Rep[Option[Element]]. The **for** expression contains a sequence of statements that are executed in order, as long as the previous statement returned a Rep[Some[Element]] value.

```
for {
  loginWidget <- document.find("div.login")
  loginButton <- loginWidget.find("submit.button")
} loginButton.on(Click)(handler)
```

Listing 7. Handling null references in js-scala

Such a monadic API brings both safety and expressiveness to developers manipulating optional values but usually involves the creation of an extra container object holding the optional value. In our case, the monadic API is used in the initial program but generates code that does not wrap values in container objects but instead checks if they are **null** or not when dereferenced. So the extra container object exists only in the initial program and is removed during code generation: Listing 7 produces a code equivalent to Listing 6.

Listing 8 shows the JavaScript code generator for methods isEmpty (that checks if the optional value contains a value) and foreach (that is called when the **for** notation is used, as in Listing 7). The emitNode method handles OptionIsEmpty and OptionForeach nodes returned by the implementations of isEmpty and foreach, respectively. In the case of the OptionIsEmpty node, it simply generates an expression testing

---

[7] However, one could alleviate the syntax burden by using a language such as CoffeeScript [1], that suppports a special notation for optional values dereferencing and desugars directly to JavaScript.

```
override def emitNode(sym: Sym[Any], rhs: Def[Any]) =
  rhs match {
    case OptionIsEmpty(o) =>
      emitValDef(sym, q" $o === null")
    case OptionForeach(o, b) =>
      stream.println(q"if ($o !== null) {")
      emitBlock(b)
      stream.println("}")
    case _ =>
      super.emitNode(sym, rhs)
  }
```

Listing 8. JavaScript code generator for null references handling DSL

if the value is **null**. In the case of the OptionForeach node, it wraps the code block dereferencing the value within a **if** checking that the value is not **null**.

The IR nodes are not tied to the JavaScript code generator, so we are able to make this abstraction available on server-side by writing a code generator similar to the JavaScript code generator, but targeting Scala. So the same abstraction is efficiently translated on both server and client sides.

4.3 DOM Fragments Definition

This section shows how we define an abstraction shared between clients and servers, as in the previous section, but that has different native counterparts on client and server sides. The challenge is to define an API providing a common vocabulary that generates code using the target platform native APIs.

```
var articleUi = function (article) {
  var div = document.createElement('div');
  div.setAttribute('class', 'article');
  var span = document.createElement('span');
  var name =
    document.createTextNode(article.name + ': ');
  span.appendChild(name);
  div.appendChild(span);
  var strong = document.createElement('strong');
  var price = document.createTextNode(article.price);
  strong.appendChild(price);
  div.appendChild(strong);
  return div
};
```

Listing 9. JavaScript DOM creation native API

```
def articleUi(article: Article) =
  <div class="article">
    <span>{ article.name + ": " }</span>
    <strong>{ article.price }</strong>
  </div>
```

Listing 10. Scala XML API

A common task in Web applications consists in computing HTML fragments representing a part of the page content. This task can be performed either from the server-side (to initially respond to a request) or from the client-side (to update the current page). As an example, Listing 9 defines a JavaScript function articleUi that builds a DOM tree containing an article description. Listing 10 shows how one could implement a similar function on server-side using the standard Scala XML library. The reader may notice that the client-side and server-side APIs are very different and that the client-side native API is very low-level and inconvenient to use. We could use a library on client-side to get a higher level API

for DOM fragment creation, but that would decrease the runtime performance. Instead, we want to define a high-level API that compiles to code as efficient as if it was written using the native APIs on both platforms.

Our first step consists in capturing, in a high-level API, the concepts common to the JavaScript and Scala APIs. Though they are different, both APIs define HTML elements with attributes and content. We propose to have a function el to define an HTML element, eventually containing attributes and children elements. Any children of an element that is not an element itself is converted into a text node. Listing 11 shows how to implement our example with our DSL. The children elements of an element can also be obtained dynamically from a collection, as shown in Listing 12.

```
def articleUi(article: Rep[Article]) =
  el('div, 'class -> 'article)(
    el('span)(article.name + ": "),
    el('strong)(article.price)
  )
```

Listing 11. DOM definition DSL

```
def articlesUi(articles: Rep[Seq[Article]]) =
  el('ul)(
    for (article <- articles)
    yield el('li)(articleUi(article))
  )
```

Listing 12. Using loops

The el function returns an Element IR node that is a tree composed of other Element and Text nodes. The JavaScript and Scala code generators traverse this tree and produce code building an equivalent DOM tree and XML fragment, respectively. When the children of an element are constant values (as in Listing 11) rather than dynamically computed (as in Listing 12), the code generators unroll the loop that adds children to their parent, for better performance. As a result, Listing 11 generates a code equivalent to Listing 9 on client-side and equivalent to Listing 10 on server-side.

Listings 13 and 14 show the relevant parts of the code generators for this DSL. They basically follow the same pattern: they visit Tag and Text IR nodes and produce the corresponding elements in the target language.

5. Evaluation

Our goal is to evaluate the level of abstraction provided by our solution and its performance, by comparing it with common approaches. We take the number of lines of code as an inverse approximation of the level of abstraction. We also evaluate the ability to share code between client and server sides.

We realized two micro-benchmarks involving programs using the selectors DSL and the optional value DSL, and we benchmarked a real world program. In each case we have written several implementations of the program, using plain JavaScript, Java/GWT, HaXe and js-scala (in each case we tried to write the application in an idiomatic way). The performance benchmarks measured the execution time of the generated JavaScript code. The tests were executed on a DELL Latitude E6430 laptop with 8 GB of RAM, on the Google Chrome v27 Web browser.

All our charts show three kinds of measures: the first group is the speed execution in operations per second (higher is better), the second group is the number of lines of code (lower is better) and the last group is the execution speed to number of lines of code ratio (higher is better). We normalized the values so the three groups can be shown within a same chart without scale issue.

```
case Tag(name, children, attrs) =>
  emitValDef(sym, q"document.createElement('$name')")
  for ((n, v) <- attrs) {
    stream.println(q"$sym.setAttribute('$n', $v);")
  }
  children match {
    case Left(children) =>
      for (child <- children) {
        stream.println(q"$sym.appendChild($child);")
      }
    case Right(children) =>
      val x = fresh[Int]
      stream.println(q"for (var $x = 0; $x < $children.length; $x++) {")
      stream.println(q"$sym.appendChild($children[$x]);")
      stream.println("}")
  }
case Text(content) =>
  emitValDef(sym, q"document.createTextNode($content)")
```

Listing 13. JavaScript code generator for the DOM fragment definition DSL

```
case Tag(name, children, attrs) =>
  val attrsFormatted =
    (for ((name, value) <- attrs)
      yield q" $name={ $value }").mkString
  children match {
    case Left(children) =>
      if (children.isEmpty) {
        emitValDef(sym, q"<$name$attrsFormatted />")
      } else {
        emitValDef(sym,
          q"<$name$attrsFormatted>{ ${children.map(quote)} }</$name>"
        )
      }
    case Right(children) =>
      emitValDef(sym, q"<$name$attrsFormatted>{ $children }</$name>")
  }
case Text(content) =>
  emitValDef(sym, q"{xml.Text(content)}")
```

Listing 14. Scala code generator for the DOM fragment definition DSL

5.1 Micro-Benchmarks

The micro-benchmarks measure the performance of our implementation of the selectors and optional value abstractions[8].

5.1.1 Selectors

We could not implement this abstraction in GWT or HaXe as efficiently as we did in js-scala because it relies on the staging mechanism: the best we could do in GWT or Haxe is to expose the native high-level API (querySelector and querySelectorAll). So we directly compared the execution time of the JavaScript code generated by Listing 4 with a JavaScript program equivalent to Listing 1 but using the high-level native API (querySelector and querySelectorAll) instead. The code was executed in a Web page containing a few elements: 4 fieldset elements, each containing 0 to 2 elements with class word.

Figure 4 shows the benchmark results. The JavaScript-opt version is Listing 1, which uses low-level native APIs, the JavaScript version is the equivalent listing using the high-level native API, and the jQuery version is Listing 2. The js-scala version is slightly slower than the JavaScript-opt (by 14%), but is 2.88 times faster than the JavaScript version, and 28.6 times faster than the jQuery

---

[8] The source code of the benchmarks is available at https://github.com/js-scala/js-scala/tree/master/papers/gpce2013/benchmarks

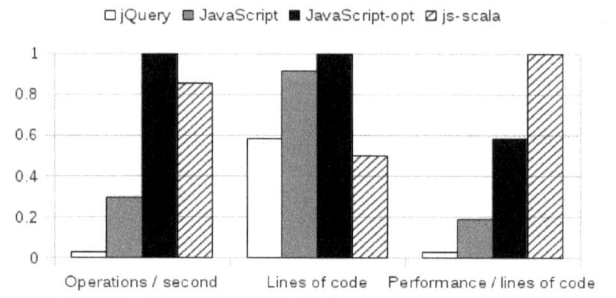

Figure 4. Micro-benchmark on the selectors abstraction

version. Finally, the js-scala version has a performance to lines of code ratio more than 1.72 times higher than others.

5.1.2 Optional Value

We reimplemented the optional value abstraction in plain JavaScript, Java and HaXe and wrote a small program manipulating optional values. Listing 15 shows the js-scala version of this program. The maybe function is a function partially defined on Int values.

Figure 5 shows the benchmark results. The js-scala version of the program runs between 3 to 10 times faster than other ap-

58

```
val maybe = fun { (x: Rep[Int]) =>
  some(x + 1)
}

def benchmark = for {
  a <- maybe(0)
  b <- maybe(a)
  c <- maybe(b)
  d <- maybe(c)
} yield d
```

Listing 15. Micro-benchmark code for the optional values abstraction

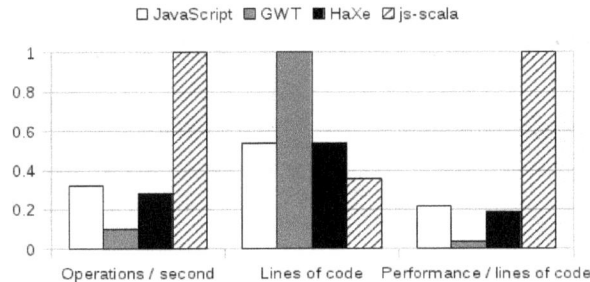

Figure 5. Micro-benchmark on the optional values abstraction

proaches. This version also takes less lines of code than others (this result is almost due to the special **for** notation, that has no equivalent in other benchmarked languages). Finally, the js-scala program has a performance to lines of code ratio more than 4 times higher than others.

5.2 Real World Application

Chooze [9] is an existing complete application for making polls. It allows users to create a poll, define the choice alternatives, share the poll, vote and look at the results. It contains JavaScript code to handle the dynamic behavior of the application: double-posting prevention, dynamic form update and rich interaction with the document. The size of the whole application (server and client sides) is about one thousand lines of code.

The application was initially written using jQuery. We rewrote it in vanilla JavaScript (low-level hand-tuned code without third-party library), js-scala, GWT and HaXe.

5.2.1 Performance

The benchmark code simulates user actions on a Web page (2000 clicks on buttons, triggering a dynamic update of the page and involving the use of the optional value monad, the selectors API and the HTML fragment definition API). Figure 6 shows the benchmark results.

The runtime performance of the vanilla JavaScript, HaXe and js-scala versions are similar (though the js-scala version is slightly slower by 6%). It is worth noting that the vanilla JavaScript and the HaXe versions use low-level code compared to js-scala, as shown in the middle of the figure (lines of code): the js-scala version needs only 74 lines of code while the vanilla JavaScript version needs 116 lines of code (57% bigger) and the HaXe version needs 148 lines of code (100% bigger). The jQuery JavaScript version, which code is high-level (54 lines of code, 27% less than js-scala) runs 10 times slower than the js-scala version.

---

[9] Source code is available at http://github.com/julienrf/chooze, under the branches vanilla, jquery, gwt, haxe and js-scala

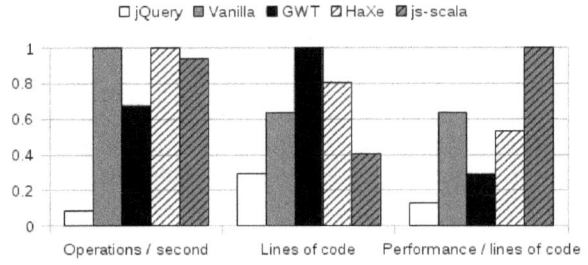

Figure 6. Benchmarks on a real application

The last part of the figure compares the runtime performance to lines of code ratio. Js-scala shows the best score, being 1.48 times better than the vanilla JavaScript version, 1.88 times better than the HaXe version, 3.45 times better than the GWT version and 7.82 times better than the jQuery JavaScript version.

5.2.2 Code Reuse

We were able to share some DOM fragment definitions between server-side and client-side only in the js-scala version. In the GWT version we don't have a choice: dynamic DOM fragments are always built only on client-side (a practice that makes it more difficult to make the pages content crawlable by search engines and may increase the initial display time). In the other versions the code for building the DOM fragment is duplicated between client and server sides, representing 20 lines of JavaScript code (17% of the total) and 15 lines of HTML (5% of the total) in the JavaScript version, and 19 lines of HaXe code (13% of the total) and 15 lines of HTML (5% of the total) in the HaXe version. In the js-scala version the DOM fragment definitions shared between clients and servers represent 22 lines of Scala code (30% of the total) and save 15 lines of HTML (5% of the total).

5.2.3 Threats to Validity

Our goal was to put the runtime performance in perspective with the level of abstraction. We are aware that the indicator we chose as an inverse approximation of the abstraction level, the number of lines of code, is not scientifically established and may be subject to discussion. However, we think it is a reasonable approximation in our case because all the candidate languages we use have a similar syntax, inherited from the C programming language.

Another weakness of our validation may come from the fact that our application does not make a heavy use of client-side code and thus may not be representative of the way large Web applications are written. However, we think that a richer application would have more parts of code susceptible to be shared between client and server sides, thus giving even better results on the code reuse statistics.

Finally, the GWT version may not have been written in an as idiomatic as possible way. Indeed, we mainly catch the events directly on the HTML DOM, as we do in JavaScript, without reusing all the GWT widgets. We do not build the application as a blank page with a set of widgets. However, this way of developing using GWT has no impact on the performance and a minor impact on the number of lines of code.

6. Discussion

We implemented our solution as compiled embedded DSLs in Scala. Generating code from our DSLs is a two step process: an initial Scala program first evaluates to an intermediate representation of the final program that is traversed by code generators to produce the final JavaScript code. Domain-specific optimizations can happen during the IR construction (as shown in section 4.1) or during the code generation (as shown in section 4.2).

An important consequence of the implementation as compiled embedded DSLs is that defining a DSL that can be shared between server and client sides requires a low effort: compiled embedded DSLs are simply defined as libraries but let developers specialize the generated code according to each target platform (as shown in section 4.3).

In other words, the compiled embedded DSL approach gives us a way to exploit the Scala host language to define high-level language units that integrate seamlessly together and bring domain-specific knowledge to the code generation scheme to produce efficient code for client and server sides.

These characteristics allowed us to capture some Web programming patterns as high-level abstractions, making the code of our application simpler to reason about and making some parts of the code reusable between client and server sides, while keeping execution performance on client-side as high as if we used hand-tuned low-level JavaScript code.

7. Conclusion

High-level abstractions for Web programming, which are useful to decrease the complexity of the code and to abstract over the differences between the client and server environments, must be implemented in a way to efficiently run on hardware with limited capabilities.

In this paper we showed how to leverage staging to implement high-level abstractions for Web programming that are efficiently compiled for heterogeneous platforms such as Web clients and servers that differ in their technical API. We also showed how these abstractions can be shared between client and server sides.

Our two kinds of benchmarks, (i) micro-benchmarks to evaluate one abstraction and (ii) a benchmark on a real application using these abstractions, show performance similar to hand-optimized low-level code.

In a future work we may investigate more coarse-grained optimizations like smart DOM updates minimizing the number of browser reflows.

References

[1] J. Ashkenas. Coffeescript, 2011.

[2] B. Bibeault and Y. Kats. *jQuery in Action*. Dreamtech Press, 2008.

[3] K. J. Brown, A. K. Sujeeth, H. J. Lee, T. Rompf, H. Chafi, M. Odersky, and K. Olukotun. A heterogeneous parallel framework for domain-specific languages. In *Parallel Architectures and Compilation Techniques (PACT), 2011 International Conference on*, pages 89–100. IEEE, 2011.

[4] N. Cannasse. Using haxe. *The Essential Guide to Open Source Flash Development*, pages 227–244, 2008.

[5] P. Chaganti. *Google Web Toolkit: GWT Java Ajax Programming*. Packt Pub Limited, 2007.

[6] E. Cooper, S. Lindley, P. Wadler, and J. Yallop. Links: Web programming without tiers. In *Formal Methods for Components and Objects*, pages 266–296. Springer, 2007.

[7] C. Elliott, S. Finne, and O. De Moor. Compiling embedded languages. *Journal of Functional Programming*, 13(3):455–481, 2003.

[8] R. Griffith. The dart programming language for non-programmers-overview. 2011.

[9] T. Hoare. Null references: The billion dollar mistake. *Presentation at QCon London*, 2009.

[10] J. Huang, Q. Xu, B. Tiwana, Z. M. Mao, M. Zhang, and P. Bahl. Anatomizing application performance differences on smartphones. In *Proceedings of the 8th international conference on Mobile systems, applications, and services*, pages 165–178. ACM, 2010.

[11] P. Hudak. Building domain-specific embedded languages. *ACM Computing Surveys*, 28, 1996. URL http://dsel.ps.

[12] U. Jørring and W. L. Scherlis. Compilers and staging transformations. In *Proceedings of the 13th ACM SIGACT-SIGPLAN symposium on Principles of programming languages*, pages 86–96. ACM, 1986.

[13] G. Kossakowski, N. Amin, T. Rompf, and M. Odersky. JavaScript as an Embedded DSL. In J. Noble, editor, *ECOOP 2012 – Object-Oriented Programming*, volume 7313 of *Lecture Notes in Computer Science*, pages 409–434, Berlin, Heidelberg, 2012. Springer Berlin Heidelberg. . URL https://github.com/js-scala/js-scala/.

[14] J. Kuuskeri and T. Mikkonen. Partitioning web applications between the server and the client. In *Proceedings of the 2009 ACM symposium on Applied Computing*, SAC '09, pages 647–652, New York, NY, USA, 2009. ACM. ISBN 978-1-60558-166-8. . URL http://doi.acm.org/10.1145/1529282.1529416.

[15] M. McGranaghan. Clojurescript: Functional programming for javascript platforms. *Internet Computing, IEEE*, 15(6):97–102, 2011.

[16] T. Mikkonen and A. Taivalsaari. Web applications - spaghetti code for the 21st century. In *Proceedings of the 2008 Sixth International Conference on Software Engineering Research, Management and Applications*, pages 319–328, Washington, DC, USA, 2008. IEEE Computer Society. ISBN 978-0-7695-3302-5. . URL http://dl.acm.org/citation.cfm?id=1443226.1444030.

[17] M. Nanda and S. Sinha. Accurate interprocedural null-dereference analysis for java. In *Software Engineering, 2009. ICSE 2009. IEEE 31st International Conference on*, pages 133–143. IEEE, 2009.

[18] J. C. Preciado, M. L. Trigueros, F. Sánchez-Figueroa, and S. Comai. Necessity of methodologies to model rich internet applications. In *WSE*, pages 7–13. IEEE Computer Society, 2005. ISBN 0-7695-2470-2.

[19] R. Rodríguez-Echeverría. Ria: more than a nice face. In *Proceedings of the Doctolral Consortium of the International Conference on Web Engineering*, volume 484. CEUR-WS.org, 2009.

[20] T. Rompf. *Lightweight Modular Staging and Embedded Compilers: Abstraction without Regret for High-Level High-Performance Programming*. PhD thesis, ÉCOLE POLYTECHNIQUE FÉDÉRALE DE LAUSANNE, 2012.

[21] T. Rompf, A. Sujeeth, N. Amin, K. Brown, V. Jovanovic, H. Lee, M. Jonnalagedda, K. Olukotun, and M. Odersky. Optimizing Data Structures in High-Level Programs: New Directions for Extensible Compilers based on Staging. Technical report, 2012.

[22] S. Souders. High-performance web sites. *Communications of the ACM*, 51(12):36–41, 2008.

[23] A. Van Deursen, P. Klint, and J. Visser. Domain-specific languages: an annotated bibliography. *ACM Sigplan Notices*, 35(6):26–36, 2000.

[24] E. Visser. WebDSL: A case study in domain-specific language engineering. In R. Lämmel, J. Visser, and J. Saraiva, editors, *Generative and Transformational Techniques in Software Engineering II, International Summer School, GTTSE 2007*, volume 5235 of *Lecture Notes in Computer Science*, pages 291–373, Braga, Portugal, 2007. Springer. ISBN 978-3-540-88642-6. .

Reified Type Parameters Using Java Annotations

Prodromos Gerakios   Aggelos Biboudis   Yannis Smaragdakis

Department of Informatics
University of Athens
{pgerakios,biboudis,smaragd}@di.uoa.gr

Abstract

Java generics are compiled by-erasure: all clients reuse the same bytecode, with uses of the unknown type erased. C++ templates are compiled by-expansion: each type-instantiation of a template produces a different code definition. The two approaches offer trade-offs on multiple axes. We propose an extension of Java generics that allows by-expansion translation relative to selected type parameters only. This language design allows sophisticated users to get the best of both worlds at a fine granularity. Furthermore, our proposal is based on Java 8 Type Annotations (JSR 308) and the Checker Framework as an abstraction layer for controlling compilation without changes to the internals of a Java compiler.

Categories and Subject Descriptors   D.1.5 [*Programming techniques*]: Object-oriented programming; D.3.4 [*Programming languages*]: Processors—Code generation; D.3.2 [*Programming languages*]: Language Classifications—Extensible languages

Keywords   mixins, reification, type annotation, pluggable types

1. Introduction

Java generics are compiled via the technique of *type erasure* or just *erasure*: Type parameters are removed by the compiler and replaced by their bound (`Object` or other, if specified). The generated bytecode contains no generic information and all instantiations share a single classfile. This approach satisfies the crucial requirement of backward compatibility and avoiding alterations of the JVM specification. The erasure technique also succeeds in lowering the code generation burden: the generic's code is not replicated on every type-instantiation. Type erasure has often been criticised in the research literature and developer communities. Firstly, the compiler inserts type casts where erasure happened to ensure compatibility with the JVM. Furthermore, data structures instantiated by primitive types like `int`, must suffer from the cost of boxing. The greatest issue, however, is the limited capabilities of reflective operations, as type parameter information is not retained after type-instantiation. As a result, Java generics cannot support important generic code patterns and declarations such as `T element = new T();` or `class Serial<T> extends T` or `T.class`, where `T` is a type parameter. To address the limitations of erasure, some solutions use clever tricks

based on reflection following a library approach [5] but with cumbersome syntax or others extend directly the `javac` compiler [11].

The alternative to erasure is an *expansion*-based translation, where the generic code is replicated at every type-instantiation site. This addresses the expressiveness shortcomings of erasure, but at the cost of replicating generic code. C++ templates are translated by expansion and they also suffer from another significant drawback: type-checking and code generation is not performed on the generic code but only after expansion, separately for each type instantiation. The Pizza language [8], which is often considered the predecessor and inspiration of the Java generics mechanism, defined both erasure and expansion as possible translation strategies for generics.

In this paper we propose a preliminary language design that combines erasure and expansion of generics at a fine granularity. Each type parameter can specify whether it is to be erased or not. For instance, a generic class C can be defined as:

```
class C<@reify X,Y> { ... }
```

In this case, type parameter Y is to be erased, while type parameter X will not be. As can be seen, type parameters are selected for expansion by use of a Java type annotation. In total, the new elements of our approach are as follows:

- A fine grained language design for controlling expansion or erasure of generic type parameters.

- An extension of the Java language entirely using advanced (upcoming, in Java 8–JSR 308) annotations and the Checker Framework. This is a case study of the expressiveness of these facilities for language extensions that are both fundamental and obtrusive (i.e., the presence of an annotation changes the semantics of code).

- A translation technique that performs expansion, yet strives to minimize code replication by also leveraging delegation.

Our work is currently in the design stage, with full implementation to follow. However, we have conducted preliminary feasibility studies and have high confidence that the mechanics of the extension to the language is realizable as described, using the advanced annotations of JSR 308 and the Checker Framework.

2. Background

We next discuss some necessary background for our work. First, we introduce the concept of mixins, which we will use as a motivating example and demonstration of non-erased type parameters throughout the paper. Next, we present the JSR 308 Java Type Annotations and the Checker Framework—both essential parts of our proposal.

Mixin-Based Programming.   (Template-based) mixins are an important, well-known pattern in generic programming. Mixins allow programmers to express component-based designs with clean

GPCE '13,   October 27–28, 2013, Indianapolis, Indiana, USA.
Copyright is held by the owner/author(s). Publication rights licensed to ACM.
ACM 978-1-4503-2373-4/13/10. . . $15.00.
http://dx.doi.org/10.1145/2517208.2517223

and concise class-based modules. A mixin is a standalone entity that can be composed with other entities or mixins, thereby enabling modular behavior sharing. A typical declaration of a mixin class in most OO languages is: class M<T> extends T. That is, the mixin generic class, M, inherits from its unknown type parameter, T. Such a mixin, M, is often called an *abstract subclass*. Mixins can be combined to form other mixins and can be composed with other classes. The mixin pattern is one that has appeared many times in the literature—e.g., [2, 12–15]. Mixins cannot be supported when generics are subject to type erasure such as in Java programs and adding mixin support to Java is a non-trivial task [4]. Our proposal is not the first to enable mixin support in Java. However, mixins are simply a use case for demonstrating our more general selective reification approach that permits fine-grained control over expansion and erasure of generics.

Use of Type Annotations and the Checker Framework. The recent addition of JSR 308 permits annotating any use of a type, such as generic type arguments, casts and type declarations. The Checker Framework [3, 9] is an abstraction layer built on top of JSR 308. This framework allows the implementation of our proposal employing Java annotations and integrating a pluggable type system and code generator/transformer. Our language extensions are intrusive to standard Java: the program does not have the same meaning (and in fact may not even compile) when our annotations are erased from the source code. The main advantage of the Checker Framework is that it automatically propagates annotations to compilation units where no annotation appears, thereby enabling type checking and code generation for these units. Additionally, it allows us to use a uniform programming model for AST transformations. A similar technique has also been employed in EnerJ by Sampson et al. [10].

3. Safe Reification for Java Generics

The standard type-erasure semantics of Java generics ensures that the run-time behavior of programs does not depend on type information. This abstraction principle allows generic classes to be compiled exactly *once*, allowing client classes to reuse the *same* bytecode with distinct compile-time type instantiations. However, the type erasure property prohibits the use of mixins. On the contrary, the lack of type erasure in C++ templates enables the use of mixins, but sacrifices separate compilation and implementation abstraction, as well as leads to code duplication. Our proposal reconciles these two approaches, by enabling selective reification and mixins in a modular manner.

Selective reification. Our proposal preserves the default behavior and properties of generic types: the programmer must explicitly state that a type variable must persist, otherwise the type variable is subject to type erasure. Therefore, we maintain backwards compatibility with standard Java code and permit selective code generation or transformation for types instantiating reified type variables.

The following example illustrates a class definition having two generic variables X and Y respectively. However, only the latter type variable, Y, is subject to type erasure. X is not erased, thus, for example, it can be passed to a new operator to create a new instance of X. Notice that classOfX will be instantiated to the object representing the class type instantiating type variable X. In the case of ReifiedGeneric<String,Integer>, classOfX is equal to String.class.

```
1  class ReifiedGeneric<@reify X,Y> {
2    Class classOfX = X.class;
3    Y id(Y y) { return y; }
4    X newInstance() { return new X(); }
5  }
```

Mixin support. Type variables annotated with @reify can be used within an extends clause, thereby enabling the formulation of mixin classes. The following example illustrates the mixin classes Serial and TimeStamped. The Serial mixin class declaration is equivalent to what we can already express in C++ with template<class T> class Serial : public T. In method placeOrder, the customer object is an instance of the bottom class in the following hierarchy: TimeStamped◁Serial◁Customer, where ◁ is a shorthand for "extends". Therefore, customer has the functionality of Customer along with a unique serial number and a timestamp indicating its creation time.

```
1  class Serial<@reify T> extends T {
2    static long counter = 1;
3    long serialN = counter++;
4    public long getSerialNumber() {
5      return serialN;
6    }
7  }
8
9  class TimeStamped<@reify T> extends T {
10   long timestamp = new Date().getTime();
11   public long getTimestamp() {
12     return timestamp;
13   }
14 }
15 ...
16   void placeOrder(){
17     TimeStamped<Serial<Customer>> customer =
18       new TimeStamped<Serial<Customer>>();
19     long x = customer.getSerialNumber();
20     long y = customer.getTimestamp();
21     ...
22     customer.order();
23   }
```

4. Safe and modular type system

Our main goal is to enable *modularly safe* type-checking for our language extension: *code generation of a valid program with reified types can never fail.* The inclusion of reification as a language feature requires careful treatment of type variables and type instantiation so as to preserve modular type checking. We informally describe the constraints enforced by our proposed type checker in order to guarantee validity. Let us define class GenericFactory as follows:

```
1  class GenericFactory<@reify X> {
2    X newInstance() { return new X(); }
3  }
```

Reified type invariants. Substituting a standard type variable for a reifiable type variable is an invalid operation as there is insufficient type information for performing code generation. For instance allowing an ordinary type variable Y to indirectly flow to the instantiation point of GenericFactory will inevitably lead to code generation failure and thus violate our safety invariant. The same argument applies when substituting *interfaces* or *abstract* classes where reified types are expected. In order to guarantee modular type checking, we place the restriction that type variables annotated as @reify can only be instantiated with another @reify type variable or a concrete type. In the later case, the type must provide a public constructor accepting no arguments.

Mixin invariants. The above constraints are sufficient for guaranteeing modular reified type validity. However, they are insufficient when inheritance polymorphism (i.e., mixins) is introduced to the language. Let us assume that GenericFactory<String> indirectly flows to ObjectFactory through type instantiations.

```
1  class ObjectFactory<@reify X> extends X {
2    Object newInstance() {
3      return new Object();
4    }
5  }
```

ObjectFactory<GenericFactory<String>> is not a well-formed Java type as there exist two *overloaded* methods newInstance with distinct return types Object and String respectively.

To address non-modular type errors emerging from the propagation of invalid mixin instantiations, we employ *structural* type constraints over reified type variables appearing in extend clauses. Structural constraints are expressed in terms of ordinary nominal types T at the definition of reified type variables. More specifically, the reified type variable declaration @reify(T.class) X denotes that T<X> extends X is a well-formed type for any X. Any class having a subset of the methods implied by T<X> is a structural supertype of T<X>. Thus, a structural type T<X> acts merely as a macro definition for describing a set of methods rather than as a nominal type. Consequently, @reify(T.class) X is implied by @reify(T'.class) X, when T<X> is a structural supertype of T'<X>. Notice that only a constrained reified type can instantiate another constrained type variable. We restrict types representing structural constraints to standard Java types without reification.

```
1   interface Constraint<X> {
2     Object newInstance();
3     Long getTimestamp(String);
4   }
5   class ObjectFactory<@reify(Constraint.class) X>
6   extends X {
7     Object newInstance() {
8       return new Object();
9     }
10  }
```

In the example above, X is constrained by Constraint<X>, which is a structural supertype of ObjectFactory<X>: if any X implementing Constraint<X> is a well-formed type, then X extended with ObjectFactory<X> is also well-formed. Using nominal types as macros for structural constraints allow us to minimize the amount of annotations required and makes our constraint specifications modular: it suffices to alter the definition of Constraint<X> in order to add constraints as opposed to having to perform explicit inter-module modifications of @reify constraints. Finally, when a type parameter X is not constrained, we issue a compiler warning (which the user can ignore at her own risk): type safety is not guaranteed modularly.

5. Code Generation

Once the type checking stage is complete, AST transformations are performed in order to lower generic object allocation, type variable type information and mixins to standard Java. The non-trivial part of our translation is that it tries to combine traditional expansion with reuse of the generic's code: most functionality is translated into indirect calls, delegating to a common implementation, rather than always expanding the code in-place. The feasibility of this approach in a full language setting (which, notably, includes overloading resolution) will be a challenge in our future work.

5.1 Transforming classes with reified generics

The transformation process of reified classes entails the erasure of reification annotations from the original class, substitution of type variable allocation expressions with method invocations and declarations and finally a unique interface that contains all methods of the translated class. This interface must be implemented by the translated class. The following example shows the code emitted by the transformation process of our earlier GenericFactory class:

```
1   interface iface$GenericFactory<X> {
2     X new$X();
3     X newInstance();
4   }
5   class GenericFactory<X>
6   implements iface$GenericFactory<X> {
7     X new$X() { return null; }
8     X newInstance(){ return new$X(); }
9   }
```

A new method new$X() with no implementation and a subsequent invocation replace the original allocation expression new$X(). A new interface iface$GenericFactory is generated containing all methods implied by the original class in addition to the generated methods. Class GenericFactory implements iface$GenericFactory and has no reification annotations.

There are two alternatives for instantiating reified type variables:

Instantiation with other reified variables. In this case, types containing reified type variables are substituted for the generated interfaces described above. A class instantiating a reified type with a type variable X has no information regarding X except its upper bound, which may be included in the generated interface signature (i.e. in the case of mixins), thus it is safe to substitute the instantiated reified type with its instantiated interface. Similar arguments apply to the environment of the class containing the reified type, thus the generated interface is also employed when accessing class members (i.e. no downcasts are required).

Instantiation with nominal types. Reified variable instantiations with concrete types are transformed to a new class, where reified variables have been substituted for the concrete type. The following example illustrates the generated class code corresponding to type GenericFactory<Integer> in the original source program:

```
1   class GenericFactory$Integer
2   extends GenericFactory<Integer> {
3     Integer new$X() {
4       return new Integer();
5     }
6   }
```

The generated class GenericFactory$Integer extends GenericFactory<Integer> and overrides method new$X, which is unimplemented, by returning an allocation expression on the concrete type instantiating X.

Translation of fields. Field member declarations are translated by adding getter and setter methods to the generated interface. Field accesses are substituted for invocations to appropriate interface methods.

5.2 Mixins and constrained reification.

Let us modify the GenericFactory of the previous example to be a mixin and declare an interface Constraint as a structural supertype of GenericFactory:

```
1   interface Constraint<X> {
2     X newInstance();
3   }
4   class GenericFactory<@reify(Constraint.class) X>
5   extends X {
6     X newInstance(){ return new X(); }
7   }
```

The transformation process is then modified accordingly.

Instantiation with other reified variables. As in the case of simple reified types, constrained reified types of the form GenericFactory<Y> are replaced by the generated interfaces instantiated with the same type variable Y. However, the environment of the class containing a mixin instance may be aware of its concrete parent, therefore downcasts from the generated interfaces to the expected types are performed.

Instantiation with nominal types. Assume we generate code for `GenericFactory<Integer>` as in the previous example. The code generation for `GenericFactory` and `iface$GenericFactory` are identical to the previous example. Let us rename the class of `GenericFactory$Integer` of the previous example to `GenericFactory$$Integer` in order to use it here. The code generation for `GenericFactory<Integer>` differs:

```
1  class GenericFactory$Integer extends Integer
2  implements iface$GenericFactory<Integer> {
3    iface$GenericFactory<Integer> mixin =
4          new GenericFactory$$Integer();
5    Integer new$X() {
6      return mixin.new$X();
7    }
8    Integer newInstance() {
9      return mixin.newInstance();
10   }
11 }
```

The key difference is that the generated class is a subtype of both `Integer` and `iface$GenericFactory` and employs delegation on the *mixin* instance in order to avoid code duplication (i.e., in-place substitution of the mixin). Thus, although every mixin is expanded once per instantiation, the actual code content of a mixin (i.e., the bodies of methods) is only generated once.

6. Related work

NextGen [11] retains parametric type information of generics at runtime to support type dependent operations supported by a custom class loader that generates template instantiations at runtime. Our language extension is merely a pluggable module to the `javac` compiler. Additionally in our work we avoid replication by a compile-time generational step to wire class instantiations with mixin code implementations.

Scala [7] supports limited selective reification (but no "abstract-subclass" style mixins) with runtime reflection, a mechanism based on a combination of implicit parameters and `TypeTag` objects carrying implicit type information.

There are many independent projects that overcome the limitations of type erasure. Similarly to our approach, Gafter [5] preserves generic types by declaring anonymous classes at instantiation points. Other works aim to support mixins directly as a language feature by extending Java. Java Layers [2] supports mixins by adopting a source-to-source approach from a custom compiler to valid Java. Jam [1] adopts the same implementation strategy as Java Layers, but suffers from code duplication. Both Java Layers and Jam suffer from non-modular compilation. McJava [6] is an extension of Java allowing for mixin composition with classes and other mixins. McJava does not support modular type checking as mixin well-formedness is validated at type instantiation without imposing intra-procedural constraints. McJava code generation performs copying of mixin declarations to instantiation points. Our approach only generates code for each mixin *once* and performs wiring with specific instantiations, thereby avoiding code duplication.

7. Summary

In this work, we presented the `@reify` annotation that extends Java generics with by-expansion translation relative to selected type parameters only. We demonstrate the translation schemes of classes having both reified and standard generic parameters. We support mixins and allocation expressions using generic types in a modular manner. The logic behind type checking and generation is based on a pluggable type system, without modifying the Java compiler.

Acknowledgments

We gratefully acknowledge funding by the Greek Secretariat for Research and Technology under the "MorphPL" Excellence (Aristeia) award; and by the European Union under a Marie Curie International Reintegration Grant and the "SPADE" European Research Council Starting/Consolidator grant.

References

[1] D. Ancona, G. Lagorio, and E. Zucca. Jam-Designing a Java Extension with Mixins. *ACM Transactions on Programming Languages and Systems (TOPLAS)*, 25(5):641–712, 2003.

[2] R. Cardone, A. Brown, S. McDirmid, and C. Lin. Using Mixins to Build Flexible Widgets. In *Proceedings of the 1st International Conference on Aspect-Oriented Software Development (AOSD)*, pages 76–85, New York, NY, USA, 2002.

[3] W. Dietl, S. Dietzel, M. D. Ernst, K. Muşlu, and T. W. Schiller. Building and using Pluggable Type-Checkers. In *Proceedings of the 33rd International Conference on Software Engineering*, pages 681–690, 2011.

[4] B. Eckel. Mixins: Something Else You Can't Do With Java Generics? http://www.artima.com/weblogs/viewpost.jsp?thread=132988, Oct. 2005.

[5] N. Gafter. Super Type Tokens. http://gafter.blogspot.gr/2006/12/super-type-tokens.html, Dec. 2006.

[6] T. Kamina and T. Tamai. McJava - A Design and Implementation of Java with Mixin-Types. In *Proceedings of the Programming Languages and Systems: Second Asian Symposium, (APLAS)*, pages 4–6, Taipei, Taiwan, 2004.

[7] M. Odersky. The Scala Language Specification, 2013.

[8] M. Odersky and P. Wadler. Pizza into Java: translating theory into practice. In *Proceedings of the 24th ACM SIGPLAN-SIGACT symposium on Principles of Programming languages (POPL)*, POPL '97, pages 146–159, New York, NY, USA, 1997. ACM.

[9] M. M. Papi, M. Ali, T. L. Correa,Jr., J. H. Perkins, and M. D. Ernst. Practical Pluggable Types for Java. In *Proceedings of the 2008 International Symposium on Software Testing and Analysis*, ISSTA '08, pages 201–212, New York, NY, USA, 2008. ACM.

[10] A. Sampson, W. Dietl, E. Fortuna, D. Gnanapragasam, L. Ceze, and D. Grossman. EnerJ: approximate data types for safe and general low-power computation. In *Proceedings of the 32nd ACM SIGPLAN conference on Programming Language Design and Implementation (PLDI)*, pages 164–174, San Jose, California, USA, 2011.

[11] J. Sasitorn and R. Cartwright. Efficient First-Class Generics on Stock Java Virtual Machines. In *Proceedings of the 2006 ACM symposium on Applied computing*, SAC '06, pages 1621–1628, New York, NY, USA, 2006. ACM.

[12] Y. Smaragdakis and D. Batory. Implementing Layered Designs with Mixin Layers. In *Proceedings of the 12th European Conference on Object-Oriented Programming (ECOOP)*, pages 550–570. Springer-Verlag LNCS 1445, 1998.

[13] Y. Smaragdakis and D. Batory. Mixin-Based Programming in C++. In *Generative and Component-Based Software Engineering Symposium (GCSE)*, pages 163–177. Springer-Verlag, LNCS 2177, 2000.

[14] M. VanHilst and D. Notkin. Using C++ Templates to Implement Role-Based Designs. In *JSSST International Symposium on Object Technologies for Advanced Software*, pages 22–37. Springer Verlag, 1996.

[15] M. VanHilst and D. Notkin. Using Role Components to Implement Collaboration-Based Designs. In *Proceedings of the 1996 ACM SIGPLAN Conference on Object-Oriented Programming Systems, Languages and Applications (OOPSLA)*, pages 359–369, San Jose, California, USA, 1996.

Does the Discipline of Preprocessor Annotations Matter? A Controlled Experiment

Sandro Schulze

Technische Universität Braunschweig
Braunschweig, Germany
s.schulze@tu-braunschweig.de

Jörg Liebig, Janet Siegmund,* Sven Apel

Universität Passau
Passau, Germany
{joliebig,siegmunj,apel}@fim.uni-passau.de

Abstract

The C preprocessor (CPP) is a simple and language-independent tool, widely used to implement variable software systems using conditional compilation (i.e., by including or excluding annotated code). Although CPP provides powerful means to express variability, it has been criticized for allowing arbitrary annotations that break the underlying structure of the source code. We distinguish between *disciplined* annotations, which align with the structure of the source code, and *undisciplined* annotations, which do not. Several studies suggest that especially the latter type of annotations makes it hard to (automatically) analyze the code. However, little is known about whether the type of annotations has an effect on program comprehension. We address this issue by means of a controlled experiment with human subjects. We designed similar tasks for both, disciplined and undisciplined annotations, to measure program comprehension. Then, we measured the performance of the subjects regarding correctness and response time for solving the tasks. Our results suggest that there are no differences between disciplined and undisciplined annotations from a program-comprehension perspective. Nevertheless, we observed that finding and correcting errors is a time-consuming and tedious task in the presence of preprocessor annotations.

Categories and Subject Descriptors [*Software and its Engineering*]: Preprocessors; [*Software and its Engineering*]: Software product lines; [*General and reference*]: Experimentation

Keywords variability; C preprocessor; controlled experiment; program comprehension; disciplined annotations

1. Introduction

The *preprocessor* CPP, developed over 40 years ago, is widely adopted in the practice of software development to introduce variability in software systems [6, 26]. Being a simple and language-independent text-processing tool, CPP provides powerful and expressive means to implement variable source code [26]. Program-mers use preprocessor annotations (e.g., #ifdef directives) to implement optional and alternative code fragments. Since CPP is language-independent, programmers can use annotations at a fine grain, for instance, by annotating single tokens, such as an opening bracket. CPP is often criticized for this capability, as fine-grained annotations are a major source of errors. For instance, practitioners report from maintainability and understandability problems with arbitrary preprocessor usage [3, 34]. Furthermore, preprocessor usage, especially at a fine grain, hinders tool support for code analysis or restructuring tasks [7, 8, 14–16]. Hence, the source of all problems is the lack of discipline of annotations (i.e., their usage at a fine grain), and how programmers understand code in their presence.

In earlier work, we analyzed the discipline of annotations and distinguished *disciplined* and *undisciplined* annotations [27]. Disciplined annotations align with the underlying structure of the source code by targeting only code fragments that belong to entire subtrees in the corresponding abstract syntax tree. For example, we consider an annotation enclosing a whole function definition to be disciplined. In contrast, undisciplined annotations include arbitrary annotations of code fragments, for instance, an annotation of a single function parameter. One reason for why we consider the latter annotation undisciplined is that such fine-grained annotations are difficult to refactor using tool support [8, 15].

Another reason is experience from practice: Some software developers are aware of problems related to CPP and introduced coding guidelines for preprocessor usage. For instance, one guideline for developers of the Linux kernel for using the CPP states:[1]

> *Code cluttered with ifdefs is difficult to read and maintain. Don't do it. Instead, put your ifdefs in a header, and conditionally define static inline functions, or macros, which are used in the code.*

In fact, this guideline advises developers to use disciplined instead of undisciplined annotations, such as annotating only entire functions instead of annotating parts of the function definition. This and similar guidelines express long-term experiences and opinions of developers. However, while these guidelines rely on experience, they are not the result of a sound empirical investigation. Hence, several questions regarding the interaction of programmers with annotated code are still open:

1. Do programmers understand code with disciplined annotations better than code with undisciplined annotations?

2. Are maintenance tasks, such as adding or modifying code, more difficult or even more error-prone in the presence of undisciplined annotations than with disciplined annotations?

---

* Janet Siegmund has published previous work as Janet Feigenspan.

GPCE '13,   October 27–28, 2013, Indianapolis, Indiana, USA.
Copyright is held by the owner/author(s). Publication rights licensed to ACM.
ACM 978-1-4503-2373-4/13/10... $15.00.
http://dx.doi.org/10.1145/http://dx.doi.org/10.1145/2517208.2517215

---

[1] see /Documentation/SubmittingPatches in the Linux source

3. How does the discipline of annotations influence the detection and correction of errors?

4. Generally speaking, are there differences in the programmers' performance or correctness (regarding the tasks) with respect to disciplined and undisciplined annotations in source code?

To answer these questions, we conducted a controlled experiment with 19 undergraduate students from the University of Magdeburg. We designed seven different tasks that aim at understanding and maintaining annotated source code, including the detection and correction of errors.

In a nutshell, the results of our experiment do *not* support the assumption that the discipline of annotations has an observable effect on comprehension of annotated code. For both types of annotations, the respective groups performed similarly regarding correctness and response time. However, we made the general observation that detecting and fixing errors in the presence of annotations is a tedious and time-consuming task with only minor success.

The remainder of the paper is organized as follows: In Section 2, we introduce preprocessor annotations and how they are used for expressing variability. In Section 3, we describe our experimental setting. We present the results of our experiment and interpret them in Section 4. In Section 5, we discuss threats to validity, followed by a discussion of related work (Section 6). Finally, we present our conclusions and suggestions for future work in Section 7.

2. Preprocessor Annotations in Action

The C preprocessor CPP is a simple text-processing tool that provides metaprogramming facilities, and that is used by programmers to implement variable source code. Programmers use it to mark optional or alternative code fragments in the programming language of their choice (host language), and to include and exclude these code fragments on demand (controlled by macro constants).[2] Since the preprocessor is a language-independent tool and works on the basis of tokens of the target language, it allows programmers to annotate variable source code at any level of granularity. For example, in the programming language C, annotations may be on single tokens (e.g., an opening or closing bracket), expressions, statements, or type definitions. In earlier work, we analyzed CPP's annotation capabilities and distinguished between disciplined and undisciplined annotations [27]:

> In C, annotations on one or a sequence of *entire functions* and *type definitions* (e.g., struct) are disciplined. Furthermore, annotations on one or a sequence of *entire statements* and annotations on *elements inside type definitions* are disciplined. *All other annotations are undisciplined.*

Disciplined and undisciplined annotations are in the center of a larger discussion about expressiveness, replication, and comprehension of source code (Figure 1). While the first two aspects have been discussed already elsewhere [27, 31], we focus on program comprehension, which has not been investigated yet systematically (to the best of our knowledge).

We explain the trade-off between the aforementioned properties by means of a variable stack implementation (with or without synchronization). To this end, we show the respective source code of a disciplined and an undisciplined version in Figure 2. The implementation of synchronization using undisciplined annotations requires to add a function parameter (Figure 2a; Line 4), to extend an existing expression (Figure 2a; Line 9), and to add statements in the middle of a function body (Figure 2a; Lines 14 and 18). By using undisciplined annotations, we can omit code replication, but have

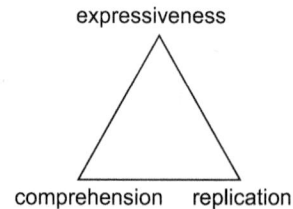

Figure 1. Trade-off between expressiveness, comprehension, and replication

to use four different annotations. In contrast, the disciplined stack implementation (Figure 2b) has only two annotations (#ifdef and #else branches), but contains several replicated code fragments: the declaration of function push with the object parameter o (Figure 2b; Lines 3 and 14), the null pointer check and the return statement (Figure 2b; Lines 5 and 14), the assignment to the array (Figure 2b; Lines 8 and 16), and the function call fireStackChanged (Figure 2b; Lines 10 and 17).

```
1  class Stack {
2    void push(Object o
3  #ifdef SYNC
4    , Transaction txn
5  #endif
6    ){
7      if (o==null
8  #ifdef SYNC
9    || txn==null
10 #endif
11   )
12     return;
13 #ifdef SYNC
14   Lock l=txn.lock(o);
15 #endif
16   elementData[size++] = o;
17 #ifdef SYNC
18   l.unlock();
19 #endif
20   fireStackChanged();
21  }
22 }
```
(a)

```
1  class Stack {
2  #ifdef SYNC
3    void push(Object o,
4      Transaction txn)
5    {
6      if (o==null || txn==null)
7        return;
8      Lock l = txn.lock(o);
9      elementData[size++] = o;
10     l.unlock();
11     fireStackChanged();
12   }
13 #else
14   void push(Object o) {
15     if (o==null)
16       return;
17     elementData[size++] = o;
18     fireStackChanged();
19   }
20 #endif
21 }
```
(b)

Figure 2. Undisciplined (a) and disciplined (b) stack implementation

Generally, undisciplined annotations can *always* be transformed into disciplined ones (at the extreme end by replicating a whole source file), and vice versa. Consider the undisciplined annotation of the subexpression '|| txn==null' in our stack implementation (Figure 2; Line 9).[3] To transform this undisciplined annotation, we lift the annotation to the upper if-statement. The result are two differently annotated if-statements, one with the subexpression '|| txn==null' and one without (cf. Figure 2). Both annotations are disciplined according to our definition. The result are two disciplined annotations that form an alternative [27].

In general, by using undisciplined annotations, programmers are able to reduce the amount of code replication. Although recent studies show that code replication is not intrinsically harmful [17, 21], it can be a source of errors and influence the underlying software systems and its development in a negative way, such

---
[3] The different annotations of the undisciplined stack implementation overlap when we transform them into disciplined annotations. Therefore, in our case, we only have two large annotations (#ifdef – #else – #endif; Lines 7, 10, and 13) instead of multiple, more fine-grained annotations.

```
 7 │   if (o==null        ┐              7 │ #ifdef SYNC
 8 │ #ifdef SYNC           │              8 │   if (o==null || txn==null)
 9 │   || txn==null   ● expansion         9 │     return;
10 │ #endif                │             10 │ #else
11 │   )                   │             11 │   if (o==null)
12 │   return;             ┘             12 │     return;
                                         13 │ #endif
```

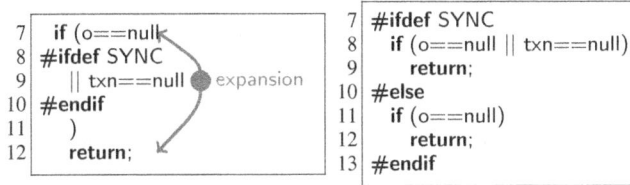

Figure 3. Transformation of an undisciplined annotation into a disciplined one

as increased maintenance effort or error propagation [2, 20]. By using undisciplined annotations, differences in code fragments can be factored out at a fine grain. However, reducing the amount of code replication comes at the price of introducing undisciplined annotations, which are considered to be more difficult to understand. For instance, preprocessor annotations obfuscate the source code and make it difficult to differentiate and locate source code [11, 22].

Beside the influence on program comprehension, an undisciplined use of the preprocessor has further implications. For instance, analysis tools (e.g., data-flow analysis) or transformation tools (e.g., source-code refactoring) require a structural representation of the code in form of an abstract syntax tree. With undisciplined annotations, such a representation is difficult to create, because fine-grained annotations, such as an annotated opening bracket, cannot be represented in terms of the abstract syntax of the host language. The reason is that single tokens, such as an opening bracket, may not have counterparts in the abstract syntax tree. As a consequence, many current IDEs struggle with software projects that make use of preprocessors. Typically, in such IDEs, the preprocessor annotations are removed, which causes a loss of variability information. To shed light on the preprocessor discipline, in previous work we analyzed the usage of disciplined and undisciplined preprocessor annotations in 40 software projects from different domains and sizes [27]. Except for one small project, we found undisciplined annotations in all projects. In summary, undisciplined annotations sum up to 16 % of all annotations.

Although the major part of preprocessor usage is disciplined, undisciplined annotations are still frequently used, despite their disadvantages. This raises the question of whether programmers perform differently using undisciplined or disciplined annotations. More precisely, are there differences in program comprehension for common programming tasks, such as maintenance, with respect to the discipline of annotations? To answer this question, we designed a controlled experiment. Next, we give a detailed description of the experiment and the material we used.

3. Experiment

By means of an experiment, we evaluate whether the kind of annotation (disciplined vs. undisciplined) has an influence on program comprehension. To this end, we let subjects solve programming tasks on several open-source systems and analyzed the correctness and response time. According to the work of Dunsmore et al., these tasks can be categorized as *maintenance* and *mental-simulation* tasks, both requiring program comprehension [5]. Next, we give a detailed description of our experimental setting, whereas we present and discuss the result in Section 4. Both sections are structured according to the guidelines of Jedlitschka et al. [19].

3.1 Objectives

The main objective of our experiment is to evaluate whether the discipline of preprocessor annotations has an influence on program comprehension. There is an ongoing debate about the discipline of preprocessor annotation, and the result is yet open. Some people argue in favor of disciplined annotations, because they ease automated analysis and thus tool support for the respective programs [6, 15]. Other people, in turn, prefer undisciplined annotations, because they provide flexibility, expressiveness, and avoid bloated code. As a matter of fact, undisciplined annotations are commonly used by professional developers [27]. Some developers argue that they have no problem with understanding their own code that contains undisciplined annotations.[4] While this may be reasonable for small, one-man software systems, it may become a problem in large systems, in which several developers are involved.

Due to these opposing positions regarding the discipline of annotations, we do not state a hypothesis in favor for a particular kind of discipline, but rather we formulate two research questions, which reflect the essence of the four open questions, which we posed in Section 1:

RQ.1 Does the discipline of annotations influence the correctness of program-comprehension and maintenance tasks?

RQ.2 Does the discipline of annotations influence the time needed to solve program-comprehension tasks?

Based on these research questions, we define two dependent variables: response time and correctness. To ensure, that these variables are not influenced or biased by other factors, we also have to control potential confounding parameters [33]. In Table 3.1 we show the five parameters we found to be most important to control for our experiment, together with the control technique we used to control them and the corresponding measurement.

Table 1. Confounding parameters, how we controlled them and which measurement we used

Conf. parameter	Control technique	Measurement
Motivation	Analyzed afterwards	Questionnaire
Difficulty	Analyzed afterwards	Questionnaire
Programming experience	Balancing	Questionnaire
Domain knowledge	Kept constant	—
Tool familiarity	Kept constant	Proprietary editor w. typical functions

We controlled the first two parameters, because different levels of motivation or an unbalanced difficulty between tasks may bias the results. We analyzed both parameters after completion of the tasks (participants had to complete a questionnaire), because it is not possible to evaluate these parameters in advance. Next, we controlled programming experience by forming two balanced groups based on a questionnaire (cf. Section 3.2). Finally, we had to control the level of domain knowledge (with respect to subject systems and participants), and how familiar the participants are with the tool that they used during the experiment.

3.2 Subjects

We recruited 19 undergraduate students from an operating-system course of the University of Magdeburg, Germany. As part of the lecture, the students had to implement a basic operating system, and thus were familiar with C/C++ and the CPP. However, the participants were neither aware of the different types (disciplined/undisciplined) of annotations nor the discussions about them. As a motivation, the participants had the chance to win one of several Amazon gift cards and could omit a mandatory exercise for participating in the experiment.

---

[4] This statement is an outcome of several discussions with professional C developers, e.g., Daniel M. German at PASED Summer School 2011.

Prior to the experiment, participants completed a questionnaire to measure their programming experience, which has been designed and evaluated carefully [10], based on state-of-the-art guidelines for empirical research. Within this Web-based questionnaire we asked the participants to estimate their programming experience regarding different languages, paradigms, and their participation in software projects. The participants had to assess their skills on a five-point Likert scale for each question [28]. In particular, participants had to respond on different questions by assessing their skills from 1 (low) to 5 (high). Finally, we computed the experience rank for each participant as a weighted sum based on the answers of the questionnaire. For this computation, we decided to give the experience with the C programming language a higher priority than for other languages, such as Java or Haskell, which is reflected by a higher weighting during computation. The reason is that, because the subject systems are written in C, knowledge of C is essential to obtain meaningful results.

Based on the results, we formed two homogeneous groups for our experiment, by applying a matching on the computed experience rank of the participants [18]. The goal of forming homogeneous groups was to have two comparable groups with a similar experience rank. As a result, we obtained groups with 8 and 11 participants, respectively (see Section 3.7 for explanation of the different group size). The smaller group had an experience rank of 20.8, on average (standard deviation: 6.89), and is referred to as *undisciplined group* in the remainder, because this group worked on the source code with the undisciplined annotations. Likewise, the other group had an experience rank of 16.8, on average (standard deviation: 5.26), and is referred to as *disciplined group*. Note that due to the different group size, the experience between both group differs. Nevertheless, it is still similar enough so that we can consider both groups to be comparable regarding their programming experience. We show the detailed experience rank for each participant of both groups in Table 2.

Table 2. Experience rank for disciplined and undisciplined group (descending order)

Participant	Rank discip. group	Rank undiscip group
#1	29	40
#2	27	28
#3	20	22
#4	20	19
#5	17	19
#6	16	14
#7	13	12
#8	13	12
#9	13	–
#10	10	–
#11	7	–
Distribution	0 10 20 30 40	0 10 20 30 40

3.3 Material

To be as close as possible to real applications, we used real code from four open-source systems from different domains. Particularly, we used parts of *boa* (a web server), *dia* (a chart/diagram application), *irssi* (an IRC client), and *xterm* (a terminal emulator) as material. Due to their diversity (e.g., different domains, different programmers), we argue that these system are sufficiently representative for real-world software systems. However, since we aimed at analyzing program comprehension for different tasks and for different types of annotations, we had to prepare the code manually (e.g.,

removing files/lines of code). Otherwise, it would be infeasible for the participants to understand all the systems in detail, and to solve the respective tasks. Furthermore, by narrowing down the sample systems, we were able to emphasize the code that is of interest for our experiment and to mitigate side effects that may influence the result of our empirical study such as that participants sift through irrelevant code.

For selecting appropriate files for each task, we relied on our experience and former studies on preprocessor annotations [11, 27]. Consequently, we selected files that contain not only an average amount of annotated code (according to [26, 27]), but especially *undisciplined* annotations. Subsequently, we created a second version of each file by transforming undisciplined annotations to disciplined annotations using the expansion technique by Liebig et al. [27]. For instance, in our stack example in Figure 2b, we have disciplined annotations at the function level, but both annotated code fragments are replicated. Note that we explicitly avoided source code with mixed annotations, that is, disciplined and undisciplined annotations in the same place. Although such tangling may occur in real-world systems, it would render our results meaningless to some extent, because we could not measure *which* kind of annotation has an influence on our measurements (i.e., response time and correctness). Finally, we shortened some files, such that they fit to the time constraints of our experiment. This step of preparation was mainly initiated by feedback from our pre-tests with masters and PhD students, which we present in Section 3.4.

Next, we computed two code metrics: discipline of annotation and code clones (i.e., replicated code) [27, 30, 31], which we summarize in Table 3. We specifically computed the amount of code clones, because in recent studies we have shown that the discipline of annotations comes at the cost of replicated code (cf. Figure 1), which may influence the programmer's performance in maintenance tasks [31]. Additionally, code clones may affect program comprehension, because they may hinder the developer in building a mental model of the underlying code [24]. Regarding the discipline metric, we computed the number of disciplined annotations compared to all annotations in the system under study. As a result, we observed for the undisciplined version of the material, that the number of disciplined annotations differs from 33% to 91% with respect to all preprocessor annotations in the code (cf. Table 3).

3.4 Pilot Study

To assess whether our material is appropriate for our experiment (e.g., regarding time or difficulty), we conducted a pilot study, involving undergraduate and graduate students. Three students (1 master, 2 PhD) from the University of Passau and six students (4 master, 2 PhD) from the University of Magdeburg confirmed their participation. All of them worked with a similar setting as the participants in the experiment: They had to complete seven tasks within 90 minutes (to avoid fatigue effects). In contrast to the experiment, the pilot study took place at different times and different places (e.g., in office or at home). In addition to solving the tasks, we asked the subjects to make immediate comments on each task with pen & paper or within the form that is used to type in the solution for the respective task. Finally, we conducted interviews with each pilot tester to ask for her opinion regarding the material as well as the tasks. Based on the pilot study, we revised our material according to the comments of the pilot tester. In particular, we rephrased task descriptions that have been ambiguous to make them more understandable. Furthermore, for certain tasks, the pilot testers complained that the source code was too long for the given time. Hence, we shortened the respective files by removing parts that contain no preprocessor annotations.

Table 3. Summary of the material used for the tasks of the experiment, including annotation discipline and code clone metrics

Task	System	Version	SLOC D	SLOC UD	Discipline in % D	Discipline in % UD	Clones in % D	Clones in % UD	Task
T1	*boa*	0.94.13	1 405	1 404	100	90	5.9	5.9	Identifying all (different) preprocessor variables
T2	*xterm*	2.4.3	1 047	961	100	91	11.7	0.0	Determining the max. depth of #ifdef nesting
T3	*vim*	7.2	233	135	100	33	77.8	0.0	Determining the number of possible variants
T4	*vim*	7.2	606	475	100	41	0.0	0.0	Identifying code fragments that belong to a variant
T5	*irssi*	0.8.13	287	282	100	69	0.0	0.0	Add a new variant by modifying existing code
T6	*irssi*	0.8.13	457	447	100	86	0.0	0.0	Delete code that belongs to a given variant
T7-d	*xterm*	2.4.3	100	100	79	79	0.0	0.0	Correct an error
T7-u	*xterm*	2.4.3	100	100	79	79	0.0	0.0	Identify, whether an error occurs

D – disciplined group, UD – undisciplined group; All software systems are available on the Web: http://freecode.com.

3.5 Tasks

For our experiment, we created seven tasks, each of them related to one of two categories [5]: mental simulation or maintenance. Additionally, for each task, we provided the relevant material (source code), as explained in the previous subsection. Moreover, the tasks had a fixed order.[5]

The first four tasks T1–T4 correspond to mental simulation, each of them requires a grasp of how variability is expressed with preprocessor annotations. With these tasks, we measure how participants understand variability introduced by annotations. For instance, we asked the participants in task T1 to identify all the different preprocessor variables in the given piece of code. Another example is task T3, in which we asked participants for the number of possible variants of a certain function. Although such tasks may rarely occur explicitly in practice, programmers often face such tasks implicitly, for example, when trying to reproduce internals of source code (in our case, variability).

Tasks T5 and T6 (cf. Table 3) correspond to maintenance: We let participants modify and delete annotated code, which also requires understanding the respective source code. This may be necessary due to changed user requirements, which is quite common in software maintenance. For example, in task T6, participants had to remove all code that is related to a certain preprocessor variable.

Finally, with task T7 (related to mental simulation), we aim at discovering how developers detect and correct (syntax) errors in the presence of preprocessor annotations. This task is different, compared to the previous tasks, in two ways. First, the corresponding source code is identical for both the disciplined and undisciplined group. Second, the task itself is different for both groups. The reason is that, for disciplined annotations, syntax errors can be detected (by definition) *before* the preprocessing step of the CPP (e.g., by the parser) [23, 27]. Hence, with disciplined annotations, programmers do not need to detect syntax errors manually. In contrast, for undisciplined annotations, one can detect syntax errors automatically only after this preprocessing step. Hence, we focused solely on undisciplined annotations within task T7.

For the disciplined group, we provided the information (within the task description) that the code contains a syntax error and in which situation this error occurs (cf. T7-d in Table 3). Based on this information, the task was to rewrite the code to *fix the error*. In contrast, the task for the undisciplined group was to check whether the source code is syntactically correct for all configurations of preprocessor variables (i.e., to *detect the error*). We discuss the

implication of this task design in Section 5. In Figure 4, we show the respective code snippet that contains the error.[6]

For all tasks, we created sample solutions in advance to compare the subjects' answers to it. This way, we aim at eliminating the possibility that the assessment of the solutions of the experiment is biased.

```
1   #if defined(__GLIBC__)
2   // additional lines of code
3   #elif defined(__MVS__)
4   result = pty_search(pty);
5   #else
6   #ifdef USE_ISPTS_FLAG
7       if (result) {
8   #endif
9       result = ((*pty = open("/dev/ptmx", O_RDWR)) < 0);
10  #endif
11  #if defined(SVR4) || defined(__SCO__) || \
12      defined(USE_ISPTS_FLAG)
13      if (!result)
14          strcpy(ttydev, ptsname(*pty));
15  #ifdef USE_ISPTS_FLAG
16      IsPts = !result;
17  }
18  #endif
19  #endif
```

Figure 4. Example of undisciplined annotation in *xterm* (task T7)

3.6 Execution

We conducted the experiment in November 2011 in a computer lab at the University of Magdeburg, with standard desktop machines and 19 inch displays. At the beginning of the experiment, we gave a short introduction to the experiment in the form of a presentation. Furthermore, we used PROPHET as tool infrastructure, which has been specifically developed for supporting program-comprehension experiments [10, 13]. PROPHET provides the basic functionalities of an Eclipse-like IDE, including as a file explorer, an editor with syntax highlighting, as well as a project and file search. Additionally, PROPHET has a dedicated dialog to show the task description to participants, and it provides a form for typing the respective answers. Beside this, we enabled source-code editing of the text editor for tasks T5 to T7.

With the help of PROPHET, we were able to track the activities of the participants and thus to use the resulting data for the analysis of the experiment. Basically, PROPHET records the answers and

---

[5] The concrete tasks, together with the source code, for both control groups are available on the Web: http://www.fosd.net/experimentIfdef.

[6] The error occurs in the case that the preprocessor variables __GLIBC__ and USE_ISPTS_FLAG are defined.

time needed for each task. Furthermore, it logs the participants' activities while solving tasks. In particular, it logs different activities within the text editor, such as searching, scrolling, or editing. This, in turn, allows us to reason about peculiarities that we observe during the experiment and its analysis.

We conducted the experiment with a time limit of 90 minutes. If this limit was reached, we asked the participants to quit, but they were allowed to finish the task they were currently working on. We presented the tasks to participants in sequential order, one at a time. For each task, we recommended a time as a guideline for participants. However, participants were free to spent as much time as they wanted for an individual task. Finally, we asked participants about the difficulty and their motivation for each task using a questionnaire.

3.7 Deviations

During the execution of our experiment, two deviations occurred. First, two students took the experiment before all other participants (same day, but different time). Hence, they could have talked to other participants about the experiment, which may bias our results. However, they credibly assured that they did not disseminate any information about the experiment to the other participants. Second, three students did not complete the questionnaire prior to the experiment. Consequently, we could not assign them to any group in advance. Hence, these participants completed the questionnaire directly before the experiment. Subsequently, we randomly assigned them to a group by a coin toss. Nevertheless, we argue that this deviation does not influence our results for two reasons. First, the experience rank is similar for both the disciplined as well as the undisciplined group (cf. Section 3.2). Second, our analysis did not reveal any peculiarities regarding the performance of these three participants.

4. Analysis and Interpretation

In this section, we present the analysis of our experiment and interpret the results. First, we discuss the results of the statistical analysis. Then, we relate the results to the research question(s) and discuss peculiarities that we detected during the analysis. We discuss task T7 separately, because it diverges in its design from the other tasks (cf. Section 3.5).

4.1 Analysis of Correctness & Response Time

For the analysis of our data, we differentiate between two aspects, according to our research questions: Correctness of solutions and response time for each task. Additionally, we manually analyzed the log data that we collected during the experiment. We used SPSS[7] and R[8] for analysis.

4.1.1 Correctness

For correctness, we used a 3-point scale. A solution could either be completely correct (2), almost correct (1), or wrong (0). We decided to use a 3-point scale, because we found that subjects often solved a task almost correct, such that we can be sure that comprehension has taken place correctly. To this end, we analyzed the log data to filter out minor mistakes that do not depend on the discipline of annotations. For example, in task T1, subjects should count the number of #ifdef variables and one participant used the PROPHET search facility only for one (of two) folders. Hence, she detected only 15 instead of 17 #ifdef annotations (i.e., the corresponding preprocessor variable). Nevertheless, we can be sure that the participant worked seriously on the task, but only made

[7] http://www.ibm.com/software/analytics/spss/

[8] http://www.r-project.org/

Table 4. Overview of correctness for each task

Task	Type of annotation	0	1	2	χ^2	p
Task 1	Disciplined	5	4	2	1.679	0.432
	Undisciplined	5	3	0		
Task 2	Disciplined	1	1	9	1.082	0.598
	Undisciplined	2	1	5		
Task 3	Disciplined	6	0	5	0.038	0.845
	Undisciplined	4	0	4		
Task 4	Disciplined	7	2	2	1.360	0.507
	Undisciplined	3	2	3		
Task 5	Disciplined	4	4	3	1.337	0.512
	Undisciplined	2	5	1		
Task 6	Disciplined	3	4	4	2.796	0.247
	Undisciplined	1	6	1		
Task 7	Disciplined	9	0	2	0.130	0.719
	Undisciplined	6	0	2		

0 – wrong, 1 – almost correct, 2 – completely correct

a mistake in using the tool. Besides this example, there are similar cases for the other tasks. Additionally, we defined a threshold for the answers that we found to be almost correct, so that we can guarantee that an answer is (almost) correct. As a result, we decided that only if at least 90% of the task has been solved correctly, we assess the answer with "almost correct".

Furthermore, two authors double-checked their evaluation of the results as follows: Each of the two authors has been assigned a group. First, they checked all tasks of this groups participants, respectively. Afterwards, they hand out their assessment each other. Then, they checked the solutions of the participants and the assessment of the other author. In the case that their assessment for a certain task diverged, this task was discussed together and another author should have been asked. However, for all tasks of both groups, both authors agreed on the assessment of each other, respectively.

In Table 4, we give an overview of the correctness of the answers of the subjects. Task T2 seems to be easiest, because it was solved correctly by most subjects. In contrast, task T7 seems to be rather difficult, because there are only a few correct answers, which may be caused by the different design of the task. Overall, the distribution of correct answers is similar in both groups. We conducted a χ^2 test to evaluate whether significant differences between the correctness of tasks exist. Although having a small number of participants, χ^2 is an appropriate test, because researchers have shown that χ^2 is even applicable (and robust) to low expected values [4]. Our test revealed no significant difference between the disciplined and undisciplined group: the χ^2 values are smaller than 2.796 and the p values are larger than 0.247. Hence, we found *no significant evidence* that the kind of annotation has an effect on correctness.

4.1.2 Response Time

In Table 5, we give an overview of the mean response times for each task and group. To analyze the effect of the kind of annotation on response time, we conducted a t test for independent samples [1], because the data have a metric scale and are normally distributed (as shown by a Kolmogorov-Smirnov test [1]). We did not correct the response times for wrong answers, which we discuss in Section 5. Our data reveal that, for the tasks T1 to T6, the difference in the response time is negligible (according to a t test; the t values vary from 1.197 to 1.952; all p values are larger than 0.068). In contrast, the difference between response times for the last task T7 is significant (t value: -3.239; p value < 0.05), with the disciplined group being faster. However, we have to take into account that the task for both groups was different. Hence, the response time should not be compared with those from task T1 to T6.

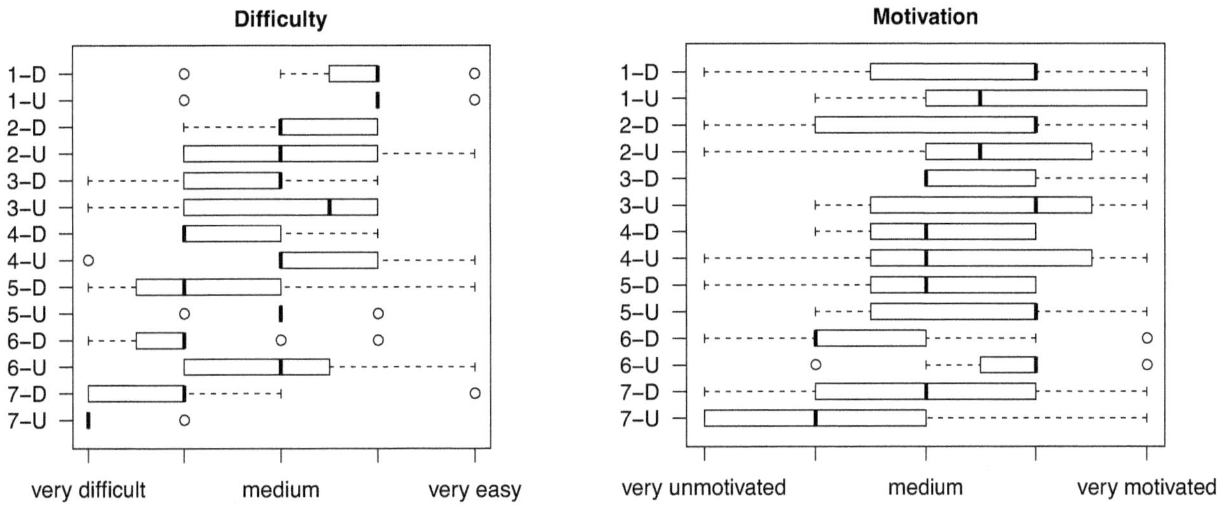

Figure 5. Difficulty (left) and motivation (right) of the tasks (assessed by participants): D – disciplined group, U – undisciplined group

4.2 Motivation and Difficulty

For all tasks, we asked the participants to assess the difficulty of the tasks and their motivation to solve them on a five-point Likert scale. The reason for gathering these measures is to eliminate the possibility that neither motivation nor difficulty (of the tasks) may bias our results. We show the results in Figure 5. Overall, the results coincide with those we measured for correctness and response time: There is *no* significant difference between the disciplined and undisciplined group for tasks T1 to T6, and thus there is no influence of these factors on our results. However, the results of task T6 vary compared to the other five tasks in that the motivation of both groups differs considerably, which we cannot explain entirely.

Table 5. Overview of response time for each task

Task	Version	Response time Distribution	Mean	N	t value
Task 1	Discip		10.69	11	1.504
	Undiscip		8.21	8	–
Task 2	Discip		10.59	11	1.197
	Undiscip		9.57	8	–
Task 3	Discip		4	11	1.526
	Undiscip		3.07	8	–
Task 4	Discip		12.44	11	1.698
	Undiscip		9.98	8	–
Task 5	Discip		8.13	11	1.952
	Undiscip		6.46	8	–
Task 6	Discip		11.96	11	1.745
	Undiscip		8.61	8	–
Task 7	Discip		11.64	11	-3.239
	Undiscip		22.29	8	–

N: number of subjects per group; t value: result of t test ($p < 0.05$)

The differences correspond to the result of the experiment in so far as the undisciplined group performed slightly better than the disciplined group (cf. Figure 4), which may explain our observation to some extent.

Finally, there is an observable difference in motivation and difficulty for the last task T7, which corresponds to the results of our analysis, specifically regarding response time.

4.3 Research Questions

The analysis of our experimental data revealed no significant differences between the disciplined and the undisciplined group, neither for correctness nor for response time. Next, we interpret our results with respect to the research questions we formulated in Section 3.1. Additionally, we put emphasis on error handling, which mainly encompasses our results of task T7. Finally, we present findings that result from a detailed analysis of the log data we recorded during the experiment.

RQ.1 – Does the discipline of annotations affect the correctness of program comprehension and maintenance tasks?

Based on the results of our analysis, we conclude that the discipline of annotations has *no* significant influence on mental simulation or maintenance tasks. Nevertheless, we observed some minor tendencies regarding correctness. First, we observed a considerable difference between the first four tasks, regardless of the respective group. For instance, the second task has been solved correctly[9] by most participants in both groups (disciplined: $\sim$ 90%, undisciplined: 75%), as we show in Table 4. In contrast, for the other three tasks (T1, T3, and T4), the ratio of correct answers is 60% or less for both groups (cf. Table 4). Additionally, we observed the tendency that participants of the undisciplined group performed slightly better with respect to correctness than participants of the disciplined group regarding maintenance tasks ($\sim$ 80% compared to $\sim$ 70%, on average) (cf. Table 4).

Second, while the disciplined group performed slightly better for the first four tasks (i.e., mental simulation tasks), the undisciplined group achieved better results for tasks T5 and T6 (i.e., maintenance tasks). This observation is reflected in the number of wrong answers (relatively to all participants for each of the two groups, see Table 4) and may indicate that the compressed representation of variability by means of undisciplined annotations may be advantageous for making changes to the source code. However, this

---

[9] either completely or almost correct

71

is only a conjecture and not supported by our statistical analysis. More research with a specific focus on certain tasks such as maintenance is necessary to evaluate this assumption. Specifically, it is of interest to evaluate whether this observation holds for large-scale maintenance tasks, where the comprehensibility of a program may outweigh the compressed presentation.

RQ.2 – Does the discipline of annotations influence the time needed to solve mental simulation and maintenance tasks?

Similar to the correctness of the answers, our statistical analysis reveals that there is *no* significant difference regarding response time, either. Nevertheless, the mean time for each task shows that the disciplined group tends to need more time throughout all tasks, without being significant. For some tasks, such as T3 or T4, the increased code size could be responsible, because this leads to more code that has to be investigated by the participant. However, we have currently no general explanation for this observation. Overall, we conclude that the kind of annotation does not seem to affect the response time of subjects at all.

Detecting/Fixing errors in the presence of #ifdefs

Because T7 differs from all other tasks in both design and focus of the task the results are difficult to compare to the other tasks. Hence, we discuss the results of this task separately. Generally, we made two interesting observations when considering the results of this task: First, *detecting* an error in the presence of preprocessor annotations is a difficult and time-consuming task. This observation is reflected by the high response time of the undisciplined group that is significantly higher than the time of the disciplined group. Second, even with the knowledge that an error exists, it is complicated to *remove* this error in the presence of preprocessor annotations. This is reflected by the high number of wrong answers, even for the disciplined group (where we provided information that an error exists). Although these observations confirm the assumption of other researchers [6], we support this assumption for the first time by means of our experiment.

Nevertheless, both observations have a limited generalizability. First, detecting and correcting errors is a complicated and time-consuming task in general, even without preprocessor annotations. Hence, our results may be influenced by this fact, and we cannot entirely conclude to what extent the preprocessor annotations are the reason for our observations.

4.4 Log Data/Manual Analysis

To get deeper insights into *how* subjects solved the tasks, we analyzed the behavior of subjects during each task. The reason is that we wanted to investigate whether certain patterns occur when solving tasks. As a result, we can reason about wrong answers or exceeding response time and how both are related to the discipline of preprocessor annotations. To this end, we analyzed the comprehensive log data (recorded by PROPHET) and the edited source files (for T5 and T6). Next, we present our observations.

Task T1 to T4 (Mental Simulation): For the first four tasks, the log data reveal that *all* participants had an idea of how to solve each task. For instance, all of them used similar and appropriate search terms. Additionally, we observed a similar scroll behavior, such as time spent on certain code fragments while investigating the source code. Nevertheless, in particular cases (and independent of the respective group), some participants failed to solve the task at all, by proposing a solution that was entirely wrong, or they submitted only a partial or even no solution. We hypothesize that other reasons are responsible for this diverging results, such as time spent on a certain task. But this observation could also indicate that identifying relevant code fragments is generally complicated in the presence of preprocessor annotations and complex tasks. Overall, our log data support the analysis result that the discipline of anno-

tations does not influence correctness.

Task T5 and T6 (Maintenance): For the two tasks related to maintenance, our analysis revealed that four participants had no idea how to solve the tasks. For T5, three participants of the disciplined group provided a solution that was not even close to correct. In fact, they made changes to code that actually had nothing to do with the problem, as stated in the task description. Interestingly, two of these participants did not use the code-search facilities of PROPHET to identify the right place within the code, which could be a reason for their wrong solution. Furthermore, we observed that most of the participants who provided a solution that was partially correct made the same mistakes. That is, while they introduced a new preprocessor variable in the right place, they neglected to remove certain statements or fields from the code that is surrounded by this newly introduced variable. This, in turn, may lead to errors, and thus we decided to classify these solutions as only partially correct. Finally, two participants of the undisciplined group introduced syntax errors, which we assume were caused by the undisciplined nature of annotations. More precisely, the participants omitted and misplaced a bracket, respectively.

For task T6, we identified one participant who failed to remove the source code related to the preprocessor variable IP_V6 (as specified in the task). Since she used the code search with the same search terms as the other participants, we hypothesize that she did not understand the task at all and thus used a wrong search term.

Overall, we could not detect a clear pattern for one of the groups. However, regarding the minor mistakes for T5, we assume that preprocessor annotations in general (i.e., independent of the discipline) have a (negative) effect on source code changes.

Task T7 (Detecting/Fixing Errors): Finally, for task T7, we have to distinguish between the disciplined and undisciplined group, because they had to solve considerably different tasks. For the disciplined group, the log data revealed that five (out of eleven) participants tried to fix the error stated in the task description at a totally different position in the source code than expected. Hence, we assume that, although we provided information to localize the root of the error, half of the participants did not understand the interrelation between the preprocessor annotations and the syntax error caused by them.

In conclusion, when considering the detailed behavior of subjects, we could not find an influence of the kind of annotation on program comprehension. Nevertheless, we explicitly mention that this does not necessarily mean that there are no (significant) differences. In fact, our conclusion is valid for our experiment, but may not be generalizable regarding further studies. Beyond that, for different tasks and independent of the discipline, our observations indicate that the presence of preprocessor annotations in general has a (negative) influence on program comprehension. Further research on this topic using screen and video-capture facilities could provide deeper insights.

5. Threats to Validity

Next, we discuss threats to internal and external validity, which helps other researchers to interpret our results and to put them into relation to experiments with similar focus. Internal validity refers to how well we controlled influences on what we observed, that is, program comprehension. External validity describes the generalizability of our results [32].

5.1 Internal Validity

The participants had to work in an unfamiliar environment (i.e., PROPHET), specifically designed to support experimental studies.

Still, we argue that this environment is easy enough to use, because it contains standard features of a modern IDE, such as syntax highlighting. Moreover, with the help of PROPHET, we can rule out that other factors, such as outstanding knowledge about tools or techniques (e.g., the preferred IDE or regular expressions), bias our results.

Furthermore, there are some limitations regarding the execution and analysis of our study. Three students did not complete the questionnaire prior to the experiment, which we used to assign participants to the groups. Hence, we randomly assigned these students to the groups. However, both groups are comparable, as the similar experience ranks show that we computed for each group.

Additionally, we did not filter out wrong answers when analyzing the response time, because this would reduce our already small sample size further [36]. However, by manual inspection of our log data, we found no information indicating that a participant did not answer a task seriously (e.g., response times did not deviate too much toward zero).

5.2 External Validity

First, all participants of our experiment are undergraduate students and thus have less programming experience than professional developers. Hence, our results are only valid for this level of programming experience and should only be carefully interpreted with respect to experienced developers. Nevertheless, previous studies demonstrate that even students can be treated similar to professional programmers [35].

Second, participants had to complete the tasks on code snippets of different systems, whereas in a real-world scenario, programmers work on large-scale systems that consist of thousands of lines of code. In addition, the particular tasks were rather small, so that they fit the time constraints of the experiments. Both, the amount of source code and complexity of tasks may limit the generalizability of our study, because they do not reflect the real world in its entirety. However, regarding the tasks, we decided to define *micro tasks* to measure different aspects of preprocessor annotations and program comprehension. The effect of the kind of annotation in larger tasks has to be evaluated empirically, for which our experimental design can be reused.

Third, we created all disciplined annotations manually, by transforming undisciplined ones. This may render the disciplined code artificial and thus limit the generalizability of our case study. However, the disciplined annotations that result from our transformation coincides with those, typically found in C systems [26]. Hence, we argue that creating the disciplined annotations does not affect our case study.

Finally, in our study, we considered only the CPP usage in C programs, while the CPP is used with other languages such as C++ as well. However, all tasks and code examples have been chosen without making heavy use of underlying language mechanisms (i.e., standard imperative mechanisms). Hence, the tasks could be applied to programs in different target languages in the same way.

6. Related Work

Prior to this paper, several other researchers addressed the usage of preprocessor annotations in source code.

Spencer and Collyer investigated the usage of preprocessor annotations to support the portability of systems [34]. They found that a moderate usage of #ifdefs is acceptable, whereas an overly extensive usage leads to severe problems regarding maintenance and understanding of source code. However, compared to our work, they solely rely on experiences with the C News system (and how to avoid unnecessary #ifdefs), whereas we conducted an empirical experiment. Furthermore, they do not distinguish between disciplined and undisciplined annotations.

Feigenspan et al. addressed the problem of comprehensibility of preprocessor annotations [9, 11, 12]. They conducted experiments to measure whether background colors are useful to support program comprehension in the presence of preprocessor annotations. Similarly, Le et al. propose a prototype that provides facilities to manage software variation within a GUI [25]. They present a user study to evaluate differences between using common CPP directives and their prototype, confirming that the prototype is more effective for implementing variability. While both approaches focus on comprehension of annotated code in general (including possible alternatives to CPP), we focus on program comprehension of *different types* of annotations (disciplined and undisciplined), which are often discussed in the literature.

Medeiros et al. analyzed preprocessor-based systems with respect to syntax errors [29]. They conducted experiments on 40 systems and observed that only few errors occur, which particularly remained for years in the system. While this coincides with our observations that syntax errors are hard to detect, our work is different in that we conducted an experiment to determine the favorable annotation discipline, using humans.

Furthermore, in prior work, we analyzed the discipline of annotations with respect to code replication [31]. In particular, we investigated whether the discipline of annotations has an effect on the number of code clones. Within our analysis, we found evidence that systems with entirely disciplined annotations contain more code clones than systems with undisciplined annotations. However, we neither considered program comprehension nor maintenance issues of the analyzed system.

7. Conclusion and Future Work

The C preprocessor CPP is widely used to express variability in source code. Despite its expressiveness and usage even in large-scale systems, the CPP is criticized for obfuscating source code, making it difficult to understand. We concentrated on the issue of how the discipline of preprocessor annotations influences program comprehension, by means of a controlled experiment with human subjects. We created two groups, each of which had to solve seven tasks related to maintenance and mental simulation on source code with disciplined and undisciplined annotations, respectively. Then, we measured their performance in terms of correctness and response time. Our results indicate that the discipline of annotations has *no influence on program comprehension and maintenance*, neither for correctness nor for performance (in terms of response time). Although we observed some tendencies, they are not supported by our statistical analysis. However, our experiment confirms that finding errors in the presence of preprocessor annotations is a tedious and time-consuming task. More research on this topic is needed, especially with a focus on certain aspects that were out of scope of this study such as large-scale maintenance tasks or error detection in the presence or absence of preprocessor annotations. In future work, we aim at addressing these aspects based on the results of this study as a starting point.

First, we plan an experiment to evaluate whether the current results hold for large-scale maintenance tasks. In such an experiment, participants have to solve one task concerned with maintenance, which is more complex than the tasks in the present experiment. Second, we will use a complete system rather than small parts of different systems. In a similar way (e.g., similar experimental setup), an experiment for measuring program comprehension in the presence of different types of annotations is part of our future work.

Acknowledgment

Siegmund's work is funded by BMBF project 01IM10002B. Apel's work is funded by the DFG grants AP 206/2, AP 206/4, and AP 206/5. Schulze would like to thank Bram Adams for initial discussion on that topic during PASED summer school 2011. Finally, we are grateful to Christoph Steup for support in acquiring participants for the experiment and comments on earlier versions of this paper.

References

[1] T. Anderson and J. Finn. *The New Statistical Analysis of Data.* Springer, 1996.

[2] B. Baker. On Finding Duplication and Near-Duplication in Large Software Systems. In *Proc. Work. Conf. Reverse Engineering (WCRE)*, pages 86–95. IEEE, 1995.

[3] I. Baxter and M. Mehlich. Preprocessor Conditional Removal by Simple Partial Evaluation. In *Proc. Work. Conf. Reverse Engineering (WCRE)*, pages 281–290. IEEE, 2001.

[4] G. Camilli and K. D. Hopkins. Applicability of Chi-square to 2×2 Contingency Tables with Small Expected Cell Frequencies. *Psychological Bulletin*, 85(1):163, 1978.

[5] A. Dunsmore and M. Roper. A Comparative Evaluation of Program Comprehension Measures. *Journal Sys. and Soft. (JSS)*, 52(3):121–129, 2000.

[6] M. Ernst, G. Badros, and D. Notkin. An Empirical Analysis of C Preprocessor Use. *IEEE Trans. Software Engineering (TSE)*, 28(12):1146–1170, 2002.

[7] J.-M. Favre. The CPP Paradox. In *Proc. European Workshop Software Maintenance*, 1995. http://equipes-lig.imag.fr/adele/Les.Publications/intConferences/EWSM91995Fav.pdf.

[8] J.-M. Favre. Understanding-In-The-Large. In *Int. Workshop Program Comprehension (IWPC)*, pages 29–38. IEEE, 1997.

[9] J. Feigenspan, C. Kästner, S. Apel, J. Liebig, M. Schulze, R. Dachselt, M. Papendieck, T. Leich, and G. Saake. Do background colors improve program comprehension in the #ifdef hell? *Empirical Software Engineering*, pages 1–47, 2012.

[10] J. Feigenspan, C. Kästner, J. Liebig, S. Apel, and S. Hanenberg. Measuring Programming Experience. In *Proc. Int. Conf. Program Comprehension (ICPC)*, pages 73–82. IEEE, 2012.

[11] J. Feigenspan, M. Schulze, M. Papendieck, C. Kästner, R. Dachselt, V. Köppen, and M. Frisch. Using Background Colors to Support Program Comprehension in Software Product Lines. In *Proc. Int. Conf. Evaluation and Assessment in Software Engineering (EASE)*, pages 66–75. Institution of Engineering and Technology, 2011.

[12] J. Feigenspan, M. Schulze, M. Papendieck, C. Kästner, R. Dachselt, V. Köppen, M. Frisch, and G. Saake. Supporting Program Comprehension in Large Preprocessor-Based Software Product Lines. *IET Software*, 6(6):488–501, 2012.

[13] J. Feigenspan, N. Siegmund, A. Hasselberg, and M. Köppen. PROPHET: Tool Infrastructure to Support Program Comprehension Experiments. In *Proc. Int. Symp. Empirical Software Engineering and Measurement (ESEM)*, 2011. Poster.

[14] A. Garrido and R. Johnson. Challenges of Refactoring C Programs. In *Proc. Int. Workshop Principles of Software Evolution (IWPSE)*, pages 6–14. ACM, 2002.

[15] A. Garrido and R. Johnson. Refactoring C with Conditional Compilation. In *Proc. Int. Conf. Automated Software Engineering (ASE)*, pages 323–326. IEEE, 2003.

[16] A. Garrido and R. Johnson. Analyzing Multiple Configurations of a C Program. In *Proc. Int. Conf. Software Maintenance (ICSM)*, pages 379–388. IEEE, 2005.

[17] N. Göde and J. Harder. Clone Stability. In *Proc. European Conf. Software Maintenance and Reengineering (CSMR)*, pages 65–74. IEEE, 2011.

[18] C. Goodwin. *Research in Psychology: Methods and Design.* Wiley Publishing, Inc., second edition, 1999.

[19] A. Jedlitschka, M. Ciolkowski, and D. Pfahl. Reporting Experiments in Software Engineering. In *Guide to Advanced Empirical Software Engineering*, pages 201–228. Springer, 2008.

[20] E. Jürgens, F. Deissenböck, B. Hummel, and S. Wagner. Do Code Clones Matter? In *Proc. Int. Conf. Software Engineering (ICSE)*, pages 485–495. IEEE, 2009.

[21] C. Kapser and M. W. Godfrey. "Cloning Considered Harmful" Considered Harmful. In *Proc. Work. Conf. Reverse Engineering (WCRE)*, pages 19–28. IEEE, 2006.

[22] C. Kästner, S. Apel, and M. Kuhlemann. Granularity in Software Product Lines. In *Proc. Int. Conf. Software Engineering (ICSE)*, pages 311–320. ACM, 2008.

[23] C. Kästner, S. Apel, S. Trujillo, M. Kuhlemann, and D. Batory. Guaranteeing Syntactic Correctness for all Product Line Variants: A Language-Independent Approach. In *Proc. Int. Conf. Objects, Models, Components, Patterns (TOOLS)*, pages 174–194. Springer, 2009.

[24] T. D. LaToza, G. Venolia, and R. DeLine. Maintaining Mental Models: A Study of Developer Work Habits. In *Proc. Int. Conf. Software Engineering (ICSE)*, pages 492–501. ACM, 2006.

[25] D. Le, E. Walkingshaw, and M. Erwig. #ifdef Confirmed Harmful: Promoting Understandable Software Variation. In *Proc. IEEE Symp. Visual Languages and Human-Centric Computing (VL/HCC)*, pages 143–150. IEEE, 2011.

[26] J. Liebig, S. Apel, C. Lengauer, C. Kästner, and M. Schulze. An Analysis of the Variability in Forty Preprocessor-Based Software Product Lines. In *Proc. Int. Conf. Software Engineering (ICSE)*, pages 105–114. ACM, 2010.

[27] J. Liebig, C. Kästner, and S. Apel. Analyzing the Discipline of Preprocessor Annotations in 30 Million Lines of C Code. In *Proc. Int. Conf. Aspect-Oriented Software Development (AOSD)*, pages 191–202. ACM, 2011.

[28] R. Likert. A Technique for the Measurement of Attitudes. *Archives of Psychology*, 140:1–55, 1932.

[29] F. Medeiros, M. Ribeiro, and R. Gheyi. Investigating Preprocessor-Based Syntax Errors. In *Proc. Int. Conf. Generative Programming and Component Engineering (GPCE)*. ACM, 2013. to appear.

[30] C. Roy and J. Cordy. A Survey on Software Clone Detection Research. Technical Report 2007-541, Queen's University at Kingston, 2007.

[31] S. Schulze, E. Jürgens, and J. Feigenspan. Analyzing the Effect of Preprocessor Annotations on Code Clones. In *Proc. Work. Conf. Source Code Analysis and Manipulation (SCAM)*, pages 115–124. IEEE, 2011.

[32] W. R. Shadish, T. D. Cook, and D. T. Campbell. *Experimental and Quasi-Experimental Designs for Generalized Causal Inference.* Houghton Mifflin Company, 2002.

[33] J. Siegmund. *Framework for Measuring Program Comprehension.* PhD thesis, University of Magdeburg, 2012.

[34] H. Spencer and G. Collyer. #ifdef Considered Harmful, or Portability Experience with C News. In *Proc. USENIX Technical Conf.*, pages 185–197. USENIX Association Berkeley, 1992.

[35] M. Svahnberg, A. Aurum, and C. Wohlin. Using Students as Subjects – An Empirical Evaluation. In *Proc. Int. Symp. Empirical Software Engineering and Measurement (ESEM)*, pages 288–290. ACM, 2008.

[36] J. Yellott. Correction for Fast Guessing and the Speed Accuracy Trade-off in Choice Reaction Time. *Journal of Mathematical Psychology*, 8:159–199, 1971.

Investigating Preprocessor-Based Syntax Errors

Flávio Medeiros

Federal University of Campina Grande
Campina Grande, Brazil
flaviomedeiros@copin.ufcg.edu.br

Márcio Ribeiro

Federal University of Alagoas
Maceió, Brazil
marcio@ic.ufal.br

Rohit Gheyi

Federal University of Campina Grande
Campina Grande, Brazil
rohit@dsc.ufcg.edu.br

Abstract

The C preprocessor is commonly used to implement variability in program families. Despite the widespread usage, some studies indicate that the C preprocessor makes variability implementation difficult and error-prone. However, we still lack studies to investigate preprocessor-based syntax errors and quantify to what extent they occur in practice. In this paper, we define a technique based on a variability-aware parser to find syntax errors in releases and commits of program families. To investigate these errors, we perform an empirical study where we use our technique in 41 program family releases, and more than 51 thousand commits of 8 program families. We find 7 and 20 syntax errors in releases and commits of program families, respectively. They are related not only to incomplete annotations, but also to complete ones. We submit 8 patches to fix errors that developers have not fixed yet, and they accept 75% of them. Our results reveal that the time developers need to fix the errors varies from days to years in family repositories. We detect errors even in releases of well-known and widely used program families, such as *Bash*, *CVS* and *Vim*. We also classify the syntax errors into 6 different categories. This classification may guide developers to avoid them during development.

Categories and Subject Descriptors D.3.4 [*Programming Languages*]: Processors

Keywords Program Families, Preprocessors, Syntax Errors

1. Introduction

A program family is a set of programs whose commonality is so extensive that it is advantageous to study their common properties before analyzing individual members [1]. In this context, developers often use the C preprocessor to handle variability and implement these individual members [2]. The C preprocessor is a simple, effective, and language independent tool. However, despite their widespread use in practice, preprocessors suffer of several drawbacks, including no separation of concerns, which obfuscate the code and hampers understanding [3–5].

In particular, preprocessors also ease the introduction of subtle syntax errors [4, 6–8], like when we annotate an opening bracket without its correspondent closing one. Although this claim is pretty reasonable due to the problems that preprocessors may cause, we still lack studies to investigate preprocessor-based syntax errors and quantify to what extent they occur in practice. Notice that categorizing the syntax errors and investigating the way developers introduce them is important to aid developers on minimizing these errors during their development tasks, improving quality and reducing effort.

To formulate the theory that preprocessors cause syntax errors, we define a technique to identify preprocessor-based syntax errors in releases and commits of C program families. Our technique considers a syntax error as an incorrect output of the preprocessing task [9], i.e., it generates an invalid program according to the C grammar. To consider variability during our analysis, we rely on TypeChef, a variability-aware parser that checks all possible configurations of the source code [8].

To evaluate to what extent preprocessor-based syntax errors is a problem in practice, we use our technique to conduct a comprehensive empirical study. In particular, we answer research questions related to the occurrence of syntax errors in releases and commits, whether the errors arise in valid configurations, how developers introduce the syntax errors, the time developers need to fix the errors, the percentage of commits with errors, and if we can classify the syntax errors in type categories.

To answer our research questions, we analyze releases of 41 C program families and more than 51 thousand commits of 8 families. We select these families inspired by previous work [7, 10, 11]. Besides, the majority of families are well-known and used in industrial practice. In this context, however, notice that analyzing many families with thousands of commits seems unfeasible, since it is a time consuming task. Our technique minimizes this problem sufficiently to enable us to analyze several program families while still providing reasonable results.

Our study reveals that preprocessor-based syntax errors are not common in family releases. We roughly conclude the same when considering commits. In particular, we find 33 preprocessor-based syntax errors, out of which only 24 happen in valid configurations. To conclude that 9 errors arise in invalid configurations, we rely on answers—from e-mail and bug reports—of the actual program families developers. Further, we detect that developers introduce syntax errors mainly by changing existing code and adding preprocessor directives, for example, to support a different operating system. Regarding the time that developers need to fix the errors, we detect that it varies from days to years. Moreover, we identify some errors that developers took more than five years to fix, and some errors still not fixed. So, we submit patches with suggestions to fix the errors, and developers accept 6 and reject 2 patches.

Also, we observe that the percentage of commits with syntax errors vary significantly as well. We find files that contain errors only in 0.43% of commits. In contrast, we also find files that contain errors in all commits. Last but not least, we categorize the 24 syntax errors we find into six types of errors. The results reveal that the majority of syntax errors occur because of ill-formed constructions,

GPCE '13, October 27–28, 2013, Indianapolis, Indiana, USA.
Copyright © 2013 ACM 978-1-4503-2373-4/13/10...$15.00.
http://dx.doi.org/10.1145/2517208.2517221

e.g., an `else` without its correspondent `if` statement, and missing brackets. In summary, the main contributions of this paper are:

- We perform an empirical study using 41 C program families and more than 51 thousands commits to quantify and better understand preprocessor-based syntax errors;

- We classify preprocessor-based syntax errors and study the way developers introduce them;

- We present a technique that makes feasible the task of analyzing the syntax of several program families.

We organize the remainder of this paper as follows. In Section 2, we show a real example of preprocessor-based syntax error that motivates our study. Then, in Section 3, we describe our technique to find preprocessor-based syntax errors. Afterwards, we present the empirical study settings in Section 4, and discuss the results in Section 5. Last, we present the related work in Section 6 and the concluding remarks in Section 7.

2. Motivating Example

Developers often use preprocessors to handle variability in C program families. For instance, *libpng*[1] is a program family implementing the official PNG reference library. Figure 1 presents part of the *libpng* program family related to progressive display style, which is useful to read images from the network. Figure 1 contains a preprocessor macro that implements a progressive display style, i.e., `PNG_READ_INTERLACING_SUPPORTED`. The macro uses the interlacing method, which is responsible for encoding a bitmap image. During the download process, we can already see a copy of the whole image despite the incompleteness. It is useful for transmitting images over slow communication links.

```
 1. // Other includes..
 2. #include <fenv.h>
 3. // Other function definitions..
 4. static void progressive_row(png_structp ppIn, png_bytep new_row){
 5.     // Code Here..
 6.     if (new_row != NULL) {
 7.         // Code Here..
 8.         if (y >= dp->h)
 9.             png_error(pp, "invalid y to progressive row callback");
10.         row = store_image_row(dp->ps, pp, 0, y);
11. #ifdef PNG_READ_INTERLACING_SUPPORTED
12.         if (dp->do_interlace){
13.             // Code Here..
14.         } else
15.             png_progressive_combine_row(pp, row, new_row);
16.     } else if (dp->interlace_type == PNG_INTERLACE_ADAM7)
17.         png_error(pp, "missing row in progressive de-interlacing");
18. #endif
19. }
20. // More function definitions..
```

Figure 1. Code snippet of *libpng* with a syntax error when we do not define macro `PNG_READ_INTERLACING_SUPPORTED`.

Developers of C program families like *libpng* use existing compilers, such as *GCC* and *clang*. However, these compilers do not have a good support to check whether all configurations contain syntax errors. For example, preprocessing Figure 1 without `PNG_READ_INTERLACING_SUPPORTED` generates an invalid program according to the C grammar. It contains a preprocessor-based syntax error since it opens the `if` statement block at line 6, but it does not close at line 16. The error presented in Figure 1 we find in release 1.5.14 of *libpng*, which contains 360 preprocessor macros. If there is no forbidden configuration, we might have 2^{360} possible configurations, where 50% of them contain the preprocessor-based syntax error we discuss here. We report this error by submitting a patch to *libpng* developers, and they accepted and fixed the error. To identify this error, developers have to check each configuration

individually to detect this error using the existing compilers. However, it is unfeasible in several cases due to the high number of possible configurations. Developers need a better tool support to detect such kinds of errors. In this context, there are some variability-aware parsers to detect preprocessor-based syntax errors in C program families [8, 12] to help developers.

Previous studies [4, 6–8, 10] refer to syntax errors similar to the one we describe in Figure 1. However, they do not provide a comprehensive study to better understand to what extent these errors happen in practice, if they happen in valid configurations, or even if we can classify syntax errors into type categories. In this paper, we present a technique to find preprocessor-based syntax errors in program families (Section 3) and an empirical study to answer research questions on this topic (Sections 4 and 5).

3. A Technique to Find Preprocessor-Based Syntax Errors

In this section, we present a technique to identify syntax errors in program families. To parse the program families and check all configurations, we use the TypeChef variability-aware parser [8]. Without a variability-aware parser, we need to check each configuration separately, which is unviable for program families with many configurations. To better explain our technique, we refer to Figure 2, and detail its four steps in what follows.

The goal of the first step is to enable us to analyze several program families. In this step, our technique excludes all external libraries from the program family by eliminating `#include` directives. Notice that we still consider the header files of the program families, but exclude the external ones. For example, the C file depicted by Figure 1 includes the *fenv.h* library, which is not available in standard C compilers and it is not part of the program family code. In addition, the program families use specific external dependencies for different operating systems, e.g., we cannot use a package-building mechanism from a *Linux* system to install the external *windows.h* library. Because finding and downloading the correct library version is a manual and time consuming task, considering these external libraries would hind our analysis. In this way, we only focus on the program family code.

By excluding `#include` directives, Step 1 may leave some types and macros undefined in the program family. We generate stubs using C/C++ Development Tooling (CDT) with the default configuration to replace the original types and macros. Then, we create a `stubs.h` file to contain these stubs (Step 2) and now TypeChef is able to parse the source code. We use the CDT parser to generate an Abstract Syntax Tree (AST) for each source code file. Then, we navigate through the AST, get the types and macros that CDT identifies, and add them to the `stubs.h` file. We include this file into the program family source code.

Step 3 generates a shell script that calls TypeChef for each source code file. We built an Eclipse *plug-in* that automates Steps 1-3. Finally, we run the script our technique generates in Step 4. When TypeChef reports an error, we perform a manual check to verify whether the error is related to preprocessors. After fixing the error, we may continue to analyze the program family, i.e., depending on the error, we add a missing bracket, or remove an additional comma, and so on. This way, TypeChef continues to analyze the file. In case of a preprocessor-based syntax error, we create an error report with information like the *problematic configuration*[2] and code snippet with the syntax error.

We use our technique to analyze *Git* and *Mercurial* software repositories. For each set of files of a given commit in the reposi-

---

[1] http://www.libpng.org

---

[2] By problematic configuration we mean a valid configuration, according to the feature model constraints, that contains a syntax error.

Figure 2. A technique to identify preprocessor-based syntax errors in program families.

tory, we apply the technique to find preprocessor-based syntax errors. In the first commit of a given program family, we analyze all files. In the following commits, we only consider the updated and added files. In this way, we avoid the overhead of analyzing files that have not changed. We use the *Git* and *Mercurial* diff tools to identify the changed files. Figure 3 depicts this process.

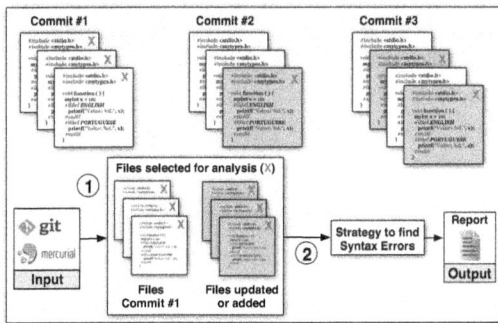

Figure 3. Analyzing software repositories using our technique.

It is important to mention that our technique may generate false positives and negatives. For example, CDT may not identify all types and macros. Additionally, external libraries defining macros may influence the program family code. Finally, our commits retrieval may miss to detect updates to a file that affect other files. Section 5.4 discusses these topics in details.

4. Study settings

In this section, we present the settings of our empirical study to investigate syntax errors. Our study considers 41 C program families and more than 51 thousand commits. To better structure our study, we use the Goal, Question, Metrics approach [13].

4.1 Definition

The goal of this empirical study is to analyze program families for the purpose of evaluation with respect to verifying the presence of preprocessor-based syntax errors in the context of the C language. In particular, this study addresses the following research questions:

- **Question 1.** Do program families releases contain preprocessor-based syntax errors?

- **Question 2.** Do commits to the program families repositories contain preprocessor-based syntax errors?

- **Question 3.** Do preprocessor-based syntax errors arise in valid configurations?

- **Question 4.** How do program families developers introduce the preprocessor-based syntax errors?

- **Question 5.** For how long a preprocessor-based syntax error remains in commits of a particular source file?

- **Question 6.** What is the percentage of commits with preprocessor-based syntax errors for each file?

- **Question 7.** What are the types of preprocessor-based syntax errors we find in practice?

To answer Questions 1 and 2, we count the number of syntax errors in releases and the number of syntax errors in commits for each family we analyze. To answer Question 3, we analyze each syntax error to verify whether it arises in a valid configuration. In this question, we consider feedbacks from the actual developers.

In Question 4, we investigate each syntax error to identify how developers introduce it. For instance, we investigate whether developers introduce the syntax error in a new source file, or in an existing one by altering a function code, and so on. Here we also detect whether developers add or remove preprocessor directives.

Regarding Question 5, we analyze two metrics: Date of Commit that Fixes the syntax Error ($DCFE$) and Date of Commit that Introduces the syntax Error ($DCIE$). Now we can measure the time in-between, the Time to Fix the syntax Error:

$$TFE = DCFE - DCIE$$

To better explain it, we refer to Figure 4 that depicts these metrics. In this context, *developer 2* introduces a syntax error in file `example.c` on June 02, 2013 (commit #2). Then, *developer 1* fixes this error on June 10, 2013 (commit #4). Thus, $TFE = 8$ days.

To answer Question 6, we measure the Percentage of Commits with syntax Errors (PCE) for each source file. We compute this metric in the following way:

$$PCE\,(file) = \frac{Number\,of\,Commits\,with\,Errors\,(file)}{Total\,Number\,of\,Commits\,(file)}$$

This way, we count the number of updates with errors in a particular file and the total number of commits that changes the specific file. For instance, as we show in Figure 4, we have one update in `example.c` with the syntax error (commit #2), and developers update this file four times (commits #1, #2, #4 and #5). Thus, PCE (`example.c`) $= 1/4 = 25\%$.

Regarding Question 7, we classify all errors. For example, Section 2 illustrates a syntax error in which developers incorrectly annotate an `else if` statement. A similar error appears in other program families. We classify them into a type of error (category).

4.2 Planning

Next, we describe the subjects and the instrumentation of our study.

4.2.1 Subjects Selection

We analyze 41 program families written in C ranging from 2,681 to 1,536,979 lines of code. These families are from different domains, such as operating systems, web servers, text editors, games, and databases. We select these program families inspired by previous work [4, 6, 7]. We also randomly select program families that run on different operating systems and use the C preprocessor from Source Forge.[3] We present the details of each family in Table 1.

4.2.2 Instrumentation

We use the technique presented in Section 3 to investigate syntax errors. We use TypeChef version 0.3.3 to parse all possible config-

---

[3] http://sourceforge.net/

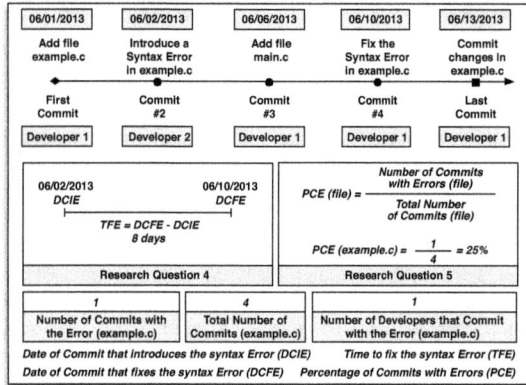

Figure 4. Scenario illustrating commits timeline and how we compute our metrics.

urations and CDT version 8.1.2 to create the stubs. Further, to automatize our technique, we use Eclipse Classic 4.2.2 to implement and run a *plug-in* to analyze the program families. We use Terminal version 2.3 on Mac OS X to run the scripts. We also count the number of lines of code and the number of files of each program family using the Count Lines of Code tool version 1.56, which eliminates blank lines and comments. Finally, we use *Git* version 1.7.12.4 and *Mercurial* version 2.5.4 tools to identify changes in files and get information about program families repositories.

4.3 Operation

We execute the empirical study on a MacBook Pro 2.4GHz dual-core Intel Core i5 8GB, running Mac OS X 10.8 Mountain Lion. As a first part of our analysis, we execute our technique to find syntax errors in releases of all 41 C program families we consider in this study. The analysis of all releases considers 9,064 files and almost 4 Million Lines of Code (MLOC). Then, we investigate syntax errors in commits. However, performing this analysis in all families is a very time consuming task, since the fourth step of our technique is semi-automatic. This way, we decide to analyze the commits only on the families we identify syntax errors in their releases. If some program family does not have *Git* or *Mercurial* repositories, we select another one. To perform this selection, we consider well-known families that several people use, and receive a considerable support from the open source community. During the analysis of the repositories, we consider only the trunk, i.e., we do not analyze the individual branches.

Next, we interpret and discuss the results of this empirical study to investigate preprocessor-based syntax errors.

5. Results and Discussion

In this section, we answer the research questions (Section 5.1), examine the directives that cause the syntax errors (Section 5.2), discuss the patches we submit (Section 5.3), and present the threats to validity (Section 5.4). The artifacts necessary to execute this empirical study are available at the project's web site.[4]

5.1 Research Questions

Next we answer and discuss the research questions.

---

[4] http://www.dsc.ufcg.edu.br/~spg/gpce2013/

5.1.1 Do program families releases contain preprocessor-based syntax errors?

Usually developers make a release available after code reviews and testing activities to minimize errors and improve quality. Nevertheless, our results reveal that preprocessor-based syntax errors still occur in releases. We find 14 syntax errors in 7 program families: *Bash* (2), *CVS* (1), *libpng* (1), *libssh* (4), *Vim* (3), *Xfig* (1), and *XTerm* (2). See more details in Table 1.

Next, we discuss some reasons that may lead to the syntax errors. Firstly, existing C compilers like *GCC* and *clang* are not variability aware. Developers identify syntax errors only when compile the program family using the problematic configuration. So, these errors may be difficult to detect using existing compilers.

Moreover, programs containing preprocessors are difficult to read and understand [3, 4, 6–8]. For example, the error we describe in Section 2 has been fixed immediately after our patch submission. In this case, it seems that the *libpng* developers did not fix the error earlier because they had not identified it during their maintenance tasks. On the other hand, although developers can identify the error earlier, they may decide to fix it later, setting this fixing task as low priority. For example, the syntax error may happen in a not deliverable configuration (consequently not exercised by the compilers), meaning that it is not important at least for now. However, notice that the error can still hamper reading and understanding activities.

5.1.2 Do commits to the program families repositories contain preprocessor-based syntax errors?

To perform the study in repositories, we select four out of seven program families in which we find errors in releases (see Section 5.1.1): *Bash, libpng, libssh, Vim*. We do not select all seven because we do not find the *git* or *mercurial* repositories of three of them. To increase the number of repositories to analyze, we also consider other four program families in which we do not find syntax errors in their releases: *Apache, libxml2, Dia*, and *Gnuplot*.

We analyze 51,035 commits and identify 27 preprocessor-based syntax errors, out of which 8 syntax errors also belong to releases. We find syntax errors in all repositories we analyze. Table 2 presents the commits results, indicating the number of developers that submitted commits, total number of commits for each program family, date of the first commit, date of the last commit, and total number of syntax errors.

Not surprisingly, here we find more errors than in releases, since the source code in commits is still under development. Nevertheless, our results reveal that preprocessor-based syntax errors are not common in the repositories we analyze. We identify in total 33 distinct preprocessor-based syntax errors in releases and commits as we can see in Figure 5.

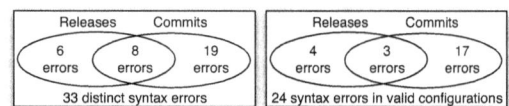

Figure 5. Syntax errors in releases and commits.

5.1.3 Do preprocessor-based syntax errors arise in valid configurations?

In this section, we analyze whether the errors we find in commits and releases happen in valid configurations. To answer this question, we rely on answers of the actual developers of each family we analyze. We get feedback via email and bug track systems.

We find 33 distinct preprocessor-based syntax errors in releases and commits, out of which 24 errors arise in valid configurations (72%) as we can see in Figure 5. In releases, we find 14 syntax

Table 1. Subject Characterization and Number of Syntax Errors in Releases

Family	Version	Application Domain	LOC	Number of Files	Syntax Errors	Errors in Valid Configurations
apache	2.4.3	web server	144,768	362		
atlantis	0.0.2.1	operating system	2,681	103		
bash	4.2	command language interpreter	44,824	138	2	2
bc	1.03	calculator	5,177	27		
berkeley	4.7.25	database system	185,111	580		
bison	2	parser generator	24,325	129		
cherokee	1.2.101	web server	63,109	346		
clamav	0.97.6	antivirus	107,548	377		
cvs	1.11.21	version control system	76,125	236	1	1
dia	0.97.2	diagramming software	28,074	132		
expat	2.1.0	XML library	17,103	54		
flex	2.5.37	lexical analyzer	16,501	41		
fvwm	2.4.15	windows manager	102,301	270		
gawk	3.1.4	GAWK interpreter	43,070	140		
ghostscript	9.05	postscript interpreter	1,536,979	3,230		
gnuchess	5.06	chess player	9,293	37		
gnuplot	4.6.1	plotting tool	79,557	152		
gzip	1.2.4	file compressor	5,809	36		
irssi	0.8.15	IRC client	51,356	308		
kin db	0.5	database system	64,120	119		
libieee	0.2.11	IEEE standards for VHDL library	5,323	27		
libdsmcc	0.6	DVB library	5,453	30		
libpng	1.6.0	PNG library	44,828	61	1	1
libsoup	2.41.1	SOUP library	40,061	178		
libssh	0.5.3	SSH library	28,015	125	4	
libxml2	2.9.0	XML library	234,934	162		
lighttpd	1.4.30	web server	38,847	132		
lua	5.2.1	programming language	14,503	59		
lynx	2.8.7	web browser	80,334	117		
m4	1.4.4	macro expander	10,469	26		
mpsolve	2.2	mathematical software	10,278	41		
mptris	1.9	game	4,988	29		
prc-tools	2.3	C/C++ library for palm OS	14,371	142		
privoxy	3.0.19	proxy server	29,021	67		
sendmail	8.14.6	mail transfer agent	91,288	243		
sqlite	3.7.15.2	database system	94,113	134		
sylpheed	3.3.0	e-mail client	83,528	218		
rcs	5.7	revision control system	11,916	28		
vim	7.3	text editor	288,654	178	3	2
xfig	3.2.4	vector graphics editor	70,493	192	1	1
xterm	2.4.3	terminal emulator	50,830	58	2	2
Total			3,860,078	9,064	14	9

Table 2. General Information about the Program Families Repositories

Project Name	Total Number of Developers	Total Number of Commits	First Commit	Last Commit	Syntax Errors	Errors from valid Configurations
apache	108	24,719	Jul-3-1996	May-3-2013	3	3
bash	2	68	Aug-26-1996	Mar-7-2013	2	2
dia	217	5,397	Jan-3-1997	May-5-2013	2	2
gnuplot	16	7,611	Apr-15-1998	May-6-2013	5	5
libpng	5	2,179	Jul-20-1995	Apr-25-2013	2	2
libssh	26	2,569	Jul-5-2005	Apr-5-2013	7	2
libxml2	169	4,179	Jul-24-1998	May-9-2013	2	2
vim	2	4,313	Jun-13-2004	May-4-2013	4	2
Total		51,035			27	20

errors, out of which 7 errors (50%) happen in valid configurations. We find 27 syntax errors in commits, out of which 20 (74%) arise in valid configurations. Tables 1 and 2 summarize the results.

We identify 9 syntax errors in *invalid configurations*[5] of *libssh* (5), *Vim* (2), and *XTerm* (2). Figure 6 illustrates part of a function of *libssh*. If we do not define macros HAVE_LIBGCRYPT and HAVE_LIBCRYPTO, our technique identifies a function with no signature in this configuration. However, it is not valid according to the developers. The *libssh* building process checks that these macros are alternative and we must define exactly one of them. Similar problems happen in the *Vim* program family. Some macros (FEAT_GUI_W32, FEAT_GUI_MOTIF, and FEAT_GUI_GTK) are alternative as well and we must define exactly one of them.

```
1. #ifdef (HAVE_LIBGCRYPT)
2.     static void dsa_public_to_string(gcry_sexp_t key, BUFFER *buffer){
3. #elif defined (HAVE_LIBCRYPTO)
4.     static void dsa_public_to_string(DSA *key, BUFFER *buffer){
5. #endif
6.         // Code Here..
7. }
```

Figure 6. Syntax error in *libssh* family in an invalid configuration.

As another example, Figure 7 illustrates a code snippet of *XTerm*. Notice that configuration __GLIBC__ and USE_ISPTS_FLAG does not open the if statement bracket at line 5, but it closes the bracket at line 14. However, according to the *XTerm* developers, this configuration is invalid. They use USE_ISPTS_FLAG to handle macro ISC (long obsolete), which predated __GLIBC__.

Despite happening in invalid scenarios, we argue that this situation makes the task of understanding and maintaining the code cumbersome. It can confuse developers unaware of particular configuration constraints and lead them to wrongly suppose that there is a syntax error in valid configurations.

5.1.4 How do program families developers introduce the preprocessor-based syntax errors?

In this section, we investigate how developers introduce 20 preprocessor-based syntax errors in commits that happen in valid configurations. We identify four categories:

1. *Changing existing code and adding preprocessor directives:* developers modify existing syntactical units by changing tokens. In addition, they introduce new preprocessor macros, for example, to support different operating systems;

2. *Changing existing code and removing directives:* developers change existing syntactical units by changing tokens. Further, they remove preprocessor macros;

3. *Changing existing code without adding or removing preprocessor directives:* developers modify existing syntactical units by only changing tokens;

4. *Adding completely new code:* developers introduce new code, e.g., adding new syntactical units, functions, and files.

In our study, developers introduce more syntax errors when changing existing code and adding preprocessor directives. In this category, they introduce 7 errors (35%). Further, developers introduce 5 errors (25%) when modifying code without adding or removing preprocessor directives. Finally, they introduce 2 errors (10%) when adding completely new code, and 1 error (5%) when changing code and removing directives. Developers may introduce more errors when changing code because preprocessor directives

---

[5] By invalid configuration we mean that it is not valid according to the feature model constraints.

make the tasks of reading and understanding the source code more difficult [3, 4].

We could not classify 5 errors (25%), since we find these errors in the very first commit available for analysis. So, we miss information. For instance, if developers migrated the program family from one repository to the current one, our analysis does not consider the information with respect to the former repository.

```
1. #ifdef __GLIBC__
2.     // Code Here..
3. #else
4.     #if defined (USE_ISPTS_FLAG)
5.         if (result) {
6.     #endif
7.     result = ((*pty = open("/dev/ptmx", O_RDWR)) < 0);
8. #endif
9.     // Code Here..
10. #if defined (SVR4) || defined (__SCO__) || defined (USE_ISPTS_FLAG)
11.     if (!result)
12.         strcpy(ttydev, ptsname(*pty));
13.     #ifdef USE_ISPTS_FLAG
14.         }
15.     #endif
16.     // Code Here..
17. #endif
18.     // Code Here..
```

Figure 7. Syntax error in an invalid configuration of *XTerm*.

5.1.5 For how long a preprocessor-based syntax error remains in commits of a particular source file?

In this section, we investigate the time required to fix errors in valid configurations. In our study, the time developers need to fix the errors varies from days to years. For example, developers fixed the *Vim* error in file ex_cmds2.c in a few days after introducing it. In contrast, developers took more than 5 years to fix the error in parser.c of *Gnuplot*. Table 3 depicts each syntax error we find during the analysis of commits, indicating the file name that contains the error, the date of the first commit containing the error, the date of commit that fixes the error, and time to fix the error.

There are some reasons why developers may take a long time to fix these errors. As described before, this might happen because developers do not identify the errors. They may not use variability-aware parsers or may have difficulties when reading and understanding preprocessor-based code. On the other hand, even if they find an error, they might take some time to fix it, since the error may arise in not exercised or deliverable configurations, leading developers to set lower priority to these errors when compared to semantic ones, for example.

In our study, we do not find a correlation between the file size—see Column "*Lines of Code (LOC)*"—and the time developers need to fix the errors (we remove errors developers have not fixed). There are some syntax errors in files with thousands lines of code fixed in two days, such as the file xpath.c in *libxml2*. On the other hand, we also find the opposite: errors in smaller files like parser.c (468 LOC) in *Gnuplot* fixed after more than 5 years.

Finally, we do not find a correlation between the time to fix errors and the number of developers that commit a file with syntax error (we also remove errors developers have not fixed). Table 3 indicates the number of developers that commit a file with syntax error (see column "*Developers*"). For instance, 13 different developers committed 77 times the file mod_include.c containing a syntax error in *Apache*. They took almost a year to fix the error. As another example, we also find an error in os_unix.c (*Vim*) that still needs fixing, in spite of 131 commits in 9 years. Only two developers committed this file. Nevertheless, it is important to note that our study cannot conclude if the developers were aware of these syntax errors before fixing them.

Table 3. Results of the Analysis of Commits per Syntax Error (only in valid configurations)

Project Name	File Name	Lines of Code (LOC)	Date of Commit that Introduce the Error	Date of Commit that Fix the Error	Time to Fix the Error (TFE) in days	Total Number of Commits	Number of Commits with the Error	Number of Developers that Commit with the Error	Percentage of Commits with Errors (PCE)	Directive Type
apache	ssl_util_ssl.c	365	Jun-28-2001	Apr-2-2002	278	62	15	4	24.19%	Complete
apache	ab.c	751	Abr-24-2000	May-16-2000	22	222	4	1	1.80%	Complete
apache	mod_include.c	2105	Oct-16-2000	Set-10-2001	329	353	77	13	21.81%	Complete
bash	getcppsyms.c	401	Aug-26-1996	Dec-23-1996	119	1	1	1	100%	Complete
bash	execute_cmd.c	2578	Jul-27-2004	Not Fixed	-	23	12	2	52.17%	Incomplete
dia	app_procs.c	429	Sep-3-2001	Nov-1-2001	59	232	1	1	0.43%	Complete
dia	preferences.c	645	Sep-3-2001	Sep-23-2002	385	100	10	5	10%	Incomplete
gnuplot	plot.c	450	Apr-15-1998	Sep-22-1998	160	180	5	1	2.78%	Incomplete
gnuplot	util.c	505	Jun-2-1999	Jun-9-1999	7	123	2	1	1.63%	Incomplete
gnuplot	parse.c	468	Apr-15-1998	Jul-22-2003	1924	89	27	3	30.34%	Complete
gnuplot	graph3d.c	2211	Oct-21-2002	Jan-7-2003	78	293	3	2	1.02%	Incomplete
gnuplot	datafile.c	3662	Feb-23-2008	Apr-13-2009	414	268	34	1	12.69%	Incomplete
libpng	pngtest.c	1198	Mar-14-2001	May-14-2001	0	1204	8	1	0.66%	Incomplete
libpng	pngtrans.c	186	May-16-1997	Jan-30-1998	259	738	4	1	0.54%	Incomplete
libssh	server.c	910	Jul-5-2005	Jul-5-2005	0	173	1	1	0.58%	Complete
libssh	channels.c	715	Jun-12-2008	Jun-16-2008	4	229	1	1	0.44%	Complete
libxml2	xmlregexp.c	2790	Apr-20-2002	Sep-17-2002	150	98	3	1	3.06%	Complete
libxml2	xpath.c	7659	Apr-18-2004	Apr-20-2004	2	370	2	1	0.54%	Complete
vim	ex_cmds2.c	3088	Jan-19-2010	Jan-19-2010	0	99	2	1	2.02%	Incomplete
vim	os_unix.c	4520	Jun-13-2004	Not Fixed	-	131	131	2	100%	Incomplete

5.1.6 What is the percentage of commits with preprocessor-based syntax errors for each file?

In this section, we analyze the percentage of commits with preprocessor-based syntax errors for each file. We only consider errors in valid configurations. As can be seen, the percentage of commits with errors also varies significantly, from 0.43% to 100% (see column *"Percentage of Commits with Errors"* (PCE) in Table 3). For instance, *Dia* developers committed the app_procs.c file 232 times but only once with the syntax error ($PCE = 0.43\%$).

We also identify two syntax errors that developers have not fixed, e.g., in os_unix.c (*Vim*), and execute_cmd.c (*Bash*). Regarding the syntax error in *Vim*, we find it in all commits (100%) with the specific file, totaling 131 commits. It may arise only in configurations that users do not use in practice. It is probably the reason why developers did not fix it yet. Regarding the syntax error in *Bash*, we find it in 57 commits (52.17%). However, this syntax error may not be affecting the users of *Bash* as well, since it is in the repository since 2004. This way, *Bash* and *Vim* developers may not be worried about these syntax errors despite the fact that they arise in valid configurations.

We do not observe correlation between PCE and LOC, TFE, or the number of developers (again, we remove the errors not fixed yet). Nevertheless, our results suggest a tendency that with few commits, developers fix the errors.

5.1.7 What are the types of preprocessor-based syntax errors we find in practice?

In this section, we categorize the preprocessor-based syntax errors we find in valid configurations in our study. We classify them in 6 types: missing/additional array separator, ill-formed construction, missing bracket, missing logical operator, missing parenthesis, and missing semicolon. Our results reveal that the types of errors ill-formed construction and missing bracket are the most common ones. We present the number of errors of each type in Table 4.

We find two errors in the missing/additional array separator type. For example, Figure 8 illustrates a syntax error of the *Gnuplot*

Table 4. Syntax Errors for each type.

Type of error	Number of Occurrences	Percentage
Array Separator	2	8.33%
Ill-Formed Construction	7	29.16%
Missing Bracket	6	25%
Missing Logical Operator	2	8.33%
Missing Parentheses	4	16.66%
Missing Semicolon	3	12.5%

family. This code snippet generates an invalid C program when we have EAM_OBJECTS and !WITH_IMAGE. In this configuration, we have two array separators, one at line 3 and another at line 9.

```
1. df_bin_default_columns default_style_cols[LAST_PLOT_STYLE + 1] = {
2.     // other elements here
3.     {HISTOGRAMS, 1, 0},
4. #ifdef WITH_IMAGE
5.     {IMAGE, 1, 2},
6.     {RGBIMAGE, 3, 2}
7. #endif
8. #ifdef EAM_OBJECTS
9.     , {CIRCLES, 2, 1}
10. #endif
11. };
```

Figure 8. Code snippet of *Gnuplot* with a syntax error when we define EAM_OBJECTS and !WITH_IMAGE.

We also find some syntax errors related to ill-formed construction type. The code snippet in Figure 9 generates an invalid C program when we have START_RSH_WITH_POPEN_RW and !SHUTDOWN_SERVER in *CVS*. In this configuration, we introduce an else if without its corresponding if.

Regarding the missing bracket type, we present an example of *libpng* in Section 2. In this example, we show a directive that causes a syntax error, i.e., a missing bracket, when we do not define PNG_READ_INTERLACING_SUPPORTED. We find 6 errors of this type. Figure 10 depicts an error we find in *Vim*, where we classify as missing logical operator type. In this example, if we define WIN32, an error arises, since there is a missing logical operator at line 4.

```
1.  // Code here..
2.  #ifdef (SHUTDOWN_SERVER)
3.     if (current_parsed_root->method != server_method)
4.  #endif
5.  #ifndef (NO_SOCKET_TO_FD)
6.     {
7.        if (S_ISSOCK (s.st_mode))
8.           shutdown (fileno (bc->fp), 0);
9.     }
10. #endif
11. #ifdef (START_RSH_WITH_POPEN_RW)
12.    else if (pclose (bc->fp) == EOF){
13.       error (1, errno, "closing connection to %s");
14.       closefp = 0;
15.    }
16. #endif
17. // Code continues here..
```

Figure 9. Code snippet of *CVS* with a syntax error when we define START_RSH_WITH_POPEN_RW and !SHUTDOWN_SERVER.

```
1.  // More code here..
2.  int fd_tmp = mch_open(filename, O_RDONLY
3.  #ifdef WIN32
4.     O_BINARY | O_NOINHERIT
5.  #endif
6.     , 0);
7.  // Code continues here..
```

Figure 10. Code snippet of *Vim* with a syntax error at line 4 when we define WIN32.

Next, we present in Figure 11 a syntax error in *Apache* of the missing opening parentheses type. In this example, there is a syntax error when we define SSL_EXPERIMENTAL_PROXY. There is a missing opening parentheses at the if statement condition.

```
1.  #ifdef SSL_EXPERIMENTAL_PROXY
2.  // More code here..
3.  if (apr_dir_open(&dir, pathname, sp)) != APR_SUCCESS) {
4.     apr_pool_destroy(sp);
5.     return FALSE;
6.  }
7.  // Code continues here..
8.  #endif
```

Figure 11. Code snippet of *Apache* with a syntax error at line 3 when we define SSL_EXPERIMENTAL_PROXY.

Finally, Figure 12 presents another syntax error in *Apache* of the missing semicolon type. We find a syntax error at line 8 in configurations defining NOT_ASCII. In this case, developers do not include a semicolon at the end of line 8.

```
1.  // More code here..
2.  #ifdef NOT_ASCII
3.     status = ap_xlate_open(&to_ascii, "ISO8859-1", cntxt);
4.     if (status) {
5.        fprintf(stderr, "ap_xlate_open(to ASCII)->%d\n", status);
6.        exit(1);
7.     }
8.     status = ap_xlate_open(&from_ascii, "ISO8859-1", cntxt)
9.     if (status) {
10.       fprintf(stderr, "ap_xlate_open(from ASCII)->%d\n", status);
11.       exit(1);
12.    }
13. #endif
14. // Code continues here..
```

Figure 12. Code snippet of *Apache* with a syntax error at line 8 when we define NOT_ASCII.

Notice that making developers aware of these types might be useful to avoid these errors. For example, when defining optional array elements, they can pay more attention to either not add unnecessary or miss separators. So, they may avoid the code constructions related to these types.

5.2 Verifying the Type of the Preprocessor Directives that causes the Syntax Errors

The C preprocessor is expressive enough so that we can encompass any code snippet. Developers can annotate part or a complete syntactical unit using preprocessor directives. For example, the if

statement in Figure 11 represents a complete annotation, since the preprocessor completely encompasses the statement. As another example, Figure 10 presents the #ifdef directive that separates the parameters of the mch_open function call. In this case, it is an incomplete annotation [6].

In our study, we find 24 distinct errors in valid configurations in commits and releases (we find 3 common errors in both analyses). We observe that 10 syntax errors (41.67%) are related to complete annotations, and 14 to incomplete ones (58.33%). Table 3 details these results considering commits and valid configurations. Regarding only the commits results, 10 errors (50%) happen in incomplete annotations. On the other hand, we have 7 errors in releases, out of which 6 (85.71%) happen in incomplete annotations.

In this context, related approaches [3, 4, 6, 7] suggest that the use of incomplete annotations may be more error prone. Although this hypothesis seems reasonable due to difficulties of reading and understanding incomplete annotations, we find that 41.67% of the syntax errors occur in complete annotations.

5.3 Submitting Patches to Fix the Syntax Errors

We submit 8 patches—for each syntax error not fixed—to 6 families: *Bash* (1), *CVS* (1), *libpng* (1), *libssh* (2), *Vim* (2), and *Xfig* (1). In each patch, we also suggest how to fix the error. To the best of our knowledge, *Xfig* and *Vim* do not use bug track systems, so we submit patches to these families via email. Regarding patches to the other 4 families, we submit them via bug track systems.

We consider that developers accept a patch when they mention that it is an error by email, or keep the patch open after updating information like its priority. On the other hand, we consider that developers reject the patch when they mention it is not an error by email, or update this information on the patch. Thus, developers accepted 6 out of 8 patches. We present information about the patches we submit in Table 5, illustrating the family name, the file name with the error, and the patches status and priority.

Two out of six patches accepted have been set as low priority because the errors happen in invalid configurations. Figure 6 illustrates one of them. To fix it, we suggest to add an #else directive followed by the #error directive, making the source code explicit regarding the definition of exactly one of the macros. Next, we quote one of the *libssh* developers in response to our suggestion:

> *"Yes, we could add an error in this case. But the configure step takes care of making sure either libcrypto or libgcrypt is available."*

Notice that the *libssh* developers accepted our patch even occurring in invalid configurations. Therefore, it seems that it is worthwhile to change the source code so it becomes more readable and understandable regarding configuration constraints. The second patch of *libssh* is in the same file (keys.c), and it is very similar to the one we present in Figure 6.

We submit a patch to *libpng* and developers fixed the error immediately after our patch submission (see Section 2). Regarding two patches we submit to *Bash* and *CVS*, developers accepted and the patches are still with the open status and normal priority. Developers accepted another patch to *Vim* as well, but they set no priority explicitly since we submit patches to *Vim* via email.

Vim developers rejected one patch by just arguing that it arises in an invalid configuration. Developers rejected a patch we submit to the *Xfig* program family as well. In this case, developers mention they do not use (at least for now) the erroneous macro we identify. According to the following quotation, it seems that the macro will be used when they decide to distribute the *Xfig* manual in Japanese. So, we still count this as an error, since it may arise in the future.

Table 5. Patches we submit to Program Families.

Family	File	Configuration	Status	Priority
bash	execute_cmd.c	valid	open	normal
cvs	buffer.c	valid	open	normal
libpng	pngvalid.c	valid	fixed	normal
libssh	keys.c	invalid	new	low
libssh	keys.c	invalid	new	low
vim	os_unix.c	valid	open	-
vim	if_mzsch.c	invalid	not a bug	-
xfig	w_cmdpanel.c	valid	not a bug	-

5.4 Threats to Validity

Construct Validity. It refers to whether the preprocessor-based syntax errors we find are indeed errors in valid configurations. We minimize this threat by getting feedback from the actual developers. They accepted 6 out of the 8 syntax errors we report.

Internal Validity. Our technique excludes `#include` directives to eliminate external libraries in order to scale. However, notice that we may face false negatives due to the exclusion of these `#include` directives, which makes our technique unsound. In some cases, the external libraries can introduce additional code through macro definitions that may cause preprocessor-based syntax errors into the family source code. In this context, our technique may miss some syntax errors. Moreover, our technique may yield false positives due to types and macros that the CDT parser does not identify, i.e., these types and macros may not be included in our `stubs.h` file. So, we add the type or macro manually, which is an error-prone task. Still, in our study, our technique found 33 syntax errors in 26.83% of the program families we analyze. Moreover, we detect that 24 out of 33 syntax errors arise in valid configurations.

Our technique analyzes only updated and added files in software repositories from the second to the last commit, as described in Section 3. However, this approach may lead to false negatives. For instance, developers may update a macro definition in a file A, which leads to errors in a different file B. In our approach, because only A has been modified, we only analyze A. However, later, if developers modify B, our technique may catch the syntax error. Further, we may miss some syntax errors during the analysis of the repositories since we analyze only the trunk, i.e., branches may contain syntax errors as well.

Finally, the last step of our technique is semi-automatic, which is an error prone activity. However, it is important to be semi-automatic. For example, due to several C standards such as ANSI C, C99, and C11, TypeChef might not parse some C constructions, arising false positives easily recognizable by humans.

External Validity. We analyze 41 releases of different domains, sizes, and different number of developers. Moreover, we analyze more than 51 thousands commits of 8 families from small to mid sizes. We select well-known and active C families used in industrial practice. The families communities exist for years and seem very active: there are commits in 2013. In this way, we alleviate this threat. However, the small number of errors we identify makes it hard to apply inference statistics. Thus, the results are initial measurements and we should not use them to any direct comparison.

6. Related Work

Analysis of C Preprocessor Usage. Some approaches studied the way developers use the C preprocessor in practice. Liebig et al. [7] analyzed 40 program families, and suggested that developers can introduce subtle syntax errors, for example, by annotating a closing bracket but not the opening one. They define this kind of annotation as *undisciplined*. According to their study, undisciplined annotations correspond to 15.6% of the total number of annotations. Undisciplined annotations are similar to incomplete annotations [6, 14, 15] we use in this paper. In our work, we found 24 syntax errors related to undisciplined and disciplined annotations.

Baxter and Mehlich proposed DMS, a source-code transformation tool for C and C++ [16]. In a more recent work, these authors used DMS and emphasized the problem of using unstructured annotations [3], similar to incomplete annotations as well. Further, the authors presented an example with a syntax error related to the missing bracket error type we discuss here. In our work, we perform an empirical study investigating the presence of syntax errors in program families different from their approach.

Ernst et al. [4] presented an empirical study on how the C preprocessor is used in practice. They analyzed 26 packages comprising 1.4 MLOC. They found that most C preprocessor usage follows simple patterns. It also discussed about the undisciplined use of the C preprocessor and its problems, such as that it makes the program more difficult to understand. However, it focused mainly on macro definitions using `#define` directives. In this sense, our work complements the analysis of using the C preprocessor and presents findings about problems related to syntax errors in practice.

Others approaches also complemented these studies providing more information about the preprocessor usage. In a previous work, Ribeiro et al. [11] analyzed how often methods with preprocessor directives contain feature dependencies. Liebig et al. [10] proposed and collected some metrics to analyze the feature code scattering and tangling when using preprocessor directives. They analyzed 40 families implemented in C. However, none of them investigated the presence of syntax errors in C program families.

Variability-Aware Parsers. There are some strategies to parse C code with preprocessor directives. Some approaches [6, 17, 18] applied the strategy of preprocessing or modifying the code before parsing it. However, this strategy is not interesting to analyze variability since we lose information about the preprocessor directives.

Kästner et al. [8] proposed a variability-aware parser, i.e., a parser that analyze all possible configurations of a C program at once. In addition, it performs type checking analysis [19, 20]. In our work, we use TypeChef to identify errors in C program families.

Gazzillo and Grimm [12] proposed a variability-aware parser called SuperC. This parser is faster than TypeChef, but it does not perform type checking analysis. Since SuperC does not recognize some C constructions of different standards, we did not use it in our work. It does not parse some families that we use in this study.

Extracting Variability Information. Others proposed techniques to extract variability information from C program families. Some researches considered the Linux kernel in their studies and analyzed its source code files, Kconfig files, and Makefiles [21–23]. Other researches analyzed the rapid evolution of the Linux configurations. The number of features had doubled in the period analyzed [24]. She et al. [25] analyzed different operating systems, such as FreeBSD and eCos. In our work, we decide to contact the developers of the program families to check configuration constraints. This way, we avoid the effort of gathering information about configuration constraints for each family.

Tartler et al. [26] revealed the presence of zombie configurations, i.e., macros that cannot be either enabled or disabled at all, in the Linux kernel. Besides, others researches found several inconsistencies in the Linux kernel by analyzing source files, Kconfig and makefiles [27, 28]. In our work, we focused only on syntax errors in source code files and their presence in valid configurations. To the best of our knowledge, there is no existing work that investigated the impact of syntax errors in many C program families.

7. Concluding Remarks

In this paper, we presented an empirical study to investigate preprocessor-based syntax errors in C program families. Firstly, we defined a technique to identify syntax errors. Then, we analyzed 41 C program families and more than 51 thousands commits to answer our research questions. In summary, we found 24 distinct syntax errors (7 syntax errors in releases and 20 errors in commits). Moreover, we detected 9 errors that arise only in invalid configurations.

The results showed that preprocessor-based syntax errors are not common in practice. Furthermore, the results revealed that developers introduce syntax errors mainly by modifying existing code and adding preprocessor directives, e.g., adding new directives to support other operating systems. We detected that the time developers need to fix syntax errors varies from days to years. In this context, we could not find correlation with the LOC of the file that contains the error, or even with the number of developers modifying that particular file. The percentage of commits with syntax errors varies as well. We found files in which 0.43% of the commits with them contain the syntax error, but also files that contain the syntax error in all commits. Regarding the types of errors, we identified that we can categorize the syntax errors we found in 6 different types. We presented them using real code snippets of the program families we consider in this study. Finally, our empirical study presented findings that may be helpful to actual program families developers minimize the problem of syntax errors in practice.

Acknowledgments

We gratefully thank Christian Kästner for helpful comments. This work was partially supported by the National Institute of Science and Technology for Software Engineering (INES), funded by CNPq grants 573964/2008-4 and 480160/2011-2.

References

[1] D. Parnas, "On the design and development of program families," *IEEE Transactions on Software Engineering*, vol. 2, pp. 1–9, 1976.

[2] H. Spencer, "Ifdef considered harmful, or portability experience with C news," in *USENIX Annual Technical Conference*, pp. 185–197, 1992.

[3] I. Baxter and M. Mehlich, "Preprocessor conditional removal by simple partial evaluation," in *Proceedings of the Working Conference on Reverse Engineering*, WCRE '01, pp. 281–290, IEEE Computer Society, 2001.

[4] M. Ernst, G. Badros, and D. Notkin, "An empirical analysis of C preprocessor use," *IEEE Transactions on Software Engineering*, vol. 28, pp. 1146–1170, 2002.

[5] C. Kästner and S. Apel, "Virtual separation of concerns – a second chance for preprocessors," *Journal of Object Technology (JOT)*, vol. 8, no. 6, 2009.

[6] A. Garrido and R. Johnson, "Analyzing multiple configurations of a C program," in *Proceedings of the 21st IEEE International Conference on Software Maintenance*, ICSM '05, pp. 379–388, IEEE Computer Society, 2005.

[7] J. Liebig, C. Kästner, and S. Apel, "Analyzing the discipline of preprocessor annotations in 30 million lines of C code," in *Proceedings of the 10th Aspect-Oriented Software Development*, AOSD '11, pp. 191–202, ACM, 2011.

[8] C. Kästner, P. Giarrusso, T. Rendel, S. Erdweg, K. Ostermann, and T. Berger, "Variability-aware parsing in the presence of lexical macros and conditional compilation," in *Proceedings of the 26th ACM SIGPLAN Object-Oriented Programming Systems Languages and Applications*, OOPSLA '11, ACM, 2011.

[9] IEEE, "Standard Glossary of Software Engineering Terminology," *IEEE Std 610.12-1990*, pp. 1–84, 1990.

[10] J. Liebig, S. Apel, C. Lengauer, C. Kästner, and M. Schulze, "An analysis of the variability in forty preprocessor-based software product lines," in *Proceedings of the 32nd International Conference on Software Engineering*, ICSE '10, pp. 105–114, ACM, 2010.

[11] M. Ribeiro, F. Queiroz, P. Borba, T. Tolêdo, C. Brabrand, and S. Soares, "On the impact of feature dependencies when maintaining preprocessor-based software product lines," in *Proceedings of the 10th Generative Programming and Component Engineering*, GPCE '11, pp. 23–32, ACM, 2011.

[12] P. Gazzillo and R. Grimm, "SuperC: parsing all of C by taming the preprocessor," in *Proceedings of the 33rd Programming Language Design and Implementation*, PLDI '12, pp. 323–334, ACM, 2012.

[13] V. Basili, G. Caldiera, and D. H. Rombach, "The goal question metric approach," in *Encyclopedia of Software Engineering*, Wiley, 1994.

[14] A. Garrido and R. Johnson, "Challenges of refactoring C programs," in *Proceedings of the International Workshop on Principles of Software Evolution*, IWPSE '02, pp. 6–14, 2002.

[15] A. Garrido and R. Johnson, "Refactoring C with conditional compilation," in *Proceedings of the 18th Automated Software Engineering*, ASE '03, pp. 323–326, IEEE Computer Society, 2003.

[16] I. Baxter, "Design maintenance systems," *Communication of the ACM*, vol. 35, no. 4, pp. 73–89, 1992.

[17] S. Somé and T. Lethbridge, "Parsing minimization when extracting information from code in the presence of conditional," in *Proceedings of the International Workshop on Program Comprehension*, IWPC '98, pp. 118–125, 1998.

[18] Y. Padioleau, "Parsing C/C++ code without pre-processing," in *Compiler Construction*, vol. 5501 of *Lecture Notes in Computer Science*, pp. 109–125, Springer Berlin Heidelberg, 2009.

[19] A. Kenner, C. Kästner, S. Haase, and T. Leich, "Typechef: toward type checking #ifdef variability in C," in *Proceedings of the 2nd Feature-Oriented Software Development*, FOSD '10, pp. 25–32, ACM, 2010.

[20] C. Kästner, S. Apel, T. Thüm, and G. Saake, "Type checking annotation-based product lines," *ACM Transactions on Software Engineering and Methodology*, vol. 21, pp. 14:1–14:39, July 2012.

[21] J. Sincero, R. Tartler, D. Lohmann, and W. Schröder-Preikschat, "Efficient extraction and analysis of preprocessor-based variability," in *Proceedings of the 9th Generative Programming and Component Engineering*, GPCE '10, pp. 23–32, ACM, 2010.

[22] N. Andersen, K. Czarnecki, S. She, and A. Wasowski, "Efficient synthesis of feature models," in *Proceedings of the 16th Software Product-Line Conference*, SPLC '12, pp. 106–115, ACM, 2012.

[23] C. Dietrich, R. Tartler, W. Schröder-Preikschat, and D. Lohmann, "A robust approach for variability extraction from the linux build system," in *Proceedings of the 16th Software Product-Line Conference*, SPLC '12, pp. 21–30, ACM, 2012.

[24] R. Lotufo, S. She, T. Berger, K. Czarnecki, and A. Wasowski, "Evolution of the linux kernel variability model," in *Proceedings of the 14th Software Product-Line Conference*, SPLC '10, pp. 136–150, Springer-Verlag, 2010.

[25] S. She, R. Lotufo, T. Berger, A. Wasowski, and K. Czarnecki, "Reverse engineering feature models," in *Proceedings of the 33rd International Conference on Software Engineering*, ICSE '11, pp. 461–470, ACM, 2011.

[26] R. Tartler, J. Sincero, W. Schröder-Preikschat, and D. Lohmann, "Dead or alive: finding zombie features in the linux kernel," in *Proceedings of the 1st Feature-Oriented Software Development*, FOSD '09, pp. 81–86, 2009.

[27] R. Tartler, D. Lohmann, J. Sincero, and W. Schröder-Preikschat, "Feature consistency in compile-time-configurable system software: facing the linux 10,000 feature problem," in *Proceedings of the 6th Computer Systems*, pp. 47–60, ACM, 2011.

[28] R. Tartler, J. Sincero, C. Dietrich, W. Schröder-Preikschat, and D. Lohmann, "Revealing and repairing configuration inconsistencies in large-scale system software," *International Journal on Software Tools for Technology Transfer*, vol. 14, no. 5, pp. 531–551, 2012.

Using Document-Oriented GUIs in Dynamic Software Product Lines

Dean Kramer, Samia Oussena,
Peter Komisarczuk

School of Computing and Technology
University of West London, United Kingdom
{dean.kramer,samia.oussena,peter.komisarczuk}@uwl.ac.uk

Tony Clark

School of Engineering and Information Sciences
Middlesex University, United Kingdom
t.n.clark@mdx.ac.uk

Abstract

Dynamic Software Product Line (DSPL) Engineering has gained interest through its promise of being able to unify software adaptation whereby software adaptation can be realised at compile time and runtime. While previous work has enabled program logic adaptation by the use of language extensions and platform support, little attention has been placed on Graphical User Interface (GUI) variability. Different design patterns including the Model View Controller are commonly used in GUI implementation, with GUI documents being used for declaring the GUI. To handle dynamic GUI variability currently, the developer needs to implement GUI refinements using multiple techniques. This paper proposes a solution for dealing with GUI document variability, statically and dynamically, in a unified way. In our approach, we currently use a compile time method for producing GUI variants, and code transformations to handle these variants within the application at runtime. To avoid GUI duplicates, only GUI variants that are unique, and related to a valid product configuration, are produced. To validate our approach, we implemented tool support to enable this for Android based applications.

Categories and Subject Descriptors D.2.2 [*Software Engineering*]: Design Tools and Techniques—User interfaces; D.2.9 [*Software Engineering*]: Management—software configuration management

Keywords Graphical User Interfaces; Dynamic Software Product Lines

1. Introduction

Smart phones in recent years have seen high proliferation, allowing more users to stay productive while away from the desktop. This proliferation has seen the increasing amount of mobile applications being developed and becoming available to consumers through centralised application repositories. It has become highly predictable for these devices to have an array of sensors including GPS, accelerometers, digital compass, proximity sensors, sound etc. Using

these sensors with other equipment already found in phones, a wide set of contextual information can be acquired.

This contextual information can be used in Context-Aware Self Adaptive (CASA) software. This software can monitor different contextual parameters and dynamically adapt at runtime to satisfy the user's current needs [17]. These behavioural variations can be seen to share similarities with features in Software Product Lines (SPL), where product commonality and variability is handled, providing higher asset reuse. Within SPLs, Feature-Oriented Software Development (FOSD) has emerged as a method for modularising the features of a system [8]. The one fundamental difference between these two concepts is that while SPLs conventionally manage static variability which is handled at compile time, adaptive software requires dynamic variability to be handled at runtime.

Dynamic Software Product Lines (DSPL) enables the SPL to be reconfigurable at runtime [22]. By using DSPLs, variability can be static, adapted at compile time, or dynamic and adapted at runtime. This allows for greater reuse as variability can be implemented for both static and dynamic adaptation, as different products may require the adaptation to be applied at different times [28]. Previous work has enabled the program logic adaptation to be handled at runtime, but there is little known how to handle Graphical User Interface (GUI) variability statically or dynamically.

Using GUI documents in GUI development is becoming more widespread, with their use in many development platforms. Using GUI documents, GUIs are implemented in a declarative fashion outside of the application code. While previous DSPLs approaches have been prominently centred around support for logic adaptation [19, 29, 35], they mostly centre around the use of single language situations. However, little attention has been paid to using GUI documents in static, and dynamic adaptation. The problem we wish to consider is how GUI adaptation, be it static, and dynamic, can be written using GUI documents. This paper seeks to address the issue and presents an approach to handle both, static and dynamic, variabilities of GUI documents.

In the proposed approach, the unified adaptation principles of previous DSPL work are followed, where the developer has the ability to use a single code base, and choose at a later stage when the adaptation should be applied. To test our approach, we implemented a solution for use with DSPL applications deployed on the Android platform.

The remainder of this paper is structured as follows: Background to the area, along with a motivating scenario application is presented in Section 2. In Section 3, we propose our approach on dealing with static and dynamic variability of GUI documents, with details of tool support implemented to validate the approach. Next, we evaluate and discuss the limitations of our approach in Section 4. Later in Section 5, we discuss related work in the fields

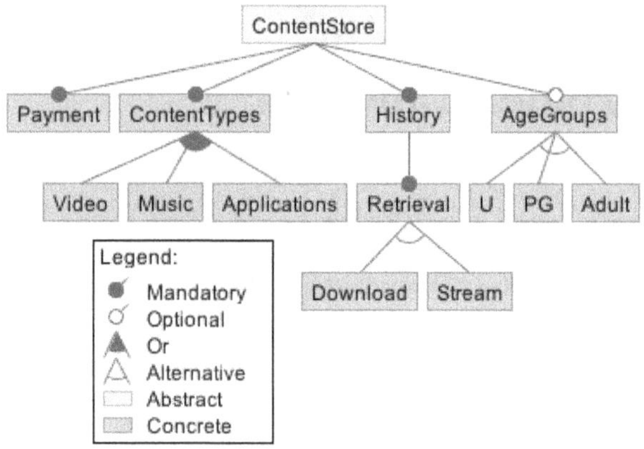

Figure 1. Scenario Application

Figure 2. Variability of the main screen

of DSPLs, GUIs in SPLs, and Adaptive User Interfaces. Finally, our paper is concluded in Section 6.

2. Background

When using SPLs, variability and commonality are expressed in terms of *features*. A feature of an SPL has been defined as *"a prominent or distinctive user-visible aspect, quality, or characteristic of a software system or systems"* [23]. Features can be implemented in feature modules, incrementing software functionality [33], by extending the base functionality of a program with additional logic.

Functionality in terms of program logic may not be the only crosscutting software artefact in an SPL. Just like specific business logic may be associated with a given feature, so too can be GUIs or GUI refinements [31]. By handling GUI variability within features, greater reuse can be achieved with this type of artefact. Variability in the GUI can be a number of differences. Examples of this include specific widgets needed for particular features. Therefore, if a feature is not included in a product, that widget/GUI element is not needed. Other variability can be found in widget property differences, including colour differences, size, text styles etc. This variability can be expressed in the feature model in different ways, whether its explicitly with specific feature trees for each GUI [39], more implicitly by features of the system that can cross cut many GUI screens, or a combination of both [30].

Unlike conventional SPLs, DSPLs can reconfigure at runtime, driven by context changes. Context can be described as *"information that can be used to characterise the situation of an entity. An entity is a person, place, or object that is considered relevant to the interaction between a user and an application, including the user and applications themselves"* [1]. On reconfiguration, the running application is altered by the addition and removal of program logic. Additionally the GUI may need to be altered to suit the new configuration.

2.1 Scenario

To illustrate our motivation, consider a DSPL example of a content store application for a mobile device. This application may provide different content for the user including applications, movies, music etc. Different content is organised into different categories. A simplified feature model of the DSPL can be seen in Figure 1. This application provides content for different age groups, and also the application can be tailored to suit these different groups.

In the feature model, we can see that the features *Payment, ContentTypes, History,* and *Retrieval* are required in every configuration

of this DSPL. The *Payment* feature handles all payment transactions when content is bought or rented. The *ContentTypes* feature contains the different components for browsing, and buying different types of content. Because different regions in the world may require different content distribution licenses, it may not be possible to sell content in every region, so depending on the location of the user, different content type features including *Video, Music,* and *Applications* will be bound or unbound. In the *History* feature, all bought content is found, which can be retrieved in *Retrieval*. There are two primary methods in which content can be retrieved, downloaded or streamed. Certain content including video maybe downloaded or streamed. Depending on how much storage is available on the device, it may be not be possible to download the movie, so only the *Streaming* feature is bound. In Figure 2, we can see the variability of the screen according to content type features. If you consider the video feature, there is a button that takes the user to a set of screens for video content, and also a containership of widgets for advertising popular movies.

2.2 GUIs as Documents

Historically, GUIs have been described and implemented within code. Different elements of the GUI including visual properties and controls are created using program statements. This approach requires programming knowledge from the developer creating the GUI.

Within recent years, we have seen the emergence of GUI representation being implemented using documents instead of code [18]. Using this approach, GUI representation is implemented in a more declarative fashion, commonly in markup based languages [25]. GUI documents are often used in conjunction with different UI design patterns for example the Model-View-Controller (MVC) [26]. When using these patterns, the GUI documents are used as a method of implementing the View. Examples of these languages includes Mozilla XUL, QML used in QT, Microsoft XAML, Apple XNib, and Android XMLBlock. While there are differences in capabilities across these implementations, all essential share the ability to declare the layout of different GUI screens in terms of GUI elements/widgets, and their positions. Once the document has been created, it is normally referenced within the main application code, and at runtime, the document is interpreted.

By using a document-oriented approach, there are many advantages discussed in [18] including separation of concerns, compatibility, editibility, non-universality and abstraction. Also, with many development platforms, *What You See Is What You Get* (WYSIWYG) editors are included for the GUI documents, allowing developers to preview their GUI without the need for compilation and testing.

For illustration, we show an excerpt of a GUI document used for the main menu screen of the content application for Android shown in Figure 3. This GUI can be seen to having a number of widgets including buttons and containership widgets used for aiding layout in the window. The XML node type refers to the widget type, with widget properties e.g. size, text, background contained within the XML node attributes. Widget containerships are handled by all contained widgets being placed as child XML nodes of their parent. As we see in the feature model, different content types can be offered in the store, and depending what content types can be provided in a given product variant, certain buttons and advertisements should be visible to the user.

```
1   <FrameLayout
2          android:id="@+id/mainFrame"
3          android:layout_width="match_parent"
4          android:fitsSystemWindows="true"
5          .....>
6          ....
7          <Button
8              android:id="@+id/applications"
9              android:layout_width="160dp"
10             android:text="@string/apps"
11             android:background="@drawable/apps"/>
12  <LinearLayout
13         android:id="@+id/adverts"
14         ....>
15         <TextView
16             android:id="@+id/appAdsTitle"
17             android:text="@string/PopularFreeAppss"/>
18             ...
19  </LinearLayout>
20  </FrameLayout>
```

Figure 3. A excerpt of a GUI document for the main screen in Android

3. Static and Dynamic Support

Using prior DSPL approaches, to handle dynamic GUI variability, the developer would have to implement the GUI within the program host language. Using this approach, the developer can not use GUI documents for both static and dynamic variability. This either leads a developer to either use different implementation for static and dynamic, or they choose not to use GUI documents at all. In our approach, we consider how static and dynamic support can be reached while using GUI documents to implement GUIs. It is our goal to support a single code base for GUI variability using GUI documents.

3.1 Document Refinement

Variability in the GUI documents is implemented via document refinements. Refinements of a document can include GUI widget addition, but also additions or alterations in widget properties, for example colour, and size. These refinements are implemented using physical separation of concerns, whereby each refinement is contained within its own file. Refinements are then held together within a feature module. A feature module can be seen a folder designed to contain assets for a given feature in the SPL. By having

GUI documents also kept in feature modules, we can ensure feature cohesion, keeping all feature specific assets together.

Using the scenario application introduced in the previous section, let us consider the video feature. In this feature, for the main screen, a button that leads to that content type needs to be added, and also a relevant suggestion container, which can container several suggested videos for the particular user, shown in Figure 4. For the refinement, the parent nodes of the refinement must be stated, using a unique identifier, in the case of android GUIs, `android:id`. The other properties of the parent nodes are not required, unless a refinement or override is being used.

```
1   <FrameLayout
2          android:id="@+id/mainFrame">
3          <LinearLayout
4              android:id="@+id/mainlayout">
5              <LinearLayout
6                  android:id="@+id/contenttypes">
7                  <Button
8                      android:id="@+id/videos"
9                      android:layout_width="160dp"
10                     android:text="@string/videos" />
11             </LinearLayout>
12         </LinearLayout>
13  <LinearLayout
14         android:id="@+id/adverts">
15         <LinearLayout
16             android:id=@+id/videoAd
17             ....>
18             <TextView
19                 android:id="@+id/TopMovies"
20                 android:text="@string/TopMovies"
21                 ..../>
22         </LinearLayout>
23  </LinearLayout>
24  </LinearLayout>
25  </FrameLayout>
```

Figure 4. Video Refinement

3.2 Static Variability

Static variability of the GUI is handled using the principles of *superimposition*. Superimposition has been a successful feature composition technique in many different approaches [2–5, 8]. By superimposing a GUI refinement on top of an existing GUI document, we can generate a GUI document in a stepwise fashion. To superimpose GUI documents, we consider GUIs conceptually as trees. In Figure 5, we try to illustrate how the trees are superimposed, producing a composite tree. With the opening screen of the content store, various buttons are used for adverts and to specific content types e.g. video, music etc. As we introduced in the Section 2.1, because of different distribution rights, not all content types may be accessible in every country of use. We handle this change by adding the buttons designed to take the user to that specific content. While superimposition has been acknowledged as not being a silver bullet, it has also been applied to other non programming languages including UML [2].

As there will be features that require binding at runtime based on certain contextual conditions, there can also be features that can be statically bound. An example of where this can be of use include the age group set of features in our scenario application. The content store can be derived to suit a different set of users. As part of a program variant designed for school devices, the GUI and functionality can be designed to suit that group of users. This variability may not need to be decided at runtime, and therefore can be statically bound. By combining static and dynamic feature binding, we can apply an approach used in FOP, whereby features are joined to create composite features, also known as dynamic binding units

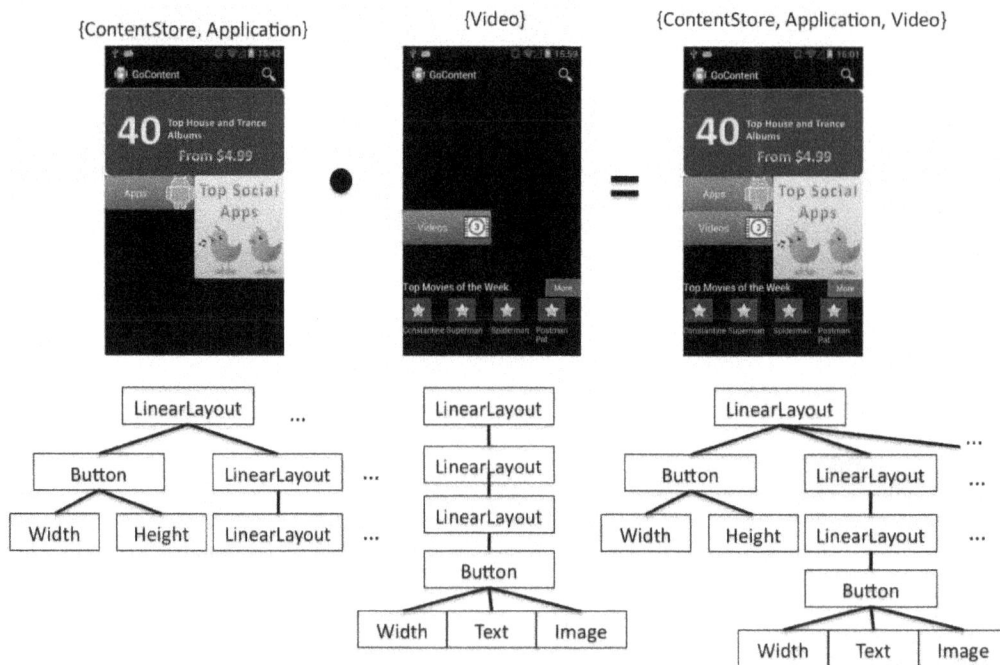

Figure 5. Composition of Home screen

[34]. Using dynamic binding units can be seen to follow a staged configuration [15], whereby product derivation is not carried out within a single step, but more over a number of steps, each specialising the product more. This staged configuration leads to a final feature model, which exhibits only dynamic variability needed by the system.

3.3 Dynamic Variability

As said before, GUI variability is not only a static issue, but can also be a dynamic issue. To handle this dynamic GUI variability in the GUI documents, there are two different times in which this can be carried out, dynamically at runtime, or at compile time.

For dynamic composition, after the deployed DSPL contains the base source and the source refinements. Then at runtime, the DSPL composes each of the sources when appropriate. To dynamically compose GUI documents at runtime, all composition tools need to be integrated with the main DSPL meta-program. While mobile device processing power is increasing, runtime composition is not ideal due to a number of reasons. Firstly, mobile devices run on battery power, which can be drained far faster if the processor is stressed more. Secondly, it is common that GUI documents are preprocessed to an internal format during application compilation, for example XMLBlock in Android, Nib in iOS, and QML in the QT Framework. Much of this can be attributed to performance optimising for faster parsing. Therefore, to handle runtime composition, pre-processing tools would also be needed to be included with the application. This can cause further storage overhead, and performance overhead, as these tools would need to run after composition.

Compile time composition on the other hand entails that all composition is carried out during the compilation of the application. Using this approach, all variations of the GUI documents are derived. Different variants are then chosen at runtime, depending on the configuration of the DSPL. This then helps reduce the need for composing and preprocessing the source files at runtime.

3.3.1 Variant Generation

Based on the feature model that is to be deployed with the DSPL, all GUI variants are generated. To do this, it is not simply enough to compute every possible valid configuration of the feature model and compose the GUI variants based on this. This is because its more likely that a refinement for every GUI will not be present in every feature. So, by generating every valid configuration and compose a GUI document based on that, it is likely we will produce duplicate documents, whereby the content is actually identical. This can be prevented by using the algorithm proposed below. In this algorithm, firstly, we get all GUI refinements (line 1). This is handled by tracing the feature modules in the feature order. A two way mapping between GUI documents and the features that refine them is created. Then for every GUI document (line 2), all refinement combinations for that particular document are generated (line 3). This can be carried out using a simple combination algorithm against a list of values, in this case, feature names.

Not only should GUI documents be unique in content, but they should only be generated if that needed feature configuration is satisfiable with the feature model. Each combination is checked for feature satisfiability (line 4). To do this, we start by creating a new configuration with the combination as the initially selected features (line 5). Following that, all related features are propagated

Algorithm 1 Generate all GUI variant configurations

Input: A set of relative ordered *Features*
1: $Guis \leftarrow$ GETALLGUIREFINEMENTS(Features)
2: **foreach** Gui in $Guis$ **do**
3:     $combinations \leftarrow$ GETREFINEMENTCOMBINATIONS(Gui)
4:     **foreach** $comb$ in $combinations$ **do**
5:         $config \leftarrow$ NEWCONFIGURATION(comb)
6:         $config.propagateFeatures()$
7:         $valid \leftarrow config.isValid()$
8:         **if** valid **then**
9:             ADDCONFIGURATION($Gui, Config$)
10:         **end if**
11:     **end foreach**
12: **end foreach**

(line 6). By feature propagation, we mean selecting features that are related either by the tree structure itself, or due to inter-tree constraints between features. Examples of these include feature parents if they are not selected, or selecting/deselecting a feature because of a feature model constraint. After this, the configuration is then analysed by a SAT solver in order to check its satisfiability against the feature model (line 7). This can be carried out using existing approaches for mapping a configuration to a SAT problem [9], and then checked using a standard off-the-shelf SAT solver like SAT4J [1]. Only if the configuration is evaluated to be valid, is it then added to a list of feature combinations to be composed for a given GUI document.

Just like cross-cutting features in programming languages, two or more features can interact, in a derivative. These derivatives are handled in the variant generation process, much the same way as any other feature. Derivative features are handled during configuration propagation, so that any derivatives needed in a configuration are added to that refinement combination before composition.

After each valid configuration for a given GUI document is created, that configuration is composed using the same approach used for composition of static variability. The variants that generated from this composition are then named by the document name, and variant number, needed for the runtime variant management, discussed next.

Finally, GUI documents that are contained within a feature module, but contain no variability, are simply copied over. Examples of theses documents include the document for displaying video titles in the video advertisements, found in the *Video* feature. Each video advertised has a set layout including a picture of the movie, and its name. This document is used at runtime to be dynamically added to the advertisement section, and therefore not referenced in the main GUI document. Business logic for adding instances of this layout for each movie advert can be implemented within the main source code refinements.

3.3.2 Code Generation and Transformation

In addition to variant generation, variant management code is generated to handle at runtime which GUI document variants should be used. Within this class, for every GUI document there are two data structures, one containing a list of the features that refines each GUI document, and a map containing the given feature combinations and their variants. When a document is requested, the correct variant is returned by comparing the currently selected features with the feature combinations found within the GUI documents variant map. After a match is found, that variant reference is returned to be used by the calling object. If a resource requested only has a single variant, then the original reference is returned.

[1] http://www.sat4j.org/

Code transformation is then carried out on each controller class. Because the management class can handle all GUI resources, managed, and not managed, a simple transformation can be carried out on every class making specific method calls. For Android, two method calls including `setContentView`, and `inflate` take the GUI document as a parameter. The `inflate` method reads the GUI documents and returns a GUI tree which can be then be applied to the current GUI visible to the user. Whereas, `setContentView` can be seen to both inflate the GUI document, and then set the currently visible GUI to that inflated GUI tree. It is therefore these method calls that require the current GUI document variant. If these specific method calls are found within any class or class refinement, we can simply alter the parameter to instead get the variant from the management class, as shown in Figure 6. These refinements can then be developed using existing adaptation approaches for example dynamic binding FOP langauges like FeatureC++ [33] and rbFeatures [21], Context Oriented Programming (COP) languages [40], or SOA approaches [29].

```
1   //Original Implementation of onCreate() method
2   @Override
3   protected void onCreate(Bundle savedInstanceState) {
4         super.onCreate(savedInstanceState);
5         setContentView(R.layout.activity_main);
6   }
7
8   //Implementation after transformation
9   DSPLResourceGetter dsplrg = (DSPLApp)getApplicationContext().
10        getDSPLRG();
11
12  @Override
13  protected void onCreate(Bundle savedInstanceState) {
14    super.onCreate(savedInstanceState);
15    setContentView(dsplrg.getResourceVariant(
16        R.layout.activity_main));
17  }
```

Figure 6. Code transformation of an Android method

3.3.3 Runtime Behaviour

At runtime, depending on which features are bound, when a GUI document is needed, the correct variant needs to be chosen. For this the variant manager needs its list of bound features to be updated by the middleware when a feature binding change occurs. This list of active features can either be requested from the meta-program, or alternatively be updated by the meta-program automatically. When a feature binding change occurs, our middleware updates the list of active features within this management class either directly or using interprocess communication when used external to the application sandbox.

In Figure 7, we illustrate an example from the scenario application with the main screen. In this example, different contextual events (e) can be received by the main middleware that handles the main feature and configuration management. This can cause a change in what features are bound active in a system. After a valid feature reconfiguration has taken place, the middleware can update the currently bound business logic refinements, and also the list of actively bound features in the GUI document variant manager. Also, when a GUI document is needed by a class, in this case, the `MainScreen` class, a document is requested from the variant manager. Based on the currently bound features, the variant manager returns the correct document variant, which is then used by `MainScreen`.

3.4 Implementation

In the previous section, we have discussed an approach for which GUI document variability can be handled statically and dynami-

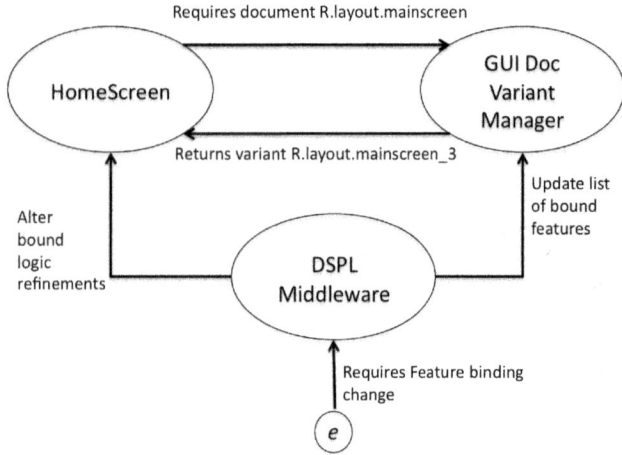

Figure 7. Graphical illustration of the runtime behaviour for the main screen

cally by variant generation at compile time, combined with code generation transformations can bring dynamic configuration of GUIs. To validate our approach, tool support was implemented on top of FeatureIDE [24] to handle DSPL applications for the Android platform. In this tool support, we implemented the component for variant generation, along with the code transformation component. Because of the extensive use of documents for use of different aspects of the application including menus, style etc, it is possible our approach can apply to those documents also. Checking configuration satisfiability is handled using the inbuilt configuration management tools of FeatureIDE.

Composition of the GUI documents is handled using *Feature-House*[2] [3]. FeatureHouse provides a language independent solution to software composition. When FeatureHouse composes a project, it creates a Feature Structure Tree (FST) model. Within a FST model, different FST nodes represent different elements of a given artefact, for example package imports, classes, and methods. There are specifically two types of nodes, *nonterminal*, the inner nodes of the tree with recursively further nodes and *terminal*, the leaves in the tree. These FSTs are then composed by superimposition, in a stepwise fashion. Because of the tree structure form of GUIs, it is straight forward to create FSTs of GUIs. Within the GUI, different GUI widgets and layout holders are nonterminal nodes, and each widget property is a terminal node. During composition, widget properties are either added, or replaced if a new property value is found.

3.4.1 Document Management

In Android, resources including GUI documents are referenced using static integer values that are within a generated class named R. For every handled GUI document by the manager, a generated method is added. Because GUI document are referenced using integers, we can delegate which method is required by use of a simple switch statement. This method does the variant lookup for a specific GUI document, by which it gets the list of active features that are known to refine that GUI document, and then do a map lookup. Only the active features that refine GUI document are used because as said earlier, it is possible to have duplicate variants for multiple configurations. This would require far more variants to configuration maps, which is unnecessary. By only storing configurations of features that actually refine a specific GUI document, and its variant, we can greatly reduce the overall map structure.

---
[2] https://github.com/deankramer/featurehouse

The document manager is retained within the *Application* class object. An Application class object is an application singleton that is created when the application starts, and is accessible in any application Activity. The compile-time tool checks if a class of type Application already exists. If one does not exist, an Application class is created with the code needed to instantiate the resource manager, as shown in Figure 8. Where an Application class already exists, the additional statements required for the manager instantiation are added. A DSPL management middleware has also been

```
 1  public class DSPLApp extends Application {
 2
 3      DSPLResourceGetter dsplrg;
 4
 5      @Override
 6      public void onCreate()
 7          super.onCreate()
 8          dspl = new DSPLResourceGetter();
 9          ...
10      }
11
12      public DSPLResourceGetter getdsplrg() {
13          return dsplrg;
14      }
15      .....
16
17  }
```

Figure 8. Generated Android Application Singleton

developed for handling feature selection at runtime. This middleware is designed to function as part of a DSPL application, or be used externally by many applications. When feature change for the application happens, the active feature list within the resource manager are updated either by Inter process communication when used externally, or by direct object alterations when used as part of the DSPL application.

While our implementation has been designed for the Android platform, it is possible that this approach could be applied to other types of GUI documents for different platforms using a modified implementation.

4. Discussion and Evaluation

Our goal is to bring support to handling static and dynamic variability of GUI documents, within a DSPL. In this section we discuss some of the limitations of our approach, and test our approach in terms of performance and storage consumption. While there are FOP extensions C++ [36] and Ruby [21], we are unaware of a FOP language extension of Java that enables runtime adaptation. Because of this reason, for controller and other source code refinements, we have used the Context-Oriented Programming (COP) language JCOP for dynamic adaptation [6]. COP share similar goals with FOP, but concentrate only with runtime adaptation [13]. Because our research concentration does not focus on dynamic composition of classes, only a basic implementation for test purposes has been created.

4.1 Limitations

While our approach proposes a solution to dealing with GUI variability at runtime, there are limitations to this solution. Currently, tackling these limitations is considered as future work.

4.1.1 Configuration Timing

Configuration timing is an important issue regarding GUI reconfiguration. Within the lifecycle of a GUI, there are two main phases in which a refinement could be applied, on *inflation* or while it is *active*. The inflation of a GUI can be regarded as when the GUI is being constructed during the transition from one screen to another. In contrast, the active phase of a GUI is while the screen or GUI is currently active and visible to the user.

Currently, GUI changes are only realised during the inflation of an interface. Changes in the GUI may be required after a GUI is displayed to the user. Work is currently being carried out to bring adaptation while a GUI is active. We can foresee that GUI document variants will be used, updating the current GUI tree based on new variant. This can be carried out by inflating the new variant and only adding or switching the widgets required in that refinement. Unlike completely recreating the GUI based on the new variant, this method should lead to a faster and less noticeable transition.

An issue surrounding active GUI changes includes handling of state. Other than static applications that do not handle dynamic data or data input, widget state is important to maintain during change. Examples of widget state include text entered by a user into a textfield, labels and images added from dynamic source etc. We believe this can tackled using code templates for each widget, which can be used to generate source code for copying the state between the old and new widget instances.

4.1.2 Composition

This work attempts to follow a unified feature-oriented approach for refining GUI documents and handle variants needed at runtime. The first limitation in composition is regarding widget ordering. When new widgets are added in a refinement, depending on their order within a layout widget, we can determine their position on the screen. While widget ordering can be handled using relative feature ordering within the feature model, it is currently not possible to place a widget before an already existing widget. This is not always a problem, particularly in situations where absolute position coordinates are used with widgets. Also, in some platforms, it is possible to have widget properties stating its position relative to other particular widgets, but this solution is not universal, and therefore a limitation. To alleviate this limitation, we believe a hooking mechanism is needed. This mechanism needs to allow for elements to be placed *before* or *after* other elements. This can be carried out by the use of special keywords in the refinements, along with the widget name in question. Adding this capability is currently being carried out.

The second composition limitation is regarding the need for view hierarchy retention in refinements. To compose two FSTs, FeatureHouse compares FSTNodes in both trees. For it to compose two FSTNodes, it needs to be aware of all of the parent nodes back to the root. The effect of this is normally not a problem with other languages supported in FeatureHouse because of the limited depth normally found in source code. This though may not always be true in GUI documents. Because of the potential complexities and view hierarchy depth in terms of View tree, its possible to have potentially deep FSTs. Ways of controlling a very deep View tree is by decomposing it into smaller trees, refining only the decomposed trees, and then, at runtime, compose the inflated views. This though can make it more difficult to be able to preview and develop a screen as a whole.

4.1.3 Artefact Inconsistencies

Using GUI documents helps provide separation of concerns by implementing the view external from the data, and business logic, normally using a MVC like pattern. This then means that there are multiple linked software artefacts. Because of this, it is important to make sure that no inconsistencies between the different elements occur. Examples of these errors include attempting to add an event listener to a non existent button, or even declaring an event listener that is not implemented within that controller. When implementing

the View in code, it is possible to have some form of static checking. When using GUI documents, this is not always possible, as many approaches mean the documents are interpreted at runtime, and therefore not statically checked. Within a SPL, it is possible that different features can refine different software artefacts, like the GUI documents, or the business logic within the controller/presenter classes. This can make it increasingly difficult to check the dependencies between each of the elements, and therefore problems can arise. To help find some of these inconsistencies, we suggest the following checks:

- Controller to View: This checks the consistency between view references made in the controller to the view. In this check, we attempt to ensure widgets referenced in controllers exist within the GUI document that is used.

- View to Controller: This checks the consistency between controller references made in the view to the controller. In this check, we attempt to ensure that, event handlers declared within the GUI documents are implemented within the controller.

If any check finds a potential issue, a warning to the developer should be present. It is possible that a developer has already considered these issues within their code. For this reason, we only place a warning, which can be ignored. Currently, a prototype implementation is considered future work. We are interested to see how feasible it is to run these checks over a project regarding performance, as one could understand such a task to be computationally intensive.

4.2 Performance and Storage Consumption

Because of the particular approach taken, one of the areas we wish to examine is *application bloat*. For our research, we describe application bloat as the amount of storage needed by repetitive code found in more than one GUI variant. To gain a sense of the size of the GUI documents, we consider both before preprocessing, and afterwards, where they would be part of a compiled application. To obtain the size of the preprocessed documents, we compile the Android application to an application APK ready for deployment, to which we then inspect the file contents of the application resources. Non preprocessed GUI documents were all reduced to a condensed format using a single line, thus avoiding discrepancies due to differences in XML tag formatting, and indentation. As a running example, here we consider how much bloat is found related to the Home screen GUI, shown earlier. In this example, we consider the age groups to be set static, and only content type to be dynamically variable, based on the location of the user. Because there are 3 refining "Or" features, *Applications, Music,* and *Video*, this equates to 7 variants of this GUI.

The size of each variant varies from 1.8 KB (2 KB when preprocessed), when only Applications or Music are bound, up to 3.2KB (3.3KB when preprocessed) when all 3 features are bound. This combined size can be considered the optimal amount of storage required for this variability. When considering that the size of all the variants is 17.6KB (18.7KB preprocessed), and the size of the base GUI document and the refinements are 4KB, we can assume there is 13.6KB of bloat. This means that of the space required to store those different variants, 77% of that space is actually repetitive source. While these results can appear as not very encouraging in terms of scale, we should put these sizes in perspective with the general size of mobile applications, which can be larger than several megabytes.

When considering runtime performance, there are two main areas that we can consider, resource manager initialisation, and GUI lookups. Resource management initialisation is carried out when the application starts, during which, the data structures containing the GUI variants are filled. How long this initialisation takes really depends on how many GUI documents are being managed, and how many variants are there of each GUI document being managed. The GUI lookup is purely the task of the GUI document reference being queried and looked up. To compare static selection of GUIs with the resource manager, we set up a micro-benchmark on a Samsung Nexus S running Android 4.2.1. When comparing lookup times from the resource manager to a purely static solution, we found it took on average 4ms longer for the manager. At least in this simple case, this is close to negligible regarding our target use. It is foreseeable that it will be slower if there are more features that it needs to check against, but we do not expect more GUI documents to affect speed considerably. This is because for each managed GUI, a separate lookup method is used. When a resource is requested, depending on which GUI type e.g. home screen, will determine which lookup method to use. Since GUI references on Android are stored as Integers, we can carry this out within a simple switch.

4.2.1 Scaling

Scaling within SPLs is a very important issue regarding any approach. Any approach that generates variations of artefacts should take into consideration the issue of scaling. There are some possible methods that can be adopted to help lower the amount of bloat when developing GUIs. Because the GUI is essentially a tree of different widgets and layout containers, GUI decomposition is possible. Decomposing a GUI essentially breaks a GUI document down in to multiple parts, that can be joined together at runtime. If much variability of a GUI is concentrated only on particular elements, this method can help lower bloat considerably. This is because there is less repetitive code across the GUI variants. To fully understand the effects of scaling on this approach to a more real life size, a case study in future will need to be carried out.

To summarise, while performance in our limit tests show that this approach is not a problem in terms of choosing the right GUI at runtime, it does show that storage could become an issue. This is particularly true if there is a lot of runtime variability across the GUI of an application. Due to the combinatory nature of this approach, it can be seen that the amount of bloat that can arise from this approach is not linear within regards to the number of features refining a GUI, but more exponential. While this is far from optimal, how limiting this is really depends on scenario in which this approach is being used.

4.2.2 Threat to Validity

Our largest threat to validity can be attributed to that only a limited test was carried out on a single GUI document in a synthetic application. This application was created as a synthesis of different types of variability that can exist in the GUI. Sizes in GUI documents can vary considerably depending on the complexity of what they represent, and the area of screen they associated with. We believe this GUI represented a GUI of medium complexity and size, when comparing to different GUI documents in open source Android applications. The feasibility of this approach largely depends on the amount of dynamic variation for each document, and their size.

5. Related Work

Research into adaptive, customisable GUIs is not a new field [7], and has been an interest for many years. Recent approaches proposed include [42]. In this work, a middleware is presented to support model-based UI design and reconfiguration. Depending on context on the device, a server sends an XML based presentation of the GUI, which is then displayed on the device. Other recent work include [10], an approach using executable models consisting of design information, runtime state, and execution logic. A implementation was proposed, which can build multimodel user interfaces for smart homes. In [37], the authors present a method of refactoring code to make existing GUIs adaptive. In their approach, the authors carry out a stepwise, incremental approach, and treat adaptive behaviour as a crosscutting concern. A toolkit for handling transparent GUI migration and adaptation was proposed by [20]. Their approach was designed to be used with the Mozart Programming System, based on the Oz language providing declarative, object oriented, and constraint programming. This approach requires a specialised virtual machine to be used, limiting its use to platforms that can run that virtual machine. Model-driven software engineering (MDSE) methods have also been popular for applying runtime GUI adaptations [14, 32]. These adaptations are applied using model-to-model transformations against GUI architectural models.

While these approaches propose different methods to GUI adaptation and customisation, they are not concerned with systematic software reuse that SPLs bring. Our research aims to handle these GUI cross-cutting concerns in a more modular way. Many also only deal with runtime adaptation, and fail to consider compile-time adaptation.

Other forms of adaptive GUIs include *Plastic User Interfaces* (PUI) [12]. This proposed framework was based on a model-based GUI approach, but designed to incorporate the ability to deal with context change. A tool to support reification was presented. In [41], it was proposed to use MDSE in to create PUIs. With this approach, a mapping meta-model is proposed, with mappings for specifying transformation specifications, and properties. While PUIs do consider both static and dynamic adaptation, PUIs are concerned predominately with usability preservation under different contexts. Variability in the GUI may not just include differences in layout, but may also include functionality differences. These methods also do not support families of products, which we attempt to tackle.

5.1 GUIs and SPLs

GUI research within the scope of SPLs has been limited. Some of first related work includes those of Schlee and Vanderdonckt using generative programming techniques with GUIs [39]. In that work, it was proposed to model abstract parts of a GUI using feature models, and then generate GUIs from that model. GUIs were generated using the ANGIE-Based GUI Generator, taking an XML specification of the GUI from a dialog-based graphical-interactive DSL. In [31], a case study was carried out to investigate the GUI variability found in a commercial web-based information system. An analysis tool based on Selenium was used to extract data from the HTML and CSS documents mapping elements to the reference application. Their results show large amounts of non trivial variability in the GUIs, of which much could not be handled by stylesheet changes, with not one GUI element being used.

Furthermore in [30], an approach to handle UI customisation in model-driven SPLs is presented. In this approach, they provide a solution to tackle the need for manual customisation. The authors proposed a methodology for handling UI within domain and application engineering. This approach though has only been applied to static interfaces that do not change at runtime.

Other work considers how to re-engineer configurators [11]. In this work, the authors present challenges regarding the reverse engineering of existing configurators analysing GUI, webpage source, and code base to extract variability information. The second challenge was then regarding forward engineering and generating a tailored GUI and codebase.

To summarise, there has been limited research regarding GUIs and SPLs, and also, what work has been done, has been a concentration only on static variability. In our research we wish to go further, and achieve the ability of handling this variability statically and dynamically.

5.2 DSPL Implementation Support

There has been two main methods proposed to help support DSPL implementation, by language extensions, or by larger services and component architectures.

Language support including Feature-Oriented Programming (FOP) languages like FeatureC++ [35] have been proposed. In FeatureC++, logic within the dynamic feature modules is modularised using the decorator pattern. Using this pattern, decorators wrap classes at runtime to alter the behaviour of an application. Other work has included the emergence of Delta-Oriented Programming (DOP), particularly DeltaJava [38] and its dynamic form, Dynamic Delta Oriented Programming (DDOP) [16]. In DOP, feature refinements are implemented in *Delta Modules*. A delta module though similar to feature modules in that it can increment a base program functionality, it can also remove functionality. Delta Modules are implemented as single files, instead of each class refinement being a class file as in FOP.

While these language extensions bring very good support for runtime business logic and class member changes, they support a single language only. This then limits the developer in following particular design patterns and other tools to aid the developer.

Components and services have also been proposed as a method to producing DSPLs. Service Oriented Architectures (SOA) recently has been a popular domain for DSPL research [19, 27, 28]. In [27], a mobile DSPL was proposed, but GUI adaptation appears to have been handled via business logic, and not using a document-oriented approach. Parra proposed a unified approach to implementing logic variability in [28], whereby it should not matter if the variability is compile time or runtime, it should be seen and implemented as the same, an approach we intend to follow for the GUI.

6. Conclusions

GUIs of an application, like the rest of the software, can exhibit static variability that is derived at compile time [30, 31], and dynamic variability that must be realised at runtime. In this paper, we presented an approach to support static and dynamic variability of a single code base of GUI documents within features. Because of this, we can alter when variability is realised, without having to change the codebase. Also, when dynamic configuration is required, runtime management code is generated, along with code transformations to automate what GUI variant is required in a set condition. Furthermore, tool support was implemented to validate this approach.

Limited tests of the approach were carried out, showing that the approach has the potential to not scale well, when used with large amounts of dynamic variability. While there are limitations to our approach, this solution is a step forward for implementing runtime GUI changes, while being able to use GUI documents for its representation. This will provide greater flexibility to the developer, by which they are not tied to single language solutions.

References

[1] G. D. Abowd, A. K. Dey, P. J. Brown, N. Davies, M. Smith, and P. Steggles. Towards a better understanding of context and context-awareness. In *Proceedings of the 1st international symposium on Handheld and Ubiquitous Computing*, HUC '99, pages 304–307, London, UK, 1999. Springer-Verlag.

[2] S. Apel, F. Janda, S. Trujillo, and C. Kästner. Model superimposition in software product lines. In *Proceedings of the 2nd International Conference on Theory and Practice of Model Transformations*, ICMT '09, pages 4–19, Berlin, Heidelberg, 2009. Springer-Verlag.

[3] S. Apel, C. Kastner, and C. Lengauer. Featurehouse: Language-independent, automated software composition. In *Proceedings of the 31st International Conference on Software Engineering*, ICSE '09, pages 221–231, Washington, DC, USA, 2009. IEEE Computer Society.

[4] S. Apel, T. Leich, M. Rosenmüller, and G. Saake. Featurec++: on the symbiosis of feature-oriented and aspect-oriented programming. In *Proceedings of the 4th international conference on Generative Programming and Component Engineering*, GPCE'05, pages 125–140, Berlin, Heidelberg, 2005. Springer-Verlag.

[5] S. Apel, C. Lengauer, B. Möller, and C. Krästner. An algebra for features and feature composition. In J. Meseguer and G. Rosu, editors, *Algebraic Methodology and Software Technology*, volume 5140 of *Lecture Notes in Computer Science*, pages 36–50. Springer Berlin / Heidelberg, 2008.

[6] M. Appeltauer, R. Hirschfeld, H. Masuhara, M. Haupt, and K. Kawauchi. Event-specific Software Composition in Context-oriented Programming. In *Proceedings of International Conference on Software Composition*, Lecture Notes in Computer Science, pages 50–65, Berlin, Heidelberg, Germany, 2010. Springer-Verlag.

[7] L. Balint. Adaptive interfaces for human-computer interaction: a colorful spectrum of present and future options. In *Systems, Man and Cybernetics, 1995. Intelligent Systems for the 21st Century., IEEE International Conference on*, volume 1, pages 292–297 vol.1, 1995.

[8] D. Batory, J. Sarvela, and A. Rauschmayer. Scaling step-wise refinement. *IEEE Trans. Softw. Eng.*, 30:355–371, June 2004.

[9] D. Benavides, S. Segura, and A. Ruiz-Cortés. Automated analysis of feature models 20 years later: A literature review. *Inf. Syst.*, 35:615–636, September 2010.

[10] M. Blumendorf, G. Lehmann, and S. Albayrak. Bridging models and systems at runtime to build adaptive user interfaces. In *Proceedings of the 2nd ACM SIGCHI symposium on Engineering interactive computing systems*, EICS '10, pages 9–18, New York, NY, USA, 2010. ACM.

[11] Q. Boucher, E. Abbasi, A. Hubaux, G. Perrouin, M. Acher, and P. Heymans. Towards more reliable configurators: A re-engineering perspective. In *Product Line Approaches in Software Engineering (PLEASE), 2012 3rd International Workshop on*, pages 29 –32, june 2012.

[12] G. Calvary, J. Coutaz, and D. Thevenin. A unifying reference framework for the development of plastic user interfaces. In M. Little and L. Nigay, editors, *Engineering for Human-Computer Interaction*, volume 2254 of *Lecture Notes in Computer Science*, pages 173–192. Springer Berlin Heidelberg, 2001.

[13] N. Cardozo, S. Günther, and T. DHondt. Feature-oriented programming and context-oriented programming: Comparing paradigm characteristics by example implementations. In *International Conference On Software Engineering Advances (ICSEA'11)*, pages 130–135. IARIA, 2011.

[14] J. Criado, C. Vicente-Chicote, N. Padilla, and L. Iribarne. A model-driven approach to graphical user interface runtime adaptation. In *Proceedings of the 5th Workshop on Models@run.time at the ACM/IEEE 13th International Conference on Model Driven Engineering Languages and Systems*, pages 49–59, 2010.

[15] K. Czarnecki, S. Helsen, and U. W. Eisenecker. Staged configuration through specialization and multilevel configuration of feature models. *Software Process: Improvement and Practice*, 10(2):143–169, 2005.

[16] F. Damiani and I. Schaefer. Dynamic delta-oriented programming. In *Proceedings of the 15th International Software Product Line Conference, Volume 2*, SPLC '11, pages 34:1–34:8, New York, NY, USA, 2011. ACM.

[17] L. M. Daniele, E. Silva, L. F. Pires, and M. Sinderen. A soa-based platform-specific framework for context-aware mobile applications. In W. Aalst, J. Mylopoulos, M. Rosemann, M. J. Shaw, C. Szyperski, R. Poler, M. Sinderen, and R. Sanchis, editors, *Enterprise Interoperability*, volume 38 of *Lecture Notes in Business Information Processing*, pages 25–37. Springer Berlin Heidelberg, 2009.

[18] D. Draheim, C. Lutteroth, and G. Weber. Graphical user interfaces as documents. In *Proceedings of the 7th ACM SIGCHI New Zealand*

chapter's international conference on Computer-human interaction: design centered HCI, CHINZ '06, pages 67–74, New York, NY, USA, 2006. ACM.

[19] H. Gomaa and K. Hashimoto. Dynamic software adaptation for service-oriented product lines. In *Proceedings of the 15th International Software Product Line Conference, Volume 2*, SPLC '11, pages 35:1–35:8, New York, NY, USA, 2011. ACM.

[20] D. Grolaux. *Transparent Migration and Adaptation in a Graphical User Interface Toolkit*. PhD thesis, Université catholique de Louvain, 2007.

[21] S. Günther and S. Sunkle. rbfeatures: Feature-oriented programming with ruby. *Sci. Comput. Program.*, 77(3):152–173, Mar. 2012.

[22] S. Hallsteinsen, M. Hinchey, S. Park, and K. Schmid. Dynamic software product lines. *Computer*, 41:93–95, April 2008.

[23] K. Kang, S. Cohen, J. Hess, W. Nowak, and S. Peterson. Feature-Oriented Domain Analysis (FODA) Feasibility Study. *Technical Report CMU/SEI-90-TR-21*, 1990.

[24] C. Kastner, T. Thum, G. Saake, J. Feigenspan, T. Leich, F. Wielgorz, and S. Apel. Featureide: A tool framework for feature-oriented software development. In *Proceedings of the 31st International Conference on Software Engineering*, ICSE '09, pages 611–614, Washington, DC, USA, 2009. IEEE Computer Society.

[25] J. Kim and C. Lutteroth. Multi-platform document-oriented guis. In *Proceedings of the Tenth Australasian Conference on User Interfaces - Volume 93*, AUIC '09, pages 27–34, Darlinghurst, Australia, Australia, 2009. Australian Computer Society, Inc.

[26] G. E. Krasner and S. T. Pope. A cookbook for using the model-view controller user interface paradigm in smalltalk-80. *J. Object Oriented Program.*, 1(3):26–49, Aug. 1988.

[27] F. Marinho, F. Lima, J. Ferreira Filho, L. Rocha, M. Maia, S. de Aguiar, V. Dantas, W. Viana, R. Andrade, E. Teixeira, and C. Werner. A software product line for the mobile and context-aware applications domain. In J. Bosch and J. Lee, editors, *Software Product Lines: Going Beyond*, volume 6287 of *Lecture Notes in Computer Science*, pages 346–360. Springer Berlin / Heidelberg, 2010.

[28] C. Parra. *Towards Dynamic Software Product Lines: Unifying Design and Runtime Adaptations*. PhD thesis, INRIA Lille Nord Europe Laboratory, March 2011.

[29] C. Parra, X. Blanc, and L. Duchien. Context awareness for dynamic service-oriented product lines. In *SPLC '09: Proceedings of the 13th International Software Product Line Conference*, pages 131–140, Pittsburgh, PA, USA, 2009. Carnegie Mellon University.

[30] A. Pleuss, B. Hauptmann, D. Dhungana, and G. Botterweck. User interface engineering for software product lines: the dilemma between automation and usability. In *Proceedings of the 4th ACM SIGCHI symposium on Engineering interactive computing systems*, EICS '12, pages 25–34, New York, NY, USA, 2012. ACM.

[31] A. Pleuss, B. Hauptmann, M. Keunecke, and G. Botterweck. A case study on variability in user interfaces. In *Proceedings of the 16th International Software Product Line Conference - Volume 1*, SPLC '12, pages 6–10, New York, NY, USA, 2012. ACM.

[32] D. Rodríguez-Gracia, J. Criado, L. Iribarne, N. Padilla, and C. Vicente-Chicote. Runtime adaptation of architectural models: an approach for adapting user interfaces. In *Proceedings of the 2nd international conference on Model and Data Engineering*, MEDI'12, pages 16–30, Berlin, Heidelberg, 2012. Springer-Verlag.

[33] M. Rosenmuller. *Towards Flexible Feature Composition: Static and Dynamic Binding in Software Product Lines*. PhD thesis, Otto-von-Guericke-University Magdeburg, June 2011.

[34] M. Rosenmüller, N. Siegmund, S. Apel, and G. Saake. Flexible feature binding in software product lines. *Automated Software Engg.*, 18(2):163–197, June 2011.

[35] M. Rosenmüller, N. Siegmund, M. Pukall, and S. Apel. Tailoring dynamic software product lines. *SIGPLAN Not.*, 47(3):3–12, Oct. 2011.

[36] M. Rosenmüller, N. Siegmund, G. Saake, and S. Apel. Code generation to support static and dynamic composition of software product lines. In *Proceedings of the 7th international conference on Generative programming and component engineering*, GPCE '08, pages 3–12, New York, NY, USA, 2008. ACM.

[37] A. Savidis and C. Stephanidis. Software refactoring process for adaptive user-interface composition. In *Proceedings of the 2nd ACM SIGCHI symposium on Engineering interactive computing systems*, EICS '10, pages 19–28, New York, NY, USA, 2010. ACM.

[38] I. Schaefer, L. Bettini, F. Damiani, and N. Tanzarella. Delta-oriented programming of software product lines. In *Proceedings of the 14th international conference on Software product lines: going beyond*, SPLC'10, pages 77–91, Berlin, Heidelberg, 2010. Springer-Verlag.

[39] M. Schlee and J. Vanderdonckt. Generative programming of graphical user interfaces. In *Proceedings of the working conference on Advanced visual interfaces*, AVI '04, pages 403–406, New York, NY, USA, 2004. ACM.

[40] C. Schuster, M. Appeltauer, and R. Hirschfeld. Context-oriented programming for mobile devices: Jcop on android. In *Proceedings of the Workshop on Context-Oriented Programming (COP) 2011*, Lancaster, UK, July 2011.

[41] J.-S. Sottet, G. Calvary, J. Coutaz, and J.-M. Favre. A model-driven engineering approach for the usability of plastic user interfaces. In J. Gulliksen, M. B. Harning, P. Palanque, G. C. Veer, and J. Wesson, editors, *Engineering Interactive Systems*, volume 4940 of *Lecture Notes in Computer Science*, pages 140–157. Springer-Verlag, Berlin, Heidelberg, 2008.

[42] K. Yaici and A. Kondoz. A model-based approach for the generation of adaptive user interfaces on portable devices. In *Wireless Communication Systems. 2008. ISWCS '08. IEEE International Symposium on*, pages 164–167, 2008.

Family-Based Performance Measurement

Norbert Siegmund   Alexander von Rhein   Sven Apel

University of Passau, Germany

Abstract

Most contemporary programs are customizable. They provide many features that give rise to millions of program variants. Determining which feature selection yields an optimal performance is challenging, because of the exponential number of variants. Predicting the performance of a variant based on previous measurements proved successful, but induces a trade-off between the measurement effort and prediction accuracy. We propose the alternative approach of *family-based performance measurement*, to reduce the number of measurements required for identifying feature interactions and for obtaining accurate predictions. The key idea is to create a variant simulator (by translating compile-time variability to run-time variability) that can simulate the behavior of all program variants. We use it to measure performance of individual methods, trace methods to features, and infer feature interactions based on the call graph. We evaluate our approach by means of five feature-oriented programs. On average, we achieve accuracy of 98 %, with only a single measurement per customizable program. Observations show that our approach opens avenues of future research in different domains, such an feature-interaction detection and testing.

Categories and Subject Descriptors   C.4 [*Performance of Systems*]: Measurement techniques;   D.2.13 [*Reusable Software*]: Domain engineering

Keywords   Family-based Analysis, FeatureHouse, Performance Prediction

1. Introduction

Customizability is a critical success factor in software engineering. A customizable program gives rise to a *family* of *program variants* that can be tailored to the requirements of individual stakeholders. The customization process is simple: Select the *features* that satisfy your requirements, map the selected features to their respective implementation artifacts, and generate the corresponding program variant based on the artifacts. However, despite this simplicity, it is often unclear what the *best* feature selection is to satisfy all requirements, including non-functional requirements.

Especially, performance is critical. Often, a user wants to know the influence of a feature on performance of the generated program variant. For example, in the data-management domain: a customer has a specific workload for which she wants to determine the best feature selection of a given customizable data-management system

(i.e., with the fastest response time). Considering the huge space of possible variants (33 optional and independent features give rise to a unique variant for each human on the planet), a brute-force approach that measures all variants does not scale.

Recent solutions to this problem aim at *predicting* a variant's performance based on the feature selection [17, 34]. This requires a performance model of the customizable program, which either must be trained via a number of measurements [11, 15, 17, 32] or inferred based on code analyses [24] and architectural knowledge [5, 38]. Both approaches have their benefits. Measurement-based performance models produce accurate performance predictions, but at the cost of time-consuming measurements. With code analysis, one does not have to actually measure individual program variants, reducing prediction accuracy, because the environment and other side-effects cannot be considered. Clearly, there is a trade-off between measurement effort and prediction accuracy [33].

We focus on measurement-based performance modeling. Our goal is twofold. First, we collect precise information on the performance behavior of individual features and their interactions based on the customer's workload. Second, we aim at minimizing the measurement effort to produce a performance model. To reach our goals, we propose *family-based performance measurement*. The key idea is not to measure individual program variants, but to execute a *variant simulator* that subsumes the individual behavior of all program variants.

Technically, family-based performance measurement consists of three steps: First, it generates a variant simulator for a given customizable program. In this step, it tracks which methods belong to which feature. Second, it executes the variant simulator with a given user-defined benchmark, logs the method execution times, and creates a corresponding call graph. Third, it analyzes the call graph to determine how much time has been spent within feature code and which of the paths in the call graph are visited only for a specific feature combination (which indicates a feature interaction). Then, times for each feature and feature interaction are aggregated in a performance model, in the form of a *choice-calculus* expression [14].

Family-based performance measurement relies on tracing information that is obtained when creating the variant simulator, by translating compile-time variability (e.g., feature modules [3]) to run-time variability (conditional execution). However, it can be applied also to programs that are variable at run time, but, in this case, tracing information needs to be provided externally.

We argue that family-based performance measurement is a promising alternative to the state of the art:

- It executes and measures only one variant simulator per customizable program and workload.
- It determines which features are actually used by the respective workload.
- It identifies performance-critical features and feature interactions of any order. [1]

---

[1] The *order* of a feature interaction specifies how many features interact (minus one) [28]. For example, an interaction between two features is first-order.

GPCE '13,   October 27–28, 2013, Indianapolis, Indiana, USA.
Copyright © 2013 ACM 978-1-4503-2373-4/13/10. . . $15.00.
http://dx.doi.org/10.1145/2517208.2517209

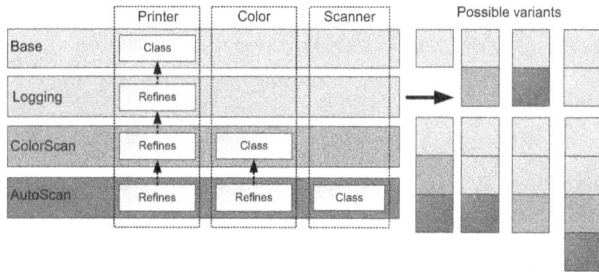

Figure 1. Decomposition of classes (vertical bars) with respect to features (horizontal layers) in the printer driver

Being a novel approach, it has some limitations (e.g., no multi-threading support), which we discuss in Section 5.2. Furthermore, we concentrate on feasibility in the evaluation. How accurate are predictions based on a variant simulator? What is the role of feature interactions, and how can they be detected, independently of their order? To answer these questions, we developed a tool chain for family-based performance measurement based on FEATUREHOUSE [3], in which features are implemented with statically composable feature modules. We evaluate our approach using five feature-oriented programs taken from a standard repository. Our experiments show that we achieve a prediction accuracy of 98 %, on average, while measuring only a small fraction of the variant space (we need only a single execution). We detected many feature interactions, up to the order of five, which cannot be found by current approaches that rely on pair-wise sampling [34].

2. Feature-oriented Programming

We demonstrate feasibility of our approach with *feature-oriented programming (FOP)* [6]. Programmers implement features in distinct, physically separated modules, called *feature modules*, whose composability facilitates customization. A feature module encapsulates source code otherwise scattered across different classes inside a single unit of composition. It can introduce new classes and extend existing classes (*class refinements*). A composer, such as FEATUREHOUSE [3], incrementally composes a set of given feature modules to obtain a final program variants.

In Figure 1, we show the layered design of a feature-oriented printer driver. Horizontal layers represent the feature modules of the driver, and vertical bars represent JAVA classes. Starting from a base implementation of a class, multiple refinements belonging to different features are applied. Refinements add new members to classes, such as methods and fields, or extend existing methods by overriding. For example, if a user selects feature *ColorScan*, class `Printer` is composed of the base implementation and a refinement to scan paper with colors.

In Figure 2, we show the code of the four feature modules of the printer driver. Technically, composition is implemented by superimposition [3]. Superimposition composes feature modules, based on nominal and structural similarity. It starts at the top of the hierarchical structure of the feature modules; if two program elements match in name and type they are merged; then, it proceeds recursively.

In our example, the composition starts with the feature modules *Base* and *Logging*. Both declare a class `Printer`. Since the names match, the content of the classes is superimposed, meaning that the composed class `Printer` contains the union of all their members. Then, superimposition proceeds with the individual class members. If two methods have the same signature in both feature modules, one method overrides the other method, in composition order (method `print` of feature *Logging* overrides method `print` of feature *Base*), a mechanism called *method refinement*. Keyword **original** refers to the overridden method. In our example, we extend the base implementation of `print` by adding a statement and calling the overridden

Feature: *Base*

```
1  class Printer {
2    public static void main(String[] args){
3      Printer p = new Printer();
4      p.print((Page)args[0]);}
5    public void print(Page p) {
6      ... // 2s
7    }
8    public Page scan() {
9      ... // 1s
10  }}
```

Feature: *Logging*

```
11  class Printer {
12    public void print(Page p) {
13      log("Execute printer job."); // 1s
14      original(p);}
15    public Page scan() {
16      ... // 0.5s
17      return original();}
18  }
```

Feature: *ColorScan*

```
19  class Printer {
20    public void print(Page p) {
21      ... // 5s
22      scan();
23      original(p);}
24    public Page scan() {
25      return original();}
26  }
```

Feature: *AutoScan*

```
1  class Printer {
2    // scans one page and prints it
3    public void print(Page p) {
4      ... // 1s
5      scan();
6      original(p);}
7  }
```

Figure 2. A feature-oriented printer driver (the class declarations of *Logging*, *ColorScan*, and *AutoScan* refine the corresponding declaration of *Base*)

Program variant: {*Base, Logging, ColorScan, AutoScan*}

```
1  class Printer {
2   public static void main(String[] args){
3     Printer p = new Printer();
4     p.print((Page)args[0]);}
5   public void print(Page p) {
6     ... // 1s by AutoScan
7     ... // 5s by ColorScan
8     log("Execute printer job."); // 1s by Logging
9     ... // 2s by Base
10    scan(); // by ColorScan
11    scan(); // by AutoScan
12   }
13   public Page scan() {
14     ... // 0s by ColorScan
15     ... // 0.5s by Logging
16     ... // 1s by Base
17  }}
```

Figure 3. Variant with the features *Base*, *Logging*, *Scan*, and *Copy*

method. The result of the composition of all features of our example is shown in Figure 3.

Note that, using the program variant of Figure 3, we can measure the performance of all features in combination (because the example does not include mutually exclusive features). But, this way, we cannot infer to what extent individual features contribute to the measured performance and how they interact. To quantify the influence of each feature, we would need to measure individual combinations, using a brute-force or sampling approach. As an alternative to this approach, we propose a family-based approach, which relies on a variant simulator.

Variant Simulator. A *variant simulator* subsumes the behavior of all variants of the customizable program. Technically, we generate

Variant simulator: {*Base*, *Logging*, *ColorScan*}

```
1  class Printer {
2   static boolean _HighColor_enabled;
3   @Feature(name="Base")
4   public static void main(String[] args){
5    Printer p = new Printer();
6    p.print((Page)args[0]);}
7   @Feature(name="Base")
8   public void print_role_Base(Page p) {
9    ...// 2s by Base
10  }
11  @Feature(name="Logging")
12  public void print_role_Logging(Page p) {
13   ...// 1s by Logging
14   print_role_Base(p);
15  }
16  @Feature(name="FeatureSwitch")
17  public void print_role_before_Logging(Page p) {
18   if (_Logging_enabled) {
19    print_role_Logging(p);
20   } else {
21    print_role_Base(p); }
22  }
23  @Feature(name="ColorScan")
24  public void print_role_ColorScan(Page p){
25   ...// 5s by Logging
26   print_role_before_Logging(p);
27  }
28  @Feature(name="FeatureSwitch")
29  public void print(Page p) {
30   if (_ColorScan_enabled) {
31    print_role_ColorScan(p);
32   } else {
33    print_role_before_Logging(p); }
34  }
35 }
```

Figure 4. Excerpt of the variant simulator for the features *Base*, *Logging*, and *ColorScan*

a variant simulator using *variability encoding* [2], which essentially translates compile-time variability to run-time variability. A variant simulator contains the code of all features as well as information on which feature combinations are valid. It invokes feature-specific behavior based on enabling and disabling guards around feature code. The guards are controlled by boolean variables that represent the presence and absence of individual features and that can be set at run time. For each method refinement, there is a new method introduced, called *feature switch*, that dispatches between the refined methods and the refining method. Finally, each method and each feature switch is annotated with information on their origin (i.e., the feature it belongs to).

Figure 4 shows the variant simulator of our example. Each method is annotated; the annotation in Line 3 states that this method belongs to feature *Base*; the annotation in Line 16 states that the method is a feature switch, included by variability encoding.

Note how the original methods have been renamed to implement method refinement. Each method refinement is translated to two new methods, one method that implements the actual refinement and one method (a feature switch) that dispatches between the refined method and the actual refinement. For example, `print_role_Logging` implements a method refinement (Line 12) and `print_role_before_Logging` a feature switch (Line 17). The base method does not need a feature switch (Line 8), and the last method refinement in chain receives the original name of the method (Line 29).

3. Family-based Measurement

Family-based measurement is inspired by related work on family-based analysis of software product lines [36], type checking [20, 23], static analysis [8, 27], model checking [4, 13], and deductive verification [37]. The idea is simple: Do not measure each program variant (or a subset thereof) individually, but execute a corresponding variant simulator to build a performance model. Clearly, there are

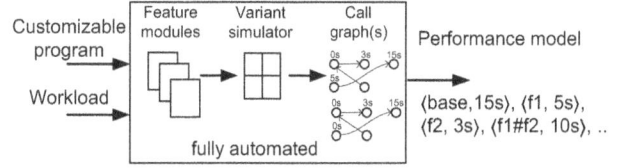

Figure 5. Process of family-based performance measurement

several challenges that arise when using a variant simulator, such as how to handle alternative features and how to identify feature interactions. Hence, we begin with discussing requirements and goals of family-based measurement:

- When measuring performance, we need a specific workload or benchmark. For instance, to determine performance of a customizable database system, we need a representative workload that simulates the target application scenario of the fully-customized program variant. Such a workload may be standardized (e.g., TPC-H in the database domain) or given by the user to represent the intended use case.
- Beside the workload, we require a variability model (e.g., a feature model) to encode run-time variability properly. We reason only about the valid execution paths across features, and disregard invalid feature combinations. Furthermore, the variability model is used to optimize the performance model, for example, by stating which features are mandatory.
- The third requirement is measure all valid execution paths in the variant simulator. That is, we aim at full feature coverage according to the given workload.
- Finally, we want to fully automate the whole process, as illustrated in Figure 5. The inputs are the customizable program and the workload for which we generate the performance model.[2] Next, the variant simulator is generated and executed on the workload. From this measurement, we automatically extract execution times and feature interactions, and produce the corresponding performance model.

3.1 Performance Model

Our goal is to produce a performance model that captures the times that the variant simulator spent in the respective features' code. Clearly, the model should incorporate interactions among features, because feature interactions can have a substantial influence on performance [33]. The output is a variable performance model that computes, for any given feature selection, a performance value, which is used to predict the performance when actually executing the corresponding variant. We express the performance model using the *choice calculus* [14], in which each term holds a feature name and the time consumed by the feature when selected. The performance model Π for a customizable program p with the features $f_1, \ldots, f_n$, and a workload w is defined as follows:

$$\Pi_p^w = \sum_{i=1}^{n} \langle f_i, t_i^w \rangle \quad | \quad f_i \in p, t_i^w \in \mathbb{R} \tag{1}$$

For a workload w, we log the time t_i^w that a feature f_i contributes to the execution of p. A simple performance model of our running example is:

$$\langle Base, 5s \rangle + \langle Logging, 1.5s \rangle + \langle ColorScan, 5s \rangle$$

With this performance model, we can predict the execution time of all valid program variants by adding the corresponding performance values (considering feature *Base* is mandatory and *Logging* and *ColorScan* are optional):

---

[2] Note, in our scenario, we assume that the customizable program can be automatically generated.

Variant	Time in s
Base	5.0
Base, Logging	6.5
Base, ColorScan	10.0
Base, Logging, ColorScan	11.5

Note that we can have additional terms in the performance model representing feature interactions. A feature-interaction term represents the execution time that is consumed when the interacting features are present in a program variant, in addition to times of the individual features. If we identify a feature interaction between n unique features, we add a corresponding term to the performance model, denoted with operator # [7]:

$$\langle f_1 \# \ldots \# f_n, \ t_{1\#\ldots\#n} \rangle$$

For example, if the features *Logging* and *ColorScan* interact, we write *Logging#ColorScan*. Adding the feature-interaction term $\langle Logging\#ColorScan, 2s\rangle$ to the performance model of our example, would change the predicted performance of configuration {*Base, Logging, ColorScan*} from 11.5s to 13.5s, because we must add 2 seconds for program variants that contain both *Logging* and *ColorScan*.

3.2 Approach

The overall approach of family-based performance measurement consists of four steps:

1. Generate the variant simulator and weave code into the variant simulator to trace and measure feature code;
2. Execute the variant simulator to build a call graph that consists of methods with annotated feature names and measured execution times;
3. Identify feature interactions based on the call graph;
4. Aggregate performance values per feature to build a performance model;

In the remaining section, we explain the four steps in detail. For illustration, we use our running example, where *Base* is mandatory and *Logging*, *ColorScan*, and *AutoScan* are optional. Furthermore, we assume the times the features consume as specified in the comments of Figure 3.

3.2.1 Call Graph with Feature Annotations

The first step of family-based performance measurement is to measure the execution time of each individual feature. We need to extract the following information from the running variant simulator:

- Which methods are executed?
- To which features do these methods belong?
- What is their execution time?
- What is the sequence of method calls?[3]

To obtain this information, we weave code around each method when compiling the variant simulator, as shown in Algorithm 1. First, we measure the execution time of each method and log the time together with the name of the corresponding feature (or feature combination). To this end, when visiting a method, we automatically start a measurement (Line 9) and log the visit (Line 3). After returning from this method, we stop the measurement and log the result (Lines 11 and 12). Second, we build a call graph to trace the control flow, as illustrated in Figure 6. To this end, we log which feature calls which other feature, and we distinguish between a call due to a method refinement (via `original`) and a normal method call (Lines 4–7). By storing the name of the visited feature, we can keep track of that we visit all features (required by feature-coverage requirement), and we can identify feature interactions by analyzing the control flow across features.

By applying Algorithm 1 to the variant simulator of our running example, we obtain the call graph shown in Figure 6. Horizontal

---

Algorithm 1: Build call graph

```
Data: CallGraph callGraph, Method parent
Result: CallGraph callGraph
1  When executing Method method
2  begin
3    callGraph.add (method, method.featureName);
4    if method.isRefinement() then
5      | callGraph.createRefineEdge(parent,method);
6    else
7      | callGraph.createCallEdge(parent,method);
8    parent = method;
9    startTime = startMeasurement();
10   method.execute() ;     // continue method execution
11   measuredTime = endMeasurement() - startTime;
12   method.time = measuredTime;
13   parent = method.parent;
14   return callGraph;
15 end
```

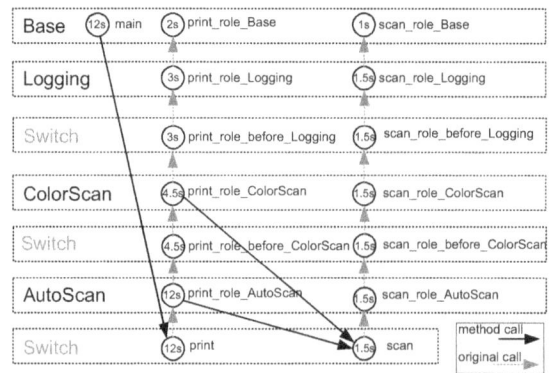

Figure 6. Call graph of our running example

layers denote features, nodes denote methods and method refinements, and edges denote method calls (both normal calls and calls due to `original`). For example, method `print_role_Base` contains the code contributed by feature *Base*; it is is refined three times, which results in three feature switches and three actual refinement implementations.

Although every node holds the time that the corresponding method has consumed, we do not know yet the actual time spent in a feature. This is because the measured time comprises also all execution times of methods that have been called from this method. For example, if we measure the execution time of method `print_role_ColorScan`, we measure 9.5s, which is only half the story, because we spent only 5s in this method, and the remaining 4.5s in `print_role_Logging`, `scan`, etc. Another important information that we do not have yet is on which features the execution of a method depends. To gain this information, we have to identify feature interactions, as we explain next.

3.2.2 Identifying Feature Interactions

Our approach to identify feature interactions is based on the observation that a call from one method to another always induces an interaction between the calling feature and the called feature. With "interaction", we mean that the called feature would never be executed, if the calling feature was not present.[4] For example, in Figure 6, there is an interaction between *Base* and *AutoScan*, as with-

---

[4] There are also features a code level, referred to as *derivatives* [28]. We treat derivatives similar to features. If the execution of interaction code leads to an alternative call sequence, we treat this similar to mutually exclusive features (see Section 3.3).

out *Base*, method `print_role_AutoScan` would not be executed. Likewise, there is an interaction between *AutoScan* and *ColorScan*, because `print_role_AutoScan` calls `scan`; *ColorScan*'s method refinement is executed only because *AutoScan* made this call.

In general, the execution of a method in a feature f_n may depend on a whole set $f_1, \ldots, f_{n-1}$ of other features. We define this set as the *prefix* $f_1\#\ldots\#f_{n-1}$ of feature f_n in the corresponding interaction term. In our algorithm, prefixes grow when traversing the call graph.

In Algorithm 2, we show how to identify feature interactions. When entering a method, we determine whether this is due to a normal method call or a method refinement (Line 4). In the case of a normal call, we protocol a feature interaction between the calling feature and the called feature by adding the corresponding prefix to the call graph (Line 7). The prefixes are passed from the calling feature to the called feature and extended in each step (Lines 4–7).

Algorithm 2: Detect feature interactions

Data: CallGraph callGraph, Method parent
Result: CallGraph callGraph

```
1  // When entering Method method
2  begin
3  │   String currentFeature = method.getAnnotation();
4  │   if method.isRefinement() then
5  │   │   method.prefix = parent.prefix;
6  │   else
7  │   │   method.prefix
   │   │       = parent.prefix + currentFeature + "#";
8  │   callGraph.addPrefix(method, method.prefix);
9  │   ...
10 │   method.execute() ;      // continue method execution
11 │   ...
12 │   return callGraph;
13 end
```

There are two important facts to consider that are not obvious. First, an **original** call does not cause a feature interaction, because the execution of the method that has been refined does not depend on the feature that applied the refinement. Second, the execution of *all* refinements of a method depends on the feature that calls the method (via a normal method call).

In Figure 6, method `print` and all of its refinements depend on the presence of feature *Base*, which calls `print` from `main`. Based on this call, we identify four feature interactions: *Base#AutoScan*, *Base#ColorScan*, *Base#Logging*, and *Base#Base*. So, all features that refine method `print` obtain the prefix *Base#* to keep track of the interaction. Furthermore, all measured times will be included in the performance model with the prefix and the feature name. As the program execution continues, the prefix grows. For example, the two calls to method `scan` from *AutoScan* and *ColorScan* result in two sets of feature interactions:

{*Base#AutoScan#ColorScan*, *Base#AutoScan#Logging*, *Base#AutoScan#Base*}

{*Base#ColorScan#ColorScan*, *Base#ColorScan#Logging*, *Base#ColorScan#Base*}.

Simplifying Interaction Terms. The interaction terms created by Algorithm 2 are quite verbose, so we simplify them, according to a standard model of feature composition by Batory [7]. In particular, we define two rules for simplification. First, if a feature interacts with itself, then we can shrink the prefix accordingly, because the execution of the feature's methods depends on the presence of itself, which is always satisfied:

$$f_i \# f_i \longrightarrow f_i \qquad \text{(S-Ref)}$$

Second, mandatory features are always present, so a feature interaction between an optional and a mandatory feature depends only on the presence of the optional feature:

$$\frac{mandatory(f_i) \qquad prefix(f_i) = \emptyset}{f_i \# f_j \longrightarrow f_j} \qquad \text{(S-Mand)}$$

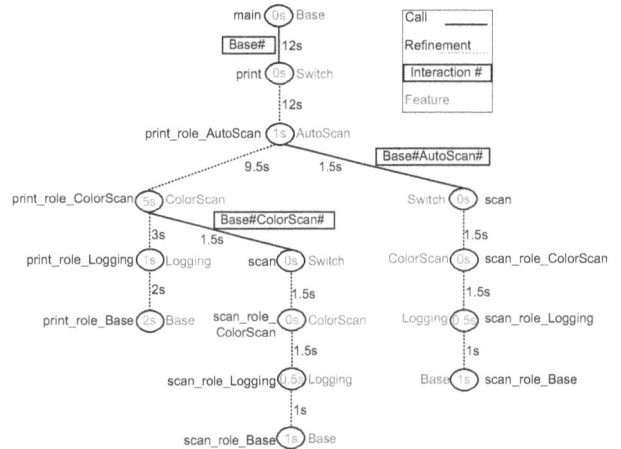

Figure 7. Reachability tree of our running example (with omitted feature switches). Times inside methods represent the time spent by the method itself. Times on edges represent actually measured times

Note that $\#$ is not commutative, and this rule does not apply if f_j is mandatory and f_i is optional, because, in this case, we execute a method of the mandatory feature f_j only if the optional feature f_i is present. Consequently, the time spent in this method influences performance only when both features are present.

When applying these simplifications to our running example, we obtain the following feature combinations in the performance model:

Base, AutoScan, ColorScan, Logging, AutoScan#ColorScan, AutoScan#Logging, ColorScan#Logging

Note that, even in this simple example, we identify three pair-wise feature interactions, indicating the potential of this approach to detect feature interactions. Next, we explain the remaining task to obtain a performance model: aggregating the execution times of individual methods.

3.2.3 Aggregate Execution Times

As said previously, when we log the time at the end of a method execution, we measured not only the time consumed by the method itself, but also the time spent in other methods it called. We have to subtract these times from the current measurement to compute the actual performance of this method.[5] For example, we measured an execution time of 9.5 seconds for method `print_role_ColorScan`, but we visited the method only for 5 seconds and spent the remaining time in the methods `print_role_Logging` (1 second), `print_role_Base` (2 seconds), and in four additional methods (1.5 seconds), as illustrated in Figure 7.[6]

Technically, we solve this problem by representing the call graph as a *reachability tree* similar to reachability trees in model checking [12]. Nodes in the tree represent executed methods and edges represent calls to other methods. Using this tree, we compute the actual time t_m spent in method m with the measured time T_m as follows:

$$t_m = T_m - \sum_{i=1}^{n} T_i \mid \forall i \in children(m) \qquad (2)$$

with n being the number of children of method m in the reachability tree.

---

[5] Since we use a call graph and not a dynamic call tree, we handle also recursive methods by representing it only a single time in the graph and aggregating the executing time of all executions.

[6] Note that we omitted some feature switches in Figure 7, for readability.

In Figure 7, we show the corresponding tree for our example. For each method, we know the corresponding feature, and after the execution of each method, we know the time spent. This time is annotated to the corresponding edges of the tree and subsumes the whole time spent below the current node. Using Equation 2, we compute for method `print_role_ColorScan` the time:

$$
\begin{aligned}
t_{print\_role\_ColorScan} &= T_{print\_role\_ColorScan} \\
&- \sum_{i=1}^{n} T_{print\_role\_ColorScan} \\
&= 9.5s - (3s + 1.5s) = 5s
\end{aligned}
$$

Next, we aggregate the method times t_i to build the performance model. For this task, we have to consider feature interactions. That is, it is not sufficient to take only the annotated feature names and sum the times up for each feature. If we do so, we lose the information under which condition a feature's method is executed (i.e., which features must be present to execute a certain method). The outcome would be a performance model that expresses the *maximal* execution time per feature, but not the actual execution time depending on a given feature selection. To solve this problem, we use the identified feature interactions encoded with the prefixes in order to create the correct performance terms for the performance model, as shown in Algorithm 3.

Algorithm 3: Build performance model

Data: `CallGraph callGraph, PerformanceModel model`
Result: `PerformanceModel model`

```
1 foreach Method m in callGraph do
2     Term t = m.prefix + m.featureName ; // from Alg 2
3     t.time = m.clearedTime ;            // from Equation 2
4     model.addOrUpdate(t) ;              // add term to model
5 end
6 return model;
```

3.2.4 Putting the Pieces Together

So far, we have described the four steps of family-based performance measurement: (1) the algorithm to build the call graph, (2) the algorithm to identify feature interactions, (3) the simplification rules, and (4) the algorithm to build the performance model. Next, for a better overview, we explain how these pieces interplay using on the example of Figure 7.

We enter the program from method `main`, so all preceding methods in the call graph depend on the presence of *Base*. *Base#* is passed as the prefix when considering method `print`. Next, we reach method `print_role_AutoScan` and subtract from the measured 12s all times coming from the corresponding child nodes (9.5s and 1.5s).[7] As a result, we store the term $\langle Base\#AutoScan, 1s \rangle$ in our performance model (12s − 9.5s − 1.5s = 1s). Then, we continue with the left child, which is method `print_role_ColorScan` of feature *ColorScan*. Since this call is a method refinement, we do not extend the prefix. We measure 9.5s for this method, whereas 3s are consumed by the first child and 1.5s are consumed by the second child. Hence, we include the term $\langle Base\#ColorScan, 5s \rangle$ in our performance model (9.5s − 3s − 1.5s = 5s). When entering the second child of method `print_role_ColorScan` (which is method `scan`), we have to extend the current prefix by *ColorScan*. That is, we store for method `scan_role_ColorScan` the term $\langle Base\#ColorScan\#ColorScan, 0s \rangle$, and so on. The term amounts to 0s, because the child nodes consume the whole execution time (the method simply delegates the call).

---

[7] In practice, we first compute the performance terms of all child nodes, because the method is recursive. We explain the algorithm in the order of program execution to ease understanding.

By applying the simplification rules and by removing terms with a zero performance value, we obtain the following performance model:

$$
\begin{aligned}
&\langle Base, 2s \rangle + \langle Logging, 1s \rangle + \langle ColorScan, 6s \rangle \\
+ \; &\langle AutoScan, 2s \rangle + \langle ColorScan\#Logging, 0.5s \rangle \\
+ \; &\langle AutoScan\#Logging, 0.5s \rangle + \langle ColorScan\#Base, 1s \rangle \\
+ \; &\langle AutoScan\#Base, 1s \rangle
\end{aligned}
$$

Finally, the performance model is then used as follows: Based on a valid feature selection, the model computes the performance value by removing all terms that do not contain any feature in the selection; then, the sum of the times of the remaining terms represents the performance value of the corresponding program variant.

3.3 Mutually Exclusive Features

So far, we did not consider the case in which features are mutually exclusive, say two alternative implementations of logging. While mutually exclusive features can be integrated into a single variant simulator, they can never be active in the same execution (incorporating the variability model, we consider only valid execution paths). A simple solution to this problem is to execute the variant simulator once per mutually exclusive alternative, and to compute the times consumed by the corresponding features. While this increases the number of measurements, this measurement applies only to sets of mutually exclusive features, not to all kinds of feature combinations, as in brute-force or sampling approaches [17]. Furthermore, since we assume that the method execution time is constant, we do not have to measure all combinations of alternative features. We discuss this issue further in Section 5.

4. Evaluation

The aim of our evaluation is to explore whether family-based performance measurement is feasible. To this end, we evaluate the accuracy of the predictions of our approach, compared to the actual performance that is measured. Furthermore, we compare the measurement effort of family-based measurement with state-of-the-art sample-based prediction approaches [34]. Finally, we discuss to what extent our approach can identify feature interactions.

Based on these goals, we formulate three research questions:
1. How accurate are the predictions of our approach?
2. What is the measurement effort of our approach compared to brute-force and state-of-the-art sampling approaches (i.e., feature-wise and pair-wise measurement)?
3. What kinds of feature interactions is our approach able to detect?

The complete tool chain (i.e., the extension of FeatureHouse and the measurement infrastructure) as well as all experimental data are publicly available: `http://fosd.de/Family`.

4.1 Experimental Setup

Next, we explain the customizable programs we used for our evaluation and the measurement procedure.

Subject Programs. As subject programs, we selected five feature-oriented programs from a public repository.[8] The selection criteria were that these programs can be processed by our tool chain (i.e., FeatureHouse) and that they can run a benchmark automatically without user intervention, to obtain reproducible results. For each subject program, we executed either a standard benchmark (deployed with the program) or a typical workload (e.g., we analyzed a substantial code base with AJStats). We give an overview of subject programs in Table 1.

In the following, we describe each subject program briefly, including the changes we made to run a benchmark:

- AJStats is a customizable code-analysis tool for AspectJ programs. Depending on the configuration, it collects different statis-

---

[8] `http://fosd.de/fuji/`

Program	Domain	# Features	# Variants	LOC
AJSTATS	Code Analyzer	20	131 072	14 782
ELEVATOR	Simulator	6	10	2 488
EMAIL	E-mail Client	9	40	1 455
ZIPME	Compression Lib	14	10	5 355
MBENCH	Micro Benchmark	11	1 014	120

Table 1. Overview of the subject programs

tic, including the number of aspects, pointcuts, etc. As a workload, we analyzed Orbacus, a customizable CORBA implementation.

- ELEVATOR models an elevator with varying optional conditions, such as weight limitations and priority service. It has been used before as a benchmark for (functional) feature-interaction detection [4, 29]. We extended the model by realistic timing information (e.g., how long different functions of the elevator need). As a workload, we use a scenario, applied by other researchers for verification.
- Much like ELEVATOR, EMAIL has been used before to verify the behavior of differently customized e-mail clients [4, 18]. Again, we included timing information into the model. We used a typical e-mail scenario as workload.
- ZIPME is a compression library that allows users to customize it by selecting different compression algorithms. As a benchmark, we use a file of 6 MB size generated by UIQ, a standard benchmark generator for compression algorithms.[9]
- We wrote a micro benchmark, called MBENCH, to test corner cases of family-based measurement. For example, it (a) calls methods from within a refined method, (b) it calls `original` within a loop, to simulate complex call graphs, (c) it defines methods in a feature that are called only by other features, etc.

We performed all measurements for a single customizable program exclusively either on a Intel Core2 Quad CPU, Win7 64Bit professional system with 8 GB RAM or on an Intel Core i7 2GHZ, Win7 64Bit professional with 4 GB RAM.

Experimental Procedure. We extended FEATUREHOUSE such that it generates a proper variant simulator for a given feature-oriented program. It generates (i) feature-name annotations for each method and (ii) methods to switch between alternative features. We implemented the measurement infrastructure and construction of the call graph using ASPECTJ, by weaving advice around each annotated method.

The measurement process is simple: We run the variant simulator to log the execution times and to compute the performance model. Then, we create and measure all variants of the respective program and compute the error rate of our prediction as the relative difference between predicted and actually measured performance: $\frac{|actual-predicted|}{actual}$. For AJSTATS, we could not measure all variants in a reasonable time. Instead, we measured 30 256 randomly selected configurations, requiring two weeks of measurement.

4.2 Results

Prediction Accuracy and Measurement Effort. We present the measurement results in Table 2, including the error rate for each program, the distribution of the error rate using box plots, as well as mean and standard deviation. On average, the error rate is 1.7 %, which is well within the general measurement error of 2 %.[10] In short, to answer research question 1, we achieve very accurate predictions.

To learn about the feasibility of our approach, we quantify the measurement effort. Actually, we had to run each variant simulator only once, because no alternative features were present (research question

---

[9] http://mattmahoney.net/dc/uiq/

[10] In our experiments, measuring the same program multiple times results in variations of up to 2 %. That is, a prediction error rate of below 2 % is as accurate as actually measuring the program variants.

Program	Time (BF)	Error Rate (in %)	
		Distribution	$\mu \pm \sigma$
AJSTATS	15s (53d)		3.2± 2.5
ELEVATOR	46s (220s)		0± 0
EMAIL	60s (882s)		0.4± 0.5
ZIPME	40s (405s)		3.1± 3.0
MBENCH	50s (4h)		2.0± 1.3

Table 2. Accuracy and measurement effort of the subject programs; BF refers to time needed for the brute-force approach. μ: arithmetic mean; σ: standard deviation

2). This is far less than in the brute-force approach and in all sample-based approaches (i.e., linear number of measurements for feature-wise sampling and quadratic for pair-wise sampling with respect to the number of features). Also note that the times presented in the table do not include repeating a measurement several times, which is, however, required to reduce measurement bias. Increasing the robustness and reliability of measurements would mean to multiply the times by a factor of 10 or higher. Even feature-wise measurement (as explained next) requires more measurements for our subject programs, but with a higher error rate, as it does not consider feature interactions at all [34].

For illustration, we depict in Table 2 the times needed for family-based performance measurement in relation to the times needed to measure all variants (in brackets). The benefit of family-based measurement increases with the number of optional features (but decreases with the number of mutually exclusive features, as we discuss in Section 5).

Comparison against Sampling. Does family-based performance measurement outperform state-of-the-art sampling approaches: (a) feature-wise and (b) pair-wise measurement [34]? *Feature-wise measurement* samples the customizable program to quantify the influence of each feature on performance. To this end, we measure two variants that differ only in a single feature. By computing the delta of both measurements, we quantify the impact of this feature on performance. *Pair-wise measurement* aims at improving prediction accuracy of feature-wise measurement by keeping track of all pair-wise (i.e., first-order) feature interactions. To this end, we measure for each pair of features an additional variant and compare predicted against measured performance [32]. In Table 3, we compare family-based performance measurement with feature-wise and pair-wise measurement regarding prediction error rate and measurement effort. In all cases, family-based measurement outperforms or is, at least, equally accurate as feature-wise and pair-wise measurement. Considering the substantial reduction of measurement effort, we conclude that family-based performance measurement is a promising alternative to existing sampling approaches.

Feature Interactions. To answer research question 3, we analyzed the interaction terms of the generated performance models. In Figure 8, we show the distribution of interaction terms depending on their order. Terms with an order of zero represent the influence of a single feature on performance. With an increasing order, the terms are more difficult to detect.

In ELEVATOR, we could not identify any feature interaction. Considering the perfect prediction accuracy, we assume that there are, in fact, no interactions present in this program. For all other programs, we identified a considerable number of feature interactions. More than 80 % of all terms represent feature interactions. For ZIPME, we found interactions up to an order of four and, for AJSTATS, up to an order of five. These results demonstrate that, in principle, there is no limit to detect interactions of arbitrary orders, which is not the case

Program	Appr.	Effort #M	Effort Time	Error Rate (in %) Distribution	Error Rate (in %) $\mu \pm \sigma$
AJSTATS	Family	1	15s		3.2 ± 2.5
	FW	18	486s		2.4 ± 2.1
	PW	115	2 425s	0 5 10 15 20 25 30	8.9 ± 6.9
ELEVATOR	Family	1	46s		0 ± 0
	FW	5	147s		0 ± 0
	PW	9	178s	0 5 10 15 20 25 30	0 ± 0
EMAIL	Family	1	60s		0.4 ± 0.5
	FW	7	149s		12.4 ± 13.3
	PW	27	586s	0 5 10 15 20 25 30	0 ± 0
ZIPME	Family	1	40s		3.1 ± 3.0
	FW	5	192s		4.3 ± 3.7
	PW	8	246s	0 5 10 15 20 25 30	1.8 ± 2.5
MBENCH	Family	1	50s		2.0 ± 1.3
	FW	11	205s		24.2 ± 18.7
	PW	67	1 885s	0 5 10 15 20 25 30	10.5 ± 11.9

Table 3. Comparison of family-based measurement with sampling approaches. #M: number of measurements; FW: feature-wise; PW: pair-wise; μ: arithmetic mean; σ: standard deviation

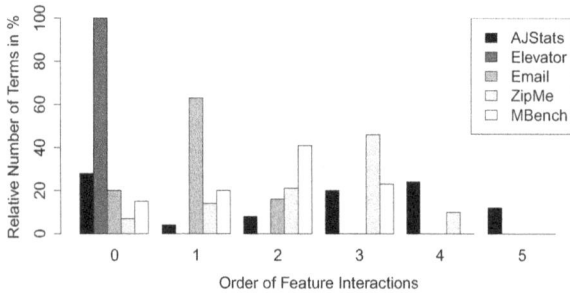

Figure 8. Number of identified performance terms for each customizable program. An order higher than zero indicates a performance term representing a feature interaction

for sample-based approaches (e.g., pair-wise is able to detect only first-order interactions).

In Figure 9, we show how much time we spent in determining interactions terms of different orders during the execution of the variant simulator. This illustrates the influence of feature interactions on the overall execution time. We see that the higher the interactions the less influence they have on the execution times. But, still, higher-order interactions exist! This finding confirms heuristics used in previous work [33].

Figure 9. Relative time contributed by interaction terms of different orders

5. Discussion

5.1 Threats to Validity

A threat to external validity is certainly the limited selection of subject systems. This is due to the novelty of our approach and the fact that the tool chain still imposes certain technical requirements on the subject systems. Nevertheless, we argue that our experiments demonstrate, at least, the potential of our approach, which, of course, shall be evaluated with more rigor in the future.

Our approach detects feature interactions based on the control flow only, not considering the data flow. The presence of additional data-flow interactions may change the results, but not the big picture, because of the already quite accurate results. In further work, we plan to combine family-based performance measurement with family-based data-flow analysis [27].

Furthermore, the aspect that performs the measurement and that creates the call graph may induce an overhead in execution time. To reduce this effect, we (a) measured the overhead of the aspect when visiting a method and (b) how often we visit a method per feature. Based on this information, we subtract the overhead for each feature. Note that the overhead varies depending on the subject program.

Our conclusions can be transferred to other customization and implementation techniques only with care. Our approach traces the execution of a method to the feature it belongs to. For feature-oriented programs, this information is available at compile time, and can be transferred to run time. For related compile-time customization techniques, this information can be obtained in a similar way, for example, for aspect-oriented programming and component systems. Results on analyzing C programs with preprocessor directives demonstrates that even fine-grained, undisciplined annotation-based customization techniques can be used for tracing [22, 27]. Furthermore, there is ongoing work on translating preprocessor directives to conditional statements [31].

Finally, performance is important, but not the only non-functional property of interest. Instead of measuring the execution time, we can measure memory usage, energy consumption, throughput. We expect our approach to be applicable to all other non-functional properties that are measurable like performance.

5.2 Applicability and Limitations

As a novel approach, we face some limitations and focus on certain application scenarios. Next, we discuss each limitation and highlight how to overcome it in further research.

Mutually Exclusive Features. An issue that we largely set aside is how to handle mutually exclusive features. In our experiments, we needed only a single run per subject program, as they do not contain any mutually exclusive features. As explained in Section 3.3, with an increasing number of mutually exclusive features, the effort for family-based measurement (and also other sampling-based approaches) increases, because alternative execution paths must be visited to cover all possible program paths. However, previous studies suggest that only a small fraction of features in real-world customizable programs are mutually exclusive [26]. Furthermore, in the presence of mutually exclusive features, our approach needs substantially fewer runs than state-of-the-art sampling-based approaches, as for them the number of variants increases not only with the number of mutually exclusive features, but also with the number of optional features. In fact, even in the worst case that all features are mutually exclusive, we require only a linear number of measurements (given our assumption that a method's execution time is constant), which is the lower bound of existing sampling approaches.

Program-Flow Analysis and Context Sensitivity. Our approach assumes that a method has a constant execution time no matter what optional feature is called before. The time can change only if the data used by the method depends on previously executed functions. Identifying such a change would require a program-flow analysis, which is a direction of future research. However, despite this limitation, we observed a high prediction accuracy. We assume that, in most cases, a changing workload has more significant influence on method execution times than feature selection. Furthermore, features in our evaluation usually implement a modular piece of functionality that does not depend on data manipulated by other features. For instance, applying an additional CRC check, signing an e-mail message, or additionally counting static members in an aspect in AJSTATS introduces a constant execution time for a static workload. Clearly, there may be cases in which feature execution times depend on other features' functionality and program-flow analysis is important, but our experiments suggest that focusing on control-flow can be often sufficient.

Determining the execution time of a single multi-threaded program is already challenging, but multi threading in the context of customizable programs imposes even more challenges, because we may encounter temporal dependencies among features. For instance, a feature may be executed in parallel to another feature. This means that depending on the feature selection, we may have an overlapping execution time. We invite the community to jointly tackle this problem.

Granularity and Implementation Techniques. Currently, we support only FeatureHouse-style programs, because we rely on the transformation of compile-time variability to run-time variability. An interesting question is whether we can apply these transformations also for other implementation techniques, supporting a finer granularity (e.g., #ifdefs in C). In a parallel line of research, we currently develop means to transform also #ifdef-based customizable programs to variant simulators, including type changes of variables and so forth. Furthermore, Kästner and others have shown that an automated transformation of an #ifdef-based program to a corresponding set of feature modules is possible [21]. An alternative way which makes our approach independent of the variant simulator is to make current profilers feature-aware. That is, if we can trace which statements belong to which feature at runtime, we can certainly create our call graph and subsequently our performance model.

To sum up, we expect that our assumptions (e.g., constant method execution time, no program-flow analysis) are usually met by feature-oriented programs, because features often implement coarse-grained and cohesive pieces of functionality. This picture may change when more fine-grained configuration options are considered as features, for instance, a feature that enables 64 bit support or doubles the precision of certain computations.

6. Related Work

The term 'family-based' stems from a recent classification of analysis techniques for product lines [36]. Currently, family-based analysis is performed mainly in the context type checking [20, 23], static analysis [8, 27], model checking [4, 13], and deductive verification [37]. We use a family-based approach for performance prediction, which

imposes unique challenges, in particular, tracing and aggregating execution times, identifying and incorporating feature interactions, as well as making performance models themselves variable.

Performance Prediction. Chen and others [11] use a combined benchmarking and profiling approach to predict the performance of component-based applications. Based on a JAVA profiling tool, a performance model is constructed for application-server components. In contrast, we correlate the measurements to the feature selection and have to perform the measurement only a single time.

Guo and others predict performance of software product lines using classification and regression trees [17]. They measure multiple configurations and classify the performance results by means of selected and deselected features. When predicting performance of a configuration, they use the most similar feature selection for which they have already measured the corresponding configuration.

In our previous work, we proposed an approach to quantify the influence of each feature on performance [34]. To this end, we measure two variants that differ only in a single feature and interpret the delta of the measurements as the performance impact of the differing feature. We refined this approach to detect feature interactions by using several heuristics [33]. While improving prediction accuracy, this also increased the number of measurements.

Family-based measurement differs form all these approaches in that it requires a principally lower number of measurements, while it achieves slightly improved prediction accuracy in our experiments. However, family-based measurement is not a black-box approach. We require the source code of the program.

Feature Interactions. Feature-interaction detection has been addressed in a substantial body of previous research (see Calder et al. [10] for a comprehensive overview). There are measurement-based approaches, such as by Calder and Miller, who use pair-wise measurement based on linear temporal logic to detect feature interactions [9]. Another approach to identify feature interactions is iTree [35]. It aims at reducing the complexity of combinatorial testing of customizable programs by identifying sets of features that are most likely to interact, especially, for higher-order interactions. Other techniques can be classified as model-based detection, for example, reachability graphs [30] and model checking [2, 13]. In contrast to previous work, we concentrate on performance feature interactions and analyze the control flow of a variant simulator to identify interactions. The relation to other kinds of feature interactions shall be explored in further work.

Performance Profiling Performance profiling has a long tradition and has similar equal goals. *Calling context trees* are related to our annotated call graphs [1]. They allow us to handle different execution times of the same method depending on the calling context. We believe this technique can be combined with our approach. There are a number of approaches that use profiling data to create a performance model of a program [25]. For instance, Jovic and others analyze samplings of call stacks of deployed versions of a program to find performance bugs [19]. Grechanik and others propose to learn rules for the generation of workloads that reveal program paths with a degraded performance [16]. However, these approaches tackle workload variability rather than program variability.

7. Conclusion

Most of today's software systems are customizable in terms optional and alternative features. The selection of features can affect the performance of a program substantially, and often users need to customize a program to maximize performance or to satisfy certain performance requirements. Measuring the performance of all program variants is usually infeasible due to the combinatorial explosion of possible feature combinations. Instead of measuring all variants, we predict their performance based on the feature selection and with as few measurements as possible.

We proposed family-based performance measurement—an approach that uses a variant simulator to measure performance of each feature with only few runs. The variant simulator encodes compile-time variability at run time, such that it subsumes the behavior of all program variants. When executing the simulator, we log the execution time of each method, the features to which the methods belong, and the features from which the method calls came from. Based on this information, we analyze the call graph to determine interactions among features and to aggregate execution times for each method to produce a performance model. Then, we use this model to predict the performance of a certain feature selection.

We evaluated our approach by means of five customizable programs implemented with feature-oriented programming. The results show that our predictions reach an accuracy of 98%, on average, while requiring only a single measurement per program. On a final note, this work is not intended to be complete. Instead, we want to open a door to further work on the analysis of feature interactions and the prediction and optimization of non-function properties.

Acknowledgments

The work of Siegmund is supported by the German ministry of education and science (BMBF), number 01IM10002B. The work of Apel and von Rhein is supported by the German Research Foundation (AP 206/2, AP 206/4, AP 206/5, and AP 206/7).

References

[1] G. Ammons, T. Ball, and J. Larus. Exploiting hardware performance counters with flow and context sensitive profiling. In *Proc. PLDI*, pages 85–96. ACM, 1997.

[2] S. Apel, H. Speidel, P. Wendler, A. von Rhein, and D. Beyer. Detection of feature interactions using feature-aware verification. In *Proc. ASE*, pages 372–375. IEEE, 2011.

[3] S. Apel, C. Kästner, and C. Lengauer. Language-independent and automated software composition: The FeatureHouse experience. *IEEE Transactions on Software Engineering*, 39(1):63–79, 2013.

[4] S. Apel, A. von Rhein, P. Wendler, A. Größlinger, and D. Beyer. Strategies for product-line verification: Case studies and experiments. In *Proc. ICSE*, pages 482–491. IEEE, 2013.

[5] S. Balsamo, A. Di Marco, P. Inverardi, and M. Simeoni. Model-based performance prediction in software development: A survey. *IEEE Transactions on Software Engineering*, 30(5):295–310, 2004.

[6] D. Batory, J. N. Sarvela, and A. Rauschmayer. Scaling step-wise refinement. *IEEE Transactions on Software Engineering*, 30(6):355–371, 2004.

[7] D. Batory, P. Höfner, and J. Kim. Feature interactions, products, and composition. In *Proc. GPCE*, pages 13–22. ACM, 2011.

[8] C. Brabrand, M. Ribeiro, T. Tolêdo, J. Winther, and P. Borba. Intraprocedural dataflow analysis for software product lines. *Transactions on Aspect-Oriented Software Development*, 10:73–108, 2013.

[9] M. Calder and A. Miller. Feature interaction detection by pairwise analysis of LTL properties: A case study. *Formal Methods in System Design*, 28(3):213–261, 2006.

[10] M. Calder, M. Kolberg, E. H. Magill, and S. Reiff-Marganiec. Feature interaction: A critical review and considered forecast. *Computer Networks and ISDN Systems*, 41:115–141, 2003.

[11] S. Chen, Y. Liu, I. Gorton, and A. Liu. Performance prediction of component-based applications. *Journal of Systems and Software*, 74 (1):35–43, 2005.

[12] E. Clarke, O. Grumberg, and D. Peled. *Model Checking*. MIT Press, 1999.

[13] A. Classen, P. Heymans, P.-Y. Schobbens, A. Legay, and J.-F. Raskin. Model checking lots of systems: Efficient verification of temporal properties in software product lines. In *Proc. ICSE*, pages 335–344. ACM, 2010.

[14] M. Erwig and E. Walkingshaw. The choice calculus: A representation for software variation. *ACM Transactions on Software Engineering and Methodology*, 21(1):1–27, 2011.

[15] C. Ghezzi and A. Sharifloo. Model-based verification of quantitative non-functional properties for software product lines. *Information and Software Technology*, 55(3):508–524, 2013.

[16] M. Grechanik, C. Fu, and Q. Xie. Automatically finding performance problems with feedback-directed learning software testing. In *Proc. ICSE*, pages 156–166. IEEE, 2012.

[17] J. Guo, K. Czarnecki, S. Apel, N. Siegmund, and A. Wasowski. Variability-aware performance prediction: A statistical learning approach. In *Proc. ASE*. IEEE, 2013. to appear.

[18] R. Hall. Fundamental nonmodularity in electronic mail. *Automated Software Engineering*, 12(1):41–79, 2005.

[19] M. Jovic, A. Adamoli, and M. Hauswirth. Catch me if you can: Performance bug detection in the wild. In *Proc. OOPSLA*, pages 155–170. ACM, 2011.

[20] C. Kästner and S. Apel. Type-checking software product lines - a formal approach. In *Proc. ASE*, pages 258–267. IEEE, 2008.

[21] C. Kästner, S. Apel, and M. Kuhlemann. A model of refactoring physically and virtually separated features. In *Proc. GPCE*, pages 157–166, 2009.

[22] C. Kästner, P. Giarrusso, T. Rendel, S. Erdweg, K. Ostermann, and T. Berger. Variability-aware parsing in the presence of lexical macros and conditional compilation. In *Proc. OOPSLA*, pages 805–824. ACM, 2011.

[23] C. Kästner, S. Apel, T. Thüm, and G. Saake. Type checking annotation-based product lines. *ACM Transactions on Software Engineering and Methodology*, 21(3):14:1–14:39, 2012.

[24] S. Kolesnikov, S. Apel, N. Siegmund, S. Sobernig, C. Kästner, and S. Senkaya. Predicting quality attributes of software product lines using software and network measures and sampling. In *Proc. VaMoS*, pages 25–29. ACM, 2013.

[25] Y. Kwon, S. Lee, H. Yi, D. Kwon, S. Yang, B.-G. Chun, L. Huang, P. Maniatis, M. Naik, and Y. Paek. Automatic generation of efficient performance predictors for smartphone applications. In *Proc. USENIX*, pages 297–308. Usenix Association, 2013.

[26] J. Liebig, S. Apel, C. Lengauer, C. Kästner, and M. Schulze. An analysis of the variability in forty preprocessor-based software product lines. In *Proc. ICSE*, pages 105–114. ACM, 2010.

[27] J. Liebig, A. von Rhein, C. Kästner, S. Apel, J. Dörre, and C. Lengauer. Scalable Analysis of Variable Software. In *Proc. ESEC/FSE*. ACM, 2013.

[28] J. Liu, D. Batory, and C. Lengauer. Feature-oriented refactoring of legacy applications. In *Proc. ICSE*, pages 112–121. ACM, 2006.

[29] M. Plath and M. Ryan. Feature integration using a feature construct. *Science of Computer Programming*, 41(1):53–84, 2001.

[30] K. Pomakis and J. Atlee. Reachability analysis of feature interactions: A progress report. In *Proc. ISSTA*, pages 216–223. ACM, 1996.

[31] H. Post and C. Sinz. Configuration lifting: Verification meets software configuration. In *Proc. ASE*, pages 347–350. IEEE, 2008.

[32] N. Siegmund, M. Rosenmüller, C. Kästner, P. Giarrusso, S. Apel, and S. Kolesnikov. Scalable prediction of non-functional properties in software product lines. In *Proc. SPLC*, pages 160–169. IEEE, 2011.

[33] N. Siegmund, S. Kolesnikov, C. Kästner, S. Apel, D. Batory, M. Rosenmüller, and G. Saake. Predicting performance via automated feature-interaction detection. In *Proc. ICSE*, pages 167–177. IEEE, 2012.

[34] N. Siegmund, M. Rosenmüller, C. Kästner, P. Giarrusso, S. Apel, and S. Kolesnikov. Scalable prediction of non-functional properties in software product lines: Footprint and memory consumption. *Information and Software Technology*, 55(3):491–507, 2013.

[35] C. Song, A. Porter, and J. Foster. iTree: Efficiently discovering high-coverage configurations using interaction trees. In *Proc. ICSE*, pages 903–913. IEEE, 2012.

[36] T. Thüm, S. Apel, C. Kästner, M. Kuhlemann, I. Schäfer, and G. Saake. Analysis strategies for software product lines. Technical report, University of Magdeburg, Nb.: FIN-04-2012, 2012.

[37] T. Thüm, I. Schaefer, S. Apel, and M. Hentschel. Family-based deductive verification of software product lines. In *Proc. GPCE*, pages 11–20. ACM, 2012.

[38] I. H. Witten and E. Frank. *Data mining: Practical machine learning tools and techniques*. Elsevier, Morgan Kaufman, 2. edition, 2005.

ShadowVM: Robust and Comprehensive Dynamic Program Analysis for the Java Platform

Lukáš Marek

Faculty of Mathematics and Physics
Charles University, Czech Republic
lukas.marek@d3s.mff.cuni.cz

Stephen Kell   Yudi Zheng

Faculty of Informatics
University of Lugano, Switzerland
firstname.lastname@usi.ch

Lubomír Bulej   Walter Binder

Faculty of Informatics
University of Lugano, Switzerland
firstname.lastname@usi.ch

Petr Tůma

Faculty of Mathematics and Physics
Charles University, Czech Republic
petr.tuma@d3s.mff.cuni.cz

Danilo Ansaloni   Aibek Sarimbekov

Faculty of Informatics
University of Lugano, Switzerland
firstname.lastname@usi.ch

Andreas Sewe

Software Technology Group
TU Darmstadt, Germany
andreas.sewe@cs.tu-darmstadt.de

Abstract

Dynamic analysis tools are often implemented using instrumentation, particularly on managed runtimes including the Java Virtual Machine (JVM). Performing instrumentation robustly is especially complex on such runtimes: existing frameworks offer limited coverage and poor isolation, while previous work has shown that apparently innocuous instrumentation can cause deadlocks or crashes in the observed application. This paper describes ShadowVM, a system for instrumentation-based dynamic analyses on the JVM which combines a number of techniques to greatly improve both isolation and coverage. These centre on the offload of analysis to a separate process; we believe our design is the first system to enable genuinely full bytecode coverage on the JVM. We describe a working implementation, and use a case study to demonstrate its improved coverage and to evaluate its runtime overhead.

Categories and Subject Descriptors   D.3.3 [*Programming Languages*]: Language Constructs and Features—Frameworks

Keywords   Dynamic analysis; JVM; instrumentation

1. Introduction

To gain insight about how to optimise, debug, extend and refactor large systems, programmers depend on analysis tools. One popular class of tools is *dynamic program analysis* tools, which observe a program in execution and report additional data about that execution. Many popular bug-finding and profiling tools are of this form, including the Valgrind suite [19], DTrace [2], and GProf [12]. Meanwhile, research continues to devise more complex and specialised tools, for race detection [10], white-box testing [25], security policy enforcement [28] and more.

Developing dynamic analyses is difficult. One approach is to invasively modify the host runtime system, but this is an expert task yielding a non-portable solution. Alternatively, instrumentation frameworks including Pin [6] and DynamoRIO [5] (exporting a roughly compiler-style intermediate representation), and also Javassist [7], Soot [21] and DiSL [16] (targeting Java bytecode), are highly general. However, using them can be challenging, since they require deep understanding of both the intermediate representation and the host runtime environment. More constrained frameworks [2, 11] provide stronger properties with less user effort, but each caters to a smaller set of use cases. Outwith these use cases, developing a *high-quality* dynamic analysis remains a Herculean task, plagued by the recurrence of three mutually antagonistic requirements: *isolation*, meaning roughly that observing the program does not cause it to deviate from the path it would ordinarily take; *coverage*, meaning the ability to observe all relevant events during execution, including both user code and system code; and *performance*, meaning the minimisation of slowdown caused by the analysis.

In this paper we present ShadowVM[1], a system for dynamic analysis of programs running within the Java Virtual Machine (JVM) which advances on prior work by simultaneously combining strong isolation and high coverage. Analyses execute asynchronously with respect to the observed program, allowing parallelism to mitigate isolation-induced slowdowns. To our knowledge, ours is the first complete dynamic analysis framework offering asynchronous execution without effectively serializing heavily instrumented workloads. It does so by exploiting heterogeneity among dynamic analyses, which typically only need to preserve the order of observed events for particular *subsets* of events. In summary, this paper presents the following contributions:

- We describe an architecture and programming model for dynamic analyses of Java bytecode which enforces isolation by performing all analysis computation in a separate process. This enables *asynchronous* remote evaluation while permitting a familiar programming model similar to that of existing instrumentation frameworks.

- We summarise the state of the art regarding *coverage* on the JVM, identifying challenges which so far limit the coverage available under existing systems, and explaining how our implementation

---

[1] Sources available at http://disl.ow2.org

circumvents these challenges. We believe our system to be the first offering truly complete bytecode coverage on the JVM.

- We evaluate the isolation and coverage of our implementation compared to classic in-process analysis and provide experimental evidence of reduced perturbation and improved coverage. To quantify the cost of the improved isolation in terms of performance, we evaluate the runtime overhead and scalability of our solution with parallel workloads.

We begin by motivating our approach in greater depth.

2. Motivation

A popular mechanism used by dynamic analysis tools to observe applications on the Java platform is *bytecode instrumentation*. The analysis tool inserts "hooks", in the form of bytecode snippets, into locations of interest in the application code. When the application execution reaches a particular location, the corresponding hook is executed as a part of the application. Compared to alternative observation mechanisms, such as debugging interfaces or virtual machine modifications, bytecode instrumentation is often more portable, less complex, and offers higher performance. However, observation through bytecode instrumentation also exhibits two significant problems: one concerning the safety of *high coverage* analyses, and another concerning the semantics of *asynchronously executing* analysis tools. We discuss these in turn.

2.1 Coverage versus isolation

Observation through bytecode instrumentation necessarily mixes the application code with (at least some of) the analysis code. This can lead to problems achieving high coverage in analyses, i.e. to observe program activity in all code, including sensitive bytecode regions such as system-level libraries. Java analysis tools usually cannot avoid calling these libraries from within the analysis code, because the libraries offer the standard or even the only means of performing many essential operations—including input and output (e.g. for exporting the analysis results), reflective acquisition of metadata (e.g. for inspecting the class and field information pertaining to the instrumented event), and keeping references to program objects (e.g. through the weak reference mechanism). When the libraries offering these functions are themselves instrumented, library-internal resources become shared between the application and the analysis in an uncoordinated way. Consequently, even very basic instrumentation scenarios can suffer from subtle problems including state corruption (from introduced reentrancy), deadlocks (from lock order violations), and memory exhaustion (from sharing the weak reference queue handler) [22].

A cheap way to avoid this interference, i.e. to improve the *isolation* between analysis and the application, is to exclude common library code from instrumentation. This exclusion technique is commonly used in various dynamic analysis frameworks; Figure 1 shows three examples from well-known frameworks. Exclusion limits the observation power of the analysis, since it can no longer analyse library operations—resource usage by library code is invisible, data flow through library code cannot be tracked, and so on. Managed runtimes, notably the Java platform, suffer particularly because core functionality, including class loading and some aspects of memory management, is implemented in bytecode and cannot be cleanly and effectively replaced or virtualized to isolate the base program from the analysis.

Instead of sacrificing coverage by using exclusion to achieve isolation, we prefer to perform the analysis "outside" the observed program. Doing so in native code appears feasible (given appropriate care to inadvertent sharing of state through native method implementations). Unlike bytecode, native code can safely perform input and output operations through the operating system interfaces,

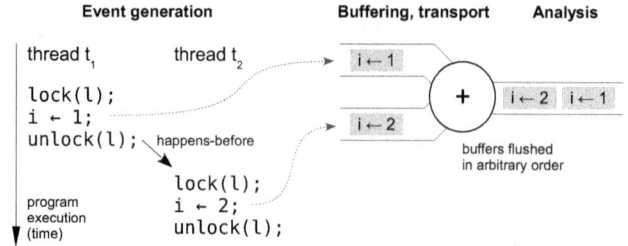

Figure 2. Multiple buffering can cause reordering of observations. Here, two assignments ordered by synchronization in the program are nevertheless reordered in the event stream fed to the analysis.

access object references through the virtual machine API, and implement out-of-band reflection. We pursue this approach; details in the context of our tool are in §4.2 and §6.

Writing analyses in native code requires knowledge of C or C++ and the associated virtual machine and system API. This can become a practical obstacle for Java developers. We therefore seek a programming environment where analyses are written at the same level of abstraction as when using plain bytecode instrumentation, but with improved coverage and isolation. For example, it should be possible to safely perform Java-style reflection, to keep references to objects in the observed program, and to freely use existing library code when implementing the analysis. This environment should also provide specialised mechanisms for common analysis tasks, such as associating analysis state with application objects. We describe such an environment in §4.

2.2 Resource lifecycle events

Even with the best coverage possible, bytecode instrumentation can only observe bytecode execution events. In some cases this is incomplete—not only because the application can execute native code, but also because the events of interest can occur inside the code of the virtual machine itself, rather than in the application. Some events are not associated with particular bytecode execution (such as virtual machine startup and shutdown) yet are highly relevant to analyses (e.g. for purposes of state management). Frameworks focusing solely on bytecode instrumentation neglect such events. This class of events can be viewed as events in the *lifecycles* of the basic system resources: program objects, threads, and the virtual machine itself. They contrast with the usual state transitions *within* a given system resource, such as within objects (field updates) and within threads (calls, returns, computations on the operand stack), which are cleanly captured by bytecode. Although hooks for several lifecycle events are available through either the Java API or the virtual machine API, their use from within the analysis is complicated by isolation and synchronization issues. For example, with the standard JVM shutdown notification API (in `java.lang.Runtime`), the shutdown hooks run concurrently with other hooks and with daemon threads, which execute application code. An analysis therefore cannot rely on the virtual machine shutdown event being the last event observed. Another example is the JVM reference handling mechanism, used for notification of object death. This mechanism cannot be safely used by analysis that also observes the application reference handling behavior [22]. In general, the problem is that these hooks are neither isolated from the application nor ordered relative to other observed events. §4.4 explains how our programming model avoids these problems by introducing lifecycle event ordering guarantees.

```
# RoadRunner's default exclusion  list        // Chord's  implicit  exclusion  logic :                        // BTrace excludes " sensitive "  classes
java..*                                         public boolean isImplicitlyExcluded (String cName) {          private  static  boolean  isSensitiveClass (String  name) {
javax..*                                          return cName.equals("java.lang.J9VMInternals") ||              return  name.equals("java/lang/Object") ||
com.sun..*                                         cName.startsWith("sun.reflect.Generated") ||                   name.startsWith("java/lang/ThreadLocal") ||
org.objectweb.asm..*                               cName.startsWith("java.lang.ref.");                            name.startsWith("sun/reflect") ||
sun..*                                          }                                                               name.equals("sun/misc/Unsafe") ||
                                                                                                                name.startsWith("sun/security/") ||
                                                                                                                name.equals("java/lang/VerifyError");
                                                                                                            }
```

Figure 1. Exclusion lists from the RoadRunner [11], Chord [18] and BTrace (http://kenai.com/projects/btrace) frameworks. Such exclusions are found in prevailing bytecode-level dynamic analysis frameworks, limiting the coverage available to tools built with them.

2.3 Asynchronous analysis

To exploit modern multiprocessor hardware, designs which relax synchronisation between application and analysis are increasingly desirable. Several existing systems and techniques, such as Shadow Profiling [26], SuperPin [29], and CAB [14], support offloading the analysis to separate cores for parallel processing. So far, however, little attention has been paid to the impact of asynchronous analysis design on the ability to observe application event ordering.

With a synchronous design, the hooks inserted through bytecode instrumentation execute the analysis code as a part of the application, synchronously (with respect to the thread running the inserted bytecode). The virtual machine applies the semantic rules governing program execution to both the analysis and the application together— in particular, the analysis actions are ordered with the program actions using the intra-thread semantics of the Java language and the happens-before relation of the Java Memory Model.

In contrast, an asynchronous analysis design separates the hooks from the analysis code. The hooks still execute as a part of the application and are therefore still ordered with the program actions. However, instead of executing the analysis code directly, the hooks notify the analysis code through asynchronous communication. The analysis code executes in a separate thread or even a separate process, and the communication involved may easily change the order in which the individual actions are ultimately observed by the analysis. Figure 2 shows an example of this reordering, where the instrumentation uses multiple thread-local buffers to avoid contention. Since these are flushed to an output stream in a non-deterministic order (e.g. when the buffer is full), the original program ordering is lost. Dynamic program analyses differ in their sensitivity to these changes: count-based analyses tend to work with any ordering; thread-local analyses may require ordering guarantees from the thread perspective; other analyses are yet more demanding. Because additional ordering guarantees bring additional costs, an efficient instrumentation framework should exploit the heterogeneity of the analyses and provide only the ordering that is required. We consider this further in §4.3.

3. ShadowVM design goals

ShadowVM addresses some of the issues that make the development of high-quality dynamic analyses difficult. It has several goals, each corresponding to one or more features in the design.

Isolation. We wish to avoid sharing state with the observed program to the greatest extent possible. This is necessary both generally to reduce perturbation and specifically to avoid various known classes of bugs which less well-isolated approaches inherently risk introducing [22]. Our design's **hook–analysis separation** achieves this by factoring analyses into a remotely executed part and short local "hooks" inserted by bytecode instrumentation, which trap immediately to native code. Although this pattern has been advocated, e.g. in the JVMTI documentation, we know of few dynamic anal-

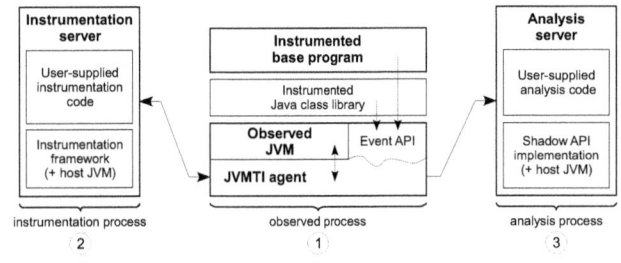

Figure 3. ShadowVM architecture at a high level.

yses which actually follow it. This undoubtedly owes to a lack of supporting infrastructure—a lack which our work addresses.

High coverage. We wish to allow instrumentation of both user-level application code and system-level core libraries. Previous approaches have provided only partial solutions. There is a fundamental tension with isolation, since achieving coverage deep in the system-level libraries risks perturbing core JVM behaviour. We explore these difficulties in §5. Our approach combines several implementation techniques, notably **out-of-process analysis** and the aforementioned "straight to native" hooks. These are able to cover all bytecode execution. To our knowledge, ours is the first system offering genuinely complete bytecode coverage on the JVM.

Performance. We require dynamic analyses to perform well in spite of the additional level of isolation provided by our system. To this end, our **asynchronous analysis** design exploits the availability of spare CPU cores. Meanwhile, our **flexible ordering models** help extract latent parallelism while preserving the event ordering relationships on which the analysis' functional correctness depends.

Productivity. We wish to allow instrumentation and analysis to be free of unnecessary constraints on how they may be programmed. In particular, it must be possible to implement them in Java code, rather than only in native code. We also require that they may be expressed in terms of a well-defined and convenient API. We define a "shadow API" for this purpose. Two notable features are its convenient **associative shadow state** abstraction and the **ordering guarantees** it offers, which reflect the selected ordering model.

4. Writing analyses using ShadowVM

Writing a dynamic analysis using ShadowVM is in many ways similar to the use of a bytecode-level instrumentation system such as DiSL, BTrace or (the dynamic analysis part of) Chord. However, our design differs to improve the robustness of the resulting tool. The most significant difference is a "hook–analysis separation": since analysis code does not run in the same process as the observed program, instrumentation is strongly separated from analysis by a generated stub layer which notifies the remote analysis of events of interest. Figure 3 shows the high-level architecture of the system.

```
1  // ————— runs in the observed VM
2  public class AllocCounterStub {
3      // instrument: snippet inserted after each "new" bytecode
4      @AfterReturning(marker=BytecodeMarker.class , args="new")
5      public static void allocSnippet(
6          DynamicContext dc, AllocationSiteStaticContext sc) {
7          // transmit event to analysis
8          AllocCounterRE.onAlloc(
9              dc.getStackValue(0, Object.class), // object allocated
10             sc.getAllocationSite() );           // alloc site
11     }
12 }
13 // ————— runs in the analysis VM
14 public class AllocCounter implements AllocAnalysis {
15     AtomicLong counter = new AtomicLong();
16     public void onAlloc(
17         ShadowObject o, ShadowString allocSite) {
18         counter.incrementAndGet();
19     }
20 }
```

Figure 4. This simple analysis counts object allocations by allocation site. For simplicity, this code only instruments the **new** bytecode. Other bytecodes allocating objects would require similar treatment.

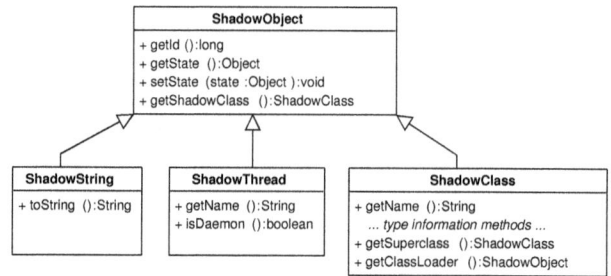

Figure 5. The Shadow API provides an analysis-friendly view of objects and threads in the observed program. Shadow objects are in bijection with the subset of objects in the observed program that have been passed to the analysis. Each object allows association of shadow state, which can be used to store arbitrary data.

Whereas the instrumented base program is executed by the JVM within the *observed process*, a second process performs all bytecode instrumentation. This process separation is essentially hidden from the user. A third process performs the analysis itself; this separation is much more apparent. Finally, we note that since in our implementation, both analysis and instrumentation are implemented in Java, each process runs its own JVM.[2]

Three other distinctions of our programming model are: its flexible approach to analysis-visible object state (in which the user controls how objects in the observed program are represented for analysis); notification ordering (in which more relaxed orderings can be requested, offering improved performance); and resource lifecycle events, which allow notifications not directly available through Java bytecode instrumentation. We discuss each of these, beginning with an example.

4.1 Introductory example

Figure 4 shows a simple example analysis implemented using ShadowVM. It consists of an instrumentation part and an analysis part. The instrumentation part, lines 2–12, uses a pre-existing annotation-based instrumentation language, DiSL [16], to define a "hook" as a code snippet woven into the program on the events of interest (here execution of the **new** bytecode). This hook simply extracts the information from the instrumentation context (here the object allocated, retrieved from the top of the stack using getStackValue(0, Object.class)) and calls into an onAlloc method of the AllocCounterRE class. The definition of this method is not shown because it is a stub routine generated from the AllocAnalysis interface exposed by the analysis part. The stub simply notifies the analysis VM of the event. The analysis part, lines 14–20, defines the analysis computation, its interface being a single onAlloc method.

The hook runs in the observed VM, whereas the analysis runs in the analysis VM. Unlike other bytecode instrumentation systems, under our design the hook only invokes native notification calls, which marshal their arguments into a wire representation that is sent over a socket to the analysis VM. The analysis VM runs an event loop which receives the notifications and dispatches them to the appropriate analysis method. (The dispatch logic is also responsible for creating analysis threads; we describe this in §6.4.)

4.2 Shadow API and object representation

In the analysis VM, analyses are clients of the *Shadow API*, shown in Figure 5. This API provides methods for reflecting on the class

metadata in the observed program, and for associating analysis state with objects in the base program. Each object is reified as a *shadow object* which provides an associative API but (by default) does not replicate the fields of the original object—only object identity and class information are available by default. This design reflects the fact that object contents are not required by many analyses (e.g. most profilers). Meanwhile, many that *are* sensitive to object contents (e.g. a shape analysis over heap structure) may benefit from a customised representation of the fields (e.g. only recording distinct pointer fields, rather than every field). To replicate object contents, the analysis must receive field write events from the observed VM, and associate these field values with the shadow objects.

The use of distinct "shadow" object, thread and string classes necessitates some translation in the mapping from analysis APIs to notification (stub) APIs. Whereas the analysis API's method signatures must be in terms of **ShadowObject**, **ShadowString** etc. (and primitive types), in the observed VM these will appear as the usual **Object**, **String**, etc. Instances of **java.lang.Class** are also shadowed specially: every class loaded in the observed VM has corresponding "shadow class" metadata available in the analysis VM. This is essential because many analyses generate output in terms of the structure of the program (profiles per class or per method, backtraces on events of interest, etc.).

4.3 Threading and ordering

Analysis code runs according to a particular threading model, where different models are suitable for different analyses. The analysis VM creates threads for processing incoming notifications. Different analyses have different requirements concerning in what order they must process notifications. These requirements reflect the dependency structure of the analysis computation. For example, just as profilers rarely require object contents, many profilers are insensitive to reordering of events of the same kind, because they effectively perform counting (counter increments are commutative).

In general, the developer needs to be aware of the ordering requirements of a particular analysis, and choose an appropriate implementation strategy for the analysis code. ShadowVM's most conservative ordering yields similar behaviour to the existing dynamic analysis frameworks such as Chord, where the observed program is effectively serialized for analysis.[3] However, ShadowVM also provides higher-performance (but more relaxed) ordering configurations, for use when appropriate.

---

[2] We use "instrumentation VM" and "instrumentation process" interchangeably. Similarly, the "observed" and "analysis" processes are also "VMs".

[3] Although strictly speaking, nothing in Chord's design serializes the program, ordering is handled by contending for a lock on a unique shared buffer. Frequent contention for this lock in all threads, as generated by any moderate or heavy instrumentation, effectively serializes the program.

We describe ordering using the following terminology. *Program actions* are state transitions in the observed process. A subset of these are of interest to the analysis, so are hooked. This generates an *event*, which is a message encapsulating the values gathered by the hook code, and which is transmitted to the analysis VM. *Notification* is the receipt of an event by the analysis VM from the observed VM. We say that the hooked program action in the observed VM *triggers* a notification in the analysis VM. The ordering of notifications is not, in general, the same as the ordering of the program actions that triggered them. The different ordering models we now describe cause different subsets of the ordering of program actions to be preserved in the ordering of notifications. (We note that the "ground truth" ordering of program actions is determined by the behaviour of the host system. In our case, since the host system is a JVM, this behaviour is circumscribed by the Java standard.)

Per-thread configuration. In this configuration, notifications are ordered by the (per-thread) program order in the observed program. Events from each thread are stored in a dedicated FIFO buffer pool by the agent, the pools are flushed in arbitrary order with respect to each other. Notifications are dispatched to multiple analysis threads corresponding to the threads that trigger the events in the observed program.

Per-group configuration. This is the most flexible configuration. The developer specifies a group identifier to be used with each hook. Each group has its own FIFO buffer pool for notifications. It can be seen as a generalisation of per-thread ordering where pools need not map to threads. For example, a group could map to a set of threads, a single object, code in a particular set of classes, and so on. Similar to the per-thread configuration, the analysis server dispatches notifications to the corresponding analysis methods in multiple threads, one thread per group.

Global-ordering configuration. This is the most conservative configuration. Conceptually, it can be thought of as per-group configuration with a single group identifier. A single buffer pool is used, and the analysis server dispatches all notifications to the corresponding analysis methods in a single thread.

4.4 Resource lifecycle events

ShadowVM analyses can request notifications for special events which do not correspond to execution of bytecodes. Rather, they relate to some unit of *resource* in the program, where these resources can be threads, objects or the VM itself. These special events mark the end of resource *lifetimes*. For example, the user can request notification of object death (which occurs in the garbage collector, so has no corresponding bytecode). Our attention to ordering guarantees extends to these events. Specifically, we guarantee that following a notification of the death of a thread, object or the VM, no further notifications referencing that entity will occur. In the case of the VM, a "VM death" notification is the last one of the execution.

This contrasts with existing APIs which might be used for such purposes, such as finalizers, or the Java library's `Runtime.addShutdownHook` method. These APIs offer few or no guarantees about the scheduling of hook code, making them difficult to employ from analyses without risking loss of coverage. For example, although an analysis could register its own shutdown hook, there is no guarantee that some user-supplied hook would not run after it. A similar lack of guarantee applies to object finalizers (which, in any case, need not mark the end of an object's lifetime, owing to resurrection [4]). Meanwhile, there is no portable way to identify the bytecode representing the precise end of a thread's execution.

As with other notifications, these ordering guarantees are enforced in the buffer management code. For all ordering configura-

tions, ShadowVM ensures that the lifecycle events are delivered in proper order related to the notifications produced by hooks.

5. Coverage challenges

In any instrumentation-based design, isolating the analysed program from the analysis is inherently in tension with coverage, because the inserted code necessarily shares an execution context with the analysed program code. By default, therefore, it is not isolated from it. Isolation can only be provided by adopting a discipline which restricts what is done from the inserted code, yet still provides analyses with essential functionality such as allocating memory, keeping references to objects in the observed program, and performing I/O. In this section we summarise the specific difficulties of achieving this on the Java platform, and the extent to which existing solutions have (and have not) overcome them.

Exclusion list. A simple way to avoid isolation difficulties is to sacrifice coverage, by omitting instrumentation of core classes. This avoids bootstrapping problems, interference between program and analysis (through shared library state), and infinite regress (if these libraries are used from instrumentation). We saw some exclusion lists in Figure 1.

Load–instrument gaps. High coverage relies on intercepting the loading of a high proportion of the base program code, so that an instrumented version can be substituted. Many naive instrumentation implementations on the Java platform miss some coverage by missing load events (therefore never instrumenting the loaded code), or by allowing execution of uninstrumented versions of the code for some time. The Java instrumentation API in `java.lang.instrument` suffers from this problem because it does not allow applying the instrumentation during JVM start. Moreover, since the Java code performing the instrumentation may itself trigger additional classes to be loaded (which cannot be transformed at that point), it leaves the untransformed version available for use by other threads. We avoid this by performing instrumentation outside the observed VM (in a separate process) using JVMTI's `ClassFileLoad` hook (which does not lead to concurrent use of the uninstrumented code).

Missed initializers. Possibly the most obvious problem with instrumenting core libraries is infinite regress when those libraries are invoked from the inserted code. It is easily avoided using a per-thread "bypass" flag [17]. However, a side-effect of bypass is that initializers for classes used by the analysis are run while the bypass is active and so are not analysed; if the same classes are used later by the program, their initializers will not be re-run, and so will not be covered. ShadowVM does not suffer from this problem because the only classes referenced by its implementation are `Object` and `String` which are preloaded by the JVM bootstrap long before the first bytecode is executed.

Avoiding bootstrap bypass. Special-case handling is inevitably required for instrumentation affecting the very earliest bytecode that the JVM executes, a.k.a. the "bootstrap phase". The hook code snippets as well as our generated stub classes are carefully restricted to a safe subset of bytecode operations. For example, it is not safe to allocate objects in inserted code that might be invoked from `Object.< clinit >` (causing a stack overflow). Since our stubs need only call a static native method, this careful construction is possible—the fact that calls to our native stub code can be called so early owes to the fact that an initial set of classes, including `Object` and `Class`, is necessarily special-cased by the JVM.[4]

---

[4] The JVM's definition of a class being "loaded" implies that a `Class` object exists for it [13, §12.2]—yet, to instantiate the `Class` object for class `Object` under these rules, both `Class` and its superclass `Object` would (circularly)

Reference handling. The standard way for an analysis to maintain references to objects in the observed program is to use `WeakReferences`. Usually, one shared reference handler thread (or a garbage collection thread) processes cleared reference objects (`WeakReference`, `SoftReference`, `PhantomReference`) on behalf of all other threads. If this thread's code is instrumented, it may create a self-sustaining allocation cycle, because the inserted code within the reference handler may allocate more `WeakReferences`. Excluding the reference handling code avoids this problem, but loses coverage of reference handling on behalf of the observed program. Our design avoids using `WeakReferences` and thus avoids this problem.

6. ShadowVM Architecture

We have summarized the high-level, multi-process architecture of ShadowVM earlier in §4. Here, we review the key architectural elements in greater detail. In general, the architecture is driven by the design goals elaborated in §3, and the ShadowVM responsibilities are split between three processes, as shown in Figure 3.

Firstly, the observed VM (augmented with a JVMTI agent) contains the instrumented base program and class library. The inserted hook code is responsible for producing base program events that are of interest to the analysis. The agent has two key responsibilities: installing instrumented base program code in the observed VM, and forwarding events produced by the hooks in the base program to the analysis.

A second VM contains the instrumentation server, itself written in Java. The instrumentation server performs all bytecode instrumentation, communicating Java bytecode with the observed VM's agent via a socket.

The third VM contains the analysis server, which hosts the analysis written against the Shadow API. The analysis server is responsible for dispatching event notifications received via socket from the observed VM's agent to the analysis code, while respecting the selected ordering configuration.

We now review the various responsibilities in turn.

6.1 Load-time instrumentation

To ensure load-time instrumentation of the base program, the agent intercepts all class loading events in the observed VM and requests instrumented versions from the instrumentation VM. The use of a separate VM to perform instrumentation avoids the substantial perturbation which would be caused if instrumentation were performed within the observed VM. For example, doing so would bring forth a significant amount of class loading and initialization activity, which would then not be analysed at the proper point in the observed program's execution. Besides reducing perturbation, this separation is also essential to enable high-coverage instrumentation encompassing the Java Class Library (JCL).

6.2 Base-program event generation

The user-defined hooks in the base program are responsible for generating the events of interest for a particular analysis. The hooks are expressed as DiSL [16] snippets. However, unlike conventional analyses based on bytecode instrumentation (including ordinary uses of DiSL), the hook code is always of the same restricted form: invoking a native helper method (event API) provided by the observed VM's agent, passing as arguments values capturing the program state that is relevant to the instrumented event. Beyond this point, the reified event is the responsibility of the agent, and in this paper we do not concern ourselves further with how the instrumentation itself is expressed or performed. We simply assume

that the events of interest at bytecode level can be intercepted and handled appropriately, and to simplify hook development, we provide a library of snippets for various event types.

6.3 Event forwarding

The agent natively implements an *event API*, into which hooks call during the execution of the instrumented base program, producing base program events. The methods of this API marshal their arguments into buffers and the agent delivers the event notifications in an asynchronous manner to the analysis server executing on the analysis VM. This separation is crucial to achieve high coverage and isolation, because it allows instrumenting the base program without any bypass mechanisms. It also allows using extra computing power for analysis without perturbing the base-program execution.

The communication between observed and analysis processes requires carefully designed buffering and threading strategies in order to yield high-performance asynchronous analyses while respecting ordering constraints (introduced in §4.3). Events produced by base program threads are stored and marshaled into buffers in the context of the event API invocations. Object references in the buffers are processed by a separate thread that ensures, with the help of object tagging, that objects have unique identity and that it is preserved on the analysis server. Another thread then sends the completed buffers to the analysis VM.

6.4 Notification delivery

Recall that the analysis code runs in a separate JVM (*analysis VM*). Base program event notifications are sent via socket to the analysis server. Dispatch logic in the analysis server consumes from this socket, performs appropriate unmarshaling, and invokes methods of the analysis.

Apart from the threading model described in §4.3, which is exposed to the analysis, the analysis server has to cooperate with the agent to maintain notification ordering mandated by the selected ordering configuration. The internal threading model of the analysis server was designed to properly order resource lifecycle notifications with respect to base program event notifications. In addition to the threads dispatching base program notifications, the analysis server also creates a dedicated thread to deliver resource lifecycle event notifications to the analysis.

7. Evaluation

We consider the high degree of isolation and full bytecode coverage to be the key benefits of ShadowVM. We therefore aim at evaluating the difference in perturbation and analysis coverage when a base program is subjected to a heavy-weight dynamic analysis—once implemented in the classic in-process manner, and once implemented using ShadowVM.

With respect to performance, the distributed nature of the ShadowVM approach comes with an inherent overhead due to reification and forwarding of events to the analysis VM. However, the ShadowVM approach also has an inherent scaling potential, which hinges on the ability of a particular analysis to execute in multiple threads mirroring the base-program threads. We therefore aim at quantifying the overhead of a ShadowVM-based analysis compared to classic in-process analysis and to assess the scalability of ShadowVM with parallel workloads.

As case study for our evaluation, we chose the field immutability analysis (FIA) by Sewe et al. [1][5]. In summary, FIA tracks all object allocations and field accesses and maintains a per-field "state-machine" that describes the mutability of that field. If a field is written outside the dynamic extent of an object's constructor, it is

---

already need to be loaded and initialized. All JVMs therefore employ some kind of special-casing to avoid this circularity.

[5] The sources are available at http://www.disl.scalabench.org/modules/immutability-disl-analysis/.

Benchmark	Uninstrumented	In-process FIA	ShadowVM FIA
avrora	1020	1221	1022
batik	2042	2248	2044
fop	1868	2129	1870
h2	919	1120	921
jython	2651	2828	2653
luindex	783	984	785
lusearch	680	886	682
pmd	1194	1387	1196
sunflow	938	1104	940
xalan	1168	1389	1170

Table 1. Comparison of class loading perturbation. The table presents the number of classes loaded by the observed VM.

marked mutable. Explicit field initialization during construction and reliance on implicit zeroing of fields by the VM are taken into account. Overall, the analysis is relatively heavy-weight and would be a typical candidate for offloading to a separate VM.

We recast the original in-process FIA to ShadowVM and evaluate the differences in perturbation, coverage, and performance. To assess scalability of FIA under ShadowVM, we run it with both per-thread (which suffices for FIA) and global ordering configurations. The base programs for our evaluation come from the DaCapo suite [23] (release 9.12). Of the fourteen benchmarks in the suite, we excluded tomcat, tradebeans, and tradesoap due to well known issues unrelated to ShadowVM.[6] We also excluded eclipse, which exhibits too non-deterministic behaviour under instrumentation and thus prevents fair comparison.

All experiments were run on a 64-bit multi-core platform with Oracle Hotspot Server VM[7], and with all non-essential system services disabled.

7.1 Perturbation

With respect to perturbation, the ShadowVM approach should improve on classic in-process analysis thanks to the isolation from the observed VM. Consequently, a ShadowVM-based analysis should exhibit minimal (if any) influence on class loading or garbage collections triggered by the base-program.

7.1.1 Class loading perturbation

We first evaluate the class loading perturbation caused by a dynamic analysis. To this end, we simply capture the sequence of classes loaded by the observed VM in response to base-program execution. The data collected when running the uninstrumented base program serve as a reference for comparison with the data collected when running with either the in-process or ShadowVM-based FIA implementation.

Table 1 lists the numbers of classes loaded by the observed VM when running base programs from the DaCapo suite. We note that in the case of the ShadowVM-based FIA implementation, the observed VM loads exactly two more classes than the uninstrumented version. These two classes wrap the native methods designated for reifying the base-program events in the observed VM's agent. In contrast, the in-process FIA implementation loads significantly more classes, because it is implemented using those classes.

7.1.2 Garbage collection perturbation

Next, we evaluate the perturbation in garbage collection behavior. Ideally, an analysis should not influence the memory allocation

[6] See bug ID 2955469 and 2934521 in the DaCapo bug tracker at http://sourceforge.net/tracker/?group_id=172498&atid=861957.

[7] 2x Intel Xeon X5650 2.67GHz with 24 cores, 48 GB of RAM, OpenJDK 1.7.0_09-icedtea 64-Bit Server VM (build 23.2-b09) running on Fedora 18

patterns imposed on the JVM by the observed base program. The experimental setup is similar to that of the previous evaluation, except we collect information on garbage collections performed by the JVM during the execution of the base program. The maximum heap size is limited to two gigabytes and the actual heap size never reaches the limit. Apart from the maximum heap size, the JVM is in default configuration. Again, the data collected when running the uninstrumented base program serve as a reference for comparison.

Table 2 lists the numbers of garbage collections in the young and old generation spaces, the amount of allocated (garbage collected) memory, and the final heap size including the sizes of the young and old generation spaces.

We note that regarding memory consumption and garbage collection, the ShadowVM FIA implementation exhibits very similar behavior compared to that of the uninstrumented base program. There is a slight increase in the total amount of allocated memory, which can be attributed to the FIA tracking each allocated object and passing its reference to the native space. This slightly increases the lifetime of the base program's objects and, more importantly, effectively disables the JIT compiler optimization that converts certain heap allocations to stack allocations, resulting in increased heap consumption. In contrast, the optimization can be still used in the uninstrumented base program.

The in-process FIA implementation reveals a significantly higher memory consumption, because the analysis keeps its state on the heap shared with the base program. Consequently, the allocation rate increases, resulting in a higher number of garbage collections.

7.2 Coverage

With respect to coverage, a ShadowVM-based analysis should improve on classic in-process analysis, because there is no need for a "bypass" mechanism, which enables complete instrumentation of the base program, including the JCL, and including the JVM bootstrap phase. To evaluate the difference in coverage between the two FIA implementations, we compare the total number of object allocations observed by the respective implementation, along with a breakdown of allocations observed by one and not the other implementation. Since the original in-process FIA implementation uses DiSL for base-program instrumentation, it already has a near-complete coverage, with only a small exclusion list. We therefore expect the difference to be small, but still in favor of the ShadowVM-based FIA implementation.

Even though the designers of the DaCapo suite took great care to avoid non-determinism in the benchmarks [23], the allocation profiles vary slightly between benchmark runs, regardless of the FIA implementation used to analyze them. To assess the variability, we have configured the benchmarks for small workload and executed each benchmark ten times with both FIA implementations, collecting the allocation profiles observed during the first iteration in each of the ten runs.

Table 3 shows the number of object allocations observed by both FIA implementations for each of the benchmarks. The variation in the allocation volume is under 0.5% in all benchmarks except h2, where it fits under 0.7%. With the exception of jython, the ShadowVM-based FIA implementation observes slightly more object allocations than the original in-process implementation.

However, in all cases, there are several thousands of objects that are observed by one FIA implementation and not the other. This effect is visible in Table 4 and there are several reasons for the difference, each contributing to the result.

First, there is a slight variability in the allocation profiles between benchmark runs, indicating that the benchmarks do not always allocate the same objects.

Second, the in-process analysis starts tracking object allocations only after the JVM has been initialized, does not track allocations

Benchmark	Uninstrumented			In-process FIA			ShadowVM FIA		
	GC young/old	Allocated memory	Final heap size	GC young/old	Allocated memory	Final heap size	GC young/old	Allocated memory	Final heap size
avrora	1/1	65 906	740 480	218/1	26 675 365	639 456	1/1	66 548	740 480
batik	1/1	122 865	740 480	10/1	2 230 259	997 792	1/1	127 293	740 480
fop	1/1	62 600	740 480	4/1	887 367	856 371	1/1	68 568	740 480
h2	3/1	956 686	933 632	92/1	49 247 450	1 124 621	5/1	1 076 014	740 480
jython	1/1	172 068	740 480	73/1	12 023 437	1 075 930	1/1	177 161	740 480
luindex	1/1	32 029	740 480	2/1	450 167	740 480	1/1	39 170	740 480
lusearch	4/1	729 793	933 632	14/1	6 835 034	1 168 493	4/1	721 823	740 480
pmd	1/1	35 912	740 480	2/1	271 791	740 480	1/1	38 070	740 480
sunflow	2/1	306 649	740 480	22/1	11 953 069	1 174 035	2/1	218 245	740 480
xalan	1/1	190 011	740 480	11/1	5 083 672	1 163 386	1/1	192 811	740 480

Table 2. Memory characteristics presented as mean over ten runs. Final heap size and allocated memory shows the size in kilobytes.

Benchmark	In-process FIA		ShadowVM FIA	
avrora	830 972 ±	0.32 %	849 675 ±	0.42 %
batik	376 728 ±	0.29 %	383 638 ±	0.27 %
fop	352 346 ±	0.00 %	359 032 ±	0.00 %
h2	15 999 644 ±	0.66 %	16 028 646 ±	0.57 %
jython	2 449 022 ±	0.00 %	2 443 509 ±	0.00 %
luindex	38 528 ±	0.01 %	42 317 ±	0.01 %
lusearch	840 635 ±	0.00 %	843 682 ±	0.00 %
pmd	69 697 ±	0.01 %	75 985 ±	0.01 %
sunflow	2 303 802 ±	0.00 %	2 307 116 ±	0.00 %
xalan	694 117 ±	0.02 %	699 041 ±	0.03 %

Table 3. Average number of allocations observed (± sample mean standard deviation)

Benchmark	Objects observed only by			
	In-process FIA		ShadowVM FIA	
avrora	506	0.06 %	19 209	2.26 %
batik	676	0.18 %	7586	1.98 %
fop	872	0.25 %	7559	2.11 %
h2	163 690	1.02 %	192 692	1.20 %
jython	9483	0.39 %	3971	0.16 %
luindex	350	0.91 %	4139	9.78 %
lusearch	386	0.05 %	3434	0.41 %
pmd	603	0.86 %	6891	9.07 %
sunflow	376	0.02 %	3690	0.16 %
xalan	3616	0.52 %	8540	1.22 %

Table 4. Average number of objects observed only by one implementation of the field-immutability analysis but not the other (percentages relative to number of objects observed by the respective implementation)

originating in daemon threads to avoid triggering undefined behavior when manipulating weak references, and bypasses the instrumentation when using JCL classes. The ShadowVM implementation, on the other hand, tracks allocations during the whole run of the benchmark, including JVM initialization. Therefore, even if the same objects are observed later, the in-process analysis cannot determine their allocation site and they appear distinct in the comparison.

Third, the in-process analysis may perturb the benchmark state through sharing JVM resources with the base program, resulting in allocations unique for that analysis.

And finally, the two analyses do not have a common point at which they stop tracking object allocations. The ShadowVM-based implementation stops upon receiving the "VM Death" event, while the in-process implementation ends when the JVM executes a pre-registered shutdown hook. Unfortunately, there is no documented relation between the two events—we observe the JVM to still execute some bytecode after emitting the JVMTI "VM Death" event.

In our experiments, the input data of Table 4 for avrora and h2 exhibit high variability, suggesting the reported mean value for those benchmarks is not informative. Still, the huge difference in observed events between the in-process and the ShadowVM FIA implementation for avrora reflects the fact that the number of events observed by ShadowVM is orders of magnitude higher than by in-process analysis.

For h2, the situation is more complicated. In two thirds of the runs, the ShadowVM FIA observes more events than the in-process version. However, for some runs, the number of events observed by the in-process FIA can be up to 5 times higher than in the ShadowVM version. This might indicate some kind of state perturbation in the in-process version, causing more objects to be allocated.

The behavior of jython is also unexpected. It is the only benchmark, where the number of observed allocations is higher with the in-process FIA. The instrumentation coverage of the in-process version is lower compared to the ShadowVM version. We were unable to find the reason for five thousand unique allocations among two and half million, and again we suspect that the in-process FIA may cause some shared state perturbation.

In summary, the ShadowVM FIA implementation is able to capture class loading events and daemon thread events missed by the in-process version. The behavior of some of the benchmarks, when observed using the in-process FIA leads us to believe that our goal of reducing perturbation in the observed system makes sense.

7.3 Performance

In this section, we evaluate the steady-state performance of the in-process and ShadowVM FIA implementations with the DaCapo benchmarks. As mentioned earlier, the ShadowVM FIA implementation is used with both per-thread and global ordering to evaluate the two main ordering configurations.

The experimental setup is identical to the previous evaluations. To obtain mean execution time, we execute each benchmark 5 times in a new process. To obtain steady-state results, we collect the execution time of the fifth iteration of the benchmark during each execution. Measuring execution time after reaching the steady-state provides time for the JIT compiler to optimize the base program code. The measured overhead can be then attributed only to the execution of the inserted hook code and event forwarding.

Table 5 shows the runtime overhead of the steady-state scenario, with the in-process FIA as the baseline. The steady state performance of the ShadowVM FIA is typically about two times worse than the in-process analysis, the worst observed slowdown being a factor

| | | ShadowVM | | | |
Benchmark	In-process [ms]	per-thread ordering [ms]	overhead	global ordering [ms]	overhead
avrora	141 307	851 782	6.03	849 792	6.01
batik	9563	19 796	2.07	26 734	2.80
fop	5072	6240	1.23	8619	1.70
h2	82 831	157 781	1.90	233 792	2.82
jython	14 473	27 681	1.91	34 989	2.42
luindex	1491	3922	2.63	5219	3.50
lusearch	23 693	360 220	15.20	250 892	10.59
pmd	1430	1774	1.24	2359	1.65
sunflow	57 466	133 843	2.33	158 307	2.75
xalan	18 631	276 160	14.82	232 416	12.47

Table 5. Average steady-state execution time of the in-process FIA and the ShadowVM FIA using per-thread and global ordering configurations. The overhead of the ShadowVM FIA uses the execution time of the in-process FIA as a reference.

| | | ShadowVM concurrent tagging | | | |
Benchmark	In-process [ms]	4 bench. threads [ms]	overhead	8 bench. threads [ms]	overhead
avrora	141 307	606 356	4.29	600 930	4.25
lusearch	23 693	47 843	2.02	27 130	1.15
xalan	18 631	37 322	2.00	18 951	1.02

Table 6. Average steady-state execution time of the in-process FIA and an experimental (concurrent tagging) ShadowVM FIA using per-thread ordering. The ShadowVM overhead is calculated with the in-process FIA as a reference.

of fifteen. Besides the overhead of marshaling inherent to the ShadowVM design, the main sources of overhead are related to object tagging and creation of global references in native code. Both facilities are provided by the JVM, but their implementation represents a major bottleneck for the ShadowVM use case.

A small but systematic difference is visible when comparing per-thread and global-ordering configurations. In most cases, the relaxed synchronization of the per-thread configuration is beneficial, however, for a few benchmarks the per-thread configuration performs worse than global-ordering. After further investigation, we believe this effect is caused by excessively fine-grained synchronization between the benchmark threads inside the native code executed as a part of the inserted analysis hooks.

To separate the synchronization effects due to Hotspot JVM from the performance of ShadowVM, we have modified the Hotspot JVM to support concurrent object tagging (the tags are normally kept in a globally locked hash map). The essence of the change was replacing the hash map with a concurrent one. Table 6 shows the performance of a ShadowVM prototype adjusted to run with concurrent tagging for the three benchmarks that exhibited the most pronounced synchronization effects. The adjustment reduces the analysis overhead significantly, unfortunately, requiring proprietary virtual machine adjustments goes against many benefits of analyses based on bytecode instrumentation. Still, we believe the illustrated benefits would justify introducing similar adjustment into the standard Hotspot VM.

8. Related Work

Binary translation systems including Pin [6], Valgrind [19], and DynamoRIO face similar issues of isolating analysis code from the observed program. By performing instrumentation directly at the machine code level, they avoid our complications in escaping

from the Java world. Conversely, they are a poor fit for observing managed runtimes, since the abstractions of the VM (such as objects, references to objects, reflective information, and VM threads if not implemented natively) are not easily visible from instrumentation code. Use of private dynamic compilation infrastructure means that baseline slowdown is high (around 2x–5x)—especially when instrumenting a JVM, where two levels of dynamic compilation are now operating.

Shadow profiling [26] and SuperPin [29] support running analysis code asynchronously in overlapping slices, which, given enough cores, can together analyse all events produced by the observed program. However, they work well only if there are no data dependencies between the work done by distinct slices. In practice, since the places where slices begin and end are dictated by rates of production and consumption, handling slice boundaries is problematic and can introduce divergence or loss of coverage [14]. The use of `fork()` to create slices also limits these systems to analysis of single-threaded applications.

Several instrumentation frameworks for Java bytecode may be used to create dynamic analyses, including Javassist [7], Soot [21], ASM[8] and DiSL [16]. These vary in details and expressiveness, but crucially, none assists in isolating the analysis from the observed VM, nor supports asynchronous processing.

BTrace[9] conservatively disallows all potentially dangerous instrumentation in its default configuration—providing a form of isolation, but also limiting its expressiveness to simple applications (e.g. its inability to perform reflection makes it unable to model object fields).

A notable exception is Chord [18], which supports piping a trace of events to a separate process for analysis. This isolates analysis from the program and allows full coverage (§2.1). However, since each instrumentation snippet contends for a shared buffer in this mode, heavy instrumentation effectively serializes the program, in contrast to our flexible approach (§4.3). In addition, Chord's "multi-JVM mode" offers less straightforward support API relative to the unisolated default mode. In particular, program metadata such as class and method names is only available by accessing files dumped from the instrumented JVM, making it more difficult to use.

The RoadRunner dynamic analysis framework [11] caters to data race detectors and closely related dynamic analyses. A key innovation is its compositional pipe-and-filter design. However, unlike Unix pipes, processing along the pipeline is still done synchronously. This makes sense since race detection is highly order-sensitive. However, as a consequence, it cannot introduce parallelism, making it unsuitable (unlike our system) for analyses with weaker ordering requirements. Moreover, the analysis developer is offered no assistance in ensuring isolation of program from analysis.

Aftersight [8] offers a platform for "decoupled" dynamic program analyses, based on the record-replay infrastructure of the VMware virtual machine monitor. Programs are observed under record, generating a log, which is analysed using a special CPU emulator (based on QEmu [3]) which replays the observed program. Observed workloads can be run "behind" the analysis for real-time monitoring, at a cost of slowdown, or else analysis can be run offline with only modest recording overhead. The main contrast with our work is that multiprocessor workloads are not supported: if a multithreaded program is observed, it is implicitly serialized.

Pipa [20] is an extension of dynamic binary translators which provides an efficient representation of profiling data suitable for fast handoff to an asynchronous (pipelined) processing stage, together with carefully optimised dynamic instrumentation code at the binary level. Meanwhile, CAB [14] provides a cache-friendly buffering

---

[8] http://asm.ow2.org/

[9] http://kenai.com/projects/btrace

design which offers further performance improvement. Since our current implementation lacks cache-aware buffering, uses fairly naive data encoding, and relies on the host JVMs for dynamic compilation, we believe CAB and Pipa to be complementary to our work, in that these techniques could be used to further increase the performance of our approach.

Problems related to full-coverage bytecode instrumentation are mentioned in the literature. The "Twin Class Hierarchy" (TCH) [9] claims to support user-defined instrumentation of the standard JCL by replicating the full hierarchy of the instrumented JCL in a separate package. This has drawbacks in that applications need to be instrumented to explicitly refer to the desired version of the JCL (original or instrumented), but more importantly, that in the presence of native code, call-backs from native code into bytecode will not reach the instrumented code [27]. TCH is therefore not suited for comprehensive instrumentation, as it fails to transparently instrument the JCL. Saff et al. [24] deem the dynamic instrumentation of the JCL to be impossible.

9. Conclusions and future work

ShadowVM allows developers to write dynamic analyses using convenient high-level languages and APIs, retaining the feel of a bytecode instrumentation system but achieving higher levels of isolation and coverage than previous systems. Its contributions include the disciplined use of native code to ensure isolation, the provision of distinct ordering models to allow efficient asynchronous analysis, and the avoidance of numerous coverage gaps that afflict previous systems. We believe it is the first system offering genuinely full bytecode coverage for the JVM. Despite the addition of a process separation, its performance is acceptable for many use cases.

Considerable future work stands to further improve ShadowVM. Coverage could be improved by allowing instrumentation of JNI interactions with the VM, and of VM-internal events currently exposed only through JVMTI callbacks. For analysing some program behaviours, particularly memory usage, a deeper understanding of VM-internal activity has previously been shown to be helpful [15]. A different transport strategy, perhaps based on shared memory instead of socket communication, could potentially also improve performance, although careful coordination with the garbage collector will be required to make shared memory work reliably. We believe that careful extensions to existing JVM implementations could significantly improve the performance of object tagging and global references, which have proven to be bottlenecks in the current implementation. More generally, the optimal observation mechanism will likely require invasive modifications to existing VM implementations and, indeed, their architectures. Meanwhile, ShadowVM constitutes (to our knowledge) the most comprehensive portable solution.

Acknowledgments

This work was supported by the Swiss National Science Foundation (project CRSII2_136225), by a Sino-Swiss Science and Technology Cooperation (SSSTC) Institutional Partnership (project IP04–092010), by the European Commission (Seventh Framework Programme grant 287746), by the Grant Agency of the Czech Republic project GACR P202/10/J042), by the EU project ASCENS 257414, and by Charles University institutional funding SVV-2013-267312.

References

[1] A. Sewe, et al. new Scala() instance of Java: a comparison of the memory behaviour of Java and Scala programs. In *Proc. ISMM '12*, pages 97–108. ACM, 2012.

[2] B. Cantrill, et al. Dynamic instrumentation of production systems. In *Proc. ATEC '04*, pages 15–28. USENIX Association, 2004.

[3] F. Bellard. QEMU, a fast and portable dynamic translator. In *Proc. ATEC '05*, pages 41–41. USENIX Association, 2005.

[4] Hans-J. Boehm. Destructors, finalizers, and synchronization. In *Proc. POPL '03*, pages 262–272. ACM, 2003.

[5] D. L. Bruening. *Efficient, transparent, and comprehensive runtime code manipulation*. PhD thesis, MIT, 2004. AAI0807735.

[6] C. Luk, et al. Pin: building customized program analysis tools with dynamic instrumentation. In *Proc. PLDI '05*, pages 190–200. ACM, 2005.

[7] S. Chiba. Load-time structural reflection in Java. In *Proc. ECOOP'00*, pages 313–336. Springer-Verlag, 2000.

[8] J. Chow, T. Garfinkel, and P. M. Chen. Decoupling dynamic program analysis from execution in virtual environments. In *Proc. ATC'08*, pages 1–14. USENIX Association, 2008.

[9] M. Factor, A. Schuster, and K. Shagin. Instrumentation of standard libraries in object-oriented languages: the twin class hierarchy approach. In *Proc. OOPSLA '04*, pages 288–300. ACM, 2004.

[10] C. Flanagan and S. N. Freund. FastTrack: efficient and precise dynamic race detection. In *Proc. PLDI '09*, pages 121–133. ACM, 2009.

[11] C. Flanagan and S. N. Freund. The RoadRunner dynamic analysis framework for concurrent programs. In *Proc. PASTE '10*, pages 1–8. ACM, 2010.

[12] S. L. Graham, P. B. Kessler, and M. K. Mckusick. Gprof: A call graph execution profiler. In *Proc. SIGPLAN '82*, pages 120–126. ACM, 1982.

[13] J. Gosling, et al. *Java(TM) Language Specification, The (Java SE 7 Edition, 4th Edition)*. Addison-Wesley Professional, 2013.

[14] J. Ha, et al. A concurrent dynamic analysis framework for multicore hardware. In *Proc. OOPSLA '09*, pages 155–174. ACM, 2009.

[15] K. Ogata, et al. A study of Java's non-Java memory. In *Proc. OOPSLA '10*, pages 191–204. ACM, 2010.

[16] L. Marek, et al. DiSL: a domain-specific language for bytecode instrumentation. In *Proc. AOSD '12*, pages 239–250. ACM, 2012.

[17] P. Moret, W. Binder, and É. Tanter. Polymorphic bytecode instrumentation. In *Proc. AOSD '11*, pages 129–140. ACM, 2011.

[18] Mayur Naik. Chord user guide, March 2011. URL http://pag-www.gtisc.gatech.edu/chord/user_guide/. Retrieved on 2013/3/28.

[19] N. Nethercote and J. Seward. Valgrind: a framework for heavyweight dynamic binary instrumentation. *SIGPLAN Not.*, 42(6):89–100, 2007.

[20] Q. Zhao, et al. Pipa: pipelined profiling and analysis on multi-core systems. In *Proc. CGO '08*, pages 185–194. ACM, 2008.

[21] R. Vallée-Rai, et al. Optimizing Java bytecode using the Soot framework: Is it feasible? In *Proc. CC '00*, pages 18–34. Springer-Verlag, 2000.

[22] S. Kell, et al. The JVM is not observable enough (and what to do about it). In *Proc. VMIL '12*, pages 33–38. ACM, 2012.

[23] S. M. Blackburn, et al. The DaCapo benchmarks: Java benchmarking development and analysis. In *Proc. OOPSLA '06*, pages 169–190. ACM, 2006.

[24] D. Saff, S. Artzi, J. H. Perkins, and M. D. Ernst. Automatic test factoring for Java. In *Proc. ASE '05*, pages 114–123. ACM, 2005.

[25] K. Sen, D. Marinov, and G. Agha. Cute: a concolic unit testing engine for c. In *Proc. ESEC/FSE-13*, pages 263–272. ACM, 2005.

[26] T. Moseley, et al. Shadow profiling: Hiding instrumentation costs with parallelism. In *Proc. CGO '07*, pages 198–208. IEEE Computer Society, 2007.

[27] E. Tilevich and Y. Smaragdakis. Transparent program transformations in the presence of opaque code. In *Proc. GPCE '06*, pages 89–94. ACM, 2006.

[28] W. Enck, et al. TaintDroid: an information-flow tracking system for realtime privacy monitoring on smartphones. In *Proc. OSDI'10*, pages 1–6. USENIX Association, 2010.

[29] S. Wallace and K. Hazelwood. Superpin: Parallelizing dynamic instrumentation for real-time performance. In *Proc. CGO '07*, pages 209–220. IEEE Computer Society, 2007.

A Comparison of Product-based, Feature-based, and Family-based Type Checking

Sergiy Kolesnikov   Alexander von Rhein   Claus Hunsen   Sven Apel

University of Passau
Germany

Abstract

Analyzing software product lines is difficult, due to their inherent variability. In the past, several strategies for product-line analysis have been proposed, in particular, *product-based*, *feature-based*, and *family-based* strategies. Despite recent attempts to conceptually and empirically compare different strategies, there is no work that empirically compares all of the three strategies in a controlled setting. We close this gap by extending a compiler for feature-oriented programming with support for product-based, feature-based, and family-based type checking. We present and discuss the results of a comparative performance evaluation that we conducted on a set of 12 feature-oriented, JAVA-based product lines. Most notably, we found that the family-based strategy is superior for all subject product lines: it is substantially faster, it detects all kinds of errors, and provides the most detailed information about them.

Categories and Subject Descriptors   D.2.13 [*SOFTWARE ENGINEERING*]: Reusable Software;   D.3.3 [*PROGRAMMING LANGUAGES*]: Language Constructs and Features

Keywords   Feature-oriented programming; product-line analysis; type checking; Fuji

1. Introduction

A *feature* is an end-user-visible behavior or characteristic of a product that satisfies a stakeholder's requirement [17]. A *software product line* is a family of related software products that share common features and differ in other features [12]. The product-line approach introduces a further dimension of complexity to software engineering: *variability*. It is this additional dimension that renders existing analysis tools impractical, for example, model checkers, static analyzers, type checkers, and so on [30]. Sure, to analyze a product line, we can use an off-the-shelf analysis tool and apply it to all of its products, which, however, requires exponential analysis effort, due to feature combinatorics (in the worst case, the number of products grows exponentially with the number of features). Alternatively, applying off-the-shelf tools to the variable code base of a

product line itself (e.g., consisting of unprocessed C code, feature modules, or aspects) is often impossible. However, a solution is to make the tools *variability-aware* [30].

Variability-aware analysis techniques that can be applied to the variable code base of a product line are called *family-based*. They take advantage of the inherent variability of a product line and can deliver sound and complete analysis results. However, they are often computationally expensive, compared to standard analyses.

To handle computational complexity, *feature-based* analyses operate on the implementation of individual features, without considering interactions across feature boundaries. While feature-based analyses are fast, they are incomplete, for example, in that they cannot catch bugs that arise from feature interactions.

Of course, using a *product-based* analysis, we could analyze each product of a product line individually. This way, we do not need to adapt existing analysis tools, but would face severe scalability problems for larger sets of products. However, a developer could analyze only a subset of all products, which is again incomplete.

Each of these three product-line analysis strategies has different strengths and weaknesses, as has been discussed conceptually in the literature (see a recent survey on product-line analysis by Thüm et al. [30]). To gain more empirical evidence, different researchers began to compare product-line analysis strategies quantitatively, for example, in terms of scalability and coverage. For example, Apel et al. compared family-based and product-based strategies in the context of model checking [7], and Liebig at al. compared family-based and product-based strategies in the context of type checking and data-flow analysis [21].

Despite existing empirical work on product-line analysis, there is no any study that compared all three strategies in a controlled setting (i.e., by means of a common set of subject systems and the same analysis tool that implements all three strategies). Our goal is to close this gap. As a concrete analysis technique, we chose type checking, as it has been used before in several studies on product-line analysis [3, 14, 18, 21]. As an implementation technique, we use feature-oriented programming [6], because we already have a proper tool infrastructure at our disposal, and we have access to a repository of subject systems for our experiments.

For our experiments, we implemented the three type-checking strategies—family-based, feature-based, and product-based—as an extension of FUJI, an extensible compiler for feature-oriented programming in JAVA [5]. Using FUJI, we compared the three strategies by applying them to 12 feature-oriented, JAVA-based product lines, from different application domains and of different sizes. Overall, we found that the family-based strategy is superior in that it is complete and takes substantially less time for type checking than the other strategies. The feature-based strategy is also quite fast, compared to the product-based strategy, but incomplete.

GPCE '13,   October 27–28, 2013, Indianapolis, IN, USA.
Copyright © 2013 ACM 978-1-4503-2373-4/13/10... $15.00.
http://dx.doi.org/10.1145/2517208.2517213

Based on the experimental results, we discuss a number of issues regarding the ability to detect and report errors, the role of optimization for family-based strategies, the influence of factors such as the size of a product line, and the trade-off between analysis coverage and time.

To summarize, we make the following contributions:

- We implemented a type checker for feature-oriented, JAVA-based product lines that supports family-based, feature-based, and product-based type checking. This is the first time that all three analysis strategies have been integrated within a single tool.

- We compare the three type-checking strategies regarding different aspects, such as the ability to detect different kinds of type errors and the quality of the provided information about errors.

- We present and discuss the results of a comparative performance evaluation that we conducted on a set of 12 subject product lines. Most notably, we found that the family-based strategy is the most efficient strategy for all of them. It is substantially faster, detects all kinds of errors, and provides the most detailed information about the errors found, but it requires adaption of the standard type-checking tools.

The implementation of the strategies (in the form of a FUJI compiler extension), the subject product lines, and the experimental data are available online: http://fosd.de/fuji/ .

2. Product-Line Type Checking

By means of a running example and type checking as a concrete analysis technique, we illustrate product-based, feature-based, and family-based strategies for product-line analysis.

2.1 Running Example

The example in Figure 1 is a very simple product line of list data structures. It consists of two features: *Base* and *Batch*. The mandatory feature *Base* provides two basic implementations of lists: SingleList for singly-linked lists, and DoubleList for doubly-linked lists. It also provides a test class TestCase. The optional feature *Batch* provides a special list implementation BatchList for scheduling batch jobs that uses class SingleList of feature *Base*.

In practice, not every combination of features is valid. Feature models are commonly used to describe the conditions of the absence and presence of features, including dependencies among features [17]. In Figure 2, we show the feature model of our example. It states that feature *Base* is mandatory (i.e., it must be present in every product) and feature *Batch* is optional (i.e., it may be present in a product). Consequently, our running example consists of two valid products: {*Base*} and {*Base*, *Batch*} .

If we take a closer look at the code of feature *Base*, we see that it refers to class BatchList in Line 9 of Figure 1. If we attempt to compile a product with *Base* and without *Batch*, we get a type error, because BatchList is declared only in *Batch*. This dangling reference is a simple example of an error that involves multiple features. The cause of this type error is an inconsistency between the feature model and the implementation of the product line: The feature model suggests that feature *Base* is independent from feature *Batch*, but the implementation requires these features to be selected together.

To resolve the inconsistency, we can make *Batch* mandatory or move the test case from *Base* to *Batch*. The key point is that, in large-scale product lines, such inconsistencies may go unnoticed for a long time and show up only late in the development cycle [28].

Another kind of type error is illustrated in Line 17 of Figure 1. There, the undeclared variable resutl is accessed. This type error is caused by a simple typo. It is an example of a *feature-local* error

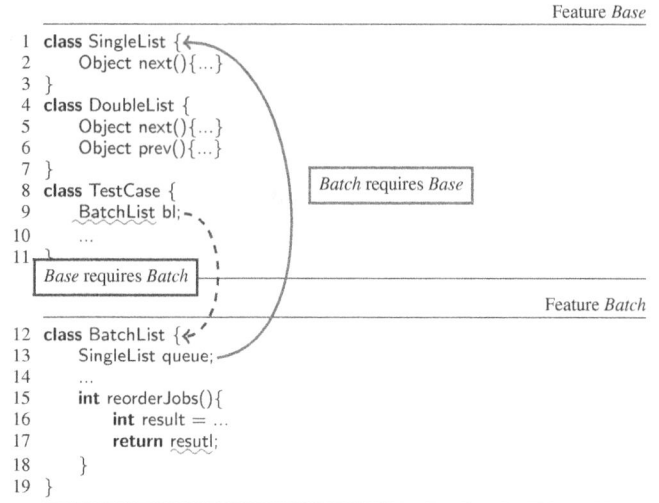

```
 1   class SingleList {
 2       Object next(){...}
 3   }
 4   class DoubleList {
 5       Object next(){...}
 6       Object prev(){...}
 7   }
 8   class TestCase {
 9       BatchList bl;
10       ...
11   }

12   class BatchList {
13       SingleList queue;
14       ...
15       int reorderJobs(){
16           int result = ...
17           return resutl;
18       }
19   }
```

Feature *Base*

Batch requires *Base*

Base requires *Batch*

Feature *Batch*

Figure 1. Running example: two basic list implementations (feature *Base*) and a list for batch jobs (feature *Batch*); type errors are underlined; arrows denote references; the dashed arrow denotes a possibly dangling reference.

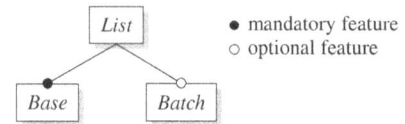

- mandatory feature
- optional feature

Figure 2. Feature model of the running example.

that can be discovered as soon as the affected feature is used in a product.

Next, we discuss which type errors can be detected by different type-checking strategies. We consider what information can be provided to a developer by a type checker to help to fix these errors. We also take a look at certain properties of the strategies that can influence type-checking performance.

2.2 Type Checking Product Lines

Our procedure for type checking of product lines consists of two steps, as illustrated in Figure 3. In the first step, *setup*, we parse the code of the considered features and compose it accordingly. In the second step, *checking*, we perform the actual type checks on the result of the first step. If a particular type-checking strategy cannot check the whole product line in a single run, the type-checking procedure is repeated. For example, the product-based strategy repeats the procedure for each product, the feature-based strategy repeats it for each feature, and only the family-based strategy checks all products simultaneously in a single run.

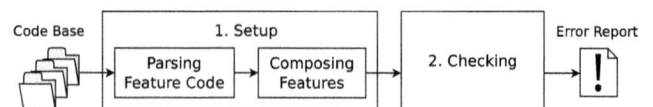

Figure 3. Steps of product-line type checking.

The performance of a type-checking strategy is the total time t required to check the entire product line:

$$t = \sum_{i=1}^{r} t_i^{\text{setup}} + t_i^{\text{checking}}$$

The value r is the number of type-checker runs needed to verify the complete product line; t_i^{setup} is the time used by the setup in run i, and t_i^{checking} is the time used by the checking step in run i. Based on this equation, we can derive the following possibilities for optimizing the type-checking procedure, of which the tree type-checking strategies make use to different extents:

- Minimize the number of type-checker runs r
- Minimize the setup time t_i^{setup}
- Minimize the checking time t_i^{checking}

2.3 Product-based Strategy

To ensure that every product of a product line is well typed, we can apply the product-based strategy. That is, we generate and check each product individually. This way, we find every type error in all products of the product line.

We can even use an off-the-shelf type checker (or compiler) for this task, because the individual products do not contain any compile-time variability. In our setting, the products are normal JAVA programs.

However, by generating and checking individual products, we lose information about the features the products are made of as well as about their dependencies. This makes it difficult to create meaningful error messages. The error messages for our running example will only tell us that one product accesses an unknown type BatchList. A product-based type checker fails to identify the primary reason, namely, the false optionality of feature *Batch*. That is, the type checker cannot blame the feature that is responsible for the error, which is left to the user. This also applies to feature-local errors, such as for the undeclared variable resutl.

A major weakness of the product-based strategy is its poor scalability. With n optional and independent features, we have to repeat the type-checking procedure for each of the 2^n products. Therefore, the *upper bound* for the performance is

$$t = \sum_{i=1}^{2^n} t_i^{\text{setup}} + t_i^{\text{checking}} \qquad \text{(Product-based)}$$

The reason for the poor scalability are redundant analyses made in every step of the type-checking procedure (Figure 3). During the setup, we repeatedly parse and compose the same features again and again. During type checking, we repeat type checks that are similar among different products.

To avoid this redundancy, it is possible to parse the code of feature *Base* only once, because the corresponding parse tree is the same per product. Likewise, it is sufficient to perform type checks that concern code inside *Base*, such as type checking the body of method next, only once.

The remaining two type-checking strategies exploit this optimization potential, which we explain next.

2.4 Feature-based Strategy

Using the feature-based strategy, we check every feature of a product line individually. We assume that all types, declarations, and so on that a feature requires are available in all valid products. For example, if we check feature *Base*, then the feature-based type checker assumes that the required type BatchList, provided by feature *Batch*, is always available. Type BatchList becomes part of the feature's required interface. While the feature-based strategy may

seem naive at first glance, it is motivated by open-world systems, in which not all features are known at development time [20, 22].

Technically, we implement the required interface of a feature module using stubs. A *stub* is a bundle of JAVA interfaces and classes, possibly with member prototypes, that represent the types and members a feature requires from other features. Either stubs are provided by the developer to define the required interface, such as in HYPER/J [27], or they are generated using tools, such as AHEAD [29] or FEATURESTUBBER.[1] To type check feature *Base* of our example, a stub containing an empty class named BatchList is needed, possibly with proper member declarations.

While checking a feature, the feature-based strategy does not know anything about other features. Consequently, a feature-based type checker cannot detect type errors that arise between features. In our example, it cannot detect the erroneous access to the missing type BatchList, because the type is provided by the stub (i.e., the type checker simply assumes that it will be provided by another feature). Only errors that are local to a feature can be detected by the feature-based type checker, as the undeclared variable resutl.

To guarantee that all products are well typed, feature-based type checking has to be supplemented with additional type checks during byte-code feature composition (which corresponds to linking in C). The result is a mixed *feature-product-based* strategy [30].

Much like for the product-based strategy, we can use an off-the-shelf type checker for feature-based type checking, because a single feature complemented with stubs does not contain any compile-time variability.

In contrast to a product-based type checker, a feature-based type checker can provide sufficient information about feature-local errors, but it misses errors that arise from combinations of features.

Furthermore, the feature-based strategy requires one type-checker run for each feature. Thus, every feature is parsed and checked only once, and the number of the unnecessarily repeated actions is reduced compared to the product-based strategy. The strategy also completely avoids the feature-composition part of the setup (cf. Figure 3). To summarize, it utilizes the following optimization possibilities:

- The number of type-checker runs r is reduced from 2^n to n, where n is the number of features.
- The setup time t_i^{setup} is reduced by omitting feature composition.

Therefore, the performance of the feature-based strategy is

$$t = \sum_{i=1}^{n} t_i^{\text{setup}} + t_i^{\text{checking}} \qquad \text{(Feature-based)}$$

2.5 Family-based Strategy

The family-based strategy analyses the code base of a product line as a whole. Hence, it can detect all type errors and guarantee that all products of a product line are well typed.

The variability of a product line has to be incorporated into the type-checking procedure, so that the type checker can take it properly into account. The key idea is to compose all features of the product line (even mutually exclusive ones), and to keep variability information in the syntax tree (i.e., which program element belongs to which feature and depends on which other features) [29]. This way, the syntax tree does not represent only a single product or feature, but the whole product line, as illustrated in Figure 4. A family-based type checker works on these enriched syntax trees and must be able to cope with variability. For this reason, we cannot use an off-the-shelf type checker for this task.

---

[1] http://fosd.de/featurebite/

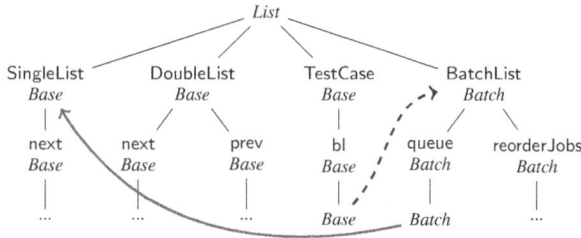

Figure 4. Syntax tree of the running example. Every node knows the feature to which it belongs. Arrows denote references; the dashed arrow denotes a possibly dangling reference (cf. Figure 1).

```
Base/TestCase.java:9:
  Type Error: 1 optional target:
    Feature Base accesses the type
    (default package).BatchList of feature Batch
```

Figure 5. Error message of the family-based type checker.

Figure 5 shows an example of an error message produced by our family-based type checker. The error message identifies the features participating in the type error. It shows in which feature and where exactly in its code the error occurs. Moreover, the error message describes the exact cause of the error, namely that feature *Base* requires feature *Batch* (because *Base* uses type BatchList introduced by *Batch*), but feature *Batch* is not present in all products in which *Base* is present; all these products contain the type error, which is useful information for debugging.

The family-based strategy parses and composes the code of all features in one run. Thus, no repetitive parsing or composition of the same source code is necessary. The resulting syntax tree represents the whole product line. Therefore, only one type-checking run is needed to cover the whole product line. To summarize, the strategy utilizes the following optimization possibilities:

- The number of type-checker runs r is reduced to the minimum of one.

- Furthermore, the time t^{checking} for type checking can be reduced by using caching, as we will explain in Section 3.6.

Therefore, the performance of the family-based strategy is

$$t = t^{\text{setup}} + t^{\text{checking}} \qquad \text{(Family-based)}$$

2.6 Summary

For a better overview, Table 1 summarizes the properties of the three strategies, regarding performance, optimization, the ability to find errors and to blame features, and the possibility to reuse off-the-shelf tools.

3. Empirical Evaluation

The main goal of our evaluation is to compare the three strategies quantitatively in terms of their performance. We believe that the family-based strategy outperforms the other two, because it reduces the number of type-checker runs to one. This way, the strategy avoids unnecessarily repeated analysis operations during the setup and checking steps. Nevertheless, a family-based type checker has to take the whole variability of a product line into account. Therefore, the respective problem is more complex and may require more time for analysis. Moreover, family-based type checkers rely on SAT solvers to determine dependencies between features [3, 18]. The corresponding SAT solver calls are expensive and may reduce

```
20  class BatchList extends SingleList {
21    ...
22  }
```

```
23  class BatchList extends DoubleList {
24    ...
25  }
```

Figure 6. Example of a variable type hierarchy: The choice between *BatchSingle* and *BatchDouble* defines the superclass of class BatchList.

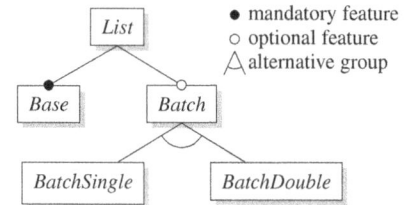

Figure 7. Feature model for the running example, extended with the two new features *BatchDouble* and *BatchSingle*.

the overall performance. Therefore, product-based type checking may be faster than family-based, especially, on product lines with a small number of products.

As for the feature-based strategy, it processes the same amount of code as the family-based strategy and completely avoids the composition part and ignores feature combinatorics. Thus, it is an open question whether it outperforms the family-based strategy when the analyzed product line has a small number of features. Of course, the potential win of the feature-based strategy would be at the expense of the number of type errors found, as it would detect only feature-local errors (see Section 2.4). To be able to detect errors occurring between features, we supplemented the strategy with additional type checks at the byte-code level, as explained in Section 2.4. These type checks run on the per-product basis when composing separately compiled feature modules, which corresponds, in fact, to a mixed feature-product-based strategy. For illustration, we also present the performance measurements for this mixed strategy.

3.1 Hypotheses

Based on our previous considerations, we state the following three hypotheses that we address in the evaluation:

- **H.1:** The family-based strategy is superior to the feature-based and product-based strategies in terms of performance.

- **H.2:** As an exception to H.1, the product-based strategy is superior to the family-based one, if the analyzed product line has a relatively small number of products.

- **H.3:** As an exception to H.1, the feature-based strategy is superior to the family-based one, if the analyzed product line has a relatively small number of features.

3.2 Implementation

We implemented the three type-checking strategies in a single type checker. The type checker is an extension of a feature-oriented JAVA compiler FUJI.[2] It operates on the abstract syntax tree, built

---

[2] http://fosd.de/fuji/

Table 1. Conceptual comparison of the three type-checking strategies.

Strategy	Performance	Optimization	Error detection	Feature blaming	Tool reuse
Product-based	$\sum_{i=1}^{2^n} t_i^{\text{setup}} + t_i^{\text{checking}}$	—	●	○	●
Feature-based	$\sum_{i=1}^{n} t_i^{\text{setup}} + t_i^{\text{checking}}$	# runs, setup	◑	●	●
Family-based	$t^{\text{setup}} + t^{\text{checking}}$	# runs, checking	●	●	○

● possible
◑ partly possible
○ impossible

by the FUJI's parser, and extends the underlying JAVA type system to implement variability-aware type checks.

To calculate dependencies between features, our type checker uses a corresponding library from the FEATUREIDE project.[3] In FEATUREIDE, the problem of determining a dependency between features is reduced to a SAT problem and solved by querying an off-the-shelf SAT solver (SAT4J). FEATUREIDE implements a caching mechanism to reduce the response time in the case of multiple identical SAT solver queries (see Section 3.6, Caching).

It is important to note that our type checker covers many but not all JAVA type rules. In a nutshell, it checks all accesses to fields, methods, constructors, and types, and verifies that the accessed elements are present in all corresponding products. The possibly variable type hierarchy of the corresponding product line is considered too, because it can influence the presence or absence of program elements, such as fields or methods. For illustration, let us assume that we decided to add two *alternative* features to our running example, as illustrated in the Figures 6 and 7. The new features refine feature *Batch*, and specify a new superclass for class BatchList. Consequently, the two alternative features define which methods are inherited by BatchList. If feature *BatchSingle* is selected, the superclass of BatchList is SingleList, and BatchList inherits method next. If feature *BatchDouble* is selected, the superclass of BatchList is DoubleList, and BatchList inherits the methods next and prev. Now, if prev is called on a BatchList object, the type checker has to determine in which feature combination method prev is inherited by BatchList (in our case, the required combination is {*Base*, *BatchDouble*}).

Further type rules cover explicit and implicit casts, which also take a possibly variable type hierarchy into account. The rules for implicit casts cover assignment expressions involving two variables, assignments of a return value of a method call, parameter passing, and so on.

3.3 Subject Systems

We conducted the evaluation of the type-checking strategies on a set of 12 feature-oriented, JAVA-based product lines. The set has been collected and prepared before for benchmarking purposes and was used in several studies [1, 5]. The subject systems belong to different application domains, and they are of different sizes: in terms of lines of code, number of features, and number of products. In Section 3.6, we use the three size categories to discuss the relation between the size of a product line and the corresponding performance of type checking. Table 2 summarizes relevant information about the systems.

3.4 Measurement Procedure

To compare the performance of the three type-checking strategies, we applied each strategy to each subject system, and we measured the time required by every step of the type-checking procedure (i.e., t^{setup} and t^{checking}). We repeated each measurement 10 times and took the average value to reduce measurement bias. The maximum relative standard error was 3.1 %, which we observed for family-

Table 2. Overview of the subject systems (LOC: number of lines of code; # F: number of features; # P: number of products).

System	Domain	LOC	# F	# P
EPL	Expression evaluation	304	12	425
GPL	Graph library	2 855	25	156
GRAPHLIB	Graph library	401	5	16
GUIDSL	Configuration tool	14 318	26	24
NOTEPAD	Text editor	2 193	10	512
PKJAB	Chat client	4 109	8	48
PREVAYLER	Persistence library	6 185	6	32
RAROSCOPE	Compression library	415	4	16
SUDOKU	Game	1 926	6	64
TANKWAR	Game	4 845	38	2 458
VIOLET	Model editor	10 866	88	$\approx 2^{88}$
ZIPME	compression library	5 076	13	24

based type checking of ZIPME. For the product-based strategy, we did not include the time needed to generate the configuration of each product, because this time was negligible compared to the time required for type checking. Likewise, for the feature-based strategy, we did not include the time used to generate stubs (Section 2.4), because stubs represent required interfaces and are part of the corresponding feature modules. We measured the performance of the family-based type checker twice, with and without caching, to investigate the influence of the caching (Section 3.2) on the overall performance.

We instrumented the code of the FUJI compiler with calls to the timer of ThreadMXBean,[4] such that we measure only the CPU time consumed by the type-checker thread. This approach eliminates the influence of other concurrent tasks (e.g., garbage collection) on the measurement results. Furthermore, we did not measure the JVM startup time for each type-checking run, because the overhead can be avoided using special tools.[5]

We conducted all measurements on a workstation equipped with an Intel Xeon CPU (2.9 GHz) and 8 GB RAM, running Ubuntu 12.04 (64-Bit) and OpenJDK 7 (u21).

3.5 Results

In Table 3 (page 10), we present the results of our measurements (in seconds). For each subject system and each strategy from our comparison, we show the setup time (t^{setup}), the checking time (t^{checking}), and the total time (i.e., the performance of the strategy, t). We also provide total times (t) for the feature-product-based strategy and the family-based strategy with caching disabled. For the feature-based strategy, we computed the speedups relative to the product-based strategy. For the family-based strategy, we computed the speedups relative to the product-based strategy and the feature-based strategy. Note that we aborted the product-based measurements for VIOLET after checking 40 random products, because it was impossible to check all of the approximately 2^{88} products in

---

[3] http://fosd.de/featureide/

[4] java.lang.management.ThreadMXBean is part of the JAVA 7 API.

[5] http://martiansoftware.com/nailgun/

reasonable time. We mark the corresponding values in the table with "X."

For comparison, we visualize the results in Figure 8 by means of bar plots. There is one bar plot per subject system, consisting of five stacked bars, divided into two groups (with different axes to compensate the considerable differences between the measured times). Each bar denotes the amount of time (in seconds) used by the corresponding type-checking strategy. The light gray part of each bar denotes the time required by the setup step; the white part denotes the time required by the check step. The crosses over the bars for VIOLET indicate that we aborted measurements at this point.

Note that, for the family-based strategy, there are two bars: the first, FM, denotes the performance of the strategy with SAT-solver caching *enabled*; the second, FM*, denotes the performance with SAT-solver caching *disabled*. FT* denotes the performance of the feature-product-based strategy; its dark gray part denotes the time required by the byte-code feature composition (Section 2.4).

As we can see, the family-based strategy is the fastest for all subject systems. Compared to the product-based strategy, the minimum *speedup* of this strategy has been measured for GUIDSL, where it is 8.8 times faster. The maximum speedup of 745.3 has been measured for TANKWAR. As we could not check all products of VIOLET in reasonable time, we do not consider the corresponding speedups (they are likely to be much higher). Compared to the feature-based strategy, the speedup of the family-based strategy lies in between 1.7 and 6.5. The feature-based strategy is the second fastest. Its speedup compared to the product-based strategy lies in between 2.2 and 129.7.

Recall that the feature-based strategy finds only feature-local errors (Section 2.4). In our evaluation, it found no errors at all. The reason is that our subject systems have been used in many previous studies. Every single feature of the product lines was type checked as part of a product at least once. Therefore, all feature-local errors have already been detected and fixed. The other two strategies detected the same 556 unique type errors. These errors occurred between features and stayed undetected, because the corresponding feature combinations have been never considered by the developers and users of the systems.

The results support our first hypothesis H.1 (Section 3.1): the family-based strategy is superior to the other two strategies in terms of performance. Although quite apparent from Table 3, we still conducted statistical tests to test all hypotheses. We used the Wilcoxon test, because the data are not normally distributed (according to a Shapiro-Wilk test). Though, we could use the non-parametric ANOVA, we decided to use the conservative double-test variant with Bonferroni correction, because it is more rigorous. For all performance comparisons, the p value is much smaller than 0.01.

We found no supporting evidence for hypothesis H.2 (i.e., product-based is superior on product lines with few products) and H.3 (i.e., feature-based is superior on product lines with few features), because, for none of our subject systems, the product-based or the feature-based strategy is superior to the family-based strategy, not even for very small product lines with few products and features (e.g., GRAPHLIB and RAROSCOPE).

A comparison of the results for the two variants of the family-based type checker shows a substantial influence of SAT-solver caching on performance.

Finally, the feature-product-based strategy is always slower than the family-based strategy (with caching) and the feature-based strategy. More interestingly, it is only in several cases slower than the product-based strategy (e.g., GUIDSL, PKJAB, ZIPME), which indicates the benefits of separate feature compilation and byte-code feature composition.

Table 4. Break-even points of the superiority of the family-based strategy for the subject systems. Total number of products #P and break-even points ⚡B (i.e., the number of products whose cumulative analysis time exceeds the time needed by the family-based strategy to check *all* products of the product line).

System	#P	⚡B	System	#P	⚡B
EPL	425	2	PREVAYLER	32	2
GPL	156	4	RAROSCOPE	16	2
GRAPHLIB	16	2	SUDOKU	64	2
GUIDSL	24	3	TANKWAR	2458	4
NOTEPAD	512	3	VIOLET	$\approx 2^{88}$	8
PKJAB	48	2	ZIPME	24	2

3.6 Discussion

Next, we discuss the results of our measurements based on the size categories of Table 2 as well as regarding the implementation of our type checker. We use the product-based strategy as the base line, and compare it to the other strategies. We subdivided this section in three parts, one part for each strategy.

Product-based strategy. The measurements of the product-based strategy support our expectations about its poor scalability. As discussed in Section 2.3, this strategy induces considerable redundant work in every step of the type-checking procedure, while the number of the unneeded repetitions increases with the number of products. An extreme example is VIOLET, which we could not even check completely, because of the sheer amount of time required to generate and check all of the approximately 2^{88} products. Nevertheless, if developers have to use a standard (non-variability-aware) type checker, product lines with few products and relatively small code bases (e.g., RAROSCOPE) can be checked in reasonable time.

Comparing the results for GUIDSL and ZIPME makes it apparent that it is insufficient to consider only the number of products when estimating the performance of the product-based strategy. Both product lines have the same number of products, but type checking GUIDSL lasts almost twice as long as type checking ZIPME. The cause is the larger code base of GUIDSL, which is almost three times larger than the code base of ZIPME. Systems with a similar number of products and a similar size of the code base (e.g., GRAPHLIB and RAROSCOPE) have similar times.

Although not in the scope of our study, one could use sampling to speed up the product-based strategy [15, 16, 23–25]. This would render the analysis incomplete, but tractable, at least. To give an impression of how the family-based strategy performs in comparison to sampling, we computed the (average) number of products one has to check with a sample-based strategy to exceed the time needed for the family-based strategy. This number marks the break-even point, at which the family-based strategy is superior without question (recall sampling is incomplete). In Table 4, we list the break-even points for the subject systems in terms of this number (and the overall number of products checked by the product-based strategy). The results are clear: Only when checking a very small number of products (less than 5 %, on average), a sample-based strategy is faster. But these small numbers also mean that the coverage will be very low and does not satisfy state-of-the-art coverage criteria (e.g., pair-wise coverage [23]). This observation is in line with previous results [21].

Feature-based strategy. A feature-based type checker parses and checks the code of each feature only once (cf. Section 2.4). The result of this optimization becomes apparent when we compare the performance of the product-based and feature-based strategies in the setup step. With a growing number of products the advantage of the feature-based strategy becomes more evident. Nevertheless,

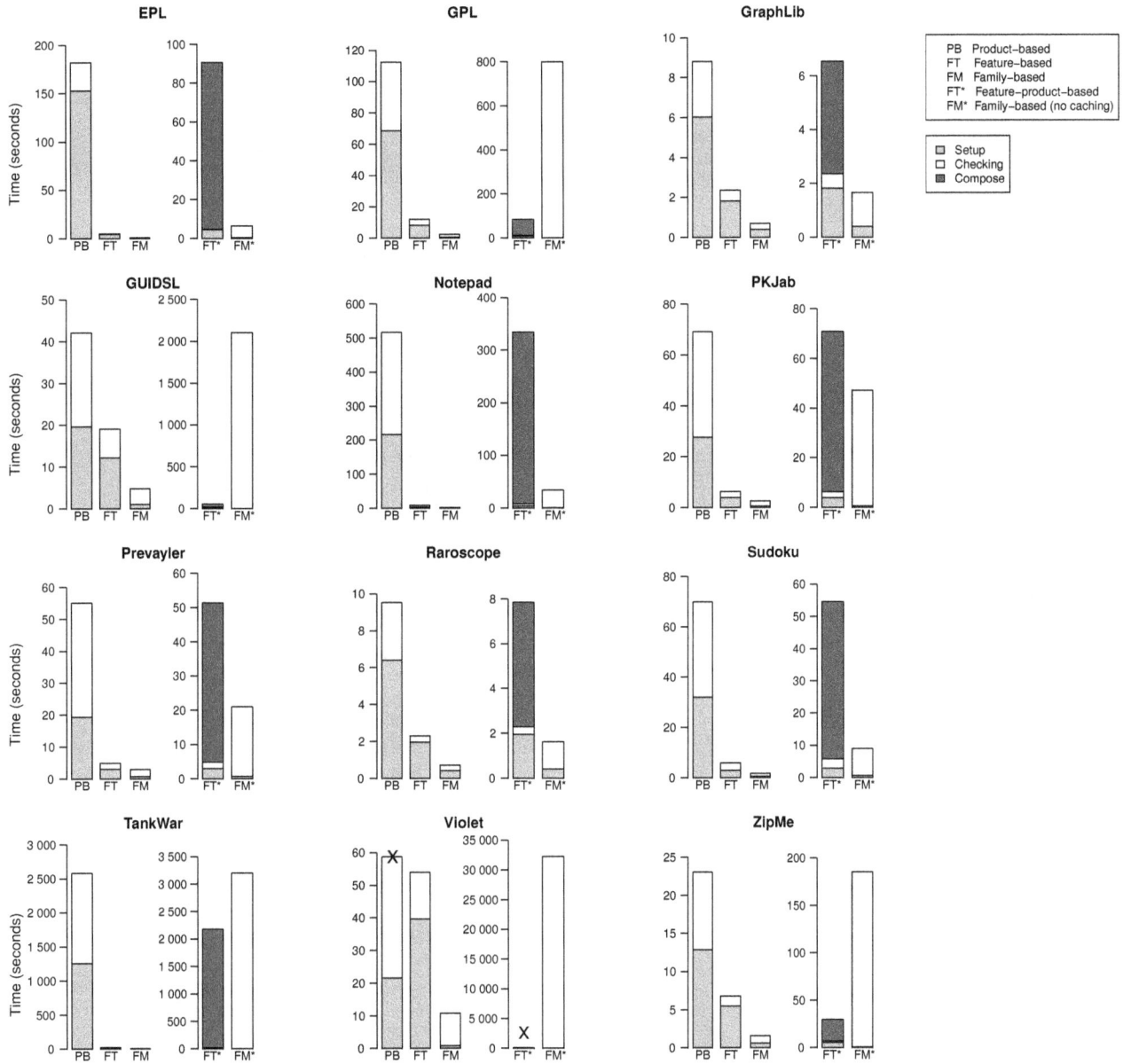

Figure 8. Type-checking times for each subject system—five bars per system. A bar denotes the time used by the corresponding type-checking strategy. Each step of the type-checking procedure (Section 2.2) is denoted by a different color inside a bar. The crosses over the bars for VIOLET indicate that we aborted the product-based measurement after checking 40 products (cf. Section 3.5).

the feature-based strategy induces an overhead for every type-checker run that is caused by instantiating internal data structures and loading classes from the JAVA run-time library. This overhead explains why setting up type checking for GUIDSL is only slightly faster using the feature-based type strategy, then using the product-based strategy. A peculiarity of GUIDSL that is responsible for this effect is that it has a relatively small number of products and more features than products.

The checking step of the feature-based strategy also consumes less time than that of the product-based strategy. Still, we have to keep in mind that the feature-based strategy is able to detect only feature-local errors (cf. Section 2.4). Our subject systems have been used in many previous studies and all eventual feature-local errors have already been fixed. Therefore, the feature-based

strategy found no errors. The inability to detect the full range of errors is the main weakness of this strategy.

We used FEATUREBITE[6]—a tool developed by us—to perform supplementary type checks when composing individually compiled feature modules to products. These additional checks at the byte-code level find type errors that arise between features (cf. Section 2.4). This way, we can achieve the same level of type safety as with the other two type-checking strategies (all 556 errors are found). However, our evaluation demonstrates that attaining type safety by combining the feature-based and product-based strategy requires considerably more effort than using the feature-based strategy alone, which was to be expected. The interesting finding is that,

---

[6] http://fosd.de/featurebite/

in all subject product lines except GUIDSL, PKJAB, and ZIPME, the feature-product-based strategy outperforms the product-based strategy.[7] The reason is that the number of products of these three product lines is relatively low compared to the number of their features, which outweighs the benefit of separate feature compilation. This result demonstrates that the intermediate steps of checking and compiling feature modules and composing them at the byte-code level can positively influence analysis performance.

Family-based strategy. The family-based strategy is the clear winner among the three strategies. It requires only one run to check all products of a product line. Consequently, it does not induce the overhead of feature-based type checking (i.e., repeated instantiation of data structures in each run) in the setup step. It also avoids the overhead of the product-based strategy (i.e., repeated type checks) in the checking step (cf. Section 2.5).

Furthermore, our results show that the family-based strategy outperforms also the feature-based strategy in the checking step, even though the feature-based strategy considers only features in isolation. We attribute this phenomenon to the same kind of overhead that the feature-based strategy induces in the setup step (i.e., repeated instantiation of data structures in each run). From Table 3 (page 10), we can see that the advantage of the family-based strategy in the checking step increases with the number of features. For product lines with a small number of features (e.g., GRAPHLIB, PREVAYLER, RAROSCOPE, SUDOKU), the family-based strategy is 1.7 to 3.5 times faster than the feature-based strategy. For product lines with larger numbers of features (e.g., GPL, GUIDSL, TANKWAR), the family-based strategy is 4.1 to 5.8 times faster than the feature-based strategy.

Caching. One property of our family-based type checker poses a principal boundary on its performance. The type checker reduces the problem of determining dependencies between features to a SAT problem (cf. Section 2.5). SAT is NP-complete, which renders family-based type checking NP-complete, as well (w.r.t. the number of features). Luckily, today's SAT solvers mitigate this theoretical boundary for practical problems. Nevertheless, the calls to a SAT solver are still expensive enough, so minimizing the number of such calls is always a good idea.

Our family-based type checker uses a caching mechanism. All queries of the type checker to the SAT solver are cached, and none of the queries is performed twice. As we can see from the measurements (the FM and FM* bars in each plot, Figure 8), the caching mechanism leads to a substantial speedup. This is due to the fact that the family-based type checker makes a considerable number of repeated, identical calls that involve the SAT solver.

A large number of features often means a more complex feature model and, consequently, more expensive SAT solver calls. A small number of products keeps the time needed for the product-based type checking relatively low. ZIPME and GUIDSL are such product-lines, and, as we can see in Figure 8, the family-based type checker without caching is slower than the product-based type checker.

The reasons for the success of caching is that the feature modules in our subject systems are relatively coarse-grained units, and checking them involves checking a large number of identical type, method, and field accesses. This may not be the case if a product line consists of many fine-grained features containing no or few identical accesses (e.g., as may be the case for preprocessor-based variability).

---

[7] We do not consider VIOLET, as we could not check all its products.

3.7 Threats to Validity

We implemented a substantial subset of type rules in FUJI, but not all type rules specified for the JAVA language. This threatens the internal validity of our study. However, the implemented rules cover a considerable number of language constructs and involve complex analyses of the possibly variable type hierarchy. We can safely assume that adding new type checking rules (e.g., checking access modifiers) will not change the overall picture substantially.

As often the case, the external validity of our study is affected by the choice of the subject product lines. In our evaluation, we used only product lines built with AHEAD/FUJI-style feature modules. The coarse-grained nature of these features is beneficial for the caching mechanism used in the family-based type checker (cf. Section 3.6, Caching). Although, we cannot draw sound conclusions for other kinds of feature implementations (e.g., based on the C preprocessor), previous work shows a similar picture, at least regarding the performance of the family-based strategy compared to the product-based strategy [21].

4. Related Work

Our classification of product-line analysis strategies is based on a recent survey by Thüm et al. [30]. Beside the classification, the authors discuss the conceptual strengths and weaknesses of the individual strategies. Based on this survey, von Rhein et al. propose the Product-Line-Analysis model [32] that describes a whole spectrum of possible combinations of product-line analysis strategies.

The family-based strategy has been applied to several analysis techniques, including type checking [3, 14, 18, 29], static analysis [9, 10, 21], model checking [4, 7, 11, 19], performance measurement [26], and deductive verification [31]. The feature-based strategy has been used before for type checking [2, 8] and verification [20] of product lines. Product-based analyses with sampling have been used in the context of product-line testing [16, 23] and performance prediction [15, 24, 25].

There are only few studies that compare product-line analysis strategies empirically. Two studies evaluated the performance of the family-based and product-based strategy in the context of product-line verification [7, 13]. Brabrand et al. compares the performance of the family-based and product-based strategy for static analysis [10]. For type checking, Liebig at al. evaluated the efficiency of several sample-based strategies, compared to the family-based strategy [21]. While their results are in line with ours, our work is the first that implements all three strategies in one tool and evaluates them using the same subject systems and measurement procedure, so that all comparisons are made in a controlled setting.

5. Conclusion

For the first time, we compared the three product-line analysis strategies—product-based, feature-based, and family-based—in a controlled setting. In our evaluation, we used feature-oriented programming as an implementation technique and type checking as an analysis technique, although the big picture of our results may be transferable to other techniques. In particular, we compared the analysis performance, but we also addressed the ability to detect different kinds of errors, and the quality of the provided information about errors. Our evaluation is based on a feature-oriented compiler that we extended with the three type-checking strategies for this purpose, and a subject set of 12 feature-oriented, JAVA-based product lines.

A main result of our study is that the family-based strategy outperforms the other strategies for all subject systems in terms of analysis time. We identified its caching mechanism as the key factor for the success, as it substantially reduces the number of

SAT-solver queries. At the same time, the family-based strategy is complete: it finds errors that are feature-local and that occur between features (556 in total), which is not the case for the feature-based strategy. Furthermore, the family-based strategy provides the most comprehensive error messages, as it has all information on features and variability at its disposal, which is not the case for the other two strategies.

Although not being in the focus of our study, we found that pursuing a sampling-based strategy (checking only a tractable subset of products) would not change the big picture. For our subject systems, the break-even point, at which the family-based strategy becomes faster, is at very low numbers of products, which means that the corresponding analysis coverage of sampling is likely to be very small, compared to the family-based strategy, which achieves full coverage.

Surprisingly, the feature-based strategy is often slower than the family-based strategy, although it ignores feature interactions and is, consequently, incomplete. Combining the feature-based with the product-based strategy makes it complete, but is substantially slower. Interestingly, such a combined strategy outperforms the plain product-based strategy in most cases in our experiments, which indicates that separate feature compilation and byte-code composition can have a positive effect on analysis performance.

An interesting avenue of further work is to combine the individual strategies and to explore trade-offs in the search for an optimal strategy [32].

Acknowledgments

We thank Peter Lutz for the implementation of the family-based strategy in FUJI. This work was supported by the DFG grants AP 206/2, AP 206/4, and AP 206/5.

References

[1] S. Apel and D. Beyer. Feature Cohesion in Software Product Lines: An Exploratory Study. In *Proc. ICSE*, pages 421–430. ACM, 2011.

[2] S. Apel and D. Hutchins. A Calculus for Uniform Feature Composition. *ACM TOPLAS*, 32(5):19:1–19:33, 2010.

[3] S. Apel, C. Kästner, A. Größlinger, and C. Lengauer. Type Safety for Feature-Oriented Product Lines. *Automated Software Engineering*, 17(3):251–300, 2010.

[4] S. Apel, H. Speidel, P. Wendler, A. von Rhein, and D. Beyer. Detection of Feature Interactions using Feature-Aware Verification. In *Proc. ASE*, pages 372–375. IEEE, 2011.

[5] S. Apel, S. Kolesnikov, J. Liebig, C. Kästner, M. Kuhlemann, and T. Leich. Access Control in Feature-Oriented Programming. *Science of Computer Programming*, 77(3):174–187, 2012.

[6] S. Apel, C. Kästner, and C. Lengauer. Language-Independent and Automated Software Composition: The FEATUREHOUSE Experience. *IEEE Trans. Software Engineering*, 39(1):63–79, 2013.

[7] S. Apel, A. von Rhein, P. Wendler, A. Größlinger, and D. Beyer. Strategies for Product-Line Verification: Case Studies and Experiments. In *Proc. ICSE*, pages 482–491. IEEE, 2013.

[8] L. Bettini, F. Damiani, and I. Schaefer. Compositional Type Checking of Delta-oriented Software Product Lines. *Acta Informatica*, 50(2):77–122, 2013.

[9] E. Bodden, M. Mezini, C. Brabrand, T. Tolêdo, M. Ribeiro, and P. Borba. SPL^{LIFT}: Statically Analyzing Software Product Lines in Minutes Instead of Years. In *Proc. PLDI*, pages 355–364. ACM, 2013.

[10] C. Brabrand, M. Ribeiro, T. Tolêdo, J. Winther, and P. Borba. Intraprocedural Dataflow Analysis for Software Product Lines. *Trans. on Aspect-Oriented Software Development*, 10:73–108, 2013.

[11] A. Classen, P. Heymans, P.-Y. Schobbens, A. Legay, and J.-F. Raskin. Model Checking Lots of Systems: Efficient Verification of Temporal Properties in Software Product Lines. In *Proc. ICSE*, pages 335–344. ACM, 2010.

[12] P. Clements and L. Northrop. *Software Product Lines: Practices and Patterns*. Addison-Wesley, 2001.

[13] M. Cordy, A. Classen, G. Perrouin, P.-Y. Schobbens, P. Heymans, and A. Legay. Simulation-Based Abstractions for Software Product-Line Model Checking. In *Proc. ICSE*, pages 672–682. ACM, 2012.

[14] B. Delaware, W. Cook, and D. Batory. Fitting the Pieces Together: A Machine-Checked Model of Safe Composition. In *Proc. FSE*, pages 243–252. ACM, 2009.

[15] J. Guo, K. Czarnecki, S. Apel, N. Siegmund, and A. Wasowski. Variability-Aware Performance Prediction: A Statistical Learning Approach. In *Proc. ASE*. IEEE, 2013.

[16] M. Johansen, Ø. Haugen, and F. Fleurey. An Algorithm for Generating t-wise Covering Arrays from Large Feature Models. In *Proc. SPLC*, pages 46–55. ACM, 2012.

[17] K. Kang, S. Cohen, J. Hess, W. Novak, and A. Peterson. Feature-Oriented Domain Analysis (FODA) Feasibility Study. Technical Report CMU/SEI-90-TR-21, Carnegie Mellon University, 1990.

[18] C. Kästner, S. Apel, T. Thüm, and G. Saake. Type Checking Annotation-Based Product Lines. *ACM Trans. on Software Engineering and Methodology*, 21(3):14:1–14:29, 2012.

[19] K. Lauenroth, S. Toehning, and K. Pohl. Model Checking of Domain Artifacts in Product Line Engineering. In *Proc. ASE*, pages 269–280. IEEE, 2009.

[20] H. Li, S. Krishnamurthi, and K. Fisler. Verifying Cross-cutting Features as Open Systems. In *Proc. FSE*, pages 89–98. ACM, 2002.

[21] J. Liebig, A. von Rhein, C. Kästner, S. Apel, J. Dörre, and C. Lengauer. Scalable Analysis of Variable Software. In *Proc. ESEC/FSE*, pages 81–91. ACM, 2013.

[22] J. Liu, S. Basu, and R. Lutz. Compositional model checking of software product lines using variation point obligations. *Automated Software Engineering*, 18(1):39–76, Mar. 2011.

[23] S. Oster, F. Markert, and P. Ritter. Automated Incremental Pairwise Testing of Software Product Lines. In *Proc. SPLC*, LNCS 6287, pages 196–210. Springer, 2010.

[24] N. Siegmund, S. Kolesnikov, C. Kästner, S. Apel, D. Batory, M. Rosenmüller, and G. Saake. Predicting Performance via Automated Feature-Interaction Detection. In *Proc. ICSE*, pages 167–177. IEEE, 2012.

[25] N. Siegmund, M. Rosenmüller, C. Kästner, P. Giarrusso, S. Apel, and S. Kolesnikov. Scalable Prediction of Non-functional Properties in Software Product Lines: Footprint and Memory Consumption. *Information and Software Technology*, 55(3):491–507, 2013.

[26] N. Siegmund, A. von Rhein, and S. Apel. Family-Based Performance Measurement. In *Proc. GPCE*. ACM, 2013.

[27] P. Tarr, H. Ossher, and S. Sutton Jr. Hyper/J: Multi-Dimensional Separation of Concerns for Java. In *Proc. ICSE*, pages 689–690. ACM, 2002.

[28] R. Tartler, D. Lohmann, J. Sincero, and W. Schröder-Preikschat. Feature Consistency in Compile-time-configurable System Software: Facing the Linux 10,000 Feature Problem. In *Proc. EuroSys*, pages 47–60. ACM, 2011.

[29] S. Thaker, D. Batory, D. Kitchin, and W. Cook. Safe Composition of Product Lines. In *Proc. GPCE*, pages 95–104. ACM, 2007.

[30] T. Thüm, S. Apel, C. Kästner, M. Kuhlemann, I. Schaefer, and G. Saake. Analysis Strategies for Software Product Lines. Technical Report FIN-004-2012, University of Magdeburg, 2012.

[31] T. Thüm, I. Schaefer, S. Apel, and M. Hentschel. Family-based Deductive Verification of Software Product Lines. In *Proc. GPCE*, pages 11–20. ACM, 2012.

[32] A. von Rhein, S. Apel, C. Kästner, T. Thüm, and I. Schaefer. The PLA Model: On the Combination of Product-Line Analyses. In *Proc. VaMoS*, pages 73–80. ACM, 2013.

Table 3. Measurement results for each subject system and type-checking strategy from our comparison, the setup time (t^{setup}), checking time ($t^{checking}$), and total time (t) are provided. We also provide total times (t) for the feature-product-based strategy and the family-based strategy with caching disabled. For the feature-based strategy, the speedups relative to the product-based strategy and the product-based strategy are provided. For the family-based strategy, the speedups relative to the product-based strategy and the feature-based strategy are provided. We rounded all values to one decimal place. × We aborted the product-based measurements for VIOLET after checking 40 random products (cf. Section 3.5).

System	Product Time (seconds)			Feature Time (seconds)			Feature Speedup w.r.t. Product	Family Time (seconds)			Family Speedup w.r.t. Product	Family Speedup w.r.t. Feature	Feature-product Time (seconds)	Family (no caching) Time (seconds)
	t^{setup}	$t^{checking}$	t	t^{setup}	$t^{checking}$	t	Product	t^{setup}	$t^{checking}$	t	Product	Feature	t	t
EPL	152.7	28.9	181.7	4.6	0.3	4.9	37.2	0.4	0.4	0.8	240.3	6.5	90.5	6.4
GPL	68.5	43.7	112.2	8.1	3.8	12	9.4	0.6	1.7	2.3	48.9	5.2	84.2	798.2
GRAPHLIB	6	2.8	8.8	1.8	0.5	2.4	3.7	0.4	0.3	0.7	12.7	3.4	6.5	1.7
GUIDSL	19.6	22.5	42.1	12.2	6.9	19.1	2.2	1	3.7	4.8	8.8	4	55.9	2102.2
NOTEPAD	216.1	300.1	516.3	3.7	4.3	8	64.5	0.5	1.6	2.1	242.2	3.8	334	34.2
PKJAB	27.6	41.6	69.2	3.9	2.4	6.3	11	0.6	2	2.6	27.1	2.5	70.8	47.2
PREVAYLER	19.3	35.7	55.1	3	1.9	4.9	11.2	0.7	2.2	2.9	18.9	1.7	51.4	21
RAROSCOPE	6.4	3.1	9.5	1.9	0.4	2.3	4.1	0.4	0.3	0.7	13.4	3.2	7.8	1.6
SUDOKU	32	37.9	69.9	3	2.9	5.8	12	0.6	1.1	1.7	41.7	3.5	54.6	9
TANKWAR	1254.4	1326.5	2580.8	12.7	7.2	19.9	129.7	0.6	2.9	3.5	745.3	5.7	2176.5	3200.9
VIOLET	21.6×	37.1×	58.7×	39.6	14.4	54	1.1×	0.8	10	10.8	5.4×	5	100.2×	32251.1
ZIPME	12.8	10.2	23	5.5	1.3	6.8	3.4	0.6	1	1.6	14.5	4.3	30.1	185.3

Spiral in Scala: Towards the Systematic Construction of Generators for Performance Libraries

Georg Ofenbeck[†]   Tiark Rompf [*‡]   Alen Stojanov[†]   Martin Odersky[*]   Markus Püschel[†]

[†]Dept. of Computer Science, ETH Zurich: {ofgeorg, astojanov, pueschel}@inf.ethz.ch
[‡]Oracle Labs: {first.last}@oracle.com   [*]EPFL: {first.last}@epfl.ch

Abstract

Program generators for high performance libraries are an appealing solution to the recurring problem of porting and optimizing code with every new processor generation, but only few such generators exist to date. This is due to not only the difficulty of the design, but also of the actual implementation, which often results in an ad-hoc collection of standalone programs and scripts that are hard to extend, maintain, or reuse. In this paper we ask whether and which programming language concepts and features are needed to enable a more systematic construction of such generators. The systematic approach we advocate extrapolates from existing generators: a) describing the problem and algorithmic knowledge using one, or several, domain-specific languages (DSLs), b) expressing optimizations and choices as rewrite rules on DSL programs, c) designing data structures that can be configured to control the type of code that is generated and the data representation used, and d) using autotuning to select the best-performing alternative. As a case study, we implement a small, but representative subset of Spiral in Scala using the Lightweight Modular Staging (LMS) framework. The first main contribution of this paper is the realization of c) using type classes to abstract over staging decisions, i.e. which pieces of a computation are performed immediately and for which pieces code is generated. Specifically, we abstract over different complex data representations jointly with different code representations including generating loops versus unrolled code with scalar replacement—a crucial and usually tedious performance transformation. The second main contribution is to provide full support for a) and d) within the LMS framework: we extend LMS to support translation between different DSLs and autotuning through search.

Categories and Subject Descriptors I.2.2 [*Automatic Programming*]: Program synthesis, Program transformation; D.3.3 [*Programming Languages*]: Language Constructs and Features – Abstract data types; D.3.4 [*Programming Languages*]: Processors – Code generation, Optimization, Run-time environments

Keywords Synthesis; Abstraction over Staging; Selective Precomputation; Scalar Replacement; Data Representation

1. Introduction

The development of highest performance code on modern processors is extremely difficult due to deep memory hierarchies, vector instructions, multiple cores, and inherent limitations of compilers. The problem is particularly noticeable for library functions of mathematical nature (e.g., BLAS, FFT, filters, Viterbi decoders) that are performance-critical in areas such as multimedia processing, computer vision, graphics, machine learning, or scientific computing. Experience shows that a straightforward implementation often underperforms by one or two orders of magnitude compared to highly tuned code. The latter is often highly specialized to a platform which makes porting very costly (e.g., Intel's IPP library includes different FFT code, likely written in assembly, for Pentium, Core, Itanium, and Atom).

One appealing solution to the problem of optimizing and porting libraries are program generators that automatically produce highest performance libraries for a given platform from a high level description. When the platform is upgraded, the code is regenerated, possibly after an extension of the generator if new features need to be supported (e.g., longer vectors in the architecture as in AVX versus SSE). Building such a generator is difficult, which is the reason that only very few exist to date. The difficulty comes from both the problem of designing an extensible approach to perform all the optimizations the compiler is unable to do and the actual implementation of the generator. The latter often results in an ad-hoc collection of stand-alone programs or scripts. These get one particular job done but are hard to extend, reuse, or further develop, which is a major impediment to progress.

We believe that a programming environment that provides suitable advanced programming concepts should offer a solution to this problem. Hence, the motivating question for this paper is: *Which tools and features provided by programming languages and environments can facilitate the development of generators for performance libraries?* First, we inspect existing generators to derive a common, systematic approach. Then we show with a case study how the components of this approach can be realized using high-level language features and programming techniques.

Program generators for performance. A few program generators have been built for mathematical functionality with highest performance as objective. Examples include the FFTW codelet generator (codegen) for small transforms [15], ATLAS [41], Eigen [1], and Build to Order BLAS [4] for basic linear algebra functions, Spiral for linear transforms [26], the OSKI kernel generator for sparse linear algebra [39], FLAME for linear algebra [16], cvxgen for optimization problems [24], and FEniCS for finite element methods [2]. In most cases, the starting point is a description in a domain-specific language (DSL); where it is not (e.g., ATLAS, which only uses parameters) porting to new platform features (e.g., vectorization) or functions is difficult. In many cases, the DSL is used only to specify the input (e.g., in cvxgen, FEniCS), in some cases to also represent the algorithm (e.g., Flame, Spiral), and sometimes also to perform optimizations through DSL rewriting (e.g., Spiral). Some generators use search over alternatives to tune (e.g., ATLAS, OSKI) some do not (e.g., FFTW codegen, OSKI kernel generator). Several performance optimizations are relevant for most domains (e.g., loop unrolling combined with scalar replacement [5], precomputation, and specialization).

GPCE '13,   October 27–28, 2013, Indianapolis, Indiana, USA.
Copyright © 2013 ACM 978-1-4503-2373-4/13/10. . . $15.00.
http://dx.doi.org/10.1145/2517208.2517228

These generators have been implemented in a large variety of environments. Some are built from scratch (e.g., ATLAS, cvxgen), others make use of a particular programming environment: e.g., OCaml (FFTW codegen), Mathematica (parts of FLAME), the computer algebra system GAP (Spiral). UFL in FEniCS is a standalone languages. Eigen is a collection of C++ templates that perform optimizations during preprocessing.

Systematic construction of program generators. Extrapolating from the commonalities of all these generators, we propose the following systematic approach to construct program generator implementations. Instantiating this approach in a problem domain (such as the ones above) is an orthogonal research question.

- *Describe problem and algorithmic knowledge through one or multiple levels of DSLs.* Program generators need to model problems and algorithms at a high level of abstraction and may need to optimize code at multiple intermediate abstraction levels. For example, FFTW codegen's input is a sum representation of FFTs but most optimizations are done on DAGs. Spiral uses three internal DSLs and rewriting for loop optimizations and parallelization. Successively lower-level DSLs are a natural choice to express these various stages of program generation.

- *Specify certain optimizations and algorithmic choices as rewrite rules on DSL programs.* DSLs can be used for high-level optimization through rewriting (e.g., parallelization in Spiral) but rewrite rules can also be used to express algorithmic choices. Doing so facilitates empirical search ("autotuning"), which in many cases is required to achieve optimal performance.

- *Design high-level data structures that can be parametrized to generate multiple low-level representations.* Often generated libraries need to support multiple input/output data formats. A common example is interleaved or split or C99 format for complex vectors, meaning there will be one library function per format. A generator should be able to abstract over this choice of low-level data formats to ensure maximal compatibility [3].

- *Rely on common infrastructure for recurring low-level transformations.* There are certain transformations common in high performance code that are necessary but particularly unpleasant to implement and maintain manually. Examples include a) unrolling with scalar replacement, b) selective precomputation during code production or initialization, and c) specialization (e.g., to a partially known input). Since these transformations are so common, they should be implemented in a portable way using suitable language features.

While the first two points, DSLs and rewriting, are well-studied topics and supported by existing tools, the latter two points have, to our best knowledge, only been realized in ad-hoc ways. It is a main contribution of this paper to demonstrate how all four points, including the last two, can be achieved with the help of high-level programming language features. To do so we utilize a case study implemented in a specific environment, which we describe in more detail in the following section. However, we emphasize that any programming environment that offers the needed language features can be used instead.

Language support for program generation. For already quite some time, the programming languages community has proposed multi-stage programming using quasi-quotation as a means to make program generation more principled and tractable [34]. However, most approaches remained a thin layer over syntactic composition of program fragments and did not offer facilities beyond serving as a type safe assembly language for program generation. We provide a more detailed discussion of related work in Section 5.

The recently introduced LMS [28, 30] framework works at a higher level than pure composition of code fragments; it is a library-based staging approach that offers an extensible compiler

framework with a rich set of features, including transformations on an intermediate representation and different code generators. LMS has already been applied successfully to implement a range of performance-oriented, high-level domain specific languages (DSLs) in the Delite framework [7, 9, 32]; however, the requirements for generators of highest performance libraries go considerably beyond the use of LMS to date. First and foremost, previous LMS DSLs were designed to be user-facing, not as internal languages for program generators. Thus, no particular support for parameterizing DSL programs over low-level generation choices was available. While LMS has been equipped with program transformation support within a single intermediate representation [31], there was no support for translating between different DSLs. Furthermore, LMS did not provide support for autotuning and had only been used to generate moderately large pieces of code. Consequently, generating code as large as several MB caused serious performance problems which had to be addressed. Finally, while LMS has always used types to denote staged expressions, programming techniques that *abstract over* whether a certain expression is staged had not been studied.

Contributions. In summary, this paper makes the following contributions:

- We conduct a case study for the systematic construction of a program generator in the sense outlined before: the implementation of a subset of Spiral and FFTW codegen inside Scala with LMS. The subset covers the generation of fixed input size C code for FFTs as explained in [12, 15, 27, 42]. It does not cover transforms other than the FFT (Spiral covers more than 30), or the generation of vectorized or parallel code as explained in [13, 14]. However, even though the latter extensions are substantial, they are all based on rewriting. Only the generation of general input size libraries as described in [38] requires new techniques and is subject of future research.

- In implementing this case study, we develop novel programming techniques to address the challenges of parameterizing data structures over code generation choices and implementing transformations like unrolling with scalar replacement. Specifically, we show that with LMS, the type class pattern [40] is a natural fit to abstract over staging decisions, i.e., which pieces of a computation are performed immediately and for which pieces code is generated. More importantly, we show that this mechanism can be applied to data structures to decide which parts of a nested data structure are staged and which only exist at code generation time. This enables us to use a single generator pipeline that abstracts over all required data layouts. A particular layout can be chosen by instantiating the pipeline with the proper types. Coupled with selective staging of loops, this directly leads to an arguably elegant and modular implementation of various loop unrolling and scalar replacement schemes.

- We pushed the LMS framework beyond what was done previously. Novel are in particular the translation between different DSLs (which are not user-facing, but internal steps in the program generation pipeline), empirical autotuning through search, and performance optimizations inside the LMS framework to support the generation of much larger programs.

The source code accompanying this paper is available at spiral.net.

2. Background

We provide necessary background on Spiral and on the LMS framework [28, 30] in Scala.

2.1 Spiral

Spiral is a library generator for linear transforms such as the discrete Fourier transform (DFT). The version we consider here gener-

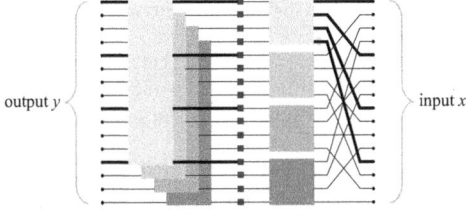

Figure 1. FFT (1) dataflow (right to left) for $n = 16 = 4 \times 4$. The inputs to two $\mathbf{DFT}_4$s are emphasized.

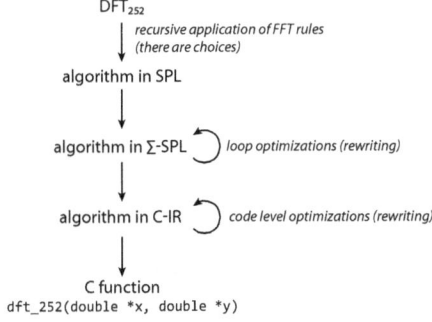

DFT$_{252}$

recursive application of FFT rules
(there are choices)

algorithm in SPL

algorithm in Σ-SPL ⤷ loop optimizations (rewriting)

algorithm in C-IR ⤷ code level optimizations (rewriting)

C function
dft_252(double *x, double *y)

Figure 2. The version of Spiral considered in this paper.

ates unvectorized single-threaded DFT code for arbitrary but fixed input sizes as explained in [12, 27, 42].

Discrete Fourier transform. The DFT multiplies a given complex input vector x of length n by the fixed $n \times n$ DFT matrix to produce the complex output vector y. Formally,

$$y = \mathbf{DFT}_n \, x, \quad \text{where } \mathbf{DFT}_n = [\omega_n^{k\ell}]_{0 \le k, \ell \le n}$$

and $\omega_n = \exp{-2\pi\sqrt{-1}/n}$.

Fast Fourier transforms (FFTs). Divide-and-conquer FFTs (the algorithm knowledge) in Spiral are represented as rules that decompose $\mathbf{DFT}_n$ into a product of structured sparse matrices that include smaller DFTs. For example, the Cooley-Tukey FFT is given by

$$\mathbf{DFT}_n \to (\mathbf{DFT}_k \otimes I_m) T_m^n (I_k \otimes \mathbf{DFT}_m) L_k^n, \quad n = km, \quad (1)$$

where I_n is the identity matrix, L_k^n is a certain permutation matrix, T_m^n is the diagonal matrix of twiddle factors, and

$$A \otimes B = [a_{k,\ell} B]_{0 \le k, \ell < n} \quad \text{for } A = [a_{k,\ell}]_{0 \le k, \ell < n} \, .$$

This formalism, called SPL, is a DSL that captures the data flow of computation. For example, (1) for $n = 16 = 4 \times 4$ is shown in Fig. 1; each gray block is a $\mathbf{DFT}_4$ that is again computed recursively using (1).

Other FFT rules in our prototype include the prime factor FFT ($n = km$, $\gcd(k, m) = 1$), and the Rader FFT (n is prime):

$$\mathbf{DFT}_n \to V_{k,m}^{-1} (\mathbf{DFT}_k \otimes I_m)(I_k \otimes \mathbf{DFT}_m) V_{k,m}, \quad (2)$$

$$\mathbf{DFT}_n \to W_n^{-1}(I_1 \oplus \mathbf{DFT}_{p-1}) E_n (I_1 \oplus \mathbf{DFT}_{p-1}) W_n. \quad (3)$$

Here, V, W are certain permutation matrices, E_n is diagonal, and $\oplus$ is the block-diagonal composition. Recursive application of FFT rules (1)–(3) yields algorithms for a given $\mathbf{DFT}_n$ and there are many choices in this recursion. All FFTs are terminated with the base rule $\mathbf{DFT}_2 \to F_2 = \begin{bmatrix} 1 & 1 \\ 1 & -1 \end{bmatrix}$.

Loop merging. Fig. 1 suggests a recursive computation in four steps: permutation, followed by a loop over smaller FFTs, followed by scaling, followed by another loop over smaller FFTs. This causes four passes over the data, which is inefficient. A better solution fuses the permutation and scaling steps with the subsequent

loops. The permutation then becomes a readdressing in the loop. This merging problem becomes more difficult upon recursion. For example, if all rules (1)–(3) are applied (e.g., for $n = pq$, q prime and $q - 1 = rs$) one may encounter the SPL fragment

$$(I_p \otimes (I_1 \oplus (I_r \otimes \mathbf{DFT}_s) L_r^{rs}) W_q) V_{p,q}.$$

The challenge here is to fuse all three permutations into the innermost loop and to simplify the resulting index expression. In Spiral, this is solved using the DSL Σ-SPL and rewriting [12]. Σ-SPL makes loops and index functions explicit. As a simple example, we consider the fragment $(I_4 \otimes \mathbf{DFT}_4) L_4^{16}$ occurring in Fig. 1. First, it is translated into Σ-SPL, then the permutation is fused into the loop, then the resulting composed index function is simplified. All steps are done by rewriting using rules provided to Spiral:

$$\left(\sum_{j=0}^{3} S(h_{4j,1}) \, \mathbf{DFT}_4 \, G(h_{4j,1}) \right) \mathrm{perm}(\ell_4^{16}) \quad (4)$$

$$\to \sum_{j=0}^{3} S(h_{4j,1}) \, \mathbf{DFT}_4 \, G(\ell_4^{16} \circ h_{4j,1}) \quad (5)$$

$$\to \sum_{j=0}^{3} S(h_{4j,1}) \, \mathbf{DFT}_4 \, G(h_{j,4}). \quad (6)$$

$G(.)$ and $S(.)$ are called gather and scatter and are containers for symbolic index functions that can be manipulated. The sum represents a possible loop, and the loop body is a $\mathbf{DFT}_4$ yet to be further expanded.

Generator. The entire generator is shown in Fig. 2 for some example size ($n = 252$). One of many possible algorithms is generated in SPL, translated to and then optimized in Σ-SPL as explained above, and then translated into a C intermediate language using partial unrolling (namely every DFT below a certain size B encountered in the recursion; we use $B = 16$) that represents the computation DAG. On this DAG, various standard and DFT-specific simplifications are done as explained in [15] (e.g., algebraic simplification, constant normalization and propagation); finally the code is unparsed into C. The entire process is wrapped into a search loop that measures runtime and finds the best recursion using dynamic programming.

2.2 Scala and Lightweight Modular Staging

Multi-stage programming (MSP, or *staging* for short) as established by Taha and Sheard [34] aims to simplify program generator development by expressing the program generator and parts of the generated code in a single program, using the same syntax. Traditional MSP languages like MetaOCaml [8] implement staging by providing syntactic quasi-quotation brackets to explicitly delay the evaluation of (i.e., stage) chosen program expressions.

Contrary to dedicated MSP languages, LMS uses only types to distinguish the computational stages. Expressions of type Rep[T] in the first stage yield computations of type T in the second stage. Expressions of a plain type T in the first stage will be evaluated and become constants in the generated code. The standard Scala type system propagates information about which expressions are staged and thus performs a semi-automatic local binding-time analysis (BTA). Thus, LMS provides some of the benefits of automatic partial evaluation [18] and of manual staging.

Example: Data and traversal abstractions. Consider a Scala implementation of a high-level vector data structure backed by an array:

```scala
class Vector[T](val data: Array[T]) {
  def foreach(f: T => Unit): Unit = {
    var i = 0; while (i < data.length) { f(data(i)); i += 1 }
}}
```

Given this definition, we can traverse a vector using its foreach method; for example to print its elements:

```
vector foreach { i => println(i) }
```

While convenient, the vector abstraction has non-negligible abstraction overhead (e.g., closure allocation and interference with JVM inlining). To obtain high performance code, we would like to turn this implementation into a code generator, that, when encountering a foreach invocation, will emit a while loop instead. Using LMS, we only need to change the method argument and return types, and the type of the backing array, by adding the Rep type constructor to stage selected parts of the computation:

```
class Vector[T](val data: Rep[Array[T]]) {
  def foreach(f: Rep[T] => Rep[Unit]): Rep[Unit] = {
    var i = 0; while (i < data.length) { f(data(i)); i+=1 }}}
```

The LMS framework provides overloaded variants of many operations (e.g. array access data(i)) that lift those operations to work on Rep types, i.e., staged expressions rather than actual data. This allows us to leave the method body unchanged.

It is important to note the difference between types Rep[A=>B] (a staged function object) and Rep[A]=>Rep[B] (a function on staged values). For example, using the latter in the definition of foreach, ensures that the function parameter is always evaluated and unfolded at staging time.

In addition to the LMS framework, we use the Scala-Virtualized compiler [29], which redefines several core language features as method calls and thus makes them overloadable as well. For example, the code

```
var i = 0; while (i < n) { i = i + 1 }
```

will be desugared as follows:

```
val i = __newVar(0); __while(i < n, { __assign(i, i + 1) })
```

The LMS framework provides methods __newVar, __assign, __while, overloaded to work on staged expressions with Rep types.

The LMS extensible graph IR. Another key difference between LMS and earlier staging approaches is that LMS does not directly generate code in source form but provides instead an extensible intermediate representation (IR). The overall structure is that of a "sea of nodes" dependency graph [10]. For details we refer to [28, 30, 32]; a short recap is provided next.

The framework provides two IR class hierarchies. Expressions are restricted to be atomic and extend Exp[T]:

```
abstract class Exp[T]
case class Const[T](x: T) extends Exp[T]
case class Sym[T](n: Int) extends Exp[T]
```

Composite IR nodes extend Def[T]. Custom nodes typically are composite. They refer to other IR nodes only via symbols. There is also a class Block[T] to define nested blocks.

As a small example, we present a definition of staged arithmetic on doubles (taken from [30]). We first define a pure interface in trait Arith by extending the LMS trait Base, which defines Rep[T] as an abstract type constructor.

```
trait Arith extends Base {
  def infix_+(x: Rep[Double], y: Rep[Double]): Rep[Double]
  def infix_-(x: Rep[Double], y: Rep[Double]): Rep[Double]
}
```

We continue by adding an implementation component ArithExp, which defines concrete Def[Double] subclasses for plus and minus operations.

```
trait ArithExp extends BaseExp with Arith {
  case class Plus(x: Exp[Double], y: Exp[Double])
    extends Def[Double]
  case class Minus(x: Exp[Double], y: Exp[Double])
    extends Def[Double]
  def infix_+(x: Exp[Double], y: Exp[Double]) = Plus(x,y)
  def infix_-(x: Exp[Double], y: Exp[Double]) = Minus(x,y) }
```

Trait BaseExp defines Rep[T]=Exp[T], whereas Rep[T] was left abstract in trait Base.

Taking a closer look at ArithExp reveals that the expected return type of infix_+ is Exp[Double] but the result value Plus(x,y) is of type Def[Double]. This conversion is performed implicitly by LMS using toAtom:

```
implicit def toAtom[T](d: Def[T]): Exp[T] = reflectPure(d)
```

The method reflectPure maintains the correct evaluation order by binding the argument d to a fresh symbol (on the fly conversion to administrative normal form (ANF)).

```
def reflectPure[T](d: Def[T]): Sym[T]
def reifyBlock[T](b: =>Exp[T]): Block[T]
```

The counterpart reifyBlock (note the by-name argument) collects performed statements into a block object. Additional reflect methods exist to mark IR nodes with various kinds of side effects (see [32] for details).

3. Implementing the Spiral Prototype Using LMS

In this section we explain the implementation of the generator, as outlined in Section 2.1, in the LMS framework. The section is organized according to the approach presented in Section 1; all of the steps are relevant for the chosen subset of Spiral. The running example will be $\mathbf{DFT}_4$ decomposed using (1):

$$\mathbf{DFT}_4 \to (\mathbf{DFT}_2 \otimes I_2)T_2^4(I_2 \otimes \mathbf{DFT}_2)L_2^4 \qquad (7)$$

3.1 Algorithmic Knowledge as Multiple Levels of DSLs

Spiral requires three DSLs: SPL, Σ-SPL, and an internal representation of C (C-IR); see Fig. 2. We focus on SPL.

DSL representation. The DSL SPL is defined inside Scala in two steps. First, basic matrices such as T_m^n, L_k^n, or $\mathbf{DFT}_2$ are defined as regular Scala classes:

```
abstract class SPL
case class T(n: Int, m: Int) extends SPL
case class DFT(n: Int) extends SPL
case class F2() extends SPL
case class I(n: Int) extends SPL
case class L(n: Int, k: Int) extends SPL
```

Then, matrix operations like product (composition) or $\otimes$ are defined using LMS. The common practice in LMS is to first provide the language interface in terms of abstract methods that operate on (staged) Rep types:

```
trait SPL_Base extends Base {
  implicit def SPLtoRep(i: SPL): Rep[SPL]
  def infix_tensor (x: Rep[SPL], y: Rep[SPL]): Rep[SPL]
  def infix_compose(x: Rep[SPL], y: Rep[SPL]): Rep[SPL] }
```

The method SPLtoRep defines an implicit lifting of SPL operands to Rep[SPL] expressions, and the methods infix_tensor as well as infix_compose define the corresponding operations. Similar to the example in Section 2, we continue with the concrete implementation in terms of the LMS expression hierarchy.

```
trait SPL_Exp extends SPL_Base with BaseExp {
  implicit def SPLtoRep(i: SPL) = Const(i)
  case class Tensor (x:Exp[SPL], y:Exp[SPL]) extends Def[SPL]
  case class Compose(x:Exp[SPL], y:Exp[SPL]) extends Def[SPL]
  def infix_tensor (x:Exp[SPL], y:Exp[SPL]) = Tensor (x, y)
  def infix_compose(x:Exp[SPL], y:Exp[SPL]) = Compose(x, y) }
```

SPLtoRep instructs the compiler to convert objects of type SPL to their staged version, whenever a compose or tensor operation is applied.

Decomposition and search. As explained in Section 2.1, FFTs are expressed as decomposition rules in SPL. We represent such a rule (e.g., (1)), using Scala's first-class pattern matching expression called *partial function*. The type in our case is

```
type Rule = PartialFunction[SPL,Rep[SPL]]
```

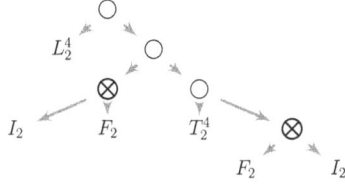

Figure 3. SPL IR representation of a staged $\mathbf{DFT}_4$ decomposition

SPL exp. S	Pseudo code for $y = Sx$	Function
$A_n B_n$	`<code: t = Bx>` `<code: y = At>`	f_{comp}

$I_n \otimes A_n$	**for** (i=0; i<m; i++)
	 `<code: y[i*n:1:i*n+n-1] =`
	 `A(x[i*n:1:i*n+n-1])>`
		f_{ItensorA}

$A_n \otimes I_n$	**for** (i=0; i<n; i++)
	 `<code: y[i:n:i+m*n-n] =`
	 `A(x[i:n:i+m*n-n])>`
		f_{AtensorI}

F_2	`y[0] = x[0] + x[1];` `y[1] = x[0] - x[1];`	f_{F2}

Table 1. SPL to code mapping and name of the emitted functions.

where SPL and Rep[SPL] are the types of the lefthand side and right-hand side of a rule like (1), respectively. The complete definition of (1) takes the following form. Note how the partial function captures the condition of applicability.

```
val DFT_CT: Rule = {
  case DFT(n) if n > 2 && !isPrimeInt(n) =>
    val (m,k) = factorize(n)
    (DFT(k) tensor I(m)) compose T(n,m)
      compose (I(k) tensor DFT(m)) compose L(n,k)
}
```

In the same fashion we represent a base rule to terminate the algorithm:

```
val DFT_Base: Rule =
  case DFT(2) => F2()
```

Partial functions provide a method isDefinedAt that matches an input against the pattern inside the function and returns true if the match succeeds. Hence, we obtain a list of all rules applicable to $\mathbf{DFT}_4$ as follows:

```
val allRules = List(DFT_CT, DFT_Base, ...........)
val applicableRules = allRules filter (_.isDefinedAt(DFT(4)))
```

Partial functions also include an apply method that returns the result of the body of the function. Using this method, all algorithms for a $\mathbf{DFT}_n$ can easily be generated. In practice, we utilize a feedback driven dynamic programming search to explore only a subspace of all possible decompositions. In our running example, there is only one algorithm shown in Fig. 3. The circles refer to the Compose class, the $\otimes$ to the Tensor class; all the leaves are subclasses of SPL. This representation can now be transformed using rewriting (see Section 3.2 later), or unparsed into the target language.

Translation. Since we need to further manipulate the generated algorithm, we do not unparse directly to target code. Rather we define a denotational interpretation of the DSL, which maps every node of the IR graph to its "meaning": a Scala function that performs the corresponding matrix-vector multiplication. The in- and output types are arrays of complex numbers. This function can immediately be used to execute the program when prototyping or debugging. In the next section we will derive translations to lower-level DSLs from the interpretation. Examples of these functions are

shown in Table 1. Conceptually, they correspond to the templates used in the original SPL compiler [42].

To implement this mapping in Scala, we define an abstract method transform in the base class SPL:

```
abstract class SPL {
  def transform(in: Array[Complex]): Array[Complex] }
```

and provide implementations for each concrete subclass (e.g., mapping F_2 to f_{F2}).

```
case class F2() extends SPL {
  override def transform(in: Array[Complex]) = {
    val out = new Array[Complex](2)
    out(0) = in(0) + in(1)
    out(1) = in(0) - in(1)
    out    }}
```

The definition of complex numbers is straightforward.

```
case class Complex(_re: Double, _im: Double) {
  def plus(x: Complex, y: Complex)
    = Complex(x._re + y._re, x._im + y._im)
  def minus(x: Complex, y: Complex)
    = Complex(x._re - y._re, x._im - y._im)  }
```

In addition to the SPL operands, we need to translate the tensor and compose operations. We provide suitable functions for each individual case, for example

```
def I_tensor_A(I_n: Int, A: (Array[Complex]=>Array[Complex]))
  = { in: Array[Complex] =>
      in.grouped(in.size/I_n) flatMap (part => A(part))  }
```

To obtain an interpretation of a given SPL program, we traverse the SPL IR graph (e.g., Fig. 3) in dependency order, call for every node the appropriately parameterized function:

```
def translate(e: Exp[SPL]) = e match {
  case Def(Tensor(Const(I(n)), Const(a: SPL))) =>
    I_tensor_A(n, a.transform)
  .....
}
```

The pattern extractor Def is provided by LMS and will look up the right-hand side definition of an expression in the dependency graph. The result of invoking translate on the topmost node in the SPL IR yields the desired DFT computation as a Scala function of type Array[Complex]=>Array[Complex]. In the running $\mathbf{DFT}_4$ example, the generated call graph takes the following form:

$$f_{\text{comp}}(f_{\text{comp}}(f_{\text{comp}}(f_{\text{AtensorI}}(f_{\text{F2}}, f_{\text{I}}), f_{\text{T}}), f_{\text{ItensorA}}(f_{\text{I}}, f_{\text{F2}})), f_{\text{L}}) \quad (8)$$

In summary, at this stage we have already constructed an internal DSL, which can be used within the native environment of Scala.

Translation to another DSL. Running an internal DSL in a library fashion is convenient for debugging and testing. However, for the generator we need to be able to translate one DSL into another DSL, to rewrite on the DSL, and to unparse the DSL into a chosen target language. Next, we show how to translate SPL into another DSL: an internal representation of a subset of C, called C-IR, for further optimization. We omit the step through Σ-SPL shown in Fig. 2 due to space limitations, but the technique used for translation is analogous.

To translate to C-IR, only a very minor change is required: the parameters of the class Complex are annotated with Rep for staging:

```
case class Complex(_re: CIR.Rep[Double], _im: CIR.Rep[Double])
```

Note that since we are now working with multiple DSLs, we need to specify which language we are referring to by using SPL.Rep or CIR.Rep. In unambiguous cases we omit the prefix and leave it to Scala's scoping mechanism. Invoking translate as defined above now yields a function that returns an IR representation of the computation, instead of the actual computation result. Enveloping the generated function within a wrapper as shown below yields the C-IR representation depicted in Fig. 4.

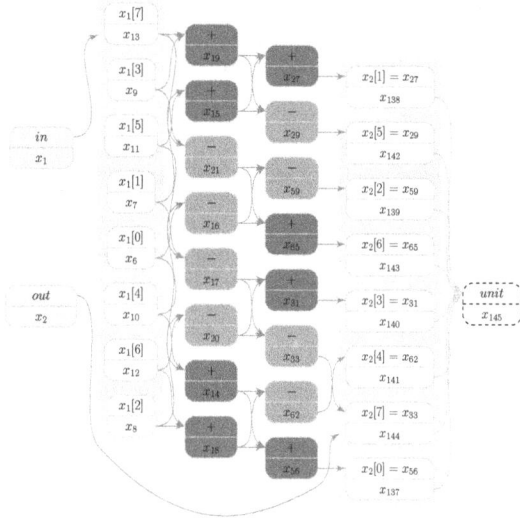

Figure 4. C-IR representation of a staged $\mathbf{DFT}_4$ decomposition for complex input.

```
def wrapper(f: Array[Complex]=>Array[Complex], dft_size: Int)
    (in: Rep[Array[Double]], out: Rep[Array[Double]]) = {
  val scalarized = new Array[Complex](dft_size)
  for (i <- 0 until dft_size)
    scalarized(i) = Complex(in(i*2),in(i*2+1))
  val res = f(scalarized)
  for (i <- 0 until dft_size) {
    out(i*2) = res(i)._re
    out(i*2+1) = res(i)._im
}}
```

This wrapper transforms a staged double array into another staged array by calling the created function f within the snippet. Note that the implementation commits to a specific encoding of complex arrays into double arrays (as shown: interleaved format). We will abstract over the choice of representation in Section 3.3.2. The `wrapper` also commits to a specific code style, namely unrolling with scalar replacement; abstraction over this choice is also explained later. The white boxes in Fig. 4 correspond to the reads of and writes to the staged array; the other boxes are arithmetic operations on staged doubles. Note how any abstraction overhead in the function callgraph is gone due to unrolling and only the operations on the staged variables _re and _im remain. Unparsing to actual C code is now straightforward.

3.2 Optimization through DSL Rewriting

Most domain-specific optimizations in Spiral are done by rewriting DSL expressions. In case of our prototype this occurs on two levels (Fig. 2): Σ-SPL and C-IR. LMS provides rewriting support through its transformer infrastructure [28]. Combined with the pattern matching support of Scala, the rewrite rule used in (5), for example, takes the following form:

```
override def transformStm(stm: Stm):Exp[Any]= stm.rhs match {
  case Compose(Const(g: Gather), Const(lperm: L)) =>
    Gather(compose(l(lperm.k,lperm.m),g.f))
  case _ => super.transformStm(stm)
}
```

The same infrastructure is used to optimize the C-IR graph. For example, the simplification of multiplications by 0 or 1 and constant folding are implemented as follows:

```
override def transformStm(stm: Stm):Exp[Any]= stm.rhs match {
  case NumericTimes(a, b) => (this(a), this(b)) match {
    case (Const(p), Const(q)) => Const(p * q)
```

```
    case (_, Const(0)) | (Const(0), _) => Const(0)
    case (e, Const(1)) | (Const(1), e) => e
    case (e1, e2) => e1 * e2
  }
  case _ => super.transformStm(stm) }
```

The operation **this**(a),**this**(b) applies the enclosing transformer object to the arguments a,b of the multiplication statement. The optimizations implemented in our prototype include common subexpression elimination, constant normalization, DAG transposition and others from [15].

Scala provides additional pattern matching flexibility with custom *extractor objects*. Any object that defines a method unapply can be used as a pattern in a match expression. An example were we use this are binary rewrite rules over longer sequences of expressions. Consider for example a putative simplification rule $H(m) \circ H(n) \to H(m+n)$. We would like to apply this rule to a sequence of $\circ$ operations, such that for example $A \circ H(m) \circ H(n) \circ B$ becomes $A \circ H(m+n) \circ B$. This can be achieved in two steps. We use type IM as a shortcut for Rep[SPL]. First, we define a custom extractor object:

```
object First {
  def unapply(x: IM): Option[(IM, IM=>IM)] = x match {
    case Def(Compose(a,b)) => Some((a, (a1 => a1 compose b))))
    case _ => Some((x, x1 => x1))  }}
```

Matching First against $A \circ B$ will extract (A, w) where w is a function that replaces A, i.e., $w(C) = C \circ B$. Matching against just A will return (A, id).

In the second step, we define a "smart" constructor for the $\circ$ operation Compose that uses First to generalize the binary rewrite:

```
def infix_compose(x: IM, y: IM): IM = (x,y) match {
  case (Const(H(m)), First(Const(H(n)), wrap)) =>
    wrap(H(m+n))
  case (Def(Compose(a,b)),c) =>
    a compose (b compose c)
  case _ =>
    Compose(x,y)
}
```

If the rewrite is not directly applicable, another case is tried that will canonicalize $(A \circ B) \circ C$ to $A \circ (B \circ C)$. Only if that fails, an IR node Compose(a,b) is created. Finally, a transformer needs to be created that invokes the smart constructor:

```
override def transformStm(stm: Stm):Exp[Any]= stm.rhs match {
  case Compose(x,y) => this(x) compose this(y)
  case _ => super.transformStm(stm)}
```

In our generator we use this feature to implement most of the Σ-SPL rewrites including those sketched in (5) and (6).

3.3 Abstracting Over Data Representations and Code Style

In this section we discuss techniques to abstract over data layouts that go hand in hand with performance transformations such as selective precomputation, unrolling with scalar replacement, and specialization. The key insight is to abstract over staging decisions: we will be able to generate data structures or code patterns where different pieces are evaluated at generation time or computed by the generated code, depending on particular type instantiations.

We will make use of the type class design pattern [25, 40], which decouples data objects from generic dispatch and thus combines naturally with a staged programming model. As an example that we use later, we define a variant of Scala's standard Numeric type class that enables abstraction over different numeric types including double, float, and complex:

```
trait NType[T] {
  def plus (x: T, y: T): T
  def minus(x: T, y: T): T }
```

It is easy to define an instance for numeric operations on doubles:

```
implicit object doubleNT extends NType[Double] {
  def plus (x: Double, y: Double) = x + y
  def minus(x: Double, y: Double) = x - y }
```
As an example of using the generic types, we extend our earlier definition of complex numbers to abstract over the component type:
```
case class Complex[T:NType](_re: T, _im: T) {
  def num = implicitly[NType[T]]
  def +(that: Complex) =
    Complex(num.plus(_re, that._re), num.plus(_im, that._im))
  def -(that: Complex) = ... }
```
We use Scala's implicitly operation to access the type class instance that implements the actual plus and minus operations. Type classes in Scala are implemented as implicit method parameters. Thus, the above class definition could equivalently be written as
```
case class Complex[T](_re: T, _im: T)(implicit num: NType[T])
```
Now that we have defined complex numbers, we can turn them into numeric objects as well:
```
implicit def complexNT[T:NType] extends NType[Complex[T]] {
  def plus(x: Complex[T], y: Complex[T]) = x + y
  def minus(x: Complex[T], y: Complex[T]) = x - y }
```
To make the generation of C-IR as flexible as possible, we employ type classes to abstract over the choice of numeric types. In our context this means changing the signatures of our transform methods on SPL objects to the following format:
```
def transform[T:NType](in: Array[T]): Array[T] = ...
```

3.3.1 Selective Precomputation

Precomputation is naturally supported by a staging framework such as LMS. Fine grain control over which parts should be precomputed is possible by using Rep types in suitable places. In many cases it is desirable to abstract over this decision, which is done using type classes as explained next. Afterwards we show as example the selective precomputation of the twiddle factors (the constants in T_m^n in (1)).

Selective staging. To abstract over the staging decision in addition to abstracting over the numeric data type as explained above, we define NType instances for each numeric type. For example, for doubles it becomes
```
implicit object doubleRepNT extends NType[Rep[Double]] {
  def plus(x: Rep[Double], y: Rep[Double]) = x + y
  def minus(x: Rep[Double], y: Rep[Double]) = x - y }
```
Using this mechanism, we can turn staging on or off by providing the corresponding type when calling the transform function. For example, we can now invoke the same definition of transform with any of the following types:

```
Array[Double]           Array[Complex[Double]]
Array[Rep[Double]]      Array[Complex[Rep[Double]]]
```
The same mechanism enables further powerful abstractions that are explained below. In particular, the abstraction over the choice between interleaved and split complex format and over the choice between scalar replacement and array computations.

Precomputation. Precomputation is a classic performance optimization. An example in the context of the FFT are the constant twiddle factors required during the Cooley-Tukey FFT (1). Those numbers require expensive sin and cos operations. It usually pays off to precompute those numbers and inline them as constants in the code or store them in a table. For very large sizes, when the FFT becomes memory-bound, a computation on the fly may be preferable. Using selective staging we can abstract over this decision by simply instantiating the twiddle computation with a suitable type. The generic computation for one twiddle factor is
```
case class E[T:NType](val n : Int, val k : Int) {
  def re(p: T): T = cos(2.0 * math.Pi * p * k, n)
  def im(p: T): T = sin(2.0 * math.Pi * p * k, n) * -1.0 }
```

Instantiating with Double or Rep[Double] controls the precomputation. The latter needs staged sin and cos implementations.

3.3.2 Abstraction over Data Representations

One of the cumbersome programming tasks in the creation of a program generator is support for different data layouts. In our case of FFTs, this would be different ways of storing complex numbers, including as interleaved, split, and C99 complex arrays. In this section, we explain how to abstract over this choice.

So far we have been using plain arrays to hold input, intermediate, and output data. To abstract over the data representation, we first define a new, abstract collection class Vector with an interface similar to arrays:
```
abstract class Vector[AR[_], ER[_], T] {
  def apply(i: AR[Int]): ER[T]
  def create(size: AR[Int]): Vector[AR, ER, T]
  def update(i: AR[Int], y: ER[T])
}
```
In contrast to arrays, however, Vector is parametric in two type constructors: AR and ER. The type constructor AR (short for AccessRep) wraps the indices that are used to access elements, and ER (short for ElemRep) wraps the type of elements. Instantiating either or both of these type constructors as Rep or NoRep (with NoRep[T]=T) will yield a data structure with different aspects staged. Moreover, ER can be instantiated to Complex to explicitly model vectors of complex numbers.

We also want to implement subclasses of Vector that abstract not only over the data layout but also over the choice of staging the internal storage or not (this is equivalent to scalarization of arrays discussed later). To do this we introduce another abstraction of arrays, which is less general, and only wraps a single type constructor AR around all operations:
```
trait ArrayOps[AR[_], T] {
  def alloc(s: AR[Int]): AR[Array[T]]
  def apply(x: AR[Array[T]], i: AR[Int]): AR[T]
  def update(x: AR[Array[T]], i: AR[Int], y: AR[T])
}
```
Instances of ArrayOps will be used as type class arguments by Vector subclasses to abstract over plain and staged internal arrays (i.e., AR=Rep or NoRep).

Finally we have all constructs to represent a variety of different data layouts. We demonstrate with split complex (real and imaginary parts in separate arrays) and C99 complex arrays:
```
class SplitComplexVector[AR[_], T:NType](size: AR[Int])
  (implicit aops: ArrayOps[AR, T])
  extends Vector[AR, Complex, AR[T]] {
    val dataRe: AR[Array[T]] = aops.alloc(size)
    val dataIm: AR[Array[T]] = aops.alloc(size)
    def create(size: AR[Int]) = new SplitComplexVector(size)
    def apply(i: AR[Int]): Complex[AR[T]] =
      new Complex(_re = aops.apply(dataRe, i),
                  _im = aops.apply(dataIm, i))
    def update(i: AR[Int], y: Complex[AR[T]]) = {
      aops.update(dataRe,i,y._re)
      aops.update(dataIm,i,y._im)
    }}
class C99Vector[AR[_],T:NType](s: AR[Int])
  (implicit aops: ArrayOps[AR, Complex[T]])
  extends Vector[AR, AR, Complex[T]] {
    val data = aops.alloc(s)
    def create(size: AR[Int]) = new C99Vector[AR,T](size)
    def apply(i: AR[Int]): AR[Complex[T]] = aops.apply(data,i)
    def update(i: AR[Int], y: AR[Complex[T]])
      = aops.update(data,i,y)
}
```

The split complex implementation abstracts over staging via the type constructor parameter `AR` and contains elements of type `Complex[AR[T]]`. Thus, it extends `Vector[AR,Complex,AR[T]]`. An implementation of interleaved storage using a single array would use the same type. In contrast, the variant that implements arrays of C99 complex numbers specifies its element type as `AR[Complex[T]]` and therefore extends `Vector[AR,AR,Complex[T]]` The vector classes manage either one or two backing arrays using the operations of the aops type class instance, which is passed as an implicit constructor parameter. The accessor methods `apply` and `update` map element from the internal data arrays to an external interface and vice versa. In the split complex case, the external representation is always a staging-time `Complex` object.

Generalizing the generating functions. To accommodate the new generalized data structures, we have to slightly extend the interface of the `transform` method that emit the staged C-IR:

```
case class F2() extends SPL {
  override def transform[AR[_],ER[_],T:NType]
      (in: Vector[AR,ER,T]) = {
    val out = in.create(2)
    out(0) = in(0) + in(1)
    out(1) = in(0) - in(1)
    out
}}
```

Calling this generalized F2 function with the input

```
val in = new SplitComplexVector[Rep, Double](2)
```

will be resolved as

```
transform[Rep,Complex,Double](in: Vector[Rep,Complex,Double])
```

In other words, the internal storage type will be `Rep[Array[Double]]`. Therefore, array operations will appear in the resulting C-IR graph. The complex class, which is mainly used to enable more concise code, does not occur in the staged IR, therefore not causing any overhead.

In addition to the staged array data representations, we can also create a scalarized version:

```
val in = new SplitComplexVector[NoRep,Rep[Double]](2)
```

In this version, the array becomes a regular Scala array that contains staged values (`Array[Rep[Double]]`). The resulting C-IR graph does not contain any of the array or complex operations performed at staging time.

3.3.3 Unrolling and Scalar Replacement

We explain how to abstract over the code style.

Looped code. Beside variables and their operations, also control structures such as loops, conditionals and functions can be staged, as briefly shown already in section 2.2. For the `I_tensor_A` function introduced in section 3.1, extended by the abstractions introduced in 3.3.2, looped code can be implemented as follows:

```
def I_tensor_A[AR[_], ER[_], T:NType](size: Int, n: Int,
    A: Vector[AR,ER,T] => Vector[AR,ER,T]) = {
  in: Vector[AR,ER,T] =>
  val out = in.create(size)
  val n_staged: Rep[Int] = n
  val frag: Rep[Int] = size/n
  for (i <- 0 until n_staged) {
    val tmp = in.create(frag)
    for(j <- 0 until frag) tmp(j) = in(i*n+j)
    val t = A(tmp)
    for(j <- 0 until frag) out(i*n+j) = t(j)
  }
  out }
```

Note that the variables `n_staged` and `frag` are annotated with a `Rep` type, therefore causing the for loop expression to be staged.

Scalarization. In mathematical high performance code, unrolling and scalar replacement in static single assigment (SSA)

form is a standard optimization. It explicitly copies array elements that are reused into temporary variables and removes false dependencies; this way, the compiler is able to rule out memory aliasing and thus to perform better register allocation and instruction scheduling. Scalarization and SSA form come very naturally with LMS as already shown in Fig. 4. By moving the data from a staged array into a Scala container-object containing single staged variables, scalarization effectively takes place. For every operation result gained from this variables, LMS creates a new variable, thus producing SSA form. Using the constructs from Section 3.3.2, scalarization is done by simply moving data between containers:

```
val staged_array: SplitComplexVector[Rep,Double]
val scalarized=new SplitComplexVector[NoRep,Rep[Double]](size)
for (i <- until size)  scalarized(i) = staged_array(i)
for (j <- until size)  SomeComputation(scalarized(j))
for (i <- until size)  staged_array(i) = scalarized(i)
```

The value `size` is a non-staged integer. Next, we combine scalarization with unrolling.

Unrolling. To perform partial unrolling to enable scalarization, we just need to combine the concepts we have seen so far. In particular we scalarize at the beginning of the code fragment we want to unroll, replacing the staged loops with regular Scala loops.

```
def I_tensor_A[AR[_],ER[_],T:NType](size: Int, n:Int,
    A: Vector[AR,ER,T] => Vector[AR,ER,T]) = {
  in: Vector[AR,ER,T] =>
  val in_scalar = new SplitComplexVector[NoRep,ER[T]](size)
  val out = in.create(size)
  val frag = size/n
  for (i <- 0 until size) in_scalar(i) = in(i) //scalarize
  for (i <- 0 until n) {  //start unrolling
    val tmp = in.create(frag)
    for(j <- 0 until frag) tmp(j) = in(i*n+j)
    val t = A(tmp)
    for(j <- 0 until frag) out(i*n+j) = t(j)
  } //end of unrolling
  out  }
```

Instead of manually implementing scalarization for each loop, we can also introduce higher level methods to perform this conversion.

3.3.4 Specialization

Specialization is another important performance optimization and an ability that can distinguish library generators from manually written libraries. In the case of FFT, relevant opportunities for specialization include the presence of symmetry in the input (e.g., the second half is a mirrored version of the first half) or fixing certain inputs (e.g., all imaginary parts are zero). In both cases operations can be reduced. In LMS and our prototype, many specialization cases can be expressed by function composition, where the inner, more general function is wrapped into an outer one that replaces parts of the generic input to make specialization patterns explicit. To illustrate, we assume a function f on complex arrays.

```
val f: Array[Complex] => Array[Complex] = ...
```

If we want to specialize `f` to an input whose first element is known to be 1.0, a specialized version `f_spec` with the same signature can be obtained as follows (in.copy hides the assignment from the caller):

```
val f: Array[Complex] => Array[Complex] = ...
val f_spec = { in: Array[Complex] =>
  val in_spec = in.copy()
  in_spec(0) = Complex(1.0, 0.0)
  f(in_spec)}
```

This pattern is detected at the C-IR optimization level and will result in the elimination of each multiplication with the real part, and each addition and subtraction with the imaginary part. Further dead code removal and opportunities for other simplifications may apply.

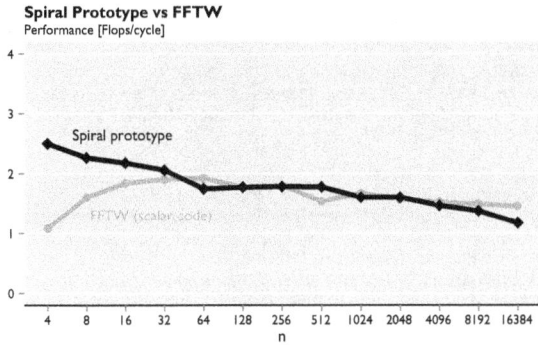

Figure 5. Our generated code versus FFTW 3.3.2

In general, in a specialization the IR graph will be pruned, leading to a simplified version of the initial graph with less operations and thus better performance. In our prototype, the specialization cases mentioned above are supported for scalarized code. This is also the case in FFTW codegen [15].

4. Experimental Results

We compare the performance of the code generated by our Spiral prototype (Fig. 2) against the performance of the carefully hand-written and hand-optimized FFTW 3.3.3 (only the base cases in FFTW are (pre)generated), known to be one of the fastest libraries available. We keep the evaluation brief since the main contribution of this paper is in the demonstration of how to use program language features to build generators.

Experimental setup. The experiments were performed on an Intel i7-2620M with Ubuntu 11.10, using icc 13.0 with flags -O3 -no-simd -no-vec -xHost. The timing is the minimum of ten repeated warm cache measurements with the TSC hardware performance counter. The code considered for both FFTW and our prototype is scalar code (no SSE/AVX vectorization) without threading and with in- and output in interleaved format. FFTW was used with its search enabled. The prototype uses a dynamic programming search and unrolls once the recursion reaches a transform of size ≤ 32. The entire code generation time was less then an hour.

Discussion. Fig. 5 shows the pseudo performance using the pseudo-flop count of $5n \log_2(n)$ on increasing two power input sizes. The plot demonstrates that our prototype yields performance comparable to the one of FFTW. The development of the generator took about 15 man months by two people with no prior experience of Spiral, Scala, or staging.

5. Related Work

There is a considerable body of work on individual program generators (as surveyed in Section 1), but systematic work on implementation methodologies for high-performance program generation is far less widespread.

The original FFTW codelet generator [15] was implemented in OCaml, whose functional programming features such as pattern matching are a good fit for symbolic manipulation. However, a key element of the FFTW simplifier is to provide a tree-like interface to an internal DAG representation. This is achieved by a monadic front-end layer, which also eliminates common subexpressions using memoization. As a consequence, the simplifier needs to be written in explicit monadic style, which adds some notational overhead.

Lisp and Scheme have for a long time supported variants of quote/unquote to compose program fragments (*quasi-quotation*). Racket [35] is a modern dialect with powerful macro facilities. However it is not clear whether sophisticated abstractions (e.g. over data layout) can be as easily achieved without a strong static type system (type classes, etc). In a statically typed setting, lan-

guage support for quasi-quotation was introduced by MetaML [34] and MetaOCaml [8]. Much of the research around these multi-stage languages focuses on extended static guarantees, such as well-scoping and well-typing of generated code. The core abstraction remains an essentially syntactic expansion facility: Composed code fragments cannot be inspected or further transformed. Thus, MetaOCaml encourages a *purely* generative approach which rules out multiple levels of DSLs. MetaOCaml has been used to develop the FFT codelets needed by FFTW [21, 22] but most of the work is performed by tailor-made front-end layers that implement custom abstract interpretations, not the staging facilities themselves. Cohen et. al. [11] demonstrate how a range of loop transformations can be implemented in a purely generative setting, but they also note the limitations, namely when it comes to composing sequences of transformations.

On the opposite end of the spectrum, there are purely transformational systems. Examples are language workbenches such as JetBrains MPS [17] or Spoofax [20] and rewriting engines such as Stratego/XT [6]. While these systems make it easy to compose and layer transformations, it takes additional steps to execute arbitrary code during a transformation. For example, using numeric libraries, or storing pieces of intermediate code in a hash table is not as straightforward as in a purely generative approach.

We believe that successful environments will most likely not be found at the extremes of the spectrum but will offer well-chosen compromises. LMS in particular provides safety assurances for common uses, but also offers an extensible IR with transformation and rewriting support. LMS is a core component of the Delite DSL framework [7, 23, 32], which has been used to implement high-performance DSLs such as OptiML [33].

Limited forms of program generation can be achieved using C++ expression templates [36]. Examples are libraries such as Blitz++ [37], POOMA[19] or Eigen [1], which implement varying degrees of optimizations. However, expressing transformations in the template language can be awkward, and there is no support for non-local transforms that operate across different template expressions or calling library functions at generation time.

Finally, the original Spiral [26] system was implemented inside the computer algebra system GAP for group theory and abstract algebra. GAP offers a rich set of transform-relevant functionality but not much beyond. Most of the required features (DSLs, rewriting, transformations) where thus implemented by extending the environment and without particular language support.

6. Conclusions

Traditionally, the community that aims for highest performance code with detailed architectural- and microarchitectural-cognizant optimizations and the community that builds programming languages and tools are somewhat separated. In the last decade, the difficulty of optimization has led the former to slowly start using DSLs and program generation; however, the implementations usually don't leverage advanced programming techniques and environments. The main goal of this paper was to show that using the proper techniques, such generators can be constructed in a more principled, systematic way with results that are easier to maintain and extend.

In our case study, a small Spiral prototype implemented in Scala using LMS, we demonstrated how to solve several key challenges involved in building generators within a staging framework. Of particular interest are the translation between multiple levels of DSLs, and the abstraction over data representations and different performance code styles with configurable types. This includes unrolling with scalar replacement, a widespread necessary but ugly transformation. The downside is the increased level of expertise required by the programmer to understand and properly use the advanced concepts. For the case study, which was started without prior Scala experience, this meant several reimplementations yielding more and more concise code and eventually the solutions presented in this paper. However, for an artifact as complex as a program generator, we believe this is a price worth paying.

Scala with LMS was one of many choices in consideration at the start of the project. Besides the obvious benefits of having the expertise of the co-authors available by choosing Scala with LMS, also other considerations drove the decision. In particular, experience with Spiral has shown that frequently auxiliary functionality is needed in building a generator; thus, the interoperability of Scala with Java, and thus access to existing Java libraries was a major advantage. In the case study, for example, we used JTransforms to verify generated code and to precompute E_n in (3) and many more libraries such as the Apache Math Commons, the Scala Language-Integrated Connection Kit, ScalaTest, Scalaz trees and Bridj. For this reason, we did not consider tool chains that provide external DSLs. We benefited from other language features in Scala; for example, we used the object-oriented paradigm to structure our implementation and to represent our DSLs, and we used the functional paradigm to express the mathematical algorithms that derive the generated code. For rewriting we benefited from the support for pattern matching and extractors. Finally, we also took into consideration the long term support of all environments in consideration, a relevant issue for long running projects such as Spiral.

References

[1] Eigen C++ template library for linear algebra. http://eigen.tuxfamily.org.

[2] G. N. W. A. Logg, K.-A. Mardal, editor. *Automated Solution of Differential Equations by the Finite Element Method*. Springer, 2012.

[3] B. Aktemur, Y. Kameyama, O. Kiselyov, and C.-c. Shan. Shonan challenge for generative programming: short position paper. In *Proc. Partial evaluation and program manipulation (PEPM)*, pages 147–154, 2013.

[4] G. Belter, E. R. Jessup, I. Karlin, and J. G. Siek. Automating the generation of composed linear algebra kernels. In *SC*. ACM, 2009.

[5] J. Bilmes, K. Asanović, C. whye Chin, and J. Demmel. Optimizing matrix multiply using PHiPAC: a Portable, High-Performance, ANSI C coding methodology. In *Proc. Int'l Conference on Supercomputing (ICS)*, pages 340–347, 1997.

[6] M. Bravenboer, K. T. Kalleberg, R. Vermaas, and E. Visser. Stratego/xt 0.17. a language and toolset for program transformation. *Sci. Comput. Program.*, 72(1-2):52–70, 2008.

[7] K. J. Brown, A. K. Sujeeth, H. Lee, T. Rompf, H. Chafi, M. Odersky, and K. Olukotun. A heterogeneous parallel framework for domain-specific languages. In *Proc. Parallel Architectures and Compilation Techniques (PACT)*, pages 89–100, 2011.

[8] C. Calcagno, W. Taha, L. Huang, and X. Leroy. Implementing multi-stage languages using ASTs, Gensym, and reflection. In *Proc. Generative Programming and Component Engineering (GPCE)*, pages 57–76, 2003.

[9] H. Chafi, Z. DeVito, A. Moors, T. Rompf, A. K. Sujeeth, P. Hanrahan, M. Odersky, and K. Olukotun. Language virtualization for heterogeneous parallel computing. In *Proc. Int'l conference on object oriented programming systems languages and applications (OOPSLA)*, pages 835–847, 2010.

[10] C. Click and K. D. Cooper. Combining analyses, combining optimizations. *ACM Trans. Program. Lang. Syst.*, 17:181–196, March 1995.

[11] A. Cohen, S. Donadio, M. J. Garzarán, C. A. Herrmann, O. Kiselyov, and D. A. Padua. In search of a program generator to implement generic transformations for high-performance computing. *Sci. Comput. Program.*, 62(1):25–46, 2006.

[12] F. Franchetti, Y. Voronenko, and M. Püschel. Formal loop merging for signal transforms. In *Programming Languages Design and Implementation (PLDI)*, pages 315–326, 2005.

[13] F. Franchetti, Y. Voronenko, and M. Püschel. FFT program generation for shared memory: SMP and multicore. In *Supercomputing (SC)*, 2006.

[14] F. Franchetti, Y. Voronenko, and M. Püschel. A rewriting system for the vectorization of signal transforms. In *High Performance Computing for Computational Science (VECPAR)*, volume 4395 of *Lecture Notes in Computer Science*, pages 363–377. Springer, 2006.

[15] M. Frigo. A fast Fourier transform compiler. In *Proc. Programming Language Design and Implementation (PLDI)*, pages 169–180, 1999.

[16] J. A. Gunnels, F. G. Gustavson, G. M. Henry, and R. A. van de Geijn. FLAME: Formal linear algebra methods environment. *ACM Trans. on Mathematical Software*, 27(4):422–455, 2001.

[17] JetBrains. Meta Programming System, 2009.

[18] N. D. Jones, C. K. Gomard, and P. Sestoft. *Partial evaluation and automatic program generation*. Prentice-Hall, Inc., Upper Saddle River, NJ, USA, 1993.

[19] S. Karmesin, J. Crotinger, J. Cummings, S. Haney, W. Humphrey, J. Reynders, S. Smith, and T. J. Williams. Array design and expression evaluation in POOMA II. In *ISCOPE*, pages 231–238, 1998.

[20] L. C. L. Kats and E. Visser. The Spoofax language workbench. rules for declarative specification of languages and IDEs. In *SPLASH/OOPSLA Companion*, pages 237–238, 2010.

[21] O. Kiselyov, K. N. Swadi, and W. Taha. A methodology for generating verified combinatorial circuits. In G. C. Buttazzo, editor, *EMSOFT*, pages 249–258. ACM, 2004.

[22] O. Kiselyov and W. Taha. Relating FFTW and split-radix. In Z. Wu, C. Chen, M. Guo, and J. Bu, editors, *ICESS*, volume 3605 of *Lecture Notes in Computer Science*, pages 488–493. Springer, 2004.

[23] H. Lee, K. J. Brown, A. K. Sujeeth, H. Chafi, T. Rompf, M. Odersky, and K. Olukotun. Implementing domain-specific languages for heterogeneous parallel computing. *IEEE Micro*, 31(5):42–53, 2011.

[24] J. Mattingley and S. Boyd. CVXGEN: A code generator for embedded convex optimization. *Optimization and Engineering*, 13(1):1–27, 2012.

[25] U. Norell and P. Jansson. Polytypic programming in Haskell. In P. W. Trinder, G. Michaelson, and R. Pena, editors, *IFL*, volume 3145 of *Lecture Notes in Computer Science*, pages 168–184. Springer, 2003.

[26] M. Püschel, J. M. F. Moura, J. Johnson, D. Padua, M. Veloso, B. Singer, J. Xiong, F. Franchetti, A. Gacic, Y. Voronenko, K. Chen, R. W. Johnson, and N. Rizzolo. SPIRAL: Code generation for DSP transforms. *Proceedings of the IEEE, special issue on "Program Generation, Optimization, and Adaptation"*, 93(2):232–275, 2005.

[27] M. Püschel, B. Singer, M. Veloso, and J. M. F. Moura. Fast automatic generation of DSP algorithms. In *International Conference on Computational Science (ICCS)*, volume 2073 of *Lecture Notes In Computer Science*, pages 97–106. Springer, 2001.

[28] T. Rompf. *Lightweight Modular Staging and Embedded Compilers: Abstraction Without Regret for High-Level High-Performance Programming*. PhD thesis, EPFL, 2012.

[29] T. Rompf, N. Amin, A. Moors, P. Haller, and M. Odersky. Scala-virtualized: Linguistic reuse for deep embeddings. In *Higher-Order and Symbolic Computation (Special issue for PEPM'12, to appear)*.

[30] T. Rompf and M. Odersky. Lightweight modular staging: a pragmatic approach to runtime code generation and compiled dsls. *Commun. ACM*, 55(6):121–130, 2012.

[31] T. Rompf, A. K. Sujeeth, N. Amin, K. Brown, V. Jovanovic, H. Lee, M. Jonnalagedda, K. Olukotun, and M. Odersky. Optimizing data structures in high-level programs. In *Proc. Principles of programming languages (POPL)*, pages 497–510, 2013.

[32] T. Rompf, A. K. Sujeeth, H. Lee, K. J. Brown, H. Chafi, M. Odersky, and K. Olukotun. Building-blocks for performance oriented DSLs. DSL, 2011.

[33] A. K. Sujeeth, H. Lee, K. J. Brown, T. Rompf, M. Wu, A. R. Atreya, M. Odersky, and K. Olukotun. OptiML: an implicitly parallel domain-specific language for machine learning. In *Proceedings of the 28th International Conference on Machine Learning*, ICML, 2011.

[34] W. Taha and T. Sheard. Metaml and multi-stage programming with explicit annotations. *Theor. Comput. Sci.*, 248(1-2):211–242, 2000.

[35] S. Tobin-Hochstadt, V. St-Amour, R. Culpepper, M. Flatt, and M. Felleisen. Languages as libraries. In *Programming language design and implementation (PLDI)*, PLDI '11, pages 132–141, 2011.

[36] T. L. Veldhuizen. Expression templates, C++ gems. SIGS Publications, Inc., New York, NY, 1996.

[37] T. L. Veldhuizen. Arrays in blitz++. In *ISCOPE*, pages 223–230, 1998.

[38] Y. Voronenko, F. de Mesmay, and M. Püschel. Computer generation of general size linear transform libraries. In *International Symposium on Code Generation and Optimization (CGO)*, pages 102–113, 2009.

[39] R. Vuduc, J. W. Demmel, and K. A. Yelick. OSKI: A library of automatically tuned sparse matrix kernels. In *Proc. SciDAC*, volume 16 of *Journal of Physics: Conference Series*, pages 521–530, 2005.

[40] P. Wadler and S. Blott. How to make ad-hoc polymorphism less ad-hoc. In *POPL*, pages 60–76, 1989.

[41] R. Whaley, A. Petitet, and J. Dongarra. Automated empirical optimization of software and the ATLAS project. *Parallel Computing*, 27(1-2):3–35, 2001.

[42] J. Xiong, J. Johnson, R. W. Johnson, and D. Padua. SPL: A language and compiler for DSP algorithms. In *Programming Languages Design and Implementation (PLDI)*, pages 298–308, 2001.

Scalaness/nesT: Type Specialized Staged Programming for Sensor Networks

Peter Chapin

University of Vermont

pchapin@cs.uvm.edu

Christian Skalka *

University of Vermont

skalka@cs.uvm.edu

Scott Smith

The Johns Hopkins University

scott@cs.jhu.edu

Michael Watson

University of Vermont

mpwatson@cs.uvm.edu

Abstract

Programming wireless embedded networks is challenging due to severe limitations on processing speed, memory, and bandwidth. Staged programming can help bridge the gap between high level code refinement techniques and efficient device level programs by allowing a first stage program to specialize device level code. Here we introduce a two stage programming system for wireless sensor networks. The first stage program is written in our extended dialect of Scala, called Scalaness, where components written in our type safe dialect of nesC, called nesT, are composed and specialized. Scalaness programs can dynamically construct TinyOS-compliant nesT device images that can be deployed to motes. A key result, called cross-stage type safety, shows that successful static type checking of a Scalaness program means no type errors will arise either during programmatic composition and specialization of WSN code, or later on the WSN itself. Scalaness has been implemented through direct modification of the Scala compiler. Implementation of a staged public-key cryptography calculation shows the sensor memory footprint can be significantly reduced by staging.

Categories and Subject Descriptors D.3.4 [*Programming Languages*]: Processors—Compilers

Keywords Staged programming; Scala; nesC

1. Introduction

A wireless sensor network (WSN) is a network of small nodes, also called *motes*, equipped with sensors or actuators, and that communicate with each other via short range radio links. Programming WSNs is challenging because the nodes are severely resource constrained in terms of memory and processor speed. This paper describes a programming language designed to support the automatic generation of runtime-efficient code for WSN nodes. The language enables *dynamic specialization* of node code on a nearby hub or other more resource-rich device, allowing adaptation to properties of a node's deployment environment such as neighborhood characteristics, network interference factors, *etc.*

* This author's work was supported by a YIP grant from the Air Force Office of Scientific Research (AFOSR).

Our system supports dynamic generation of programs for the TinyOS operating system [16], a popular platform for WSNs. It features programming abstractions for specializing WSN code, allowing on-the-fly adaptation to current WSN deployment conditions. We use a restricted form of *staging* [8, 32, 33] to achieve well founded dynamic program generation. *First stage* code is written in an extended version of Scala [30], called Scalaness. Scalaness program execution yields a residual *second stage* WSN node program written in nesT, a variant of the popular nesC programming language [12] with a stronger type checking analysis. The second stage program is constructed from module components treated as first class values, which may be *type and value specialized* during the course of first stage computation to yield more compact and efficient code. A code rewriting strategy in the implementation transforms nesT code into nesC code, which can be compiled using standard TinyOS tools.

While staging is well-studied and has been explored in a WSN context [24], our work is novel in that we achieve stronger static safety guarantees than previous work. At the point of Scalaness program compilation, our compiler can statically verify that any nesT program produced by the Scalaness runtime will be statically type-safe when deployed and run on a network node, even if module parameters are specialized during the course of nesT module composition. We call this property *cross-stage type safety*, which has been previously studied in a foundational language context [20]. In this paper we apply these concepts to the more practical Scalaness/nesT language, and illustrate how they support the implementation of efficient real-life WSN applications.

1.1 Application Setting and Contributions

The diagram in Fig. 1 provides an overview of the Scalaness/nesT language architecture. Scalaness source code is compiled in a modified Scala compiler to Java bytecode, and run in a standard JVM. At runtime this Scalaness program may generate nesT code, which is subsequently rewritten to nesC and compiled using the standard TinyOS compiler. The resulting image can then be installed on nodes in a WSN.

Another interesting feature of our intended application setting, captured in Fig. 1, is the physical platform on which different elements of the Scalaness/nesT "workflow" may be executed. Scalaness source code will typically be compiled in the lab, prior to deployment. There are two distinct deployment scenarios where compiled bytecode execution, TinyOS image generation, and mote (re)programming (the rightmost two boxes in Fig. 1) can occur. Clearly these activities can take place in the lab, where WSN motes can be easily imaged over e.g. USB connections prior to deployment. But the more interesting scenario we aim to support is generation of TinyOS images on a "hub" device *in situ*, and then to automatically reprogram WSN nodes over the air (OTA) from that hub.

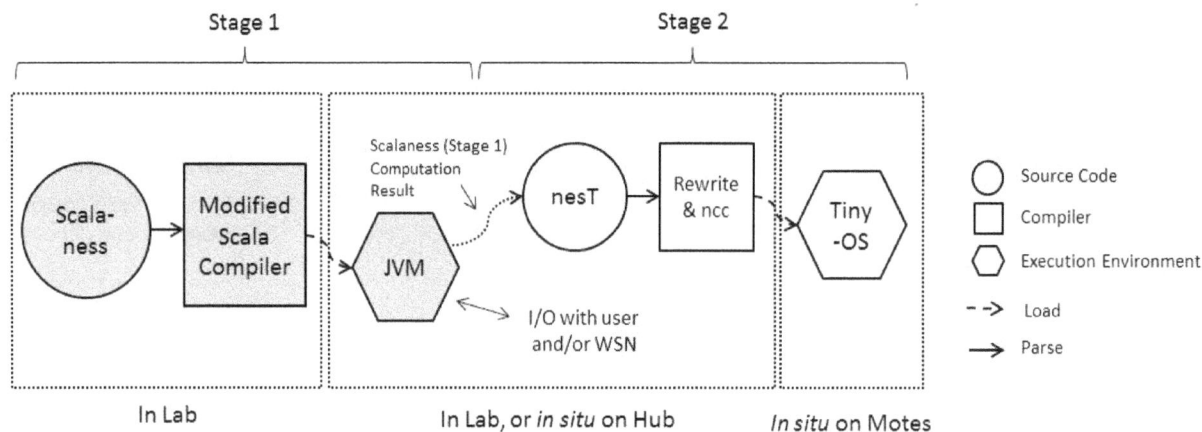

Figure 1. Scalaness/nesT Compilation and Execution Model

In WSN applications such as our Snowcloud snow telemetry system [11, 26], sensor motes report data to higher powered hubs, pictured in Fig. 2. The hub device in the figure uses a low-powered embedded Linux platform that supports a JVM, and is in direct radio communication with the sensor network via a physically attached mote. These types of devices are readily available and cheap. Such a system can execute compiled Scalaness code, and compile and deploy generated TinyOS images to nearby motes. Since the hub is in communication with the network, Scalaness/nesT is uniquely positioned to evolve network behavior based on a global view of observed data, a technique called *backcasting* [34] when used specifically for network control. In this context the benefit of cross-stage type safety is clear: type-checked Scalaness compilation in the lab ensures type safety of bytecode execution on the hub, *and* type-safety of dynamically generated TinyOS image execution on the WSN. Manual correction of type errors in generated TinyOS images in this scenario is infeasible since these systems run automatically in remote settings.

Figure 2. A Sensor Node (L,C) and Hub Device (R).

Paper Outline. The main contributions of the work presented here are the specification, implementation, and prototype application of the Scalaness and nesT languages, including their syntax, semantics, and type analysis. In Sect. 2 we summarize Scalaness/nesT via discussion of an extended example. Formal specifications of the nesT and Scalaness languages are presented in Sect. 3 and Sect. 4, respectively. Their semantics and type theory possess several novel and challenging features, which we show in Sect. 5 are grounded in principles studied in a previous foundational setting [20]. We describe our implementation and present an extended example application of our system to resource access control in WSNs in Sect. 6 and Sect. 7, along with some empirical results demonstrating efficiency benefits of our approach. We conclude with remarks on related work in Sect. 8

2. An Example: Authenticated Messaging

In this section we provide a high-level overview of Scalaness/nesT usage and applications via an example. (This example is written in DScalaness/DnesT, a simplified formalization of the implemented Scalaness/nesT, which is defined later in this paper.) The example illustrates both the type and value specializations that can occur in our system. This example needs to be very small to fit in this overview which means it alone is not complete evidence of the advantage of mote code staging, but it should point the reader to the promise of the approach.

Program description. To illustrate type specialization, we refine address size. It is well-known that minimizing address space size in WSN message packets can obtain significant energy savings by reducing message sizes, since each bit of transmission is known to consume energy similar to 800 instructions [22]. However, WSNs are "ad hoc" precisely in the sense that positions and densities of nodes in space are unpredictable, so "minimal" address space is an environmental property, where minimality may need to be determined *in situ.*

To illustrate value specialization, we define a DnesT code template that can be instantiated with specific session keys for secure communication in a WSN. We imagine that the template is instantiated on high powered hub or lab device, where session keys are generated. In previous work it has been shown how symmetric key signatures can be used to support language based resource authorization in WSNs [4, 5]. In particular, communication between security domains in a WSN is mediated by credentials implemented as keys, and nodes lying at domain frontiers can use different keys to send (to the other domain) and receive (from the other domain) over secured link layer channels. Since it is unpredictable where nodes will be physically distributed in space, appropriate keys for each node need to be established *in situ.* Defining node functionality using generic code that must be instantiated with specific keys allows adaptation to a deployment environment, and allows expensive computations for establishing session keys to be offloaded from the WSN to a higher powered device. Experience with an actual implementation of this application is discussed Sect. 7.

The Code. To distinguish Scalaness and nesT code in examples we will use a darker font for Scalaness code and a lighter font for nesT code, and line numbers for reference. We begin with the definition of a parameterized type `mesgT(t)` using the Scalaness `abbrvt` binder, where an instance `mesgT(`τ`)` denotes the ground type obtained by substituting τ for `t` in the definition of `mesgT`.

```
1  abbrvt mesgT(t) = { src : t; dest : t; data : uint8[] };
```

Next, we define a type `radioT`, which is the type of nesT modules that provide an API to the radio.

```
2  abbrvt radioT = < mt ≼ mesgT(uint) >
3            { export radio_x(mt*);
4              import handle_radio_r(mt*); };
```

The nesT module language is a simplified version of the nesC component language. In this example, any module of type `radioT` exports a `radio_x` function for sending messages, and imports a `handle_radio_r` function that allows received messages to be handled in a user-defined manner. Both functions take message references as arguments[1]. Furthermore, the module is parameterized by the type of messages `mt`, where the address type is upper-bounded by 32-bit unsigned integer. Thus, any module of type `radioT` can be dynamically specialized to a 32, 16, or 8 bit address space by type instantiation. Module type parameters are always defined with brackets $< ... >$.

Now we define another type `commT` which is the type of modules providing a QOS layer over a specialized radio.

```
5  abbrvt commT = (mt ≼ mesgT(uint)) o
6            < >
7            { export send(mt*);
8              import handle_receive(mt*); };
```

Although this type is also parameterized by a bounded message type `mt`, as is `radioT`, the parameterization is subtly different syntactically and semantically, since `commT` expects a program context where the radio has been specialized. Thus, in `commT`, `mt` is understood as being "some" type with an upper bound of `mesgT(uint)` which occurs in the module signature, whereas the module itself has no parameters to be instantiated– note the empty instance parameter brackets $<>$ in the module type after the o delimiter. This sort of type is needed in the presence of *dynamic type construction*, a useful Scalaness feature we exemplify below.

Next we define modules for sending and receiving messages that provide a layer of authentication security over the radio.

```
9   authSend = < mt ≼ mesgT(uint); sendk : uint8[],>
10            { import radio_x(mt*);
11              export send(m : mt*)
12                  { radio_x(AES_sign(m, sendk)); } };
13
14  authRecv = < mt ≼ mesgT(uint); recvk : uint8[] >
15            { import handle_recv(mt*);
16              export handle_radio_r(m : mt*)
17                  { if AES_signed(m, recvk)
18                      handle_recv(m); } };
```

Observe that in the implementation of `send` in module `authSend`, messages are signed with a key `sendk`, whereas when messages are received they must be signed with a possibly different key `recvk` before being passed on to the user's receive handler, as specified in module `authRecv`. These modules are parameterized by a message type `mt`, and also the `sendk` and `recvk` key values.

To generalize a technique for composing these modules with a radio to yield a module of type `commT`, that is abstract wrt neighborhood sizes, radio implementations, and session key material, we define the Scalaness `authSpecialize` function as follows:

```
19  def authSpecialize
20     (nmax : uint16, radioM : radioT, keys : uint8[][]) : commT {
```

---

[1] For brevity the return type on all commands is omitted. In all cases it is the TinyOS error type `error_t`

```
21     typedef adt ≼ uint = if (nmax ≤ 256) uint8 else uint16;
22     val sendM = authSend⟨mesgT(adt); keys[0]⟩;
23     val recvM = authRecv⟨mesgT(adt); keys[1]⟩;
24     (sendM ⋈ radioM⟨mesgT(adt)⟩) ⋈ recvM;
25     }
```

The first-class status of nesT modules in Scalaness is apparent here. On line 20 the function is specified to take a module parameter `radioM` of type `radioT` among its arguments, and to return a module of type `commT` as a result. It also takes an array of keys as an argument, and on lines 22 and 23 it instantiates `sendMesg` and `recvMesg` with the keys in the array. It also uses the type `adt` in the instantiations, which in line 21 is dynamically constructed on the basis of the input variable `nmax` which defines the needed address space size and bound using the Scalaness `typedef` construct. This illustrates a key novelty of our system, the ability to *dynamically* set a type to use on a mote based on a decision made in the Scalaness runtime. Since the value of `nmax` cannot be statically determined, the type analysis only knows that `adt` is some subtype of `uint`. Finally, on line 24 the instantiated radio module is composed with the instantiated send and receive modules via the Scalaness ⋈ operator. The semantics of module composition here is standard [2]; in a composition aka wiring $\mu_1 ⋈ \mu_2$, the exports of μ_2 are connected to imports of μ_1. The function result is a module of type `commT`.

To obtain a module defining a mote OS image in a program context where neighborhood size is known, a radio implementation has been provided, and session keys have been computed. We can then compose the results of an `authSpecialize` function with modules specifying top-level message send and receive behaviors, and a `main` application entry point as follows (here we assume it is known that address sizes can be limited to 8 bits, so `nmax < 256`). At line 30 a closed module is defined and a binary mote image can be produced by a call to `image`.

```
26  appMR =
27   < > { export handle_recv(m : mesgT(uint8)*) {...} };
28  appM =
29   < > { import send(mesgT(uint8)*); export main() {...} };
30  image(appM ⋈ (authSpecialize(nmax, radioM, keys) ⋈ appMR));
```

In DScalaness, `image` is an assertion that its argument is a *runnable* module, with no unresolved parameters or imports. In the Scalaness implementation, this is the point where nesT source code is actually generated. Successful Scalaness/nesT type checking (which occurs during stage 1 compilation as per Fig. 1) statically guarantees that specialized code generated at the point of `image` will run in a type-safe manner when it is eventually loaded and run on a mote.

3. The nesT Language Distilled

In this section we summarize a *D*istilled version of nesT, called DnesT, that isolates novel elements of nesT, specifically parametric types, subtyping, type safety, and modules. DnesT serves as a formal specification for the nesT implementation—given the novel type theory a specification is crucial as a guide for the implementation. Due to limited space we summarize only the top-level structure of DnesT modules and our type checking algorithm, in order to focus more on the more central technical issues of module composition, instantiation, and typing at the Scalaness level.

The goal of nesT is to be a type-safe variant of nesC, and DnesT serves as the specification for how type safety is achieved. Our approach is another species of "safe C" language design projects such as [29]. In particular, in DnesT all array bound accesses are checked at run-time, and pointer arithmetic and casting are restricted to safe forms only. We have developed a new type checking algorithm that incorporates subtyping, which supports bounded type parameters in DnesT module definitions and a more accurate static analysis of Scalaness code in the presence of type construction and nesT module instantiation.

$$\varsigma, \tau \quad ::= \quad t \mid \top \mid \textbf{uint8} \mid \textbf{uint16} \mid \textbf{uint} \mid \qquad\qquad types$$
$$\textbf{uninit} \mid \{\bar{l} : \bar{\tau}\} \mid \tau[] \mid \tau\star$$

T	$::=$	$\bar{t} \preccurlyeq \bar{\tau}$	*type parameters*
V	$::=$	$\bar{x} : \bar{\tau}$	*value parameters*
c	$::=$	$\textsf{f}(V) : \tau = \{e\}$	*command definition*
s	$::=$	$\textsf{f}(V) : \tau$	*command signature*
ι	$::=$	$\bar{s}$	*imports*
ξ	$::=$	$\bar{c}$	*exports*
ε	$::=$	$\bar{s}$	*export types*
d	$::=$	$\tau\, x \,=\, e \mid \tau\, x \,=\, [\![\bar{e}]\!] \mid$	*declarations*
		$\tau\, x \,=\, \{\bar{l} = \bar{e}\} \mid c$	
μ	$::=$	$<T; V>\{\iota; \bar{d}; \xi\}$	*module definitions*
$\mu\pi$	$::=$	$<T; V>\{\iota; \varepsilon\}$	*module signatures*

Figure 3. Syntax of DnesT Types and Modules

3.1 Syntax and Semantics of DnesT

Module definitions rely on a notion of lists aka sequences of syntactic entities, so we begin with a definition of relevant notation.

Notation and identifiers. *Sequences* are notated $x_1, \ldots, x_n$, and are abbreviated $\bar{x}$; $\bar{x}_{(i)}$ is the i-th element, $\emptyset$ denotes the empty sequence, and $|\bar{x}|$ is the size. We write $x \in \bar{x}$ to denote membership in sequences, and $x\bar{x}$ denotes a sequence with head x and tail $\bar{x}$. We denote append as $\bar{x}@\bar{y}$. For relational symbols $R \in \{\preccurlyeq, =, :\}$, we use the abbreviation: $\bar{x}\, R\, \bar{y} = x_1\, R\, y_1, \ldots, x_n\, R\, y_n$. So for example, $\bar{x} : \bar{\tau} = x_1 : \tau_1, \ldots, x_n : \tau_n$. We will use metavariable f (of set $\mathcal{F}$) for function names, l (of set $\mathcal{L}$) for field names, x (of set $\mathcal{V}$) for term variables, t (of set $\mathcal{T}$) for type variables.

Module syntax. The syntax of DnesT modules is defined in Fig. 3. Modules μ are written $<T; V>\{\iota; \bar{d}; \xi\}$ with T and V being generic type and term parameters, $\bar{d}$ being module scope identifier declarations, including function definitions, and ι and ξ being imports and exports. In Sect. 2 and elsewhere we use the keywords `import` and `export` as sugar indicating this categorization.

All type parameters are assigned an upper bound, and term parameters are explicitly typed. Imports and export types are sequences of imported and exported command type signatures. Exports are sequences of command definitions. Exports are defined in terms of expressions e, the syntax of which we omit here for brevity. Declarations $\bar{d}$; are a sequence of typed variable declarations. Base values, arrays (in brackets $[\![\cdot]\!]$), structs (in braces $\{\cdot\}$), and commands may all be declared, and the scope of declared variable names is restricted to the module. Declarations are important to include in DnesT, as they support serialization of value parameters during Scalaness instantiation as we describe in Sect. 4.3.

While we have elided the specifics of DnesT syntax from this shortened presentation, we now give a high-level summary of its largely standard features. Expressions include standard C-like conditional branching, looping, sequencing of expressions, function calls, arrays, structs, numeric base data types and basic arithmetic operations. As in nesC, no dynamic memory allocation is possible; all memory layout is established by static variable declarations. DnesT disallows pointer arithmetic, to support stronger type safety guarantees. Type casting and array access have run time checks imposed: types may never be cast to a pointer, and array accesses are always checked to be in bounds at runtime. As in nesC, DnesT includes a **post** operation for posting tasks, although we make no syntactic distinction between tasks and commands. The meaning of **post** corresponds to the "run-to-completion" model of TinyOS tasks. Interrupts are omitted from DnesT since they do not significantly affect the typing issues we are concerned with here.

Module semantics A "runnable" module – one without imports or generic parameters – is the DnesT model of a node OS image. The declarations in the module defines a *load sequence* establishing an initial machine configuration, and the application entry point is defined in a required command `main`.

DEFINITION 3.1. *A module of the form* $<\emptyset; \emptyset>\{; \bar{d}; \xi\}$, *where* $\text{main}() : \textbf{uninit} \in \xi$, *is called runnable.*

This model is consistent with nesC, where an application is defined as a top-level component that establishes an initial configuration through variable declarations, and requires user definition of an entry point (an event handler called `Booted`). Formally speaking, type safety in nesT is a dynamic property of runnable modules.

3.2 Type Checking and Subtyping

The type system for DnesT combines a standard procedural language typing approach with subtyping techniques adapted from previous foundational work [13, 20].

At the heart of our system is a decidable subtyping judgment $T \vdash \tau_1 \preccurlyeq \tau_2$, where T is a *coercion* and defines a system of upper bounds for type variables. This establishes a subtype ordering on base types, and also allows for width subtyping of records. The relation is defined in Fig. 4. Algorithms for deciding the relation and integrating it with dynamic type construction and other Scalaness (stage 1) type features was a central topic of [20].

REFLS
$$T \vdash \tau \preccurlyeq \tau$$

TOPS
$$T \vdash \tau \preccurlyeq \top$$

TRANSS
$$\frac{T \vdash \tau_1 \preccurlyeq \tau_2 \qquad T \vdash \tau_2 \preccurlyeq \tau_3}{T \vdash \tau_1 \preccurlyeq \tau_3}$$

UINTS
$$T \vdash \textbf{uint8} \preccurlyeq \textbf{uint16} \preccurlyeq \textbf{uint}$$

STRUCTS
$$\frac{T \vdash \bar{\tau_1} \preccurlyeq \bar{\tau_3}}{T \vdash \{\bar{l_1} : \bar{\tau_1} \uplus \bar{l_2} : \bar{\tau_2}\} \preccurlyeq \{\bar{l_1} : \bar{\tau_3}\}}$$

Figure 4. Subtyping Rules

The type checking algorithm for DnesT expressions is a combination of standard procedural type systems and standard subtyping systems. Module typing is obtained by type checking module exports, using a coercion obtained from the module type parameters and a typing environment obtained from a combination of module value parameters, imports, and variable type declarations. A valid module type checking judgment is written as:

$$<T, V>\{\iota; \bar{d}; \xi\} : <T, V>\{\iota; \varepsilon\}$$

Where ε is just the type signatures of ξ, and each of the command bodies in ξ is proven to respect its type signature.

EXAMPLE 3.1. *The module* `authSend` *defined in Sect. 2 code line 9 can be assigned the following type in DnesT:*

```
< mt ≼ mesgT(uint); sendk : uint8[] >
  { import radio_x(mt*), export send(mt*)  }
```

4. The Scalaness Language Distilled

Scalaness serves as the language for nesT module composition in the same manner as nesC configurations serve to compose nesC modules, but Scalaness is a much more powerful metalanguage since modules are treated as a new category of first class values in Scalaness. Instantiation, composition (aka wiring), and imaging of modules are defined as operations on module values. Because instantiation of modules with both types and values is allowed, types and values may migrate from the Scalaness level to the nesT level after programmatic refinement, realizing a disciplined form of code specialization.

L	::=	class C⟨X̄ <: N̄⟩ extends N {T̄ f̄; K M̄}	*classes*
K	::=	C(T̄ f̄){super(f̄); this.f̄ = f̄; }	*constructors*
M	::=	T m(T̄ x̄){return e; }	*methods*
e	::=	x | e.f | e.m(ē) | new C⟨T̄⟩(ē) | (N)e |	*expressions*
		l | e.f = e | def x : T = e in e |	
		abbrvt X(X̄) = T in e |	
		μ | e ⋉ e | e⟨ē; ē⟩ | image e	
T	::=	X | N | T ∘ μ_σ	*types*
N	::=	C⟨T̄⟩	*class types*
l	::=	(p, N)	*references*

Figure 5. The Syntax of DScalaness

Our goal in this Section is to describe the Scalaness syntax and semantics realized in our implementation. Since Scala is too large to easily formalize, we define here a *Distilled Scalaness*, DScalaness, that extends a core typed object-oriented language to include syntax and semantics for defining and composing DnesT modules. The particular object-oriented core calculus we use is a combination of two Featherweight Java variants: Featherweight Generic Java (FGJ) [17] and Assignment Featherweight Java (AFJ) [27].

4.1 Syntax of DScalaness

The DScalaness language syntax is presented in Fig. 5. We refer the reader to [17, 27] for details on the FGJ and AFJ object oriented calculi, which are represented in the languages of class definitions, constructors, methods, and the first line of expression forms defined in Fig. 5. DScalaness extends these features with a typed variable declaration form def x : T = e₁ in e₂ where the scope of x is e₂, a dynamic type construction form typedef x <: T = e₁ in e₂ with similar scoping rules (although this is defined as syntactic sugar in Definition 4.1). For programmer convenience a simple parameterized type abbreviation binder abbrvt is also provided. We include DnesT modules μ in the DScalaness expression and value spaces: instantiation is obtained via the form e₁⟨ē₁; ē₂⟩, where ē₁ are type parameters· and ē₂ are value parameters. Wiring of modules is denoted e₁ ⋉ e₂. Imaging of modules, denoted image e, ensures that e computes to a runnable DnesT module.

4.2 Semantics of DScalaness

The semantics of DScalaness is an extension of the semantics of AFJ and FGJ to incorporate DnesT modules and operations. Computations assume a fixed class table CT allowing access to class definitions via class names, which always decorate an object's type. A *store* ST is a function from memory locations p to object representations. Objects are represented in memory by lists of object references l̄, which refer to the locations of the objects stored in mutable field values. A reference l is a pair (p, N) where p is the memory location of an object representation and N is the nominal type of the object, including its class name. Hence, given an object reference (p, C⟨T̄⟩), we can access and mutate its fields l̄ = ST(p), and access and use its methods via the definition CT(C).

Following AFJ, the semantics of DScalaness is defined as a *labeled transition system*, where transitions are of the form e−{s = ST, s' = ST'} → e'. Intuitively, this denotes that given an initial store ST and expression e, one step of evaluation results in a modified store ST' and contractum e'. We write e → e' as an abbreviation when the store is not altered.

The primary novelty of DScalaness is the formal semantics of type and module construction. We begin with type construction, which is provided to allow programmers to dynamically con-

struct module type instances. The appropriate behavior is obtained by treating dynamically constructed types as extensions of a basic class of objects, and declarations of DnesT level types via a typedef construct as syntactic sugar for ordinary object construction. We define a LiftableType class as the supertype of all types of objects that can be used to instantiate a module, and dynamically constructed types are defined as instances of a generic MetaType class.

DEFINITION 4.1. *Any DScalaness class table CT comprises the following definitions:*

CT(LiftableType) =
class LiftableType⟨⟩ extends Object {...}
CT(MetaType) =
class MetaType⟨X <: LiftableType⟩ extends Object {...}

And we take as given the following syntactic sugar:

typedef x <: T = e₁ in e₂ ≜ def x : MetaType⟨T⟩ = e₁ in e₂

Class type MetaType is generalized on a single type variable. For brevity of notation, we define:

$$\text{MetaType}⟨\bar{T}⟩ \quad \triangleq \quad \overline{\text{MetaType}⟨T⟩}$$

A crucial fact of DScalaness type construction is that any dynamically constructed type cannot be treated as a type at the DScalaness level. This is a more restrictive mechanism than envisioned in our foundational model [20], however it allows us to define DScalaness as a straightforward extension to Scala, especially in terms of type checking.

Module instantiation, shown in Fig. 6, is the only point where specialization of DnesT modules is allowed. Since DScalaness and DnesT are two different language spaces, some sort of transformation must occur when values migrate from DScalaness to DnesT via module instantiation. This *lifting* transformation involves both data mapping and serialization since the process spaces also differ. We aim to be flexible and allow the user to specify how values are lifted and how types are transformed. We only require that lifting and type transformation are coherent, in the sense that the lifting of an object should be typeable at the object's type transformation. We formalize this in the following definition.

DEFINITION 4.2. *We assume given a relation $\overset{lift}{\hookrightarrow}$ which transforms a DScalaness reference l into DnesT declarations d̄ and expression e. We also assume given a DScalaness-to-DnesT transformation of types $[\![\cdot]\!]$. To preserve type safety, we require in all cases that $(p, N) \overset{lift}{\hookrightarrow} \bar{d}, e$ implies both of the following for some type environment G:*

$$\varnothing, \varnothing \vdash \bar{d} : G \qquad and \qquad G, \varnothing \vdash e : [\![N]\!]$$

The full definition of serialization and an example are given and discussed below in Sect. 4.3.

Module wiring is given a standard component composition semantics. We only allow wiring of instantiated modules, which is consistent with nesC and simpler to implement. In a wiring e₁ ⋉ e₂, the exports of e₂ are wired to the imports of e₁. This is specified in the MODWIRE rule in Fig. 6, which relies on the following auxiliary definition of operations for combining mappings.

DEFINITION 4.3 (Special Mapping Operations). *Let m range over vectors with mapping interpretations, in particular T, V, ι, and ξ. Binary operator $m_1 \curlyvee m_2$ represents (non-exclusive) map merge, i.e. $m_1 \curlyvee m_2 = m_1 @ m_2$ with the requirement that $id \in \text{Dom}(m_1) \cap \text{Dom}(m_2)$ implies $m_1(id) = m_2(id)$. The mapping m/S is the same as m except undefined on domain elements in set S, and the mapping $m \mid_S$ is the same as m except undefined on elements not in S.*

MODINST

$$\frac{\mu = <\bar{t} \preccurlyeq \bar{\tau}; \bar{x} : \bar{\varsigma}>\{\iota; \bar{d}; \xi\} \qquad serialize(\bar{x}, \bar{\varsigma}, \bar{I}) = \bar{d}'}{\mu\langle(\bar{p}, \mathtt{MetaType}\langle\bar{T}\rangle)); \bar{I}\rangle \rightarrow <>\{\iota; \bar{d}'@\bar{d}; \xi\}[[\bar{T}]]/\bar{t}]}$$

MODWIRE

$$\frac{\iota = (\iota_1/\mathrm{Dom}(\xi_2))@\iota_2 \qquad \bar{d} = \bar{d}_2@\xi_2|_{\mathrm{Dom}(\iota_1)}}{<>\{\iota_1; \bar{d}_1; \xi_1\} \ltimes <>\{\iota_2; \bar{d}_2; \xi_2\} \rightarrow <>\{\iota; \bar{d} \curlyvee \bar{d}_1; \xi_1\}}$$

MODIMAGE

$$\frac{\mathrm{main} \text{ defined in } \xi}{\mathtt{image} (<>\{; \bar{d}; \xi\}) \rightarrow <>\{; \bar{d}; \xi\}}$$

Figure 6. DScalaness Module Semantics

Finally, the MODIMAGE rule in Fig. 6 shows that imaging it is an assertion requiring its arguments to be a runnable module.

EXAMPLE 4.1. *Given code definitions in Sect. 2 and an invocation* `authSpecialize(50, radioM, [|k₁, k₂|])`, *where* `radioM : radioT`, *and* k_1, k_2 *are keys, the evaluation of the expression on line 24,* `sendM ⋉ radioM⟨mesgT(adt)⟩`, *will evaluate to the following module:*

```
< > ( { import handle_radio_r(mesgT(uint8)*); ...;
        export send(m : mesgT(uint8)*)
            { radio_x(AES_sign(m, k₁)); } }
```

where the elided declarations include a definition of a command `radio_x` *imported from* `radioM` *also with argument type* `mesgT(uint8)*`.

4.3 Serialization and Lifting

Serialization generates a flattened DnesT source code version of a DScalaness object in memory. At the top level, serialization binds the value parameters of a module to the results of flattening, aka lifting, via a sequence of declarations. Here is the precise definition.

DEFINITION 4.4 (Serialization). *Assume given a store ST which is implicit in the following definitions. We define serialization of DScalaness references as follows, along with an extension of the user defined lifting relation to sequences of references:*

$$\varnothing \overset{lift}{\hookrightarrow} \varnothing, \varnothing$$

$$\frac{\bar{I} \overset{lift}{\hookrightarrow} \bar{d}, \bar{e}}{serialize(\bar{x}, \bar{\tau}, \bar{I}) = \bar{d}@ \bar{\tau} \bar{x} = \bar{e}} \qquad \frac{1 \overset{lift}{\hookrightarrow} \bar{d}, e \qquad \bar{I} \overset{lift}{\hookrightarrow} \bar{d}', \bar{e}}{1\bar{I} \overset{lift}{\hookrightarrow} \bar{d}@\bar{d}', e\bar{e}}$$

Although lifting is user defined, a standard strategy is to introduce a new declared variable for each memory reference in the lifted object, and bind the variable to the lifted referent. Hence, lifting will typically be defined recursively. In our implementation, we have adapted a "default" lifting which follows this strategy, and also transforms objects by just transforming the fields into a representative struct, and ignoring methods. We will illustrate this with an example in Sect. 6. We can formally capture the essence of this transformation with the following definitions. It is easy to see that these definitions will satisfy the requirements of Definition 4.2.

EXAMPLE 4.2. *In this example we allow lifting of any object references, and transform the object o into a structure containing the transformed fields of o. Methods are disregarded by the transformation. Here is the specification of the type transformation:*

$$\frac{CT(\mathtt{C}) = \mathtt{class} \ \mathtt{C}\langle\bar{X} <: \bar{S}\rangle \ \mathtt{extends} \ \mathtt{N} \ \{\bar{R} \ \bar{f}; \ K \ \bar{M}\}}{[[\mathtt{C}\langle\bar{T}\rangle]] = \{\bar{f} : [[\bar{R}[\bar{T}/\bar{X}]]]\}}$$

MODT

$$\frac{\mu : \mu\tau \text{ in DnesT type checking}}{\Gamma \vdash \mu : \varnothing \circ \mu\tau}$$

MODIMAGET

$$\frac{\Gamma \vdash \mathtt{e} : T \circ <>\{\iota; \varepsilon\} \qquad \mathrm{main}() : \tau \in \varepsilon}{\Gamma \vdash \mathtt{image} \ \mathtt{e} : T \circ <>\{\iota; \varepsilon\}}$$

MODINSTT

$$\frac{\Gamma \vdash \mathtt{e} : \varnothing \circ <\bar{t} \preccurlyeq \bar{\tau}_1; \bar{x} : \bar{\tau}_2>\{\iota; \varepsilon\} \quad \Gamma \vdash \bar{\mathtt{e}}_1 : \mathtt{MetaType}\langle\bar{T}_1\rangle}{\Gamma \vdash \mathtt{e}\langle\bar{\mathtt{e}}_1; \bar{\mathtt{e}}_2\rangle : \bar{t} \preccurlyeq [[\bar{T}_1]] \circ <>\{\iota; \varepsilon\}}$$

with middle premises $\Gamma \vdash \bar{\mathtt{e}}_2 : \bar{\tau}_2 \quad \vdash [[\bar{T}_1]] \preccurlyeq \bar{\tau}_1 \quad \vdash [[\bar{T}_2]] \preccurlyeq \bar{\tau}_2$

MODWIRET

$$\frac{\Gamma \vdash \mathtt{e}_1 : T_1 \circ <>\{\iota_1; \varepsilon_1\}}{\Gamma \vdash \mathtt{e}_1 \ltimes \mathtt{e}_2 : T_1 \curlyvee T_2 \circ <>\{\iota; \varepsilon_1\}}$$

with premises $\Gamma \vdash \mathtt{e}_2 : T_2 \circ <>\{\iota_2; \varepsilon_2\} \quad \iota = (\iota_1/\mathrm{Dom}(\varepsilon_2))@\iota_2$

Figure 7. DScalaness Module Typing Rules

and here is the specification of lifting.

$$\frac{ST(\mathtt{p}) = \bar{I} \qquad fields(\mathtt{C}) = \bar{T} \ \bar{f} \qquad \bar{I} \overset{lift}{\hookrightarrow} \bar{d}, \bar{e} \qquad x \ fresh}{(p, \mathtt{C}\langle\bar{R}\rangle) \overset{lift}{\hookrightarrow} \bar{d}@([[\mathtt{C}\langle\bar{R}\rangle]] \ x = \{\bar{f} = \bar{e}\}), x}$$

4.4 DScalaness Type Checking

The primary novelty of DScalaness are the rules for DnesT module typing and composition, and that is the focus of this section. We adopt the typing rules of FGJ in their entirety, and refer the reader to [17] for relevant details.

DScalaness syntax for expressing DnesT module types is $T \circ \mu\tau$, where $\mu\tau$ is a DnesT module type. The T in this form represents the type bounds of dynamically constructed types that have been used to instantiate the module; we refer to this part of the type as the *instance coercion*. Because these types are dynamically constructed, their identity is not known statically, hence the need to treat them as upper-bounded type names in the static type analysis. This subtle technical point of our type system is discussed at more length in Sect. 5. It is important to note that the type names in T will be fully resolved at run time, so that any module generated by a DScalaness program execution will have a fully reified DnesT type. Throughout this paper, we abbreviate $\emptyset \circ \mu\tau$ as $\mu\tau$ for brevity.

This is reflected in the MODT rule in Fig. 7, which connects the DnesT typing system with the DScalaness type system. Since in this case we are typing an uninstantiated module definition its instance coercion is empty. An instance coercion in a module type is directly populated when a module is instantiated, as in the MODINSTT rule. Here, the type instances $\bar{\mathtt{e}}_1$ are all dynamically constructed, so they define the upper bounds of the instantiated module's instance coercion. We also expect all type and value parameters to respect the typing bounds specified in the module definition. The MODWIRET typing rule for module wiring is a straightforward reflection of the operational rule for module wiring, as is the MODIMAGET rule for module runnability imaging.

EXAMPLE 4.3. *Returning to the code and type examples in Sect. 2, we may assign the following typing:*

$$G \vdash \mathtt{authSpecialize}(50, \mathtt{radioM}, [|k_1, k_2|]) : \mathtt{commT}$$

Given $\mathtt{radioM} : \mathtt{radioT}, k_1 : \mathtt{uint8}[], k_2 : \mathtt{uint8}[] \in G$.

5. Scalaness/nesT Foundations

The Scalaness/nesT type system design is based on principles studied in the foundational calculus $\langle\text{ML}\rangle^2$ [20]. $\langle\text{ML}\rangle$ comprises $F_\le$, state, dynamic type construction, and staging features. In this section we describe how the design of modules and module operations in Scalaness can be modeled in $\langle\text{ML}\rangle$. Although the correspondence is informal, these models directed the design of Scalaness semantics and type checking, and provide confidence in its soundness. While our choice of modules as the basic unit of nesT code is based on obvious software engineering concerns and the need for a tight relation with nesC, Scalaness modules are well correlated with certain structures in $\langle\text{ML}\rangle$ and so are also technically appealing.

The model of a module. Code as a datatype is available in $\langle\text{ML}\rangle$ as expressions of the form $\langle e\rangle$. While code as a datatype is a standard feature of staged/generative programming, $\langle\text{ML}\rangle$ has adapted staged programming to a setting where different code levels are intended for execution on different machines with distinct process spaces. In particular, values, including code values, must be closed. If a type or term variable occurs free in $\langle e\rangle$, it must be Λ or λ bound, respectively, for closure. Hence, if a type variable t is free in $\langle e\rangle$, then $\Lambda t \preceq \tau.\langle e\rangle$ binds it, and provides parametric subtyping polymorphism for $\langle\text{ML}\rangle$ terms.

If the term variable x is free in $\langle e\rangle$, then $\lambda x : \tau.\langle e\rangle$ binds it. Furthermore, the type τ in the term $\lambda x : \tau.\langle e\rangle$ *must* be of the form $\langle\varsigma\rangle$, because the type discipline requires that x is of code type, since it occurs within code. If the programmer wishes to pass a value residing at the current execution stage to such a function, it must be explicitly "lifted" in the now-standard style of [33]. However, in $\langle\text{ML}\rangle$, lifting a value entails serialization of it, which is non-trivial in case the value is stateful.

We use $\langle\text{ML}\rangle$ type and term bindings to model Scalaness type and term parameters. This is a standard strategy, in fact FGJ typing [17] is based on it as well. Hence the basic analog of a module is:

$$\Lambda t \preceq \tau.\lambda x : \langle\varsigma\rangle.\langle e\rangle$$

where t is a bounded type parameter and x is a value parameter.

The model of instantiation. Most of the interesting parts of Scalaness typing happen at instantiation. Given the above model of a module, the $\langle\text{ML}\rangle$ analog of instantiation is a term of the form:

$$(\Lambda t \preceq \tau.\lambda x : \langle\varsigma\rangle.\langle e\rangle)(\tau')(\text{lift } v)$$

where all parameters are instantiated. Note in particular that the value parameter v must be explicitly lifted, since the model must reflect that values passed in to modules are always constructed at the first stage in a Scalaness program. This means that v must be assumed to not be a code value, while the type annotation on x requires that it be lifted. There is no explicit lift operation in Scalaness, but the DSCalaness semantics (Fig. 6) specifies that serialization is always implicit at module instantiation. Scalaness typing of instantiation thus treats value instantiation as λ application with implicit lifting of the argument, and type instantiation as Λ application, i.e. a form of bounded $\forall$-elimination.

Type construction and variable escape. A central technical novelty and core feature of DScalaness is dynamic type construction for module instantiation. As we discussed in Sect. 2, this feature is technically challenging since constructed types can escape their scope of declaration. Similarly, in $\langle\text{ML}\rangle$, types may be dynamically constructed that can escape their declaration scope, in particular if they are used as function type annotations. An $\exists$ type binder was introduced in $\langle\text{ML}\rangle$ for this purpose; intuitively a type of the form $\exists t \preceq \tau.\varsigma$ is a type containing a dynamically constructed type term t with upper bound τ. $\langle\text{ML}\rangle$ includes a "tlet" expression form for

---

constructing types, so for example:

tlet $t \preceq \textbf{uint16} = $ if e then $\textbf{uint8}$ else $\textbf{uint16}$ in $(\lambda x : t.x)$:

$$\exists t \preceq \textbf{uint16}.t \to t$$

Here a type t is dynamically constructed to be either **uint8** or **uint16**, and then used in the type annotation of a type-specialized identity function. Furthermore, t escapes its declaration scope since it annotates a function argument. Since e is some arbitrary computation, we cannot statically predict what t will be, other than "some type with upper bound **uint16**". Note also that since t can appear in contravariant positions, it is unsound to perform a covariant substitution of **uint16** for t, so the $\exists$ bound is needed. Although this usage of $\exists$ types is somewhat non-standard, an eigenvariable interpretation of the bound type variable is sound and also consistent with standard existential type interpretations.

Inspired by these foundations, in DScalaness the type form:

$$T_1 \circ <T_2; V>\{\iota; \varepsilon\}$$

captures the same typing mechanisms, in particular the instance coercion T_1 is the analog of $\exists$ bound type variables, in contrast to the type parameters T_2 which are implicitly $\forall$ bound, as discussed above. The static semantics of T_1 and T_2 are distinguished appropriately, especially in the treatment of the typing rules for module instantiation and module wiring in Fig. 7.

6. Implementation

Scalaness is implemented as a modification to the open source Scala compiler. Scala was chosen as a basis for our first stage language because the Scala compiler supported a plug-in architecture, and we originally envisioned implementing Scalaness as a plug-in. We also wanted to create a practical programming system, and Scala's easy access to Java libraries and broad community support were attractive.

Keeping the Scala and Scalaness type checking well separated in the implementation had useful software engineering benefits as well. It simplifies the problem of tracking the evolving Scala compiler. It also promotes a clear separation of first and second stage concerns in the mind of the Scalaness programmer. Unfortunately we found that the needed modifications to the type checker could only be made by direct modification of the compiler code base.

In addition to type checking, runtime support is needed to implement Scalaness module operations. Also, facilities are required to read nesT modules from the file system and parse them into ASTs, and to write TinyOS image source code files defined by constructed nesT modules at `image` invocations.

6.1 Online Repository and Examples

The Scalaness/nesT compiler and several code examples, including applications discussed in Sect. 2 and Sect. 7, are available for download from the following URL:

    http://tinyurl.com/a85z8cu

6.2 nesT Type Checking and Program Transformation

The nesT language is treated by two major components in the implementation, the type checker and the nesT-to-nesC rewriting transformation. The nesT type checker was written from the ground up, in contrast to the Scalaness type checker which was defined as an extension to the Scala type checker. The rewriting transformation yields TinyOS2-compliant source code, which can be separately compiled.

The nesT language is defined as a subset of the nesC language. An AST yielded by parsing is type checked by our algorithm, which incorporates subtyping and other features not present in nesC type

---

^{2} Pronounced "framed ML."

checking. This algorithm is a nearly direct encoding of the type discipline described in Sect. 3. Following type checking, the AST is submitted to a rewriting transformation that imposes semantic disciplines discussed in Sect. 3, in particular type safe casting and array bounds checks, also in nesC. For example, a statement of the form x = a[e] will be rewritten to:

```
int _x = e; if (_x >= a_SIZE) fail(); x = a[_x];
```

where a_SIZE is an automatically generated variable containing the size of a and fail is some user-defined function that handles array bounds check failure.

Source code for nesT module definitions is written in separate files that are included in Scalaness code, as discussed below. This separation is mainly for software engineering purposes, to avoid modifying the Scala compiler to parse intermingled Scala and nesT syntax.

6.3 Scalaness Module Language Syntax

In order to limit modifications of the Scala compiler and reduce engineering problems in our implementation, we have avoided modifying Scala syntax to represent Scalaness features. Hence, modules are represented as class instances, which must satisfy the following trait:

```
trait NesTModule {
  def image(): Unit    // Generates residual nesC program.
  def +>(m: NesTModule): NesTModule    // Wires this to m.
}
```

This trait is implemented by a NesTModule class that provides the appropriate semantics for wiring and TinyOS image generation, including translation to nesC and file output. This class also manages parsing and storage of nesT ASTs from source code files, and type checking of nesT ASTs.

Any nesT module definition is a subclass of NesTModule. Some subtleties are involved in supporting first class *generic* modules. Instantiation is implemented by method call, but since type and value parameters vary per module, particular modules must define their own parameters and instantiation methods. For example, we would represent the authSend component definition from Sect. 2, line 9 as follows:

```
class authSend extends NesTModule {
  var mt        : MetaType[LiftableType] = _
  var sendk  : LiftableType = _
  def instantiate(m: MetaType[LiftableType], k: LiftableType) =
    { val result=new authSend; result.mt=m; result.sendk=k }
  "authSend.nt"
}
```

Although the instantiate method and parameter fields must be defined in the implementation at the time of this writing, compiler generation of these definitions is a topic for future work; any modules instantiate method can be easily inferred from its type annotation. Note that the types at which parameters are declared are as general as possible (e.g. s and n are not declared as uints but as LiftableTypes). This is because class definitions support the semantics of Scalaness, not Scalaness type checking (discussed below), and declaring generic parameters at a maximally general type removes interference related to Scala type checking. Finally, note the string literal "authSend.nt" at the end of the definition. This is the file containing the nesT source code definition of the module. The Scala compiler has been modified to input and parse the specified source code when this literal is encountered during the Scala type checking phase.

6.4 Type Annotation and Checking

Scalaness typing relies on native Scala syntax for terms, specifically Scala annotations and singleton types are utilized. Scala annotations allow metadata to be associated with definitions. A mod-

ule type annotation is of the form @ModuleType("$\mu\tau$"), where $\mu\tau$ is defined using the syntax of Fig. 3. The compiler-defined ModuleType class automatically associates the type with the identifier immediately following it. In the case of module class definitions, the type is assigned as a class field. In the case of variable definitions, the type is assigned as a Scala singleton type of the object. For example, the declaration of authSend on line 9 in as in Sect. 2 would be preceded by such an annotation where $\mu\tau$ is the type specified in Example 3.1, and sendM as on line 22 would be annotated with an instance of that type. Similarly, annotations are required on method parameter and result types, if those methods expect nesT modules as arguments or return them, as for the radioC parameter of the authSpecialize method defined in Sect. 2, and the method's commT return type. These requirements reflect the type discipline in Scalaness as specified in Sect. 4, which requires module type annotations at these points.

Scalaness type checking has been implemented as an analysis of these annotations during Scala type checking, piggybacking on that process. When type checking a class that extends NesTModule, the compiler uses its type annotation to perform nesT type checking on the underlying AST representation of the module. When type checking module operations (i.e. at invocations of instantiate, +>, or image), the Scala compiler has been modified to examine operand types for Scalaness type annotations, and to decorate resultant singleton types of these operations with new Scalaness annotations, reflecting the typing rules in Fig. 7. A type checking exception is raised in case this analysis fails. Scalaness type checking does not modify Scala type checking in any other way, so it is a conservative extension of Scala typing.

6.5 Importing nesC Libraries

Our preliminary experiments with nesT show that it is expressive enough to write useful program components. However, any realistic application will need to interact with various libraries written in nesC. One library of critical importance is the TinyOS operating system itself. Our current solution is to allow non-generic nesC components to be treated as nesT modules as long as they only use or provide commands, which are interpreted as nesT imports and exports. Support for specializable generic nesC library components is a topic for future work. Events can be accessed through "shim" modules provided by the user, since used or provided events are really just syntactic sugar for provided or used commands respectively. A library component defined in a file LibraryC.nc can be defined as a nesT module as follows:

```
object LibraryC extends NesTModule { external("LibraryC.nc") }
```

Note that nesC code imported in this way is not type checked by the Scalaness/nesT compiler, since nesT is a strict subset of nesC. Rather, the programmer type annotates the shimmed module using a @ModuleType annotation as for other module definitions, and the compiler trusts that the annotation is correct. This introduces a possibility for type safety failure in our system, if the imported code contains a type error. A possible long term goal would be a complete re-write of TinyOS in nesT, yielding full type safety of all sensor code, but this is well beyond our current scope.

7. Example: Authorization and Access Control

In [5] the SpartanRPC architecture for link-layer resource authorization in TinyOS-based WSNs is developed (as an extension of [4]). In SpartanRPC, resources are accessed by link-layer remote procedure calls (RPC) which require authorization. Users are authorized by communicating credentials to the provider, expressed in an authorization logic based on RT [18] and implemented using TinyECC [19] public key signatures. SpartanRPC supports an "open world" security model, allowing WSNs in different security

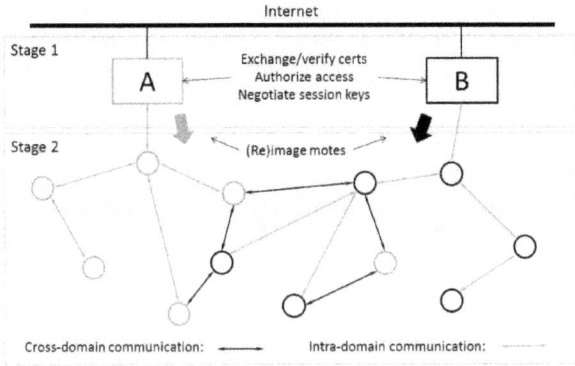

Figure 8. Staging Authorization and Authorized Access in a Multi-Domain WSN.

domains to interact without sharing secrets *a priori*. However, public key encryption and signature verification is very expensive in a WSN. Hence, session keys are negotiated for ongoing resource access (using a TinyECC-based Diffie-Hellman protocol).

In this section we describe a re-implementation of the Spartan-RPC protocol in Scalaness/nesT that addresses several shortcomings of SpartanRPC, and will thus serve to illustrate the power of Scalaness/nesT. The central idea, illustrated in Fig. 8, is that responsibility for authorization on the basis of public key credentials is offloaded from the WSN to a Scalaness program running on a hub device or lab computer. We assume a WSN comprising two subnetworks under control of distinct security domains A and B. Each domain also controls a lab or hub device which is in communication with WSN nodes in their domain, either prior to or during deployment. These devices are in communication with each other over the Internet, and exchange authorization credentials for their domain over that medium in the first-stage Scalaness program. Each device then confirms authorization for resource access according to their own domain's policies, and subsequently they negotiate session keys over the Internet. These keys are then used to specialize nesT code for imaging on WSN nodes. The overall architecture of this application represents a concrete realization of the ideas of Fig. 1, and also expands on and implements the idealized example presented in Sect. 2.

Note that our current implementation assumes nodes are programmed in the lab since we have no secure OTA program dissemination library; the Deluge protocol has such an extension [9] that we plan on using in the future.

Evaluation on Snowcloud To empirically evaluate the staged implementation of SpartanRPC in Scalaness/nesT, we have implemented and tested both the original SpartanRPC as well as the Scalaness/nesT staged version in our deployed Snowcloud WSN system architecture. Mobile gateway devices as pictured in Fig. 2 are provided to Snowcloud system users for data gathering, and are also used by system administrators for controlling sampling rates. The hardware for both of these so-called "harvester" devices, the same for users and administrators, is equipped with a mote for establishing network communication. When the device is introduced to the sensor network, the two together comprise a single network with two distinct security domains – the sensor node subnetwork, and the subnetwork of the single device mote. The mote on harvester devices provided to system users is supplied with credentials for collecting data, but not modifying network control, whereas system administration harvester motes are supplied with stronger credentials for both functions.

The original and Scalaness/nesT versions of this application can be compared both in terms of performance and user experience. In the unstaged version, the SpartanRPC protocol requires an initial network configuration period when credentials are exchanged and verified. Since a single TinyECC signature requires at least 90 seconds to verify on the Crossbow TelosB platform [5] with a fully dedicated processor, there is an initial network "warmup" period of at least a few minutes. Also, in the unstaged version, upon first invocation of an RPC service Diffie-Hellman is used in the network to negotiate a session key. In the staged version, credential exchange, validation, and session key negotiation are all performed on the high-powered hub. For this reason, mote code size in ROM is significantly reduced. There are differences in RAM usage as well, due to authorization overhead in the unstaged version and also the storage of key material in RAM vs. ROM, since specialization of code with key material in the staged version allows the latter. Note that this difference is intensified by scale and the number of keys (i.e. RPC services) needed by an application. Lower RAM and ROM usage can have significant performance impacts on deployed code. In the following table we summarize RAM and ROM usage for the harvester and sensor node images for three software versions: one with no security mechanisms in place, one with unstaged SpartanRPC protocols in place, and one generated by Scalaness evaluation in our staged version of the SpartanRPC protocol.

		Unsecured	Unstaged	Staged	Savings
Sensor:	ROM	36254	48616	36596	25%
	RAM	2868	5417	3038	44%
Harvester:	ROM	24316	35834	24436	32%
	RAM	2274	4771	2402	50%

The "Savings" are the percent reduction from unstaged to staged secure implementation, and these numbers show the potential for saving both RAM and ROM space is significant. From the perspective of user experience, the staged version of this application is more convenient, since no initial authorization period is needed when the harvester is first introduced to the network. The staged version also exposes the system to fewer bugs and failures that would be obstacles to the primary goal of data collection.

8. Conclusion

We have introduced Scalaness/nesT, a two stage programming system for wireless sensor networks. Our system provides a powerful programming environment for dynamically specializing and composing nesC modules in a type safe way; any type correct Scalaness program will generate only type correct residual programs.

8.1 Related Work

We do not review the broader topic of sensor network programming here; the reader is referred to [28] for a broader perspective.

We follow the foundational ⟨ML⟩ work in our language design [20]; Sect. 5 discusses how it serves as the theoretical underpinning of our approach. The primary aim of this work is to make the theoretical insights of ⟨ML⟩ more practical. We accomplish this by making a sensor language nesT that is based on the design of nesC, and by implementing Scalaness and nesT and testing the framework on examples.

The potential of applying metaprogramming to sensor networks was explored in the functional sensor language Flask [24]. Flask allows FRP-based stream combinators to be pre-computed before network deployment, but it is possible to generate ill-typed Flask object code since cross-stage static type checking is not performed. Hume [15] is a DSL for real-time embedded device programming.

It includes a metaprogramming layer but that layer is more like nesC's configuration files in that there is a very restricted syntax for a few special metaprogramming operations including component wiring, macros, and code templating.

MetaML [32, 33] and MetaHaskell [23] are a foundations we build on; they do not address type specialization or dynamic type construction.

Lightweight Modular Staging [31] describes a method of expressing staged computations using a Scala host framework without any compiler modifications. The approach allows cross-stage type safety but does not support dynamic type construction.

Actor based sensor metaprogramming has been studied in [6]; this work shares our focus on high level dynamic reprogrammability but is untyped. More broadly, meta programming is known to be useful for increasing the efficiency of systems applications. One example is Tempo [8], a system that integrates partial evaluation and type specialization for increasing efficiency of systems applications. Ur [7] allows for type safe meta programming for web applications.

The units of staged code composition in nesT programming are *modules*. Countless different module systems exist, but they are primarily designed to achieve separate compilation and sound linking [2]. Our different design goal leads to different design choices in nesT modules. For example, data crossing nesT module boundaries needs to conform to the property of process separation, a non-issue in standard module system designs. In addition, nesT modules allow values/types across the boundary of modules to be flexibly constructed, including dynamic construction of types, to achieve maximal flexibility of cross-stage specialization. Module systems such as ML modules [21] and Units [10] allow types to be imported/exported as we also support; there are several features of ML modules including type hiding that we do not aim to support. nesT modules are more expressive in their support of first class modules as values and the possibility of dynamic construction of "type exports." That said, first class modules are not new [1, 25], we only claim novelty in their application to program staging and the incorporation of dynamic type construction.

The type parametricity of System F and $F_\leq$ [3], and the practical type systems it inspired such as Java's generics, do not treat types as first class values as we do. C++ templates support types as meta values in template expansion, but type safety of generated code is not guaranteed without full template expansion. Concepts [14] improves on this, but types are still not first class values.

Acknowledgments

We acknowledge Yu David Liu for early contributions to this work.

References

[1] D. Ancona and E. Zucca. A calculus of module systems. *Journal of functional programming*, 11:91–132, 2002.

[2] L. Cardelli. Program fragments, linking, and modularization. In *POPL*, pages 266–277, 1997.

[3] L. Cardelli and P. Wegner. On understanding types, data abstraction, and polymorphism. *ACM Comput. Surv.*, 17(4):471–523, 1985.

[4] P. Chapin and C. Skalka. SpartanRPC: Secure WSN middleware for cooperating domains. In *MASS*, November 2010.

[5] P. Chapin and C. Skalka. Spartan RPC. Technical report, University of Vermont, 2013. Submitted. http://www.cs.uvm.edu/~skalka/skalka-pubs/chapin-skalka-spartanrpctr.pdf.

[6] E. Cheong. *Actor-Oriented Programming for Wireless Sensor Networks*. PhD thesis, University of California, Berkeley, 2007.

[7] A. Chlipala. Ur: Statically-typed metaprogramming with type-level record computation. In *PLDI*, 2010.

[8] C. Consel, L. Hornof, R. Marlet, G. Muller, S. Thibault, E.-N. Volanschi, J. Lawall, and J. Noyé. Tempo: specializing systems applications and beyond. *ACM Comput. Surv.*, 1998.

[9] P. K. Dutta, J. W. Hui, D. C. Chu, and D. E. Culler. Securing the deluge network programming system. In *IPSN*, pages 326–333, 2006.

[10] M. Flatt and M. Felleisen. Units: Cool modules for HOT languages. In *PLDI*, 1998.

[11] J. Frolik and C. Skalka. Snowcloud: A complete system for snow hydrology research. In *RealWSN*, 2013.

[12] D. Gay, P. Levis, R. von Behren, M. Welsh, E. Brewer, and D. Culler. The nesC language: A holistic approach to networked embedded systems. In *PLDI*, 2003.

[13] G. Ghelli and B. Pierce. Bounded existentials and minimal typing. *Theoretical Computer Science*, 193(1-2):75 – 96, 1998.

[14] D. Gregor, J. Järvi, J. G. Siek, G. D. Reis, B. Stroustrup, and A. Lumsdaine. Concepts: Linguistic support for generic programming in C++. In *OOPSLA*, 2006.

[15] K. Hammond and G. Michaelson. Hume: A domain-specific language for real-time embedded systems. In *GPCE*, pages 37–56. Springer-Verlag, 2003.

[16] J. Hill, R. Szewczyk, A. Woo, S. Hollar, D. E. Culler, and K. S. J. Pister. System architecture directions for networked sensors. In *ASPLAS*, pages 93–104, 2000.

[17] A. Igarashi, B. C. Pierce, and P. Wadler. Featherweight Java. *ACM Trans. Program. Lang. Syst.*, 23(3):396–450, 2001.

[18] N. Li and J. C. Mitchell. RT: A role-based trust-management framework. In *Proceedings of the 3rd DARPA Information Survivability Conference and Exposition*, pages 201–212, 2003.

[19] A. Liu and P. Ning. Tinyecc: A configurable library for elliptic curve cryptography in wireless sensor networks. In *IPSN*, pages 245–256, 2008.

[20] Y. Liu, C. Skalka, and S. Smith. Type-specialized staged programming with process separation. *HOSC*, pages 341–385, 2011.

[21] D. MacQueen. Modules for Standard ML. In *Proceedings of ACM Conference on Lisp and Functional Programming*, 1984.

[22] S. Madden, M. J. Franklin, J. M. Hellerstein, and W. Hong. TAG: a Tiny AGgregation service for ad-hoc sensor networks. *SIGOPS Oper. Syst. Rev.*, 36(SI):131–146, 2002.

[23] G. Mainland. Explicitly heterogeneous metaprogramming with MetaHaskell. In *ICFP*, 2012.

[24] G. Mainland, G. Morrisett, and M. Welsh. Flask: staged functional programming for sensor networks. In *ICFP*, 2008.

[25] J. Mitchell, S. Meldal, and N. Madhav. An extension of standard ML modules with subtyping and inheritance. In *POPL*, 1991.

[26] C. D. Moeser, M. Walker, C. Skalka, and J. Frolik. Application of a wireless sensor network for distributed snow water equivalence estimation. In *Western Snow Conference*, 2011.

[27] T. Molhave and L. H. Petersen. Assignment Featherweight Java. Master's thesis, University of Aarhus, 2005.

[28] L. Mottola and G. P. Picco. Programming wireless sensor networks. *ACM Computing Surveys*, 2011.

[29] G. C. Necula, S. McPeak, and W. Weimer. CCured: type-safe retrofitting of legacy code. In *POPL*, 2002.

[30] M. Odersky, L. Spoon, and B. Venners. *Programming in Scala, second edition*. Artima, Inc, 2011.

[31] T. Rompf and M. Odersky. Lightweight modular staging: a pragmatic approach to runtime code generation and compiled DSLs. In *GPCE*, pages 127–136, 2010.

[32] W. Taha. Resource-aware programming. In *ICESS*, pages 38–43, 2004.

[33] W. Taha and T. Sheard. Multi-stage programming with explicit annotations. In *PEPM*, pages 203–217, 1997. ISBN 0-89791-917-3.

[34] R. Willett, A. Martin, and R. Nowak. Backcasting: adaptive sampling for sensor networks. In *IPSN*, pages 124–133, 2004.

Forge: Generating a High Performance DSL Implementation from a Declarative Specification

Arvind K. Sujeeth*   Austin Gibbons*   Kevin J. Brown*   HyoukJoong Lee*   Tiark Rompf ‡†
Martin Odersky†   Kunle Olukotun*

*Stanford University: {asujeeth, gibbons4, kjbrown, hyouklee, kunle}@stanford.edu
‡Oracle Labs: {first.last}@oracle.com
†EPFL: {first.last}@epfl.ch

Abstract

Domain-specific languages provide a promising path to automatically compile high-level code to parallel, heterogeneous, and distributed hardware. However, in practice high performance DSLs still require considerable software expertise to develop and force users into tool-chains that hinder prototyping and debugging. To address these problems, we present Forge, a new meta DSL for declaratively specifying high performance embedded DSLs. Forge provides DSL authors with high-level abstractions (e.g., data structures, parallel patterns, effects) for specifying their DSL in a way that permits high performance. From this high-level specification, Forge automatically generates both a naïve Scala library implementation of the DSL and a high performance version using the Delite DSL framework. Users of a Forge-generated DSL can prototype their application using the library version, and then switch to the Delite version to run on multicore CPUs, GPUs, and clusters without changing the application code. Forge-generated Delite DSLs perform within 2x of hand-optimized C++ and up to 40x better than Spark, an alternative high-level distributed programming environment. Compared to a manually implemented Delite DSL, Forge provides a factor of 3-6x reduction in lines of code and does not sacrifice any performance. Furthermore, Forge specifications can be generated from existing Scala libraries, are easy to maintain, shield DSL developers from changes in the Delite framework, and enable DSLs to be retargeted to other frameworks transparently.

Categories and Subject Descriptors D.3.2 [*Programming Languages*]: Language Classifications—Concurrent, distributed and parallel languages, Extensible languages; D.3.4 [*Programming Languages*]: Processors—Code generation, Optimization, Runtime environments

Keywords Code Generation; Multi-Stage Programming; Domain-Specific Languages; Parallel Programming

GPCE '13, October 27–28, 2013, Indianapolis, Indiana, USA.
Copyright is held by the owner/author(s). Publication rights licensed to ACM.
ACM 978-1-4503-2373-4/13/10. . . $15.00.
http://dx.doi.org/10.1145/2517208.2517220

1. Introduction

In order to achieve high performance on modern hardware, software must be parallel, heterogeneous, and distributed [36]. Unfortunately, developing software that meets these goals is complex, and high performance applications are often cobbled together in a piecemeal fashion. For example, an expert application developer may rewrite a performance-critical portion of her application in CUDA [29] in order to leverage a GPU, and rewrite a different portion in Hadoop [1] to scale out to a large number of cores. Each of these tasks requires expertise both in the idiosyncrasies of the programming model and in the characteristics of the underlying hardware. Worse, rewriting parts of the application for performance obscures the high-level algorithm and intent, making code harder to read and maintain and increasing the complexity of the overall system.

General-purpose languages have so far been unable to maintain a high level of abstraction and still provide efficient automatic compilation to parallel and heterogeneous hardware. State-of-the-art solutions like OpenCL [38] are relatively close in abstraction layer to C and still require careful programming to achieve good performance on a particular device. On the other hand, dynamic languages like Python and Ruby provide succint, high-level abstractions that lead to great productivity benefits, but compile (in a standard installation) only to sequential processors and are much slower than their low-level counterparts.

Domain-specific languages (DSLs) are a promising means of maintaining high-level abstractions while automatically compiling to parallel, heterogeneous, and distributed hardware [10]. The key advantage that DSLs have over general-purpose languages is the ability to reason about data structures and operations at the level of domain abstractions (e.g. Matrix or Graph vs. Array). By exploiting this high-level structure, it has been shown that DSL applications can be compiled from a single source to multicore CPUs, GPUs, and even clusters [5, 14, 21]. However, DSLs have two substantial drawbacks: they are usually more difficult to construct than a high-level library, and because they use specialized tool-chains, DSL applications are harder to prototype and debug.

In our previous work, we proposed the Delite framework [4] to mitigate these problems. Delite is a library for developing compiled, embedded DSLs inside the general-purpose programming language Scala. We showed that using a common host language and compilation framework enables reuse of the Scala tool-chain and important infrastructure like optimizations and code generators, thereby substantially reducing the effort to create a new DSL. Furthermore, we demonstrated that Delite DSLs can generate code for different devices and are competitive with or exceed the performance of alternate systems in different domains [35]. While we believe Delite to be the state-of-the-art in high performance embedded DSL development, there are still two main issues:

1. *DSL authors* must have considerable expertise with Scala and Delite in order to implement expressive, safe, and efficient DSLs. Delite is a highly flexible architecture for heterogeneous code generation, but this expressiveness adds boilerplate and complexity to the common case. As a result, developing compiled embedded DSLs with Delite, while easier than external DSLs, requires more programming language and software engineering expertise than the average domain expert has.

2. *DSL users* must have at least some knowledge of the Delite stack. Even though DSLs are embedded in Scala, only parts of the Scala tool-chain can be used when executing user programs: generating code at runtime that is executed on heterogeneous devices makes prototyping and debugging difficult. For example, it is no longer possible to step through the program or set a breakpoint in an interactive IDE debugger.

In this paper, we present Forge, a new meta DSL for high performance embedded DSL development that addresses these issues by capturing recurring patterns in high performance DSL development. Forge provides a high-level, declarative API for specifying DSL data structures and operations in a manner similar to an annotated high-level library. Unlike a high-level library, Forge builds an IR of the DSL specification itself, which enables it to generate different concrete implementations of the DSL. We generate both a high productivity implementation (a pure Scala library version), and a high performance implementation (a Delite version). In the future, if a different backend is desired, it is straightforward to generate a new implementation without modifying the DSL specification. From a DSL user's point of view, the Forge-generated library can be used very similarly to any other Scala library. DSL applications can be prototyped interactively in a REPL or developed in any IDE that supports Scala (e.g. Eclipse) using standard debugging techniques like breakpoints. When an application has been tested on a small dataset, the DSL user can then "flip the switch" and run the exact same source code in Delite on multicore CPUs, GPUs, or clusters. Therefore, by raising the level of abstraction and adding a level of code generation, Forge both simplifies the development of high performance embedded DSLs and makes them more accessible to end users.

Languages and frameworks for declaratively specifying DSLs are not new [16, 17, 24, 26]. Forge follows in the footsteps of these efforts by focusing on abstractions and code generation for high performance, heterogeneous computing. To our knowledge, Forge is also the first embedded meta DSL. It is implemented using staging, and therefore shares the same infrastructure as existing Delite DSLs. Staging also provides additional benefits: Forge specifications are Scala programs, and any Scala modularity feature (objects, classes, traits) can be used to compose specifications. We can also make use of staging to perform computation inside the specification itself. For example, the DSL specification can be parameterized over configuration flags, implemented as regular Scala values. This enables generating multiple variants of a DSL–essentially implementing a product line approach to DSL development. Furthermore, since Forge is staged, its IR can be constructed by invoking methods in the Forge API. This enables us to develop external parsers that call Forge methods to build the Forge IR. A key use case is to use reflection to parse existing Scala classes. Forge can then be used as an identity transformer, generating a Forge specification from the IR that can be further modified by a DSL developer. This scaffolding ability allows DSL developers to start with an existing library implementation and automatically generate a skeleton Forge specification as a starting point for a Forge DSL.

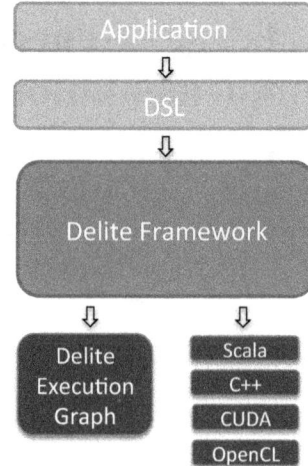

Figure 1. An overview of the Delite compilation pipeline. Applications are written in one or more DSLs. Each DSL can perform analyses and optimizations at the domain level. Delite then performs its own set of generic analyses and transformations before finally generating code for various low-level hardware programming models.

The rest of this paper is structured as follows. In Section 2, we provide essential background on Delite required to understand how the Forge-generated compiled version works. In Section 3 we provide an overview of the Forge language and show how DSLs are written in Forge. Section 4 describes how Forge is implemented internally and describes the artifacts that Forge generates in more detail. Section 5 presents case studies on three DSLs we have implemented in Forge (including two that were first implemented as stand-alone Delite DSLs and one that was implemented from scratch). Finally, Section 6 summarizes the related work and Section 7 concludes.

Forge is open-source. The source code, including examples presented in this paper, is available at:

`http://github.com/stanford-ppl/Forge/`

2. Background

Delite is a compilation framework for high performance DSLs embedded in Scala, built on top of Lightweight Modular Staging (LMS) [31]. Figure 1 depicts the Delite compilation pipeline.

Applications are written in a DSL embedded in Scala. For example, consider a toy application using a `SimpleVector` DSL:

```
trait MyApp extends SimpleVectorDSLInterface {
  def main() {
    val v: Rep[Vector[Int]] = Vector[Int](10)
    val y = v+2
    print(y(1))
  }
}
```

The DSL syntax (e.g. **val**,+) is legal Scala, although implicit conversions and curried functions can be used to emulate external DSL syntax [9]. However, unlike normal Scala library code, we use staged metaprogramming (*staging*) to defer key computations to a later time. The main idea behind LMS is that future-stage computation is encoded by wrapping types in an abstract type constructor Rep[T]. DSLs internally define Rep[T] to be Exp[T], an expression in an intermediate representation (IR). The IR is built during Scala run-time (also known as *staging time*), by implementing methods on the abstract Rep[T] types to construct IR nodes rather than imme-

146

```scala
// abstract interface exposed to DSL users
trait Base {
  type Rep[+T]
  implicit def unit[T](x: T): Rep[T]
}

// using staging to build an IR
trait BaseExp extends Base {
  abstract class Exp[+T:Manifest]
  abstract class Def[+T]
  type Rep[T] = Exp[T]

  case class Const[+T:Manifest](x: T) extends Exp[T]
  case class Sym[+T:Manifest](id: Int) extends Exp[T]

  implicit def unit[T](x: T) = Const(x)
  implicit def toAtom(d: Def[T]): Exp[T] =
    findOrCreateDefinition(d) // elided

  // a Delite IR node representing a parallel operation
  abstract class DeliteOpMap[Col](in: Exp[Col]) extends Def[Col]
}

// defines how to generate target (low-level) Scala code
trait ScalaCodegen {
  val IR: BaseExp; import IR._

  // constructs a program schedule of the IR by traversing
  // dependencies backwards, and calls emitNode in order
  def emitBlock(b: Exp[T]): Unit

  // implements code generation for individual IR nodes
  def emitNode(sym: Sym[T], rhs: Def[T]): Unit = rhs match {
    case _: DeliteOpMap => // emit parallel code
  }
}
```

Listing 1. Simplified core of LMS/Delite

```scala
trait SimpleVectorDSLInterface extends Base {
  trait Vector[T] // an abstract DSL data type
  object Vector {
    // SourceContext has debugging info (e.g. line # of call-site)
    def apply[T:Manifest](n: Rep[Int])(implicit ctx: SourceContext)
      = vector_new[T](n)
  }

  // indirection required for abstract static method
  def vector_new[T:Manifest](n: Rep[Int])
    (implicit ctx: SourceContext): Rep[Vector[T]]
  // sugar for infix operators in Scala-Virtualized
  def infix_+[T:Manifest:Numeric](x: Rep[Vector[T]],
                                  y: Rep[T]): Rep[Vector[T]]
  // an overloaded version. due to type erasure, we need to use
  // an implicit to statically disambiguate the method signature
  def infix_+[T:Manifest:Numeric](x: Rep[Vector[T]],
    y: Rep[Vector[T]])(implicit o: Overloaded1): Rep[Vector[T]]
  def print(x: Rep[Any]): Rep[Unit]
  // infix_apply (element access) elided for space
}

trait SimpleVectorDSLImpl extends SimpleVectorDSLInterface
  with BaseExp {
  // parallel domain-specific IR nodes
  case class VPlusS[T:Manifest:Numeric](x: Exp[Vector[T]], y: Exp[T])
    extends DeliteOpMap[Vector[T]] { def func = a => a+y }
  // sequential domain-specific IR nodes
  case class Print(x: Exp[Any]) extends Def[Unit]

  // construct IR node when method is called
  // vector_new, overloaded infix_+ elided
  def infix_+[T:Manifest:Numeric](x: Exp[Vector[T]], y: Exp[T])
    = VPlusS(x,y)
  def print(x: Rep[Any]) = reflectEffect(Print(x))

  // constructs transformed IR nodes
  override def mirror[A:Manifest](e: Def[A], f: Transformer) =
    e match {
      case VPlusS(x,y) => infix_+(f(x),f(y))
      // ...
      case _ => super.mirror(e,f)
    }
}

trait SimpleVectorDSLCodegen extends ScalaCodegen {
  val IR: SimpleVectorDSLImpl; import IR._

  override def emitNode(s: Sym[Any], r: Def[Any]) = r match {
    case Print(x) => emitValDef(s, "println("+quote(x)+")")
    case _ => super.emitNode(s,r)
  }
}
```

Listing 2. SimpleVector DSL implementation using core

diately evaluate a result. Note that while LMS uses Exp[T] to represent staged computation, the representation of the abstract types is polymorphic and DSLs can in principle be implemented in multiple ways using different implementations of Rep[T] (a fact that Forge relies heavily on, as discussed later). This technique is known as polymorphic embedding [7, 20]. After the IR is constructed, Delite traverses it to perform optimizations and generate code. The user then invokes the Delite runtime to run the generated code. Compared to running a pure Scala library, the generated code is efficient (abstractions have been programmatically removed by staging), heterogeneous, and parallel, which can lead to orders of magnitude improvement in performance [35]. Key optimizations performed by LMS and Delite include code motion, fusion, struct unwrapping, and array of struct to struct of array (AoS to SoA) conversion. Unlike general-purpose compilers, these optimizations are performed at the granularity of domain operations and data structures.

In order to demonstrate what this looks like under the covers, we show a bare-bones core of LMS and Delite in Listing 1, and the SimpleVector DSL implemented with this core in Listing 2. The core LMS traits define IR building blocks, such as expressions, definitions, and particular types of leaf expressions (e.g. constants and symbols). Delite adds on top of these to provide specialized classes of IR nodes that represent parallel patterns (e.g. DeliteOpMap). Although not shown here, LMS and Delite also provide facilities to construct *structs*. Structs are simple aggregate data types consisting of high performance primitives (e.g. scalars, arrays, and other structs) that Delite automatically optimizes and generates code for.

The DSL implementation traits extend the core traits to actually construct IR nodes when a method is called, to define helper methods required by LMS and Delite (such as mirror, which defines how to construct a transformed node), and to provide code generators for any node that is not a predefined pattern. A real implementation would use much more sophisticated versions of these IR building blocks provided by LMS and Delite, but the basic principle is the same.

Listing 2, although simplified, still demonstrates key productivity pitfalls. First, there is a significant amount of boilerplate (e.g. mirror), which makes the DSL implementation verbose and hinders readability. The boilerplate is required to perform functions that Delite cannot easily infer; for example, in the mirror case,

Delite does not know the name or arguments of the smart constructor that it needs to invoke to clone a node while still triggering any domain-specific rewrites that may be defined (which can be defined as overrides of the smart constructor). Second, DSL authors must be experts in Scala library development. They are exposed to implicit conversions, case classes, Manifest and SourceContext (which are Scala compiler-constructed types that carry around metadata), and even must know how to handle overloaded static method resolution in the presence of type erasure.

These issues arise because of the details of implementing a compiled embedded DSL in Scala. In other languages, there are different issues; for example, developing an external DSL requires DSL authors to actually deal with the entire process of lexing, parsing and type-checking. The key observation that we exploit with Forge is that by raising the level of abstraction, we can shield DSL developers from these implementation details.

3. Language Specification

Forge, as a meta DSL, provides methods to directly declare DSL constructs like types and operations that we saw in the previous section. Forge abstracts over the key concerns of high performance DSL development: front-end syntax, data structures, operation semantics, and parallel implementation. Forge aims to simplify DSL development by narrowing the gap between a DSL specification, which may be written as a text document, and the DSL implementation, which depends on the language and frameworks that the DSL compiler is implemented in. In the next section, we describe the implementation internals of Forge. In this section, we introduce its surface syntax and key abstractions.

To introduce Forge, we show how we can write the SimpleVector DSL example from Section 2 (including the struct definitions that were previously elided):

```
trait SimpleVectorDSL extends ForgeApplication {
  def dslName = "SimpleVector"

  def specification() {
    val T = tpePar("T")
    val Vector = tpe("Vector", T)
    data(Vector, ("_length", MInt), ("_data", MArray(T)))
    static (Vector) ("apply", T, MInt :: Vector(T), effect = mutable)
      implements allocates(Vector, ${$0}, ${ Array[T]($0) })
    direct (Vector) ("print", Nil, MString :: MUnit, effect = simple)
      implements codegen(scala, ${ println($0) })

    withTpe(Vector) {
      compiler ("vector_raw_data") (Nil :: MArray(T))
        implements getter(0, "_data")

      infix ("apply") (("n",MInt) :: T)
        implements composite ${ vector_raw_data($self)($n) }

      infix ("+") (("y",T) :: Vector(T), TNumeric(T))
        implements map((T,T), 0, ${ a => a+$y })

      infix ("+") (Vector(T) :: Vector(T), TNumeric(T))
        implements zip((T,T,T), (0,1), ${ (a,b) => a+b })
    }
  }
}
```

Every Forge specification must implement two methods: dslName is simply the DSL name, and specification is a method that contains all the DSL declarations (which could be spread across multiple files and dynamically invoked). In this example, we first declare a named type parameter, T, and a generic type Vector[T]. The **data** statement says that Vector is a struct containing two fields, _length and _data. The static method apply constructs a new Vector; **static**

specifies that the user syntax for this method will be of the form Vector(args), where args are the arguments to the op that are specified by the signature MInt :: Vector(T). This signature says that the op takes a single argument of type Int (the length of the Vector), and returns a value of type Vector[T]. The **effect** = mutable annotation specifies that this op has the semantics of allocating a mutable data structure. Finally, **allocates** is an implementation pattern that constructs a new instance of Vector by initializing each field in the struct to an appropriate value. The ${..} syntax is a marker for the Forge preprocessor, which quotes the argument as a formatted string, replacing argument names (specified with a preceding "$") with their synthetic names. Although these formatted strings are not type-checked when compiling or running Forge, the code in them *is* type-checked when compiling the generated DSL. The preprocessor handles tricky string escape issues while enabling users to benefit from syntax highlighting in an IDE. The last interesting construct in this example is **withTpe**, which introduces a Forge *syntactic scope*. Inside this scope, shorter versions of the op declaration methods are injected into the current lexical environment. The shorter versions implicitly take the enclosing **tpe** as the first argument (as well as its corresponding tpePars), which mimics the declaration style of instance methods in OO programming languages.

The other ops in the SimpleVector specification are defined in a similar fashion to apply, using other Forge method styles and implementation patterns. Listing 3 presents an overview of the Forge language constructs. The two most important groups abstract over computation and data structures, respectively, and correspond to concise versions of the Delite abstractions of Delite ops and Delite structs. Note that implements is an infix method that simply invokes the Forge construct **impl** on the result of the op invocation. In this way, Forge separates DSL interface from DSL implementation. Implementations may be defined in a completely different file, and DSL specifications can extend other DSL specifications and override behavior by defining new implementations.

DSL metaprogramming at this level also enables opportunities for programmatically-controlled reuse. Delite DSLs are typically statically dispatched, as this is most efficient and not all target platforms support dynamic dispatch (although tagged unions can be used as an alternative). Code generation provides an alternate mechanism for code reuse in this context. We can define a common Vector interface as follows:

```
def addVectorCommonOps(v: Rep[DSLType], T: Rep[DSLType]) {
  val VectorCommonOps = withTpe(v)
  VectorCommonOps {
    infix ("first") (Nil :: T) implements single ${ $self(0) }
    for (rhs <- List(DenseVector(T),DenseVectorView(T))) {
      infix ("+") (rhs :: DenseVector(T))
        implements zip((T,T,T), (0,1), ${ (a,b) => a+b })
      // ..
    }
    // other common ops
  }
}
```

The **for** statement in this example is statically evaluated during staging, so we can call addVectorCommonOps for different types of Vectors and replicate the common interface on each type. This enables each method to be invoked efficiently by end users on different types of Vectors without requiring implicit conversions, dynamic dispatch, or type classes. The trade-off, of course, is the potential for code explosion, which can negatively impact DSL compile time. This method is also insufficient for DSL users to write generic methods over Vectors. However, in DSLs with limited class hierarchies, this can be a sufficient, and concise, replacement for full-blown polymorphism.

Types:

ftpe(args, ret, **freq**)
  define a new function type (args) => ret
tpePar(name)
  define new type parameter
tpe(name, tpePars, **stage**)
  define new type
tpeClass(name, tpePars)
  define new type class
tpeClassInst(name, tpePars, **tpeClass**)
  define new type class instance

Data structures:

data(tpe, (fieldName,fieldTpe)*)
  associate tpe with the given struct
impl(op, **allocates**(tpe))
  implementation pattern to allocate a struct
impl(op, **getter**(tpe,field))
  implementation pattern to read a field
impl(op, **setter**(tpe,field))
  implementation pattern to write a field

Annotations:

effect ::= simple | mutable | write | error
  declare an op has the corresponding effect semantic
freq ::= hot | cold | normal
  code motion hints
stage ::= now | future
  declare whether a generated type should be T or Rep[T]
aliasHint ::= nohint | contains(**arg**) | copies(**arg**)
  declares relationships between operations and inputs

Methods:

arg(name,**tpe**,default)
  define a new op argument
static | **infix** | **direct** | **compiler** | **fimplicit**
  (**grp**, name, tpePars, signature, **effect**, aliasHint)
  defines a new op with the specified syntax style and parameters
(args :: retTpe)
  defines a new method signature
impl(op, **codegen** | **single** | **composite** | **map** | **filter** |
        groupby | **reduce** | **zip** | **foreach**)
  defines the implementation for an op based on a predefined pattern

Miscellaneous:

grp(name)
  declares a group of ops that do not belong to a type
extern(name)
  declares an op group implemented in external code
lift(grp)(tpe)
  declares a conversion from the given tpe to a Rep[.]
lookupOp | **lookupGrp** | **lookupTpe** (name)
  returns a previously declared DSL construct
withTpe(tpe)
  construct a new syntactic scope

Parallel Collections:

parallelize(tpe) as ParallelCollection | ParallelCollectionBuffer (ops)
  declares that the provided type implements a ParallelCollection
  interface with the given ops

Listing 3. Forge Language Overview

While Forge tries to make declaring DSL semantics simple and concise, it is important to remember that Forge is meant for high performance embedded DSL *compilers*. It is not a goal of ours to reproduce exactly a sequential library interface. Instead, the Forge abstractions are intended to capture the critical semantics required to implement parallel DSLs on multiple hardware devices. Unsurprisingly, since Forge is based on our experience with developing DSLs in Delite, the Forge abstractions are a high-level version of concepts in Delite (like parallel patterns, effects, and alias / code motion hints). By designing Forge as a new language, we gain the flexibility to easily add and refine these abstractions over time.

4. Compilation Pipeline

Forge is implemented as an embedded LMS DSL. Implementing it as an external DSL (or within an alternative DSL definition environment like Spoofax [26]) could make its syntax cleaner (e.g., we would not need to wrap names in strings), but would require more development effort compared to simply reusing the existing LMS infrastructure. One interesting aspect of Forge's implementation that mitigates the need for an external grammar is its unique use of Scala-Virtualized *scopes*. Scala-Virtualized is an experimental branch of the Scala compiler with additional support for DSL embedding [32]. A scope is a Scala-Virtualized construct that desugars a lexical block of code to an instantiation of a pre-defined Scala class, wrapping the block's contents inside a method of the class and then invoking the class constructor. We previously used this technique to implement coarse-grained DSL interoperability; the scope isolated the DSL interface inside the block, allowing DSL code to be invoked from within ordinary Scala programs [35]. In Forge, we use scopes to implement the **withTpe** construct from the previous section, injecting new method signatures into a lexical scope while maintaining type safety. This is an example of using

Scala-Virtualized to enable expressive embedded syntax in a way that would not normally be possible in a statically typed language. As described in Section 1, using staging also provides Forge with other benefits (such as the use of Scala composition, uniformity with the generated DSLs, and the ability to use staging time computations to statically manipulate DSL fragments). Like other LMS DSLs, Forge specifications are legal Scala, except for the blocks denoted with ${..} which are preprocessed before compilation as described in Section 3. The preprocessor is implemented as a pre-compile hook in SBT (Simple Build Tool) [40], the predominant build tool for Scala. It is small (around 300 lines of code) and performs a simple forward pass to quote next-stage code in DSL methods using Scala string interpolation.

Figure 2 illustrates the Forge compilation pipeline. When run, Forge constructs an IR of the DSL consisting of types, operations, data structures, etc. Whereas Delite DSLs traverse the IR and use different code generators to generate code for different platforms, Forge traverses the IR and uses different code generators to generate different DSL implementations. Since the information required to generate a sequential Scala library is a subset of that needed to generate the Delite DSL, it is simple to generate the library version. It is also relatively straightforward to add a new code generator to Forge to retarget a DSL to a new back-end (for example, an alternative runtime) without changing the DSL specification or Forge internals.

Along with an input Forge specification, Forge also allows external Scala code that should be added to the DSL implementations. This code is placed in a configurable directory, and copied by Forge automatically to the generated directory. External code provides an escape hatch for any situation that Forge does not support. Domain-specific optimizations, such as pattern rewrites and transformations, are defined as external code using Delite APIs directly, and made visible to the generated DSL using Forge's **extern**

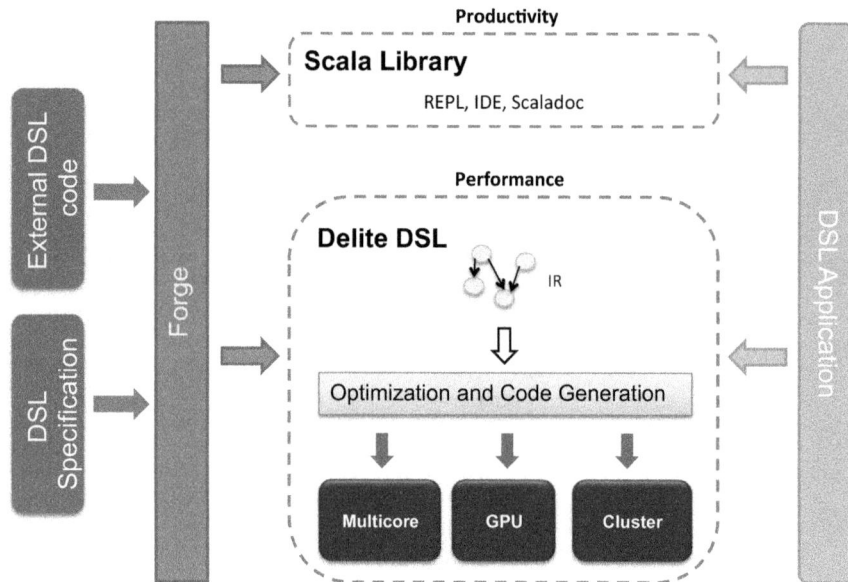

Figure 2. An overview of the Forge compilation pipeline. Forge takes as an input a DSL specification, as described in Section 3, and optional external DSL code. Forge generates two DSL implementations from these components: a high-productivity pure Scala version and a high-performance Delite version.

command. We chose this method because Delite's APIs for pattern rewriting and transformers [33] are already high-level and declarative; it is not obvious how we could abstract over these APIs in a useful way. Furthermore, these sorts of optimizations are impossible to implement in the Scala library version, so are only relevant to the Delite version.

Once the DSL implementations are generated, there is no further dependency on Forge, and DSL users can use either one. An important aspect of Forge's code generation is that it leverages polymorphic embedding not only for the Delite implementation, but also for the library implementation. In the Delite version, Rep[T] = Exp[T] as in normal Delite DSLs, but in the library version, Rep[T] = T, and Forge generates concrete classes and methods on those classes for DSL types. The key point is that DSL users now use exactly the same interface when writing their application, and need only run a different Scala object to switch between versions:

```
object MyAppInterpreter extends SimpleVectorApplicationInterpreter
  with MyApp
object MyAppCompiler extends SimpleVectorApplicationCompiler
  with MyApp

trait MyApp extends SimpleVectorApplication {
  def main() = {
    val v = Vector.rand(10)
    println("v.sum: " + sum(v))
  }
}
```

Running scala on MyAppInterpreter after compiling will run the Scala application, while running MyAppCompiler will run the Delite version to stage it and generate code for different devices. When Forge generates a DSL, it also generates the SBT project file for the DSL. A DSL user simply has to run sbt; console, and they will be dropped into a Scala REPL with all interpreter DSL dependencies pre-loaded. This provides DSL users a way to prototype their application in the Scala REPL (they can even copy and paste app code as normal) and debug their applications inside Scala IDEs in the ordinary way. In the development cycle, this also means that DSL users can also avoid expensive compilation and

staging time until they actually require high performance. When a user has finished debugging, he can switch to a larger dataset and invoke the Delite DSL. Therefore, although we have added an additional compilation step in the multi-stage compilation pipeline for DSL authors, the development cycle for DSL users can be considerably shortened. Since there are far more users than authors, this is normally a good trade-off. In order to maintain incremental compilation across the multiple stages while developing the DSL, Forge uses rsync to copy files to the generated directory.

In addition to supporting DSL construction from scratch, Forge includes a *scaffolding* code generator that allows DSL developers to bootstrap off of regular Scala classes. This generator serializes the Forge IR to re-emit a Forge specification (i.e., from an existing Forge specification, it acts like an identity generator). In order to generate a skeleton Forge specification using reflection, we use staging to build the Forge IR by simply calling the appropriate Forge methods while traversing the class. After the specification is generated, a DSL author can then fill in the gaps by adding semantic annotations (e.g. effects) and alternate code generators. As an example, if we reflect the standard String class using:

```
importAuto[java.lang.String]
```

Forge will generate a skeleton specification like the following:

```
val String = tpe ("java.lang.String")
val StringOps = grp ("String")

infix (StringOps)("trim", Nil,
  ((String) :: String), effect = simple) implements
  (codegen(scala, ${ $0.trim }))

infix (StringOps)("toLowerCase", Nil,
  ((String) :: String), effect = simple) implements
  (codegen(scala, ${ $0.toLowerCase }))

infix (StringOps)("replaceAll", Nil,
  ((String,String) :: String), effect = simple) implements
  (codegen(scala, ${ $0.replaceAll($1) }))

...
```

150

The implementation of importAuto is straightforward. It uses Scala reflection to traverse the methods of the given class and stages the corresponding Forge commands on the fly:

```
def importAuto[T:TypeTag] = {
  val scalaType = typeTag[T].tpe
  val forgeType = toForgeType(scalaType)
  val forgeClass = grp(scalaType.toString)
  lift (forgeClass) (forgeType)

  for (m <- scalaType.members if m.isMethod) {
    val methType = method.asTerm.typeSignature
    val args = toForgeArgs(methType.params)
    val ret = toForgeType(methType.resultType)

    infix (forgeClass) (m.name.toString, Nil,
      ((forgeType :: args)) :: ret, Nil, simple) implements
        (codegen(scala, quotedArg(0) + "." + m.name + argList(args)))
  }
}
```

This approach could easily be extended to read other Forge constructs from Scala or Java method annotations. With a sizable coverage of the Forge language, such annotations could provide a lightweight alternative front-end, at least for classes for which the developer is in control of the source code.

In the future, we plan to add additional code generators to Forge to generate additional artifacts. For example, if we allow users to specify Scaladoc annotations in the spec, we can generate the Scaladoc annotations in the Scala library implementation and leverage Scaladoc to generate the HTML API docs. In contrast, with ordinary Delite, there are no concrete classes in the DSL implementation and no place to put the Scaladoc annotations. We also plan to explore generating versions of the DSL that are less human readable, but are faster to compile (for example, by passing all implicits and specifying all types explicitly).

5. Evaluation

We have implemented three DSLs with Forge: OptiML (machine learning) [34], OptiQL (data querying) [35], and OptiWrangler (data transformation). Two of these (OptiML and OptiQL) were based on existing Delite DSLs, and we show that Forge significantly simplified their implementation without sacrificing performance. Furthermore, the new Forge implementations automatically produce library versions as we have discussed, so for the first time, OptiML and OptiQL can be used in a lightweight interactive way. OptiWrangler is a new implementation of Wrangler [25], and was implemented directly in Forge instead of ported from an existing Delite DSL.

For each DSL, we show that Forge lives up to the promise of DSL authors being able to write their DSL once, DSL users being able to write their application once, and being able to run efficiently on heterogeneous, parallel devices. We compare the performance of the Forge-generated DSL implementations to hand-optimized C++, to Spark [41], a Scala library for multicore and cluster computing, and to the previous Delite implementation (when available). In general, the hand-optimized C++ code is low-level and complex while the Spark version is high-level Scala that is much easier to read and to use. These two data points provide a strong measure of where the embedded DSL implementations stand in terms of productivity and performance for end users. The DSL application code is single-source and high-level, but Delite uses staging and also performs key optimizations like fusion and struct unwrapping to generate kernels that are low-level and first-order (either Scala or CUDA). In most cases, the generated Delite code closely resembles the hand-optimized C++.

DSL	Forge specification	Delite (manual)	Forge generated
OptiML	1322	7416	11743
OptiQL	301	862	1287
OptiWrangler	343	n/a	1814

Table 1. LOC for Forge implementations of each DSL vs. existing Delite implementations.

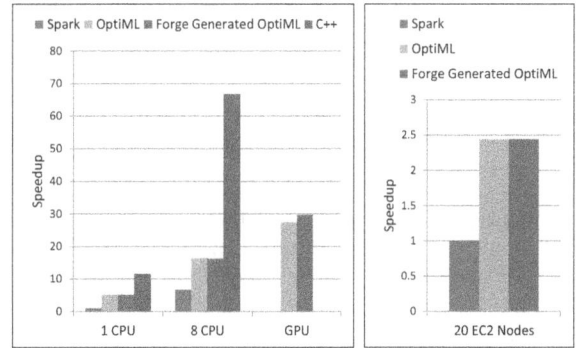

Figure 3. Speedup of Delite versions and manually-written C++ over Spark with LR on a 500k x 100 element dataset (multicore) and 10M x 100 (cluster).

Experimental Methodology   We ran Forge on each DSL to generate a Scala library version and the Delite version. For each DSL application, Delite generated parallel Scala code for the CPU and CUDA code for the GPU (when possible). We ran the generated Scala code over a cluster using the Delite runtime's support for distributed computing [5], which uses Apache Mesos [19] and Google Protocol Buffers [18] as the underlying communication layer. The Spark experiments were run with Spark 0.7.0.

Multicore CPU and GPU experiments were performed on a Dell Precision T7500n with two quad-core Xeon 2.67 GHz processors, 96GB of RAM, and an NVidia Tesla C2050. The Scala code was executed on Oracle's Java SE Runtime Environment 1.7.0 and the HotSpot 64-bit server VM with a maximum heap size of 40GB. The generated CUDA code was executed with CUDA v3.2. The C++ implementations were compiled using g++ 4.4.7 with -O3. The cluster CPU experiments were performed on Amazon EC2 using 20 m1.xlarge instances. Each machine contained 4 virtual cores, 15GB of memory, and 1Gb Ethernet connections between the 20 machines. We used the default JVM available on Amazon Linux, Java 1.6.0b24 with default options, for all three systems. We ran each application ten times (to warm up the JIT) and report the average of the last 5 runs.

When counting lines of code (LOC) to compare Forge specifications of OptiML and OptiQL to the previous Delite versions, we used CLOC [13], and counted only the subset of features of the original DSLs that we re-implemented in the Forge spec.

5.1 OptiML

OptiML is a DSL for machine learning built around a linear algebra core, which we call OptiLA. OptiML provides implicitly parallel vectors, matrices, and graphs that support bulk collection operators (e.g. **map**, **filter**) as well as standard math operators when used with numeric types. OptiML also supports control structures for iterative algorithms (such as untilconverged and gradient descent) that are common in machine learning. The Forge implementation of OptiML includes the dense data types (DenseVector, DenseMatrix), most OptiML mathematical functions, and the control structures. Row 1 of Table 1 shows the LOC count of the OptiML specification vs. the corresponding subset of the original implementation, as well as the LOC generated by Forge. Forge provides nearly a 6x reduction in LOC over the original implementation, while generating roughly 50% more LOC because it also generates the library version, which was not a part of the original OptiML. The savings comes mainly from reducing boilerplate and automatically generating the embedded DSL structure and appropriate calls into the Delite API (as discussed in Section 2). We also gain some savings by using staging and code generation to implement common Vector operations on different kinds of Vectors, whereas the previous implementation used a verbose packaging of type classes to achieve (almost) the same functionality. Qualitatively, the OptiML specification is also simpler to read and modify than the previous version, primarily because there is much less clutter than in the original embedding implementation.

To evaluate performance, we ran Logistic Regression (LR), a simple classification algorithm for predicting the discrete value of a data sample (for example, whether a particular email is spam or not). Figure 3 shows the results running on multicore CPUs, a GPU, and across the 20 node EC2 cluster. The Delite version of Forge-generated OptiML achieves the same performance as the original OptiML implementation because we are able to generate the same code from the Forge specification. The Delite versions are about 2x slower than the low-level C++, but 2.5x faster than the high-level Spark. This C++ implementation is optimized to manually fuse all loops; it allocates an output buffer per thread in order to parallelize, but otherwise contains no intermediate allocations. Furthermore, the C++ code is byte-padded to prevent false sharing, which initially caused a 3x slow-down when naïvely parallelized using OpenMP. The Delite versions fail to reach this level of performance because the fusion algorithm misses one opportunity between different parts of a reduction kernel; we believe in the future we can extend the algorithm to cover this case, which will result in the generated Delite CUDA code outperforming the manual C++ even when starting from the high-level DSL code.

In the distirbuted setting, Delite is also able to run more efficiently across nodes than Spark for the same reasons it performs better in the multicore case: fusion eliminates intermediate allocations and staging generates more efficient code than Spark, which uses high-level Scala abstractions. It is important to note that Spark, in general, is extremely efficient; it has been shown to achieve order of magnitude speedups over equivalent Hadoop implementations by intelligently keeping data in memory across multiple iterations. Delite also keeps data in memory, but at this time does not provide the same fault-tolerance guarantees as Spark.

Finally, note that the Forge-generated library version did not finish on either dataset. This version uses identical code to the pre-staged Delite version (by construction), but since it is not staged or optimized, it suffers heavily from boxing and uses far more memory. In particular, the use of polymorphic embedding in its interface imposes more dispatch and boxing overhead than the Spark version, and since it is sequential, it cannot run on multiple processors. This demonstrates that the library version is suited for interactive prototyping with small datasets, but not for high performance or large-scale execution.

5.2 OptiQL

OptiQL is a LINQ-like [27] DSL for data querying. Its primary data type is a Table, and it provides query operators (e.g. Select, Where, Sum) over them. Like OptiML, we started from an existing Delite implementation of OptiQL, and ported it to Forge. The Forge version contains all of the supported features of OptiQL, but rewrite optimizations were implemented as external DSL code

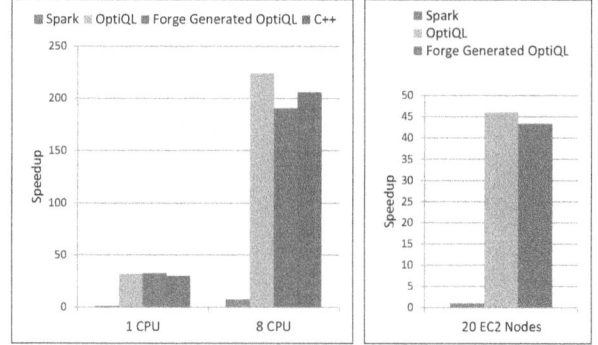

Figure 4. Speedup of Delite versions and manually-written C++ over Spark on TPC-H Q1 on a 1 GB table (multicore) and 5 GB (cluster).

directly using Delite. The rewrites performed by OptiQL perform additional fusion of query operators that go beyond the generic fusion provided by Delite.

Row 2 of Table 1 shows that the Forge OptiQL specification is about 3x shorter than the original Delite implementation. The difference is less dramatic than OptiML because OptiQL is a smaller DSL and a significant portion of its code is for the rewriting optimizations. Figure 4 shows the results of running the TPC-H benchmark suite query 1 (Q1) on multicore CPUs and on the cluster. TPC-H is a well-known database benchmark suite and Q1 consists of a single query containing Select, Where, GroupBy, and aggregate (e.g. Sum) statements. In the Delite version, the programmer-friendly array-of-struct representation is automatically converted to a more efficient struct-of-array representation, and then all of the operators are fused into a single, compact loop. Furthermore, fields that are part of the input dataset that are not used in the query are automatically eliminated from the generated code via dead field elimination. As a result, the Delite versions perform roughly the same as hand-optimized C++ and outperform Spark by 30x. In this case the speedup is magnified because the Delite optimizations have multiplicative effects; AoS to SoA enables fusion and struct unwrapping, which in turn enable dead-field elimination and the stack allocation of primitives. The same optimizations help Delite scale efficiently on the cluster, achieving 43x speedup over Spark. The increase is due to the fact that although the overall dataset is larger, the data per node is less in this experiment, and efficiency matters more. Similarly to OptiML, the Forge-generated Delite OptiQL version performs as well as the manual Delite version, while the Forge-generated library version is unable to finish for the same reasons as before (the lack of optimizations combined with polymorphic embedding and boxing overheads).

5.3 OptiWrangler

OptiWrangler is a DSL for structured string transformations and cleansing operations based on the interactive Wrangler system [25]. OptiWrangler exposes a single data element, Wrangler, and offers high level primitives (e.g. cut, split) that act over rows and columns of tabular data. In addition to managing a single table, OptiWrangler abstracts gracefully over multiple tables, allowing users to partition and merge tables without restructuring an application designed for a single table. We implemented OptiWrangler as both a Forge DSL and as a library with Spark. Unlike the other DSLs, OptiWrangler has not been previously implemented in Delite, so we use Spark as a comparison for productivity (note that in Subsections 5.1 and 5.2 the Spark implementations were for the application only, while for OptiWrangler, we implemented the entire DSL in Spark). Row 3 of Table 1 shows the code generated expansion of

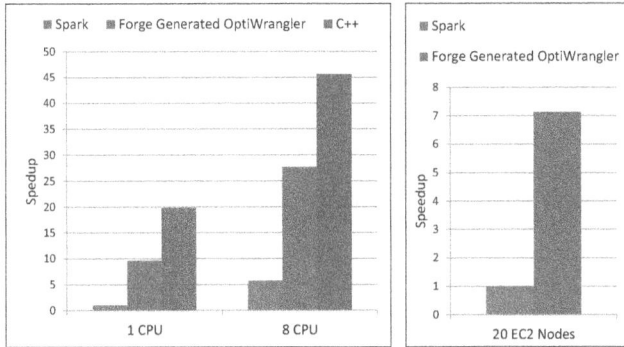

Figure 5. Speedup of Delite versions and manually-written C++ over Spark on the gene processing application with 3M sequences (multicore) and 25M (cluster).

the Forge implementation into a Delite DSL. OptiWrangler falls in between OptiML and OptiQL in terms of generated code size with a roughly 5x expansion. The Spark implementation of OptiWrangler (not shown in the table) is 253 LOC. Even though Spark is a pure Scala library, the Forge implementation is only 1.36x larger, and the difference is magnified because Forge specifications have a slightly higher fixed cost in LOC than Spark. For larger DSLs, this initial overhead would be amortized.

We evaluate performance on an application provided by a geneticist common in his workflow. Geneticists perform many types of structured-to-structured string operations, such as removing "barcodes" from gene sequences, separating genes by type, and extracting interesting subsequences. This application tests one kind of these structured transformations. Figure 5 shows the application performance with Forge-generated Delite vs. Spark and C++ (no manual Delite implementation exists). The generated Delite version unwraps all structs, leaving only a tight loop over arrays of strings. It performs approximately 2x slower than the C++ version, which heavily uses mutation to avoid allocating, for example, even new strings when constructing substrings. This requires using only a careful subset of C++ stdlib functions and makes the program harder to reason about. Like the C++ implementation of LR, this version also required byte padding to scale. On the other hand, Delite outperforms the Spark implementation by nearly an order of magnitude, which in this application is driven mostly by expensive object allocations. These benefits again translate to the cluster, resulting in a 7x speedup. This application falls somewhere in between the OptiML and OptiQL examples, since it is relatively simple (so there are not many optimizations to apply), but also not computationally heavy (so efficiency is important).

6. Related Work

The need for infrastructure to define DSLs has long been recognized and several languages and frameworks for declaratively specifying DSLs exist. The Kermeta workbench [28] is a metaprogramming environment based on metamodel engineering, which applies meta-languages to the problem of model transformations. Kermeta leverages DSLs for transforming models and the authors present common language constructs for model manipulation. The Eclipse Modeling Frameworks (EMF) [17] provide tools to generate code from a structured data model, specified in various languages (e.g. Java, XML). JetBrains MPS [24] and Spoofax [26] are language workbenches that enable developers to specify DSL grammars, static analyses and transformations (via rewrite rules, e.g. with Stratego [3]), and code generators. XText [16], JetBrains MPS and Spoofax all support automatically generating sophisti-

cated tool-chain support for custom languages, such as IDE plugins, without relying on a host language. SugarJ [15], on the other hand, does utilize a host language by enabling language developers to translate grammar extensions to the host grammar (Java), as well as apply rewrite rules and transformations. Forge follows the spirit of these efforts but focuses on code generation to make high performance, heterogeneous computing more accessible, based on our experiences with the Delite framework. Since our effort has been invested on the back-ends of optimizing DSL compilers, there is significant potential in combining Forge with a declarative framework for front-end grammars and compile-time (as opposed to staging-time) static analyses. This would enable DSL developers to have even more flexibility to define both highly expressive and high performance DSLs.

Forge is unique as a meta DSL in that it is a staged, embedded DSL, that generates other staged, embedded DSLs with specialized implementations that share a common interface using polymorphic embedding. The embedding of DSLs in a host language was first described by Hudak [22]. Tobin-Hochstadt et. al. extend Racket, a Scheme dialect, with constructs to enhance the embeddability of other languages [39]. We also use an enhanced version of the Scala compiler (Scala-Virtualized [32]) to allow for a deeper embedding of DSLs. Feldspar [2] is an instance of an embedded DSL that combines shallow and deep embedding of domain operations to generate high performance code. Taha et. al. pioneered the field of multi-stage programming with MetaML [37] and MetaO-Caml [6], extensions of ML and OCaml with staging annotations to demarcate future stage code. Forge, through LMS, uses type-directed staging instead of explicit annotations.

Forge was designed to target the Delite framework as a high performance back-end. In the field of parallel and heterogeneous computing, there have been numerous programming language and compilation approaches that have explored similar issues as, and contributed ideas to, Delite. Many of these systems are also good candidates for Forge-generated implementations, with different usability and performance trade-offs for end users of the DSL. For example, it is straightforward to generate an OpenMP [12] parallel C++ library implementation from Forge, which may integrate better with existing code bases, but would also miss out on the substantial optimizations implemented in the Delite framework (which can also generate C++ code, but at the application kernel, rather than DSL, level). OpenCL [38] is an industry-led standard for a relatively low-level, but uniform, programming model for heterogeneous devices. Forge DSLs (via Delite) can generate OpenCL from applications, allowing them to leverage the OpenCL compiler to target supported devices instead of performing low-level code generation manually. FlumeJava [11] and Dryad [23] have similar, data-flow based execution models as Delite, and also perform sophisticated optimizations on data parallel pipelines. Copperhead [8] and FirePile [30] perform run-time compilation for GPUs from Python and Scala, respectively. Forge DSLs share some of the embedding aspects of these approaches, but use staging for static whole-program analyses and generation rather than dynamic compilation, and can run in distributed environments as well as on multicore CPUs and GPUs.

7. Conclusion

We presented Forge, a meta DSL for high performance embedded DSL development. Forge is unlike previous language construction approaches in that it is embedded, staged, and generates multiple DSL implementations oriented towards simplifying heterogeneous parallel processing. Forge improves on the previous state of the art of compiled embedded DSLs by generating two versions of a DSL, a Scala library implementation that can be used for prototyping and debugging, and a Delite framework implementation that outperforms alternative systems and can run on multicore CPUs,

GPUs, and clusters from a single application. Forge can also generate itself, so it can be used with an external parser, or reflection, to generate a skeleton specification from existing libraries. We have demonstrated that Forge simplifies the process of developing and using Delite DSLs, achieving up to 6x reduction in LOC compared to existing Delite DSLs while still providing order of magnitude speedups compared to library-based approaches. We believe that a declarative specification enables new opportunities for compiled embedded DSLs, such as the ability to transparently modify the underlying high performance framework or retarget the DSLs to alternate backends.

Acknowledgments

We are grateful to the anonymous reviewers for their suggestions which improved this paper. This research was sponsored by DARPA Contract, SEEC: Specialized Extremely Efficient Computing, Contract # HR0011-11-C-0007; DARPA Contract, Xgraphs; Language and Algorithms for Heterogeneous Graph Streams, FA8750-12-2-0335; NSF grant, SHF: Large: Domain Specific Language Infrastructure for Biological Simulation Software, CCF-1111943; Stanford PPL affiliates program, Pervasive Parallelism Lab: Oracle, AMD, Intel, NVIDIA, and Huawei; and the European Research Council (ERC) under grant 587327 "DOPPLER". Authors also acknowledge additional support from Oracle. The views and conclusions contained herein are those of the authors and should not be interpreted as necessarily representing the official policies or endorsements, either expressed or implied, of DARPA or the U.S. Government.

References

[1] Apache. Hadoop. http://hadoop.apache.org/.

[2] E. Axelsson, K. Claessen, M. Sheeran, J. Svenningsson, D. Engdal, and A. Persson. The Design and Implementation of Feldspar: An Embedded Language for Digital Signal Processing. IFL'10, 2011.

[3] M. Bravenboer, K. T. Kalleberg, R. Vermaas, and E. Visser. Stratego/XT 0.17. A language and toolset for program transformation. *Sci. Comput. Program.*, 72(1-2):52–70, June 2008.

[4] K. J. Brown, A. K. Sujeeth, H. Lee, T. Rompf, H. Chafi, M. Odersky, and K. Olukotun. A Heterogeneous Parallel Framework for Domain-Specific Languages. PACT, 2011.

[5] K. J. Brown, A. K. Sujeeth, H. Lee, T. Rompf, C. D. Sa, M. Odersky, and K. Olukotun. Big Data Analytics with Delite. http://ppl.stanford.edu/papers/delite-scaladays13.pdf, 2013.

[6] C. Calcagno, W. Taha, L. Huang, and X. Leroy. Implementing Multistage Languages Using ASTs, Gensym, and Reflection. GPCE, 2003.

[7] J. Carette, O. Kiselyov, and C. chieh Shan. Finally tagless, partially evaluated: Tagless staged interpreters for simpler typed languages. *J. Funct. Program.*, 19(5):509–543, 2009.

[8] B. Catanzaro, M. Garland, and K. Keutzer. Copperhead: compiling an embedded data parallel language. PPoPP, 2011.

[9] H. Chafi, Z. DeVito, A. Moors, T. Rompf, A. K. Sujeeth, P. Hanrahan, M. Odersky, and K. Olukotun. Language Virtualization for Heterogeneous Parallel Computing. Onward!, 2010.

[10] H. Chafi, A. K. Sujeeth, K. J. Brown, H. Lee, A. R. Atreya, and K. Olukotun. A domain-specific approach to heterogeneous parallelism. PPoPP, 2011.

[11] C. Chambers, A. Raniwala, F. Perry, S. Adams, R. R. Henry, R. Bradshaw, and N. Weizenbaum. FlumeJava: easy, efficient data-parallel pipelines. PLDI, 2010.

[12] R. Chandra, L. Dagum, D. Kohr, D. Maydan, J. McDonald, and R. Menon. *Parallel programming in OpenMP*. Morgan Kaufmann Publishers Inc., San Francisco, CA, USA, 2001.

[13] A. Danial. CLOC–Count Lines of Code. *Open source*, 2009.

[14] Z. DeVito, N. Joubert, F. Palacios, S. Oakley, M. Medina, M. Barrientos, E. Elsen, F. Ham, A. Aiken, K. Duraisamy, E. Darve, J. Alonso,

and P. Hanrahan. Liszt: A Domain Specific Language for Building Portable Mesh-based PDE Solvers. SC, 2011.

[15] S. Erdweg, L. C. Kats, T. Rendel, C. Kästner, K. Ostermann, and E. Visser. SugarJ: library-based language extensibility. OOPSLA, 2011.

[16] M. Eysholdt and H. Behrens. Xtext: implement your language faster than the quick and dirty way. SPLASH '10, 2010.

[17] T. E. Foundation. Eclipse Modeling Framework Project (EMF). http://www.eclipse.org/modeling/emf/, 2013.

[18] Google. Protocol Buffers Data Interchange Format. http://code.google.com/p/protobuf, 2011.

[19] B. Hindman, A. Konwinski, M. Zaharia, A. Ghodsi, A. D. Joseph, R. Katz, S. Shenker, and I. Stoica. Mesos: A platform for fine-grained resource sharing in the data center. NSDI, 2011.

[20] C. Hofer, K. Ostermann, T. Rendel, and A. Moors. Polymorphic embedding of DSLs. GPCE, 2008.

[21] S. Hong, H. Chafi, E. Sedlar, and K. Olukotun. Green-Marl: A DSL for Easy and Efficient Graph Analysis. ASPLOS, 2012.

[22] P. Hudak. Building domain-specific embedded languages. *ACM Computing Surveys*, 28, 1996.

[23] M. Isard, M. Budiu, Y. Yu, A. Birrell, and D. Fetterly. Dryad: distributed data-parallel programs from sequential building blocks. EuroSys, 2007.

[24] JetBrains. Meta Programming System. http://www.jetbrains.com/mps/, 2009.

[25] S. Kandel, A. Paepcke, J. Hellerstein, and J. Heer. Wrangler: interactive visual specification of data transformation scripts. CHI '11, 2011.

[26] L. C. Kats and E. Visser. The spoofax language workbench: rules for declarative specification of languages and IDEs. OOPSLA '10, 2010.

[27] E. Meijer, B. Beckman, and G. Bierman. LINQ: Reconciling Object, Relations and XML in the .NET framework. SIGMOD, 2006.

[28] P.-A. Muller, F. Fleurey, D. Vojtisek, Z. Drey, D. Pollet, F. Fondement, P. Studer, J.-M. Jézéquel, et al. On executable meta-languages applied to model transformations. MTiP, 2005.

[29] NVIDIA. CUDA. http://developer.nvidia.com/object/cuda.html.

[30] N. Nystrom, D. White, and K. Das. Firepile: run-time compilation for GPUs in scala. GPCE, 2011.

[31] T. Rompf and M. Odersky. Lightweight modular staging: a pragmatic approach to runtime code generation and compiled DSLs. *Commun. ACM*, 55(6):121–130, 2012.

[32] T. Rompf, N. Amin, A. Moors, P. Haller, and M. Odersky. Scala-Virtualized: Linguistic Reuse for Deep Embeddings. Higher-Order and Symbolic Computation (Special issue for PEPM'12, to appear).

[33] T. Rompf, A. K. Sujeeth, N. Amin, K. Brown, V. Jovanovic, H. Lee, M. Jonnalagedda, K. Olukotun, and M. Odersky. Optimizing Data Structures in High-Level Programs. POPL, 2013.

[34] A. K. Sujeeth, H. Lee, K. J. Brown, T. Rompf, M. Wu, A. R. Atreya, M. Odersky, and K. Olukotun. OptiML: an Implicitly Parallel Domain-Specific Language for Machine Learning. ICML, 2011.

[35] A. K. Sujeeth, T. Rompf, K. J. Brown, H. Lee, H. Chafi, V. Popic, M. Wu, A. Prokopec, V. Jovanovic, M. Odersky, and K. Olukotun. Composition and Reuse with Compiled Domain-Specific Languages. ECOOP, 2013.

[36] H. Sutter. The Free Lunch Is Over: A Fundamental Turn Toward Concurrency in Software. *Dr. Dobb's Journal*, 30(3):202–210, 2005.

[37] W. Taha and T. Sheard. MetaML and multi-stage programming with explicit annotations. *Theor. Comput. Sci.*, 248(1-2):211–242, 2000.

[38] The Khronos Group. OpenCL 1.0. http://www.khronos.org/opencl/.

[39] S. Tobin-Hochstadt, V. St-Amour, R. Culpepper, M. Flatt, and M. Felleisen. Languages as libraries. PLDI '11, 2011.

[40] Typesafe. Simple Build Tool. http://www.scala-sbt.org.

[41] M. Zaharia, M. Chowdhury, T. Das, A. Dave, J. Ma, M. McCauley, M. Franklin, S. Shenker, and I. Stoica. Resilient distributed datasets: A fault-tolerant abstraction for in-memory cluster computing. NSDI, 2011.

On the Simplicity of Synthesizing Linked Data Structure Operations

Darya Kurilova

Carnegie Mellon University

darya@cs.cmu.edu

Derek Rayside

University of Waterloo

drayside@uwaterloo.ca

Abstract

We argue that synthesizing operations on recursive linked data structures is not as hard as it appears and is, in fact, within reach of current SAT-based synthesis techniques—with the addition of a simple approach that we describe to decompose the problem into smaller parts. To generate smaller pieces of code, *i.e.*, shorter routines, is obviously easier than large and complex routines, and, also, there is more potential for automating the code synthesis.

In this paper, we present a code generation algorithm for synthesizing operations of linked data structures and, as an example, describe how the proposed algorithm works to synthesize operations of an AVL tree.

Categories and Subject Descriptors   D.1.2 [*Programming Techniques*]: Automatic Programming; F.3.1 [*Logics and Meanings of Programs*]: Specifying and Verifying and Reasoning about Programs

General Terms   Languages

Keywords   code generation algorithm, program synthesis, SAT-solver, linked data structures, AVL trees

1.   Introduction

Software synthesis has received renewed attention in recent years. Advances in SAT/SMT solvers and verification technology have been directed at synthesis challenges. Great progress has been made; nevertheless, synthesizing operations on linked data structures appears just out of grasp as such operations usually require either recursion or loops.

We demonstrate that a careful decomposition of the problem can bring it within reach of current SAT-based synthesis techniques (*e.g.*, [7, 8, 10]). The key insights are:

- operations on linked data structures typically navigate only a small number of links;

- operations on linked data structures can be decomposed into a number of simple cases based on the values observable by a limited number of dereferences;

- each of these simple cases requires a limited number of straight-line statements (*i.e.*, no conditionals and no loops), the last of which might be a recursive call;

- a small number of necessary helper methods, such as pointer swaps, can be easily synthesized (and automatically specified) without regard to the specific operations to be performed on the overall structure;

- some synthesized methods might produce results that violate some invariants, which are then repaired by a different synthesized method;

- the choices of which invariants to violate (and repair) can be made automatically by grouping the data structure's invariants according to the fields that they refer to.

We demonstrate this approach with a case study of the AVL tree [1]. An AVL tree is a self-balancing tree, and as such it requires some tricky rebalancing methods [2]. It is common practice for programmers to write insert and delete operations for self-balancing trees that preserve the ordering of the tree but violate the balancing invariants; a rebalancing operation is then called to repair the balancing invariants (while preserving the ordering invariants). Our synthesis technique also follows this practice, and is able to do so automatically by grouping the invariants into those that preserve balancing and those that preserve order.

We work with programs written in Java and specifications written in JFSL [3, 13], which is a variant of the Alloy relational logic [6] suitable for specifying functional correctness properties of sequential Java programs.

The paper is organized as follows. §2 describes our approach and the observations and insights it is based on. §3 demonstrates our approach on the AVL tree example. §4 provides a discussion on applicability of our approach to other data structures. Related work is discussed in §5, and §6 concludes.

2.   Approach

In this section, we describe the common pattern that is the key to our code generation approach and present our overall algorithm. The key insights that enable this pattern are that operations on linked data structures typically navigate only one link at a time, and that therefore an operation on a linked data structure can be broken down into a finite number of cases based on the values of the immediately observable fields.

2.1   Common Pattern

One of the central findings of our work is that there exists a code pattern that can be seen in the code for all the linked data structures' operations. It is presented in Figure 1. All the operations can be represented as a sequence of if-blocks containing a number of

GPCE '13,   October 27–28, 2013, Indianapolis, Indiana, USA.
Copyright © 2013 ACM 978-1-4503-2373-4/13/10...$15.00.
http://dx.doi.org/10.1145/2517208.2517225

```
1   public return-type method-name(arguments) {
2       if (condition₁ && condition₂ && ... && condition_{N₁}) {
3           statement₁;
4           statement₂;
5           ...
6           statement_{M₁};
7           return object-of-the-return-type-or-nothing;
8       }
9       ...
10      if (condition₁ && condition₂ && ... && condition_{N_k}) {
11          statement₁;
12          statement₂;
13          ...
14          statement_{M_k};
15          return object-of-the-return-type-or-nothing;
16      }
17  }
```

Figure 1. Code Generating Pattern

```
1   class Node {
2       int value, height;
3       Node left, right, parent; }
```

Figure 2. Definition of Node Data Structure

4. For each conditional statement, use a SAT solver to generate the straight-line block of statements for it.

5. Clean up by consolidating blocks that have the same body.

The SAT solver in step 4 is searching for a sequence of statements that satisfy the method post-conditions given that the conditions for the block, the method pre-conditions, and the invariants are true. The search space contains five types of statements as was described above (subsection 2.1). These SAT solver runs are independent and may be run in parallel.

The main focus of the invariant analysis is dividing the provided invariants into groups to determine potential properties of the linked data structure that should be accounted for separately in the code of the methods to be generated. Essentially, the number of groups of invariants can correspond to the number of helper methods inside the main methods. The division of the invariants may be based on different properties, for example, on the attributes mentioned in each invariant as it is in the forthcoming example.

Code generation for different types of methods takes different values as fillers. Thus, for generating a @Pure method, *i.e.*, a method that does not modify the overall linked data structure, the template is filled only with values from the method's pre- and post-conditions. @Modifies methods may be broken into several helper methods according to the result of the invariant analysis. Then, the main method to be generated will contain that number of helper methods, even if it is just one. When generating a helper method for a main @Modifies method, the filler values for the code generation are taken from one specific group of invariants and the pre- and post-conditions for the main method. Once the helper methods are generated, the main method is essentially a correctly working permutation of the helper methods.

executable statements. The if-blocks are branched on a conjunction of several conditions that are mathematical comparisons, that is, expressions comparing the right-hand side to the left-hand side using the mathematical signs, such as ==, !=, <, <=, >, and >=. In some cases, the condition statements also might use the + and - arithmetic operations. Each statement inside the blocks of straight-line code is one of the following:

- a recursive call to the method itself,
- a call to a different method (a helper method or another method to be generated),
- an assignment of a new value to some existing variable,
- a variable declaration, or
- an assignment of a value to the introduced variable.

In the pattern, for each method, the number of conditions in each if-statement is the same for each block, but some of the conditions might be redundant and can be eliminated on refactoring. Also, the synthesized code could be automatically refactored to merge conditionals that lead to identical straight-line blocks, and such a refactoring would make the code nicer for a programmer to read.

2.2 Code Generation Algorithm

As a starting point for code generation, we need the programmer to specify the basics. The programmer should:

1. Define the basic data structures (*e.g.*, Node).

2. Write invariants for the linked data structure as a whole.

3. List method names for the methods to be synthesized and pre- and post-conditions for each of them.

After this information is provided, the following steps are taken to generate the linked data structure's operations (all of these actions can be automated):

1. Generate helper methods (and their specifications) that are based solely on the definitions of the data structures and not on the specifications of the methods to be synthesized.

   For example, when dealing with AVL trees, this step would generate a method to swap the left and right children of a node.

2. Generate helper methods (and their specifications) based on the data structure invariants.

3. Generate the conditional statements (see template in Figure 1) by taking the cross product of the possible variables and values.

3. Synthesis of AVL Tree Operations

In this section, we show in detail how our proposed code generating algorithm works to generate operations of an AVL tree in Java.

An AVL tree is a self-balancing binary search tree with the property that, for each node, the difference in height between its left child and its right child is at most one [1].

The programmer must supply the definitions of the data structures (Figure 2), the invariants, and the pre- and post-conditions for the methods to be synthesized. (Due to space limitations, the invariants and pre- and post-conditions are not shown.)

3.1 Generating Code

Once the essential information about the linked data structure is supplied, automatic code generation procedure can begin. Our current prototype is a very limited proof of concept: we construct an Alloy model and read out the results manually. All helper methods are generated in a systematic manual procedure. This prototype is not usable, but it illustrates that the essential ideas work.

'Swap' Methods Code generation starts with creating the simplest methods—'swap' methods. These methods are generated based only on the definition of the Node structure and basically take the Node's fields of appropriate types and swap their values. For example, swapChildren method, shown on Figure 3, takes a Node as a parameter and assigns its left child to be the right child and its right child to be the left child. Similar methods are gen-

```
1   @Ensures("this.right = @old(this.left) and
2           this.left = @old(this.right)"}
3   void swapChildren(Node one) {
4       Node temp = one.right;
5       one.right = one.left;
6       one.left = temp;
7   }
```

Figure 3. `swapChildren` Method

erated for the other fields of the `Node` structure. Calls to 'swap' methods are used as possible executable statements in `if`-blocks of the template for all the methods to be generated.

Specifications for these methods are also generated and then used by subsequent synthesis steps.

We can now synthesize the `contains` method according to the pattern in Figure 1. In total the contains method has 24 conditional blocks, each of which has one statement. A further refactoring could merge conditions whose blocks contain the same statement so that the code would be more human readable.

Invariants Analysis Before proceeding to generate more complicated non-pure methods (marked `@Modifies` in JFSL), *i.e.*, the methods that change the AVL tree, such as `insert` and `delete` methods, we need to determine the number of properties the data structure has. We do that by performing an invariants analysis.

The invariants analysis is done on the invariants as specified by the programmer and based on the fields names of the `Node` structure (Figure 2) also as defined by the programmer.

The invariants can be grouped according to which fields they mention. The `left` and `right` fields are used ubiquitously, but the `value` and `height` fields are used more selectively: `value` is used by invariants that control tree ordering, whereas `height` is used by invariants that control tree balancing. We treat these groups of invariants separately, as do programmers in practice.

Insertion Operation Based on the result of the invariant analysis, the non-pure `insert` method consists of two helper methods: one concerned with the order of nodes, which we call `insertHelper()`, and one concerned with maintaining the tree in balance, which we call `balanceHelper()`. First the helper methods are generated according to the template, and then the order in which to call them is determined. The main `insert` method is just two statements: calls to these helper methods.

The `insertHelper` method contains 48 conditional blocks, whereas the `balanceHelper` has 768.

Deletion Operation The synthesis of the delete operation is analogous to that for the insertion operation, with an interesting variation: the generated code for the `insert` method does not use other AVL tree operations, whereas the generated code for the `delete` method does—it uses an insertion operation.

The most tricky case to handle when deleting a node from a binary search tree is when a node to be deleted has two children. The standard coding practice uses additional helper methods to find either the node's in-order successor, *i.e.*, the left-most child of the node's right subtree, or in-order predecessor, *i.e.*, the right-most child of the node's left subtree [2]. However, our synthesis technique produced an alternative using an insert operation instead.

A code snippet simplified in the number of conditions inside the `if`-statement is shown below.

```
1   if (node.left != null && node.right != null
2       && node.value == x) {
3       node.value = node.right.value;
4       Node temp = node.right.left;
5       node.right.left = null;
```

```
6       delete(node.right.value, node.right);
7       insert(temp, node);
8       return;
9   }
```

3.2 Analysis

The key insight that facilitates our divide and conquer approach is that operations on linked data structures typically look at just one link at a time and at most at two, so the set of possible conditions that they can examine is finite and not that large. Within each of these conditional blocks only straight-line code is needed (possibly with a recursive call), and that can be synthesized with known SAT-based techniques (*e.g.*, [7, 8, 10]). By analyzing the code synthesized in this AVL case study, we can get a sense of how large the search space is. We first consider the generation of the conditionals:

- In accordance with the algorithm description, conditions statements inside the `if`-blocks use the mathematical comparison operands, such as ==, !=, <, and >. On the left- and right-hand sides, `Node` fields, `null`, and numeric values from the specification are used.

- The conjunction inside the `if`-statements usually has 3 to 5 conditions, and, only in one case (the `balanceHelper` method), it has 9 conditions. The number of conditions is determined by the variables in scope and the number of fields they have.

In this AVL case study there are, at most, on the order of 2^{10} conditional blocks generated.

The synthesis of the straight-line code within each conditional block is independent, and explores a space of the following size:

- The kinds of executable statements include:
  - a recursive call to the method itself,
  - a call to a different method (*e.g.*, 'swap' methods inside the `balanceHelper` method and the `insert` method inside the `deleteHelper` method),
  - a declaration of a variable,
  - an assignment to the declared variable, and
  - an assignment of a new value to a `Node` field.

- The straight-line code blocks usually have 1 to 6 statements, and, only in one case (the `balanceHelper` method), it has 12 statements.

- Up to three levels of dereferencing (*i.e.*, `node.child1.child2.f`) is necessary in any kind of statement. However, there is only one method where three levels of dereferencing is needed—the `balanceHelper` method; the rest of the methods need only two levels of dereferencing (*i.e.*, `node.child1.f`).

The search scope for these straight-line blocks can start small and be expanded if a solution is not found (*e.g.*, [11]). For example, starting with one statement and one level of dereferencing gives a space on the order of 2^3. Expanding to a second level of dereferencing increases the space to the order of 2^5, depending on how many fields are in the relevant classes (*e.g.*, `Node`). Increasing to six statements gives on the order of 2^{18} and 2^{30} for one and two levels of dereferencing respectively. These spaces are within reach of modern SAT solvers.

On the other hand, the `balanceHelper` method has blocks that require up to twelve statements and three levels of dereferencing. This method might push the limits of what is possible with current techniques.

The search can be guided and reduced by the order in which different types of statements are introduced. Our observation is that the following order would be effective:

1. A recursive call to the method itself.
2. An assignment of a new value to a `Node` field.
3. A call to a different generated method.
4. A declaration of a variable and an assignment to it.
5. A call to a 'swap' method.

In summary, while the number of conditional blocks might be in the hundreds, they are generated simply and easily, and provide the scaffolding for decomposing the problem into smaller cases that can be solved independently. The straight-line code within each block is usually just a few statements, and in most cases requires only one level of field dereferencing. The most complex straight-line blocks occur within `balanceHelper`, which require twelve statements and three levels of field dereferencing.

4. Applicability to Other Data Structures

We selected AVL trees as a case study of a reasonably complex linked data structure, and we expect that our approach generalizes to similar kinds of structures, such as unbalanced binary search trees and linked lists. The described code generation algorithm is suitable for recursive linked structures with known data layouts that navigate one link at a time.

Our approach, in its current form, is not suitable for array-based structures, such as array-lists or hash tables. The potentially large number of indices and the possibility of doing arithmetic on the indices both present challenges to the proposed algorithm.

Tree-like structures that make use of arrays and index computations, *e.g.*, B-trees, van Emde Boas trees, and Fibonacci heaps, are also beyond the current capabilities of our approach.

Likewise, handling structures, such as tries (prefix trees), where the data to be stored are decomposed according to some computation exceeds what the algorithm described here can do.

Skip lists, while recursive linked structures, are outside the reach of our approach because the different levels of links require more complex conditionals and loops in the code.

5. Related Work

Gulwani [4] surveys the literature on program synthesis and sees three dimensions to it: how the user's intent is expressed, the search space, and the search technique. According to these dimensions, our work classifies as follows. From the five different ways the user can express their intent, in our approach, the user expresses their intent primarily by writing specifications in the JFSL/Alloy relational logic language [3, 6, 13]. We also require the user to write the basic data layout of the classes. From the four different search spaces identified by Gulwani, our approach generates imperative programs in a stylized form: conditionals are generated according to a template; there are no loops; straight-line blocks are generated with known SAT-based techniques and may include recursive calls. Finally, from the four kinds of search techniques, our approach uses a combination of exhaustive search and logical reasoning. We exhaustively generate all possible conditionals from a finite set of combinations and, within each conditional, use logical reasoning to synthesize the appropriate block of straight-line code.

To Gulwani's classification [4] we add a fourth dimension: the data manipulated by the program. Gulwani's survey considers techniques that synthesize programs that manipulate integers, bit vectors, or sets. There was relatively little work done on synthesizing programs that manipulate heap references at the time of his survey, and this is the category that our approach falls under.

In our work, user intent is expressed in logical specifications, and we search in the space of imperative programs using logical reasoning techniques. This kind of approach has received an increasing amount of attention in recent years, *e.g.* [5, 7, 8, 12]. Even so, relatively little of this work deals with programs that manipulate heap references.

Leino and Milicevic [8] proposed a *dynamic synthesis* code generation algorithm that adopts ideas from concolic testing and combines concrete and symbolic execution, which is rather different from our approach. In addition, their algorithm works towards shrinking the possibly unbounded search space on each iteration while our algorithm starts with a smaller search space and expands it if the solution is not found on the current iteration. Furthermore, their currently presented work, although allows recursion, is limited to generating just read-only methods whereas our algorithm can generate methods modifying the underlying data structure.

Kuncak et al. [7] present a synthesis procedure for Boolean Algebra with Presburger Arithmetic (BAPA), which is used to manipulate sets and their sizes. Their approach significantly differs from ours, firstly, because it relies on integer linear arithmetic, and, secondly, because it does not go beyond sets and it is unclear whether it can be applied to other data structures. Moreover, the code generated by their synthesis procedure uses built-in libraries for sets and operations on them, which we restrain ourselves from.

In previous work [9], we took a syntactic approach to generating iterators over complex heap structures; however, these iterators do not modify the heap.

6. Conclusion

We have presented a divide-and-conquer strategy to the synthesis of operations on linked data structures. A case study on AVL trees illustrates that the problem might not be as difficult as had been previously imagined. The key insights are that operations on linked data structures typically examine a small number of links in a limited way and that within each conditional block only straight-line code is needed. These observations lead to search spaces that should be manageable by current SAT-based synthesis techniques.

References

[1] G. Adelson-Velskii and E. M. Landis. An algorithm for the organization of information. *Proceedings of the USSR Academy of Sciences*, 146:263–266, 1962. (Russian) English translation by Myron J. Ricci in *Soviet Math. Doklady*, 3(2):1259–1263, 1962.

[2] T. H. Cormen, C. E. Leiserson, R. L. Rivest, and C. Stein. *Introduction to Algorithms*. The MIT Press and McGraw-Hill, 2nd edition, 2001.

[3] G. Dennis. *A Relational Framework for Bounded Program Verification*. PhD thesis, MIT, 2009.

[4] S. Gulwani. Dimensions in program synthesis. In *PPDP*. 2010. Invited talk paper.

[5] S. Gulwani, S. Jha, A. Tiwari, and R. Venkatesan. Synthesis of loop-free programs. In *PLDI*, 2011.

[6] D. Jackson. *Software Abstractions: Logic, Language, and Analysis*. The MIT Press, revised edition, 2012.

[7] V. Kuncak, M. Mayer, R. Piskac, and P. Suter. Complete functional synthesis. In *PLDI*, 2010.

[8] K. R. M. Leino and A. Milicevic. Program extrapolation with Jennisys. In *OOPSLA*, 2012.

[9] D. Rayside, S. Montaghami, S. Leung, S. Yuen, S. Xu, and D. Jackson. Synthesizing iterators from abstraction functions. In *GPCE*, 2012.

[10] A. Solar-Lezama, L. Tancau, R. Bodik, V. Saraswat, and S. A. Seshia. Combinatorial sketching for finite programs. In *ASPLOS*. 2006.

[11] A. Solar-Lezama, C. G. Jones, and R. Bodik. Sketching concurrent data structures. In *PLDI*, 2008.

[12] S. Srivastava, S. Gulwani, and J. S. Foster. From program verification to program synthesis. In *POPL*, 2010.

[13] K. Yessenov. A light-weight specification language for bounded program verification. Master's thesis, MIT, 2009.

Generation of Conjoint Domain Models for System-of-Systems

Deepak Dhungana   Andreas Falkner   Alois Haselböck

Siemens AG Österreich, Corporate Technology, Vienna, Austria
{deepak.dhungana, andreas.a.falkner, alois.haselboeck}@siemens.com

Abstract

Software solutions in complex environments, such as railway control systems or power plants, are assemblies of heterogeneous components, which are very large and complex systems themselves. Interplay of these systems requires a thorough design of a system-of-systems (SoS) encompassing the required interactions between the involved systems. One of the challenges lies in reconciliation of the domain data structures and runtime constraints to ensure consistency of the SoS behavior. In this paper, we present a generative approach that enables reconciliation of a common platform based on reusable domain models of the involved systems. This is comparable to a product line configuration problem where we generate a common platform model for all involved systems. We discuss the specific requirements for model composition in a SoS context and address them in our approach. In particular, our approach addresses the operational and managerial independence of the individual systems and offers appropriate modeling constructs. We report on our experiences of applying the approach in several real world projects and share the lessons learned.

Categories and Subject Descriptors D.2 [*Programming Environments*]: Integrated environments; D.2 [*Interoperability*]: Data mapping; D.3 [*Language Classifications*]: Specialized application languages

Keywords System-of-systems integration, platform alignment

1. Introduction

In industrial settings, monolithic engineering approaches are often not applicable, due to the interdisciplinary nature and the sheer size and complexity of the projects. Large-scale systems such as power plants, industrial production sites or railway interlocking systems are designed and constructed by combining many components and subsystems and can be seen as *system-of-systems* (SoS) [19, 24]. All involved component systems have to be inter-operable, i.e., they need to communicate, exchange data, and be aligned, consistent and compatible to each other. According to [24], our approach is mainly applicable to *directed* and *collaborative* SoS, because those have, to a certain degree, a central management organization.

Due to the heterogeneity of the used tools concerning formalisms, languages, and formats, the necessary integration of such cross-domain networks of heterogeneous systems into one architecture introduces a crucial challenge for project success [23]. The data models of the component systems, referred to as *domain models* in this paper, must be consolidated. It requires rigorous tool integration methods to ensure model compatibility and re-usability across tool boundaries as well as to manage change and model evolution in a collaborative environment. Modelers must be able to express and enforce structural and behavioral requirements of the target platform architecture [17]. Data constraints in integrated environments pose additional maintenance challenges, as they must be adjusted to changes during the system's lifetime.

Many approaches have been proposed to deal with similar challenges, e.g., [4, 7, 18, 20, 30]. Many of them need highly trained specialists to use them effectively. Due to the lack of easy-to-use alternatives, ad-hoc processes such as point-to-point integration can be observed in reality. To deal with the obvious drawbacks (exponential increase in complexity, single points of failure), open integration strategies such as enterprise service bus architectures [25] have been proposed. These allow loose coupling between independent systems, which is often not adequate in practical settings to prevent redundancy, inconsistency or ambiguity in shared data.

System integration in the context of production system engineering can also be seen as a product configuration task. The integrated SoS is comparable to a product variant (represented by a conjoint domain model) derived from a product line where the existing component systems are the reusable core assets (product components). Product derivation in this sense implies that a common software platform encompassing selected tools must be created. While in product line engineering the focus lies on the selection of a complete and consistent set of features for a concrete product, the task of configuring a SoS is to support integration and collaboration of the different components which themselves are, to a reasonable degree, autonomous systems. Without proper reconciliation strategies, this is a manual process facing various challenges such as redundancy and inconsistency of concepts [26].

This paper presents a light-weight (i.e., easy-to-use) approach for pursuing development, integration, and interoperability of individual systems in a SoS context. We demonstrate our approach using examples from the domain of production systems for rail automation. It is based on our long term experiences on building industrial scale product configurators [14] and requirements from industrial projects dealing with integration and evolution of models [15]. In particular, the following challenges related to reconciliation of a common platform are addressed:

- Modeling individual systems and dependencies to potential peers in a SoS context.

- Generation of a conjoint domain model encompassing selected systems and ensuring correctness of generated content.

- Enforcement of constraints within and between all involved systems throughout system lifetime.

GPCE '13,   Oct. 27-28, Indianapolis, USA.
Copyright © 2013 ACM 978-1-4503-2373-4/13/10... $15.00.
http://dx.doi.org/10.1145/2517208.2517224

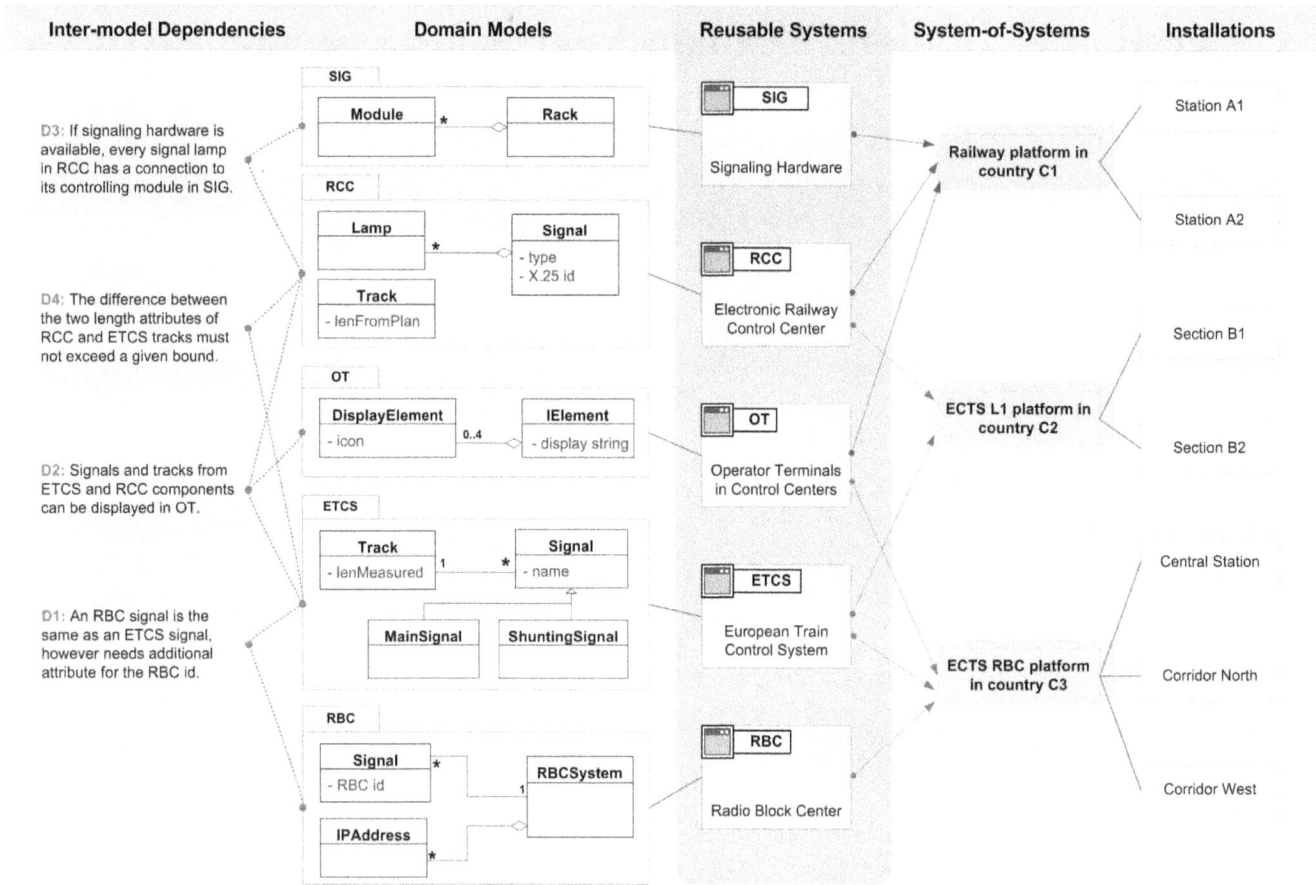

Inter-model Dependencies	Domain Models	Reusable Systems	System-of-Systems	Installations

Figure 1. Example of a system portfolio in the domain of rail automation.

- Integration of legacy tools using adapters and model translation.

This paper is organized as follows. In Section 2, we describe an industrial example and details of the challenges mentioned above. In Section 3 we present our approach to deal with those challenges: key concepts, modeling support, used tools and technology. Section 4 summarizes evaluation results. In Section 5 we relate our work to existing approaches and in Section 6 we conclude together with an outlook on future work.

2. Industrial Example and Challenges

The rail automation portfolio typically comprises a large, heterogeneous set of independent systems. Figure 1 shows a small subset of different rail automation products: signaling hardware (SIG), railway control center (RCC), operator terminal (OT), European train control system (ETCS), and radio block center (RBC). These systems represent the reusable components (i.e., the portfolio) which can be combined as needed in a system-of-systems context as long as the specified dependencies are satisfied.

A concrete rail automation solution contains a selected subset of such systems, depending on the needs of the customer and the favored technology. For example, Figure 1 sketches three such solutions in three different countries. Different component systems are integrated into one SoS based on the country-specific requirements. Based on such a SoS, different installation (for different railway stations) can be configured and deployed.

Each component system must be configured according to its special, partly significantly differing requirements, e.g., concern-ing exact locations of signals, concrete types of elements, detailed hardware wiring, monitor screen layout in control centers, etc. Therefore, each has its highly-specialized engineering tool (configurator). A modeling framework is needed for collaborative design, implementation and maintenance of domain models and configurator tools for the whole rail automation portfolio, enabling a seamless interplay of configurators for more efficient and integrated systems in product deployments. These methods are of general nature and applicable to industrial domains other than rail automation.

2.1 Challenge: Collaborative Modeling

Often, domain models of individual systems are not designed as part of a comprehensive super-model, but are built and maintained separately by different groups of experts. The result is a set of independent models/tools, each specialized for a different component system in the portfolio. However, the stakeholders responsible for modeling these systems must collaborate and communicate with each other to achieve a common understanding of the concepts.

In many cases, the domain models partly overlap (representing the same concepts from different perspectives). Different kinds of dependencies and constraints exist between the concepts of different models (see Section 2.3). Therefore, *supporting collaborative modeling* is a key requirement in this context.

Industrial state-of-practice shows that inter-system dependencies are usually resolved by data-exchange interfaces, using proprietary APIs and tools. For the rail automation domain there are efforts to standardize such interfaces, e.g., by XML-based RailML[1]. In any case, the corresponding architecture is a complicated network of engineering tools, highly cross-linked by hard-to-maintain interfaces. The users of the tools must obey a complicated error-prone process, e.g., when to configure which component and how to transfer data to which subsequent tool.

An alternative to such a complex tool architecture should therefore support *distributed modeling* of individual systems. The users should have the possibility to define shared concepts or to reuse concepts from other systems.

2.2 Challenge: Dependencies across System Boundaries

One of the toughest challenges in system integration is dealing with relationships between the participating systems. In SoS context, the systems are intrinsically independent of each other, but dependencies arise if the systems are to be integrated. Although a system can have dependencies to many other systems, not all of them need to be active in a concrete SoS - i.e., a cross-system dependency is only enabled if all its components are selected in the SoS.

Such cross-system dependencies can be structural dependencies (associations) between classes of two component systems, or reasoning expressions such as constraints or rules. In the example presented in Figure 1, these dependencies are depicted in textual form - the lines between these descriptions and model elements show the involved component systems.

D1 **Class hierarchy across systems**: An RBC signal is the same as an ETCS signal, however needs an additional attribute for the RBC id. This could be seen as a specialization (inheritance hierarchy) that goes beyond a system boundary.

D2 **Implementation of foreign concepts**: Signals and tracks from ETCS and RCC components can be displayed in OT (e.g. by implementing the IElement interface).

D3 **Conditional associations**: If signaling hardware is available, every signal lamp in RCC has a connection to its controlling module in SIG. This can be realized by an association between the two components. Note that this association does not exist if RCC and SIG are not used together.

D4 **Consistency of concepts**: Both the tools RCC and ETCS have a representation of track length, but from different sources (read from a paper plan vs. measured in the field). Automated processes should check if the differences of their values lie within an allowed range.

The possibility to define or automatically derive such cross-system dependencies is vital for the design of a system portfolio. Moreover, the target tool platform must be able to process them.

2.3 Challenge: Generation of a Conjoint Domain Model

In the proposal phase of a project, it is difficult to estimate the costs for setting up the necessary toolset for engineering and verification because of the heterogeneous landscape. In the realization phase, component systems along with their models and tools must be selected and integrated. Appropriate processes must be set up to control planning, engineering, and verification activities.

An automated or semi-automated selection and combination of the different component systems for a concrete project is needed to optimize costs and quality. The conjoint model shall minimize redundancies (to avoid duplicated and possibly conflicting user input) and avoid inconsistencies within and between models. Apart from that, models may exist in different versions and the engineers must be supported in selecting an appropriate one. The key requirement in this context is therefore supporting *automated consolidation and*

[1] http://www.railml.org/index.php/home.html

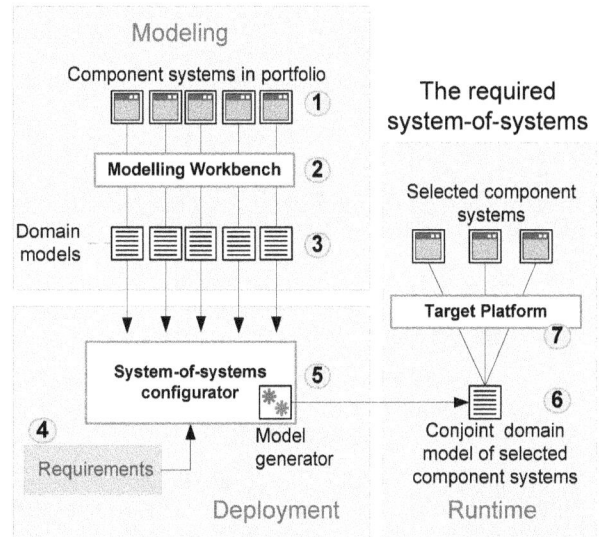

Figure 2. Overview of the approach for generating a conjoint model of involved systems in a SoS.

reconciliation of selected portfolio models and versions to a single, non-redundant model best-suited for the required variant.

In addition to the model, tools comprise code for reasoning (rules, constraints), for the user interface, for generating output in various formats, etc. It must be ensured either that this code is consistent to the conjoint domain model or that it is adapted automatically so that it will work properly on the target tool platform. The *target tool platform* is the "host" of the system-of-systems, which coordinates the individual systems based on the conjoint domain model.

2.4 Challenge: Integration of Legacy and Third-party Tools

Building up a set of engineering tools for the different products is an expensive and long-term task. Instead of creating the whole system portfolio from scratch, step-to-step modernization of the engineering tool landscape may be an effective strategy. Therefore, a powerful platform must support the integration of existing tools - legacy tools as well as third-party tools. Systems provided by an external supplier are more difficult to adapt or integrate into a common model as access to them is restricted.

A conventional approach would be to equip legacy tools with interfaces to exchange data between them. This is not feasible as it ends in the aforementioned complex and hard-to-maintain tool network. In addition, proprietary interfaces between tools would hinder integration and should be avoided.

The systems of a portfolio are continuously extended and maintained over years by different teams in various departments. Hence a monolithic approach where one modeling team is responsible for the whole set of models and their interplay is not possible. Necessary integration tasks are automated data exchange and migration, data merging, and consistency checking across tool boundaries.

3. Approach

An overview of our approach is depicted in Figure 2. It consists of a modeling step and the deployment to a runtime platform:

① Component systems represent the set of available systems in the portfolio, which can be reused to create a SoS as required in a certain domain.

2 **Modeling workbench** is a tool (called CSL Studio) we have developed to specify the domain models of the component systems, considering the dependencies among the systems.

3 **Domain models** are the textual models of the concepts supported by the component systems.

4 **Requirements for SoS** represent the set of criteria for selecting the systems from the portfolio required for building a SoS.

5 **SoS configurator** is a tool integrated in CSL Studio which ensures consistent and valid selection of input models and generates a conjoint model for the selected systems.

6 **Conjoint domain model** represents a common model of the selected components which can be used in a target platform where all selected components are deployed.

7 **Target platform** is an integration framework which is required for deploying the selected portfolio systems. This framework "interprets" the generated domain model to ensure consistency during deployment and runtime.

The data-structure of the involved systems is described using a domain-specific language designed to support the most common patterns required in industrial settings and to enable distributed modeling.

3.1 Key Concepts

A portfolio consists of individual component systems. A **system** is described by an object-oriented **domain model**, basically a network of domain classes with their features and behavioral relationships. Systems usually depend on other systems by deriving from their classes or establishing associations and dependencies to their concepts. In that case, we say that system A *uses* system B (or *is dependent on*).

A **portfolio** P is a directed graph $<S(P), E(P)>$, where the nodes $S(P)$ is the set of all systems, and the edges $E(P)$ is the set of all directed dependency links (*uses* links) between the systems $S(P)$.

A **conjoint domain model** CM induced by a selected set of systems $S' \subseteq S(P)$ is a minimal subset of $S(P)$ with the following properties:

- $S' \subseteq CM$
- if node $n1 \in CM$ and edge $n1 \rightarrow n2 \in E(P)$, then $n2 \in CM$.

In other words, a conjoint domain model of a selected set of systems represents a minimal subset of all systems of the portfolio containing the selected components and additionally all systems which are used directly or indirectly from the selected systems.

The task of specifying a conjoint domain model is straightforward: The user picks the systems she/he needs for her/his product and this set of systems can be automatically completed to a conjoint model by following the dependency links "outside" the set of selected systems, resulting in a complete and minimal set of systems needed.

3.2 Modeling Component Systems

The formal modeling language of our system models we call CSL (Configuration Specification Language). CSL is based on a standard object-oriented meta model similar to Ecore or MOF and provides all state-of-the-art features like packages, interfaces, classes with attributes of various types, associations between classes (uni- and bi-directional), inheritance and aggregation relationships, methods, constraints, rules.

The individual domain models are formulated in CSL separately by different knowledge engineers. The following snippet shows the ETCS model from Figure 1 in CSL notation. The syntax of CSL is mostly self-explanatory based on UML, so we will focus on key elements, that have been introduced to solve the model redundancy problem, i.e., similar classes which are part of different models but have overlapping properties. These concepts build the basis for tackling challenge 2.1 but only those in the next sections will cover it completely (and partly 2.2).

```
package etcs;

abstract class Signal {
    attr name: String;
    assoc onTrack[1..1]: Track;
}

class MainSignal extends Signal {
}

class ShuntingSignal extends Signal {
}

class Track {
    attr lenMeasured: Int(unit="m");
    assoc signals[0..*]: Signal oppositeOf onTrack;
}
```

3.3 Referencing Foreign Model Elements

Basic relationships between individual domain models are classical *inheritance*[2] as well as *association* and *aggregation*. The following CSL snippet shows how the dependency D1 in Figure 1 could be solved by inheritance (an RBC signal is subclass of an ETCS signal). By importing the required component, it is possible to access classes in it (thus making the uses-relation of Section 3.1 explicit).

```
package rbc;
import etcs;

class Signal extends etcs.Signal {
    attr rbcId: String;
}
```

Basic domain concepts and features can be factored out into common basis models to be reused by the individual domain models. This library of common interfaces and classes is usually provided by a supervisor team of knowledge engineers which have a general overview over all portfolio system models.

The other standard way of using model data from other models is by association or aggregation, where a link to a basic class associates its structure and behavior to a system model class. The following CSL snippets are an insufficient way to represent dependency D2 from Figure 1 (tracks and signals in ETCS can aggregate up to four display elements in OT), because such links across component borders are only unidirectional, and the (autonomous) component OT will not know the associated elements and their properties for display.

```
package ot;
enumeration ot.IconType {
    track, signalLeft, signalRight
}

class DisplayElement {
    attr icon: IconType;
}
```

---

[2] Our meta model uses single-inheritance to avoid the well-known difficulties of multi-inheritance.

```
package etcs;
import ot;

abstract class Signal {
  attr name: String;
  assoc onTrack[1..1]: Track;
  aggreg displayElements[0..4]: ot.DisplayElement;
}

class Track {
  attr lenMeasured: Int(unit="m");
  assoc signals[0..*]: Signal oppositeOf onTrack;
  aggreg displayElements[0..4]: ot.DisplayElement;
}
```

Modeling references through inheritance and association is a useful but trivial feature of the language. Industrial requirements have driven us to more sophisticated dependencies, where foreign models (peers in the SoS context) must be changed/adapted if they are included. For example, just by using references, it is not possible to define bidirectional associations (i.e., an opposite role for the aggregation `displayElements`) for the example D2 above because we do not import component ETCS to OT, avoiding circular model imports. This would violate our principle of modular, distributed modeling of the portfolio systems.

Furthermore, using only single-inheritance is too restricted because properties to be reused usually come from different neighbor or basis models, e.g., RBC signal can inherit only from ETCS signal or one of its specializations (shunting and main signal) in the example D1 above. A classical inheritance declaration is mandatory, i.e., if a class is defined to be a subclass of another class (of another model), that other class must exist. But we need to have a concept of optional inheritance, because the different systems should be reconciled to a conjoint model in a flexible way according to the needs of the customer.

So there is a need for more enhanced methods for distributed, collaborative modeling of the individual systems, with the possibility to reuse parts of other product models or stating dependencies and relationships between these product models. The two main approaches for representing such flexible interactions between different domain models are *pull injection* and *push injection*, which are described in the following.

3.4 Injecting Model Elements

The push and pull injection mechanisms are a unique contribution of this approach. In model-driven engineering, model transformation approaches like ATL [21] use concepts of injectors and projectors, but those are very specific model transformations that must be written at a fairly low level. Our idea, however, corresponds to a specification mapping from one domain or class model to another. The use of these injections are important concepts for the generation of the conjoint model. At the implementation level, push and pull injections could be realized by ATL transformation rules.

Mixins [31] and class refinements [2] in OO languages represent a similar concept and can add new data members, methods, and constructors, as well as extend existing methods and constructors of its superclass. Push and pull injections are similar concepts for SoS – it is mainly about the rights and responsibility of the modelers. With *push injection*, the modeler can change foreign components and with *pull injection*, components within her/his control are changed. A simple example is shown in Figure 3, where the domain model M2 uses concepts from model M1 by pull injection, and injects properties (like attributes or associations) into classes of model M3 by push injection.

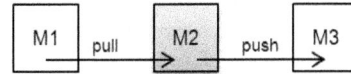

Figure 3. Schematic description of pull and push injection from the perspective of domain model M2.

3.4.1 Pull Injection

Pull injection is an operator for optional insertion of features from another domain model into a model. This injection only takes place if the referenced model is part of the final system of systems. If the referenced model is not used, no features are injected.

More formally, let C1 be a so-called injection class in model M1 with features F11 ...F1n (a feature is either an attribute, an association, a function, a constraint, or a rule). Let C2 be a class in model M2 with features F21 ...F2m.

```
Model M1:
    class C1 { F11 ... F1n }

Model M2:
    class C2 isa M1.C1? { F21 ... F2m }
```

The `isa` operator is executed during conjoint model generation time and injects the features F11 ...F1n of C1 into class C2, if and only if both models M1 and M2 are part of the SoS. After the injection, class C2 contains the union of the features F11 ...F1n and F21 ...F2m:

```
class C2 { F11 ... F1n } U { F21 ... F2m }
```

Note that the *union* of features is built (similar to the *feature refinement* operator of [2]), i.e., features with the same signature are not duplicated. Features with the same name but with different signature (e.g. attributes with different types) lead to an error during system model generation. The models must be corrected.

A class can pull injection information from more than one injection class. If the '?' is omitted at the injection operator, the model containing that injection class must be part of SoS. The conjoint model is automatically extended as described in Section 3.1.

The rest of this section demonstrates pull injection by a proper implementation of dependency D2 with CSL. The operator terminal system OT has, among others, the following concepts (cf. Figure 1:

```
package ot;

enumeration ot.IconType {
  track, signalLeft, signalRight
}

class DisplayElement {
  attr icon: IconType;
  assoc element[1]: IElement
    oppositeOf displayElements;
}

@injection
class IElement {
  attr displayString: String;
  aggreg displayElements[*]: DisplayElement;
}
```

The `@injection` annotation specifies that the properties of the class `IElement` may be injected into classes of other components.

By using the `isa` keyword, the topology elements of the ETCS domain model in the following snippet represent the fact that, if

163

an operator terminal is present, the topology elements will have connections to the OT display elements and will have an additional attribute `displayString`.

```
package etcs;
import ot;

class Signal isa ot.IElement? {
  attr name: String;
  assoc onTrack[1..1]: Track;
}

class Track isa ot.IElement? {
  attr lenMeasured: Int(unit="m");
  assoc signals[0..*]: Signal oppositeOf onTrack;
}
```

The following model is generated by our framework if systems ETCS and OT are together part of the planned SoS:

```
enumeration ot.IconType {
  track, signalLeft, signalRight
}

class ot.DisplayElement {
  attr icon: ot.IconType;
  assoc element[1]: ot.IElement
    oppositeOf displayElements;
}

interface ot.IElement {
}

class etcs.Signal implements ot.IElement {
  attr name: String;
  assoc onTrack[1..1]: etcs.Track;
  attr displayString: String;
  aggreg displayElements[*]: ot.DisplayElement
}

class etcs.Track implements ot.IElement {
  attr lenMeasured: Int(unit="m");
  assoc signals[0..*]: etcs.Signal
    oppositeOf onTrack;
  attr displayString: String;
  aggreg displayElements[*]: ot.DisplayElement
}
```

The concept of such pull injections looks very similar to standard implementations of interfaces. The main differences are: Injection declarations can be optional, allowing a flexible combination of different components to a conjoint model, and interfaces cannot have properties (like attributes or association links) but only method declarations. This serves our goal to automatically generate a consistent conjoint model which is specifically created for a concrete SoS without any redundancies[3].

3.4.2 Push Injection

Another concept for an advanced interplay of system models is push injection, where properties of a class are injected into a class definition of another model.

More formally, let `C1` be a class in model `M1` with features `F11` ...`F1n`. The push injection operator `@override` adds the features `F21` ...`F2m` from within model `M2` into model `M1`:

```
Model M1:
    class C1 { F11 ... F1n }

Model M2:
    @override class M1.C1 { F21 ... F2m }
```

---

[3] A concept which comes close to such injection classes are Scala *traits*.

When both model M1 and M2 are part of SoS, class `C1` will have the following features:

```
class C1 { F11 ... F1n } U { F21 ... F2m }
```

If model M2 is not part of SoS, class `C1` remains unchanged. Note that the *union* of features is built, i.e., features with the same signature are not duplicated. Mismatching types lead to conflicts during model generation. In CSL Studio, these conflicts are presented to the modeler similar to Java compiler error messages. References of the conflicting types are marked in the model code and the respective modeler(s) must resolve them.

Dependency D1 implies that signals in RBC shall reuse those in ETCS - but class `Signal` in component ETCS has various subclasses for each different type of signal (main signal, shunting signal, ...). Building subclasses of all those subclasses in RBC is not appropriate. The concept of push injection provides a simple and natural solution: The ETCS class `Signal` is overwritten (using the annotation `@override`) and extended in RBC:

```
package rbc;
import etcs;

@override
class etcs.Signal {
  attr rbcId: String;
  assoc rbc[1..1]: RBCSystem;
}

class RBCSystem {
  assoc signals[1..*]: etcs.Signal oppositeOf rbc;
}
```

For a SoS with both components RBC and ETCS, the generated conjoint model looks like:

```
class etcs.Signal {
  attr name: String;
  assoc onTrack[1..1]: etcs.Track;
  attr rbcId: String;
  assoc rbc[1..1]: rbc.RBCSystem;
}

class etcs.MainSignal extends etcs.Signal {
}

class etcs.ShuntingSignal extends etcs.Signal {
}

class etcs.Track {
  attr lenMeasured: Int(unit="m");
  assoc signals[0..*]: etcs.Signal
    oppositeOf onTrack;
}

class rbc.RBCSystem {
  assoc signals[1..*]: etcs.Signal oppositeOf rbc;
}
```

3.5 Ontology Alignment

Full benefit of the modeling concepts described above can only be achieved by using CSL as modeling language. But as mentioned in Section 2.4, it is also required that legacy tools along with their domain models are to be incorporated into conjoint models. Those tools are modeled using other languages than CSL, but usually follow a standard object-oriented meta model. Adapters can be written which map the legacy models to CSL models to make them available for SoS integration.

Of course, those CSL models, generated by adapters, do not make use of common basis models, or of pull or push injection.

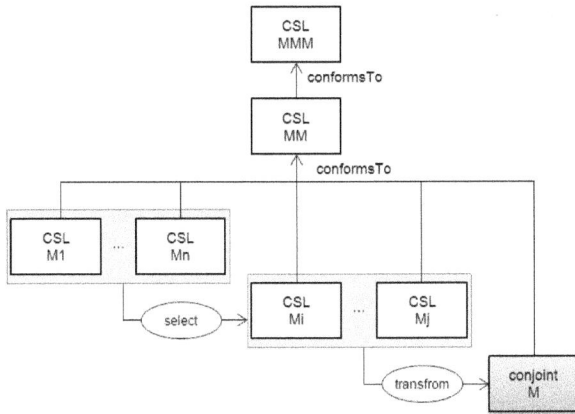

Figure 4. Generation of a conjoint domain model from a MDE point of view.

Therefore those models will redundantly contain classes and features which are also defined in models of other components. To resolve this redundancy problem for legacy tools, the semantic web technology *ontology alignment* [12] is a promising approach. With that, correspondences between concepts of different models can be found in an automatic way. Analysis and evaluation of applicability and tool support of such ontology-based methods is an on-going research focus in the CSL project.

3.6 Generation of a Conjoint Domain Model

Given a set of domain models for all systems of a portfolio and requirements for creating a concrete SoS, the first task is the identification of all components required for the concrete project. This can be done by building the transitive closure of all systems dependent on the initially selected systems. A model generator automatically builds a conjoint CSL model containing all necessary concepts (packages, classes, features, . . .) for the target system as specified in Section 3.1. All pull and push injection operators are applied. The conjoint model does not contain superfluous concepts or redundancies, and is consistent and complete (see Section 3.7).

On the implementation level, the generation of the conjoint model is realized via a specialized transformation procedure, comparable to a series of ATL transformation rules [21]. Figure 4 shows the two actions "select" and "transform". From the set of all domain models M1 . . . Mn (all conforming to the CSL metamodel, the CSL language which in turn conforms to the CSL metametamodel) the required subset Mi . . . Mj is selected and transformed to a conjoint model. This conjoint model conforms to the CSL metamodel, too.

The conjoint domain model can be seen as a condensed model, tailored for a concrete product. Configuration tools for the different parts of the product are integrated into a tool platform. All these tools work on the same model and instances. This reduces duplicated user inputs (e.g., if the user has specified the properties of a signal in one component, all other components have immediate access to those data) and avoids complicated interfaces between the different tools. This step covers challenge 2.3.

3.7 Generative Constraint Satisfaction

Constraints are an elegant way to specify logical relationships between elements. Briefly, a constraint satisfaction problem [29] consists of a set of variables along with their domains, and a set of constraint expressions restricting the set of valid value combinations. A solution to a constraint satisfaction problem is a variable assignment where no constraint is violated.

Such constraints can be restrictions (certain attribute values or element combinations are not allowed) or requirements (e.g., element A requires element B). CSL uses the *generative constraint satisfaction* formalism (GCSP, see [16]). GCSP[4] is a dynamic, object-oriented variant of classical CSP. In classical CSP, constraints are specified on instances only, while GCSP represents constraint schemata as part of the class declarations in the model. When model classes are instantiated during runtime, their GCSP constraints are instantiated, too, leading to a dynamic extension of the corresponding constraint network.

GCSP constraints are used in CSL both for intra-model logical relationships and inter-model dependencies. The latter ones are of special interest for our system portfolio environment, because they are a powerful way to maintain consistency not only within a model but also between all the models of a portfolio, and within the selected component systems of a SoS.

As an example we show CSL code for dependency D4 in Figure 1: Component RCC specifies a `Track` class with an attribute `lenFromPlan` which gets its value from a topology plan supplied by the railway company. Component ETCS specifies a `Track` which has an association relationship to the RCC track and has a similar length attribute (`lenMeasured`), but this time exactly measured in the field via GPS. Now an inter-model constraint checks, if the measured length lies within a plausible range of 10 meters around the length from the paper plan. If the ETCS track has a link to the RCC track in cases where RCC is part of the SoS, our GCSP solver automatically checks this relationship at runtime and, in case of a violation, informs the user of this violation and possible corrections. If there is no RCC track associated (RCC is not part of the SoS), the constraint is satisfied trivially.

```
package rcc;

class Track {
  attr lenFromPlan: Int;
}


package etcs;
import rcc;

class Track {
  attr lenMeasured: Int;
  assoc rccTrack[0..1]: rcc.Track;

  constraint cLen {
    (lenMeasured >= rccTrack.lenFromPlan − 5) &&
    (lenMeasured <= rccTrack.lenFromPlan + 5)
  }
}
```

It should be noted that these constraints not only are valuable at runtime of the configurators, but also at model generation time, where a selection of different model variants and versions are combined to a conjoint model. Constraints are, of course, also integrated into the conjoint model and syntactically checked. If mandatory components or referenced attributes or associations are missing or have wrong data types, the CSL compiler reports errors and the models or the model selection for the SoS must be corrected or completed.

The usage of GCSP both for intra- and inter-model constraints covers the consistency aspects of challenge 2.2.

3.8 Tool Support

Our approach is supported by a tool suite (CSL Studio), which provides a workbench for modeling individual systems, dependencies

---

[4] Siemens uses an implementation of GCSP for configuring large-scale industrial products. This implementation is not publicly available.

between them, rules and constraints. Based on these models, CSL Studio generates a conjoint model for the selected systems. The conjoint domain model specifies the SoS and is translated to different formats depending on the target platform. There it is used by persistence layers, constraint engines, and visualization components.

CSL Studio is realized as an Eclipse application, which provides a modeling language and an IDE based on Xtext [13]. A screen-shot of CSL Studio is depicted in Figure 5, which shows the common IDE elements, including visualization of component dependencies and support for generating a SoS-specific configuration. Users of CSL Studio are able to connect to a shared repository to access domain models of associated systems.

Referring to Figure 4, the CSL meta-metamodel corresponds to the Ecore metamodel, the CSL metamodel corresponds to the grammar of the CSL language written in Xtext, and each individual domain model is specified using that CSL syntax.

The concrete syntax of the language was partly shown in the examples in Section 3. In addition to modeling constructs of a standard UML class diagram, the language provides designated keywords and associated semantic to model the constructs described in the sections above. We chose a textual modeling language in contrast to a graphical notation because of pragmatic reasons: language design and implementation is much easier; collaborative work between the modelers is better supported by configuration management systems (e.g., the merging of different versions of a model); Eclipse and Xtext are very robust and rich environments for our CSL Studio implementation. Of course, to augment the CSL modeling language by a graphical UML-like editor is possible and is subject to future work.

4. Application Experiences

We evaluated the approach presented in Section 3 within the industrial environment described in Section 2. The goal of this evaluation was threefold:

- show that the approach performs sufficiently for real-world applications
- check that dependencies between systems, even legacy systems, are well covered
- ensure that knowledge engineers can easily model their domain requirements

The evaluation focused more on qualitative than quantitative aspects and proved that the approach is promising although more work on the translation of reasoning constructs (in the adapters) is to be done so that the integration of legacy tools can be automated further.

4.1 Practical Applicability

We chose a configurator for railway safety systems such as sketched in Section 2. The portfolio of systems to choose from comprises approx. 20 systems (including active versions) represented as Java libraries based on our GCSP configurator S'UPREME. The conjoint model for an interlocking system contains approx. 350 object classes with 850 attributes and 400 bi-directional associations.

Knowledge-bases of this size and complexity can be processed smoothly by CSL Studio, i.e., with response times that do not hinder the average user.

The expressiveness of CSL is adequate: The structural parts could be mapped completely without loss of information. Exemplary reasoning parts (constraints, rules) including several typical cross-system dependencies could be successfully modeled.

We conclude that CSL covers challenges 2.1 to 2.2 for the scenarios where system portfolios are designed from scratch.

4.2 Legacy Tools

An existing tool for the configuration of rail automation products is a collection of 8 independent sub-tools implemented in C++ which share parts of their data via a proprietary export/import interface. The first of those sub-tools comprises 240 object classes with 1.000 attributes and 300 bi-directional associations in total, the others are of similar size.

Within a few hours we wrote an translator (adapter) from the proprietary knowledge-base to CSL notation (only structural parts). Translation takes less than one second for each sub-tool. Therefore we expect integration of legacy tools to be sufficiently supported by our approach. This covers challenge 2.4.

Furthermore, duplicated parts of the model in the different sub-tools could easily be identified and refactored (removing redundancies). This is necessary for putting the instance data into a harmonized model while keeping the reasoning logic and other code in the legacy tools. By that, we can deal with important aspects of challenge 2.3.

4.3 Usability

As a final application test, CSL Studio was deployed to knowledge engineers at a business unit who modeled a new and comparatively small conjoint model with it (50 domain classes with 300 attributes/associations). They decided to increase hierarchical structure and re-usability (such as it is typically done in production systems' engineering) by modeling each attribute and association in its own *injection class*. The corresponding system has approx. 300 classes most of which disappear in the final conjoint model (being injected into the domain classes).

At present, the system portfolio consists of three component systems: (1) categorization of concepts (represented as interfaces), (2) collection of single attributes to be reused (each in a separated injection class) and groups of such attributes to be used together (in separated injection classes, too), (3) a domain model for the new system (i.e., classes which reuse the attributes and groups defined in (2)). This will be the base for extensions by additional domain models for other systems.

The task was executed successfully by one engineer (working part-time for a few weeks) after a short demonstration of the CSL Studio (3 hours) and with less than 5 hours of support by us (via LiveMeeting). Thus we conclude that our system is easy-to-use.

The used target tool platform was their COMOS[5] based data management system. Writing an adapter for modeling information (class structure) and instance data took several days and resulted in a working prototype. It enables to create and change data via the target platform's user interface and to store and retrieve data in its database. At present, they work on completing the modeling of the reasoning parts (rules) and on improvements of the user interface.

5. Related Work

In the area of EAI (enterprise application integration), Hohpe and Woolf [18] present fundamental patterns for integrating heterogeneous and asynchronous systems. More recently, this issue has also been addressed in the area of software and systems engineering. For instance, Moser et al. [27] propose an engineering service bus to integrate arbitrary tools in the engineering life cycle.

Bosch [6] discusses the transition from product lines to software ecosystems. He identifies three types of ecosystems (operating system-centric, application-centric, and end-user programming software ecosystems). We focus on the *configuration* of a platform architecture and integration of the implementation of selected tools,

---

[5] http://www.automation.siemens.com/mcms/plant-engineering-software/en/pages/default.aspx

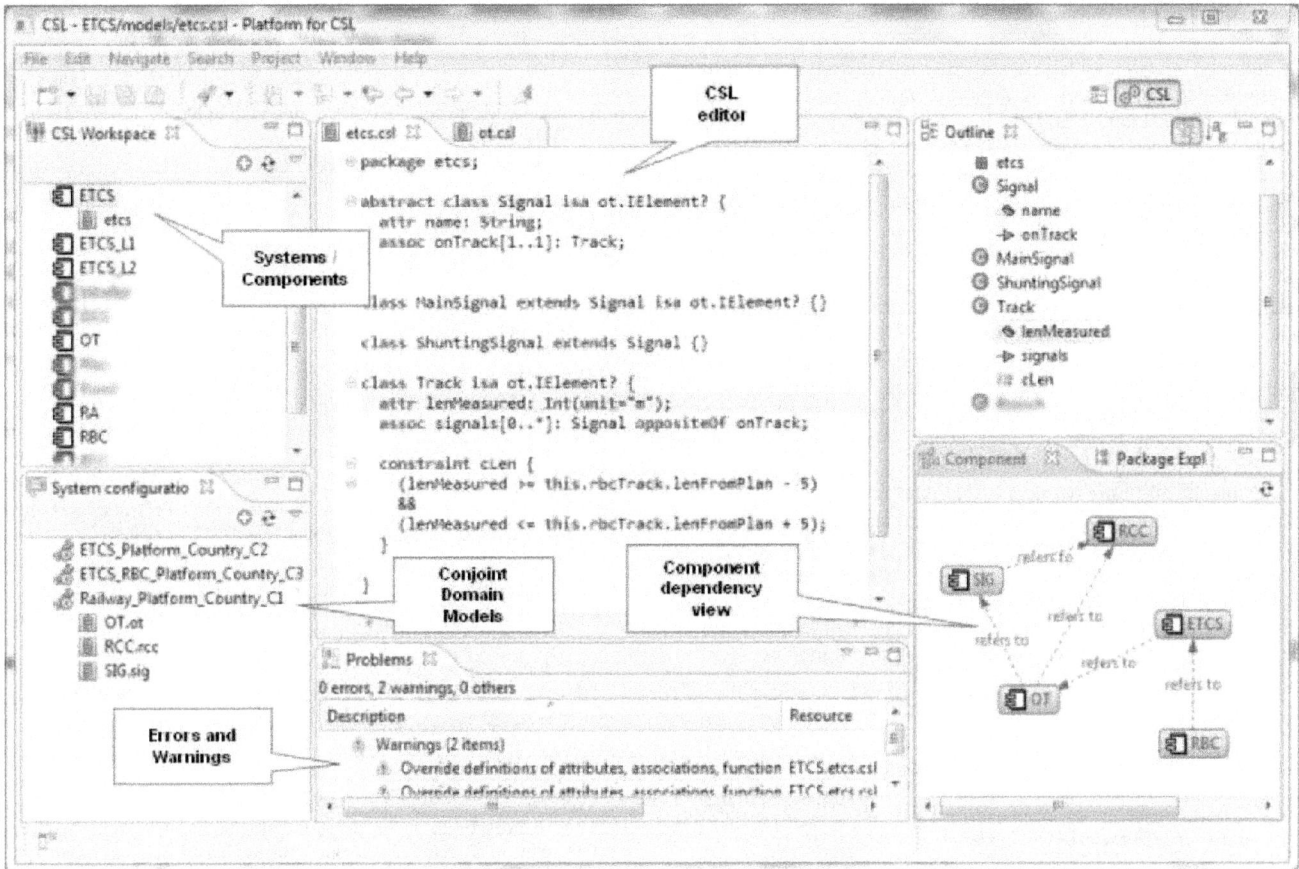

Figure 5. CSL Studio for modeling portfolio components and generating common platforms for selected components.

which relates to application-centric nature of ecosystems. Similar to the "formalization of interoperability" discussed by Bosch, our approach ensures interoperability through the generation of an integrative architecture and the interfaces between system components.

Hierarchical product lines [5] can be applied when there is a broad family with a number of focused product categories. In our approach, the individual tools intended to be reused can be seen as individual product lines. Similarly, Bühne et al. [8] extend an existing meta-model for variability modeling to structure product lines into a hierarchy.

Other related concepts and approaches include *Product Populations* introduced by Van Ommering [32]. Dhungana et al. [10] explore how to structure the modeling space for large product lines on multiple levels of abstraction. Reiser and Weber [28] suggest to model complex product lines with a hierarchy of feature models, which they call *multi-level feature trees*. Czarnecki et al. introduce the concept of superimposed variants in [9], which are used to map feature models to other kinds of models (e.g., UML class and activity diagrams).

Bruneliere et al. [7] have presented a model-based solution to overcome such interoperability issues where the internal schemas (i.e., metamodels) of each tool are used as basis for solving syntactic and semantic differences between the tools. Our approach is similar in the sense, that we generate a common scheme for all involved tools, which is the basis for interoperability. A similar approach is followed by Jossic et al [20], where predefined views on the architecture are woven together to one integrated model using

a weaving model (specifies different kinds of mappings between metamodel elements).

Moser et al. [26] present an approach for integrating heterogeneous engineering domains using tools that were not designed to cooperate seamlessly. The approach relies on data integration based on mappings between local and domain-level engineering concepts. While this approach tackles the integration problem at runtime, we deal with a similar problem at deployment time. Interoperability of models has also been addressed by the ToolBus architecture [3], where all interactions are controlled by a "script" that formalizes all the desired interactions among tools.

Ergin et al. [23] take a different approach to integrating a system of systems which is based on a generic agent-based model for analyzing behavioral dynamics of SoS. Our approach does not use agents, but a constraint engine to take care of the consistency between the behavior of the involved systems.

Dhungana et al. [11] have tackled the problem of integrating multiple product lines which together constitute a multi-product line. The Invar approach presented in this paper is based on a web-service-based composition of models at runtime. The goals of Invar are similar to CSL at runtime. There is no generation of a common model in Invar.

To some extent, concepts of aspect-oriented modeling [1, 22] can be realized by our push and pull injection approaches, thus enabling composition and verification of fragment models into target models.

6. Conclusion and Future Work

In order to ensure coherent and consistent behavior of the SoS, a common vocabulary and a shared data platform are required. Defining such a platform is a painful task in practice, consisting of several manual and tedious steps. We presented a lightweight approach for modeling systems of systems based on object-oriented and constraint-based product configuration technologies. We showed using examples, how proprietary interfaces between independent systems can be avoided through a conjoint domain model generated as required in a particular setting. In addition to the general object-oriented concepts, we presented a unique approach for modeling dependencies across system boundaries through the use of *pull injection* and *push injection* constructs.

Evaluations in an industrial environment showed that it helps engineers to model the required functionality of a distributed systems in a collaborative context. Integration with a COMOS based data management system was successfully implemented in a prototype at a business unit.

Subjects of future work are: (1) The integration of reasoning (rules and constraints) into various target platforms by defining proper semantics, specifying necessary preconditions, writing translators and/or adapters. (2) We will extend the domain model with more detailed specifications for user interfaces. (3) Typically, SoS evolves continuously, so we will investigate structural aspects of model evolution and co-evolution of dependent models.

References

[1] M. Alférez, N. Amálio, S. Ciraci, F. Fleurey, J. Kienzle, J. Klein, M. E. Kramer, S. Mosser, G. Mussbacher, E. E. Roubtsova, and G. Zhang. Aspect-oriented model development at different levels of abstraction. In *ECMFA*, pages 361–376, 2011.

[2] D. S. Batory, J. N. Sarvela, and A. Rauschmayer. Scaling step-wise refinement. In *ICSE*, pages 187–197, 2003.

[3] J. Bergstra and P. Klint. The toolbus coordination architecture. In P. Ciancarini and C. Hankin, editors, *Coordination Languages and Models*, volume 1061 of *Lecture Notes in Computer Science*, pages 75–88. Springer Berlin Heidelberg, 1996. ISBN 978-3-540-61052-6.

[4] P. A. Bernstein and S. Melnik. Model management 2.0: manipulating richer mappings. In *ICMD*, 2007.

[5] J. Bosch. The challenges of broadening the scope of software product families. *Commun. ACM*, 49(12):41–44, 2006.

[6] J. Bosch. From software product lines to software ecosystems. In *SPLC 2009*, pages 111–119, San Francisco, CA, USA, 2009. Software Engineering Institute, CarnegieMellon.

[7] H. Bruneliere, J. Cabot, C. Clasen, F. Jouault, and J. Bézivin. Towards model driven tool interoperability: Bridging eclipse and microsoft modeling tools. In *ECMFA*, pages 32–47, 2010.

[8] S. Bühne and K. Lauenroth. Modelling requirements variability across product lines. In *13th International Conference on Requirements Engineering*, pages 41– 50. IEEE CS, 2005.

[9] K. Czarnecki and M. Antkiewicz. Mapping features to models: A template approach based on superimposed variants. In *GPCE*, pages 422–437, 2005.

[10] D. Dhungana, P. Grünbacher, R. Rabiser, and T. Neumayer. Structuring the modeling space and supporting evolution in software product line engineering. *Journal of Systems and Software*, 83(7):1108–1122, 2010.

[11] D. Dhungana, D. Seichter, G. Botterweck, R. Rabiser, P. Grünbacher, D. Benavides, and J. A. Galindo. Configuration of multi product lines by bridging heterogeneous variability modeling approaches. In *SPLC*, pages 120–129, 2011.

[12] J. Euzenat and P. Shvaiko. *Ontology matching*. Springer-Verlag, Heidelberg (DE), 2007. ISBN 3-540-49611-4.

[13] M. Eysholdt and H. Behrens. Xtext: implement your language faster than the quick and dirty way. In *SPLASH/OOPSLA Companion*, pages 307–309, 2010.

[14] A. Falkner, A. Haselböck, G. Schenner, and H. Schreiner. Modeling and solving technical product configuration problems. *AI EDAM*, 25 (2):115–129, 2011.

[15] A. A. Falkner and A. Haselböck. Challenges of knowledge evolution in practice. *AI Commun.*, 26(1):3–14, 2013.

[16] G. Fleischanderl, G. Friedrich, A. Haselböck, H. Schreiner, and M. Stumptner. Configuring large systems using generative constraint satisfaction. *IEEE Intelligent Systems*, 13(4):59–68, 1998.

[17] T. Gezgin, C. Etzien, S. Henkler, and A. Rettberg. Towards a rigorous modeling formalism for systems of systems. *2012 IEEE 15th International Symposium on Object/Component/Service-Oriented Real-Time Distributed Computing Workshops*, 0:204–211, 2012. .

[18] G. Hohpe and B. Woolf. *Enterprise Integration Patterns: Designing, Building, and Deploying Messaging Solutions*. Addison-Wesley Longman Publishing Co., Inc., Boston, MA, USA, 2003. ISBN 0321200683.

[19] M. Jamshidi. *Systems of Systems Engineering: Principles and Applications*. Taylor & Francis, 2010. ISBN 9781420065893.

[20] A. Jossic, M. Del Fabro, J.-P. Lerat, J. Bezivin, and F. Jouault. Model integration with model weaving: a case study in system architecture. In *Systems Engineering and Modeling, 2007. ICSEM '07. International Conference on*, pages 79–84, 2007. .

[21] F. Jouault, F. Allilaire, J. Bézivin, and I. Kurtev. Atl: A model transformation tool. *Sci. Comput. Program.*, 72(1-2):31–39, 2008.

[22] J. Kienzle, W. Al Abed, and J. Klein. Aspect-oriented multi-view modeling. In *Proceedings of the 8th ACM international conference on Aspect-oriented software development*, AOSD '09, pages 87–98, New York, NY, USA, 2009. ACM. ISBN 978-1-60558-442-3. .

[23] N. Kilicay-Ergin, P. Acheson, J. Colombi, and C. Dagli. Modeling system of systems acquisition. In *System of Systems Engineering (SoSE), 2012 7th International Conference on*, pages 514–518, 2012. .

[24] M. W. Maier. Architecting principles for systems-of-systems. *Systems Engineering*, 1(4):267 – 284, 1999.

[25] K. Mannaro, G. Destefanis, and M. Di Francesco. The enterprise service bus as integration architecture in heterogeneous systems. pages 184–187. WSEAS, 2012. ISBN 978-1-61804-070-1.

[26] T. Moser and S. Biffl. Semantic integration of software and systems engineering environments. *Systems, Man, and Cybernetics, Part C: Applications and Reviews, IEEE Transactions on*, 42(1):38–50, 2012. ISSN 1094-6977. .

[27] T. Moser, F. Waltersdorfer, A. Zoitl, and S. Biffl. Version management and conflict detection across heterogeneous engineering data models. In *Proc. 8th IEEE International Conference on Industrial Informatics (INDIN 2010), Osaka, Japan*, pages 928–935. 2010.

[28] M.-O. Reiser and M. Weber. Managing highly complex product families with multi-level feature trees. In *14th IEEE International Requirements Engineering Conference (RE'06)*, pages 149–158, Minneapolis, MN, USA, 2006. IEEE CS.

[29] F. Rossi, P. van Beek, and T. Walsh, editors. *Handbook of Constraint Programming*. Elsevier, 2006. ISBN 0-444-52726-5.

[30] A. Schürr and H. Dörr. Introduction to the special sosym section on model-based tool integration. *Journal on Software and Systems Modeling (SoSym)*, 4(2), May 2005.

[31] Y. Smaragdakis and D. Batory. Mixin layers: an object-oriented implementation technique for refinements and collaboration-based designs. *ACM Trans. Softw. Eng. Methodol.*, 11(2):215–255, Apr. 2002. ISSN 1049-331X. .

[32] R. C. van Ommering. Software reuse in product populations. *IEEE Trans. Software Eng.*, 31(7):537–550, 2005.

Supporting Large Scale Model Transformation Reuse

Fábio P. Basso   Raquel M. Pillat
Toacy C. Oliveira

Federal University of Rio de Janeiro (UFRJ)
Rio de Janeiro, RJ - Brazil +55 21 2562-8672
{fabiopbasso,rmpillat,toacy}@cos.ufrj.br

Leandro B. Becker

Federal University of Santa Catarina (UFSC)
Postal 476 - 88.040-900 - Florianópolis - SC -
Brazil

lbecker@das.ufsc.br

Abstract

The growth of applications developed with the support of model transformations makes reuse a required practice, specially when applied to transformation assets (e.g. transformation chains, algorithms, and configuration files). In order to promote reuse one must consider the different implementations, communalities, and variants among these assets. In this domain, a couple techniques have been used as solutions to adapt reusable assets for specific needs. However, so far, no work has discussed their combined use in real software projects. In this paper, we present a new tool named WCT, which can be used to adapt transformation assets. Moreover, through lessons learned in industry, we address some reuse techniques devoted to adapt these assets.

Categories and Subject Descriptors   D.3.2 [*Software Engineering*]: Design Tools and Techniques - Computer-aided software engineering (CASE), Object-oriented design methods, Model driven development (MDD).

General Terms   Design, Theory.

Keywords   Model transformation chain, feature model, transformation reuse, product line technique, MDE.

1.   Introduction

Model Driven Engineering (MDE) [19] promotes the software development through the execution of a sequence of Model Transformations (MTs). In real world scenarios, where models can evolve attempting to new technologies, the transformation assets (e.g. MT algorithms, transformation tool configuration files, MT test cases, etc.) must be properly adapted [25]. A web survey conducted in 2011 by Hutchinson et al. [29] included 250 MDE practitioner's responses, where a huge number (67.8%) considered that source-code generation is very important. Paradoxically, in a recent study published in 2013, Petre [37] interviewed 50 industry practitioners who used the Unified Modeling Language (UML) [14] at least once in software projects. The

GPCE'13,   October 27–28, 2013, Indianapolis, IN, USA.
Copyright © 2013 ACM 978-1-4503-2373-4/13/10. . . $15.00.
http://dx.doi.org/10.1145/2517208.2517218

results show that only few practitioners (6%) used it for source-code generation purposes. Hutchinson et al. [29] addressed the difficulty related with the development of MTs as a limiting factor to disseminate the MDE, since practitioners consider that it is difficult to develop, test, and maintain transformations. Moreover, each transformation must be tailored for a particular software project, demanding expertise, time, and money [21]. Therefore, it is necessary to find solutions to easy the development of new transformation assets as well as to reuse existing ones.

Some solutions for transformation reuse divide MTs into several modules, which may be combined in configuration files known as Model Transformation Chain (TC) [49]. Some related works design transformation chains with UML [46] [20], to then generate specific MDE tool configurations. Although these solutions are helpful to manage transformation assets - independently from the adopted MDE tool - they require the design of many transformation chains in order to support alternative transformation sequences. Thus, this solution requires too much effort to design many possible transformation chains [48].

In order to reduce this effort, Aranega et al. [2] claim that TCs should support variability in transformations. Variability management is a requirement to support reuse even in different contexts [24, 39]. Accordingly, other approaches support transformation asset variability in two different scopes: a) **Runtime** variant points are checked at runtime to execute variant transformation sequences [5, 48]; b) **Generative approach** for transformation chains that are adapted to execute certain sequences [2, 46]. Our experiences show that both scopes are important and complementary.

Our main contribution in this paper is reporting a multi-year industrial effort in adapting large scale model transformation assets through the combined use of these techniques. This requires the design, composition, execution, and adaptation of transformation assets. Therefore, this paper reports experiences on using a new tool named WCT that integrates these techniques in a single toolkit. WCT has been used to adapt model transformation assets, whose technologies used to implement information systems varies [4, 6, 7].

The rest of the paper is organized as follows. Section 2 presents the related works. Section 3 introduces reuse techniques through exemplifications of variant model transformation assets designed with WCT. Results and experiences are discussed in Section 4 and Section 5 presents the conclusions. Finally, future works are pointed in Section 6.

2. Related Work

WCT is a toolkit used to adapt transformation assets both at runtime and generative approach. Due to the need of applying Product Line Architecture (PLA) reuse techniques [12], it allows associating a Feature Model (FM) [32] instance with MTs in a domain model. This domain model is then adapted to a specific MT chain or is used to dynamically re-configure the chain at runtime. In this regard, it is important to mention that the combination of FM and transformations was firstly suggested by Tekinerdoğan et al. [42], which inspired our first work in [5]. Since then, we have been applying these concepts to reuse model transformation assets through a set of reuse tools embedded into WCT.

Some reuse approaches support transformation orchestration through graphical extensions from OMG's UML [14], such as Abstract Platforms [1], MARTES UML Profile [47] and FOMDA [5]. They can all be used to generate specific transformation chains. Almeida et al. [1] proposed a solution to define MT compositions with consecutive model-to-model transformations. They defined transformation layers as abstract platforms represented with extensions of MOF packages [36]. Nevertheless, it is not possible to have notions about the transformation sequence, which makes their solution inappropriate to design TCs. In another work, van Boas [45] proposed the design of a TC using workflows to model transformation processes with UML activity diagram, but lacked more formalism used to generate real TCs as Almeida suggested. The Almeida's, Tekinerdogan's and Boas's proposals are complementary for TCs. However, none of them supports rules to assist the generation of TCs as we have done in this paper. Our contribution is complementary to such works, proposing to organize transformations in a domain ruled by feature's relationships from a platform domain model.

Aiming to generate TCs used by MDE tools, some proposals allow designing transformation compositions in high-level of abstraction to then generate specific TCs. Accordingly, Vanhooff et al. [47] proposed a TC modeling language using target platforms as part of TC designs and in Vanhooff et al. [46] a framework to execute heterogeneous transformations. Target platform and transformations are composed using UML activity diagrams, in a similar solution as we did in Basso et al. [5], using a UML Profile. These proposals were complemented by Wagelaar [49] that proposed a composition o black-box model transformations and by Etien et al. [20, 21] that suggested the use of heterogenous model transformations developed with different metamodels. Although an interesting work, Etien's, Vanhooff's and Wagelaar's did not support transformation chain executions considering target platform variants, meaning that chains must be manually changed when a different set of transformations is necessary.

Regarding the specification of target platform variability, there exist other tools such as SPLOT [35], FeatureIDE [44], Odyssey [22] and pure::variants [13]. These and other tools listed in Benavides et al. [12] and Berger et al. [13] facilitate the management of commonalities and variabilities in PLA-based applications. Therefore, PLA-based reuse techniques presented in this paper are also supported by other tools and proposals. However, similarities remains here, since these PLA-based proposals surveyed in [12, 13] cannot be compared with the current proposal. This is because our core assets are very different, what implies in the use of different techniques. In true, they are not even related works, as discussed and justified in Section 3.8. Thus, to tailor model transformation assets one must consider more specific solutions as follows.

In [5, 6] we presented the first methodology (*Features-Oriented Model-Driven Architecture*) and a tool support to add variants in model transformation processes/chains, allowing adaptations in runtime and generative approach. Völter and Groher [48] proposed a strictly runtime-based approach, where variants are programmed inside transformation chain files (e.g., an XML file that chain transformations for a specific MDE tool). In other words, a TC is not generated through a model specification, but it is manually changed in code to support variants. Accordingly, authors pointed to some important shortcomings that must be considered to apply the suggested runtime-based technique: 1) it requires a specific MDE execution engine; 2) the tracing of variant points may be difficult, since one must search for programmed instructions inside the chain's code when the feature of a FM changes. However, we consider the existence of two types of runtime-based dynamic transformation chains: one is by interpreting a model specification of a transformation chain, as we exemplified in [6], and the other one is by programming variants directly into TC code, as we exemplified in [5]. The first one not present the traceability problem, but still requires a specific MDE execution tool.

Some recent proposals have applied similar reuse techniques through generative approaches. Aranega et al. [2] uses FM to fragment some transformation assets (e.g: white-box model transformations, fragmented algorithms or "transformation rules", diverse configuration files, and so on) using aforementioned PLA tools. However, despite techniques for PLA are applicable in diverse asset types, adaptations of model transformation assets must also consider valid compositions among transformations. While in [2, 20, 21] authors seems to move in this direction, so far, only we considered the use of FM and transformation chains that allow to validate the bindings with transformation's input and output (IO) in design time. Thus, in our proposal these compositions are checked during the design of a transformation chain model, while in [2] they are checked only after the generation of a concrete model transformation chain. In comparison to the work from Aranega et al. [2], our WCT tool saves time in detecting problems that can occur while we are adapting these assets.

Considering consistency in transformation composition, Guy et al. [27] and Yie et al. [52] suggest that valid compositions must be ensured with parameter types. For example, IO parameters are checked during the design of a model transformation chain, validating rules such as metamodel data types (e.g., EMF-based metamodels compatibility), transformation languages (e.g., ATL and QVT transformations), etc. Moreover, it is important to consider that model transformation assets can evolve. In this regard, Lopez-Herrejon et al. [34] presented a proposal to automatic control the co-evolution of models, metamodels, and transformations. Although being important techniques related to model transformation assets tailoring, nor heterogeneity of model transformation composition nor co-evolution is used in this paper, figuring as a shortcoming discussed in Section 4.3.

The tailoring of transformation assets also requires a strong procedure to ensure that what was adapted leads to a working MDE-based tool. This way, it is necessary to ensure that a selected FM is consistent. This is usually made through some techniques that can be based on constraint solvers [50] or with feature selection rules, as we did in [38]. After the adaptation, test cases are critical to ensure a quick verification of wrong results. Accordingly, Küster et al. [33] suggested to develop model transformation chain with incremental steps, using automated tests. Fleurey et al. [23] presented strategies that adapt traditional test to better suit model transformations. However, such strategies are applicable to test meta-models, not to test TCs. Hervieu et al. [28] executed a similar study in industry towards execution environment variability, proposing test cases to test transformation chains. However they do not have test case support for variants. All related works contributes in many research field required to support transformation chain in some of challenges addressed by Baudry et al. [11]. As a complement, we present an extended JUnit Java API used to test model transformations considering variants.

Finally, a set of tool's features are important to apply these type of adaptations. So far, no work has tackled a combined use of the aforementioned techniques in real software projects. Moreover, only recently Guana [26] issued the need of some tasks to support maintenance in model transformation compositions. In this sense, this work is new, since we reported real experiences where a combined use of reuse techniques were applied. Accordingly, it was considered following main characteristics used to develop and to maintain model transformation assets: 1) feature modeling and transformation assets mappings, with traceability links established in transformation chain designs; 2) transformation compositions and; 3) test case support. Therefore, this work summarizes these techniques through the exemplification of WCT, relating proposals that perform a similar solution or that provide theoretical base.

3. Reuse Techniques Assisted by WCT

In this section we discuss about reuse techniques used in WCT to support tailoring of model transformation assets. It is important to mention that any technique presented in Section 3.1 to 3.6 can be started in arbitrary order considering the availability of their inputs. Accordingly, we are assuming that all the resources used by model transformation tools are model transformation assets such as: complete algorithms, fragmented algorithms, black-box Java programs [19], QVT graph-based transformations [30], white-box templates programmed with Velocity [16] or ATL [31]), model transformation chains [47], MDE tool configuration files, and so on. Finally, it is important to notice that these techniques only applies in cases where a big set of assets must be reused.

3.1 Platform Domain Analysis

Along some experiences in developing and adapting MTs to specific target architectures, we have found that variability is important to adapt transformation assets for specific needs [5]. Variability allows one to take essential decisions, e.g.: if characteristics like persistency and file are required in a software project, then one must execute a model transformer to generate file structure, otherwise executes the MT to generate database structure. Moreover, identifying a family of software project architectures is important to adapt these assets [47]. This is detailed by techniques used to analyze technical requirements as follows.

Input: New requirements (e.g., implementation technologies, patterns "design, architectural and codification", etc.) and existing model transformation assets.

Output: Platform Domain Model (PDM) and a data dictionary describing features.

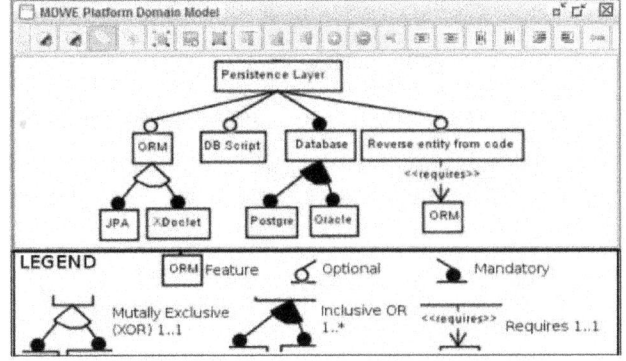

Figure 1. A Screenshot for a Platform Domain Model for a "Persistency Layer": Feature's relationships allow configuring different implementations for model transformations.

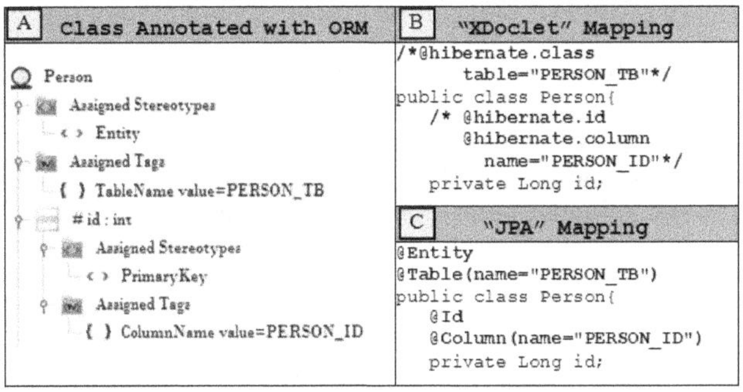

Figure 2. Source-code variants: A comparison between JPA and XDoclet implementations for tags of ORM.

Main References: Basso et al. [5], Garcia-Alonso et al. [25], Cirilo et al. [15] and Tekinerdoğan et al. [42].

The WCT toolkit merges a platform domain specification with the transformation chain specification to promote reuse. This allows the representation of a domain-oriented transformation processes [5]. This way, it uses a formalism that has been used by software engineers to define domain concepts, the so-called Feature Model (FM) [18, 42]. The FM is composed by features (representing the requirements: functional, architectural, technological, mixed, etc.) from a particular technology domain and uses relationships to configure different platform/software architectures [1]. Such possibilities allow the definition of technology variants and may be used to automate mappings between target platforms, system model input, and model transformations assets in MDE.

In this reuse technique, it is necessary to perform the domain analysis [32], which begins with the design of a Platform Domain Model (PDM) [51]. This model is also referred as abstract platform model in following works [1, 46]. Figure 1 illustrates features used to develop a persistency layer for information systems, considering those two technologies used to apply Object-Relational Mapping (ORM), as illustrated in Figure 2, in Java source-code. The model in such figure is an entity class named "Person" that owns annotations available in UML Profile (e.g.: the FrameWeb Profile [41]), allowing model-to-code transformations to generate two different implementations as illustrated in Figure 2 (B) and (C).

The platform domain model shown in Figure 1 allows one to configure some features that can be used in software projects to specify the persistence layer. The relationship between the features defines that a persistency layer must contain at least a "Database" feature. In software projects that we have produced, the Database Management System (DBMS) "Postgre" was used in some occasions and "Oracle" in other ones. However, given that more than one database can be used in the same application, we designed such relationship as an inclusive OR. Thus, both databases can be used in the same software project.

The feature "DB script" is optional, meaning that in some projects we generated the database structure with SQL scripts and in other ones we let Hibernate (the Java framework used to manage the persistence layer) to generate the structure. The ORM feature is optional to develop the persistency layer since in legacy software projects no framework for persistence layer were used. However, when object-relational mapping is present in a software project it certainly was implemented with JPA or XDoclet.

3.2 Transformation Chain Design

Model transformation chains are supported by tools such as openArchitectureware, Epsilon and AM3 (AtlanMod MegaModel Management). Transformation chain modeling is a common reuse technique where specification becomes independent from the execution tools. In this sense, the second technique is intended to design model transformation chains.

Input: Model transformation assets.

Output: Transformation Chain Domain Model (TCDM) with low-level information about model transformations associated with pre-condition rules.

Main References: Almeida et al. [1], Basso et al. [5], van Boas [45], Etien et al. [20] and Vanhooff et al. [47].

After specifying the PDM, the next step is to organize model transformations inside a Transformation Chain Domain Model (TCDM). As the name suggest, this model must specify not a single sequence of transformations, but a family of transformations that can compose model transformation chains used by more than one software project. Almeida et al. [1] and Vanhooff et al. [47] have a similar proposal to design model transformation chains, but without the link for features available in the PDM. Thus, it is necessary to constrain each transformation to a set of features, as illustrated in Figure 3, using dependency relationships stereotyped with «requires», or stereotyped with «excludes» that demands the deselection of the linked feature.

The above constraints exemplify pre-condition rules own by MTs, in which dependencies always target a feature designed in PDM. This relationship determines (in runtime and generative approach) when a MT must be used in a transformation chain derived from the TCDM. In this sense, the transformation number 2 is used only if the "DB Script" feature is selected (note, in Figure 1, that it has been specified as an optional feature). This means that if "DB Script" is not selected in PDM, then the transformation chain does not include transformation 2.

Each MT assumes at least a name, a return type (default output parameter) and a default input parameter. Besides, transformations are sequenced in TCDM through numbered back circles. Thus, Figure 3 illustrates the following sequence:

(T1 - "Apply ORM"). It is a model-to-model (M2M) transformation programmed in Java; it is classified as a Platform Independent Model (PIM) view and provides a dialog

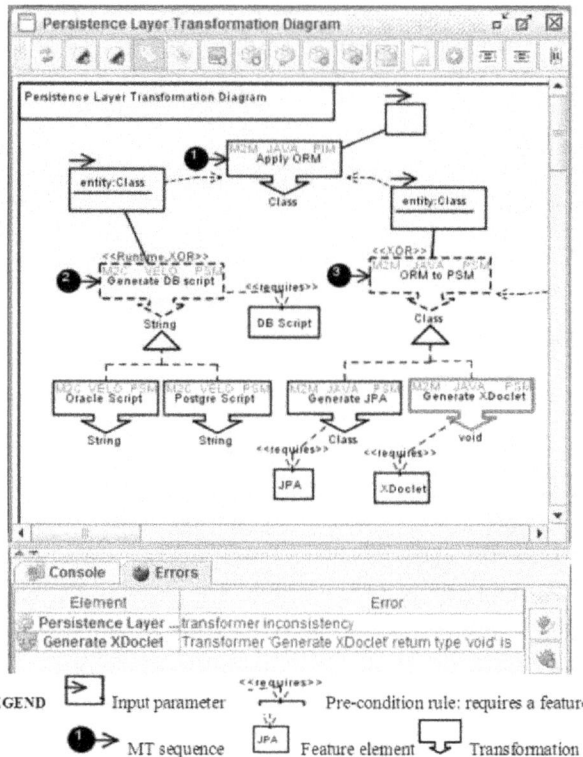

Figure 3. A TCDM screenshot. Through dependency links between transformations and features it is possible to handle variant executions in runtime as well as to adapt TCs by generating MDE tool configuration files.

to apply ORM annotations into Class elements, generating the model shown in Figure 2 (A).

(T2 - "Generate DB script"). It is an abstraction: a doted model transformation that allows generating scripts to create database structures for a specific DBMS, discussed in Section 3.3.

(T3 - "ORM to PSM"). It is also an abstraction whose transformations generate source-code embedded in Java classes known as entities. Therefore, entities own those ORM annotations exemplified in Figure 2 (B) and (C).

The second and third MTs are abstract specifications (scattered elements), which the concept was first introduced by Almeida et al. [1]. This means that they propagate a transformation for their concrete children (not dotted ones). Thus, according to the example shown in Figure 3, if "JPA" is selected then "Generate JPA" is used in the third order of execution, otherwise, if "XDoclet" is selected, then "Generate XDoclet" is used in the position number 3. The same rule is valid for "Generate DB script". However, the decision between "Oracle Script" or "Postgre Script" is tacked at runtime and not in generative approach (note the stereotype «Runtime»). Therefore, in the case of runtime decisions, the solution is strictly applied when using WCT based transformation chains and must be avoided if the intent is to tailor the TCDM for other TC tool formats.

Finally, mutual exclusion between transformations must be handled to ensure that only transformations that attempt to the selected features in a PDM are used in a resultant model transformation chain. This way, the relation between the features and transformations in a TCDM ensures the

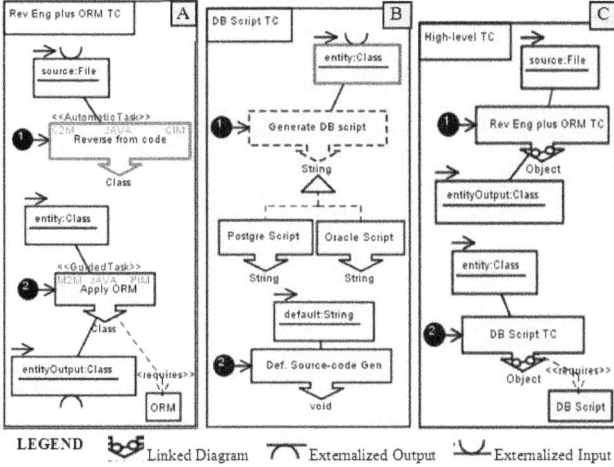

Figure 4. Screenshots from a high-level chain (in C) that is composed by the chains shown in A and B.

use of only desired execution sequences when a transformation chain is generated in Section 3.6. This is represented in a TCDM by annotating abstractions with «XOR», as illustrates those model transformers shown in Figure 3.

3.3 Transformation Composition

Through high-level specifications such as a transformation process [5] it is possible to increase the abstraction level of transformations, using it as composed software components. A transformation process is slight different from a regular transformation chain since this one execute MTs uninterruptedly [47], while with a transformation process one can execute a transformation, stop, close the MDE tool, and then back to the process to execute another MT. This way, requirements to compose transformations are depicted as follow.

Input: Model transformation assets, PDM, TCDM and, optionally, stakeholders, wizards and tool chain procedures [9].

Output: TCDM with high-level composition and composition rules (e.g., parameter matching [52] and semantic rules for chaining reuse tasks [9]).

Main References: Basso et al. [5], Basso et al. [6] (in Portuguese), Etien et al. [20], Guy et al. [27], Vanhooff et al. [46], Wagelaar [49] and Yie et al. [52].

Figure 4 exemplify two chains (A) and (B) that are included into a high-level chain (C). The first chain owns a transformation for reverse engineering: from source-code to a UML class element. Note to the "source:File" parameter: it contains an arc, representing an external parameter for this chain. This means that it is visible when the "Rev Eng plus ORM TC" is included as a high-level chain, shown in Figure 4 (C). The same is valid for the output parameter "entityOutput:Class" in Figure 4 (A) that is related with first transformer in Figure 4 (C). Also note in this chain that "DB script TC" owns a single parameter: this is because the transformation chain, shown in Figure 4 (B), externalizes only "entity" as an input (in highlight).

Moreover, Figure 4 (A) illustrates a transformation process while Figure 4(B) illustrates a regular transformation chain. Notice that "Reverse from code" is executed automatically «AutomaticTask», while "Apply ORM" is a guided procedure «GuidedTask». This one illustrates a situation

where the software engineer will specify ORM annotations shown in Figure 2 with the help of a wizard, taking the time he/she need.

In this sense, in [4] we reported experiences in using wizards and in [9] we exemplified a similar case where reverse engineering tasks are performed to allow the execution of assisted ones. In [6] we exemplify the use of a transformation tasks to execute model-to-model and model-to-code transformations to develop a web information system. In [8] we discuss procedures to transform annotated Graphic User Interface (GUI) for a UML-based model according to Model-View-Controller [41] application layers, that are refined and then used to generate a web information system source-code. Recently, in [9], we issued semantic rules specified with UML tagged values over Input and Output (IO) transformation parameters, that are useful to constraint a composition among different model transformation engines. Moreover, we also presented a metamodel and shortcomings to chain heterogeneous reuse tools.

3.4 Transformation Asset Fragmentation

While previous technique focused in compose model transformations, this technique allow split model transformation assets in small parts, also refereed as factorization [34]. These techniques are based on product line concepts, also referred in literature as Software Product Lines (SPL) [12]. In this sense, important requirements to split transformation assets are discussed along this section.

Input: Model transformation assets, PDM, TCDM, adaptation type. Transformation split must consider the adaptation type: 1) in Runtime [48] depends from an execution engine or; 2) Generative approach [2] that is independent from an execution engine.

Output: Model transformation assets are split in smaller units.

Main References: Different perspectives regarding model transformation assets factorization are found in Aranega et al. [2], Basso et al. [5] and Völter and Groher [48].

The TCDM can also be used in the context of PLA proposals, splitting and merging parts of white box transformers (e.g., ATL transformation rules) [49]. The main references listed in this section present alternatives for tools to apply the same concepts. Considering a WCT-based exemplification, the transformer T1 = "Generate DB script" needs to generate SQL scripts to create a database structure in some DBMS (Oracle and Postgres), where examples are shown in Figure 5 (A).

The source-code shown in Figure 5 (B) illustrates the transformation content, written using the Velocity template, associated to T1. In line 7, the algorithm put character (50) as data type for a column named with the return of a Velocity attribute in line 5. This code fragment is specific to generate a script file used to create table structures for Postgres DBMS.

Figure 6 shows a new TCDM element that is used to split and merge transformation fragments: a fragmentation, also called as variants [22], variant points [12] or hotspots [35], is represented by the element stereotyped with «SpecializationPoint». This element is used to cut a white box text fragment and to handle these parts in specialized units. These units implement a specialization point such as "Oracle Script", which merges the value "varchar2" with the content of "Generate DB script". As exemplified before, each MT has

Scripts to Create a Table PERSON_TB		A
ORACLE	Postgresql	

```
CREATE TABLE PERSON_TB(          CREATE TABLE PERSON_TB(
 PERSON_ID numeric(10) not null,   PERSON_ID integer not null,
 PERSON_NAME varchar2(50) not null, PERSON_NAME character(50) not null,
 PERSON_PK PRIMARY KEY (PERSON_ID)  PERSON_PK PRIMARY KEY (PERSON_ID)
);                               );
```

```
1  ##Velocity MT to generate DB Schema Supporting POSTGRESQL  B
2  #if($entity.containsStereotype("Entity"))
3    CREATE TABLE $entity.getName() {
4    #foreach($att in $entity.getAllProperties())
5    $att.getName()
6    if($att.getType().getName().equalsIgnoreCase("string"))
7        character(50)
8    #end
```

Figure 5. White-box transformer named "Generate DB Script" to generate a database schema.

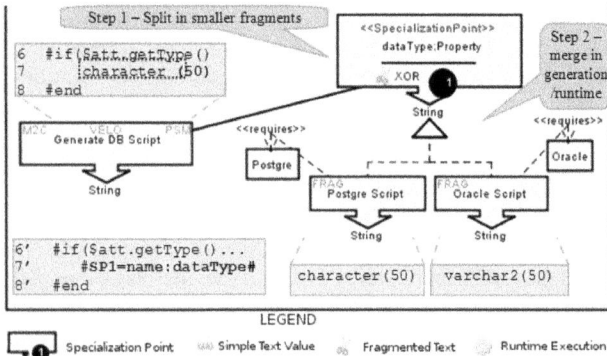

Figure 6. Fragmentation of transformations. The line 7 is replaced by a tag that is further replaced by the transformation fragment owned by "Postgre Script" OR "Oracle Script".

its own pre-condition rules in TCDM and in PDM, ensuring that the value in line 7 is: character (50) or varchar2 (50).

3.5 Development and Test Support

The development of MT is well discussed in literature [31, 51]. However, due to the necessity in combining the use of PLA and TC, a problem arises: tests must assert that adapted assets returns the correct results. This way, this section explains how to test MTs and transformation chains.

Input: Requirements for transformations and, if available, the PDM and TCDM.

Output: Model transformation rules and Test Cases.

Main References: Küster et al. [33] provide good practices for test-driven development of MT, while Cuadrado et al. [17], Jouault et al. [31] and Willink [51] provide information about MT development. Fleurey et al. [23], Hervieu et al. [28] and Baudry et al. [11] provide information about test cases applied in MTCs.

For instance, we use an approach similar to Küster et al. in [33], where MTs are developed using unit and integration tests. Accordingly, an adapted TC can be tested with the program shown in Figure 7. It is a JUnit test case derived to support the test of MT assets. Line 3 shows a Java annotation (component of WCT API) used to handle common transformation tasks, such as to open a TC, apply M2M and M2C transformation, open and save a UML model and so on. The task in Line 3 informs the test case to open a file "config/transf_chain.fomda", the TCDM, before executing the operation in line 11. This file has exemplified model transformations, such as "Generate JPA". Line 4 exemplifies an annotation used to constrain the use of this test case for

```
1  @FomdaTask{
2    tasks = {
3      @IOTask( inputFilePath = "config/transf_chain.fomda",
         kind=IOKind.INPUT, fileKind = WctFileHandlerKind.FOMDA )
4      ,@AssertFeatures(//condition to execute in a test suite
           //a rule can be IS_SELECTED, IS_NOT_SELECTED, IS_XOR,
           //IS_OR, IS_OPTIONAL, IS_MANDATORY, IS_DEPENDENCY
           rule=AssertFeatureKind.IS_SELECTED,
5         features={ @FeatureReference(featureName="ORM")})
     })
6  public class ObjectRelMappingTestCase extends FomdaTestCase {
7  /*Injects a selected transformer between those shown in Fig. 5*/
8    @InjectTransformerConfig(name = "ORM to PSM")
9    private TransformationExecutor executor;
10   @Test()//this is the unique JUnit annotation
11   public void testTransformer() throws Exception {
12     assertTrue(executor.getName().equals("Generate JPA"));
13     assertTrue(getFomdaModel().isSelectedFeature("JPA"));
14   /*Takes the input model (Figure 1 A) for transformations*/
15     Model m = getInputModel(0);
16     Class entity = m.getElementByName(Class.class,"Person");
17   /*Set the entity object into the input named entityParam*/
18     executor.getParameter("entity").setValue(entity);
19   /*Executes the model transformer*/
20     Object value = executor.execute();
21     assertTrue(value != null && ((String)value)
                                   .indexOf("@Entity") > 0);
```

Figure 7. Screenshot of a test case: 1) the test verifies if a given feature is selected (line 13); 2) then it sets the "entity" parameter in a model transformer (18); 3) and, in line 21, the test asserts that a model transformation returned the value required by the mapping shown in Figure 2 (C).

a specific selection of features in PDM. This means that in a test suite composed by many test cases, this test case is executed only if the "ORM" feature is selected in Figure 1. These details are not supported by the default JUnit framework version 4. Thus, they are important to reduce time in adapting test suites to execute tests for every time an adaptation of MT assets is necessary.

3.6 Adapting the Assets

Other reuse techniques are used in last stages of adaptations. Following we discuss about these techniques.

Input: Model transformation assets, data dictionary, PDM and TCDM.

Output: A configured MDE-based transformation tool.

Main References: Kang et al. [32] provide information about application engineering reuse technique, while in Basso et al. [5] we discuss the application of this technique in tailoring transformation processes. Related works (Aranega et al. [2] and Lopez-Herrejon et al. [34]).

After defining a PDM and a TCDM, one can configure the target platform (also referred in the literature as concrete platform) and tailor transformation assets to the configuration necessary for a given software project. The target platform definition is known as FM selection, or as instantiation process, term coming from the FORM approach [32]. The instantiation is a procedure guided by the WCT, in which it will select automatically some features considering their relationships, such as dependencies. A wizard automates this process by offering facilities to select features, considering FM's relationships, as discussed in [38].

In this moment, it is necessary to ensure that only valid selections from a PDM are acquired Thüm et al. [43]. In this this regard, due the number of a features and relations, scalability issues may be a problem. White et al. [50] proposed FAMA, a framework composed by constraint solvers to ensure the consistency in features selection and does not faces scalability problems for a model composed by up to 5000 features [50]. Alternatively, as reported in [38], we obtained good results in using a Business Rule Management System

(BRMS) to ensure consistency in features selection process using JBoss Drools [3]. Drools has been used in large scale processing software systems [3] and can be used to define features selection rules to ensure that selected features are consistent with the FM relationship syntax.

Moreover, while techniques are restrict to apply unit test for model transformations [33], other integration test cases must ensure that the adapted transformation chain contains key transformations (see line 8 in Figure 7 that inject a specific transformation in line 9). For example, the test case shown in Figure 7 searches into the adapted TC a transformation named "ORM to PSM": the abstraction shown in Figure 3 as the sequence 3. Thus, it is necessary to discover which of transformations are embedded inside a generated TC: "Generate JPA" or "Generate XDoclet". Through the suggested Java annotations, this can be made with automated tests. This subject requires in-depth discussion.

3.7 Asset management

Finally, model transformation assets, being also software assets, must be managed [24]. In this sense, in Basso et al. [10] we present a work in progress considering an asset repository to manage these assets. Moreover, through assisted reuse instructions designed as models with an extension for the Reusable Asset Specification (RAS) metamodel in [9], we are giving support to the execution of these techniques. These models are further transformed to task execution languages, that actively guide the software engineers towards the execution of tailoring tasks.

3.8 Discussions and Applicability Constraints

Our proposal can not be used to manage variants of a particular software application domain, as exemplified in many PLA-based proposals survey by Benavides et al. [12], Berger et al. [13]. For example, in [22, 32, 35, 39, 44] was applied variability analysis considering particular application domains. In a first moment, because they use PLA reuse techniques, approaches seems similar. However, the goals of our proposal and these software product line approaches are very different. While they consider variabilities for a single application domain, we consider variabilities of transformation assets used in any application domain. This imply in the use of different techniques and procedures.

In fact, proposals surveyed in [12, 13] are not much related, the reason why related works attempts to model transformation tailoring only. This is because approaches have different purposes: while the first one focuses in reuse a family of existing application assets of a particular domain (e.g. web shop or e-learning), the second one focuses in reuse "MDE tool's assets", independently from application domains. This is the same for a model transformation applicability: one develop it to be used to generate source-code independently if the target domain is a web shop or e-learning application, because the transformation rules are generic (considering they are applied in models designed with the same metamodel, such as UML models). Thus, an important question is what exactly change among model transformations to apply the suggested reuse techniques?

The answer is: target implementation can change across different software projects. A web shop can use a different framework for the controller layer than the e-learning uses, as well as e-learning applications can use different frameworks while using the same set of APIs in the View layer. It is regarding these type of features that variability arises. Accordingly, a PDM designed to specify variabilities in model transformation assets cannot contains features that are particular for web shop or for e-learning domains. The features designed in PDM must be general for both domains, because the adaptation procedure will generate configured transformation assets that can be used further to generate source-code for both applications. Therefore, this is the reason why PDM contains features related to implementation details.

For more discussions regarding these differences, see Tekinerdoğan et al. [42], Basso et al. [5], Völter and Groher [48], Aranega et al. [2] and Garcia-Alonso et al. [25].

4. Experience Report

The WCT toolkit has been improved since 2006 at Adapit, a small Brazilian company, to create MDE applications with the Java programming language. Along this time, three complete industry projects can be highlighted, where "SP^i is a software project for i in 1,2,3": (1) SP^1 - It is a web/desktop application for online auction with support to enterprise resource planning functionalities (system with 656 classes and 190 dynamic web pages), developed by the company's team; (2) SP^2 - It is a web and desktop application used internally to manage trainee (system with 789 classes and 149 dynamic web pages); (3) SP^3 - It is a web application to manage financial support for innovation projects (system with 139 java classes and 56 dynamic web pages). The latter application has been developed by a partner company with the supervision of the Adapit's team. Some measures of such application regarding software productivity are reported in [6]. It is important to notice that the developed applications have no similarities in their functionalities. Therefore, similarities and differences designed in a PDM refers to target implementation technologies, as discussed in Section 3.8.

In all these projects, transformations have been successfully used in order to generate models and code to produce multi-layered web information systems that varies in implementation technologies. Examples of application layers are: graphic user interface layer (desktop and web), data access layer, entity layer, integration or remote layer, xml configuration files, text files, Java classes, database scripts, models, etc. Garcia-Alonso et al. [25] have designed a PDM composed by a similar set of layers. Their PDM is very similar to the primary versions of our model that we have presented in [6, 7]. Besides, information about Java technologies that we have been using to produce software applications is available in [40]. These papers can be accessed to understand technical details about transformation asset variants used to generate source-code, as detailed in the next section.

4.1 Changes in Target Platforms

Our PDM defines that each software project contains the following layers: Model Layer (a conceptual model also known as entity classes); Data Access Layer (DAO classes where business logic accesses databases to retrieve and store objects); a Database Layer, a View Layer to display User Interfaces (UIs); a Controller Layer to handle user actions and, optionally; a Remote Layer, needed when the software project requires integrated applications (e.g.: UIs displayed for Desktop, Mobile and Web platforms that use business logic that run in a web server).

It is important to mention that each developed project uses a different target platform. First and second applications have had the following configuration of technologies: Hibernate, JPA (XDoclet for the first one), Dojotoolkit (the second one was migrated to jQuery), among many other technologies in support for each application layer. Dojo-toolkit and JQuery are technologies to deal with Ajax actions, they are mutually exclusive web frameworks used to develop web user interfaces for the View application layer.

In this sense, the following technologies are a part of what have been changed across projects and required modification in TCDM: a) In our first experiences, XDoclet comments that apply Hibernate mappings (ORM) were used in the model layer while in subsequent projects it was used JPA; b) The first two projects included Dojotoolkit API as the web technology used to write rich user interfaces while the last project included jQuery.

4.2 Lessons Learned

We learned that a UML Profile based solution is not de quickest alternative to design TCs, since one must specify a lot of details that are difficult when using tags and stereotypes. We have experienced UML Profiles on our first works, in the development of SP[1] as reported in [6], and have learned that it is difficult to apply bindings between model transformations and selection rules that will adapt them into a generated transformation chain. Since 2008, we have opted for an approach based on a domain specific modeling tool, presented in this paper. WCT provides facilities to design TCs and to validate bindings between transformation assets (e.g. FM, MTs, cutting rules, and other artifacts during design phase) in comparison to our previous tool prototype in [5]. However, a considerable time have been used to develop the specific diagrams (PDM and TCDM) and also to fix bugs. Therefore, a DSM is interesting to speed-up the PDM and TCDM modeling, but it is more expensive to produce than a UML Profile.

The integrated set of reuse techniques in a single toolkit allowed us to perform adaptations in an efficient way. This is supported by comparing our first experiences started in [6] with more recent ones [4, 7, 8]. In first experiences we generated transformation chains, modeled with FOMDA UML Profile [5] and mapped for FOMDA toolkit (the first prototype version [5]). This is a tiring and error-prone procedure, because tags and stereotypes can be wrongly specified in a TCDM, requiring to change it to then repeat the generation. In recent experiences, most of tags and stereotypes are replaced by specific metamodel elements. Also, dynamic runtime re-configuration of model transformation chains, exemplified in Figure 7 in line 8 and Figure 3, simplified the adaptation process. Moreover, the integrated set of tools and reuse techniques allowed to apply some validations (transformation parameter matching, unit test cases and integration test cases) more quickly. Therefore, these experiences showed us that reusable model transformation assets can be quickly constructed.

Moreover, we have experienced that changes in existing transformations must be carefully conducted. Accordingly, changes require a strong set of tests to ensure that transformations still work. This is the reason why we improved our first methodology on the FOMDA approach [5], since tests play an important role in adapting transformation assets. The use of test cases integrated in the same toolkit also helped to quickly ensure the consistency in runtime execution. Thus, through a customized JUnit engine for tests, it is ensured that transformations assets work.

Finally, we found that runtime-based approach is important, because it is quickest to apply than a generation time is. However, in order to avoid the tracing problem between features and transformation chain variants, in [6] we learned

that the best option is to interpret a transformation chain domain model stead of program variants in TC files as exemplified in [5]. Accordingly, most of our transformation compositions are at runtime because this simplifies the process to deliver working transformation assets, since runtime adaptations are quicker than to generate a model transformation chain. Thus, we prefer the use of runtime compositions.

4.3 Limitations and Open Questions

Section 3.4 discussed about important generation-time reuse techniques used adapt transformation assets, allowing to fragment model transformations through PLA concepts. Although this approach is interesting, it complicates a little bit the adaptation process, since it requires more tests to ensure that chains and transformations fragments were correctly generated. Current proposals for model transformation asset tailoring, including this one, considered model transformations that run in a single MDE tool. In this sense, an open question is how to ensure that the generated product (model transformations and chains) are valid across different model transformation engines? This question is relevant because if the intent is to tailor model transformation assets to execute in a single execution engine, it is preferable the runtime-based approach because it simplifies the adaptation process.

Moreover, in our experiences we have not considered a solution for co-evolution of model transformations, application models and metamodels. In this sense, conform the metamodel discussed in [8] evolved, transformations and application models were manually changed. This required a maintenance procedure that, in part, was facilitated by the Java compiler, because most model transformations were programmed in Java. However, since fragments of model transformations must be evolved when metamodel evolves, this figures a lack in our proposal that do not considered automatic techniques for co-evolution. In order to automatically apply changes in these three transformation assets, Lopez-Herrejon et al. [34] proposed a reuse technique for co-evolution. Although it is an interesting proposal, we find that the necessity to break transformations in fragments hampers the application of current co-evolution proposals. Thus, an open question is how to apply co-evolution reuse techniques for fragmented units of model transformations?

5. Conclusion Remarks

Model transformations are becoming the core assets of companies that produce software based on MDE techniques. Due to the growing demand of new transformations that cover new requirements, transformation assets must be changed. In this sense, this work presented the WCT toolkit as a solution to manage transformation variants in a scenario where the implementation technology used to produce software evolves together with the transformation assets. By using a set of tools available in the WCT, users are allowed to specify model transformers, transformation variants and, finally, execute model transformations and test cases that may ensure that everything is working when delivering a configured MDE tool. Thus, we presented a set of tools to deal with large scale transformation reuse.

The support for large scale transformation requires the adaptation of model transformation assets. In our work, adaptation must consider strictly variabilities of implementation solutions, but not variabilities in application domains. In other words, the set of techniques presented in this paper are not applicable to manage communalities and variabilities in a single software application domain, but are interesting to adapt model transformation assets that actually are used in more than one domain. Here relies the main differences between our proposal and the existing software product line proposals: it is general for any software application domain. Therefore, this work presented experiences in adapting model transformation assets considering the same set of implementation variants used in three software projects, each one from a different application domain.

Moreover, since a single toolkit is used to perform diverse reuse techniques, we presented WCT as an integrated solution that efficiently applies adaptation procedures. Therefore, by bringing a wider set of functionalities to allow one to customize transformation assets, we present a singular tool in comparison to the related ones.

6. Future Work

This work did not detail some important aspects to tailor model transformation assets, as follows:

A process to adapt and deliver operational MDE tools. This paper discussed about reuse techniques developed with the WCT toolkit. However, more than using an adequate tool, we consider that it is necessary to follow a production planning that assist designers of reusable MTs.

Transformation compositions with heterogeneous transformation languages. Since most transformations used in software projects reported in Section 4 are of type black-box Java programs, this work is limited for a few compositions techniques. In this sense, a more general transformation composition must be considered, with heterogeneous set of model transformation languages.

Different types of test cases. In order to facilitate the test of adapted transformation assets, our techniques discussed in Section 3.5 must be compared with the state of the practice regarding test techniques for derived PLA products.

Acknowledgments

This work was partially supported by the Brazilian agencies FINEP, CAPES and CNPq.

References

[1] J. P. Almeida, R. Dijkman, M. Sinderen, and L. F. Pires. Platform-independent modelling in mda: Supporting abstract platforms. In *Model Driven Architecture Fundations and Applications*, MDAFA'05, pages 174–188, 2005. .

[2] V. Aranega, A. Etien, and S. Mosser. Using feature models to tame the complexity of model transformation engineering. In *ACM/IEEE 15th International Conference on Model Driven Engineering Languages and Systems MODELS 2012*, pages – , 2012.

[3] M. Bali. *Drools JBoss Rules 5.0 Developer's Guide Paperback*. Packt Publishing, 2009.

[4] F. P. Basso and R. M. P. Basso. An experience report on agile software development with mda (in portuguese, um relato de experiência no desenvolvimento ágil de software com a mda). In *First Brazilian Workshop on Model Driven Development*, I BW-MDD, 2010. URL www.adapit.com.br/files/bwmdd2010.pdf.

[5] F. P. Basso, L. B. Becker, and T. C. Oliveira. Using the fomda approach to support object-oriented real-time systems development. In *Object and Component-Oriented Real-Time Distributed Computing, 2006. ISORC 2006. Ninth IEEE International Symposium on*, pages 374–381, 2006. .

[6] F. P. Basso, L. B. Becker, and T. C. Oliveira. A solution for reuse and maintenance of model transformers using fomda approach (in portuguese, uma solução para reuso e manutenção de transformadores de modelos usando a abordagem fomda). In *Simpósio Brasileiro de Engenharia de Software. Anais do 21o Simpósio Brasileiro de Engenharia de Software.*, 2007. URL www.adapit.com.br/files/sbes2007.pdf.

[7] F. P. Basso, R. M. Pillat, and R. Z. Frantz. Development through models: Software architectures managed by models (in portuguese, desenvolvimento com modelos: Arquiteturas de software gerenciadas por modelos). *Java Magazine*, 59, 2008. URL www.adapit.com.br/files/jm2008.pdf.

[8] F. P. Basso, R. M. P. Basso, and T. C. Oliveira. Towards a web modeling environment for a model driven engineering approach. In *In Third Brazilian Workshop on Model Driven Development*, III BW-MDD, 2012. URL www.adapit.com.br/files/MockupToMe.pdf.

[9] F. P. Basso, C. M. L. Werner, R. M. Pillat, and T. C. Oliveira. A common representation for reuse assistants. In *13th International Conference on Software Reuse*, ICSR 2013, pages 283–288. 2013. .

[10] F. P. Basso, C. M. L. Werner, R. M. Pillat, and T. C. Oliveira. How do you execute reuse tasks among tools? a ras based approach to interoperate reuse assistants. In *25th International Conference on Software Engineering and Knowledge Engineering, SEKE 2013, Boston, USA, June 27-29 2013*, pages 721–726, 2013.

[11] B. Baudry, S. Ghosh, F. Fleurey, R. France, Y. L. Traon, and J.-M. Mottu. Barriers to systematic model transformation testing. *Communications of the ACM*, 53(6), 2010.

[12] D. Benavides, S. Segura, and A. Ruiz-Cortés. Automated analysis of feature models 20 years later: A literature review. *Inf. Syst.*, 35(6):615–636, Sept. 2010. ISSN 0306-4379. .

[13] T. Berger, R. Rublack, D. Nair, J. M. Atlee, M. Becker, K. Czarnecki, and A. Wąsowski. A survey of variability modeling in industrial practice. In *Proceedings of the Seventh International Workshop on Variability Modelling of Software-intensive Systems*, VaMoS '13, pages 7:1–8, 2013. .

[14] G. Booch, J. Rumbaugh, and I. Jacobson. *The Unified Modeling Language User Guide (2nd Edition)*. Addison-Wesley, 2005.

[15] E. Cirilo, U. Kulesza, A. Garcia, D. Cowan, P. Alencar, and C. Lucena. Configurable software product lines - supporting heterogeneous configuration knowledge. In *13th International Conference on Software Reuse*, ICSR 2013, pages 176–191, 2013. .

[16] J. Cole and J. D. Gradecki. *Mastering Apache Velocity*. Wiley; 1 edition, 2003.

[17] J. S. Cuadrado, E. Guerra, and J. Lara. Generic model transformations: Write once, reuse everywhere. 6707:62–77, 2011. .

[18] K. Czarnecki and U. Eisenecker. *Generative Programming: Methods, Tools and Applications*. Addison Wesley, 2000.

[19] K. Czarnecki and S. Helsen. Classification of model transformation approaches. In *OOPSLA'03 Workshop on Generative Techniques in the Context of Model-Driven Architecture*, 2003.

[20] A. Etien, A. Muller, T. Legrand, and X. Blanc. Combining independent model transformations. In *Proceedings of the 2010 ACM Symposium on Applied Computing*, SAC '10, pages 2237–2243, 2010. .

[21] A. Etien, V. Aranega, X. Blanc, and R. F. Paige. Chaining model transformations. In *Proceedings of the First Workshop on the Analysis of Model Transformations*, AMT '12, pages 9–14, 2012. .

[22] P. Fernandes, C. Werner, and L. Murta. Feature modeling for context-aware software product lines. In *International Conference on Software Engineering and Knowledge Engineering (SEKE'2008)*, SEKE 2008, pages 758–763, 2008.

[23] F. Fleurey, J. Steel, and B. Baudry. Validation in model-driven engineering: Testing model transformations. In *1st International Workshop on Model, Design and Validation*, SIVOES - MoDeVa, pages 29–40, 2004.

[24] W. B. Frakes and K. Kang. Software reuse research: Status and future. *IEEE Trans. Softw. Eng.*, 31(7):529–536, July 2005. .

[25] J. Garcia-Alonso, J. B. Olmeda, and J. M. Murillo. Architectural variability management in multi-layer web applications through feature models. In *Proceedings of the 4th International Workshop on Feature-Oriented Software Development*, FOSD '12, pages 29–36, 2012. .

[26] V. Guana. Supporting maintenance tasks on transformational code generation environments. In *Proceedings of the 2013 International Conference on Software Engineering*, ICSE '13, pages 1369–1372, 2013.

[27] C. Guy, B. Combemale, S. Derrien, J. Steel, and J.-M. Jézéquel. On model subtyping. 7349:400–415, 2012. .

[28] A. Hervieu, B. Baudry, and A. Gotlieb. Managing execution environment variability during software testing: An industrial experience. In *International Conference on Testing Software and Systems*, ICTSS 2012.

[29] J. Hutchinson, J. Whittle, M. Rouncefield, and S. Kristoffersen. Empirical assessment of mde in industry. In *Proceedings of the 33rd International Conference on Software Engineering*, ICSE '11, pages 471–480, 2011. .

[30] F. Jouault and I. Kurtev. On the architectural alignment of atl and qvt. In *Proceedings of the 2006 ACM symposium on Applied computing*, SAC '06, pages 1188–1195, 2006. .

[31] F. Jouault, F. Allilaire, J. Bézivin, and I. Kurtev. ATL: A model transformation tool. *Sci. Comput. Program.*, 72(1-2):31–39, 2008. .

[32] K. C. Kang, S. Kim, J. Lee, K. Kim, E. Shin, and M. Huh. Form: A feature-oriented reuse method with domain-specific reference architectures. *Ann. Softw. Eng.*, 5:143–168, Jan. 1998. ISSN 1022-7091.

[33] J. M. Küster, T. Gschwind, and O. Zimmermann. Incremental development of model transformation chains using automated testing. In *Model Driven Engineering Languages and Systems*, MODELS'09, pages 733–747, 2009. .

[34] R. E. Lopez-Herrejon, A. Egyed, S. Trujillo, J. de Sosa, and M. Azanza. Using incremental consistency management for conformance checking in feature-oriented model-driven engineering. In *VaMoS'10*, pages 93–100, 2010.

[35] M. Mendonca and D. Cowan. Decision-making coordination and efficient reasoning techniques for feature-based configuration. *Science of Computer Programming*, 75(5):311 – 332, 2010. .

[36] MOFM2T08. MOF model to text transformation language version 1.0 av. at http://www.omg.org/spec/mofm2t08/1.0/, 2008. URL http://www.omg.org/spec/MOFM2T08/1.0/.

[37] M. Petre. Uml in practice. In *Proceedings of the 2013 International Conference on Software Engineering*, ICSE '13, pages 722–731, 2013.

[38] R. M. Pillat, F. P. Basso, T. C. Oliveira, and C. M. L. Werner. Ensuring consistency of feature-based decisions with a business rule system. In *Proceedings of the Seventh International Workshop on Variability Modelling of Software-intensive Systems*, VaMoS '13, pages 15:1–15:8, 2013. .

[39] M. Rosenmüller, N. Siegmund, M. Pukall, and S. Apel. Tailoring dynamic software product lines. *SIGPLAN Not.*, 47(3):3–12, Oct. 2011. .

[40] T. C. Shan and W. W. Hua. Taxonomy of java web application frameworks. In *Proceedings of the IEEE International Conference on e-Business Engineering*, ICEBE '06, pages 378–385, 2006. ISBN 0-7695-2645-4. .

[41] V. E. S. Souza, R. D. A. Falbo, and G. Guizzardi. A uml profile for modeling framework-based web information systems. In *12th International Workshop on Exploring Modelling Methods in Systems Analysis and Design EMMSADt'2007*, pages 153–162, 2007.

[42] B. Tekinerdoğan, S. Bilir, and C. Abatlevi. Integrating platform selection rules in the model driven architecture approach. In *Proceedings of the 2003 European conference on Model Driven Architecture: foundations and Applications*, MDAFA'03, pages 159–173, 2005. .

[43] T. Thüm, S. Apel, C. Kästner, M. Kuhlemann, I. Schaefer, , and G. Saake. Analysis strategies for software product lines. Technical report, School of Computer Science, University of Magdeburg, Germany, 2012.

[44] T. Thüm, C. Kästner, F. Benduhn, J. Meinicke, G. Saake, and T. Leich. Featureide: An extensible framework for feature-oriented software development. *Science of Computer Programming*, (0):–, 2012. ISSN 0167-6423. .

[45] G. van Boas. From the workfloor: Developing workflow for the generative model transformer. In *2nd OOPSLA Workshop on Generative Techniques in the context of Model Driven Architecture*, 2005.

[46] B. Vanhooff, D. Ayed, and Y. Berbers. A framework for transformation chain development processes. In *Proceedings of the ECMDA Composition of Model Transformations Workshop*, pages 3–8, 2006.

[47] B. Vanhooff, S. V. Baelen, A. Hovsepyan, W. Joosen, and Y. Berbers. Towards a transformation chain modeling language. In *Proceedings of the 6th international conference on Embedded Computer Systems: architectures, Modeling, and Simulation*, SAMOS'06, pages 39–48, 2006. .

[48] M. Völter and I. Groher. Handling variability in model transformations and generators. In *In Proceedings of the 7th OOPSLA Workshop on Domain-Specific Modeling*, DSM'07, 2007.

[49] D. Wagelaar. Blackbox composition of model transformations using domain-specific modelling languages. In *Proceedings of the ECMDA Composition of Model Transformations Workshop*, pages 15–19, 2006.

[50] J. White, D. Schmidt, D. Benavides, P. Trinidad, and A. Ruiz-Cortes. Automated diagnosis of product-line configuration errors in feature models. In *Software Product Line Conference, 2008. SPLC '08. 12th International*, pages 225–234, 2008. .

[51] E. D. Willink. Umlx: A graphical transformation language for mda. In *Proceedings of Model-Driven Architecture: Foundations and Applications*, pages 13–24, 2003.

[52] A. Yie, R. Casallas, D. Deridder, and D. Wagelaar. Realizing model transformation chain interoperability. *Software & Systems Modeling*, 11(1):55–75, 2012. .

Model-driven Generative Framework for Automated OMG DDS Performance Testing in the Cloud *

Kyoungho An, Takayuki Kuroda [†],
Aniruddha Gokhale

ISIS, Vanderbilt University, Nashville, TN 37235, USA
{kyoungho, kuroda, gokhale}@isis.vanderbilt.edu

Sumant Tambe and Andrea Sorbini

RTI, Sunnyvale, CA, USA
{sumant, asorbini}@rti.com

Abstract

The Object Management Group's (OMG) Data Distribution Service (DDS) provides many configurable policies which determine end-to-end quality of service (QoS) of applications. It is challenging to predict the system's performance in terms of latencies, throughput, and resource usage because diverse combinations of QoS configurations influence QoS of applications in different ways. To overcome this problem, design-time formal methods have been applied with mixed success, but lack of sufficient accuracy in prediction, tool support, and understanding of formalism has prevented wider adoption of the formal techniques. A promising approach to address this challenge is to emulate system behavior and gather data on the QoS parameters of interest by experimentation. To realize this approach, which is preferred over formal methods due to their limitations in accurately predicting QoS, we have developed a model-based automatic performance testing framework with generative capabilities to reduce manual efforts in generating a large number of relevant QoS configurations that can be deployed and tested on a cloud platform. This paper describes our initial efforts in developing and using this technology.

Categories and Subject Descriptors   D.2.5 [*Testing and Debugging*]: Testing tools

Keywords   Model-driven Engineering, Generative Programming, Publish/Subscribe, Performance Testing

1. Introduction

The OMG Data Distribution Service (DDS) [4] is a general-purpose middleware supporting real-time publish/subscribe semantics [1] for mission-critical applications. Specifically, the OMG DDS supports real-time, topic-based, data-centric, scalable, deter-

---

* This work was supported in part by NSF CAREER Award CNS 0845789. Any opinions, findings, and conclusions or recommendations expressed in this material are those of the author(s) and do not necessarily reflect the views of the National Science Foundation.

† Author is a visiting researcher from NEC Corporation, Japan

ministic and anonymous pub/sub interaction semantics for large-scale distributed applications. To support the quality of service (QoS) requirements of a broad spectrum of application domains, OMG DDS supports many QoS configuration policies (in the form of configuration parameters) that when used in different combinations determine the delivered end-to-end QoS properties.

An important consideration with DDS QoS policies is that not all QoS policies can be combined with each other since certain combinations tend to be incompatible with each other. Similarly, the values chosen for specific QoS policies may tend to become inconsistent when combined. Both the incompatibility and inconsistency issues pose significant challenges for DDS application developers who must ensure that their deployed applications have compatible and consistent QoS configuration policies. Our prior work [2] utilized model-driven engineering (MDE) techniques to pinpoint existence of such errors at design-time.

Addressing these accidental challenges alone is not sufficient, however, towards realizing high confidence DDS-based applications. Every individual QoS policy tends to impact the end-to-end performance and behavior of the application in specific ways. When these QoS policies are combined in various combinations, it is hard to predict the outcome on QoS of combining these policies. Such a problem is faced not just by application developers but also by the OMG DDS vendors themselves, who must have an indepth knowledge of how various combinations of configuration parameters interact, and to address issues raised by their customers.

It is not possible to expect an application developer or a vendor to manually write test cases that can test every QoS policy and all possible combinations of these QoS policies (along with their values), not to mention that they must also ensure that these combinations are valid. Even if one were to develop these large number of tests, executing them sequentially is time consuming, which impacts both the application developers who aim at getting their applications to market rapidly and vendors who must address customer problems in a timely manner.

To address the combinatorial testing problem and limitations of sequential testing, this paper presents AUTOMATIC (AUTOmated Middleware Analysis and Testing In the Cloud), which is a framework we have developed that combines MDE techniques with multiple stages of generative capabilities. Specifically, AUTOMATIC provides a domain-specific modeling language that developers use to model their applications and QoS policies of interest. Generative tools synthesize essentially a product line of test cases, each testing different QoS policies for the same publish/subscribe business logic. A second set of generators synthesize cloud-based deployment logic. Finally, a testing framework automates the testing of the generated test cases in parallel in the cloud. Although a related effort called Expertus [3] uses aspect oriented weaving techniques for code generation and automated testing of applications for performance in the cloud, this effort does not address the QoS configuration combinations and their impact on performance that we address in this paper.

The rest of the paper is organized as follows: Section 2 describes the overall approach providing brief details of each stage in our approach; Section 3 provides initial insights gained in validating our solution; and finally Section 4 offers concluding remarks alluding to work needed to make the work robust and complete.

2. Design and Implementation of AUTOMATIC

Figure 1 describes the overall architecture and workflow of our automated performance testing framework called AUTOMATIC. AUTOMATIC comprises three activity domains: User, Test Automation System, and Cloud Infrastructure. The Modeling and Monitoring functions included in the User domain should be conducted by a user who prototypes DDS applications and performs performance testing of the applications. In the Test Automation System domain, Test Planning and Test Deployment functions are carried out by predefined tools in our framework. When the Test Planning is completed and ready to be deployed in a testing infrastructure, a test environment is generated for our cloud infrastructure to emulate application testing. As a result, users need to define their models of applications and test specifications with a modeling tool as inputs and obtain performance results with a monitoring tool as outputs of our framework.

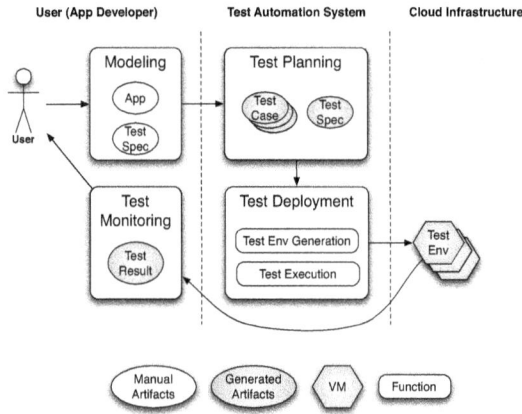

Figure 1. Framework Architecture

The rest of this section describes each activity in detail including the performance monitoring capability.

2.1 Domain-Specific Modeling Language

We developed a DSML using the Generic Modeling Environment (GME) (www.isis.vanderbilt.edu/projects/GME) that supports modeling a DDS application for emulation and testing its performance for various combinations of DDS QoS policies. GME provides a meta-modeling environment to develop DSMLs for specific domains. Our meta-model includes modeling elements for all OMG DDS entities including Domain, Topic, Publisher, Subscriber, DataWriter, DataReader, QoS, and their connections. In DDS applications, a scope or operating region of an application is determined by the Domain, and applications are isolated by different Domain IDs. DDS applications publish or subscribe via DataWriters and DataReaders through associated Topics, and therefore in the meta-model the Topic and Type elements are contained in the Domain element and Topics and Types in the Domain are accessible by DataWriter and DataReader entities running in the

same Domain. Moreover, the Domain contains a Participant element which is a concept to represent a processing unit for publishing or subscribing or both. Lastly, the modeling capability to configure QoS policies for DDS entities is contained in the Domain element. Data communications between Participants are differentiated and identified by a Topic, so a TopicConnection element is required in the Domain model to be used by DataWriters and DataReaders in Participants.

Figure 2 shows an example application defined with our modeling language. This example application examines the throughput of the application publishing octet sequence data from a Participant containing a DataWriter to a Participant involving a DataReader. Each DataWriter and DataReader are placed under the Participant element and behaves as a communicating port between Participants.

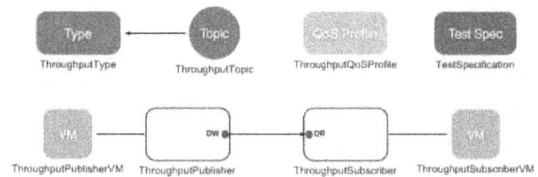

Figure 2. Example Domain-Specific Model of DDS Throughput Testing Application

The DDS Participants are deployed in virtual machines (VMs) for testing and each Participant in the model are connected to a VM element based on the deployment decision by users. In this example, each Participant is deployed in a different VM. The deployment plan (mapping of Participants and VMs) can be flexibly altered by users in the modeling language if users like to test with different deployment plans. Users can emulate their applications by setting analogous hardware specifications to find similar performance results in actual environment.

Communicating DataWriters and DataReaders are connected with directed lines which indicate communications defined by a Topic. A Topic is shown in the top of this example model. If a name of a line is the same as the name of a Topic, it means DataWriters and DataReaders connected with the link communicate data by the Topic. Each data type of a Topic is determined by a struct like data type.

In the QoS Profile element, QoS policies used by DataWriters and DataReaders are contained. For example, Reliability QoS has two kinds of policies to determine the level of reliability: RELIABILITY and BEST_EFFORT. History QoS also has two kinds of policies to set the number of history samples in a entity's cache: KEEP_ALL and KEEP_LAST. Some QoS policies need to set as numeric values such as history depth in History QoS. A QoS Profile element can be reused by multiple DataWriters and DataReaders. In our framework, QoS policies defined in a QoS Profile element are variations of generative artifacts, and the number of variations are determined by ranges of configuration parameters set by users.

Finally, the configurable parameters are set in the TestSpec element. In this element, test related information such as running duration of the test, and the number of test cases concurrently running is configured. A deployment tool uses this information to decide the number VMs in a test set and schedule the test operations.

2.2 Test Plan Generation

The Test Planning function traverses the modeled elements in a model instance via a model interpreter to generate executable applications and related test specification files.

Figure 3 shows an XML-based DDS application tree model transformed by the model interpreter based on Figure 2. Because the aim of our automatic testing framework is to analyze application performance by varying QoS configuration, elements under the QoS Library are categorized into variable elements and the rest of the elements fall into the common elements category. This approach is conducive to using generative programming to realize a product line of test cases. The QoS Library embodies QoS elements for DataWriters and DataReaders. To demonstrate our framework with a simple example, we varied only the Reliability QoS. In this example, both DataWriter QoS and DataReader QoS have Reliability QoS. BEST_EFFORT or RELIABILITY can be selected as a kind of the Reliability QoS.

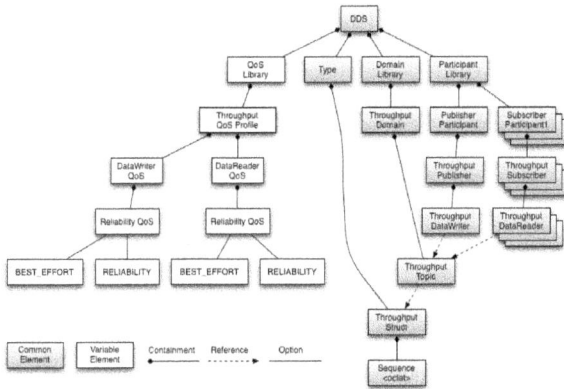

Figure 3. XML-based DDS Application Tree

The following procedure is used to form a tree shown in Figure 4 for all possible combinations of QoS configurations defined in the QoS Library. In the example, four test cases can be generated as each DataWriter and DataReader QoS has Reliability QoS that can choose from BEST_EFFORT and RELIABLE. Once the combination tree for variable elements is complete, the combination tree is traversed with depth-first search to create trees for variables elements actually used by the applications for testing.

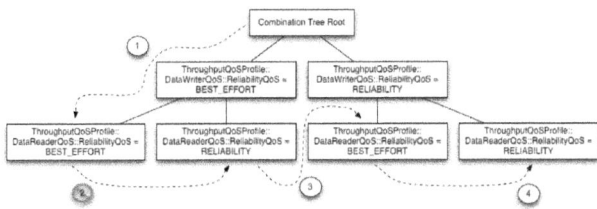

Figure 4. Variable Element Combination Tree

As a final outcome, four trees for variable elements are created as shown in Figure 5. The tree numbered 2 is discarded by the interpreter because the QoS configurations are not compatible. The reason is that if the DataWriter's Reliability QoS is BEST_EFFORT and DataReader's Reliability QoS is RELIABLE, then no communication between them is feasible according to the DDS specification.

We checked for all compatibility and inconsistency violations in the model interpreter though this task can be accomplished using the Object Constraint Language in the model itself as shown by our prior work [2] or the runtime environment may also be able to flag these cases as errors. As the final step, the trees for variable elements are combined with the tree for common elements introduced in Figure 3, and the executable applications are generated.

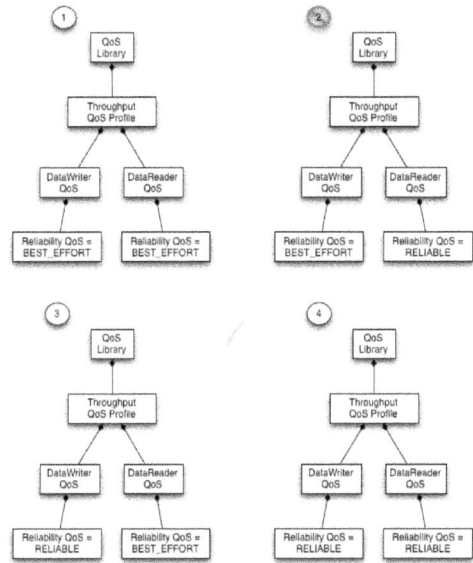

Figure 5. Variable Element Tree

2.3 Test Deployment

To deploy the XML-based DDS testing applications in a cloud-based testing infrastructure, specifications related to the deployment are also generated by the model interpreter. The specifications are composed of three parts: Test Specification, VM Specification, and Application Specification. The Test Specification describes the environment including a reference to the VM Specification, concurrency level, duration for test execution, publication period of publishers. Each test case is defined with an assigned ID and a referring specification file. The referred specification files have information about application's topology and the execution command.

The VM Specification example describes required VMs for testing and information of VMs such as VM instance type and image. These specifications are fed into our deployment tool. VM instance types indicate specifications of VM such as the number of virtual CPUs, memory size, and storage capacity. According to the user-selected VM image and VM instance type, the Test Env Generation function deploys a proper VM in a cloud infrastructure. When the VM has booted up, a SSH connection is established and a test case application is sent to the VM over the SSH connection by the Test Execution function.

We implemented our deployment tool in Python 2.7 for the Test Deployment function. Our private cloud for testing adopted OpenStack as a cloud operating system, and the Python Boto library is exploited to control cloud resources via Amazon AWS APIs. The generated XML-specified application that is moved to the deployed VM is subsequently executed on that VM using a tool provided by RTI called the RTI Prototyper (http://community.rti.com/content/page/download-prototyper).

2.4 Test Monitoring

We employed another product from RTI called the RTI Monitor to detect DDS applications' performance while it is executing on the VM. The RTI Monitor is a tool to visualize monitoring data of applications. The RTI Monitor helps users to understand their systems easily via graphical interfaces and to verify behaviors of entities as expected. Moreover, it comes to the aid of improving performance throughput provided statistics such as CPU and memory usage, and throughput. The experimental results illustrated in Section 3 were collected using this tool.

3. Technology Validation

Our efforts at validating the claims in AUTOMATIC thus far have focused on a scenario where an application developer seeks to make appropriate tradeoffs trying to balance the conflicting requirements of reliability and timeliness. To that end, the experiment evaluates performance of an example DDS application by combining the RELIABILITY, HISTORY and DEADLINE QoS policies. In this experiment, DDS applications use core libraries of RTI Connext DDS 5.0 (which is an implementation of OMG DDS) and executable scripts provided with RTI Connext Prototyper 5.0. Our OpenStack-based cloud testbed employs KVM as a virtual machine (VM) hypervisor. Each VM machine type used in this experiment consists of 1 virtual CPU and 512 MB memory.

In our example, the publisher periodically publishes a topic containing octet sequence typed data of 64K bytes to the subscriber. We chose a large packet size in the hope of congesting the network. The publishing period is decided by the DEADLINE QoS setting and was fixed at 1 millisecond. The purpose of this experiment is to understand deadline miss rate for different RELIABILITY QoS configurations. The HISTORY setting was KEEP_ALL, which means the publisher and subscriber hold on to all the data samples so they can be used for retransmissions when complete reliability is desired. The RELIABILITY setting is varied between RELIABLE (for eventual consistency) versus BEST_EFFORT (where no attempt is made to retry transmissions when samples are lost). The generated test cases are shown in Figure 5.

Figure 6 shows deadline miss counts of DataReader's (an entity on the subscriber side) in the test cases. If a sample is not arrived in a DataReader within 1 millisecond, it is counted as a missed deadline. Each test case runs for 4 minutes and values are monitored every 5 seconds. The X axis indicates time and Y axis presents deadline missed samples for 5 seconds.

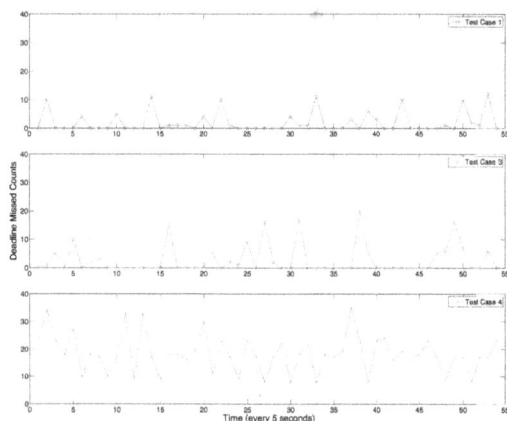

Figure 6. Deadline Miss Counts for Different Reliability QoS Settings

In test case 1, most samples do not miss the deadline and the range of the samples spans up to 10 as maximum. If Reliability QoS is set to BEST_EFFORT, a DataWriter keeps publishing data regardless of the status of a DataReader and therefore it is beneficial to be used for applications demanding low latency. In a congested network environment, it would possibly lose samples, however, since our test network is not congested, there were no lost samples.

In test case 3, deadline miss counts are monitored from 9 to 35 where they keep occurring during the entire testing period. If the

data cache of a DataWriter with the RELIABLE Reliability QoS is filled with unacknowledged samples, the DataWriter's write operation is blocked for a while to control the sending rate to avoid congestion which increases the latency of samples delivered. Accordingly, high latency causes deadline miss counts on the DataReader side. However, samples can reliably arrive at the DataReader due to the middleware supporting the retransmissions.

4. Concluding Remarks

Modern middleware, such as the OMG Data Distribution Service (DDS), provide substantial flexibility to applications by virtue of supporting a large number of configuration options. These configuration options when combined in different ways can lead to vastly different performance and behavioral characteristics for the applications. Although some intuition is always available on the potential impact of individual configurations, and some guidelines do emerge after a few years of experience using multiple configurations on real applications (*e.g.*, community.rti.com/best-practices), application developers continue to face numerous challenges deciding the right combinations of options they must use for their application for the chosen deployment environments. It is infeasible for developers to manually create and test each possible scenario to understand the impact of the configuration options.

To address these challenges in the context of OMG DDS middleware, this paper combines model-driven engineering (MDE) and generative programming techniques to provide a tool called AUTOMATIC (AUTOmated Middleware Analysis and Testing In the Cloud). MDE helps application developers with intuitive abstractions to rapidly describe their scenarios. Generative programming is needed since the test cases that combine configuration options can be considered a product line where the DDS application business logic remains common while the configurations can vary. Deployment and testing in the cloud is chosen as an approach because of its elastic nature where we can automate the parallel execution and collection of test statistics for a large number of generated tests from our tooling. Although the presented technology is showcased for the OMG DDS middleware, the principles behind AUTOMATIC are applicable to other middleware. Moreover, our technology has significant practical utility to both application developers and middleware vendors.

The presented work illustrates the feasibility of such an idea. Our ongoing work is focusing on making AUTOMATIC complete and robust for OMG DDS, and test it on a large number of deployment scenarios. Future work is also looking into generating application business logic. Current artifacts in AUTOMATIC are available for download from www.dre.vanderbilt.edu/~kyoungho/AUTOMATIC/.

References

[1] Patrick Th. Eugster, Pascal A. Felber, Rachid Guerraoui, and Anne-Marie Kermarrec. The many faces of publish/subscribe. *ACM Computer Survey*, 35:114–131, June 2003.

[2] Joe Hoffert, Douglas Schmidt, and Aniruddha Gokhale. A QoS Policy Configuration Modeling Language for Publish/Subscribe Middleware Platforms. In *Proceedings of International Conference on Distributed Event-Based Systems (DEBS)*, pages 140–145, Toronto, Canada, June 2007.

[3] D. Jayasinghe, G. Swint, S. Malkowski, J. Li, Qingyang Wang, Junhee Park, and C. Pu. Expertus: A Generator Approach to Automate Performance Testing in IaaS Clouds. In *Cloud Computing (CLOUD), 2012 IEEE 5th International Conference on*, pages 115–122, 2012.

[4] Object Management Group. *Data Distribution Service for Real-time Systems Specification*, 1.2 edition, January 2007.

Author Index

www.ingramcontent.com/pod-product-compliance
Lightning Source LLC
Chambersburg PA
CBHW081525220326
41598CB00036B/6338